MW01126153

Praise for *Walking the Ancient Paths*

— ◆ —

This commentary on the profoundly theological but relevant prophetic book of Jeremiah is vintage Kaiser. Few scholars are as gifted as the author of this fine volume in getting to the heart of the message of biblical texts and communicating its enduring theology with such clarity and verve. For those who seek a commentary to help them understand the "weeping prophet" and his message, this is the place to start.

Daniel I. Block
Gunther H. Knoedler Professor Emeritus of Old Testament
Wheaton College

Jeremiah lived at a crucial time in Israel's history and is certainly one of the most significant of her prophets. Having a sure guide through his work is a gift. That is what this commentary is, taking us through ancient paths with a skilled student of the word. Kaiser's work is solid and revealing, opening up the key teachings of this important book of the Scripture.

Darrell L. Bock
Executive Director for Cultural Engagement
Howard G. Hendricks Center for Christian Leadership
and Cultural Engagement

This long-awaited commentary by one of our leading evangelical Old Testament scholars delivers the expected thorough exegetical and theological analysis, but much more. There are also the added practical insights gained from a lifetime of study of this most important prophetic book coupled with decades of classroom experience. For scholars, pastors and students looking to "walk the ancient paths" (Jer 6:16), there is no more informed and balanced guide than Walter C. Kaiser, Jr.

Randall Price
Distinguished Research Professor of Biblical & Judaic Studies
Rawlings School of Divinity, Liberty University

Thankfully for all of us, whether scholar, student, or pastor-teacher, Walt Kaiser is still in the business of sharing his insightful and inspiring perspectives on Scripture. This commentary on Jeremiah opens our ears to the voice of God in the dark and drifting world of Israel's history, which is a history not unlike the world we live in today. All of us who have been blessed and deeply challenged by Walt's writing in the past will be grateful for this addition to our libraries and thankful for its mind-expanding and heart-instructing impact on our lives.

Joe Stowell
President
Cornerstone University

Walking the Ancient Paths expands Kaiser's clear view of the Hebrew Bible's messianic theme by a penetrating analysis of the book of Jeremiah. The authors present a readable yet technically sound commentary. Anchored in Kaiser's own annotated translation of the Hebrew text, the commentary resolves interpretive issues and offers theological insight. Preachers and teachers of Jeremiah's prophecies will find here a dependable guide to lead them through the ancient text proclaiming a message applicable to our own paths.

William D. Barrick
Emeritus Professor of Old Testament
The Master's Seminary

WALKING THE
ANCIENT PATHS

— ◆ —

WALKING THE ANCIENT PATHS

— ◆ —

A COMMENTARY ON JEREMIAH

WALTER C. KAISER, JR.

WITH TIBERIUS RATA

LEXHAM PRESS

Dedicated to Nancy Elizabeth Kaiser
—Song of Songs 8:6-7

Walking the Ancient Paths: A Commentary on Jeremiah

Copyright 2019 Walter C. Kaiser, Jr., and Tiberius Rata

Lexham Press, 1313 Commercial St., Bellingham, WA 98225
LexhamPress.com

Unless otherwise indicated, English quotations from Jeremiah are the authors' own translation.

Unless otherwise indicated, Bible quotations outside of Jeremiah are taken from the Holy Bible, New International Version®, NIV®. Copyright © 1973, 1978, 1984, 2011 by Biblica, Inc.™ Used by permission of Zondervan. All rights reserved worldwide. www.zondervan.com The "NIV" and "New International Version" are trademarks registered in the United States Patent and Trademark Office by Biblica, Inc.™

Print ISBN 9781683592679
Digital ISBN 9781683592686

Lexham Editorial: Derek R. Brown, Russell Meek, Jim Weaver, Ronald van der Bergh
Cover Design: Lydia Dahl
Typesetting: Abigail Stocker

CONTENTS

ACKNOWLEDGMENTS

The book of Jeremiah is a delight to read, study, and share with the people of God. Its arguments are so plain and straightforward, there often is very little space for puzzlement. But Jeremiah also has a message that was for former generations; it is a word that is solidly fixed on the future as well. His message about the new covenant will forever be enshrined in the hearts and lives of all believers worldwide.

May our Lord bless each of you who ponder this prophet's word from God as he has blessed the hearts and lives of both of us as co-authors of this word.

It remains to thank those who have helped us in the editing and publishing process: Derek R. Brown, Russell Meek, Jim Weaver, Ronald van der Bergh, Lydia Dahl, and Abigail Stocker.

Walter C. Kaiser, Jr.

I want to thank my wonderful wife, Carmen, for her unconditional love and support.

I am grateful for godly men like Ioan Buda (my grandfather), Pitt Popovici (my first mentor), Mihai Mihut (my first pastor), and Jeff Gill (my first dean/shepherd). They walked the ancient paths and modeled for me what it means to be faithful like Jeremiah.

I can't say "thank you" enough to my teaching assistant Chad Shively for all of the hard and meticulous work he put into this project.

Tiberius Rata

ABBREVIATIONS

1	first person
2	second person
3	third person
abs.	absolute
acc.	accusative
ACCS	Ancient Christian Commentary on Scripture
AD	anno Domini
adj.	adjective/adjectival
ANET	J. B. Pritchard, ed., *Ancient Near Eastern Texts Relating to the Old Testament*, 3rd ed.
aor.	aorist
AUSS	*Andrews University Seminary Studies*
b. Bat.	Baba Batra
BA	*Biblical Archaeologist*
BAR	*Biblical Archaeology Review*
BASOR	*Bulletin of the American Schools of Oriental Research*
BC	before Christ
BHS	*Biblia Hebraica Stuttgartensia*
Bib	*Biblica*
BibInt	*Biblical Interpretation*
BN	*Biblische Notizen*
BSac	*Bibliotheca Sacra*
c.	common
ca.	circa
CBQ	*Catholic Biblical Quarterly*
cf.	*confer*, compare
chap(s).	chapters

coh.	cohortative
conj.	conjunction
consec.	consecutive
const.	construct
COS	W. W. Hallo, ed., *The Context of Scripture*
DSS	Dead Sea Scrolls
Dtr	Deuteronomistic History
ed(s).	editor(s)
Eng.	English
ESV	English Standard Version
etc.	*et cetera*, and the rest
ExpTim	*Expository Times*
fem., f.	feminine
fut.	future
gen.	genitive
Gk.	Greek
HALOT	L. Koehler, W. Baumgartner, and J. J. Stamm, *The Hebrew and Aramaic Lexicon of the Old Testament*, trans. and ed. M. E. J. Richardson et al., 4 vols.
haplogr.	haplography
HAR	*Hebrew Annual Review*
Heb.	Hebrew
HTR	*Harvard Theological Review*
HTS	Harvard Theological Studies
ICC	International Critical Commentary
impf.	imperfect
impv.	imperative
indic.	indicative
inf.	infinitive
J.W.	Josephus, *Jewish War*
JBL	*Journal of Biblical Literature*
JBQ	*Jewish Bible Quarterly*
JETS	*Journal of the Evangelical Theological Society*
JNSL	*Journal of Northwest Semitic Languages*
JQR	*Jewish Quarterly Review*
JSOT	*Journal for the Study of the Old Testament*

JSS	*Journal of Semitic Studies*
JTS	*Journal of Theological Studies*
juss.	jussive
KJV	King James Version
lit.	literally
LXX	Septuagint
masc., m.	masculine
ms(s)	manuscript(s)
MT	Masoretic Text
NAC	New American Commentary
NASB	New American Standard Bible
NET	New English Translation
NIV	New International Version
NJPS	*New JPS Translation*
NKJV	New King James Version
NRSV	New Revised Standard Version
NT	New Testament
obj.	object
OT	Old Testament
OTE	*Old Testament Essays*
pass.	passive
pf.	perfect
pl.	plural
prep.	preposition
pres.	present
ptc.	participle
RB	*Revue Biblique*
ResQ	*Restoration Quarterly*
REV	Revised English Version
sg.	singular
SJOT	*Scandinavian Journal of the Old Testament*
suf.	suffix
Tg.	Targum
TLOT	Ernst Jenni et al., eds., *Theological Lexicon of the Old Testament*
TynBul	*Tyndale Bulletin*

v(v).	verse(s)
Vg.	Vulgate
vol(s).	volume(s)
VT	*Vetus Testamentum*
WBC	Word Biblical Commentary
WMANT	Wissenschaftliche Monographien aum Alten und Neuen Testament
WTJ	*Westminster Theological Journal*
ZAH	*Zeitschrift für Althebräistik*
ZAW	*Zeitschrift für die alttestamentliche Wissenschaft*
α´	Aquila
θ´	Theodotion
σ´	Symmachus

INTRODUCTION

Jeremiah wrote the longest of all the sixteen Old Testament latter prophetic books. In fact, Jeremiah is the longest book in all the Scripture, with a total of 21,673 words, compared to 20,512 words in Genesis, 19,479 words in Psalms, 19,123 words in Ezekiel, and 16,920 words in Isaiah (Brown, 25). He was sent as a young man to preach to Judah in the final decades of the seventh century and the opening years of the sixth century BC.

His book holds a consistent position (throughout all order traditions) in the Heb. canon between Isaiah and Ezekiel, although in the rabbinical tradition Jeremiah occupies the first position in the prophetic books.[1] In a number of French and German mss, Jeremiah also begins the Latter Prophets. In the Gk. Septuagint (LXX), Jeremiah occupies second position in the Latter Prophets, as he does in today's English versions. However, in the Syriac Peshitta his book comes right after the twelve Minor Prophets.

His book is not only the longest of all the latter prophetic books, 1,364 verses in all, but it also is the most difficult in which to detect a pattern of organization. It has no clearly stated chronological pattern, outline, or organized series of topics. Only Jer 37–44 appears to be in chronological order.

The precise meaning of the name Jeremiah (יִרְמְיָהוּ, *yirmĕyāhû*) is unknown, but some suggestions include "Yahweh founded," "Yahweh exalts," or "Yahweh throws down."[2] Jeremiah reveals much about his emotions and reactions throughout the book (cf. 9:1). For this reason he has earned the nickname "the weeping prophet." He is also considered the "most 'human' of all the prophets precisely because he reveals so much about himself

---

1. b. Bat. 14b.
2. See Heyink; Thomson and McConville, 550.

throughout the book" (Huey, 32). Jeremiah's "humanness" is summarized
well as follows:

> Jeremiah exhibited qualities of courage, compassion, and sensi-
> tivity. He also revealed a darker side of moodiness, introspection,
> loneliness, doubt, and retribution toward his personal enemies
> (11:20). He could call for vengeance on those who attacked him but
> also intercede passionately for God to spare his people. He could
> stand his ground against personal threats but also weep uncon-
> trollably as he considered the suffering of his own people. Though
> frequently called the "weeping prophet," his tears should be inter-
> preted not as evidence of inner weakness but as proof of his love
> for his people. He must have gained a reputation for courage during
> his lifetime, for centuries later comparisons were made between
> Jesus and Jeremiah (Matt 16:14). (Huey, 23)

Jeremiah's companion and amanuensis was "Baruch son of Neriah,"
whose name means "Blessed" (בָּרוּךְ), son of "Yahweh Is My Light" (נֵרִיָּה
36:4, 32). Baruch faithfully recorded Jeremiah's messages (36:4) and even
read the oracles to crowds (36:8), as well as assisting Jeremiah with other
functions (32:12-14). Though he was an often-silent helper throughout
Jeremiah's ministry, a personal struggle of Baruch's is recorded (45:1-5),
which shows that even Baruch faced great stress in Jeremiah's ministry
and needed comfort at times. Later Baruch even accompanied Jeremiah
as he was forced to go to Egypt by his own countrymen following the fall
of Jerusalem (43:3-6).

JEREMIAH'S EARLY LIFE

Jeremiah was born in a priestly home in the town of Anathoth, two to three
miles northeast of Jerusalem (1:1). His father was "Hilkiah, from the priests
who were in Anathoth, in the land of Benjamin" (1:1). There is a good possibility that he descended from the family of Abiathar, a priest in the line
of Eli, who cared for the ark of God at Shiloh (1 Sam 4:12-18). If so, then
this Abiathar was the same one who served under David and Solomon but
who fell into disfavor for backing the wrong candidate to the throne (1 Kgs
2:26) during the rebellion of David's son Adonijah (instead of Solomon).

We have no information about Jeremiah's childhood, but his later years bear witness to his knowing the law of God along with the ritual of the temple quite well. There is no word that he ever trained for the priesthood or functioned in that role, but he surely knew what the law required, as his frequent citations from the book of Deuteronomy show.

Jeremiah complained that he was too young when he was called, but God assured him of his own divine presence and help. He was also later told that he was not to marry (16:1-4), for this was to be part of his symbolic messages to Judah. This was followed by instructions that he must not attend any funerals of his loved ones or of the people of his village as a reminder that God had removed his comfort from them, and neither was he to attend any feasts, because God would remove their rejoicing (16:5-9). Needless to say, besides his unpopular messages, Jeremiah's life as a young, single prophet who would not join in major social functions likely set him apart from those around him.

Jeremiah is best known as a preacher of righteousness. Some of his earliest recorded preaching is in 2:5 and 3:1-4:1 as he adamantly decries Judah's idolatry, paganism, and empty ritualism. The nation was guilty of spiritual prostitution and must turn from being "faithless Israel" and immediately return to the Lord in repentance (3:12-13, 19-22; 4:1). But what troubled Jeremiah more than most things was the gross ingratitude of the people, as the nation literally changed its gods (2:11), a duplicitous trend unknown even among the Gentile nations (2:10), an event that was likewise contrary even to nature (5:20-25). God's people were so bent on chasing after these foreign gods that they were acting like camels or wild donkeys in sexual heat that could not be diverted from their pursuit of sensual satisfaction (2:23-25). These faithless peoples could just as well forget about being delivered by any kind of political alignments with foreign nations (2:18-19), which also were unreliable. Moreover, Judah had acted as an adulterous wife who constantly betrayed her husband, the Lord, as she kept presuming time after time on God's forgiveness as the solution to her problems (3:1-5), though she gave no evidence of repentance.

There are no precisely dated prophecies in Jeremiah for the period from the finding of the book of the law in 622/621 BC until the tragic death of King Josiah in 609 BC (though some undated prophecies could theoretically date to that period). Jeremiah would have been around twenty-two years old as Josiah launched the main part of his reform with the discovery of the book of the law in the house of God. The names of the men who assisted Josiah in carrying out the reform match the names of those who later protected Jeremiah (they are possibly the names of their sons). These men included Ahikam ben Shaphan (26:24), Gemariah ben Shaphan, and Elnathan ben Achbor (36:12).

We next hear from the prophet at the beginning of the reign of Jehoiakim (26:1; the fourth year of Jehoiakim [605/604 BC]). However, it would be incorrect to assume that Jeremiah had ceased preaching during this period after he had started so well in his early ministry. In fact, Jer 25:3 counters that idea: "for twenty-three years—from the thirteen year of Josiah, son of Amon king of Judah until this very day—the word of the LORD [had] come to [him] and [he had] spoken to [Judah] again and again, but [they had] not listened" (NIV). This seems to indicate that Jeremiah had prophesied during Josiah's reign, though those prophecies do not appear to have been recorded in this book.

After Jeremiah gives his "temple sermon" (7:1–34), more information about him begins to be included in the book (605 to 587 BC). The temple sermon became a marker in the life and ministry of the prophet, as life in Judah under a young but self-possessed King Jehoiakim was more adamantly selfish, arrogant, and openly pagan, in spite of the prophet's urging to return to the Lord and his ways. Living under such a king brought much tension into Jeremiah's life, and much grief and agony.

THE HISTORICAL PERIOD OF
JEREMIAH'S PROPHESYING

Jeremiah began his ministry under King Josiah, but to understand the significance of the events of Jeremiah's days one needs to look at the history of the kingdom. Young King Josiah had come to the throne of Judah at a most remarkable time, some thirteen years before Jeremiah commenced his ministry. Earlier, Hezekiah also had begun, at the tender age of eleven years, as a co-regent with his father, Ahaz, later beginning his sole reign at twenty-five years old (715 BC). Hezekiah was able to reverse the spiritual bankruptcy he had inherited from his father as he initiated a return to Yahweh, reopened and repaired the temple his father had closed, and destroyed the foreign **cults**[3] that had been installed during the time of Ahaz's subservience to his Assyrian overlords. Hezekiah ruled for a total of forty-two years (729–686 BC).

But all of this spiritual emphasis came to a halt under the reign of Hezekiah's son Manasseh, who reigned for over a half a century (696–642 BC) after also sharing with his father eleven years of co-regency (696–686 BC). A total lack of godliness characterized his reign—one that went in the exact opposite direction of his father. Manasseh embraced and zealously promoted the foreign **cults** of Canaan and all their trappings. Altars to Baal were erected, and the image of Asherah could be found everywhere. The arts and practices of sorcery, divination, witchcraft, spiritists, and necromancy reappeared, as in the days of northern Israel's Ahab and Jezebel, in the southern two tribes. Manasseh even offered his own sons in the Valley of Hinnom to the god Molech as human sacrifices.

Even though Manasseh had a late-in-life conversion to Yahweh after he was taken to Babylon, it was too late to affect his son Amon, who succeeded him for two years as king (642–640 BC). Even the name of this son ("causing to forget") was a symbolic indication that a relationship existed at this time in Judah between paganism and the people of Judah. Judah had forgotten their God. Manasseh was followed by King Josiah, whose reign was a bright period in Israel's relationship with God. During this time Jeremiah began to prophesy.

Jeremiah prophesied during the reigns of five kings (Josiah, Jehoahaz, Jehoiakim, Jehoiachin, and Zedekiah) and one governor (Gedaliah), but he only mentions three of the five kings, since two of them had short reigns, of only three months each (Jehoahaz and Jehoiachin). King Josiah, who began his rule in 640 BC, reigned for eighteen years after Jeremiah began his ministry in 627/626 BC, lasting until 609 BC, when Josiah led his army his up to the Megiddo Pass to prevent Pharaoh Necho II from disturbing the balance of power in the Near East. Josiah was killed by the Egyptians at thirty-nine years of age, and so ended one of the more brilliant reigns of a Judean king.

Josiah was followed by his son Jehoahaz, who reigned a mere three months in 609 BC before Necho II replaced him with his older brother

---

3. Words in bold type appear in the glossary on page 591.

Eliakim, whom Necho renamed Jehoiakim. Jehoiakim reigned for twelve years (609–597 BC), but he would have no part of continuing his father's spiritual reformation and revival. Instead, as the word of God was read to him from Jeremiah's scroll in his winter apartment, he brazenly took his knife and cut off each section as it was read to him and tossed it into the burning fireplace (Jer 36). Jeremiah had little more than a total disdain for him, declaring he would have "a donkey's funeral" (Jer 22:19).

Jehoiakim's eighteen-year-old son, Jehoiachin, was placed on the throne for only three months (598–597 BC); in March of 597 BC the Babylonians came and took Jehoiachin, the queen mother, the princes, and ten thousand leading citizens, smiths, and crafts people into captivity to Babylon. The Babylonian king Nebuchadnezzar installed Jehoiachin's uncle, Josiah's third son, Mattaniah; Nebuchadnezzar renamed him Zedekiah (just as Necho had changed Eliakim's name to Jehoiakim). Zedekiah ruled from 597 to 587/586 BC. After the capture and destruction of Jerusalem, Nebuchadnezzar appointed Gedaliah (587/586–582?) as governor over the land, but anti-Babylonian conspirators assassinated him, leading to a third deportation to Babylon while others fled to Egypt, taking the prophet Jeremiah with them.

Three especially noteworthy historical events occurred during Jeremiah's era of ministry: first, the battle at the Megiddo Pass between Judah and Egypt that terminated the rule and life of King Josiah in 609 BC; second, the battle at Carchemish in 605 BC between Egypt and Babylon, which Babylon won, handing the region's overlordship to Babylon and away from Assyrian hegemony; and third, the fall of Jerusalem in 587/586 BC, the final note of collapse for the Judean Empire.

In addition to these three events, the year Jeremiah was called to spiritual service (627 BC) was filled with key events in the lives of those in the ancient Near East. For example, Asshurbanipal died (668–627 BC), signaling the beginning of the total collapse of the Assyrian Empire. By 609 BC a power change had occurred in the Near East, with Assyria now gone forever and Babylon taking the lead under Nabopolassar (626–605 BC), who had seized the throne in Babylon in 626 BC and had taken the empire away from the Assyrians. Jerome writes that Jeremiah prophesied for forty years. "In addition, he prophesied one year beyond this time when he was led away to Egypt, where he prophesied in Tahpanhes" (Jerome, 2).

THE COMPOSITION OF JEREMIAH

It is not unreasonable to assume that the text of Jeremiah, as we have it, was in existence somewhere around 580 BC, with the possible exception of Jer 52, which probably came later. (In fact, note Jer 51:64c, "The words of Jeremiah end here.") But this does not mean that there is a chronological order to all the contents of this book. Chapters 36 and 45 are both dated "in the fourth year of Jehoiakim" (605/604 BC), but the intervening chapters, 37–44, report incidents that occurred in 586/7 BC and following.

There still is the issue of the two scrolls. Clearly, chapter 36 tells how Jeremiah was ordered by Yahweh to prepare a scroll with "all the words I have spoken to you concerning Israel, Judah, and all the [other] nations from the time I began speaking to you in the reign of Josiah until now" (Jer 36:2). Baruch, the son of Neriah, assisted Jeremiah in this task: "Baruch, at Jeremiah's dictation, wrote in a scroll-book all the words of Yahweh which [Jeremiah] spoke to him" (36:4). When it was read several months later in the presence of the king, he nonchalantly tossed away each section, after it was read, into his winter fireplace (36:22).

Jeremiah, however, as a result of King Jehoiakim's insolence, was ordered by God to prepare a second scroll, and "write on it all the former words that were on the original scroll, which Jehoiakim, king of Judah, burned up" (36:28). So that is exactly what Jeremiah did, but 36:32 notes "And in addition to that, he added *many words similar to them.*" But in what sense were these words added? Were they an appendix to the contents of the first scroll? Or were they inserted into the body of what had been the existing material of the first scroll? This has opened the tempting prospect that perhaps scholars can trace the origins of both of these scrolls in our existing text. Due to the late setting for chapter 21, the search for distinguishing the two scrolls has focused on the earlier section of the book of Jeremiah (for example, chaps. 1–20), but no scholarly consensus has been achieved. Those who have attempted to trace such minute distinctions have ended up with results that appear to be too elaborate and complex to be convincing, but a generality from this research might plausibly conclude that the first scroll ended with Jer 7:15, and the second extended it to the end of Jer 10. The most convincing mark of such a distinction between the two scrolls may be found in the fact that the prophet is told, "Do not pray for this people; do not lift up a plea or prayer on their behalf; do not plead with me, for I will not listen to you" (7:16). The logic here is that at 36:3 there still was a possibility that "perhaps if the citizens of Judah hear of all the evil that I plan to do to them, each of them will turn from his wicked way, and then I can forgive their wickedness and their sin." Even though this may not be an absolute change, it could be the place where the second scroll came into being.

The content of Jer 11–20 dates to the time up to the end of Jehoiachin's reign and has also been assigned to the period when Jeremiah and Baruch were in hiding and secluded from the public, even though the events it records took place years prior. But nothing definite can be determined on this matter either. The only point worth mentioning about this section is that it ends in chapter 20 on a very pessimistic note and might fit the mindset of one who believes all is now lost after the king's infamous penknife antics as he read the newly discovered book of the law. But again, it is a case based on assumptions, not explicit texts.

There has been a long tradition in Jeremian scholarship that has focused on the poetic oracles of Jeremiah as distinct from the prose sayings and oracles, especially those poetic portions of Jer 2–25. Already in 1901 Duhm (xi–xx), positing a link between prophetic inspiration and the so-called gift of poetic inspiration, limited the original sayings of Jeremiah to 280 verses of poetry. The prose sections Duhm attributed mainly to Baruch (220 verses) and to a long line of exilic supplementers (850 verses). Sigmund Mowinckel[4] attempted to improve on Duhm's work by identifying four literary sources for Jeremiah's work: Source "A" was the poetry in the book; source "B" was the biographical prose narratives, mostly in 19:1–20:6; 26–29; 36–45; source "C" was late Deuteronomistic additions; and source "D" was the late additions of hope, such as those found in chapters 30–31. Many scholars have accepted Mowinckel's undocumented sources with some variations.[5]

However, the separation of poetry and prose in any of the prophets' works, as we have already noted, depended on old distinctions that have

---

4. S. Mowinckel, *Zur Komposition de Buches Jeremia* (Kristiania, 1914).

5. For example, see J. P. Hyatt, "The Deuteronomic Edition of Jeremiah," in *A Prophet to the Nations*, ed. L. G. Perdue and B. W. Kovacs (Winona Lake, IN: Eisenbrauns, 1984), 251. See also E. W. Nicholson, *Preaching to the Exiles: A Study of the Prose Tradition in the Book of Jeremiah* (New York: Schocken, 1971).

largely been rejected or forgotten. Jeremiah's prose seems to accord quite well with the ordinary Heb. written in this period, as seen, for example, on the archaeological find of the Lachish ostraca.

JEREMIAH AND DEUTERONOMY

Many scholars working in the book of Jeremiah have observed the large number of passages in Jeremiah in which the style, vocabulary, and perspective are similar to the book of Deuteronomy. As far back as 1895, S. R. Driver listed sixty-six passages in Deuteronomy that Jeremiah used some eighty-six times.[6] This included not only distinctive phrases but also, in some cases, extended passages such as Jer 3:1 and Deut 24:1-4, or Jer 34:8-14 and Deut 15:2. So there seem to be strong patterns of thought, and even a structure or outline for teaching, linking the two books.

How should we explain this linkage? Conservative scholars have maintained that the book of Deuteronomy was much earlier, since it claims to have been written by Moses. Moreover, if Deuteronomy was part or the whole of what was discovered in the scroll found in the temple in 622/621 BC, it would be strange if it had little or no impact on the people or the prophets of that day. This, then, would be part of the evidence that Jeremiah was aware of the finding of the book of the law and that he presumably used parts of it in his ministry (cf. Huey, 26-28).

However, for those who take a literary-critical approach, the book of Deuteronomy does not have a Mosaic **provenance**. Moreover, what was found in Josiah's day was not simply the book of Deuteronomy but the "Deuteronomistic History" (Joshua, Judges, Samuel, Kings, referred to by scholars as "Dtr"). Accordingly, the stress on the broken covenant found in Jer 11:1-17 is paralleled by the message of Deuteronomy and the concerns of Dtr. However, it is amazing that there is no reference to the prophet Jeremiah in the whole book of Kings, yet Kings has such extensive references to the prophet Isaiah (2 Kgs 19-20), a forerunner to Jeremiah. Jeremiah 52 also strongly resembles the ending of Dtr (2 Kgs 24:18-25:30). So why is there no reference to Jeremiah in the conclusion to 2 Kings, which goes over most of the events surrounding the fall of Jerusalem, despite Jeremiah being most certainly one of the major figures in the events that

---

6. S. R. Driver, *Deuteronomy*, ICC (New York: Charles Scribner's Sons, 1895), xciii.

led up to the fall of Jerusalem? This is puzzling indeed! Could it be that Jeremiah was the author of that final section in 2 Kings and therefore modestly deferred from making any mention of his own presence or contributions during that time? Or is there some other reason for his absence in the book of Kings?

Some argue that there was a real difference between the optimistic view of Jeremiah, of a final divine, gracious regathering in the future of Israel and Judah, and the more pessimistic view of Kings, which could be seen as taking the opposite position. Nevertheless, J. G. McConville argues that the hope Jeremiah expresses for the future is close to what Deut 30:1–10 holds out as well (McConville, 20). So Dtr fails to hold out hope for a return to the promised land of Israel, whereas Jeremiah, Deut 30:1–10, and Hosea express confidence and a strong hope for the future.

But even that conclusion seems to run counter to John Bright's analysis. Bright argues that "both Jeremiah and his opponents [generally the people of Judah] were moved by strong theological convictions."[7] Bright sees Jeremiah's experiences as the result of a collision in theology, wherein the people "stressed God's election of Israel, his enduring purposes for her, and his sure promises to her, which nothing could cancel; the other [theological tack—Jeremiah's emphasis] stressed the righteous commandments which [God] had laid before his people, and which they were obligated to obey if the covenant bond was to be maintained."[8]

On this basis Bright sees Jeremiah as rooted in the theological tradition of the Mosaic covenant, while the people relied on the surety of the Abrahamic/Davidic promises from God. This may explain where the people were coming from, but it is not a good explanation of the actual position found in the Scriptures.

Finally, the literary-critical reconstruction, over against a conservative position, calls for fairly late dates—into exilic and postexilic times—for some Jeremian sections, referred to in this commentary as sections of comfort, and all too often fails to explain why they were originally written the way they were. Moreover, Deuteronomy's preoccupation with pagan idolatry would not make sense if it were written in exilic or postexilic times,

---

7. J. Bright, *Covenant and Promise* (Philadelphia: Westminster, 1976), 165.
8. Ibid., 171.

since by then it had ceased to be an issue. By then, Judah wanted nothing
to do anymore with idols. The times had seen to that.

THE SEPTUAGINTAL TEXT OF JEREMIAH

The book of Jeremiah is unique in that two separate text-types exist for
this book. The Heb. text is represented by the Masoretic Text (MT), and a
shorter text is represented in the Gk. translation found in the Septuagint
(LXX). The key differences between these two texts are:

1. The LXX is substantially shorter, with approximately one-sev-
    enth to one-eighth of the MT not represented in the LXX (about
    2,700 words found in the MT).

2. The LXX arranges the material of Jeremiah differently, mainly
    by placing the prophecies against the Gentile nations in the
    middle of the book (25:14–31:44) instead of the MT's order, near
    the end of the book (46–51).

The MT also has some significant passages missing from the LXX, such as
33:14–26; 39:4–13; 51:44b–49a; and 52:27b–30.

However, these differences may be due to the fact that the LXX is a
translation and not an original text. The MT exhibits more sensitivity to
the context and therefore is to be followed more closely. Most of the words
omitted singly by the LXX appear to result from the translator's policy of
abridgement. For example, the MT introductory formula, "Thus is what
Yahweh Almighty, the God of Israel says," is frequently shortened in the
LXX to "This is what the Lord says." Likewise, personal descriptors in the
MT, such as "king of Babylon," are dropped in the LXX.[9] Jeremiah is not the
only book in the LXX where this happens; therefore, it would not be wise to
adopt the general text of the LXX over the MT Hebrew text only in the book
of Jeremiah. Moreover, the LXX omitted passages regarded as doublets, as
well as the fourth line or fourth colon of a four-line Hebrew parallelism;

---

9. G. Archer, "The Relationship between the Septuagintal Translation and the Massoretic
Text of Jeremiah," *TJ* 12, no. 2 (Fall 1991): 139–50. Archer went on to show that the Alexandrian
translators apparently tried to reduce the ponderous style of the Heb. document to make it
flow somewhat more smoothly.

the translators may have thought it added very little if anything to what was already said.

From the excavations of Cave 4 at Qumran, three mss of Jeremiah have emerged (4QJer[a], 4QJer[b], 4QJer[c]). Of these, two (4QJer[a], 4QJer[c]) represent a text very similar to the Hebrew text; however, 4QJer[b], though very fragmentary, agrees with the LXX in spots.

Even so, this does not account for all the divergences between the MT and the LXX. For example, the six fragmentary mss that make up 4QJer[b] among the DSS appear to support the view that the LXX translators were sincerely attempting to render a different Hebrew text from the original text used for the MT. 2QJer, 4QJer[a], and 4QJer[c] substantially reflect the MT text, but 4QJer[b], showing a number of verses from Jeremiah 9–10, and 4QJer[d], containing parts of Jeremiah 43:2–10, seem to preserve a text with a word and verse order that favors the LXX rendering. So the conclusion is difficult to avoid: by the third century BC there appear to be two text forms in existence for Jeremiah. But one must be careful not to overstate the differences. Most scholars still depend on the Hebrew text rather than the LXX as their basic text.[10]

THEOLOGICAL EMPHASES IN JEREMIAH

THE GOD OF CREATION

Certainly, God is one of the key actors in the book of Jeremiah; therefore, he should head the list of theological observations. Foundational to the prophet's description of God is his role in creation. God "made the earth" (33:2; cf. 10:12–13 = 51:15–16; 27:5; 32:17). He also continues to uphold the operation of the earth (31:35–36; 33:20, 25). It is this Creator Lord who "made the sand a boundary for the sea, a perpetual barrier it cannot cross. Though the waves toss to and fro, they cannot prevail; though they roar, they cannot pass over it" (5:22c–f). Such restraint on the part of the created order of nature only highlights the exasperating conduct of Jeremiah's compatriots, who show no restraint at all when judged against the moral and ethical demands of God. Nevertheless, it is this same divinely imposed order in nature that

---

10. See T. Rata, *The Covenant Motif in Jeremiah's Book of Comfort: Intertextual Studies in Jeremiah 30–33* (New York: Peter Lang, 2007), 11–16.

continues to serve as the assurance that God can be depended on to maintain his word in all areas of life (31:5; 33:21). Therefore, if it is possible to break God's covenant with the day and his covenant with the night, then by the same token God's covenant with David and his seed might likewise be broken (33:21), and Israel and Judah will not be led back and restored to the land of Israel. However, both actions are impossible from the perspective of the promises of God!

God not only was a deity "far away" in his transcendence but was also a God "nearby" in his immanence (23:23). As further attestation, he is able to "test the heart and the mind" of individuals (11:20). In fact, "Nothing is too hard" for him (32:17, 27). He is able to work miracles and do what others think is impossible. He is the Lord of all creation and sovereign over all events and actions on earth.

THE GOD OF LOVE

Just as Hosea emphasizes the love of God for his wayward people (Hos 11:1, 8–9), so Jeremiah describes Israel as "the one I love" (Jer 12:7), or even as "my beloved" (11:15). All the previous signs and wonders done on behalf of Israel were further evidence that Israel was an object of the love of God (31:3; 32:20-22). This, of course, is not to infer that Yahweh was some sort of national deity with no concern or love for other nations. Israel did have a special role in being the agents through whom light of God's revelations would flow to all the nations, but Yahweh was just as much "king of the nations" (10:7) as "the God of all flesh" (32:27). That is why God appointed Jeremiah not only to the nation of Judah but also as "a prophet to the nations" (1:5, 10), for he had Jeremiah deliver his "burden messages" against the nations (46-51) as well as to Judah and Israel.

THE GOD OF PATHOS

Probably more than in most other biblical books, Jeremiah presents God as one having deep feelings, emotions, and passions (pathos). Yahweh shows his love and affection for Israel and the peoples of the earth, but he also shows his deep anger and wrath for all the moral degradation and flaunting of his law. This is hard for many contemporaries to understand, for we have forgotten that it is a matter of evil to stand in the presence of wickedness or sin and not be moved to hate that evil with a passion.

Our problem with God's anger is to be located in our definition of anger. We tend to identify anger with a desire to "get even" or to retaliate against someone who has hurt us. But God's anger doesn't involve that desire; instead, it is the passion of his soul and his total being stirred up against all that is wrong, unjust, unfair, evil, and wicked. If mortals loved righteousness and goodness like God loves it, then we would better understand his revulsion against all that stands opposed to that sense of right, truth, goodness, and justice.

God's anger is provoked when his mortals sin in word or in deed (7:18; 8:19; 32:29-32). Anger must be God's *response*, but it is not one of God's attributes. His response is his expression of grief and dismay over the ruptured relationship that had, or could have, existed otherwise, had it not been for sin, evil, wrong, and injustice. God's grief and sorrow are great in the presence of sin and wickedness. Even though God's sorrow and grief must be distinguished from his anger, the two cannot be separated. But the matter never rests at that point, for his grace and mercy are greater than the aggregate deeds and words of unrighteousness by mortals. To the amazement of all, this Lord can also atone for the sins of those who persistently err and sin against him, so that his grace and mercy might eventually triumph for all who call on him in faith. This would be the sticking point of interpretation for those in Jeremiah's day as well as in our own day: how could God simultaneously hate our sin, yet love the sinner? But all who make this objection have never thought about the way they regard themselves; they oftentimes hate some of the stuff they do, but that does not keep them from having a decent regard for themselves. If we can do that for ourselves, then we ought to withdraw the objection when God does the same: he does indeed love us, yet he also totally dislikes some of our actions.

SIN AND JUDGMENT

It is clear that as a result of Judah's "wickedness" (רָעָה, *rāʿâ*), "disaster" (רָעָה, *rāʿâ*) would break out on the people. This is merely to say that evil has a distinctive "fruit" that was associated with it (1:14, 16; 6:19; 12:2). In fact, the verb for "to punish" (פָּקַד) is the same verb meaning "to visit" on the people the fruit, or results, of their own deeds, whether they were evil doings or good actions (5:9; 14:10; 21:14). In so doing, God allows the consequences that are already present in the people's wicked situation to be the method he uses to judge them.

GOD'S USE OF HISTORICAL MEANS TO ACCOMPLISH HIS WILL

Often what is ascribed to God is actually what he permits to take place. We moderns are more concerned to state the differences between primary and secondary causes, but what God *allows* may also be directly attributed to him as the One in control of providence. Thus, God brought judgment in the book of Jeremiah by means of the king of Babylon, which was through Nebuchadnezzar, just as God brought deliverance through King Cyrus. In order to do this, God may use the method of "stirring up" the spirit of these kings and their movements (6:22; 25:32; 50:9, 41; 51:1, 11). This entails that God must use an imperfect mortal character to carry out his perfect will. These kings and generals act as God's "servants" (25:9; 27:6; 43:10) because they do indeed serve God and his purposes, even though they are culpable and responsible for the wrong and evil they perpetuate.

This does not mean, however, that anything and everything one of his servants does can be an evil *directly* attributed to God, for even though God used Nebuchadnezzar to carry out the destruction of Jerusalem, it did not mean that *all* Nebuchadnezzar did was thereby approved by God or that God was the immediate cause of what he did. Nebuchadnezzar, in fact, often overreached and exceeded the limits God had set for him (25:11–14; 51:24), even though he was on a mission from God. Thus, the Babylonian king was not a puppet in the hands of God whose will and actions were predetermined by God and over which he had no control, for God could still be angry with him for going *over* and *beyond* what he had been authorized to do.

Mortals are still responsible for what they do, even when they are on a mission for God. Some have wanted to infer from these observations that God is not as all-knowing or omniscient as Scripture has often described him, but that God has left a sort of openness about the future (also sometimes called recently "open theism"), so that there is room left by God for our human freedom in cases where the Lord seemed to deliberately express no preferences. But this is an incorrect conclusion; it fails to note that along with divine sovereignty there is just as strong a case to be made for human responsibility and human culpability. God has both a directive and a permissive will.

GOD'S WORDS OF SALVATION

Throughout the whole book of Jeremiah there is the repetition of the ancient words of promise given to the patriarchs and David intermingled with words of judgment (3:15-18; 12:14-16; 16:14-15; 23:5-8; 24:4-7). God will in the end rebuild and replant his people in their land, despite all that has happened in their horrible history of disobedience (7:5-7; 18:7-8; 22:1-5; 24:8-10; 38:17-18; 42:10). The future of Judah will not depend on their own works but will depend on God himself, who had long ago made "an ever-lasting covenant" with them that he will never draw back from doing good to them (32:40). In order to accomplish this, God himself "will give them one heart and one way, that they may fear [him] for all time" (32:39 NRSV). This salvation will be possible because of the new covenant that will be internalized and written on people's hearts (31:31-34).[11]

OUTLINE OF JEREMIAH

The book of Jeremiah is notoriously difficult to outline, for there are few chronological indicators, much less a clear grouping of topics. However, on three different occasions Jeremiah calls special attention to the fourth year of Jehoiakim: 25:1; 36:1; and 45:1. The year of 605/604 BC was most determinative for Judah and for the affairs of the Near East. This was the year in which Babylon, after previously defeating the Assyrians at the Battle of Nineveh in 612 BC, went on to defeat Pharaoh Necho, the only remaining rival for the world empire that Babylon now aspired to attain. 605/604 BC was also the year that Nebuchadnezzar got news in Egypt that his father, Nabopolassar, had died. Nebuchadnezzar quickly returned home to ascend the throne. All this happened in that crucial fourth year of King Jehoiakim of Judah, 605 BC. Thus, while these few dates allow for a placement of some portions of Jeremiah chronologically, the discussions on this year are spread out among other prophecies indicates that the book itself is not

---

11. See Rata, *Covenant Motif in Jeremiah's Book of Comfort*, 41-48.

the strict chronology that modern readers desire. A chronological outline is not possible.

The best suggestion for outlining this book comes from Laetsch's commentary on Jeremiah. Laetsch (12–15) suggests that the call of the prophet in chapter 1 can be divided into three notable sections: 1:4–10; 1:11–16; and 1:17–19, which in turn correspond to three sections containing conclusions to texts that began in the only dated chapters—25; 36; and 45. In these three sections Jeremiah is promised:

1. God's protection, as he was called to be God's spokesperson, regardless of his personal feelings or desires (1:4–10 = 2:1–25:38)

2. the complete destruction of Judah by an enemy from the north, later identified as Babylon (20:4–6; 25:1, 9–12) in (1:11–16 = 26:1–36:32)

3. that God would provide his help and deliverance to Jeremiah despite opposition to Jeremiah increasing, as would unbelief in God's call for repentance (1:17–19 = 37:1–45:5)

Using these three sections from chapter 1 in Jeremiah as a starting point, each is matched with the main content of the book of Jeremiah by noting how chapters 25, 36, and 45 are appropriate conclusions to each of the motifs established in the introductory chapter and its call to Jeremiah. Laetsch's proposal has slight adaptions below, namely, that his second section is further divided here into three sections: 26–29; 30–33; 34–36. Even though these chapters have been further divided (focuses: unbelief, restoration of the land, and a call for faithfulness), these three sections are understood as working together as Laetsch described. The resulting outline is as follows:

I. Prologue: The Call of Jeremiah (1:1–19)
A. The Dateline of Jeremiah's Call (1:1–3)
B. God's Appointment to Faithfulness (1:4–10; foreshadowing 2:1–25:38)
1. His Authorization (1:4)
2. His Commission (1:5)

---

12. The outline follows the versification of the English text; verse ranges in square brackets denote the Hebrew versification when it differs from the English.

COMMENTARY BIBLIOGRAPHY

Works in the commentary bibliography are cited in parentheses throughout this commentary.

Brown, M. "Jeremiah." In *Expositor's Bible Commentary*, vol. 7, 21–572. Grand Rapids: Zondervan, 2010.

Brueggemann, W. *A Commentary on Jeremiah: Exile and Homecoming.* Grand Rapids: Eerdmans, 1998.

Craigie, P., P. H. Kelley, and J. F. Drinkard. *Jeremiah 1–25.* WBC 26. Dallas: Word, 1991.

Dyer, C. H. "Jeremiah." In *The Bible Knowledge Commentary: An Exposition of the Scriptures*, edited by J. F. Walvoord and R. B. Zuck, vol. 1. Wheaton, IL: Victor, 1985.

Fretheim, T. E. *Jeremiah.* Smyth and Helwys Bible Commentary. Macon, GA: Smyth and Helwys, 2002.

Holladay, W. I. *Jeremiah 1: A Commentary on the Book of the Prophet Jeremiah (Chapters 1–25).* Hermeneia. Minneapolis: Fortress, 1986.

———. *Jeremiah 2: A Commentary on the Book of the Prophet Jeremiah (Chapters 26–52).* Hermeneia. Minneapolis: Fortress, 1986.

Huey, F. B. *Jeremiah, Lamentations.* NAC 16. Nashville: Broadman &

Holman, 1993.

Hyatt, J. P. "Jeremiah." In *The Interpreter's Bible*, edited by G. A. Buttrick, vol. 5, 777-1142. New York: Abingdon, 1956.

Jerome. *Commentary on Jeremiah.* Translated by Michael Graves. Edited by Christopher A. Hall. Ancient Christian Texts. Downers Grove, IL: IVP Academic, 2011.

Keown, G. L., P. J. Scalise, and T. G. Smothers. *Jeremiah 26-52.* WBC 27. Waco, TX: Word, 1995.

Laetsch, T. *Commentary on Jeremiah.* St. Louis: Concordia, 1952.

Thompson, J. A. *The Book of Jeremiah.* New International Commentary on the Old Testament. Grand Rapids: Eerdmans, 1980.

Voth, S. "Jeremiah." In *Zondervan Illustrated Bible Background Commentary*, edited by J. H. Walton, vol. 4, 228-358. Grand Rapids: Zondervan, 2009.

Wenthe, D. O., ed. *Jeremiah, Lamentations.* Edited by T. C. Oden. ACCS 12. Downers Grove, IL: InterVarsity Press, 2009.

PROLOGUE:
THE CALL OF JEREMIAH (1:1–19)

Call or consecration narratives in the Old Testament exhibit parallel elements even if they are not always completely identical. Norman Habel finds six constituent literary elements in the calls of four prophets and one leader in Israel.[1] Those who are called include Moses (Exod 3:1–4:17), Gideon (Judg 6:11–23), Isaiah (Isa 6:1–13), Jeremiah (Jer 1:4–10; 40:1–11), and Ezekiel (Ezek 1:1–3:11). The six literary elements that form the shape of their calls, though not every element is present in each call, are:

1. a "divine confrontation"

2. an "introductory word"

3. a "commission"

4. an "objection"

5. a "reassurance"

6. a "sign"[2]

But there are differences as well:

1. Jeremiah's call does not exhibit the first two elements in Habel's list.

---

1. N. Habel, "The Form and Significance of the Call Narratives," *ZAW* 77, no. 3 (1965): 297–323.
2. Ibid.

2. The calls of Isaiah and Ezekiel are accompanied by strong visual features in which they see themselves as being in the heavenly presence.

3. Gideon is called in the same general way, but he is not called to be a prophet, as the others are.

4. Both Moses's and Gideon's calls include a description of the circumstances of their call, while Jeremiah's, for example, simply begins with the divine call without any circumstances surrounding it.

However, looking at the last four elements of the call and omitting the calls of Isaiah and Ezekiel results in this table, as constructed by William I. Holladay (1986, 26-27), of elements in the calls of Jeremiah, Moses, and Gideon:

	Jeremiah	Moses	Gideon
Commission	Jer 1:5	Exod 3:10	Judg 6:14
Objection	Jer 1:6	Exod 3:11	Judg 6:15
Reassurance	Jer 1:7–8	Exod 3:12	Judg 6:16
Sign	Jer 1:9	Exod 3:12	Judg 6:17–22

There is, however, one distinctive factor in Jeremiah's call: he was to be a prophet "to the nations" (1:5, 10) as well as to Judah. Moreover, Jeremiah had been called even prior to his birth, which is another distinctive in the Old Testament; it is matched in the New Testament by the call of the apostle Paul (Gal 1:15).

THE DATELINE OF JEREMIAH'S CALL (1:1–3)

TRANSLATION

1 The words of Jeremiah,[3] son of Hilkiah, from the priests who were in Anathoth, in the land of Benjamin, **2** to whom the word of Yahweh came in the days of Josiah, son of Amon king of Judah, in the thirteenth year of his reign. **3** It was [also] in the days of Jehoiakim, son of Josiah, king of Judah, until the end[4] of the fifth month of the eleventh year of Zedekiah, son of Josiah, king of Judah when [the people of] Jerusalem went into exile.

COMMENTARY

The opening lines introduce both the man Jeremiah and his book, supplying a brief description of Jeremiah's family, residence, and times, and the date of his call to the ministry.

1:1 Jeremiah came from the priestly family of Hilkiah, in a town named Anathoth, which was north of Jerusalem by about two or three miles. Anathoth was the town where Abiathar, one of the two priests under King David, had been exiled for backing David's son Adonijah, who rebelled against his father (1 Kgs 2:26–27). Jerusalem was in the territory of Judah, but Anathoth was in the tribe of Benjamin. Today it is usually thought to be Anata, a name originally derived from the Canaanite goddess Anat. Albrecht Alt, however, locates Anathoth on the rocky promontory the Arabs call Ras el-Harrubeh, "summit of the carob-beans," a few hundred meters southwest from the present Arab village.[5] Soundings[6] at this site suggest that it began with an Israelite settlement in the Israelite monarchy.

---

3. LXX has τὸ ῥῆμα τοῦ θεοῦ ὃ ἐγένετο ἐπὶ Ιερεμιαν, "The word of God which came to Jeremiah."

4. LXX omits םח, "end," in the phrase "until the end of the fifth month." This could be because the regnal year differed from the calendar year.

5. A. Bergman and W. F. Albright, "Soundings of the Supposed Site of Old Testament Anathoth," *BASOR* 62 (1936): 22–26; A. Bergman and W. F. Albright, "Anathoth?," *BASOR* 63 (1936): 22–23. The modern village of Anata preserves the name of the ancient village; A. Negev and S. Gibson, eds., *Archaeological Encyclopedia of the Holy Land*, rev. ed. (New York: Continuum, 2001), 33.

6. Archaeologists take "soundings" of an area suspected of hiding archaeological treasures by digging test pits without fully excavating the area. This provides them with a sample of what lies underground and enables them to determine whether the area would be a fruitful place to conduct a full excavation.

1:2–3 If the word of Yahweh came to Jeremiah during the thirteenth year of Josiah's reign, that would mean that Jeremiah was called about 627 BC, five years prior to finding the "book of the law" in Josiah's eighteenth year, in 622/621 BC. But does the "thirteenth year" point to the year of Jeremiah's birth or the year of his calling?

J. Philip Hyatt and William L. Holladay (1986, 9–15) emphasize that even before Yahweh formed Jeremiah in the womb, he had known him and set him apart as one he had appointed to be a preacher to Judah and to the nations (1:5). On this reading, then, 627 BC was the year of Jeremiah's *birth*, not the year of his *call* to serve God. They give three reasons for their preference for this view:

1. There are no Jeremian oracles that can be confidently dated to the days of Josiah, according to some.

2. There is no direct word from Jeremiah about any of the reforms of Josiah.

3. There is no good candidate for the "foe from the north" (1:14) in 627 BC.

A later ministry, as proposed by Hyatt and Holladay, would solve all three of these difficulties, since Jeremiah would have begun his ministry in the early days of King Jehoiakim's reign, about 609–598 BC, after King Josiah had been killed, in 609 BC. However, this view is problematic because "this would be an uncommon use of the expression 'the word of Yahweh came'" (Huey, 48). It also "confuses the events of the coming word in vv. 2–4 with that of the Lord's forming in v. 5. The latter verse only says God set him apart before birth" (Huey, 48).

Another view, representing the majority of the commentaries, identifies the thirteenth year as the date of Jeremiah's calling (cf. Huey, 48). This places the prophet's birth around 643 BC and sets the date of his call when he was somewhere around fifteen or sixteen years of age, in 627 BC. This would mean that he had lived through some of the reforms that had already begun and through the exciting days of the finding of the book of the law in 622/621 BC in the house of God.

A third view, espoused by T. C. Gordon,[7] but one that has not found many adherents, is that the "thirteenth year" (1:2) is a scribal error for "twenty-third" year. The difference between the two spellings in Heb. is simply the pl. ending on the word for "ten" (an םי-, -im, ending form), making it the word for "twenty" plus the word for "three." If this view is correct, then Jeremiah began his preaching in the year 617 BC, just as Nabopolassar of Babylon began his attack on Assyria and initiated what would become the end for the Assyrian domination in the Near East and the commencement of a Babylonian hegemony. But there is no textual support for this supposition of "twenty-three" instead of "thirteen," and thus it fails.

The first and third views present the most problems; therefore, it is best to go with the second option, the prevailing view, that Jeremiah was called by God in 627 BC and that he began his ministry as a lad—somewhere around sixteen years of age. In support of the view are the two chronological references to Josiah's reign in 1:2 and 25:3, the specific reference to King Josiah in 3:6–14, and the presumption in 2:18 that Assyria is still a power to deal with, which would no longer be true if Jeremiah had begun his ministry in Jehoiakim's time.[8]

During that time things were changing quickly in the Near East. Judah was determined to act exactly opposite to what they had been taught in the Torah. The capital city of the Assyrians, Nineveh, had fallen in 612 BC, and the Babylonian armies were on the move to take over where Assyria had left off. This and more would lead to the fall of Jerusalem to the Babylonians as they returned several times to Judah and finally captured Jerusalem and took the people into exile in Babylon. But behind all these changes there was the word of Yahweh (1:2) that would guide the prophet and mark it all as more than mere happenstance.

The content of what Jeremiah had to teach us came as a word from God himself. This is what gave that word its authority and its power, which lasts even to our own day. While men and armies were on the move, the word of God was even more effective in challenging the directions mortals wanted to take history. But God's word would be much more successful and

---

7. T. C. Gordon, "A New Date for Jeremiah," *ExpTim* 44 (1932–33): 562–65.

8. On the chronology of Jer 1:3 see R. C. Young, "When Did Jerusalem Fall?," *JETS* 47, no. 1 (March 2004): 21–38.

would endure over all. God's word must never be demeaned and reduced to a secondary or subordinate position in our understanding and living.

GOD'S APPOINTMENT TO FAITHFULNESS (1:4-10)

TRANSLATION

4 The word of Yahweh came to me,[9] saying,

5 "Before I formed you in the womb, I knew you. Before you came out of the womb, I set you apart; I appointed you as a prophet to the nations."

6 I said, "Alas, Lord Yahweh, I do not know what to say, for I am a child."

7 But Yahweh said to me,

"Do not say I am [only] a child,[10]

For everywhere I send you,[11] you must[12] go,

And you must say all that I command you.

8 Do not be afraid in their presence,

For I am with you and will rescue you, declares Yahweh."

9 Then Yahweh stretched out his hand,[13] and touched my mouth and said to me,

"Behold, I have put my words in your mouth.

10 See, this [very] day I have appointed you

Over nations and over kingdoms,

To uproot and to tear down,

To destroy and to overthrow,[14]

To build and to plant."

---

9. LXX has πρὸς αὐτόν, "to him," instead of "to me."

10. Some LXX mss add "for" before "I am only a child."

11. Since עַל and אֶל are used interchangeably in Jeremiah, "everywhere I send you" can mean "wherever" or "to whomever."

12. The modal "must" translation is prompted by the preceding juss. verb. This yiqtol verb continues the modality already established.

13. LXX adds πρός με, "to me," after "stretched out his hand."

14. Some commentators see the verbs וּלְהַאֲבִיד וְלַהֲרוֹס, "to destroy" and "to overthrow," as additions. The Tg., the Syr., and the Vg. follow the MT.

COMMENTARY

His Authorization (1:4)

The prophet begins as he had in 1:2, "The word of Yahweh came to me." Jeremiah uses this clause or its equivalent phrase ("Thus says Yahweh") some 157 times out of a total of 349 such examples in the Old Testament.[15] Accordingly, in the four call elements noted above, it would appear we need to add a fifth element: that is, his authorization.[16] Had Jeremiah not been given a word from the living God, what could he have offered in the drastic situation of such strong opposition to which he was going to be called?

It was God who took the initiative to summon young Jeremiah to a lifetime of service on behalf of the high calling of heaven itself. The text reports this event as an actual experience of Jeremiah. Some have recently tried to lessen the personal aspect of this call by suggesting that it was more of a liturgical experience, similar to an ordination service (Brueggemann 1998, 23). Robert Carroll understands this call narrative as a literary device constructed editorially to supply the needed authority for what was to follow in this book.[17]

Nevertheless, the prophet uses the typical prophetic-word formula (as in 1 Sam 15:10; 1 Kgs 6:11; Hos 1:1; Joel 1:1; Mic 1:1; Zeph 1:1) to demonstrate that what he had to say was indeed from God alone. Jeremiah is sent as God's messenger.

His Commission (1:5)

The text teaches: "Before I formed you in the womb, I knew you. Before you came out of the womb, I set you apart." Even before Jeremiah was "formed" in the womb or "[was] born" or "[was] coming out" (impf. verb forms of יָצַר and יָצָא), God "knew" (יָדַע) him. Thus, both prior to his conception and while he was still a developing embryo, God had already decided to choose him and "set him apart" (קָדֵשׁ). This last act of setting him apart is from the Heb. root "to be holy, to be set apart." Therefore, God gave more than

---

15. J. G. S. S. Thompson, *The Old Testament View of Revelation* (Grand Rapids: Eerdmans, 1960), 60–61.

16. See also E. H. Roshwalb, "Jeremiah 1.4–10: 'Lost and Found' in Translation and a New Interpretation," *JSOT* 34, no. 3 (2010): 351–76.

17. R. P. Carroll, *From Chaos to Covenant* (New York: Crossroad, 1981), 49–58.

intellectual properties of divine knowledge to the prophet; he also granted him an intimate relationship. He would be wholly given over to the work for which God was now dedicating him.

God "appointed" (נָתַן, "to give") him as a "prophet to the nations." This verb is used four times in this chapter (vv. 5, 9, 15, 18).[18] Clearly God's sovereign hand can be seen in Jeremiah's personal life, as it will be seen in the panorama of history itself.

The etymology of the word "prophet" (נָבִיא) is still disputed, but it does not mean, as was formerly claimed—based on an incorrect Heb. root of נָבַע, meaning "to boil over"—"to bubble up," as if the word were pointing to a person who had lost control of himself and was giving some supernatural, automatic verbalizations that were not typical of his own personality under normal circumstances. It is better to see the word meaning "prophet" as coming from an Akkadian cognate with the pass. meaning of "one who is called."[19]

The call to be a prophet to the nations[20] was a distinctive appointment to say the least. Instead of what might otherwise be regarded as a provincial message appropriate only for Israel, here was an appointment and a message for the Gentile nations at large as well.

His Objection (1:6)

Jeremiah protested that he was only a "child" (נַעַר), a word meaning anything from an "infant" (Exod 2:6) to a "boy/child" (1 Sam 3:1) or even someone up to young manhood, a "young man" (Gen 14:24; 22:3; 34:19).[21] His point, similar to the one Moses made at his call (Exod 4:10–16), was that he felt inadequate to the task of speaking God's word to these nations and peoples. His feelings of unworthiness and incompetence for such a high office are clear. Furthermore, given his inexperience and youthfulness, he simply

---

18. We have translated it slightly differently each time ("appointed," "put," "set up," and "made").

19. *TLOT* 2:697; *HALOT* 1:661.

20. See W. Vischer, "The Vocation of the Prophet to the Nations: An Exegesis of Jeremiah 1:4–10," *Interpretation* 9, no. 3 (1955): 310–17.

21. See B. A. Strawn, "Jeremiah's In/Effective Plea: Another Look at נער in Jeremiah I 6," *VT* 55, no. 3 (2005): 366–77.

did not know how to "speak" (דָּבַר), a verb commonly used of proclaiming God's word publicly (for example, Exod 4:14; 6:29; Jer 35:2).

His Assurance (1:7–8)

"I am with you and will rescue you." Jeremiah's objection is rejected by Yahweh, who counseled him, "Do not say, 'I am only a child.'" Since the origin of the message was not Jeremiah himself, the objection missed the point. The content of the message was to be God's business, not the prophet's. That should have lifted the burden off Jeremiah's shoulders. But Yahweh went on to promise his presence and his deliverance. "I will be with you" is the oft-repeated divine promise, found over one hundred times in the OT. The living God would personally stand alongside this young man; however, God's standing will not be as some would understand this expression in other circumstances, where standing "with" someone means to be available in general, or as we mortals so often say, "I'm with you" or "I am behind you" (though we never say how far behind that person we actually are). That understanding of this promise would not be correct.

This same strong support statement appears in Exod 3:12 and in Judg 6:16, for example, as it does in many promises elsewhere (Isa 30:10–11; 41:10; 43:5). God will repeat this promise to his prophet in Jer 1:19 and 15:20. Moreover, God will "rescue" him just as he had "rescued" Israel from Egypt (Exod 3:8; 5:23; 12:27) or as he had rescued David from the lion (1 Sam 17:37).

His Sign (1:9)

"Then Yahweh reached out his hand and touched my mouth." Just as Yahweh touches Isaiah's mouth with a burning coal from off the altar (Isa 6:6–7), and Ezekiel is commanded to eat the written scroll (Ezek 3:1–3), so Yahweh reaches out his hand and causes (hiphil stem) it to touch Jeremiah—a deliberate and purposive act of God that he explains immediately. God "had put" (pf. verb form of completed action) his own words into the mouth of his prophet. This is why there was no point in Jeremiah protesting his inexperience or his youthfulness; the work is the sovereign, but gentle, work of God, not the work of the prophet.

The Summary of the Commission (1:10)

"See, this [very] day I have appointed you over nations and kingdoms." Moreover, Yahweh promises: "Now, I have put my words in your mouth." This promise is reminiscent of the almost-identical words given to Moses in Deut 18:18: "I will put my words in his mouth." There is no clearer way of saying that God will personally be the source of Jeremiah's message, even though it takes an anthropomorphism to say it, for remember: "God is spirit" (John 4:24). The word of God in the prophet's mouth will act like a sledgehammer; it will pulverize the rock (Jer 23:29), which symbolizes the hardness of the hearts of the people to whom Jeremiah would minister during his many years of service.

This completes a ministerial installation service; it will be finalized on that very day! The word "to appoint" (פָּקַד, meaning "to visit, inspect, supervise," in the causative hiphil stem) means Jeremiah has been made an inspector. He will be God's vice-regent, as viewed from our earthly point of view; yet when viewed from God's perspective, it is God who is the sovereign inspector and Judge over all.

Six metaphors dominate the substance and heart of Jeremiah's message to Judah and to the Gentile nations: four of them are negative: "to uproot, to tear down, to destroy, and to overthrow," and two of them are positive: "to build and to plant." Some or all of these purpose statements appear throughout the whole book (Jer 12:14–17; 16:19–21; 18:7–9; 24:6; 25:9–32; 31:28, 40; 42:10; 45:4). Necessarily, his words would need to dislodge entrenched evil throughout all Judah and in all the nations; but his word would also contain the content for rebuilding and replanting a new era of God's grace.

Our day shares with Jeremiah's seventh-century BC times some of the same leading indicators of our need for a new word from God: (1) rampant moral and spiritual decay, (2) more evidence of external religiosity and formal ritualism than a truly, heart-felt evidence of the real power and presence of God, (3) increased apostasy and departure from the revealed doctrines of Scripture, (4) increased international conflicts and economic tensions among the nations, and (5) increased evidences of divine judgment and warnings seen in families, the world about us, and our national leaders.

But just as God took Jeremiah and gave him and his teaching as a gift to Judah and the nations, and just as he had taken the Levites (Num 8:16, 19) as his special captives years ago, so God is still taking individuals today and giving them as "captives" for the work of the ministry, even though the titles and times may be different (Eph 4:7–15).

Those who know themselves best feel as terribly inadequate to serve when they are called to do so by God as Jeremiah felt. But all of us, along with Jeremiah, can likewise know the assurance and blessing of the presence and power of the word of God that is now found in Scripture, whose source and reception of those words was distinctive and unique. Therefore our call will differ in that area from what is demonstrated in the life of Jeremiah, since he was the recipient of the revelation from God. Yet the other elements of Jeremiah's call narrative will remain the same for us, for is that not what the call of Gideon also exemplifies and encourages us to personally experience (see Judg 6)?

THE PREDICTION OF A CONQUEROR
FROM THE NORTH (1:11–16)

TRANSLATION

11 The word of Yahweh came to me: "What do you see, Jeremiah?"[22] I replied: "A branch of an almond tree [is what] I am seeing." **12** Yahweh said to me, "You have seen correctly, for I am watching over my word to fulfill it." **13** The word of Yahweh came to me, again, saying: "What do you see?" "I see a boiling pot; its lip is [tipped] from the sides of the north," I responded. **14** Then Yahweh said to me: "From the north disaster will be poured out[23] on all the inhabitants of the land, **15** for I am about to summon all the families of the northern kingdoms,"[24] declares Yahweh.

"[Their kings] will come and each will set up his throne at the entrance to the gate of Jerusalem, against all her surrounding walls and against all the cities of Judah. **16** And I will declare my judgment over them concerning

---

22. The LXX omits "Jeremiah."
23. The LXX has ἐκκαυθήσεται, "will be kindled," instead of "will be poured out."
24. The LXX has "kingdom" where the MT has "families of the kingdoms."

all their wickedness in which they have forsaken me, when they burned incense to other gods, and they worshiped what their hands had made."

COMMENTARY

This section of the opening chapter records two visions: the first of an almond branch in vv. 11–12 and the second of a "boiling [cooking] pot" in vv. 13–16. These two visions have some of the same elements in the visions recorded in Jer 24:1–10 and Amos 7:7–9; 8:1–3. The objects seen are found in everyday life, but whether they are actually experienced externally or just seen inwardly cannot be established from what is said. A vision is different from a dream in that a recipient of a vision is not asleep, as one would be in a dream revelation, but fully awake and conscious of his mental faculties.

The purpose of the visions, however, is clear: to provide reassurances to Jeremiah over against the large amount of opposition that he would encounter in his ministry. God once again assures him that he will be with the prophet and that his word will be effective. The prophet will not need to bring about the fulfillment of his own words; God will take care of that.

1:11–12 At the center of the first vision is a wordplay on the name of the "almond tree" (שָׁקֵד, shāqēd) and that the Lord himself would be "watching" (שֹׁקֵד, shôqēd) "to see that [his] word [was being] fulfilled" (v. 12b). The focus here is not on the "branch" or "twig" (מַקֵּל), which could be made into a stick or a staff (1 Sam 17:40, 43), implying a "threatening rod of castigation." Instead, the focus is on the wordplay of the name for this amond tree, nicknamed "the watcher" or "the wakeful," and God's persistent care in "watching" over his word to see that it would not go unfulfilled.

But there is more to this vision; the almond tree is the first to bloom in spring, with its white blooms coming in January or early February. Accordingly, the almond "watches" for the spring. Jeremiah uses this same verb, "watching" (שֹׁקֵד, shôqēd), three other times (Jer 32:28; 44:27; 5:6). God's "watching" would be "to uproot, tear down, destroy, and bring disaster" as well as "to build and to plant" (31:28). This means that despite all the maneuvering of Judahites in the days of Jeremiah's preaching, Yahweh still controlled the shape, flow, and direction of history.

1:13–16 The next vision, in vv. 13–16, begins, for the third time (vv. 4, 11, 13), with "The word of the Yahweh came to me," but this time adds "again." Once again he asks, "What do you see?" This time it is a "cooking pot" used for cooking food or boiling water (v. 13). Most interpreters render the Heb. word נָפוּחַ as "boiling," but this word by itself does not imply that any water was involved. The word instead is a qal pass. ptc. of the Heb. root meaning "to blow, to fan, to breathe." This pot was "tipped away" or "its lip/rim was away from the north." The meaning, then, is that disaster will come from the north, the very route that most invaders had to take to invade Israel and Judah, since invasions could hardly come from the east through the desert to the east of Israel and the Transjordan. There is no name or identity given to this attacking foe until we come to Jer 25:9, where Babylon is cited for the first time. For the time being, the foe is only identified as "the peoples of the northern kingdoms" (v. 15). The "kings" from these northern lands, which at this time would also include Assyria, would come "and set up their thrones in the entrance to the gates of Jerusalem" (v. 15b), which was especially true of Babylon, and these northern kingdoms would come against "all the towns of Judah" (v. 15e).[25]

The reason for both of these announcements of these impending judgments is in v. 16: Judah's idolatry. Judah's worship of other gods flew right in the face of the first and second commandments (Exod 20:3–4; Deut 5:7–8). God would bring "calamity, disaster" (רָעָה, $rā'â$) on them for all the "wickedness" (רָעָה, $rā'â$, v. 16) they had done. In other words, the "calamity and disaster" came from the "wickedness" of "forsaking [God]."

Both of these visions were mercifully given as warnings to Judah to repent and turn back to God. That God constantly observes all that we do and all that is happening on our planet should make us aware that nothing is hidden from our God. He sees everything, so why do we think we are hiding something from God's sight? So, if we cannot hide from God, let us be open and forthcoming in all that he commands those who love him to do!

Our Lord also promised that he would be with Jeremiah. The powerful presence of our Lord is no small favor, both to his messengers and to all his people. Praise God for the assurance of his presence.

---

25. See S. L. Harris, "The Second Vision of Jeremiah: Jer 1:13–15," *JBL* 102, no. 2 (1983): 281–88.

THE FIERCE OPPOSITION AGAINST
JEREMIAH (1:17–19)

TRANSLATION

17 "But you, gird up your loins for battle, stand up and announce to them everything I command you. Do not be terrified of them, lest I terrify you in front of them. **18** For my part, behold I have made you today a fortified city, an iron pillar, a bronze wall [to stand] against the whole land, against the kings of Judah,²⁶ its officials, its priests,²⁷ and the people of the land. **19** They will fight against you, but they will not overcome you, for I am with you to deliver you," declares Yahweh.

COMMENTARY

1:17–18 As a result of the call narrative, which installed the prophet, and with two confirming visions concerning what God would carry out, in this final section of the first chapter the prophet is told to "Gird up your loins for battle" (v. 17a). This is the language of one who is to prepare to go into the fray, which apparently awaits the prophet from those who dislike his message. All long-flowing garments were to be lifted up and tucked securely around the waist under a belt, either physically in a real battle or metaphorically for those in the kind of battle in which Jeremiah will find himself.²⁸ Jeremiah's part is to "stand up" and get ready to speak God's word (v. 17b), while God's part was to make him "a fortified city, an iron pillar and a bronze wall" so that Jeremiah could "stand against the whole land" (v. 18). This division of labor is set forth clearly in the Heb. text, which has "for your part" (וְאַתָּה, wĕʾattāh, v. 17) set over against Yahweh's saying "for my part" (וַאֲנִי, waʾănî, v. 18). The prophet is "not to be panicked" (אַל־תֵּחַת, v. 17c). Therefore, the city of Jerusalem may be vulnerable, but Jeremiah will be an invulnerable fortress secured by God. But the prophet could not say anything other than what Yahweh commanded him to say, regardless of whether it was popular or not.

---

26. The MT has "against all the land of the kings of Judah," while the LXX only has "to the kings of Judah."

27. The LXX omits "its officials, its priests."

28. See K. Low, "Implications Surrounding Girding the Loins in Light of Gender, Body, and Power," *JSOT* 36, no. 1 (2011): 3–30.

1:19 The kings of Judah, the officials, the priests, and the populace in general may "fight against" him (v. 19), but none will be successful. God will be "with [him]" and will "deliver [him]" (v. 19b), so the results are a foregone conclusion. However, should Jeremiah have a failure of nerve and start being frightened by them, God will "terrify [him] in front of them" (v. 17d).

The Bible frequently urges believers to gird up the loins of their mind so that they might be ready to confront all the various insidious attacks of the evil one. In a similar way, God's messenger is told to get ready for action, for even though God would be powerfully present with Jeremiah, that did not mean there was nothing for him to do by way of preparing for the onslaught that he would face in serving the Lord.

Yes, officialdom and the populace itself might try to take on Jeremiah and all of us who attempt to serve the Lord day after day, but our Lord notifies them in advance that none of them will be successful against Jeremiah, nor will any of the hosts arraigned against any of us be any more successful, for God is our refuge and strength, a very present help in time of trouble.

THE PERSONAL STRUGGLES
OF THE PROPHET (2:1–25:38)

For the explanation behind grouping these chapters together as one large section, see "Outline of Jeremiah" in the general introduction.

IT'S TIME TO ACKNOWLEDGE THE
NATION'S APOSTASY (2:1–37)

This is one of Jeremiah's earlier prophecies, perhaps even his first. Even though there is no formal evidence to that effect, there are some indications that this is the case. For example, nowhere does it record that Jeremiah accepted the call of God, as he most assuredly did—though not as Isaiah directly answered, "Here am I, send me!" (Isa 6:8). Yet his acceptance of this call must be tacitly understood, for it is is presumed when the message to him begins with the divine commission to "Go and proclaim" (Jer 2:1). There are no questions asked and no protests noted. Also, Jer 2 refers to both "Israel" and "Judah" (vv. 3, 4, 14, 26), which would seem to indicate an earlier day when the memory of the northern tribes was still fresh in the minds of Jeremiah's listeners. Moreover, it is noticeable that there no threats on the horizon in this chapter, and the land seems to be enjoying a time of peace and quiet, which would distinctly fit the reign of Josiah, for in that day there seems to be have been a great deal of support for Josiah's reform movement (cf. 2 Kgs 23:1–4), even if that popular support was not always accompanied by a genuine allegiance to Yahweh. Instead that support may have come from a resurgent nationalism after years of living under the Assyrian hegemony. People seemed to have quietly acquiesced to Josiah's call for change in the matters of religion, because that also matched the national mood at the time.

Because there is no evidence declaring that the prophet Jeremiah actively supported Josiah's reforms one way of the other, it might be assumed that the prophet was not in favor of the reforms and revival. Rather, the prophet believed that a reformation in religious structures and rituals alone did not go far enough. The people were content merely to observe the outward performances of the **cultic** acts that were pressed on them without any change in their hearts or with any repentance toward God. Rather than opposing Josiah's reforms, Jeremiah spoke to the need for radical change in the hearts of the people.

Therefore, if Jeremiah's call came in the thirteenth year of King Josiah's reign, then Jeremiah ministered in circumstances of comparative tranquility from the time of his call until the death of Josiah in 609 BC, eighteen years later. After that, however, a tumult broke out around the prophet. To review King Josiah's life, he began to reign when he was eight years old. In his sixteenth year of life he began to seek Yahweh; four years later, in the twelfth year of his reign, he began to campaign against the horrible idolatry in Judah. In fact, at that time he also crossed over the borders of Judah and went through the cities of Manasseh, Ephraim, Naphtali, and Simeon, many of which now lay in ruins from what the Assyrian armies had done in previous days. There, among the remnant of Israel, Josiah carried out the same iconoclastic campaign that struck at the heart of Israel's idolatry. When he had been reigning for thirteen years, Jeremiah began his ministry. Five years later, in 622/621 BC, the book of the law was found, accompanied by a campaign of cleansing the temple. Sometime between this date and the date of Josiah's death in 609 BC, this chapter seems to have originated.

FROM HONEYMOON TO APOSTASY (2:1–13)

TRANSLATION

1 The word of Yahweh came to me: **2** "Go and proclaim in the hearing of Jerusalem, thus says Yahweh[1]:

'I remember the devotion of your youth,
As a bride you loved me,
And followed me in the wilderness,

---

1. The LXX has only "And he said, 'Thus says the Lord.'"

Through a land that was not sown.[2]
    3 Israel was holy to Yahweh,
The first of his harvest,
    All who devoured her were guilty,
And disaster overtook them,'" declares Yahweh.
4 Hear the word of Yahweh, O house of Jacob, and all the families of the house of Israel. **5** This is what Yahweh says:
    "What perversity did your fathers find in me,
That they strayed from me?
    They went after [those] evanescent [idols],
And they themselves became evanescent.
    6 They did not ask,
'Where is Yahweh,
    Who brought us up from the land of Egypt,
And led us through the desert,
    Through a land of deserts and gorges,
A land of drought and the shadow[3] of death,
In a land where no one crosses over it, and where no one lives?'
    7 I brought you into a garden-like land,
To eat its fruit and its good things.
    But you came and defiled my land,
And you made my inheritance an abomination.
    8 The priests did not ask: 'Where is Yahweh?'
The ones handling the Law did not know Me,
    The leaders transgressed against me,
And the prophets prophesied by Baal,
Going after other gods that did not benefit them.
    9 Therefore, I again press charges against you, declares Yahweh,
And against your children's children,
    10 For, cross over to the island of Cyprus and see,
And send to Kedar and observe closely;
    And see if there has even been anything like this:

---

2. The LXX omits "in the wilderness, through a land that was not sown"; instead, it has "following the Holy One of Israel."

3. The word "shadow" could have been mistaken for "barren," as the LXX suggests; this seems to fit better with the previous word, "drought."

11 Has a nation ever exchanged its gods?
(Yet they are not gods at all.)
But my people have exchanged their glory,[4]
For what has no worth.
12 Be awestruck at this, O heavens,
And bristle with a great horror,[5] declares Yahweh,
13 For my people have committed two sins:
They have forsaken me, the fountain of living water,
And they have dug their own cisterns,
Broken cisterns that are not able to hold water."

COMMENTARY

2:1 Josiah's finding of the book of the law may have introduced a time of reform, but the reform on the people's part was mostly superficial, even though the king himself was completely sincere. Jeremiah begins his message with a reminiscence of the nation's days during their wilderness wanderings (2:1–3). His message, the text announces, originated with Yahweh, and it ends as well in an inclusion that it is indeed God's own word (2:1a, 3e). That relationship between God and the nation is depicted as a marriage, with a happy honeymoon period in the desert (cf. Deut 8:2–4). This happy relationship is continued under another metaphor of a harvest offering (v. 3b).

2:2 The prophet begins poetically in v. 2 using covenantal language, wherein the nation of Israel had had a time of "devotion" (חֶסֶד) to Yahweh, expressed by saying that as "a bride" she had "loved" (אָהֲבַת) and "followed" (לְכְתֵּךְ) Yahweh. But if Israel had pledged such loyalty and fidelity, as one does in a marriage, what had happened to entitle her to pervert it and to disregard it after that time in the wilderness?[6]

---

4. Copyists changed "my glory" to "their glory" in order to circumvent what seemed to be a direct expression of a divine title (Craigie, 19).

5. Lit. "be very desolate."

6. For the meaning of "wilderness" see M. V. Fox, "Jeremiah 2:2 and the 'Desert Ideal,'" *CBQ* 35, no. 4 (1973): 441–50; and also M. DeRoche, "Jeremiah 2:2–3 and Israel's Love for God during the Wilderness Wanderings," *CBQ* 45, no. 3 (1983): 364–76.

The nation should resemble the first produce that is offered from the harvest of the land; it belongs to Yahweh (Lev 25:23). As Yahweh's possession, he was entitled to expect an early presentation from the firstfruits from the land. The nation was to be "holy" to Yahweh (v. 2a). Therefore, as a wife belongs to her husband, and as firstfruit belongs to Yahweh, Israel existed so that she might belong exclusively to Yahweh (Exod 19:6; Deut 7:6).[7]

2:3 All of a sudden, however, an unexpected and troublesome turn of events is noted: "disaster (רָעָה) overtook them." Why? Because anyone who eats this produce that was holy to Yahweh would themselves be guilty, and therefore they would receive "evil/disaster" (v. 3d). Due to the unfaithfulness of Israel, the honeymoon certainly was over and the marriage disrupted; it seemed it all was beyond any repair!

2:4 What follows is, as it is called elsewhere in the Prophets, a prophetic lawsuit (רִיב, v. 9).[8] Verse 4 is the only place in Jeremiah where the people are addressed as "Jacob" and "Israel" in a judgment message. Four other times this combination of names occurs (10:16; 30:10; 31:7; 46:27); however, these are all in messages of promise and restoration or with a positive note. So why are they addressed this way in this negative oracle? Jeremiah uses these titles because they recall God's previous gracious dealings with them. These names also stress how far they had gone away from God, if not also from the endearing grace of God, which still lay just below the surface should they choose to repent.

2:5 The lawsuit begins with an initial question that sounds more like the words of a wounded partner in a marriage: "What fault did your fathers find in me, that they strayed so far from me?" (v. 5b). Even more disturbing is that the nation has now followed gods who really were "nothings/evanescent" (הֶבֶל, *hebel*, v. 5d), resulting in the people themselves "becoming nothing/evanescent" or "becoming a vapor" as well (הָבַל, *hābal*, v. 5e). The whole situation is beyond comprehension, as A. Heschel notes: "What a sublime

---

7. For the imagery of Israel as the unfaithful wife see G. E. Yates, "Jeremiah's Message of Judgment and Hope for God's Unfaithful 'Wife,'" *BSac* 167 (April–June 2010): 144–65.

8. See H. B. Huffman, "The Covenant Lawsuit in the Prophets," *JBL* 78 (1959): 285–95.

paradox for the Creator of heaven and earth to implore the people so humbly!" (Brown, 7). But even more to be pitied are the people, who now become like the gods they serve: they too are now unsubstantial, evanescent, and like "fog" and "mist," which disappear and keep changing.

2:6-8 "They did not ask" is repeated twice (vv. 6a, 8a) as further evidence of their forgetting their Lord. It just did not occur to them to ask "Where is Yahweh?" (vv. 6b, 8b). Everyone in leadership, including the priests ("those who deal with the law," Jer 18:18; Hos 4:6; Hag 2:11; Mal 2:6-9), the rulers (lit. "the shepherds"), and the prophets, chose to rebel against Yahweh. Gone was any part of the credo that recalled Yahweh's promise to grant the "land" to Israel. The word "land" dominates vv. 6-7 (five times). Let Israel come to her senses, for where the story of the "land" is lost, soon to follow will be the actual loss of the "land" as well.

2:9-11 In light of these accusations, Yahweh is ready to take the nation to court. The word *therefore* (v. 9) concludes the historical summary of vv. 4-8. However, the actual complaint in the suit is delayed until v. 11: "Has a nation ever exchanged its gods? ... But my people have exchanged their glory for what has no worth" (יוֹעִיל; that is, worthless idols). Frequently in prophetic speeches the word *therefore* introduced the divine judgment. Here, however, it links the past action of Israel/Judah with the formal complaint that is lodged against the nation. The "charges" (found in the רִיב, v. 9a) that Yahweh "continually raised" (impf. verb) here span the generations ("against you ... and against your children's children," v. 9b). But sassy Judah will bring her own charges against Yahweh later (in v. 29).

So ludicrous is the charge of the nation's unexpected unfaithfulness that one could go from west (Kittim, which is Cyprus) to east (Kedar, which refers to the nomadic tribal people in northern Arabia) without finding a case of "god swapping" or "deity abandonment" as was illustrated by Israel's dropping her "partner," Yahweh. Was Israel's action a result of her feeling Yahweh demanded too much from her? What was her problem? Whatever her excuse, it was all totally out of character for her to abandon her God and to substitute for him so-called deities that were no gods at all. The whole thing smacked of insolence, hubris, and stupidity!

2:12-13 Under these conditions, it is hard to find a terrestrial jury or witnesses that have not been involved in the problem; therefore, Yahweh calls on the cosmic powers of the heavens above to act as his witnesses (v. 12). Surely the heavens knew who was the eternal God and they would have heard Israel's disgusting response to Yahweh. So here is the nub of the issue: "My people have committed two sins: they have forsaken me, the spring of living water, and have dug their own cisterns, broken cisterns that cannot hold water" (v. 13). Yahweh is described under the metaphor of "living water" (again in 17:13) and the people under another metaphor of "broken cisterns."[9] What Yahweh had previously supplied was what was needed, but they substituted defective replacements that were not able to perform the basic tasks that they were supposed to accomplish.

How tragic! Judah had been so wonderfully favored by its Lord for so many years, yet now the people have just plain abandoned him for what were "nothings," idols, and no gods at all! Yahweh, the source of life itself, has been "thrown under the bus" in favor of imitations that held no content and supplied none of their needs. What an insult and what hubris! Judah found itself unable to perform some of the basic tasks of life, for its dependence on these zero gods did not enable them to accomplish any of the grand purposes for which they had been created.

Didn't anyone in that day ask, "Where is Yahweh?" Judah had become clueless and unaware of how desperate its situation really was. This is a wakeup call for us in our day to "smell the coffee" and change our lifestyles before the threatened judgment comes on us as well. Can't we see that the judgment of God is coming very soon on us, as it came on Judah? Can't we see that all of our trust in our technology, our economy, our military hardware, and our wisdom is doomed to fail if we do not come to Christ, who alone is the source of real living? We must change and turn to God in repentance, or the handwriting is already on the wall for our nation and all the nations of the world!

---

9. DeRoche mistakenly suggests that Yahweh is the rejected wife. See Michael DeRoche, "Israel's 'Two Evils' in Jeremiah II 13," VT 31, no. 3 (1981): 369-71.

ISRAEL IS A SLAVE OR PREY FOR THE TAKING (2:14–19)

TRANSLATION

14 "Is Israel a servant, a slave in that house?[10]
Why has he become booty?
15 The young lions have roared,
They have growled at him.
They have made his land a waste.[11]
His cities are destroyed and without inhabitants.
16 Also the cities of Memphis and Tahpanhes
Have shaved[12] the crown of your head.
17 Is this not what you have done to yourselves,
By forsaking Yahweh your God,
When he led you in the way?[13]
18 And now, why do you go back to Egypt
To drink the waters of Shihor?[14]
And why do you go back to Assyria
To drink from the Euphrates?
19 Your wickedness will chastise you,
Your apostasy will rebuke you.
Acknowledge and realize how evil and bitter
Is your forsaking Yahweh your God
When you do not fear me,"[15] declares the Lord, Yahweh
of hosts.

---

10. Lit. "one born of the house," meaning that he was not bought, but born and raised in the household.

11. The verb translated "waste" appears in the 3 f. sg., נִצְּתָה, but should be read as 3 c. pl., נִצְּתוּ.

12. The LXX misreads יָדַע, "to know," instead of רָעָה, "to graze."

13. The LXX omits the phrase בְּעֵת מוֹלִיכֵךְ בַּדָּרֶךְ, "when he led you in the way."

14. The Shihor is a branch of the Nile River. The LXX translates Shihor as "Geon." Most English versions translate it as "Nile."

15. "When you do not fear me" is translated "I have taken no pleasure in you" in the LXX.

COMMENTARY

2:14 The prophet raises two rhetorical questions, both of which assume the answer is "no": "Is Israel a servant, a slave by birth? Why then has he become plunder?" (v. 14). Indeed, Israel had never been targeted to be someone else's slave or a prey to the nations at large. Instead, as a people and nation, they were loved and destined to be heirs of the gracious gifts of God.

2:15–17 Where did the foes of the nation come from? "Lions" (v. 15a) is a natural metaphor for destructive and fierce opponents to both persons and the nation. The "lion" was a long-standing symbol of Assyria as well, Israel's longtime enemy from the east, who had made the northern kingdom a waste in 722/721 BC and continued, though weakly, to be a threat up to this moment to others in the ancient Near East. "Memphis" (v. 16a) was fifteen miles south of Cairo, Egypt, on the banks of the Nile River, and had been the former capital of that land. "Tahpanhes" was likewise in Egypt as an outpost on the eastern delta region of the Nile bordering on the Sinai. These two cities are likened to ones who had "shaved the crown of [Israel's] head" (v. 16b). Some have attempted to render this expression as "have cracked your skull" (NET), but there is nothing that fits that harsh metonym unless it is a reference to Josiah's death in 609 BC. Better is the understanding that it refers to the utter humiliation of Judah due to her departure from Yahweh. All this had brought deep humiliation on their own heads at the very time that Yahweh had been trying to lead them in the best way they should go (v. 17). But they had consistently refused this divine direction.

2:18 But if that is so, why are they on the road in a way leading back to Egypt and to Assyria again (v. 18)? "Shihor" is an Egyptian phrase meaning "the pond of Horus"[16] and probably refers to one of the eastern branches of the Nile or one of the lakes in that part of the delta. The name Shihor would point to a part of the Nile that depicted the whole, that is, the Nile as a whole, of which Shihor was just a part.[17] Thus, the people wanted to

---

16. *HALOT*, 2:1477.

17. By using a branch of the Nile to refer to the whole Nile, Jeremiah is using a figure of speech called **synecdoche**, where a part of something is used for the whole thing.

drink the water from the Nile rather than quench their thirst from the "living water" Yahweh would supply. Israel's attempt to get relief by turning to other nations and various types of alliances had proven disastrous time after time, yet she was still inclined to go that way rather than to trust Yahweh.

2:19 However, their sin would produce their own reproof. Israel's sin was called "wickedness/evil" (רָעָה) and "backsliding" (מְשׁוּבָה, v. 19). Not only is Israel depicted as an adulterous wife and a prostitute, but now she acts like an unmanageable child. What the nation lacked was this: the fear (פַּחְדָּה) of Yahweh" (expressed elsewhere with the Heb. root יָרֵא; Job 1:1; Prov 1:7; Ps 34:11).

Neither Israel nor Judah had ever been intended to be a slave and in bondage, yet both nations allowed themselves to be bound up by their idolatry and wickedness against God. This was in the face of the Lord who loved them and had poured out his blessings on them without limit. Such actions are similar to those of all of God's unbelieving creatures worldwide—we have gone off on our own paths and tried to gain on our own what Yahweh has freely offered to us in his mercy and grace.

To help Judah get back on the right way again, God sent one nation after another against Judah to call her back to the Lord so that, in suffering, misery would finally find a voice and cry out to God for deliverance. But Judah, like all too many of us, continued to be extremely slow to get the point. They—and we, all too often—remain adamant in rejecting the God of heaven. What is needed is the fear of God, which is not to be understood as the terror of meeting Yahweh; it is instead an attitude of trust that begins with faith in him and then is seen in an outworking of that faith in obedience to what he calls us to do. When oh when will Judah and the nations, including us, turn back to the Lord?

THE CHARGES IN THE LAWSUIT (2:20–28)

TRANSLATION

20 "For long ago I broke your yoke,

And I burst your bonds[18];
But you said, 'I will not serve.'[19]
        Indeed, on every lofty hill,
And under every leafy tree,
        You laid down as a prostitute.
        21 I myself had planted you as a choice vine,
Wholly of pure stock.
        Then, how have you turned against me,
To become a degenerate and wild vine?
        22 Though you wash yourself with soap,[20]
And use much alkali,[21]
        The stain of your guilt will[22] still be in front of me, declares the
            Lord[23] Yahweh.
        23 How can you say, 'I am not unclean,
I have not run after the Baals'?
        See how you behaved in the valley;[24]
Realize what you have done—
A swift she-camel running about on her own way,
        24 A wild donkey accustomed to the desert,
While in heat she sniffs the wind!
Who can restrain her?
        None [of the males] who seek her need weary themselves;
They will find her in her month![25]

---

18. The LXX suggests 2 m. sg. verb forms, "you broke … you burst," but the context fits the MT better.

19. Some mss suggest the reading "I will not transgress/cross over" instead of "I will not serve." This seems to be a classic case of unintentional scribal error.

20. Lit. "[cleansing] soda/lye."

21. Another type of cleansing element, a soap.

22. The niphal ptc. could also be translated as pres. tense, "your guilt is before me."

23. The word אֲדֹנָי, "Lord," is missing in the LXX.

24. The MT has רְאִי דַּרְכֵּךְ בַּגַּיְא, "look at your way in the valley," where the LXX has ἰδὲ τὰς ὁδούς σου ἐν τῷ πολυανδρίῳ, "look at your way in the burial ground."

25. The MT has בְּחָדְשָׁהּ יִמְצָאוּנְהָ, "they will find her in her month," where the LXX has ἐν τῇ ταπεινώσει αὐτῆς εὑρήσουσιν αὐτήν, "they will find her at the time of her humiliation." It seems that the LXX was translating a different verb.

25 Restrain your feet from going unshod,
And your throat[26] from becoming parched.

But you said, 'It's no use,
Because I have loved foreign [gods],
And after them I will go.'

26 As a thief is ashamed when he is caught,
So the house of Israel[27] is ashamed—

They, their kings and their officials,
Their priests, and their prophets.

27 They say to wood, 'You are my father,'
And to a stone, 'You gave me birth.'[28]

For they have turned their backs to me
And not their faces;

Yet in the time of their trouble, they say,
'Come and save us!'

28 Where, then, are the gods that you made for yourselves?
Let them come if they can save you when you are in trouble!

For as the number of your cities,
So are [the number of] your gods, O Judah."[29]

COMMENTARY

2:20–22 Each of the five charges proffered against the nation in the divine lawsuit can be gathered from the accompanying words "You/they say" (vv. 20c, 23a, 25c, 27a, 27d). It all began when long ago the nation broke off its bonds of serving Yahweh (v. 20). Judah had so distorted reality that it was the opposite of what she now affirmed.

She began her path of abandonment of God by saying boldly: "I will not serve [you, Yahweh]" (v. 20c). Accordingly, she sinned under "every leafy tree … [and she] laid down as a prostitute" (v. 20d–f). In place of those

---

26. The word written is גְּרוֹנֵךְ, "threshing floor," but it should be read גְּרוֹנֵךְ, "throat."

27. The MT has בֵּית יִשְׂרָאֵל, "the house of Israel," while the LXX has οἱ υἱοὶ Ισραηλ, "the children of Israel."

28. The word written is יְלִדְתִּנִי, "you gave me birth," but it should be read as the pl. pronominal suf. יְלִדְתָּנוּ, "you gave us birth."

29. The LXX adds καὶ κατʼ ἀριθμὸν διόδων τῆς Ιερουσαλημ ἔθυον τῇ Βααλ, "according to the number of Jerusalem's streets they sacrificed to Baal," to the end of the verse.

early days of honeymooning, she now had adopted the style of a brazen harlot and nymphomaniac. Previously, to change the metaphor again from a marital image to an agricultural one, God had planted her as a "choice vine" (v. 21). This imagery might have been stimulated by Isaiah's famous vineyard message in Isa 5:1–7. This vine was "pure stock" (v. 21b), but it turned against Yahweh and became a "degenerate and wild vine" (v. 21c). Now Israel acted as if she were foreign and alien to her Lord. Sensing that something was not pure or spiritually clean, Israel tried to purify herself using soda and soap, but her guilt was so "ingrained" (NJPS) in her that she remained stained before Yahweh (v. 22).

2:23–24 But there was a second thing Israel said: "I am not unclean; I have not run after the Baals!" (v. 23a). It is difficult to tell whether this is simply self-deception or just plain lying! But Yahweh could point to the Valley of Hinnom (v. 23c), to the southwest of Jerusalem, for there Israel had practiced the abominable rites connected with the worship of the god Molech (7:31; 2 Kgs 23:10). Israel was to think about how they had acted in that valley—as they sacrificed their children alive as an offering to this pagan god. Moreover, Judah is so unrestrained and so unpredictable that she is like a young she-camel that cannot yet walk straight. When she gets loose in the marketplace, all scramble to get out of her way, for there is no predicting which way she will lurch next (v. 23e–f). Likewise, "a wild donkey" (v. 24) is just as intractable, headstrong, and independent, as it too abandons all convention and finds that only its own self-satisfaction is her sexual goals, from which she is rarely dissuaded. Judah fits this description, for once she has focused on her infatuation, she too refuses to be persuaded otherwise.

Can such people be persuaded from taking such a reckless and exhausting way of life? Hardly! They are more like a female donkey in heat that picks up the scent of a male donkey, and it is then impossible to turn her back, and neither does the male need to trouble himself too much in looking for her as a partner. She will have her way! What is true of these animal metaphors is also true of Judah's obsession with searching for foreign allies or possible partners. She will find them, make no mistake, whether they are appropriate or not, whether they are approved by God or by those who are on the path to Yahweh or not.

2:25 Therefore, it is useless to seek to dissuade Judah. You will sooner wear holes in your sandals and make your throat dry (apparently calling for Judah to return to Yahweh) as attempt to divert Israel from such foreign alliances or partners (v. 25a–b). They are like female camels and donkeys in sexual heat in their persistence to do evil!

Once more, in a third assertion, the audience Jeremiah is addressing amazingly concludes by saying: "It's no use! Because I have loved foreign [gods], and after them I must go" (v. 25c–e). The whole thing seems hopeless, for their impulse to continue on the path they had taken is so strong that any warnings of any potential dangers that may lie ahead were already too late. Their addiction is without remedy, or so it would seem.[30]

2:26 The plain fact is that the "house of Israel" had been "ashamed" (v. 26b). The Heb. hiphil form of the verb has the special sense here of "bringing on oneself shame and disgrace" (הֹבִישׁוּ). How humiliating it must be to see Israel's "kings," "officials," "priests," and "prophets" bow down to idols. How the mighty had fallen! It was not just a reference to the northern kingdom, for as v. 28 will show, the people of the southern kingdom of Judah were just as guilty as they now have become in this context as representatives of the whole community to whom God had given the Abrahamic-Davidic covenant.

2:27 The fourth declaration is even more amazing: "They [kept on] say[ing] (אֹמְרִים) to the wood, 'You are my father,' and to a stone, 'You gave me birth'" (v. 27a–b). It is not as if this were simply a momentary lapse; it had become a habitual practice. The "wood" likely[31] refers to the wooden pole of Asherah, the female fertility deity, while the "stone" probably points to the standing stone that was in form, or at least in meaning, associated with the male pagan Canaanite deity. Jeremiah seems to have ironically and deliberately inverted the two Canaanite symbols for these deities by mockingly addressing the "wood" as "father" and the "stone" as the one

---

30. See K. E. Bailey and W. L. Holladay, "The 'Young Camel' and 'Wild Ass' in Jer. II 23–25," *VT* 18, no. 2 (1968): 256–60.

31. While an Asherah pole is the most likely referent, there is also the possibility that it could refer to an idol made of wood (cf. Hab 2:19).

who "gave [them] birth." The result, however, was clear: "They have turned their backs to me and not their faces" (v. 27c), thus indicating a complete dissociation from Yahweh.

The fifth and final affirmation from this nation is: "when they are in trouble, they would say:[32] 'Come and save us'" (v. 27d–e). This is a type of "foxhole religion," but it is also a testimony to the complete bankruptcy of Canaanite religion. While Judah and Israel had been attracted to the Canaanite gods because they imposed few if any moral restraints on them, when times got tough, they felt it was time to revert to Yahweh and to the way they had previously acted before they abandoned God in favor of their current list of discount gods.

2:28 For this Jeremiah rightly thunders, "Where are the gods you made for yourselves?" (v. 29a). Judah surely had a large enough number of such gods, for they were as plentiful as the number of their towns (v. 28c). Why not ask your gods, Jeremiah ironically chides, to help you when you are in trouble. In fact, all such gods were absolutely powerless and worthless — and they knew it too!

It is frightening how this section, with its five indictments against Judah, closely fits us in the modern scene, when allowance is made for our modern equivalents for the ancient idols of wood and stone. One wonders how God in heaven was able (and still is able) to put up with all such intransigence and outright defiance of him and his name. May our hearts be softened and our awareness of the greatness of God temper our words and thoughts about the Most High God! He is to be trusted and feared above all other persons, forces, institutions, and claims of mortals.

SELF-DECEIVED ISRAEL PURSUED IDOLATRY
AND INJUSTICE (2:29–37)

TRANSLATION

29 "Why do you lodge these charges against me?
All of you have rebelled against me,
            declares Yahweh.

---

32. This is an impf. verb, which here indicates continued past habits.

30 In vain I have punished your people;[33]
They took no correction.

Your sword has devoured your prophets
Like a ravening lion.[34]

31 And you, O generation, look at the word of Yahweh:
'Have I been a desert to Israel,
Or a land of thick darkness?'

Why do my people say, 'We are free to roam[35];
We will not come any more to you?'

32 Does a maiden forget her jewelry,
Or a bride[36] her attire?

Yet my people have forgotten me
Days without number.

33 How well you direct your course to seek love!
Therefore, even the wicked women,[37]
Can learn from your ways.

34 Also on your skirts[38] can be found
The lifeblood of the innocent poor;
You did not find them breaking in.

Yet in spite of all these things[39]
35 you say, 'I am without blame,
Surely his anger has turned from me.'

Behold, I will bring judgment on you
For saying 'I have not sinned.'

---

33. Lit. "sons."

34. The LXX adds καὶ οὐκ ἐφοβήθητε, "but you were not afraid," to the end of the verse.

35. The LXX has οὐ κυριευθησόμεθα, "we will not be ruled over," where the MT has נֵרוּד, "we are free to roam." This could be a classic case of haplography. See A. J. O. van der Wal, "Jeremiah II 31: A Proposal," VT 41, no. 3 (1991): 360-63.

36. The word בְּתוּלָה can be translated "virgin, young woman," where I have chosen "bride."

37. The text has a simple substantival adj., "wicked" (fem.).

38. The word בִּכְנָפַיִךְ, "on your skirts" (the hem of your robes), is translated ἐν ταῖς χερσίν, "in your hands," in the LXX. See J. A. Soggin, "Einige Bemerkungen Über Jeremias ii 34," VT 8, no. 4 (1958): 433-35.

39. Some scholars suggest a different division of consonants that results in a possible translation of "indeed your yoke has become execrable" instead of "Yet in spite of all these things." See W. L. Holladay, "Jeremiah 2:34b—A Fresh Approach," VT 25 (1975): 221-25.

36 How lightly you treat changing your way!
You will be put to shame by Egypt
As you were put to shame by Assyria.
    37 From it too you will go out
With your hands on your head,
      For Yahweh has rejected those in whom you trust;
      You will not prosper by[40] them."

COMMENTARY

2:29–30 After God proffers his charges, he gives his rebuttal to what the people have said as they have professed innocence and insolently sought to justify their way of life. In fact, the first action that the people have taken is that they instead have brought counter-accusations against Yahweh (v. 29). Even though Judah is as guilty as can be, they insisted on boldly declaring: "I am without blame. … I have not sinned" (v. 35a, d). The amount of self-delusion is amazing to say the least. Instead of recognizing the truthfulness of the charges leveled against them, they felt hurt that Jeremiah would even suggest that this fitted them at all. The protested: "Why do you lodge these charges against me?" (v. 29a). But as rebels they had no basis for protesting God's declarations. Moreover, the people had the gall to infer that the root of their problem is that God had undeservedly brought all these calamities over them (v. 30). Amazingly, however, there was no response to any of this correction (v. 30b). Instead of humbling themselves under the word of God, "[their] swords devoured [their] prophets" (v. 30c)—the very ones whom God had sent to correct them. That is what had happened during Manasseh's reign (2 Kgs 21:16) and later in King Jehoiakim's treatment of the prophet Uriah (2 Kgs 26:20–23), exactly as Jezebel had also acted in an even earlier time (1 Kgs 19:10, 14). The people had acted against the prophets "like a ravening lion" (v. 30d). John L. Mackay comments appropriately:

> This is an aspect of their behavior that Jeremiah had not previously mentioned. Those who present themselves as tolerant of the beliefs of others frequently respond quite differently when exposed to the searching critique of divine truth. Then it is seen that their

---

40. The -ל prep. specifies who will not aid in their prosperity.

inclusiveness extends only to all varieties of error, not to the truth.
(Mackay, 164)

2:31-32 Jeremiah appends his own comments in v. 31—and not, as the LXX
inserts in this place, the standard formula for God's speaking, "Thus says
Yahweh"—with "Hear the word of Yahweh," by which the prophet calls
his generation to "consider" afresh what God had done in the past. His
challenge is set forth in a three questions:

1. "Have I been a desert to Israel or a land of thick darkness?"
   (v. 31b–c)

2. "Why do my people say, 'We are free to roam; we will not come
   any more to you?'" (v. 31d–e)

3. "Does a maiden forget her jewelry, a bride her attire?" (v. 32a–b)

As recalled in v. 6, the desert was a most inhospitable place during their
wilderness journeys. Few would have wanted to return to those days or to
that place. But that is why God asked his people: Is that how you think of
me—a place that is dark, foreboding, and inhospitable? The question is
much as it was in v. 5: What did you find that was so wrong with me that
you forsook me and replaced me with other gods? Why would Israel come
to Yahweh no more as their God? But the answer was just the opposite of
the expected response: "Of course not!" This nation wanted to go off and
do as she pleased rather than adhering to a Lord who expected a holy life.
By implication, Yahweh likened himself to a maiden's jewelry and a bride's
ornaments. How could these women forget things as important as those
tokens of their past relationships?—but Judah had easily forgotten all of
that and more. The question and the desire for an opposite answer could
not have been put with an air of greater disappointment on the part of
Yahweh, who loved them and had redeemed them from Egypt. But God's
love was totally unrequited.

2:33 Not only had Israel and Judah abandoned Yahweh, but they had exhibited real, marked skills in teaching others how to be promiscuous (v. 33a–b)
as well. They were in the unfavorable position of being able to pass on
quite a few tips to **cult** prostitutes who plied their trade as part of pagan

worship of the idols they served. They had sunk to some of the very lowest depths possible.

2:34–35 There was more than the sin of idolatry to cope with in Israel; there was also the moral degeneration that such idolatry introduced. A number of moral and social evils could be attributed to the corrupting influence of such pagan concepts of worship. Israel and Judah claim they are "innocent" (v. 35a) and had "not sinned" (v. 35d), but their hands[41] are full of the blood of the "innocent poor" (v. 34b). God's mercy will not extend to covering and excusing them for the social and moral blight that had caused the poor to become even more weakened by their poor examples. The Israelites themselves may not have been aware of the bloodstains on their garments, but the misuse of their call to lead the nations in the worship and praise of the only one true God carried a heavy burden. Just think of the implications of the guilt that fell on Israel because of those who had followed Israel and Judah in the practice of child sacrifice! In fact, there were no excuses or extenuating circumstances that could possibly have provided an explanation for what Israel had done. Just as a thief dies for breaking through a wall at night and the defender is not guilty of bloodshed as he acts in self-defense of this unrecognizable intruder (Exod 22:2), such circumstances as these could have been a basis for God extending mercy to his people, but such was not the case (v. 34c). If the nation had come to Yahweh in repentance, there might have been some hope for them; however, their bald-faced denials that they had done anything wrong and were instead innocent send the opposite signal to Yahweh.

2:36–37 The charge is the same as in the beginning of this chapter: this nation simply flitted from one wrong decision to another (v. 36). First they were off to Assyria (for example, when King Ahaz of Judah sought Assyria's help in the Syro-Ephraimite War), or later down to Egypt to counter the effects of Assyrian oppression and heavy, taxing tribute to her enemy. All of these decisions were policies of failure and were destined to lead to no good end. But those who went off to "that place," probably Egypt, returned "with their hands on their heads" (v. 37b), which usually meant the shame

---

41. Lit. "the folds of her garments."

of captivity, but here it at least means the gesture of awful shame and deep sorrow and anguish. The Jewish delegation was not able to work out an agreement with Egypt, so they had to return frustrated. But the deeper reason was that Yahweh had "rejected those [they] trust[ed]" (v. 37c). No help could be expected from that source either. Israel was being forced to recognize that if Yahweh did not help them, deliverance was not going to come from any other source.

Can you imagine how brash and how brazen Judah's responses to the living God were? It is almost unbelievable, especially after all he had done for them. But I am afraid that many of these same responses are similar to those we make in our day to the same Almighty Lord. May our Lord forgive us as well for acting so impudently; it is a sheer disgrace, to say the least. Here is another reason to repent and to ask for God's forgiveness.

A CALL TO RETURN TO YAHWEH (3:1–4:4)

Without a doubt, the main topic in this passage is the need for the people to "repent" and to "turn back" to Yahweh. Three of the most integrating features of this passage, which appear in both the prose and poetical passages alike, are the words "prostitute" (זָנָה, 3:1, 6, 9), "defiled" (חָנֵף, 3:1, 2, 9), and the key repeated term, "turn, repent" (various forms of the word שׁוּב, 3:1 [2x], 6, 7 [2x], 8 [2x], 10, 11, 12 [2x], 14, 22 [2x]; 4:1 [2x]). The latter is a central term in this passage, occurring sixteen times, and overall it occurs ninety times throughout Jeremiah. When "turn" is used in a theological sense it can point to a "turning back" to God in repentance. But it also can be used for "to apostatize," which meant "a turning away" from God and a rejection of him. Clearly, Jeremiah wanted the Judeans to turn back to God in repentance and change the path on which they were headed. It was time Judah experienced a revival.

CAN DIVORCED AND REMARRIED WIVES RETURN TO THEIR ORIGINAL HUSBANDS? (3:1–5)

TRANSLATION

1[42] "If a man divorces his wife,

---

42. לֵאמֹר, "Saying" (untranslated here), is missing in the LXX and the Syr. versions.

And she leaves him,

And she becomes another man's wife,

Should he return to her again?[43]

Would not the land be greatly polluted?[44]

You have lived as a prostitute with many lovers;

Would you [now] return to me? declares Yahweh.

2 Lift up your eyes to the barren heights and notice!

Where have you not been ravished?[45]

By the roadside you have sat for them,

Like a nomad in the desert.[46]

You have polluted the land with your prostitution and your wickedness.

3 Therefore, the showers have been withheld,

And the spring rain has not come.[47]

Yet you have the forehead of a prostitute;

You refuse to be ashamed.

4 Have you not just called out to me:

'My father, you are the friend of my youth

5 Will you be angry forever,

Will you maintain [it] forever?'

Behold, you have spoken,

But you have done [all] the evil you could."

COMMENTARY

3:1 Based on the divorce ethic taught in Deut 24:1-4, a metaphor is developed of God's marital relationship with his people, which relationship the prophet Hosea already explored (Hos 1-3), and which Ezekiel would

---

43. The LXX has ἀνακάμψει πρὸς αὐτόν, "will she return to him," instead of "should he return to her."

44. The LXX has ἔτι οὐ μιαινομένη μιανθήσεται ἡ γυνή, translated "will not the woman be defiled," where the MT has the land becoming polluted.

45. The Masoretic scribes propose reading שֻׁכַּבְתְּ, "you lay down," in place of שֻׁגַּלְתְּ, "you were ravished/violated."

46. The LXX reads the Heb. word כַּעֲרָבִי without the *yod* and has ὡσεὶ κορώνη ἐρημουμένη, "like a deserted crow," where the MT has a Heb. word that generally refers to a person dwelling in the desert.

47. The first part of the verse differs greatly in the LXX. It seems that its translation "And you kept my shepherds as a stumbling block for yourself" comes from a different **Vorlage**.

develop later on (Ezek 16). In Jeremiah's use of the metaphor, Yahweh is the innocent party who has been betrayed by his wife, Israel. The argument proceeds *a fortiori*: if a twice-divorced woman is prohibited by the Mosaic law from returning to her original husband, how much less can Israel return to Yahweh when she has prostituted herself to her many lovers in the Canaanite pantheon? Such a law was meant to eliminate serial marriages and warn against trivial or superficial commitments to the serious institution of marriage. Also, would not the land be defiled by such immoral activity, as Jeremiah (3:1d; Deut 24:4d) notes? Indeed, "as a result of the sin and guilt of individuals the land, too, incurs some measure of guilt and sin."[48]

At first sight Jeremiah seems to be proposing an impossible situation! Why would he invite the people of Judah to repent if he were simultaneously telling them that in effect there was no real way for them to return, given that they had deserted their marriage to Yahweh? If the analogy from Deuteronomy is in full play here, is there no way back home to their Lord?

But that is precisely the point that must be made here: Deut 24:1–4 has not been cited as a precise parallel in every way. While northern Israel had been served "a certificate of divorce" and "sent away" into exile because of all her adulteries (3:8), her sister *Judah has not yet been served her certificate of divorce*, nor has she as yet been formally divorced, nor sent into exile. This by no means lightens the seriousness of the plight in which Judah finds herself, but it still allows for a call for repentance and a summons for that generation in Judah to "turn back" to Yahweh. Moreover, how could Yahweh be in favor of denying any aspect of a reconciliation to the same people he had loved and promised his faithfulness? And the question in 3:5, "Will you be angry forever?" is answered later in 3:12 with "I will not maintain [my anger] forever." Thus, no prophet ever told his audiences, "Don't bother repenting; God has rescinded his offer of reconciliation!"

Some have cautioned that this section of Jeremiah must not be understood too narrowly, in strict legal terms (Fretheim, 75). But such caution is without support in this text or elsewhere, for it incorrectly argues that God "explicitly set aside the law in this case." The line of argument mounted here is that God was "not bound to the Torah in any static sense," for where

---

48. J. D. Martin, "The Forensic Background to Jeremiah III:1," *VT* 19 (January 1969): 83.

personal and relational factors were involved, he could and did override the strict application of the law, making his mercy greater than his justice! But to pit one aspect of the attributes of God (truth) against another (mercy) is to argue for an inconsistent God. Besides, there are better solutions without resorting to such a weak suggestion. That suggestion does not closely follow the argument of the text of this Scripture.

3:2 Israel's departure from Yahweh is easily documented by her behavior. One had only to look up to the "barren heights" (3:2), where the customary Baal shrines were located, to witness Israel's both physical and spiritual harlotry. Baal worship was dominated by rites that also were sexual in nature. Perhaps that is why the prophet's language here was so shocking, that is, "Where have you not been *ravished*" (3:2); the Heb. scribes (Masoretes) softened this word (שֻׁגַּלְתְּ), which they thought to be too vulgar, to the reading: "you lay down" (שֻׁכַּבְתְּ). Nevertheless, Israel also is depicted as sitting by the roadside "waiting for lovers" (3:2c) or for Bedouin merchant tribesmen, who passed by on the trade routes, so the nation could sell their wares (or in this case, their sexual favors) to them. But the result was disastrous, for not only did they bring discredit on themselves by their prostitution, they so defiled the land (3:2e) that "the showers have been withheld and no spring rains have fallen" (3:3a–b). Thus, their sexual and spiritual impudence affected the land itself. Showers were needed for the crops to grow, and the spring rains in particular, which fell in March and April, were key to all successful harvests in Israel; otherwise the yield would be severely reduced.

3:3 But all such signs of God's disfavor were totally lost and wasted on Israel; instead, the nation, with the "brazen look of a prostitute," continued on in their abandonment of Yahweh with no hint of any shame or blushing (v. 3). So accustomed had Israel become to such contemptuous obstinacy that she feared neither loss of honor nor loss of position anymore.

3:4–5 In 3:4, either Israel speaks in simulated endearing terms of "father" and "friend" in pretense to Yahweh, whom she repeatedly had disavowed by her behavior, or vv. 4–5 are spoken by God as he beckons his wayward people to return to him, for he does not bear a grudge forever. Israel has just called a piece of wood "my father," in 2:27, and "friend," which later expression was found in Prov 2:17 and used in a context of marital unfaithfulness. Perhaps Israel was falsely counting on God's anger not lasting forever, for they, as a nation, after all, were heirs of the covenantal promises, were they not?

Anyway, this is how they talked ("behold, you have spoken," 3:5c). They had little or no appreciation for how wide the breach was between them and their God. Despite all their prattle to the contrary, their actions were speaking louder than their words.

Since Judah had become tone-deaf to the call of God to repent and turn back to him, he spoke to them from a drought. There had been no spring rainfall, yet Judah had missed the significance of such a loss. One wonders how frequently we too miss God's attempts to speak to our generation by his Word and then by his withholding the ordinary benefits of nature and the land. Even so, if people would return to him, the invitation remains open, and God's forgiveness is still available. If they and we would return, then God would not remain hostile toward them and us forever.

WILL JUDAH LEARN ANYTHING FROM HER
APOSTATE SISTER ISRAEL? (3:6–11)

TRANSLATION

6 Yahweh said to me, in the days of King Josiah: "Have you seen what backsliding Israel has done by going up on every high hill and under every leafy tree and has committed adultery there? **7** I thought after she had done all this, she would return to me, but she did not return, but her unfaithful sister Judah saw it. **8** I saw [to it] that for all backsliding Israel's adulteries, I sent her away with a certificate of divorce I gave her.[49] Yet her treacherous sister Judah had no fear, but she too went and committed adultery. **9** Because she took her prostitution so lightly, she polluted the land[50] and committed adultery with stone and wood. **10** In spite of all this, her treacherous sister Judah did not return to me with all her heart, but [only] in

---

49. The LXX adds εἰς τὰς χεῖρας, "into her hands," after "a certificate of divorce I gave her," indicating that the LORD handed Israel the decree of divorce.

50. The clause "she polluted the land" is missing in the LXX.

pretense," declared Yahweh. **11** Yahweh said to me, "Backsliding Israel is more righteous than unfaithful Judah."

COMMENTARY

3:6 Here is the only dated message in Jer 1–20; it is placed "in the days of King Josiah" (3:6a). Exactly where it fits in the rule of Josiah we are not told, but it still is of more than passing interest that it must have been during one of the greatest revival movements in the history of Judah, yet the prophet must still reprove the people with some of the sternest words one could imagine. In fact, Yahweh himself asks the prophet to look around and tell him the answer to this question: "Have you seen what backsliding [that is, faithless] Israel has done?" (v. 6). Yahweh assumes the prophet will be astonished at what he sees. For instance, to single out just one aspect of Israel's outrageous behavior, she "[keeps] going" (הֹלְכָה; ptc.) to the top of every high hill and under every spreading tree to commit prostitution (זָנָה, v. 6). The charge is similar to the one made in 2:20. This does not sound as if the reform movement were having any deep effects on the general populace.

3:7-8 God might have expected that after Israel had gotten such rebelliousness out of her system that she would have awakened to how her whole experiment with rebellion and prostitution exposed her as to how empty and worthless the whole trip into Canaanite religion had been. But despite Yahweh's hopes that "she would return to [him]," "she did not!" (v. 7b). That is why God gave "apostate/backsliding" (מְשֻׁבָה) northern Israel her divorce papers and sent her away into the Assyrian exile (v. 8).

One would think that Judah, her sister, would learn from what she saw and would decide to take a different direction. But she seems to go one step further, as she became "treacherous" (בֹּגֵדָה); she was more than merely "unfaithful," as she committed adultery with deceit and treachery (v. 8c-d). Thus, what Judah learned from these startling events was nothing at all.

3:9 Judah simply shrugs off her sister's exile for her prostitution as if it all means very little to her (v. 9a). She too "polluted the land and committed adultery with stone and wood" (v. 9b). Neither does Judah "return" to Yahweh "with all her heart" (v. 10); she chooses to feign a spiritual return to Yahweh, but it all is "[only] in pretense" (v. 10b). The word for "pretense"

(שֶׁקֶר) means a "deception," a "lie." This is the first of thirty-seven times where Jeremiah uses שֶׁקֶר against the people he would minister to. Judah's return and repentance to the Lord ends up being only a sham and a false pretense of coming to terms with her sin. Even though Josiah's reform may have undoubtedly had some positive effects, it did not appear to have left any lasting marks on the national conduct and commitment to Yahweh.

3:10 Yahweh concluded that "backsliding Israel" was more righteous than "treacherous Judah" (v. 10). If God had divorced northern Israel, the question would seem to be, what did Judah think she had in store for her future? Judah had brazenly gone into evil with her eyes open to what had happened to her sister; she had not just blundered or fallen into evil. Her sin was all the more serious since she had failed to learn anything from her sister's experience.

Judah had indeed seen what had happened to northern Israel because of her sin, but instead of a genuine repentance and a full return to God, she put on a pretense of sincere return. But our Lord knew the difference. What we learn is that we learn very little, perhaps even nothing, from the lessons of history! God's divorce of northern Israel had no effect on Judah, and sometimes there is little or no effect on our generation even when we see the hand of God move in judgment on others for their perpetuation of wickeness and sin.

AN APPEAL FOR NORTHERN ISRAEL TO REPENT (3:12–18)

TRANSLATION

12 "Go and proclaim these words towards the north, and say:
'Return, backsliding Israel,' declares Yahweh.
'I will not frown on you [any longer],[51]
     For I am merciful,' declares Yahweh,
       'I will not maintain [my anger] forever.
    13 Only acknowledge your guilt—
For against Yahweh you have rebelled,

---

51. Lit. "I will not let my face fall against you."

You have scattered your favors among foreigners, under every
    leafy tree,
And you have not listened to my voice,' declares Yahweh.
    14 'Return, apostate people,' declares Yahweh,
'For I am your husband;[52]
    I will take you, one from a city,
And two from a family,
And I will bring you to Zion.

15 "Then I will give you shepherds after my own heart, who will feed you with knowledge and understanding. **16** And when you have increased and multiplied in the land, in those days, declares Yahweh, they will no longer say 'The ark of the covenant of Yahweh.'[53] It will not come to mind or be remembered; it will not be missed, nor will it be made again.' **17** At that time they will call Jerusalem 'the throne of Yahweh,' and all the nations[54] will assemble in Jerusalem [to honor] the name of Yahweh. No longer will they follow the stubbornness of their evil hearts. **18** In those days the house of Judah will join the house of Israel, and together they will come from the land of the north to the land that I gave as an inheritance to your [fore]fathers."

COMMENTARY

3:12-13 The prophet is instructed to "Go and proclaim these words toward the north" (v. 12). Not only was the north the direction from which disaster was going to come for Judah, but it also it could mean that Jeremiah is to go to the northern territory and minister to what is left of the ten tribes that had not been taken away in the 722/721 BC Assyrian exile. The Judean king Josiah had a real concern for those left in the north (2 Kgs 23:15-19; 2 Chr 34:5-7, 9, 33) as he attempted to reunite the two kingdoms under his rule, so it is possible that "the north" and "Israel" do refer to the northern Israel.

---

52. בְּעַלְתִּי can be translated "I was your husband" or "I was your master."

53. אֲרוֹן בְּרִית־יְהוָה, "The ark of the covenant of Yahweh," appears in the LXX as κιβωτὸς διαθήκης ἁγίου Ισραηλ, "The ark of the Holy One of Israel."

54. Cazelles argues that the nations mentioned here are not the foreign nations but tribes of Israel. See H. Cazelles, "Israel du Nord et Arche D'alliance (Jer. III 16)," VT 18, no. 2 (1968): 147-58.

But if the prophet is being instructed to preach to the northern tribes, is the call to repentance in v. 12b real, since the divorce of northern Israel seems so absolute in the preceding text? How can Jeremiah now be calling: "Turn back, backsliding (מְשֻׁבָה) Israel?" Michael Brown cites the Talmud (Megillah 14b) as affirming that Jeremiah preached in the north, for it explains that is the reason Josiah passed over Jeremiah and went instead to the prophetess Huldah for an interpretation of the book of the law when it was found in 622/621 BC. The Talmud says, "Jeremiah was not there [in Jerusalem], as he had gone to bring back the ten tribes" (Brown, 110).

The answer to the apparent absoluteness of Israel's divorce and the offer in v. 12 that God "will not frown on you [any longer]" (lit. "will not let my face fall against you") is that the northern ten tribes of that day had failed to return to Yahweh. But vv. 12–18 speak of a future day in which they would be brought to "Zion" (v. 14d). This introduces the days of the messianic era, in which the promises of Yahweh are offered to both Israel and Judah (see also v. 18). Therefore, the call to repent remains open. This was not because the Lord is fickle and capricious, but rather this offer comes from his being "merciful" (חָסִיד). Although this word is rarely used of God (Ps 145:17, "loving toward all he has made"), it is one of the messianic terms used in Ps 16:10, "nor will you let your Holy One (חָסִיד) see decay." That is why God "will not be angry forever." Even though this willingness on Yahweh's part not to retain his anger forever is precisely what gives Judah her false sense of security during her obstinacy, nevertheless it is the only basis for hope that sinners such as northern Israel could be restored to Yahweh or reunited with Judah. Thus, the analogy in the earlier part of this chapter is not now put into abeyance, but the former part of this chapter is addressed to the generation that had refused to return to Yahweh. In fact, that generation had been dealt with a century earlier, in 722/721 BC. But the sins of the fathers are not held against their children if they do not follow in the error of their parents' ways. Besides, the eschatological future burns brightly for both Israel and Judah, if they repent and believe.

3:14–15 It may be literally true, in the meantime, that some Israelites remain in the north who were drawn back to Jerusalem, perhaps by the preaching of Jeremiah in the north (v. 14). They may have found that Yahweh, not a piece of stone or some kind of wood, was their "husband" (בַּעַל, *bāʿal*), an obvious play on the word for "Baal," which also means "master" or "husband." Even though there would only be a few ("I will take [לָקַח] you, one from a city and two from a family," v. 14c), yet no aspect of the people of God, either in Israel or Judah, would be forgotten. However, they will not be returned to the old idolatrous shrines; they will all be brought to the one true place of worship in unity in "Zion." Jerusalem would be the center of the revived and restored nation in that future day (31:6, 12; 50:5). At that time ("then," v. 15a), Yahweh will give them "shepherds" (nationally, religiously, and politically) who will "lead [them] with knowledge and understanding," those who are "after [God's] own heart," a phrase that recalls God's approval of David in 1 Sam 13:14 (v. 15b–c). No longer will the people need to put up with self-willed leaders who mislead and consume Yahweh's people, such as was promised in Ezek 34.

3:16 All this is set "In those days," a time that pointed to the messianic times coming in the future, an expression distinctive to Jeremiah (3:16, 18; 5:18; 31:29; 33:15, 16; 50:4, 20; but only found four times elsewhere in the OT). Among the blessings of that future day will be a great increase in the population numbers: "they will multiply and be fruitful" (v. 16a, an allusion to the formula in Gen 1:28; 17:1–8) as they formerly did in Egypt (cf. Exod 1:7). Additionally, the "ark of the covenant," perhaps destroyed in the Babylonian fires in Jerusalem, "will not be missed," nor will it ever "enter their minds or be remembered" any more (v. 16c–e; see "Excursus: The Ark of the Covenant"). Two probable reasons why the ark will fade from memory and no longer be needed are:

1. Since the ark contained a copy of the law, it will no longer be useful, since the law will be written on the heart (31:31–34).

2. The ark served as the throne of God, but that too would now be surpassed by Yahweh being actually present in Jerusalem (3:17; cf. Ezek 48:35).

Anyway, all too many had come to think of the ark, as they did of the temple, as a religious talisman, a good-luck charm that reinforced an unwarranted optimism that God could never visit evil or judgment on Judah, for that would mean he would have to destroy what he had promised to keep and do in his covenant; how could God do this to his own place of residence?

3:17-18 That future day of repentance will witness "all the nations [not just Northern Israel] ... assembl[ing] in Jerusalem [to honor] the name of Yahweh" (vv. 17b; 16:19-21; Isa 2:1-6; Mic 4:1-5). No longer would the nations trouble Israel, nor would they gather their thrones at her gates as her conquerors had done previously (Jer 1:15). Now they will gather in repentance and humility before Yahweh. Even more startling is that the historic division between the north and the south will be ended and the two will "join ... together" in "the land [God] gave [their] forefathers as an inheritance" (v. 18b-c).

Hope for the future days when Messiah will come in all his glory back to earth was part and parcel of Israel's and Judah's prospect for the days to come. Jeremiah had apparently gone to minister in the northern tribes in hopes of preparing them for another day that will be brighter than the days when an earlier generation had been divorced from God. In that time the nation will multiply and increase in size, and the Lord will sit on his throne in the city of Jerusalem. What a glorious day that will be. No wonder all the nations will come annually to be taught directly by the Lord himself in that future day, as Isa 2 and Mic 4 teach. Meanwhile, the ark of the covenant will drop out of sight and memory, for the law of God found in the Ten Commandments and previously housed in the ark will be inscribed on the hearts of God's people. There will be no need to have it inscribed on stone any longer!

A DIVINE LAMENT (3:19-20)

TRANSLATION

>   **19** "I myself said,[55]
>   'How [gladly] would I treat you as sons,
>   And give you a desirable land,
>   The most beautiful inheritance of all the nations.'
>   I thought you would call me 'Father'

---

55. The LXX has "Amen, Lord, for I will set ... " where the MT has "I myself said."

And would not turn aside from following me.
  20 But like a woman unfaithful to her husband,

So you have dealt treacherously with me, O house of Israel," declares Yahweh.

COMMENTARY

3:19-20 Over against the promises of a bright future for the people of God in the eschaton, there is a switch back to the addressees who had been mentioned in the north earlier in this chapter, perhaps in 3:5 or 3:14. If so, then the people had given a decisive "No!" to God's call to turn back to him. God yearns for the future depicted in vv. 16-18, for inwardly, Yahweh "said": "How gladly would I treat you like sons and give you a desirable land, the most beautiful inheritance of any nation" (v. 19b-c), but this nation has been unfaithful as a woman can be to her husband (v. 20). The expected response instead is "father" (v. 19e) and that the nation does not turn away from following Yahweh. Alas, however, this is not to be in the days of Jeremiah.

Several verses in Jeremiah depict the pathos and emotions of Yahweh, such as 3:7a, 19; 36:3, 7. Michael L. Brown (114-17) has a fine excursus on "Open Theism and Jeremiah's View of the Foreknowledge of God." He correctly concludes that the language in these and similar instances is anthropomorphic language that demonstrates that God is fully able to experience these feelings in the course of their happening even though he is fully cognizant of their outcomes by virtue of his omniscience. Therefore, we must play down neither God's complete omniscience nor his emotional involvement in these events as he enters into the situations of this world. How tragic, then, that despite his sincere calls to Israel, there is no movement on Israel's part to respond to God's loving and merciful invitation.

What mercy and grace northern Israel experienced, only to have it all to be turned aside! It is hard to imagine what more God could have done to rescue that generation. In like manner, we as a nation are coming perilously close to being unresponsive, despite years of mercy and grace. What will we say to our Lord in that day for having flaunted all of his gracious acts to us as well? Of course, God is gracious, but payday must come someday, when there is no change in our ways.

SOUNDING THE CALL TO REPENTANCE (3:21–25)

TRANSLATION

21 A voice on the barren heights[56] is heard,
Weeping and pleading of the sons of Israel,
    Because they have perverted their ways,
And forgotten Yahweh their God.
    22 "Return, O backsliding people,
I will heal you from your backslidings."[57]
    Behold, we come to you,
For you are Yahweh our God.
    23 Surely, the commotion on the hills,
And mountains is a delusion,
    Surely, in Yahweh our God,
Is the salvation of Israel.

24 From our youth the shameful thing has devoured the labor of our fathers, their flocks, their herds, their sons and their daughters. **25** Let us lie down in our shame and let our dishonor cover us. For we have sinned against Yahweh our God, we, and our fathers; from our youth till this day, and we have not listened to the voice of Yahweh our God.

COMMENTARY

3:21–22 Here in v. 22 is a locus classicus for all repentance calls that originate with Yahweh. There is heard on "barren heights" (v. 21a) weeping and supplication by the "sons of Israel," a designation Jeremiah never uses for Judah alone; thus it reflects an anticipated response from northern Israel. The grief at that time will be very much like the weeping in Zech 12:10–13, for Israel will recognize her "perverted ways" (v. 21c). The wordplay in v. 22 is strong and powerful: "Return, O backsliding people; I will heal you from your backslidings." Whether there was at least some repentance at that historic point of time or not cannot be determined, but there surely

---

56. The LXX has ἐκ χειλέων, "from the lips," where the MT has עַל־שְׁפָיִים, "on the barren heights."

57. Or "apostasy."

was no national widespread repentance sufficient to halt the threatened approaching judgment.[58]

3:23 Just what v. 23 means is not entirely known, but apparently there was a renunciation of the Canaanite worship that had taken place to some degree on all the hilltops, but which was subsequently determined to be "false/a delusion," and "in pretense" only (שֶׁקֶר, a "deception"). Another interpretation of vv. 22b–25 is that, as in Hos 14:2, God is placing the appropriate words of repentance in the mouths of the people to show them what repentance really is like.

3:24 Nevertheless, whoever spoke and whenever this evaluation went on, those identified in this context confess their past experiences and agree that they had had a negative effect on "the labor of [their] fathers—their flocks and herds, their sons and their daughters" (v. 24b–c); their "shameful [gods had] devoured [them]" (v. 24a). The reference to shame is a not-too-subtle allusion to their worship of Baal (11:3; Hos 9:10).[59] Thus, all the hard work invested in Israel and Judah had come to naught, for God's judgment on them had occurred as Moses warned in Deut 28:30, 33. Baal, the fertility god whose worship was supposed to bring productivity to the land and people, had been an enormous failure.

3:25 Finally those who are speaking in v. 25 put it all together: their shameful worship of Baal and the other Canaanite gods has brought down over their heads an enormous disgrace and the corresponding judgment of God. Clearly, they had sinned against Yahweh, and they had "not listened to the voice of Yahweh, [their] God" (v. 25f). Jeremiah uses this latter phrase eighteen times out of the sixty-five in which it appears in the OT (Mackay, 201). This may be ideal language being used here, or it was the language of that future day of the end times, when Israel will finally come to her senses

---

58. Jeremiah often engages in dialogue with his audience. See J. T. Willis, "Dialogue between Prophet and Audience as a Rhetorical Device in the Book of Jeremiah," *JSOT* 33 (1985): 63–82.

59. Büchner suggests that if "Boshet is a divine title … then its occurrence in this Hebrew chant could be viewed as a denunciation in the same breath of the goddess and the royal administration." See D. Büchner, "Boshet in Jeremiah 3:24: Disenfranchisement and the Role of the Goddess in Seventh-Century Judah," *JTS* 59, no. 2 (2008): 478–99.

and come to the Lord. If only the nation had done that earlier in her history, much like the prodigal son finally did (Luke 15:21), she would have saved herself a great deal of pain. But even in her failures she was also a light to the nations, for they too could see that when a people turn their back on their own God—indeed, especially on Yahweh himself, who so dramatically revealed himself to Israel and the nations—that nation would be subject to the judgments of God just as much as they would be exposed to the prom-ises of God should they have repented. God's readiness to embrace a people who repent of their waywardness and sin demonstrates his remarkable grace. Repentance is always the way back home to the Father.

Northern Israel was better known for her "backsliding" nature than she was for her turning to the Lord. If only she would turn to the Lord, then he would heal her of her perpetual backsliding. But that nation decided it was best to go after the shameful worship of Baal. Israel knew no boundaries to her involvement in shameful worship of a pagan god. She had deserted her God from the early days of her youth, and she consistently disobeyed the Lord. One can only imagine a "what if" scenario had she responded dif-ferently. But will the future of our day be written in similar terms, "what if we had repented"?

CIRCUMCISION OF THE HEART (4:1–4)

TRANSLATION

1 "If you will return, O Israel," declares Yahweh.
"Return unto me."

"And if you will put your detestable [idols] out of my sight
And no longer waver,

2 And you swear, 'As Yahweh lives,'
In truth, justice, and righteousness,

Then the nations will be blessed by him,
And in him they will glory."

3 For thus says Yahweh to the men of Judah and Jerusalem:[60]
"Plow up your fallow ground,
And do not sow among thorns.

---

60. Some Heb. mss, the LXX, the Syr., and the Tg. add "inhabitants of" before "Jerusalem."

4 Circumcise yourselves to Yahweh,
Remove the foreskin of your hearts,
   O men of Judah and inhabitants of Jerusalem;
Lest my wrath burn against you like fire,
   With no one to quench it,
Because of the evil of your deeds."

COMMENTARY

4:1–2 Verses 1 and 2 spell out what real repentance entails if Israel and Judah are going to get it right:

1. They must return to Yahweh.

2. They must put out of their sight, and out of God's sight, those "detestable [idols]."

3. They must "no longer go astray" or waver in their commitment to Yahweh.

4. They must make their oaths only in the name of Yahweh.

If Israel does these things, then "the nations [!] will be blessed by [her]," (v. 2c) as they, together with Israel, will glorify Yahweh (v. 2d; 3:17).

Some think that no amount of theological or exegetical explanation can account for the contradictory messages calling for repentance with that same message also noting the northern nation's rejection and when her divorce is already complete and final. Explanations that attempt to answer this dilemma by assigning all the absolute promises in the Abrahamic-Davidic covenants only to a southern (read: Judean) tradition, while making just the northern tradition contingent on obedience, are contrived and without textual or theological support. Therefore, instead of assuming that there are two opposite or even contradictory strains here, the text argues for one coordinated response. For even within the Davidic covenant, each individual descendant in each generation does not automatically enjoy the blessings and promises given to the Davidic house; rather, it is true that often they must *transmit* the blessings to the next generation, but they can only *participate* in those blessings by faith, which is evidenced by obedience to the word of God (2 Sam 7:14). Thus, a whole current generation could fail to enter into the blessings of the divine promises, but that would not prevent the next or future generations from receiving what they had missed if that new generation would begin in believing hearts to God.

4:3-4 Verses 3 and 4 summarize the message of repentance and turning to Yahweh. Jeremiah uses two images to underline his emphasis on his call for repentance and turning back to Yahweh:

1. the plowing up of fallow or virgin ground (v. 3b-c; also in Hos 10:12)

2. the circumcision of the heart (v. 4a-b)

Fallow or unplowed ground is not suitable for sowing seed or for reaping a harvest; that ground, which has lain fallow and unplowed or disked for so long that thorns, briars, and young trees have now emerged over the whole plot of land, must be broken up and plowed and disked under before it can be sown. This brings to mind Jesus's parable of the four kinds of soils (Mark 4:1–20). But it is only the "soil," or the heart, that has been made tender by repentance and turning back to God that has any chance of producing a harvest that is pleasing to God. If the word is sown among the thorns, or on hard, unworked ground that has lain fallow for years, the worries of life and the cares of this world will choke out the word of God (Mark 4:18–19) and the seed will be unable to take root.

The second image Jeremiah uses is a call to circumcise their hearts (v. 4). This mark of the covenant was established in Abraham's day (Gen 17:9–14). But it calls for more than a mere external or superficial change. Already Moses had instructed: "Circumcise your hearts" (Deut 10:16; 30:6). Jeremiah's audience was luxuriating in King Josiah having brought reform into the temple and the book of the law of God being found and again being read. But little of these outward signs of change touched the personal lives of the general population, or if they did, it was only an outward mask for deep, contrary feelings of abandonment of Yahweh and his word. The "heart/mind" (לֵבָב) is used some sixty-five times in Jeremiah to call for the action of repentance and turning back to God, and it extends into the inner feelings of one's thoughts, will, and spiritual life. Men and women could not surrender partially to Yahweh; he called for a complete dedication of all of themselves to him. Repenting "lightly" (6:14) was not an option!

The consequences of refusing to repent authentically and in deep contrition of their hearts are serious, for the threats of divine wrath breaking out on them are attached to the calls for true turning to God. God's wrath will burn like an unquenchable fire (v. 4d–f). The reason for such an alarming ultimatum for those who do not wish to consecrate themselves afresh is repeated: the evil of their ways (Deut 28:20; Hos 9:15; Jer 21:12; 23:2, 22; 25:5; 26:3; 44:22). But let it be noted: when this message is given there is still time to repent. God will hold the door open for repentance and for a change in his threatened judgments all the way up to the final nanosecond before the time when the judgment is to fall. Yahweh will always send his exhortations to turn and repent prior to the bursting forth of his judgments. Unfortunately, Jeremiah's generation thinks differently; it believes it has an unprecedented divine declaration of eternal endurance that they are so blessed that no evil could or would ever happen to them. Once you are chosen, they falsely reasoned, that it is forever! But they fail to distinguish between the necessity of *transmitting* the promises and blessings of God versus the reality of their *participating* in them only by personal belief and the corresponding evidence of obedience to God's word.

The call for revival in this text is the same as had been issued earlier by the prophet Hosea (10:12): "Sow righteousness for yourselves, reap the fruit of unfailing love; and break up your unplowed ground; for it is time to seek the LORD, until he comes and showers his righteousness on you." The hearts of the people had laid fallow, and they had not been plowed and harrowed into pulverized soil for anything spiritual to take root in their lives. Instead, what came up were wild thorns, bushes, and scattered trees that left the soil hard and impervious, completely unable to sprout any seeds.

But if Israel responded, then the nations of the earth would invoke blessings on her from the Lord. So it is high time to break up the unplowed and fallow ground. Sowing thorns in place of good seed is no way to farm, nor is it a good way to prosper in the way of the Lord.

Circumcision is also called for, but it is to be a circumcision of the heart, not of the flesh. Routine liturgy and rote performance are not acceptable to God and in no way attract his mercy or favor. God wants genuine repentance and an honest turning back to himself.

TERROR AND CALAMITY FROM
THE NORTH (4:5–6:30)

Whereas chapter 2 depicts how God's love was betrayed, and 3:1–4:43 point the way for true repentance, 4:5–6:26 warns that God's judgment is extremely near if there is no repentance. The alarm sounded here reverberates through seven or eight poems of Jeremiah's agitated soul on what all of this portends for an unrepentant Judah.

This extremely long third section of Jeremiah's early ministry is divided into two parts, each beginning with these introductory words: "Announce in Judah" (4:5; 5:20). These words inaugurate a series of verbal commands for Israel and Judah to get ready for the "disaster from the north" (4:6c). So great is this attack that it is called the "great/terrible destruction" six times (שֶׁבֶר גָּדוֹל, šeber gādôl; 4:6d; 6:1; 14:17; 48:3; all with reference to Judah, but two others with reference to Babylon, 50:22; 51:54). The seriousness of this destruction is evidenced in the usage of the Heb. word šeber, which can be used of a "fractured" bone, a "shattered" piece of pottery, or "collapse or break" in a wall.

But who is this enemy from the north? Greek historian Herodotus argues that the foes from the north were Asiatic tribesmen generally equated with the Scythians, known to classical authors.[61] Herodotus says these invaders dominated the area for twenty-eight years as they marched through Israel intent on attacking Egypt. However, they were bought off by taking Egyptian gold and satisfied themselves with looting a temple in the Philistine territory at Ashkelon. There are few facts to confirm any of this, for nowhere are the Scythians identified in Scripture. The best evidence comes from Hellenistic times, when the town of Beth Shan was also known as Scythopolis. If the Scythians were present, it may have been earlier in Jeremiah's ministry, before 616 BC. Or it may just as well be that at first Jeremiah did not identify this foe with any particular power.

Once again the metaphor of a lion is used (4:7) of the enemy forces that have left the towns in ruins (v. 7d). But is this description of the savage pillage of the towns in Judah accurate? William Foxwell Albright writes:

---

61. Herodotus, *Histories* 1.103–6.

Many towns were destroyed at the beginning of the sixth century BC and never again occupied; others were destroyed at that time and partly reoccupied at some later date; still others were destroyed and reoccupied after a long period of abandonment. ... There is not a single case where a town of Judah was continuously occupied through the exilic period.[62]

John Bright, Albright's student, agrees: "The land was in shambles. ... Virtually all of the fortified towns of Judah's heartland had been razed to the ground" (Bright, liii). But in recent days this assessment has come under serious challenge as scholars such as Hans M. Barstad argue that this was more a myth than a real statement of the situation.[63] However, B. Oded shows to the contrary, the archaeological findings confirm Jeremiah's descriptions of the land of Judah after the Babylonian attacks. Interestingly enough, there is clear evidence that the Benjamites escaped this Babylonian onslaught.[64]

Older commentators, who followed Herodotus,[65] assume the invaders the prophet was referring to here were the Scythians of central Asia, whose horsemen terrorized the Middle East during this period. In fact, the Scythians did raid Ashkelon (604 BC, presumably as they served in Nebuchadnezzar's army) in the Gaza Strip of the Philistines, but there is no evidence that they also ever attacked Judah. However, none of God's revelations to Jeremiah mentions the Scythians; moreover, we may completely exclude them due to God mentioning "chariots" (4:13), which the Scythians did not possess, and siege tactics (4:16; 5:17c; 6:6), which were not part of the Scythian strategy (Kidner, 38–39). Babylon, which appears a generation later, better answers to the details mentioned here.

---

62. W. F. Albright, *Archaeology of Palestine* (Baltimore: Penguin, 1960), 160.

63. H. M. Barstad, *The Myth of the Empty Land: A Study of the History and Archaeology of Judah during the "Exilic" Period* (Oslo: Scandinavian University Press, 1996), as cited in Michael Brown, "Jeremiah," in *The Expositor's Bible Commentary* 7 (Grand Rapids: Zondervan, 2010), 124–25.

64. B. Oded, "Where Is the 'Myth' of the Empty Land to Be Found?," in *Judah and the Judeans in the Neo-Babylonian Period*, ed. O. Lipschits and J. Blenkinsopp (Winona Lake, IN: Eisenbrauns, 2003), 55–74.

65. Herodotus, *Histories* 1.103–6.

THE ENEMY IS COMING FROM THE NORTH (4:5–9)

TRANSLATION

     5 "Announce in Judah and proclaim in Jerusalem and say:
'Give a blast on the shofar throughout the land!'
     Cry out aloud[66] and say:
'Band together!
Let us flee[67] to the fortified cities!'
     6 Hoist the banner toward Zion!
Get to safety without delay!
     For I am bringing disaster from the north,
Even an immense calamity.
     7 A lion has come up from his lair;
A destroyer of nations has set out,
     He has gone out from his place
To lay waste your land.
     Your towns will fall to ruins,
Without inhabitant.
     8 On account of this, gird on sackcloth,
Lament and wail,
     For the fierce anger of Yahweh
Has not turned away from us.[68]
     9 In that day, declares Yahweh,
The courage[69] of the king and the courage of the officials
Will crumble,
     The priests will be appalled,
And the prophets will be horrified."

---

66. Lit. "Cry out and make full."

67. Lit. "flee."

68. It could be that the word מִמֶּנּוּ, "from us," has been misplaced, fitting better after לֹא־שָׁב instead of at the end of the phrase.

69. Lit. "heart/mind."

COMMENTARY

Without indicating a new start, a series of pl. commands are ordered one after another, beginning with the blast of the shofar, which would be something similar to the air raid warning alert in World War II or modern civil defense or tornado sirens, which are tested weekly or monthly in many parts of the United States. The prophet's task is to wake up those who stood under God's condemnation—they were doomed if they did not turn back to God. So with a word picture as a forerunner of what would happen, Jeremiah sounds forth God's word for all who will listen up and repent. Such blasts on the horn are sure signs that an emergency and an invasion of some kind is pending.

4:5 One can almost hear the prophet's breathless warning in more pl. impvs.: "Cry out, make full" (literally, as in "filling" the hands with a weapon), which could mean, "Go to full mobilization." Those who were scattered throughout Judah in the villages and fields must quickly "band together [assemble]" and "flee to the fortified [walled] cities."

4:6 Six times Jeremiah announces that Yahweh is going to bring a "great destruction" (שֶׁבֶר גָּדוֹל, *šeber gādôl*; 4:6; 6:1; 14:17; 48:3) on Judah and twice on Babylon (50:22; 51:54). Such a destruction will be utter and complete, as evidenced through Holladay's discussion of how *šeber* can be used in three ways (mentioned earlier; Holladay 1986, 153):

1. for a bone fracture, as a metaphorical use for the spiritual condition of the people as "broken" or "fractured" (6:14; 8:21; 10:19),

2. for the shattering of pottery (18:10),

3. for the breaking down of the physical infrastructure of a country.

The "signal" (v. 6a) was likely a flag that was hoisted on a hilltop and would confirm the alarm that the trumpet had sounded. Indeed, the reason for such prompt action is that God is going to bring disaster from the north (v. 6c). This reference to the north takes the reader back to 1:13-14.

4:7 The expected foe is described as "a lion" (v. 7a, אַרְיֵה, which is a different word for "lion" than in 2:15). But from his description, this lion is more than a threat to an individual or a group; it will emerge from its lair, where it has been sleeping to be "a destroyer of nations" (v. 7b). Thus, what can be expected is not just an isolated raid with the routine type of looting; no, this will involve real devastation that is deliberately planned rather than some random attack.

Not all interpreters accept the judgment, given by Albright in the above quote, that the land was in shambles; some even contend that the thesis of an "empty" land of Judah is a myth.[70] But as Brown argues to the contrary, Jeremiah's repeated contentions cannot be classified as hyperbole. Moreover, B. Oded has shown that while the cities of Benjamin escaped this destruction from the north, the archaeology of Judah during this period shows extensive destruction in town after town.[71] No wonder Jeremiah predicted that "your towns will lie in ruins without inhabitant" (v. 7e).

4:8 The pl. forms of the impvs. continue in v. 8. The recommended garb is "sackcloth," a coarse material made out of goat or camel hair that, in some contexts, suggests repentance was in order, as in Jonah 3:5. But often it was merely a sign of lamentation over a disaster that had occurred (6:26; 48:37). True, the disaster had not happened as yet, but given the stubbornness of the hearts of his listeners, they might just as well begin their grieving right now. The intense anger of Yahweh has not "turned away" (שָׁב, šab) from its purpose, for the people have not repented or "turned toward" God (שׁוּב, šûb); that is why God is unable to "turn away" (שׁוּב; šûb) from his threatened judgment.

4:9 The oft-repeated formula "in that day" (v. 9) does not always carry the eschatological reference that it so frequently does in Isaiah and elsewhere; here it refers to the preceding warning. Too unwisely, the kings and his officials presume immunity from all disaster; their claim rests solely on the ancient promise of God. But while each generation was required to

---

70. Barstad, *Myth of the Empty Land*, 79, quoted in Brown, 124.

71. Oded, "Where Is the 'Myth' of the Empty Land to Be Found?," 67–70, quoted in Brown, 124. Also see L. E. Stager, "The Fury of Babylon," *BAR* 22, no. 1 (1996): 56–69, 76–77.

pass on and transmit the blessings of God in the Abrahamic-Davidic covenant, there was no guarantee that each generation would personally benefit in those blessings if they failed to believe God and to faithfully obey his word. For now, there is no doubt that there will be a time of darkness and despair when God intervenes to carry out what his prophet warns will happen if there is no repentance and turning back to Yahweh. The leadership of the king, his officials, priests, and prophets all fall under the divine indictment. There is no more "courage," or "heart," for the resolve or nerve of these leaders has evaporated and crumbled in the face of the impending onslaught.

Announcing one command after another, Jeremiah warned that disaster was threatening from the north. So the people of Judah were to assemble in the fortified cities, for it was high time to flee to safety. Once again the metaphor of a lion is used to depict the conqueror. Their towns would soon be in ruins; it was now time to gird on sackcloth and to wail, for the tremendous anger of God could no longer be averted. All Judah's official leaders will be horrified at what would happen to them, and her false prophets will be downright appalled. It is time to get real with God or face the consequences.

JEREMIAH'S PROTEST (4:10)

TRANSLATION

10 Then I said, "O no, Adonai Yahweh, surely you have really deceived this people and Jerusalem, telling them, 'All will be well,' when the sword is at our throats."

COMMENTARY

4:10 Almost spontaneously the prophet reacts by saying in effect, "This is unfair!" Jeremiah's reaction is at once strong and puzzling, at least on first take. He uses the unusual name of "Adonai Yahweh," which is used almost exclusively when God refers to his promise to Abraham (Gen 15:2, 8) or his promise to David (2 Sam 7:18, 19, 20, 22, 28, 29) and the promise of the land (Jer 32:17, 25). Those are the ancient promises of peace, safety, and rest in the land, but now Jeremiah has to bring a word of destruction and a complete wipeout of Jerusalem and Judah. Therefore, unthinkingly for the moment, he charges God with having "deceived his people." Nevertheless, he begins by asserting again that God is God over everything. But he goes on to say in emphatic terms (using a hiphil inf. abs.; הַשֵּׁא) that God has completely deceived this people and Jerusalem itself. How should we understand such language? Is he speaking ironically to taunt and deride those who had prophesied falsely? However, had not God promised peace to Judah and Jerusalem a century earlier when the Assyrians had threatened to invade them (Isa 37:33–35)? But surely for these false prophets, if that is their basis for preaching peace once again, they have certainly failed to get a new word from God and to realize that these were different times from Isaiah's.

Jeremiah's words can be understood by the incident in 1 Kgs 22:2–23, where God permitted false prophets of King Ahab's day to speak lies. The Heb. mode of speaking was not always concerned to record all the secondary causes involved, so what God permitted could be directly attributed to his own doing. For example, it pleased Yahweh to bruise the Servant of Yahweh, but Peter makes it clear on the day of Pentecost that the Jews and the Romans were culpable for what occurred on Good Friday (Acts 2:23). But it is also true that such was at the same time the work of a sovereign God.

Calvin (213) takes a different approach. He understands Jeremiah's speech to be ironic, one that taunts and derides those who prophesied falsely. In this case, God had permitted the false prophets to appear and work as lying spirits, as God had done with the lying spirits of the prophets of Ahab (1 Kgs 22:2–23). Thus, it was the false prophets who had said, "You will have peace."

Once again, at the end of the age, God will allow a strong delusion to come over those who deny the truth of God (2 Thess 2:7–12). The message the false prophets brought was dead wrong for Jeremiah's times; they claimed "You will have peace" (v. 10c). Instead, "the sword" itself was at their very "throats." The word translated "throats" (נֶפֶשׁ) usually means "soul," but here means "throat," that is, the organ involved in breathing.

Whether this was a case of divine permission for the false prophets to speak lies (cf. 1 Kgs 22:20–23) to catch a disobedient people off guard or a case of ironic speech that derided those who prophesied incorrectly, we cannot determine. But on either explanation, the Lord cannot be charged with sponsoring error or falsehood since he is Lord over all and he is holy.

THE SCORCHING HOT WINDS OF JUDGMENT (4:11–18)

TRANSLATION

11 At that time, this people and Jerusalem will be told, "A scorching wind from the barren heights in the desert blows toward the daughter of my people, but not to winnow or cleanse,

12 A wind too full, for this comes from me. Now, I am the one who will pronounce judgments on them.[72]

13 Behold, he advances like the clouds,

His war-chariots like a whirlwind;

Swifter than eagles are his horses.

Woe to us, for we are ruined!

14 O Jerusalem! Wash your hearts from evil

And be saved!

How long will your wicked thoughts

Lodge within you?

15 A voice is announcing from Dan,

Proclaiming disaster from Mount Ephraim.

16 'Tell this to the nations,

Announce it to Jerusalem:

"Besiegers[73] are coming from a distant land;

Raising their war cry against the cities of Judah.

17 Like guardians of the field they surround her,

Because she has been recalcitrant against me,'''" declares Yahweh.

18 "Your [own] conduct and your actions

Have brought this upon you.

This is your punishment!

How bitter it is!

How it pierces to the heart!"

---

72. Althann argues that vv. 11–12 are poetry, not prose, and that Jeremiah is using "the pivot pattern, a poetic technique frequently employed in Jeremiah." See R. Althann, "Jeremiah IV 11–12: Stichometry, Parallelism and Translation," *VT* 28, no. 4 (1978): 385–91. Nevertheless, the meaning of the text does not change. See also W. L. Holladay, "Structure, Syntax and Meaning in Jeremiah IV 11–12A," *VT* 26, no. 1 (1976): 28–37.

73. The Heb. text has צָרִים, "besiegers," where the LXX has συστροφαί, "conspirators." The editor of the *BHS* recommends the emendation to "enemies."

COMMENTARY

4:11–12 "At that time" (v. 11) resumes the "in that day" of v. 9 and the description of an invasion in vv. 5–7. What the people will be told is a word that has been announced previously, here the day of judgment. Jeremiah here describes the coming judgment under the figure of a wind known as a *sirocco*. It is a wind that comes off the eastern desert, but rather than bringing refreshment and relief from the oppressive heat, it is altogether too dry, too hot, and too strong a wind to be of any help either for cooling or for sifting the wheat from the chaff. Instead, the wind lifted up the sand and limited the visibility of the sun, leaving only a slight shadow cast by a tent's shape. As used here, it became a metaphor for the coming destruction, which would engulf all alike without making any discrimination. Jeremiah sees it aimed at those whom God acknowledged as his own "daughter" and his own "people" (v. 11). The wind is sent from God as his judgment against his people. The wind, as a matter of fact, comes from the same "barren heights" that were associated with the places where Judah went after her adulterous and idolatrous affairs. The connection was not to be wasted or missed by those in Judah.

4:13 Oftentimes in Scripture God is depicted as advancing in judgment, as if he were riding a cloud chariot (Pss 18:7–15; 68:33; 104:3; Nah 1:3), or even using a whirlwind (Job 38:1). Here is that same imagery of impending judgment that he brings through other nations. The foe God will send could be seen gathering like a cyclone, for the war chariots were ready to swoop down like a stormy wind attached to horses that exceeded the speed of eagles, which Jeremiah announces in hyperbolic form. These images are similar to those used in Isa 5:28; 66:15; Ezek 38:16; Hab 1:8. So dreadful is the impact of all of this that the panic-stricken people declare: "We are ruined!" (v. 13d). There is no way to identify the oppressors in this case, whether Scythians, Assyrians, or Babylonians; but the judgment, wherever it is to come from, is certain!

4:14–16 However, even at this late date, there is a possible deliverance, if Jerusalem wishes to be saved (v. 14b). She must cleanse her heart of all evil (v. 14a). The juggernaut is advancing closer and closer until it reaches Jerusalem. Reports have come already from the northernmost outpost—Dan (modern Tell el-Qadi, v. 15a), at the headwaters for the Jordan River. Then word comes from the hills of Ephraim, just ten miles north of Jerusalem, that a pending disaster is on its way. Has anyone yet turned and repented by cleansing their heart of the evil residing inside them? This call for turning away from "evil," "sin," and "iniquity" repeats the same pleas Jeremiah had made in chapter 3 as he called for repentance.

4:17 The occupation forces take up their places as if they are guarding a field (v. 17a), enclosing Jerusalem all around, like farmers who act in a similar way to protect their crops and animals. But why is all of this necessary? The prophet puts it in plain terms: "Because you [Judah] have been recalcitrant against [Yahweh]" (v. 17b). So there is a strong theological reason why these things were happening.

4:18 Or to put the matter directly, all this is happening because of Judah's own conduct and her own actions against Yahweh (v. 18a). To be sure, this punishment is itself bitter, and it pierced the heart, but there is an offer of a different ending if she will only repent. But no! Jeremiah's audience is resolute in their evil and their stubbornness. They presumed they would be delivered just as Hezekiah had been delivered from the Assyrians years ago. The sour and disagreeable consequences of their failure to repent will be of their own doing.

At the very time God has decreed for judgment, an extremely strong wind will arise, announcing the judgment of God. Often in Scripture this figure of speech depicts God as arriving in a chariot made up of his clouds. What is wanted from Judah is the same thing God expects from all peoples on earth: to have their hearts washed so they might be saved. So what is necessary for Judah to hear is also important to the nations (4:16). God's demand for holiness and righteousness would always be the same for Judah and Israel, as it is for all nations of our day. The Lord requires an accountability from all nations in terms of living according to the ethical standards he has given us in his word.

THE PROPHET'S ANGUISH (4:19–22)

TRANSLATION

19 My anguish, my anguish![74]
    I writhe in pain.
Oh, the walls of my heart!
    My heart pounds within me,
I cannot keep silent,
      For the sound of the shofar in my spirit;
      The alarm of the battle.
20 Disaster follows disaster;
    The whole land lies in ruins.
Suddenly, my tents lie in ruins,
    In a moment my curtains.
21 "How long must I see the banner,
    And hear the shofar blast?
22 For my people are foolish;
    They do not know me.
Foolish children they are;
    They have no understanding.
They are wise in doing evil;
    They do not know how to do good."

COMMENTARY

4:19–22 The speaker of these verses could be Yahweh, but the verses could also fit the prophet; however, the difference is slight, for the prophet gets his messages from God. They are in the form of a lament as the physical effect of what the speaker sees coming in the future. The coming destruction is sounded in the blast of a war alarm on the shofar/trumpet. He sees the tents crumbling, the battle cry lifted, and general ruination of the land about to occur, according to his vision. But the problem still resides in the lives and hearts of the people: what fools they have been to not wake up and see the signs of the coming destruction all about them. Instead of

---

74. The word can be translated as "intestines" or "bowels," and it represents the center of one's being, the seat of emotions.

being experts in holiness and in doing good, they have majored in acting like fools and senseless idiots whose skill sets are limited to working in evil.

Despite the prophet's deep love for his people, he has been called on to announce their judgment and destruction (1:9-10). This forces his daily life into an anguished paradox, in even the words that he chooses, such as the word behind "My anguish, my anguish," which represent the Heb. word literally rendered as "bowels," that is, his inward viscera. (In ancient psychology, the organs affected by such devastating emotional experiences were in the lower part of the body, such as the bowels, whereas modern speakers would refer to the same type of wrenching experiences by pointing to their hearts as the center of their emotions.)

Already he can hear the din of war experientially, as if it has already begun. This leaves the prophet feeling alone and defenseless. He cannot imagine how much longer he will be able to hold out under these types of circumstances. Worst of all, his people simply do not know Yahweh. What intelligence left to them is exhausted as those residual skills are used instead for doing evil.

Both the Lord and the prophet pour out their grief over the disaster that is coming. One wretched experience follows hard after the previous one. It tears the deep emotions of any who are concerned for the welfare of the people. Such pain and grief did not need to happen, nor does the threatened judgment of God need to happen in our day if only we too repent and turn back to our Lord. Alas, however, we, like Judah, are like sensless children who have no understanding. Why do we think we will be able to avoid the threatened judgment somehow? It does not make sense. Our Lord will be patient, but he will act in the end!

A VISION OF THE COMING DESTRUCTION (4:23-28)

TRANSLATION

> **23** I looked at the earth,
>   And behold, it was formless and empty;
> And at the heavens,
>   And their light was gone.
> **24** I looked at the mountains,
>   And behold, they were quaking.

And all the hills were swaying.

25 I looked, and behold, there were no people;

And all the birds of the air had fled.

26 I looked, and behold, the fruitful land was a desert;

And all of its towns were broken down,[75]

Before Yahweh and his burning anger.

27 For thus says Yahweh:

"The whole land will be ruined,

Yet I will not make a full end.

28 Therefore the earth will mourn

And the heavens above will grow dark,

For I have spoken; I have purposed,

I will not relent, nor will I turn back."

COMMENTARY

4:23-26 In some of the most moving poetry in the whole Bible, the coming ruin of the land is depicted as if it involves a cosmic conflagration. The earth is described, much as in the creation narrative of Gen 1:2, as being a formless and empty void,[76] that is, still not a finished work of creation.[77] Each of vv. 23-26 begins with "I looked," followed by "behold." It envisions four aspects of the universe: earth, heavens, mountains, and hills; followed by four visions of life: people, birds, fruitful land, cities. Surely there is oriental hyperbole here, but it is not all dissimilar from the ways Jeremiah's colleagues point to divine judgment (Isa 2:12-14; Hos 4:3). Nevertheless, it is no wonder that Jeremiah is so distraught in his inner being over what he and his nation are about to face.

In a very real sense, what is to happen is a reversal of creation, especially for that part of the world inhabited by Judah. Without using the terminology of the Day of Yahweh, Jeremiah certainly uses the imagery of the same (cf. Joel 2:1-11; Amos 8:9-10; Nah 1:2-8; Zeph 1:2-3). Usually we

---

75. Many mss, including the LXX (ἐμπεπυρισμέναι), opt for נִצְּתוּ, "were burned," instead of "were broken down."

76. Some scholars believe that the original text only had "formless" while "and void" was added later to parallel Gen 1:2. See K. M. Hayes, "Jeremiah IV 23: Tōhû without Bōhû," VT 47, no. 2 (1997): 247-49.

77. Jeremiah shows a clear awareness of both creation and covenant. See H. Lalleman, "Jeremiah, Judgment, and Creation," *TynBul* 60, no. 1 (2009): 15-24.

associate stability and durability with the mountains and the hills, but when they start to move and to sway back and forth, it is time to ask, just what can a body use as a solid reference point in a world where everything moves?

4:27–28 However, even if the whole land becomes ruined, God will not make a complete end to it (vv. 27b–c). Jeremiah is given a word of hope in the midst of this description of waste and void. The reason for this caveat on God's part is his ancient promise, all the way back to the patriarchs. Divine judgment will come, but judgment will not have the last word; God will have the final word! In the meantime, there will be no changing of God's mind, for since his people will not turn back from their evil ways, then God will not turn back from his intentions to bring judgment.

God will not change his mind and relent, because he has spoken his word: unless his people repent and turn back to him, there will be no deliverance for any in that generation. Everything appears to be shaken, even the mountains that one ordinarily relied on for stability and firmness. It will be as if there had been no creation at all, for there will be no people left, and even the birds are flown away (4:25). Nevertheless, God just as firmly promises in v. 27 that he will not destroy the earth completely. What a gracious Lord! There will be a remnant.

DRESSED TO KILL (4:29–31)

TRANSLATION

> **29** From the noise of horsemen and archers,
>> Every town takes to flight.
> They go into the thickets;
>> They climb up on the rocks.[78]
> All the towns are deserted;
>> No one resides in them.
> **30** You, O desolate one,
>> What are you doing?

---

78. The LXX has a longer text, "They entered the caves, and they hid themselves in the groves," where the MT has "They climb up on the rocks."

Why do you adorn yourself in scarlet?
> Why do you deck yourself with gold jewels?

Why do you enlarge your eyes with eye paint?
> You beautify yourself in vain,

Your lovers despise you;
> They seek your life.

31 I hear the cry of a woman in labor,
> A groan of one bearing her first child—

The cry of the Daughter of Zion gasping for breath, [saying:]
"Woe is me! I am fainting;
> My life is [given over] to murderers."

COMMENTARY

4:29–31 Once again the image changes as Yahweh's "Daughter of Zion" is figuratively described, this time as a prostitute dressed up for her suitors (the enemy that is about to come); yet in reality these presumed lovers actually loathe her and are ready to murder her. All her trouble to beautify herself will be in vain!

As the Babylonian enemy arrives in that future time, already the commotion and noise of the horseman and archers fill the land. As a result, everyone in Judah starts running to hide themselves in any available cover, such as the thickets, caves in the rocks, or the stony cliffs. The result is that the land is deserted except for the fortified cities.

But silly Jerusalem, here called the "Daughter of Zion," prepares to welcome the enemy like a Jezebel of former days. Three successive clauses in v. 30, each beginning with "for/indeed" (כִּי), ask in almost unbelievable outrage, (1) What's all the scarlet dress all about? (2) Why the gold jewelry? and (3) why are you using all that eye paint to enlarge your eyes? But there is no use in going to all that trouble, for you are not going to be able to wow the enemy; they actually despise you and they will kill you as fast as look at you. Nice try … but too bad; it's too late!

In fact, you all are as vulnerable and as helpless as a woman having her first child. You can stretch out your hands in pain all you want, but your lives have been given over to plain old murderers. The title "Daughter of Zion" probably comes from the Heb. word for "city" (עִיר) and the word for "land" (אֶרֶץ) both being fem. in form, so the personification is as natural as the designations "Daughter of Tyre" (Ps 45:12) and "Daughter of Edom" (Isa 4:21) or "Daughter of Babylon" (Pss 5:42; 51:33; 137:8).

Why are humans so prone to think that all predictions of disaster will not affect them or that we will be able to get around them? This is what Judah thought, but she too was wrong. The enemy will indeed come, and our beliefs that we will be rescued at the last moment are tragically misplaced. We might think we will be able to dissuade the enemy with our charm (or something like that), but we will fall victims to our conquerors. So why don't we respond to God in the first place and save ourselves a lot of trouble? It is revival time for all people and nations.

SEARCHING FOR ONE RIGHTEOUS MAN (5:1–9)

TRANSLATION

1 Run up and down the streets of Jerusalem,
   Look now and take note!
Search through her plazas [to see],
   If you can find a person,
Who deals honestly,
   And seeks the truth,
   That I may forgive her [Jerusalem].
2 Although they swear, "As Yahweh lives,"
   Nevertheless,[79] they swear falsely.
3 Yahweh, do not your eyes look for truth?
   You struck them, but [they feel] no pain.[80]
You have crushed them,
   But they refused to take discipline.
They have made their faces harder than stone;
   They refused to turn back.
4 Then I thought, "These are only the poor;
   They are foolish,
For they do not know the way of Yahweh,

---

79. Many Heb. mss and the Syr. read אָכֵן, "surely," where the MT has לָכֵן, "therefore."
80. Lit. "They did not weaken/writhe."

The justice of our God.
5 I will go to the great [men of great station]
    And speak with them;
For they know the way of Yahweh,
    The demands[81] of our God."
However, they together had broken off the yoke,
    And torn to pieces the bonds.
6 Therefore, a lion from the forest will attack them,
    A wolf from the desert will ravage them.
A leopard will lie in wait near their towns;
    Everyone venturing out of will be torn to pieces,
For their transgressions are many,
    And their apostasies are countless.
7 Why should I forgive you [for this]?
Your sons have abandoned me,
    And sworn by gods that are not gods.
When I filled them to the full,
    They committed adultery,
    And haunted[82] the prostitute's house.
8 They were well-fed[83] and lusty[84] stallions;
    Each neighing for his neighbor's wife.
9 "Shall I not punish them for these things?" declares Yahweh.
"Should I not avenge myself,
    On a nation such as this?"

COMMENTARY

5:1 It is not every day that an offer comes along to save one's civilization, but in this case all it would take is for Jeremiah to locate in their midst just one truly righteous man—not fifty, forty-five, thirty, twenty, or even

---

81. Lit. "judgment/justice."

82. A few Heb. mss use the hithpael יתגוררו, "to seek hospitality with, to patronize," instead of the MT's יִתְגֹּדָדוּ, "they haunted."

83. The word מֻיָזָנִים is a ***hapax legomenon***, and its meaning is uncertain. It is translated "well-fed" based on context.

84. The meaning of מַשְׁכִּים is also uncertain. Based on Ugaritic, it seems to have the meaning of "lustful," as in the LXX.

ten, as was the case when Abraham argued a similar case for the possible deliverance of Sodom and Gomorrah (Gen 18:26–33). If one citizen could be found who had real integrity, and who followed Yahweh, God would "forgive" the sins of the entire city (v. 1f). This word for "forgive" (סָלַח) is used exclusively of God's forgiveness in the Old Testament; other Heb. words are used for human forgiveness.

5:2–3 Alas, there is not even a single righteous soul to be found (outside Jeremiah, apparently). Nor is the reason for the prophet's failure time strictures, for he apparently could take as long as he needed to finish the search; it is that there simply is not a single righteous soul to be found. That is a harsh indictment indeed!

5:4 Jeremiah started with the common folk, the "poor" as he called them (v. 4), but they did not understand the ethical "ways" or the "demands" (מִשְׁפַּט) of Yahweh. The poverty of these "poor" folks is not of an economic sort but a poverty of knowledge and understanding. To be sure, there still was a lot of religious jargon around, for as the prophet scoured the neighborhood for this one shining exception, he heard people take an oath, "As surely as Yahweh lives" (v. 2), but all that was only a lot of lip service with no reality: biblical and doctrinal illiteracy was rampant! It was easier to give God a lot of religious talk than it was to give him their hearts, or to exhibit "faithfulness" of life and obedience.

5:5–6 As distinct from the poor, the "great ones" that is, those who had attainted some great station in life, defiantly and knowingly had broken away from observing what was in the covenant. If King Josiah's reformation had achieved anything, there seems to have been little evidence of it left among either group.

The people are behaving as if they are a pack of wild animals. Their rebellion and outright disregard for what God had expected of them is like that of an ox that had broken loose from its yoke and like ones who have lost the protection of their master as they are attacked in the forest. It is as if they have wandered off and had been attacked by a lion, or a wolf in the desert, or even a prowling leopard. God's people will suffer the same misfortune. Based on these figures and images, Josiah's revival apparently removed some of the outward signs of falsity and irreligion, but what now passes for true religion is shallow and trivial, to say the least. The people's backslidings continued downhill unabated.

5:7–9 In light of this state of affairs, why should God withhold his punishments (v. 7)? If God needs more evidence, then what about the oaths that were being taken by Judahites, all of which were in the name of other gods? And what is to be said about their thronging the houses of prostitution? And if that isn't enough, then what about the way they are whinnying after their neighbor's wife, like well-fed and over-sexed stallions? It is well known that the gods and goddesses of Canaan offered wholesale participation in immoral conduct. That is what Solomon concludes in Eccl 7:20—"There is not a righteous man on earth who does what is right and never sins." The apostle Paul argues the same way in Rom 3:9–12, paraphrasing King David in Ps 14:1–3.

God's search for one righteous person continues. This offer is even more generous than the offer that God made to Abraham to deliver the five cities of the plain if ten righteous persons could be found in Sodom and Gomorrah. The point is clear: a righteous few are enough to deliver a whole nation. Who says one person plus God cannot make a difference? They surely can!

It is all too easy to go along with the trends of the majority, not realizing how significant a life lived to the glory of God can be—not only for the individual but also for masses of persons living in that same culture. For too long all too many of us have lived off the debentures of the few righteous in our culture. Now God is asking: what about you?

INFIDELITY LEADS TO EXILE (5:10–19)

TRANSLATION

>**10** Go up to her vineyard terraces and destroy,
>   But do not make a full end;
>   Strip off the tendrils of her vines,

For they do not belong to Yahweh.[85]

11 For the house of Israel and the house of Judah

Have certainly been unfaithful to me, declares Yahweh.

12 They have lied against Yahweh;

They said: "He will do nothing!

No evil will come upon us;

We will never see sword or famine!

13 The prophets are but wind

And the word is not in them[86];

Thus it shall be done to them."[87]

14 Therefore, thus says Yahweh, God of Hosts:

Because you have spoken this word,

Behold I am making my words in your mouth a fire

And these people the wood it consumes.

15 "Behold, O House of Israel," declares Yahweh,

I am bringing a nation from a distance against you;

It is an enduring nation,

It is an ancient nation,[88]

A nation whose language you do not understand,

Nor can you understand what they say.

16 Their quivers are like an open grave;[89]

All of them are mighty warriors.

17 They will eat up your harvests and food,

They will eat up your sons and your daughters;

They will eat up your flocks and your cattle,

They will eat up your vines and your fig trees.

---

85. Where the MT has הָסִירוּ נְטִישׁוֹתֶיהָ כִּי לוֹא לַיהוָה הֵמָּה, "strip off the tendrils of her vines for they belong to Yahweh," the LXX has the contrary, ὑπολίπεσθε τὰ ὑποστηρίγματα αὐτῆς ὅτι τοῦ κυρίου εἰσίν, "leave the tendrils of her vines."

86. The LXX has καὶ λόγος κυρίου οὐχ ὑπῆρχεν ἐν αὐτοῖς, "The Word of the Lord was not in them," where the MT has only וְהַדִּבֵּר אֵין בָּהֶם, "The word is not in them."

87. The LXX does not have the phrase כֹּה יֵעָשֶׂה לָהֶם, "Thus it shall be done to them."

88. The phrase גּוֹי אֵיתָן הוּא גּוֹי מֵעוֹלָם הוּא, "it is an enduring nation, it is an ancient nation," is missing in the LXX.

89. The phrase אַשְׁפָּתוֹ כְּקֶבֶר פָּתוּחַ, "their quivers are like an open grave," is missing in the LXX.

With the sword they will beat down,
> Your fortified cities in which you trust."

18 "But even in those days," declares Yahweh, "I will not make a full end of you. **19** And when you [yourselves] ask, 'Why has Yahweh our God done all this to us?' you will tell them, 'As you have forsaken and served foreign gods in your own land, so you will serve foreigners in a land not your own.'"

COMMENTARY

5:10 As Yahweh continues to speak, he turns to address the enemy and to urge them to get on with their future task. The enemy could just as well begin with the vineyards and the hillside terraces where the vines were growing. Israel has already been addressed as a "choice vine" in Jer 2:21, but the time has come to spoil and ruin that vineyard for reasons that Yahweh goes on to explain. There could be little doubt that the vineyard represents the nation of Israel (Jer 2:21; Isa 5:1–7; Ps 80:8; Matt 21:31–41), which was expected to bring forth fruit for the use of Yahweh, who had promised his grace to them if they would accept it and believe.

But in an amazing way this section is bracketed by an **inclusio** in vv. 10 and 18 with the theme that God will not destroy Judah completely. The people have indeed been unfaithful, but that will be no excuse for God rendering null and void the validity of his ancient promises to the patriarchs. Some commentators have resisted recognizing the negative form of "not a complete end," but that argument also needs to deny the ancient promise of God. In fact, the divine command is not to uproot or destroy the vine but merely to strip off its trailing tendrils, that is, to heavily prune it. The NIV understands "they" to refer to the people, but in context it refers more naturally to the "branches" and "trailing tendrils," as the ESV, NRSV, and NKJV understand it as well.

5:11–14 Verse 11 is the first time since 3:18 that both northern Israel and Judah are mentioned. The past performance of both parts of the nation Israel is such that they had dealt treacherously with Yahweh. The basis for this charge of treachery is that they have lied about Yahweh (v. 12a). They are convinced that he will "do nothing!" against them (v. 12b), which here literally put is, "Not he!" This is not an attempt to deny that God existed but more of a denial that God would intervene in such a way as Jeremiah depicted. Whether those who had so acted are just the false prophets or whether this is a widely held belief is not definitively sorted out in the text. However, v. 13 certainly seemed to link a good deal of this "wind"/hot air to "the prophets" (v. 13a). But the word of God was not in these prevaricators; instead, Jeremiah speaks what is equivalent to a curse as he announces: "Let what they say be done to them" (v. 13c), for v. 14c–d follows with Yahweh accepting that verdict. These false prophets have taught that evil/harm would not come to them (v. 12c) and that they will never see the sword or famine (v. 12d), but that will be exactly what they will see if there is no repentance.

While the false prophets mount their false scenarios, God promises that he will make his own words like "fire" in Jeremiah's "mouth" (v. 14c), which will burn up the unrepentant people like a fire consumes wood (v. 14d). To reject God's word is to openly court God's repudiation of the words, actions, and lives of these rejecters of God's revelation.

5:15 Where, however, will such judgments come from? God will bring a foreign nation as his agent to remedy the sin of the people (v. 15b). Not only will this nation come from "afar," but it will be an "enduring" and "ancient" nation whose speech and language Israel will not understand (v. 15c–e). All of this will only spell more trouble for communicating with the occupying forces. That they will be an "ancient" nation points to Babylon probably being intended (Gen 10:10) and not the Scythians. Moreover, the language barrier may hint at the confusion of the languages at Babel (Gen 11:9).

5:16–17 The deadly nature of that coming nation's "quivers" (v. 16a) and the reputation of their mighty warriors will only make things more drastic. The enemy will "eat up" (used four times in v. 17) everything in its path: the resources of their harvest, their food, their sons and daughters, their flocks and herds, and what their vines and fig trees produce. As a result, they will both forage (to sustain their army) and plunder (in wanton destruction) all they see. Not even the safety of their walled cities will prove to be enough of a defense (v. 17f).

5:18–19 Verses 18–19 are generally regarded as prose statements that ask again why Yahweh will do this (vv. 9–10, 18–19). But once again Yahweh assures the prophet he will not completely destroy Israel because of his ancient promise. Nevertheless, the question remains: "Why [then] has Yahweh our God done all this to us?" (v. 18b).

The answer is twofold:

1. God will not rescind his promise to his people in his covenant.

2. God will be just as faithful in his threatened judgments as he will be in all his promises.

To expand this second answer, Israel must show the truthfulness of God's judgments as they did his promises. Therefore, Israel must also show to the watching nations that God will deal with all mortals on the basis of exacting the punishment that fits the crime of rejecting him. The nations are to be instructed that what he will do to Israel is what he will do to the nations at large as they too walk in their own ways apart from him.

This is an amazing piece of text, for while it is clear judgment must come because of Judah's and Israel's sin, v. 18 clearly declares that "[God] will not destroy [them] completely." Our Lord will remember his promises to Abraham and David. His word is not up for sale or reinterpretation. However, the words of the false prophets will amount to hot air. But God will make Jeremiah's words in his mouth as a fire that will consume the people as if they are merely wood (v. 14).

God's word is not reversible and unpredictable, for it is based on his character and person. He cannot and will not lie, as the false prophets were so prone to do. Judgment will come, but the enemy will not have the final word; God will have the last word, and it will be a word of deliverance, for God pledged long ago that he will not destroy Israel completely!

A FOOLISH AND COMPLACENT PEOPLE (5:20–31)

TRANSLATION

> **20** Declare this in the house of Jacob,
>   And proclaim it in Judah, saying:
> **21** "Hear this, O foolish and heartless people,

Who have eyes, but do not see,

Who have ears, but do not hear:

22 Should you not fear me? declares Yahweh.

Should you not tremble before me?

I made the sand a boundary for the sea,

A perpetual barrier it cannot cross.

Though the waves toss to and fro, they cannot prevail;

Though they roar, they cannot pass over it."

23 But these people have a stubborn and rebellious heart;

They have turned aside and have gone away.

24 They do not say to themselves,

"Let us fear Yahweh our God,

Who gives the autumn and spring showers,

Who maintains for us the pattern of the weeks of harvest."

25 Your wrongdoings have blocked these [showers],

Your sins have deprived you of the bounty.

26 For among my people are found wicked men,

Who lie in wait like men who snare birds

And like those who set traps to catch men.[90]

27 Like cages full of birds,

Their houses are full of treachery;

And so they have become great and rich

28 And have grown fat and sleek.[91]

Their evil deeds have no limit;[92]

They do not plead the case of the fatherless to win it,

They do not defend the rights of the poor.[93]

---

90. The simile seems to compare "evil-doers to bird-hunters concealed in a blind, waiting to catch their game." See Craigie, Kelley, and Drinkard, 94.

91. The expression עָשְׁתוּ שָׁמְנוּ, "and have grown fat and sleek," is missing in the LXX. The word translated "sleek" comes from the root עשׁת, which appears only twice in the OT (Jer 5:28; Jonah 1:6). Pinker suggests that there is no support in cognate languages for the sense "be smooth, shine" for this verb, so he recommends that the semantic range be limited to the idea of "to think." Subsequently, the first line of v. 28 should be translated "they grew fat, they thought of themselves." See A. Pinker, "The Semantic Field of עשׁת in the Hebrew Bible," VT 57 (2007): 386–99.

92. The expression דִבְרֵי־רָע, "their evil deeds have no limit," is missing in the LXX.

93. The LXX has χήρας, "widow," where the MT has אֶבְיוֹנִים, "poor." This could be an unintentional scribal error.

29 Should I not punish them [for this]?" declares Yahweh.
"Should I not avenge myself
    On such a nation as this?
30 An appalling and a shocking thing has happened in the land:
31 The prophets prophesy lies,
    The priests have exercised control on their own authority,[94]
And my people love it this way.
    But what will you do in the end?"

COMMENTARY

5:20-21 Once again the prophet returns to the theme of denouncing the people for their foolishness and their failure of heart (vv. 20-21). This announcement is addressed to both houses of Israel, with the use of the "house of Judah" and the "house of Jacob"; the latter occurs only here and in 2:4 as a reference to the northern ten tribes. This may be another indication that this sermon represents one of Jeremiah's earlier sermons.

Israel has a real problem in that they are being spiritually insensitive, for though they have eyes and ears, they still do not get it. This leads to two rhetorical questions: Shouldn't you fear [Yahweh]? And shouldn't you tremble in his presence? The fear of Yahweh is the beginning of life itself. But there is no respect shown for the majesty of God and his person. Moreover, there is no appreciation for the evidences of his character and power as seen in his setting up the barriers for the sea in the sand (Job 38:11). Those waves could toss and threaten all they wanted to, but forever God had established limits and boundaries for the waves.

5:22-24 In Jer 2:6-7 Israel had failed to confess God as their Redeemer, but here in 5:22 they fail to acknowledge him as their Creator. In their persistent stubbornness and defiance, they have "turned aside" (v. 23, סוֹרֵר, sôrēr) and "gone away" from God (סָרוּ, sārû, another play on words by Jeremiah). That is why the people do not acknowledge that God sends the rains (Hos 2:8-11; Jer 5:24) and promised the seven weeks of harvest

---

94. The Heb. text translated "the priests have exercised control on their own authority" could be translated "the priests scrape out on their hands," suggesting that the priests are acting to deconsecrate themselves. See W. L. Holladay, "The Priests Scrape Out on Their Hands: Jeremiah V 31," *VT* 15, no. 1 (1965): 111-13.

between Passover and Pentecost. The spring rains that come in March and April provide the good harvest, while the autumn rains that fall mid-October to mid-December make the ground ready for sowing and planting. But all of this seems to be of no avail, for the rains are not received with gratitude or reverence for God.

5:25 Israel's infidelities are the reason these blessings, which were assumed as natural and normal, will not happen at this time. The lack of righteousness and morality will adversely affect the cosmic order and the order in nature (v. 25).

5:26–29 The list of indictments continues to grow in vv. 26–31. These scoundrels are acting like fowlers who lie low in wait to spring their hidden bird traps—only here it is to catch human beings. As a result, they have "gown fat and sleek" (v. 28), and there is no limit or end on what they are willing to do to enhance their own fortunes. Instead of pleading the case of the poor or the fatherless, they take care of only themselves. Therefore, why shouldn't Yahweh punish them for this? Wouldn't it be right for Yahweh to take vengeance on this nation, since it had failed to keep the covenant (v. 29)?

5:30–31 Even more astounding and appalling is that the prophets are handing out a pack of lies and the priests are taking control of things based on their own directions (vv. 30–31). But even more horrifying was that this is how the people love things to go! It is the popular thing to do! Forget Yahweh's censure on their immoral and outrageous behavior; everyone is in favor of this new way of operating in preaching and in rendering judicial judgments.

Israel and Judah have become "foolish and senseless." You would think they have lost their eyes and ears, for nothing God has permitted them to hear and see has struck a residual note within them; they simply refuse to believe and to fear God. For instance, haven't they ever pondered why it is that the sand along the seashore is enough to prevent the waves of the pounding sea to stop at that point? Haven't they ever wondered why autumn and spring rains failed to arrive on time for planting when evil was rampant in the nation? Is all of this just happenstance? God's people are acting like pirates or robbers, who lie in wait to spring from their hiding place on defenseless people in order to accost them and rob them to increase the criminals' own riches. So shouldn't God punish them for sins similar to these? And what should God do about all those who preached and prophesied lies and untruths about him, and the wicked priests, who ruled by their own instincts and not by the word of God? To top it all off, God's people love things the way they are, with all this crime, sin, and injustice. Amazing indeed!

THE COMING DISASTER (6:1–8)

TRANSLATION[95]

> **1** Get to safety, Benjamites,
>> Get outside of Jerusalem!
> In Tekoa blow the horn,
>> And in Beth-Hakkerem light a beacon!
> For evil peers are coming down from the north,
>> A shattering disaster.
> **2** That beautiful and daintily bred daughter of Zion,
>> I will destroy.
> **3** Shepherds with their flocks
>> Will come against her;
> They will pitch their tents around her,
>> Each grazing his patch.
> **4** Prepare for battle against her!
>> Arise, let us attack at noon.
> Woe to us, for the daylight is fading,
>> And the shadows of evening are growing long.
> **5** Come on, let us attack at night,
>> And destroy her fortresses.
> **6** For this is what Yahweh of the armies says,
>> "Cut down the trees,

---

95. The eight verses could be grouped as follows: vv. 1–3, the people are warned to flee Jerusalem; vv. 4–5, the shouts of the enemy are heard; and vv. 6–8, Yahweh himself warns the people. See S. D. Snyman, "A Structural-Historical Investigation of חמס ושד in Jeremiah 6:1–8," *HTR* 58, no. 4 (2002): 1593–1603.

Pile against Jerusalem a ramp [of earth].
This is the city[96] that must be punished;
It is filled with oppression inside her."
7 As a well keeps its waters fresh,
So she keeps fresh her wickedness.[97]
Violence and destruction are heard in her;
Ever before me are her wounds and sickness.[98]
8 Be warned, O Jerusalem,
Lest I turn away from you in disgust,
Lest I make your land so desolate
No one can live in it.

COMMENTARY

6:1 The alarm is sounded once again, but this time it is not a call to take shelter in a fortified city, for by now they will have all been deserted (4:29). But why address the entreaty to the people of Benjamin?[99] It may have been because of the assonance of terms accompanying it or because Jerusalem originally was in Benjamite territory. But an invasion was imminent, so the trumpet must be sounded in Tekoa (another instance of assonance, וּבִתְקוֹעַ תִּקְעוּ, *ûbitqôaʿ tiqʿû*, "and in Tekoa sound"). Tekoa was some eleven miles south of Jerusalem and six miles south of Bethlehem, the birthplace of the prophet Amos (Amos 1:1). Another "signal" consists of a beacon light that must be raised in "Beth Hakkerem," "house of the vineyard" (mentioned also in Neh 3:14). This is probably the site of Ramat Rachel, a village just south of Jerusalem but easily seen from the city of Jerusalem because of its height and unobstructed vantage point.

"Evil" is appearing (or, as it is ominously and dramatically put by Jeremiah, "peering down," as if it pokes its head out of a window facing

---

96. The LXX has πόλις ψευδής, "false city," where the MT only has הָעִיר, "city."

97. Richard Hess suggests that the first two lines of v. 7 should read, "As a well overflows with its water, so [Jerusalem] overflows with its evil." See R. S. Hess, "Hiphil Forms of QWR in Jeremiah VI 7," VT 41, no. 3 (1991): 347–50.

98. In v. 7 we are told in the Heb. Bible that we have come to the middle verse in the OT.

99. Joosten suggests that Jeremiah alludes to the Judg 19–20 episode and the crime of the Benjaminites in Gibeah. Thus, Jeremiah declares that those who take refuge in Jerusalem will be exterminated. See J. Joosten, "Les Benjaminites au Milieu de Jérusalem: Jérémie vi 1ss et Juges xix–xx," VT 49 (1999): 65–72.

north), for the north[100] is the traditional direction out of which all enemy invaders had come (due to the desert to the east and south of Israel). It will bring a "shattering disaster."

6:2–3 In v. 2 Jerusalem, here poetically called "Zion," is personified as the "beautiful and daintily bred daughter" who must nevertheless be destroyed. Personifying the city as a female only increases her weakened and vulnerable image. As the invasion begins "shepherds" are spoken of metaphorically for the "rulers" and their "flocks," which pictures a hostile army now laying siege to the city. Each pitches his tent and the tents of the portion of the besieged city put under his care.

6:4–5 The command is given to commence the battle at noon, a signal in itself ominous, for ordinarily battles begin at daybreak and continue until the evening light begins to fall. Perhaps the next line in v. 4c belongs to the defenders, but with the battle launched at this noon hour, the defenders are worried what the night hours will hold for them. Verse 5 seems to confirm their fears, for the order is given to attack at night as well. So confident are the Babylonian forces that they feel they can press the attack just as well under the cover of darkness.

6:6 The Sovereign Lord directs the campaign against Judah as he instructs the enemy to "cut down the trees" (v. 6). The soil and stones were to be piled up for the siege ramps, and the trees presumably were to be used as battering rams against the gates and walls, while other trees were to be used for making ladders to scale the walls of the defending city. But if God's involvement is questioned, a reason for the divine authorization of all this activity follows: "This is the city that must be punished; it is filled with oppression inside her" (v. 6d–e). Oppression violated the covenant, an abuse of power that deprived others of their property rights (Lev 19:13; Isa 30:12; 59:13).

---

100. The enemy from the north are the Chaldeans and their allies. See J. P. Hyatt, "The Peril from the North in Jeremiah," *JBL* 59, no. 4 (1940): 499–513.

6:7 But now to continue: so generous a supply of wickedness was on hand in Judah that it was like a deep well that retained its water cool and available to drink. The sights and sounds of social injustice, social unrest, and moral disruption were constantly available and a blotch before the eyes of the Yahweh.

6:8 Despite all such evidences of moral and spiritual sickness, God is still warning Jerusalem to repent (v. 8a). Yahweh himself is about to turn away in disgust and make the land so desolate that no one could live in it (v. 8b–d). It is not as if this is the outcome God desires, for that is why Yahweh has sent Jeremiah to preach to them. But it does not appear that an appropriate response is forthcoming from this hardened nation.

With Jerusalem under siege, the command is to flee for safety. Oh that Judah might have repented and turned back to God instead of suffering all of the violence and bloodshed that will come from the northern approach of the enemy!

In like manner, our Lord would rather we are wounded by his words and driven to reverse our flirting with sin, wickedness, and unrighteousness. God sees all the evil we do, and therefore we are guilty and vulnerable to similar disasters after a long stay of the judgment of God. Just as God graciously gave his warning in v. 8, so he through this text gives to us in our day a similar warning and a call to repent while there still is time.

EVERYTHING IS NOT WELL AT ALL (6:9–15)

TRANSLATION

> **9** This is what Yahweh of hosts says,
> "Glean it thoroughly as a vine,
>   The remnant of Israel;
> Pass your hand over the branches again,
>   Like one picking grapes."
> **10** To whom can I speak and give warning,
>   That they may hear?
> Look, their ears are uncircumcised,
>   And they cannot pay attention.

Look, the word of Yahweh is offensive to them,
  They find no pleasure in it.
11 So I am full of Yahweh's fury,[101]
  I am tired of holding it in.
"Pour it out on the kids in the streets,
  On the bands of youths as well;
For both husband and wife will be caught in it,
  The old and those full of days.
12 Their homes will be turned over to others,
  Their fields and wives as well;
For I will stretch out my hand,
  Against those who live in the land," declares Yahweh.
13 For, from the least up to the greatest,
  Every single one of them is greedy for profit,
From prophet up to priest,
  Everyone practices fraud.
14 They dress my people's wounds superficially,
  Saying, "It is well, well indeed!"
  When you are not well at all!
15 Were they ashamed for acting so abominably?
  No! They felt no shame at all;
  They did not even know how to blush!
Therefore, they will fall among the fallen;
  They will be brought down when I punish them, declares
    Yahweh.

COMMENTARY

6:9-10 Yahweh again speaks to Jeremiah, this time using the figure of a "vine" (v. 9; cf. 5:10), but Jeremiah is told that a small group of the people will be left after God is finished bringing judgment on the land. Grape harvesting usually came last in the summer's work, and gleaning what was left on the vine was left to the poor of the land (Lev 19:10). Thus one gleaner challenges another to make use of the grapes are that are left on the vine (v. 9c-d). Though the Heb. uses the coh. verbal forms for both "speak"

---

101. The LXX has τὸν θυμόν μου, "my fury," where the MT has חֲמַת יְהוָה, "the fury of Yahweh."

(אֲדַבְּרָה) and "give warning" (וְאָעִידָה), they appear to be used here to indicate the gravity of the situation: "Who is going to listen and who is taking any heed to the warning?" The ears of the Judeans seem to be "uncircumcised" and blocked, as if a spiritual covering were over them that prevents any reception of the message from God. In fact, they find God's word to be "offensive" or a "reproach" to them. Has anyone ever heard of something as tragic as this? Instead of holding Yahweh's word in high esteem, they treat it as contemptible and worthless.

6:11–15 Jeremiah in the meantime has had about all he all he can take (v. 11). The people are so unresponsive, and yet he senses so keenly the fury of Yahweh. But suddenly Yahweh turns to Jeremiah and enlarges the audience he is to address: all from young children who play in the street to the elderly who are full of years. Jeremiah is being told to "pour it on" rather than "hold" it in (v. 11b–c). The coming devastation will be horrendous, for God is going to "stretch out [his] hand against those who live in the land" (v. 12c–d), just as in former days he stretched it out to save Israel (Exod 3:20). The divine judgment will encompass everyone from the least to the greatest (v. 13), for they were all greedy and so anxious to get ahead of each other so that they did not care how it was done; just do it! All levels of society were taken in as well: Prophets and priests alike; it was nothing but fraud and greed—everywhere. Whatever people wanted to hear, that is what they got! This section of 6:13–15 will be repeated in 8:10–12.

For this, their religious leaders came up with the wrong remedies. They kept saying, "It's all going to be okay!" But that was not true. They declared "peace," but there was no tranquility, wholeness, or well-being in the future of an unrepentant people! How could God bless existing regimes and endorse the work of the people's hands when they despised his covenant and refused to listen to what he said?

The pity of the whole thing is that so oblivious have the people and their false teachers become that they no longer even blush or show any shame over their actions and words. Therefore, their doom is sealed. They have now become so hardened to what God is feeling about them that it does not even occur to them that their conduct is detestable to Yahweh (v. 15).

There comes a time when the patience and long-suffering of our Lord expire and become exhausted on a people who simply do not listen or heed his words. God can no longer withhold his wrath against such blatant sin, so the prophet is told to really pour it on and teach with all his heart and soul, as if such teaching is going out of fashion—and it is! Jeremiah must preach to everyone, from the children in the street to the elderly who had lived for years. Everyone from the youngest to the oldest was consumed with the goal of getting rich as quickly as possible. No different were Judah's priests and false prophets. Nobody takes God, or his word, or the threat of an approaching disaster seriously. Don't worry, they say, it will all work out! Most amazing of all is that Judah has even lost her abilty to blush or to experience any shame over her conduct and sinful ways.

A similar warning comes to our generation in our day. We too have for the most part lost our ability to blush and to experience shame over how we are acting and thinking. It no longer is all about God and his ways; no, it is instead all about us and making money! And that is how one spells disaster.

SEARCH FOR THE OLD, TRIED PATHS (6:16–21)

TRANSLATION

16 This is what Yahweh says,
"Stand at the crossroads and look,
   Ask for the ancient paths,
Where the good way is. Walk in it.
   Find for yourselves[102] rest.
But you said, 'We will not walk in it.'
17 I have appointed over you watchmen,
   Who told you, 'Pay attention to the sound of the trumpet,'
But you said, 'We will not pay any attention.'
18 Therefore, hear, O nations!
Observe, O witnesses,
   What is about to happen to them.
19 Hear, O earth! Behold, I am bringing disaster on this people,
   The fruit of their schemes,[103]

---

102. Lit. "your soul."

103. The LXX has τὸν καρπὸν ἀποστροφῆς αὐτῶν, "the fruit of their rebellion," where the MT has פְּרִי מַחְשְׁבוֹתָם, "the fruit of their schemes."

Because they have not listened to my messages,
    And my law—they have rejected it.
20 What do I care about incense from Sheba,
    Or aromatic spices from a country far away?
Your burnt offerings are not acceptable,
    And your sacrifices give me no pleasure."
21 Therefore, this is what Yahweh says:
"I am going to place obstacles before this people.
    Fathers and sons alike will stumble over them,
    Neighbors and friends will perish."

COMMENTARY

6:16 As a group of travelers who come to a juncture in the road and must decide which way to go, so Judah is here encouraged to stop and think carefully about the options before them. What is more, in this case they are given good advice: "Ask for the ancient paths" (v. 16). It is not as if one ought to automatically opt for the traditional and old ways of doing things, but when the new options are the dead opposite of what God would have wanted, then go back to the ways that one knows have already been approved by God, which is the "good way" (v. 16d). It is the way that ends up being right, the one that leads to participating in the blessings of the covenant of God. However, this is not a matter of merely knowing what is good or approved by God as the best path; it is a matter of "walk[ing] in it" (v. 16f). The only way one can find rest for his or her soul is by actually living in obedience to what God commands, not mere lip service and outward verbalization of the truth of God. Amazingly, Jeremiah's audience plainly refuses to walk in this way; they stubbornly say, "We will not ... "

6:17 Despite this impudent refusal, Yahweh "kept on appointing over [them] watchmen" (v. 17a). These watchmen were no doubt the prophets he has set as sentinels to give advance warning to the people if there is any deviation in their conduct (cf. Ezek 3:17; 33:7). Nevertheless, in spite of their warnings to "pay attention to the sound of the trumpet" (v. 17b), the people reply with bald-faced defiance, "We will not pay any attention" (v. 17c).

6:18–19 With such effrontery as the background for what follows, Yahweh turns and now calls for witnesses from the nations/Gentiles (v. 18a–b). What God is about to do has universal significance even though it is aimed at his covenantal Jewish people. Judah has dreamed up her own plans without giving any regard as to what is going to happen to them. In so doing, Judah has paid no attention to any of God's messages or his law, found in the Mosaic covenant (v. 19). Therefore the "fruit" of their evil will come to pass shortly.

6:20 Instead of following the teaching of the law, they insisted on putting in its place the presentation of "incense obtained from Sheba and aromatic spices from a country far away" (v. 20a–b). The "incense" was probably frankincense, a white substance made from the gum resin of various trees and used as an exclusive formula for the sacred incense in the tabernacle and temple (Exod 30:34). The incense came from Sheba, probably modern-day Yemen. Sweet calamus, or cane, was imported from India and was used in the oil prepared for anointing (Exod 30:23). But these rituals are not meant as a substitute for a genuine heart obedience to God. God always looks at the heart before he regards the smells, rituals, or external forms of worship. Outward performance of worship is empty and unacceptable if it is not accompanied by actions of the heart. The same thing could be said of their burnt offerings and sacrifices; if they are not accompanied by a genuine turning back to God with a loyal obedience to his word, they also are wasted time, effort, and money. There is no point in being ritually correct and inwardly bent on rebellion and a rejection of what God taught.

6:21 Given this track record, Yahweh will place "obstacles" and "stumbling blocks" in the obstinate paths of his rebelling people. Without any spiritual discrimination, the unruly will miss the significance of these circumstances and will "stumble" (v. 21). All will miss the point: fathers and sons as well as neighbors and friends; they all are one and alike; they will miss what those with spiritual eyes will pick up immediately.

When believers want to know what path or course in life they should take, it would pay them dividends to pause and stand still for a moment at the crossroads of life to look and see what have been those good ways and ancient paths that others have trodden before we arrived on the scene.

Not only were these the good and tried paths of Judah's righteous ancestors, but they are still the preferred routes we should take to find rest for our souls (see Jer 18:15; Deut 32:7; Isa 30:21). In fact, this is the text quoted by Jesus in Matt 11:29 (cf. Isa 28:12; Ps 119:165).

God had appointed "watchmen" over Judah, just as he has sent those who minister his word to us in our day. But we must listen and heed the sounds of alarm and the signs of the time as announced in the word of God. The results of many of our schemes and the fruit of our rejection of his law will end up with our being involved in one disaster after another.

God will not be overtaken by our attempt to sweet-talk him or to offer him all sorts of rituals, smells, and liturgy that have no heart or desire for obedience behind them. Such religious shame will not trick our Lord. He wants real sincerity and real faith that results in obedience.

HERE COMES THE ENEMY (6:22–26)

TRANSLATION

22 Here is what Yahweh says:
"Look out, a people is coming,
From the north country,
A great nation is being roused.
They are armed with bow and spear,
From the ends of the earth.
23 They are cruel and show no mercy,
The noise they make is like the roaring sea,
As they[104] ride on their horses,
Drawn up in battle formation against you,
O daughter of Zion.
24 We have heard the report on them,
Our hands hang limp;
With pain as a woman in labor.
25 Do not go out to the fields,
Or walk on the roads,
For the enemy has a sword,

---

104. Some Heb. mss replace "he" with "they." The Vg. and the Syr. also have "they."

> There is terror everywhere.
> **26** O daughter of my people,
> Gird on sackcloth,
>   And roll in ashes.
> Wail with bitter lamentation
>   As you would for an only son,
> For suddenly the destroyer will come upon us."

COMMENTARY

6:22-23 Verse 22 begins another new section with the introductory formula "This is what Yahweh says." If some inquiringly ask, "what is that stumbling block to look like?" the answer is ready: an invading army from the north. God will rouse up a "great nation," which will seem to the Judeans as if they are coming "from the ends of the earth" (v. 22e). But make no mistake about it, they are fearsome: "armed with bow and spear," and they are "cruel" and will "show no mercy" (v. 23a-b). An army of archers constituted the major part of an invading army, but we are not sure how to render the word here translated as "spear" (כִּידוֹן). Many render it as "javelin" in its nine appearances in the OT, but the spear was usually the weapon of choice for infantry, while a javelin was the weapon of choice for the cavalry. They will strike "terror everywhere," a warning that becomes almost a mantra for Jeremiah. The sound of the horses and the charioteers is comparable to the roaring of the sea (v. 23c), a sound that must have frightened the life out of the people of Judah, who were largely immobile.

6:24-25 Jeremiah allows time for the people to record their reaction (v. 24). To put it bluntly, they feel overwhelmed. The disaster described is so great that it is almost as if a paralysis has begun to set in. What else can they do? The "daughter of Zion" (v. 23f) feels like a woman who was about to deliver her baby (v. 24d). So the advice is this: "Do not go to the fields" (v. 25a), for the advancing enemy troops are so close that leaving the city now would not be a good idea: "terror is on every side" (v. 25d), which is one of Jeremiah's favorite phrases (6:25; 20:10; 46:5; 49:29; Lam 2:22), at first used of others, but then turned around and attached to Jeremiah.

6:26 It is time to get out the traditional clothes for mourning, for the coming tragedy is as great as if the only son were taken in death and the end of the family line is at hand. In all of this Jeremiah identifies himself with the people in this coming tragedy—"the destroyer will come upon us" (v. 26f).

The obstacles God will use this time are nothing less than the Babylonian armies that will descend on Judah. When our Lord calls and calls, and no one listens, then he finally, even if reluctantly, must bring the threatened judgment over all who disobey him. God is not a paper tiger: he will act on Judah and on us in a similar manner for the same causes and same reasons.

THE TESTER OF METAL (6:27–30)

TRANSLATION

> **27** "A tester of metals I have made you,
>   And my people are the ore,
>   That you may observe and test their ways."
> **28** All of them are the most stubborn of rebels,
>   Going about to slander.
> They are bronze and iron;
>   They all act corruptly.
> **29** The bellows blow fiercely,
>   But the lead comes whole from the fire;
> It is useless to go on refining,
>   The wicked are not removed.
> **30** They are called rejected silver,
>   Because Yahweh has rejected them.

COMMENTARY

6:27 Though called as a prophet to the nation of Judah and the nations of the world, God now adds for Jeremiah the task of a metal tester. It is Yahweh himself who will do the testing, but the prophet is asked to join in the task of scrutinizing and assaying. In this case the people are the ore (v. 27b), and as Jeremiah proclaims the word of Yahweh he will be able to observe the people's reactions.

6:28-30 If v. 27 ends Yahweh's speech, then vv. 28-30 are the prophet's report as God's assayer. The report is straightforward: all of them are hardened rebels who go about slandering. Whether the slander consists of spreading false reports or it is just plain gossiping is not clear, but the truth is that they are surely not one of the precious metals: they are more like the baser metals of bronze and iron. Their actions are corrupt (v. 28c).

In the ancient process of refining silver, the ore is super-heated along with lead. As the air is directed to the molten mass, the air oxidizes the lead, which acts as a flux to carry away the impurities. If the silver is finished in its time of being refined, the silversmith will know the precise moment the silver is ready: when he sees his reflection in the molten mass. But in this case it is all to no avail. The refining goes on and on, as the wicked, in this applied case, still are not yet purged out. They are rejected silver; Yahweh has rejected them. Reworking the refuse silver is not worth considering. It is too contaminated to be of any value or worth.

God makes his prophet a "tester of metals," that is, a prophet who is to evaluate the response of the people to the word of God. In this illustration the people are like ore that needs to be refined. However, as Jeremiah observes the lifestyles of the people of Judah, they simply do not pass the test of refining. This nation is closer to the base metals and not gold or silver. Even though the refiner pumps more and more air (in this case preaching the powerful word of God), it takes no effect, for the refining just goes on and on.

God is still in the business of inspecting how each of us who read and weekly hear the word of God in our churches are doing. But no matter how urgently God calls and no matter how many Scriptures we hear, the result is the same: very little change, or even none at all! This is a modern challenge just as it was a challenge in Jeremiah's day. Will we pass the refiner's test?

THE TEMPLE GATE SERMON (7:1-8:12)

There is a change in the mode and style of writing from chapter 6 to chapter 7; chapter 7 presents us with the first extended prose writing in the book. This chapter is also a twin chapter to Jer 26, and since that chapter is dated "early in the reign of Jehoiakim son of Josiah king of Judah" (26:1), perhaps the texts share the same date. If so, this message was given in the period between 609 BC and 605 BC, a most critical moment in the life of the nation Judah, when Jehoahaz briefly ruled, followed by Jehoiakim, who led Israel to sin and led to the invasion by Nebuchadnezzar in 605 BC.

Both Jer 7 and 26 place the location where this sermon was given as "the gate of Yahweh's house" (7:2; 26:2); both use the tabernacle's former location at Shiloh as an illustration, where it too was destroyed as a warning to the current generation, which was trusting in externals and the trappings of religion to save them (7:12, 14; 26:6, 9); and there is the double admonition of "reform your ways and your actions," which is clearly emphasized (7:3, 5; 26:13). This message is relevant not only to Judah in her day, but also to our generation in our times, for the situations and needs remain the same.

RELIGIOUS ATTENDANCE IS NO SUBSTITUTE FOR A REAL MEETING WITH GOD (7:1–15)

TRANSLATION

1 The word that came to Jeremiah from Yahweh[105]: **2** "Stand by the gate of Yahweh's house and there proclaim this message. Say, 'Listen to the message from Yahweh, all you of Judah who enter by these gates to worship Yahweh.[106] **3** This is what Yahweh of Hosts, the God of Israel, has declared:

Reform your ways and your actions, and I will let you live in this place.[107] **4** Stop putting your trust in a false slogan,[108] claiming: "Yahweh's temple, Yahweh's temple, Yahweh's temple are these."

---

105. The entire verse, "The word that came to Jeremiah from Yahweh, 'Stand by the gate of Yahweh's house and there proclaim this message, say … '" is missing from the LXX.

106. The phrase "all you of Judah who enter by these gates to worship Yahweh" is missing in the LXX.

107. Holladay believes that the word מָקוֹם, "place," is the glue that holds various sections together. Isbell and Jackson suggest that the concept of "worship" is what binds chaps. 7 and 8 together. See C. D. Isbell and M. Jackson, "Rhetorical Criticism and Jeremiah VII 1–VIII 3," VT 30 (1980): 20–26. Leuchter argues that the term has a sacred nature, "as is the spirit of deuteronomistic ideology, but the privileged status of Jerusalem and the Temple is eliminated." He suggests that "the prophet's rhetorical strategy had a dramatic effect on subsequent modes of sacral consciousness, especially during the period of Babylonian hegemony when members of the prophet's audience were scattered well beyond the precincts of Jerusalem." See M. Leuchter, "The Temple Sermon and the Term מקום in the Jeremianic Corpus," JSOT 30, no. 1 (2005): 93–109.

108. The LXX adds ὅτι τὸ παράπαν οὐκ ὠφελήσουσιν ὑμᾶς, "for they shall not profit you," after "Stop putting your trust in a false slogan."

5 [Instead,] if you really change your ways and your actions—if you behave justly one toward another— **6** If you no longer oppress the alien, the orphan, and the widow, and do not shed innocent blood in this place—and if you do not follow other gods to your own harm— **7** then I will let you go on living in this place, in the land I gave to your fathers forever and forever.

8 Look, you are putting your trust in a false slogan that will prove worthless. **9** What? Will you steal, murder, and commit adultery, and swear falsely, burn incense to Baal, and follow other gods you did not know [previously], **10** and then come and stand before me in this house, which bears my name, and say, "We are saved—just so that we can go right on doing all these abominations"? **11** Has this house,[109] which is called by my name, become in your estimation[110] a den of robbers? Look, as for me! I have been watching, declares Yahweh! **12** Go now to my place in Shiloh, where I first made a dwelling for my name and see what I did to it because of the wickedness of my people. **13** So now, because you have done all these things, declares Yahweh, when I spoke to you repeatedly, you did not listen, and when I called, you did not answer, **14** I will treat the house which bears my name, which you trust in, the place I gave to you and your fathers, just as I treated Shiloh. **15** I will throw you out of my presence, just as I threw out all your kinsmen, all the people of Ephraim.

COMMENTARY

7:1–2 It was unusual to be stopped by a sermon as one was going into the courts of the house of God to worship, but that is what Jeremiah is instructed to do. He is to stand by the gate to the house of God and proclaim this message. It is as if the people are being greeted with the message that internal preparation is needed as a prior condition for meeting with God, or even before they thought of entering the house of God, or even while they were getting ready to attempt to worship him.

---

109. The LXX has ὁ οἶκός μου, "my house," where the MT has הַבַּיִת הַזֶּה, "this house."

110. Lit. "in your eyes."

7:3 The heart of the prophet's message is "Reform your ways and your actions" (v. 3). As a result, personal holiness becomes a priority and a prerequisite to mere attendance at the house of God. Thus, both the tilt of a person's "way" of living and thinking as well as his or her actual "deeds" are open for inspection before God; both call for an appropriate change that resulted in repentance. If Judah plans on continuing to live in the land, they had better think about changing their lifestyles, their way of living, and their way of acting right away.

7:4–9 The way they are to change is spelled out in more detail in vv. 4–9. First of all, they have to stop referring to the "temple of Yahweh" as if this were some sort of a slogan or mantra, a talisman, good-luck charm, or a type of rabbit's foot for safety and protection against the wrath of God. Rather than expressing a repentance from the heart, they are trusting in externals as something they can hide behind and use as a badge of orthodoxy. However, divine things cannot be used in such a trite manner or resorted in as a substitute despite the manner of one's own way of life. Some today, in a similar manner, try to hide behind such good things as their church's missionary-mindedness, their sound evangelical doctrine, their large congregations, their Christian institutions, or something similar that could act as substitutes for an earnest, heartfelt response to God, but all of it often amounts to a false front and an obvious misuse of externals in place of a genuine heart relationship or real repentance. All such substitutions will turn out to be deceptive and false—a trusting in works and outward acts of an alleged piety! But in the end, they will sound more like heathen incantations based on magic than genuine worship of the Living God.

7:5 But the ways of reform can be spelled out even more succinctly. The first area of reform is in the way they deal with each other (v. 5). Yahweh has set out such proper responses in the Mosaic covenant he has made for the people. Since the verbs in this section are all pl. verbs, they refer equally to the king and the people. There must be just and fair legal and civil administration in the land. But to the degree that social justice has failed, reform and repentance are required and necessary if they are to continue to live in the land.

Some additional requirements of the Mosaic law are brought forward to instruct the Judeans as to how they were to live. For example, all forms of extorting things from the poor in order to accumulate wealth for the rich are to cease. Such oppression of the poor is not a prelude to worship, nor is it pleasing to God. Neither is reaping unfair benefit from the foreigner or alien in their midst allowed either, nor doing the same toward the orphan and the widow. Even though the alien is only a temporary resident in the land from another country, without relatives or family to look after his interests in this foreign country, that is no reason for making him an object of prey. In a similar way, orphans and widows have lost their natural spokesmen and are liable to be maltreated by those who have little or no conscience about God seeing all done under the sun. Yahweh has taught his people to reach out to each of these three groups (Exod 22:21–24; Lev 19:33–34; Deut 10:18; 16:11, 14; 24:17–18), but these Judeans seem to be oblivious to all of that teaching.

7:6 Another area that needs reforming is where innocent blood had been shed (v. 6c). When the king and God's people become insensitive and indifferent to this issue, it pollutes the whole land. Under the rule of King Manasseh, life was typically regarded as cheap, and the blood of the innocent victims consequently flowed copiously (2 Kgs 21:16).

Judah is also warned not to follow other pagan and foreign gods (v. 6d), for it is not enough to be correct in social justice; one has to be right in behavior toward Yahweh as well. Moreover, attractions to false gods and theological aberrations likewise open the door to other deviations from the teaching of the word of God. Rejecting the exclusive worship and love for the Lord God is one sure way for any nation to find itself in danger of impending calamity. However, if there is evidence of true repentance and a reformation of ways and deeds, the people could expect to live long lives in their land, just as Yahweh had promised Abraham (Gen 17:8).

7:9 Despite the good news in the offer just noted, however, Judeans were failing the test in every way: they are characteristically stealing, murdering, committing adultery, perjuring themselves, and burning incense to Baal, along with other gods about whom they know just about nothing (v. 9)! The first six verbs of v. 9 are all inf. abs., which lays special stress on the action of the verb.[111] That along with the rapid fire of one verb after another in this rhetorical question carries the indignation of the prophet over the laxity of the morality and ethical actions of the people. In fact, listed here are five of the Ten Commandments (Exod 20)—a real moral breakdown, to say the least, on the part of the nation of Judah.

7:10 The tragedy of the whole matter was that these Judeans think it is possible to live any way they please and then frivolously enter the house of God and think that everything will be just fine. Worse still, they even boast that they have been saved precisely so that they can practice all these detestable things without any bad consequences (v. 10)! There is little thought that such might be a duplicitous lifestyle, which is displeasing to God. Yahweh himself will take care of the political situation and guarantee the continuity of their national state, for they have an eternal covenant from God about their future, or so they falsely reason so far as their own generation is concerned. Furthermore, as long as they continue to be present at the house of God in time for the worship of God, how could it matter to God how they lived, they lamely reason?

7:11 But so indignant is Yahweh that he pointedly asks, "Aren't you making my house a hangout for thieves and robbers?" (v. 11). The similarity is evident: thieves and robbers flee to the safety of their caves and various hangouts after a heist; in like manner, the people of Judah, after acting all week like gross sinners, resort to attending Yahweh's temple without any thought of sorrow or repentance, thus God's house becomes a den of robbers and thieves. Jesus uses this same denunciation for those who were using the temple of that day in a similar way (Matt 21:13; Mark 11:17; Luke 19:46). They pretended as if no one cared; the mere attendance at the house of God was the principal idea, or so they thought.

That, however, is dead wrong, for in an emphatic form God announces, "Look, as for me! I have been watching [you]" (v. 11b). Although a different Heb. word for "watching" (רָאָה) is used here than was used in Jeremiah's

---

111. The actions stressed are: to steal, murder, commit adultery, swear falsely, make offerings, and go [after other gods].

call (1:12; שָׁקַד), it is similar to the warning God had given to Jeremiah in 1:11. God is in no way fooled by the pretense of their piety; it is all a sham.

If one believes one's mere attendance at his sanctuary grants immunity from punishment, then there are two examples one had better think about rather quickly: the destruction of Shiloh in 1050 BC and the exile of the northern kingdom in 722/721 BC. For those who would not believe until they have seen things with their own eyes, Yahweh says, "Go now to my place in Shiloh" (v. 12a); there are ashes there to kick around if they are unconvinced! Shiloh was about nineteen miles north of Jerusalem and was where the sanctuary of God was located in the days of Eli and Hannah's son Samuel (1 Sam 1:9; 3:3), around the time at the end of the period of the judges. Yet, in spite of its sacrosanct status, it had been destroyed. Though Scripture does not record that event, the archaeological evidence shows that Shiloh was hit with an overwhelming conflagration by the Philistines around 1050 BC and remained pretty much a loss even up to 300 BC, when it showed a small recovery as a small community. So the opinion that the Judeans are safe because Jerusalem was the site of the temple and they are therefore immune to any destruction permitted by God is shown to be false by what had happened at Shiloh for the same reasons. That, however, is not what Yahweh wants to happen, for he has been speaking to the people of Judah repeatedly, calling for a change and repentance even while they have been in the midst of doing all these things, but all to no avail. How much more intense and earnest can a loving God be than what these people have experienced?

7:14–15 The conclusion was not far off, for what had happened at Shiloh is going to happen to the temple again, only this time it would be the temple at Jerusalem (v. 14). Their disrespect is not only for the word of God, but it also is an outright flouting of the place where God has placed his name (v. 14b). As a result, God will cast them out of his sight, just as he had done to Samaria a little over one hundred years prior, in 722/721 BC (v. 15).

If Judah and our own generation think that merely showing up at the house of God is enough to excuse us from obedience to the word of God, there is a big surprise coming for them and for us. God cannot be used as a talisman or a rabbit's foot that brings good luck just by rattling off favorite mantras or showing up for certain services of worship. If Judah and we persist in falsely worshiping our inert idols, then judgment is not far away. Yes, God miraculously delivered King Hezekiah and the city of Jerusalem in 701 BC (2 Kgs 19:32-36), but Hezekiah was a man of prayer and faithfulness. No amount of shouting "the temple of Yahweh, the temple of Yahweh, the temple of Yahweh" (or even such good sayings as we believe in inerrancy or we are missions-minded) is going to be substitute for a real meeting with God. Those words are as hollow and empty as can be when one's fervent heart-relationship is absent from such sloganeering. God wants a heart-relationship, not a bunch of slogans and bumper-sticker theologies.

Jesus quotes the last part of Jer 7:11 along with Isa 56:7 in Matt 21:13; Mark 11:17; Luke 19:46. God's house is not going to serve as a den or a hideout for those who falsely use the temple as a good-luck charm as a pretext and substitute for confessing their sins while continuing in that sin as before. If we think our places of worship, or our nation, are so sacrosanct that calamity will never reach us, then we need to think again! Remember where God's house originally stood in Shiloh? Where is it today? It is gone! God destroyed Shiloh because of its sin, so what do we think will prevent him from touching our places of comfort?

Those who flout God's law and his word will surely face the devastating results, as they and we have been warned. Don't try to put God off by presenting him with a lot of artificial substitutes!

RELIGIOUS OBSERVANCE IS NO SUBSTITUTE FOR HEARTFELT OBEDIENCE TO GOD (7:16-29)

TRANSLATION

16 "As for you, do not pray for this people; do not lift up a plea or prayer on their behalf; do not plead with me, for I will not listen to you. **17** Don't you see what they are doing in the cities of Judah and in the streets of Jerusalem?— **18** The children are gathering up wood, and their fathers are kindling a fire, and the women are kneading the dough to make cakes for the Queen of Heaven. They are pouring out libations to other gods in order to provoke me to anger. **19** Am I the one they are provoking?" asked Yahweh. "Is it not themselves, to their own shame?" **20** Therefore, this is what Lord[112] Yahweh has said, "Look, my anger and my wrath will be poured out on this place, on man and on beast, on the trees of the field and the produce of the ground; it will burn and not be extinguished."

21 This is what Yahweh of Hosts, the God of Israel, has said: "Go ahead! Add your burnt offerings to your sacrifices, and eat meat! **22** For when I brought your fathers out of the land of Egypt, I did not speak or command them for the sake of burnt offerings and sacrifices.[113] **23** But this command I gave them: 'Obey my voice and I will be your God and you shall be my people. Walk in all the way I command you that it may be well with you.' **24** But they neither obeyed nor paid any attention, but they walked in the counsels of their wicked heart. They went backward, not forward. **25** From the day your fathers[114] came out of Egypt until the present, I sent to them all my servants the prophets, day after day, again and again. **26** But they neither heeded me nor paid any attention. They were stiff-necked and did more evil than their fathers.

27 "You are to say all these things to them, but they will not listen to you. You will call them, but they will not answer. **28** So say to them, 'This is the nation that would not obey the voice of Yahweh its God, nor accept discipline; trustworthiness has perished, it has vanished from their lips.' **29** Cut off your hair and throw it away; take up a lament on the barren heights,[115] for Yahweh has rejected and abandoned this generation that is under his wrath."

---

112. The word אֲדֹנָי, "Lord," is missing in the LXX.

113. Jeremiah does not oppose ritual worship; rather, the sacrificial system has its permanent place "in the setting of Yahweh's ethical requirement and Israel's ethical response." See J. A. Motyer, "Jeremiah VII, 22," *TynBul* 1 (1965): 4–5; and G. E. Whitney, "Alternative Interpretations of *Lō'* in Exodus 6:3 and Jeremiah 7:22," *WTJ* 48 (1986): 151–59.

114. The LXX, the Syr., and the Vg. have "their fathers" where the MT has "your fathers."

115. The LXX has ἐπὶ χειλέων, "on your lips," where the MT has עַל־שְׁפָיִם, "on your bare heights."

COMMENTARY

In this new section of the ongoing sermon at the gate of the temple, it is clear that any and all service to God without a repentant heart and obedience to Yahweh is just as bankrupt as the mere act of attendance at God's house. The point is that Yahweh never calls for sacrifices, offerings, prayers, or offerings of any kind to be done *for their own sake*. Instead, God always inspects the heart of the one making the offering before he had regard for the offering.

This section teaches us another fact about the prophets: they were intercessors in addition to being proclaimers. For example, Samuel, one of the forerunners of the long line of prophets, was asked not to stop interceding on Israel's behalf to God for Israel (1 Sam 7:9). Moses shows that same characteristic (Exod 32:11–13, 30–32; Num 14:13–25), as did Isaiah (2 Kgs 19:3–4) and Amos (Amos 7:1–6). Prayer for those who hear the message is as important as the faithful proclamation of the word; in fact, the proclamation of the word without the strong environment of prayer surrounding it is also ineffective.

7:16 But now Jeremiah is told a total of seven times not to pray or "intercede for" this people throughout his ministry (Jer 7:16; 11:14; 14:11; 29: 7; 37:3; 42:2, 20). Why? It may be worth noting that three times he uses the Heb. אַל, "not," instead of the emphatic and durative form of לֹא, "not." Therefore, only in such circumstances as these is he not to intercede. But one thing is surely clear: Yahweh is not pleased at all with Judah's conduct and he is not regarding it as a trivial matter; Yahweh will not listen to requests on Judah's behalf. We ask: Is so drastic an action the result of the impudent act of Jehoiakim, that is, his burning the recently discovered scroll of the word of God? Later this prophet will pray not for the avoidance of coming tragedy but that the circumstances of the attack may be lessened. But even that observation needs some qualifying, for Jeremiah is instructed on other occasions to pray for this people (18:20; 21:12; 37:3). It is difficult to discern the reason for what appears to be a set of exceptions. Some have conjectured that Jeremiah thought things were improving at certain points, so he added his prayers to those circumstances. One thing is clear: God cannot be bought off with sacrifices and prayers when all avenues and calls for repentance have failed, for what he wants instead is evidence of genuine repentance and a change of heart.

7:17-18 At the very time they are supposedly worshiping Yahweh, the entire family is engaged in perverted devotion to the Queen of Heaven.[116] In all the towns of Judah and streets of Jerusalem (v. 17), the children are gathering wood for her honor, the fathers are lighting the fires, and the women are kneading dough into "cakes" (Heb. כַּוָּנִים, a word of foreign origin, v. 18). It is a total family effort to honor the Queen of Heaven, possibly Ishtar, the Babylonian fertility female idol.

7:19-20 Verse 19 does not intend to contradict the idea that Yahweh is indeed provoked by all these distorted family values involved in worshiping this goddess. Surely God is grieved and deeply vexed by this whole scene, but this text emphasizes that the behavior of men, women, and children results in harm to themselves even more than to anyone else. It is getting difficult to look each other in the eye, as their participation in such idolatry directly opposed their alleged loyalty and love for Yahweh. Consequently, God surely will pour out his wrath on this place (v. 20). That includes the temple, which the people have so mechanically and automatically thought will act as a good-luck charm against all such chastening raised by divine judgment. This devastation will be all-inclusive: it will hit mortals, beasts, trees of the field, and all the produce of the ground (v. 20).

If the people's reliance on attendance at public worship as a prophylactic against punishment is completely wrong, then so too is their reliance on mere sacrifices and gifts as a talisman against future judgment. It is another attempt to put God off by offering him another substitute: mere performance of rituals rather than any heartfelt desire to please him and to obey his word.

7:21 In a deeply sarcastic and ironic tone, Yahweh urges the Judeans to "Go ahead, Add your burnt offerings to your other sacrifices and eat meat"

---

116. Cohn affirms that "it may be reasonable to speculate that the 'Queen of Heaven' mentioned in Jeremiah" is the goddess Anat. See H. Cohn, "Is the 'Queen of Heaven' in Jeremiah the Goddess Anat?," *JBQ* 32, no. 1 (2004): 55–57. See also "Excursus: The Queen of Heaven."

(v. 21). The burnt offerings, which were wholly consumed by fire on the altar, ordinarily depict the heart attitude, reflecting complete surrender and dedication to Yahweh. But how can this be, with the whole family involved in the worship of the Queen of Heaven and other deities? The whole procedure is nothing but a show and a downright sham. The ones making the offerings seem more interested in what comes at the end of the sacrifice—the eating of meal in community—than in any spiritual values. So, go on and have a good meal, Yahweh seems to say with deliberate sarcasm. You don't have the slightest concept of what you are pretending to do, Judah! All such sacrificial rituals are useless and amount to less than nothing—both for yourselves and for God.

7:22 What a radical disjuncture! When God brought Israel up from the land of Egypt and instructed about the place and reason for sacrifices, he never intended that all of this was merely "for the sake of" Yahweh getting some more offerings or sacrifices (עַל־דִּבְרֵי, "for the sake of," himself; v. 22c, cf. 14:1; Deut 4:21; 2 Sam 18:5; 2 Kgs 22:13; Ps 7:1). Yahweh is not primarily or principally interested in sacrifices per se, for they neither feed him nor personally enrich him; instead, he wants to see obedience and faithfulness to his word, not just rote performance! Critical scholars often argue that this one text is to be interpreted literally: God did not speak to the Israelites when he brought them up out of Egypt about sacrifices and offerings.[117] Therefore, these legal injunctions must not be placed in the so-called P document that comes in the postexilic era and not in Mosaic times. Such a misunderstanding can be traced in part to the scholars' inability to understand this passage, for they misunderstand what is plainly taught here: God did not speak merely *"for the sake of"* sacrifices and offerings. When this is correctly understood, one of the main verses for late-dating the Levitical instructions to the postexilic times is removed from critical scholars.

God always inspects the heart of the offerer before he inspects the offering (cf. Isa 1:11–17; Amos 5:21–24; Mic 6:6–8). King Saul had to learn the same lesson: "Does Yahweh delight in burnt offerings and sacrifices as much as in obeying the voice of Yahweh? To obey is better than sacrifice, and to heed is better than the fat of rams" (1 Sam 15:22). The psalmist says

---

117. See Lindblom 1999 for a short discussion on this issue.

as much in Ps 50:7–12: "I have no need of a bull from your stall or of goats from your pens, for every animal of the forest is mine. … If I were hungry I would not tell you, for the world is mine and all that is in it." David gives this same teaching in Ps 51:16–19, where in connection with his sin against Bathsheba he concludes, "You [Lord] do not delight in sacrifice, or I would bring it. … The sacrifices of God are a broken spirit; a broken and a contrite heart, O God, you will not despise. … Then there will be righteous sacrifices."

7:23 Unfortunately, the people are unreceptive to such teaching. Yahweh states it as plainly as he can: "Obey me and I will be your God and you will be my people" (v. 23). Once again, the promise-plan of God, often repeated throughout the Scriptures as the triple formula of the promise-plan of God, is cited here with two of its usual three parts in that formula. If only Judah will obey the living God (v. 1) he will be their God and (v. 2) they will be his people. This formula occurs almost fifty times in both the OT and NT. Judah's obedience, however, is not to be partial. They are to live obediently and faithfully according to all God had instructed them; this calls for a "total" commitment and an "exact" response to all that God has taught.

7:24–26 But Yahweh could just as well have been talking to a blank wall, for the people "did not listen or pay attention"; instead they do jolly well just as they were pleased to (v. 24). What they give priority to is the "stubborn inclinations of their evil hearts" (v. 24b). Neither is this a happening that only occurred every once in a while; no, this has been routinely taking place ever since their forefathers had left Egypt. Nevertheless, God has sent his servants the prophets time after time, but that too is to no avail (v. 25). Israel has a long track record of deliberate disobedience and tone-deafness to the commands of God. God sends the prophets in hopes that the people will hear the message and turn back to him (2 Chr 36:15–16), but instead they turn away from God. They are "stiff-necked" (Jer 7:26; 17:23; 19:15; Deut 9:6, 13), a metaphor from the farm that is used for an animal unwilling to let the farmer slip the yoke over its neck; yet without that yoke the animal is useless to the farmer, for it cannot pull any farm implement or do anything helpful.

7:27–29 Yahweh had warned Jeremiah as he began that his message would not be received by those who heard him (1:8, 17–19), so it is appropriate for Yahweh to remind him of this fact once again (7:27). This sets things up for the solemn declaration of God's approaching judgment: Since they have not responded to correction, nor obeyed Yahweh, "truth [had] perished; it [had] vanished from their lips" (v. 28b). If truth can be detected in the lives of those who practice it, then the personification of truth has expired; it has been expunged from the community. The end must be near!

What Judah is taught here is still relevant for us: sacrifice and offerings to God are valid and acceptable to God only when they are accompanied by genuine repentance and heartfelt obedience. If they or we think otherwise, then pile on meaningless numbers of sacrifices and offerings, but the message is the same as it was to King Saul: To obey is better than to sacrifice (1 Sam 15:22). God cannot be bought!

God never looks at the gifts or offerings we bring to him before he looks at our hearts; he always looks at the inner recesses of the giver and then looks to the gift. This was true in the case of the offerings of Cain and Abel, for in Gen 4:4, 5 God "had respect" to the man (the person) first and then to his offering. That theme is found all through Scripture and into our modern times as well. But when truth and authenticity are absent from the inner being of the believer, then such worship is worthless. God will not be impressed by substitutes when he has asked instead for our hearts.

POSSESSION AND KNOWLEDGE OF THE WORD OF GOD IS NO SUBSTITUTE FOR A GENUINE RESPONSE TO IT (7:30–8:12)

TRANSLATION

30 In fact, the people of Judah have done evil in my eyes, declares Yahweh. They have set up their detestable idols in the house that bears my name and have defiled it. **31** They have built the high places of Topheth in the valley of Ben-Hinnom in order to burn their sons and their daughters in the fire, which I did not command and which did not enter my mind.

32 Therefore, look out, the days are coming, declares Yahweh, when [people] will no longer call it Topheth, or the Valley of Ben-Hinnom, but the Valley of Slaughter; for they will bury in Topheth until there is no room left. **33** Then the corpses of this people will become food for the birds of the air and the beasts of the earth, and there will be no one to frighten them away. **34** And I will banish from the streets of Judah and from Jerusalem the sound of joy and jubilation, the voice of bridegroom and bride, for the land will be a desolate waste.

8:1 At that time, declares Yahweh, they will exhume the bones of the kings of Judah and the bones of its officials and the bones of the priests and the bones of the prophets and the bones of the citizens of Jerusalem from their graves. **2** And they will spread them out to the sun and the moon and to all the stars of the heavens, whom they have loved, and served, and whom they have followed and consulted and worshiped. They will never be gathered or buried, but will be like dung left on the ground. **3** And to all the remnant of the survivors[118] of all this evil family, death will seem preferable to life, declares Yahweh of Hosts.

4 Say to them, this is what Yahweh says, "Does one fall and not get up? Or go away, [does he] not come back?" **5** Why, then, has this people backslidden? [Why does] Jerusalem turn away? [Why] do they cling to deceit and refuse to come back? **6** I have listened attentively, but I have not heard [what is] right. There is not a man who repents of his evil, saying, "What have I done?" Each pursues his own course like a horse charging to battle. **7** Even the stork flying in the sky knows her appointed times; and a turtledove, the swallow, and the swift observe the time of migration. But my people do not know the justice of Yahweh. **8** How can you say, "We are wise because we have [in our possession] the law of Yahweh?" In fact, look, it has been made into a falsehood by the lying pen of the scribes. **9** The wise are shamed, defeated, and trapped. Why, look! They have rejected the word of Yahweh, so what kind of wisdom can they have? **10** Therefore, I will give their wives to others, their fields to new owners; from the least to the greatest, all of them are greedy for gain; from the prophet to the priest—all practice fraud. **11** Yet they dress the fracture of my daughter [and] people superficially say, "peace, peace," when there is no peace. **12** Are they ashamed of their loathsome conduct? No! They felt neither shame

---

118. The *BHS* editor suggests deleting the word הַנִּשְׁאָרִים, "remaining," since it could be a case of **dittography**, an unintentional scribal error, since the word occurs on the previous line. The word does not appear in the LXX or the Syr.

nor did they know how to blush. Therefore, they will fall among the fallen; at the time of their punishment they will be brought down, says Yahweh.

COMMENTARY

The Valley of Slaughter (7:30-34)

7:30-31 By this time Judah has fallen so far that there seems to be no limit to the depths of degradation she will stoop to. In fact, by popular demand, seemingly without the leadership of the officialdom, the people have gone ahead and "set up their detestable idols in the house that bears [Yahweh's] name and [thus] have defiled it" (v. 30). Whereas in the past they had been content to set up these idols under trees and out in the open high places, they now insist on bringing their idolatrous trappings right into the temple of God! Such detestable practices seem to have begun during the days of Kings Ahaz and Manasseh (2 Kgs 21:5-6; 23:10), but now in the reigns of King Jehoiakim and Zedekiah they increase and become all the more insolent and bold (Jer 44; Ezek 5:11; 8:6) after King Josiah had abolished them in Judah. Thus, these later installations are no doubt a reversal of policy and practice that King Josiah had eradicated. But Jehoiakim was not attracted to follow his father's practices in this regard. Meanwhile, the sacred precincts outdoors not only continued, but worsened. The Judeans built "high places of Topheth in Valley" (v. 31).

7:32 So resolute and absolute is Yahweh on this command against offering the firstborn to an idol that he stresses that such sacrifices not only are matters he never commanded, but they are things that never even "enter[ed his] mind" (v. 31c). Jeremiah warns, "The days are coming" (v. 32, an expression he repeats some fifteen times), when a sudden reversal will come. Instead of calling it "Topheth" or "the Valley of Ben Hinnom," it will be known as the "Valley of Slaughter" (v. 32), for that is what it has become! To be sure, they will bury the dead until there is no more room to bury any more in that valley (v. 32c). It is a disgusting disgrace! In this regard Topheth stands as a symbol in days of old much as the huge collection of aborted fetuses stands as a scream to heaven in our own day.[119]

---

119. See "Excursus: Topheth."

7:33-34 So great will be the slaughter that scavenging birds and animals will be able to eat all they want as the corpses are left unburied, a sign of a terrible curse (see 1 Sam 17:43-46). Likewise, the sounds of joy and gladness that arise from the festivities of weddings and the like will cease as the land became desolate and mute because of the offense (v. 34).

Judgment for Astral Worship (8:1-3)

8:1 Jeremiah 8:1-3 resumes the list of future divine judgments begun in 7:32-34. But whereas the dead previously had been treated to a mass burial (7:32), or to exposure of their bones (7:33), now this section declares that there will be a desecration of graves as the bones of the deceased are exhumed from their graves. Five times over the text repeats the phrase "the bones of." Presumably, the graves of the rich were always an attraction to an invader, as they were to others, but this section seems to go beyond grave robbing. It is a great humiliation to have one's bones treated in such a brutal way (2 Sam 21:12-14; Ps 53:5; Isa 14:18-19; Ezek 6:5).

8:2-3 Even more ironically, the bones will be deliberately spread out and exposed to the sun, moon, and stars that have been the object of Judah's astral worship. Evidence of such worship can be seen also in 2 Kgs 21:3, 5; 23:4; Zeph 1; 5; Ezek 8:16. This macabre display is the recompense for such stupid adoration of the creation of Yahweh rather than of the Creator himself.

In another fivefold reference, there is a repeated note beginning with the relative pronoun "which" (אֲשֶׁר). Like the steady gonging of the funeral dirge bell, Jeremiah notes that these are the gods "whom they have loved, and served, and whom they have followed and consulted and worshiped" (v. 2). The level of their commitment to these astral deities is mind-boggling in its persistence, for they not only follow or walk after them, but they consult, or seek them out, by means of a medium or prophet to learn the will of the deity, as they pledge themselves in complete submission to these powerless nothings.

The result is horrific: they will be scattered about on the ground like dung. The promised curse will be the portion of the people. One hardship after another awaits them in exile (Lev 26:36-39; Deut 28:65-67). The religious insensitivity of the people will not be left unattended to; the same God who will fulfill his promises will also keep his warnings and punishments.

Why Does No One Repent of Their Wickedness? (8:4-7)

8:4 The contrast between the people of Judah and what God might expect could not be more shocking: there is first of all the expected actions of people (vv. 4-5), then the example of a horse (v. 6), and finally the practice of migratory birds (v. 7). Thus, this section begins with a series of questions from Yahweh.

The first question is this: If someone falls, does he not try to get up again? Or again, if someone goes away from home on a trip, doesn't he return at some point in the future? The point of the question is made clearer when we understand that the verb in v. 5 is the same verb used so frequently of a spiritual return to the Lord in repentance in chapter 3.

8:5-6 So why have the people turned away from Yahweh and left their spiritual moorings? This turning away is so resolute that the cycle of apostasy seems to have no breaks or interruptions. It is just an outright spiritual "backsliding" (מְשֻׁבָה, v. 5). There are no examples of anyone who repents and suddenly comes to his or her senses and says, "What have I done?" (v. 6d). Instead, everyone just rushes headlong, charging into life following their own course and way of living (v. 6e).

8:7 Funny thing, however, is that even the birds carefully observe the times of their migratory demands and fly south when the weather begins to indicate that the cold days are coming. However, God's people, who have been endowed with wisdom and good sense, seem to say, "It will never happen here; this will be a very mild winter; there is no reason for flying all those miles just to avoid the cold." So the point again is that the birds are more observant than the creatures God made in his own image. Apparently, men and women see the signs of a coming disaster, but they think it will all blow over and that will be the end of it!

Another peculiarity is the fact that the "stork" is called in Heb. חֲסִידָה (ḥăsîdâ), which comes from the same Heb. root as the word "loving kindness" or "steadfast love" (חֶסֶד, ḥesed). So why are the birds more responsive to God's decrees than God's people, who pretend judgment will not come? One does not observe birds on electric wires down the road picketing with signs in the autumn that say, "It's a drag every year to fly south, so we refuse to flap, flap, flap on that long journey." Instead, they obey and fly south because it is going to get cold!

Why Pretend Possessing God's Word Is
Better than Obeying It? (8:8–12)

8:8–9 How is it possible to claim to be the possessors of the Word of God and ones who are so wise when these same folks do not heed what that word of God says? That the law of God is in their possession is no guarantee that they have received the necessary wisdom to heed and obey that law. Moreover, the pen of the scribes merely perpetuates a "lie" (v. 8). That is, they are not being accused of rewriting the law, but falsely interpreting that law. They use the law to say everything at the time is at peace, and the people should continue in their relaxed condition and have a complacent attitude toward the law and its demands. Such use of the law will never move anyone to ask, "What have I done?" (v. 6). Instead, the laws are used to conceal the problem at hand, when that same law had been given to reveal the problem itself. All too many teachers of the word of God use that very same word from God to say what is precisely at variance with the direct statements of that same word. But like the scribes of old, all that literary activity amounts to zero. Past, present, and future scribes will be put to shame, dismayed, and trapped (v. 9) because they have rejected and defiantly distorted the word of Yahweh (v. 9c). So what kind of wisdom do any of those ancient or modern interpreters think they have?

8:10–12 For such poor performance, the word of judgment, "therefore" (v. 10), will be noted in a series of consequences, including that their wives will be turned over to other men, as will their fields. All of the leaders, from top to bottom, from the greatest to the least, are just plain greedy for gain. This is just as true of the prophets as it is for the priests. They simply want to get rich as quick as they can. Meanwhile, they dress the wound of God's people superficially, disregarding its seriousness. They keep saying, "peace, peace"; everything will be all right, you will see! Yet, there is no peace to be found anywhere. In fact, they are not at all embarrassed by their conduct. Even when they know the word of God, it does not cause them the slightest discomfort and unease when they declare what is counter to what is written. Their sins are plainly evident, but that does not cause any blushing or embarrassment (v. 12). They feel that possession of the word of God itself is sufficient; it need not be obeyed or heeded necessarily.

It offends God to pawn off artificial acts of attendance for a genuine, heartfelt entrance into the house of God. It also offends God to exchange rote presentation of offerings that are not from a repentant heart. It is third offense to God to claim that possession of the word of God can be a legitimate substitute for authentic response to that word. The shame of all such hypocrisy is what Jeremiah labored to expose in his day and ours. God is not tricked or fooled by artificial substitutes or half-attempts at worship. He wants authentic and real responses that come from the heart rather than mere performance and external ritualism.

It is a real possibility that we honor the word of God as inspired and inerrant but never read it or heed what it says. We should be like birds that, when cold weather begins to hint at its presence early in the fall, begin to assemble for their long flight south. But we, God's creatures, made in his image, see more than hints of disaster about to arrive and adopt no change of lifestyle or being. We just keep whistling in the graveyard, telling each other such tragedy will never come to us. God loves us too much for that to happen. After all, they improperly argue, we are the real believers, for we hold to the full inspiration and authority of the word of God. But it is all talk and no response to that word or to God. Our Lord will not accept the mere act of possessing the word of God and even arguing, as we should, for its full reliability and truthfulness but never using it for our daily devotions or as the actual basis for the sermons we preach.

NO BALM OR PHYSICIAN IN GILEAD (8:13–10:25)

This is made up of three sections: 8:13–23 (Heb. 9:1); 9:2–26 (Heb. 9:1–25); and 10:1–25. The first section is largely made up of laments, both from the people (vv. 14–15, 19b, 20) and the prophet and God (vv. 18–19a, 21–22, 9:1). The reason for lament is given in 8:16–17, which describes the approach of the enemy. The key question, however, occurs in 8:22—"Is there no balm in Gilead?" Gilead was renowned as a source of physicians and healing balms from that area. Alas, alas, even they are helpless to put Judah on the road to health again.

Another lament initiates the second section (9:2), which in turn links it to another indictment (vv. 3–6), followed by a judgment (vv. 7–9). Three more laments follow this section (vv. 10–11, 17–19, 20–22), with two prose sections interposed (vv. 13–16 and vv. 23–26). The first prose section looks to the past, and the second one looks to the future.

The poem in 10:1–25 gives us one of the most scathing denunciations of idolatry. It follows so closely to similar things in Isaiah said that some attribute this section to Isaiah (cf. Isa 40:18–20; 41:7; 44:9–20; 46:5–7). There is a problem with the smoothness of this chapter, especially since v. 11 is written in Aramaic, and vv. 6–8 and v. 10 are omitted from the Septuagint altogether, which also places v. 9 after the first part of v. 5. Some have suggested that Jeremiah is here quoting aphorisms that perhaps Isaiah had coined, but there is no doubt that Jeremiah has idolatrous worship as practiced by the Canaanites as his target in this section.

LAMENTS OVER GOD'S PROMISED DISASTER (8:13–9:1 [8:13–23])[120]

TRANSLATION

13 "I will take away their harvest,"[121] declares Yahweh.
There will be no grapes on the vine.
There will be no figs on the tree,
Even the leaves are withered,
And what I gave them has passed away from them.[122]
14 Why do we sit still?
Gather together!
Let us flee to the fortified cities!
And let us perish there!
For Yahweh our God has doomed us to perish,
And given us poisoned water to drink,
Because we have sinned against Yahweh.

---

120. The outline follows the versification of the English text; verse ranges in square brackets denote the Hebrew versification when it differs from the English.

121. The meaning of the phrase אָסֹף אֲסִיפֵם is uncertain. It can be translated "I will gather them" or "I will take away."

122. The phrase וָאֶתֵּן לָהֶם יַעַבְרוּם, "And what I have them has passed away from them," is missing in the LXX.

15 We hoped for peace,

But no good has come![123]

For a time of healing,

But behold, terror!

16 The snorting of their horses is heard from Dan,

At the sound of the neighing of their stallions,

The whole land trembles.

They come and devour the land,

And all that fills it,

The city and those who dwell in it.

17 For behold, I am sending among you poisonous snakes,

That cannot be charmed,

And they will bite you, declares Yahweh.[124]

18 O my Comforter in sorrow,[125]

My heart is faint within me.

19 Listen! The cry of the daughter of my people,

From a land far away:

"Is Yahweh not in Zion?

Is her king no longer there?"

"Why have they provoked me to anger,

With their graven images,

With their worthless foreign gods?"

20 The harvest is past,

The summer has ended,

And we are not saved.

21 Since the daughter of my people is crushed,

I am crushed,

And horror[126] has gripped me.

22 Is there no balm in Gilead?

Is there no physician there?

---

123. Lit. "there is no good."

124. The phrase נְאֻם־יְהוָה, "declares Yahweh," is missing in the LXX.

125. The phrase מַבְלִיגִיתִי עֲלֵי can be translated "O my Comforter in sorrow," "My joy is gone; grief is upon me," or "My joy is beyond healing." In its current form the phrase is untranslatable. All translations are based on emendation. See Craigie, Kelley, and Drinkard, 137.

126. The LXX adds ὠδῖνες ὡς τικτούσης, "as a woman in travail."

Why then is there no healing for the daughter of my people?

9:1 [8:23] O that my head were [a spring of] water,

And my eyes were a fountain of tears!

I would cry day and night for the slain of the daughter of my people.

COMMENTARY

8:13–15 God's promised disaster begins with a description of judgment. No harvest can represent lack of income, no grapes can represent lack of joy, and no figs can represent lack of food. The last phrase, translated "and what I gave them has passed away from them," appears literally as "And I gave them, they shall pass over them" in the Heb. text.[127] The text unit continues with a question asked by the people: "Why do we sit still?" "Let us flee to the fortified cities and let us perish there" (v. 14a, c). The people instinctively sense that judgment is in the air and that they must not sit around and do nothing until disaster came. The reason is that Yahweh has already begun his work of gathering up the grain and the fruit at harvest time. Alas, however, Yahweh found that there were no grapes and no figs left (cf. 2:21); in fact, the leaves on the vines and the trees have already withered. Instead of the usual fruitfulness of the land as a gift from the gracious hand of the Creator, the land itself has been adversely affected by the people's sins and now resembles more of a wasteland than a productive area of crops (cf. 4:26; 7:34; 9:10).

The people seem to be resigned to judgment being on the way, for they feel as if they are doomed (v. 14e). They feel as if they are being given poisoned water to drink (v. 14f; cf. 23:15), which is used here as a metaphor for some lethal experience, or it may instead be an enemy tactic to poison their wells, or it even may be the image of the "cup of wrath" (25:15–16) that will come from the hand of God. Whereas they were hoping for peace, there is now only terror and despair. What a desperate state of affairs!

---

127. An proposed emendation suggests that the text originally read "I gave them a naked forest." See D. Aberbach, "*W'tn lhm Y'brwm* (Jeremiah VIII 13): The Problem and Its Solution," *VT* 27 (1977): 99–101.

8:16 The divine response to the people comes in vv. 16–17. Instead of some signs of deliverance, God is sending the armies from out of the north (the usual line of attack from Babylon and countries to the east of Israel). The enemy is so close that by now that the snorting of the horses can be heard already in Dan, in northern Israel (v. 16). Moreover, so vast is the army that the whole land trembles and vibrates with their advance. The enemy has come to eat up and consume everything (v. 16c).

8:17 The imagery then gives way from depicting stallions to dealing with poisonous snakes in v. 17. It may be literally true that God will let loose a swarm of snakes, as he once did in the wilderness march (Num 21:6; Deut 32:24). But if anyone is thinking that perhaps they might be able to charm these poisonous snakes, forget it, for this enemy's bite will prove fatal (v. 17c).

8:18 Both God and the prophet are deeply affected by the lack of response from the people. Even the repeated phrase "the daughter of my people" (vv. 19, 21, 22, 23 [9:1]; 9:2) is filled with pathos. The beginning word of v. 18 (מַבְלִיגִיתִי) is difficult to translate since it only occurs here in Scripture. Most propose dividing the word into two (מִבְּלִי גֵהֹת), which would mean "without healing," and is supported by the LXX (ἀνίατα, "incurable"; Craigie, 135).[128] What is certain is that Jeremiah is just as grieved over disaster coming to his people as Yahweh.[129] This will be no picnic!

As a result, a sickness comes to Jeremiah that goes right to his heart. What is about to happen makes him sick in his whole being. It has left his heart faint within him. He must speak the words of disaster, but he has little taste for the assignment given to him by Yahweh. There is no joy in announcing the disaster he and his people must now face because of the hardness of their hearts.

---

128. Cf. *HALOT*, 1:542.

129. There is disagreement with regard to the identity of the weeping speaker. Some suggest is Jeremiah, some Yahweh, and some both. See J. M. Henderson, "Who Weeps in Jeremiah VIII 23 (IX I)? Identifying Dramatic Speakers in the Poetry of Jeremiah," *VT* 52, no. 2 (2002): 191–206.

8:19-21 A cry goes up from the people in vv. 19-20, which plaintively asks: "Is Yahweh no longer in the land?" "Is her king no longer there?" While in the land of Judah, the temple is the signal and assurance of God dwelling in their presence, but what can they now say when they will be going to a foreign land? So with a mournful proverb, the people break out in this lament: "The harvest is past, the summer has ended, and we are not saved." Instead, the people feel "crushed" and gripped by "horror" (v. 21). Holladay puts it well: "the tragedy which Jeremiah is expressing in this oracle is not only that the people are sick and need to be made whole, but (more keenly) that they do not know Yahweh, nor recognize his voice."[130]

The word translated "I mourn" in v. 21 (קָדַרְתִּי) literally means "I am black" or "I am dark." Thus the word sets the mood as the reality of mourning. The prophet's thoughts are depressing and dark, for if only the people would acknowledge their guilt and repent, they could be spared a lot of coming trouble.

8:22 The area north of the country of Moab and east of the Jordan River was part of the Transjordan, or more specifically called Gilead. It was renowned for resin that apparently came from the balsam tree in that area. When Joseph was sold into slavery by his brothers, he was given over into the hands of a caravan that was carrying balm from Gilead down to Egypt (Gen 37:25). This aromatic resin was applied to wounds as a healing device and was said to keep the wounds from putrefying.

Many know this verse from the spiritual that begins with the words "There is a balm in Gilead, to make the wounded whole," as well as to "heal the sin-sick soul." Notice, however, that the balm Jeremiah refers to was insufficient to heal the spiritual sickness of Judah. Instead, they need a healer, no less than Yahweh himself; a balm would not be effective for the soul-sickness of these folks.

William Cowper, the hymn writer and poet (1731-1800), begins "The Time Piece" by using lines from Jer 8:18-9:2:

O for a lodge in some vast wilderness,
Some boundless contiguity of shade,

---

130. W. L. Holladay, "The So-Called 'Deuteronomic Gloss' in Jer. VIII 19b," *VT* 12, no. 4 (1962): 494-98.

Where rumor of oppression and deceit,
Of unsuccessful or successful war,
Might never reach me more. My ear is pained,
My soul is sick with every day's report,
Of wrong and outrage with which Earth is filled,
There is no flesh in man's obdurate heart,
It does not feel for man; the natural bond
Of brotherhood is severed as the flax,
That falls asunder at the touch of fire.[131]

The land, its people, and its products are crushed, and for the moment it does not look as if anyone is available to heal. What mournful words: "The harvest is past, the summer has ended, and we are not saved" (8:20). All the time, however, the great Healer stands ready to help them, and us, recover if we would only turn to him.

DECEIT AND IGNORANCE DESTROY THE LAND (9:2–26 [9:1–25])[132]

TRANSLATION

2 [1] O that I had in the desert,
   A lodging place for travelers,[133]
That I might leave my people,
   And go away from them:
For they are all adulterers,
   A crowd of treacherous men.
3 [2] They bend their tongue like a bow;
   Lies, not truth, prevail in the land.
They proceed from evil to evil,
   and do not know me, declares Yahweh.[134]
4 [3] Be on guard against one another;

---

131. W. Cowper, *Poems by William Cowper, Esq., Of the Inner Temple*, 10th ed. (New York: William L. Allison, n.d.), 273 as cited by Fretheim, 155.

132. The outline follows the versification of the English text; verse ranges in square brackets denote the Hebrew versification when it differs from the English.

133. The expression "a lodging place for travelers" appears as σταθμὸν ἔσχατον, "a most distant lodge," in the LXX.

134. The phrase נְאֻם־יְהוָה, "declares Yahweh," is omitted in the LXX in vv. 2, 5, and 21.

Do not trust your brother!
For every brother is a deceiving Jacob,
   And every friend a slanderer.
5 [4] Every one cheats his neighbor,
   And no one speaks the truth.
They have taught their tongue to speak falsehood,
   They weary themselves with going astray.
6 [5] You live in the midst of deception;
   In their deception, they refuse to acknowledge me,
      declares Yahweh.
7 [6] Therefore, this is what Yahweh of Hosts says,
   "Behold, I will refine them and test them,
   What else can I do because of [the sin of] the daughter of
      my people?
8 [7] Their tongue is a deadly arrow;
   It speaks with deceit.
With his mouth he speaks peace to his neighbor,
   But in his inner being he sets a trap for him."
9 [8] "Should I not punish them for this?" asks Yahweh.
   "Should I not avenge myself against a nation such as this?
10 [9] For the mountains I will take up a weeping[135] and a wailing,
   And for the desert pastures a dirge,
For they are desolate and without any passing through,
   And the lowing of cattle is not heard.
   The birds of the air and the animals have fled and are gone.
11 [10] I will make Jerusalem a heap of rubble,
   A haunt for jackals,
And the towns of Judah I will make a devastation
   So no one can live there."[136]
12 [11] What man is wise enough to understand this?
   And to whom has the mouth of Yahweh spoken that he
      may declare it?

---

135. Where the MT has אֶשָּׂא, "I will take up (weeping)," the LXX has the 2 pl. aor. impv. λάβετε, "take up."

136. Lit. "Without inhabitants."

Why has the land been ruined and laid waste like a desert
>that no one can cross?

13 [12] And Yahweh said, "It is because they have forsaken my law,
which I set before them; they have not obeyed me or conducted themselves
in accordance with it. **14 [13]** But they have walked after the stubbornness
of their hearts,[137] following the Baals of which their fathers taught them.
15 [14] Therefore, this is what Yahweh of Hosts, the God of Israel says,
'Behold, I will feed this people with wormwood and give them poison to
drink. **16 [15]** I will scatter them among the nations which neither they
nor their fathers have known, and I will send the sword after them until
I have destroyed them.'"

17 [16] This is what Yahweh of Hosts says,
>"Consider and call for the wailing women and they will come,
>>Send the most skilled of them, and they will come."

18 [17] Let them come quickly[138] and take up a wailing over us,
>Till our eyes overflow with tears,
>And our eyelashes stream with water.

19 [18] For the sound of wailing is heard from Zion!
How ruined we are,
>How great is our shame!
For we must leave our land
>Because our dwellings are in ruins.

20 [19] Now, O women, hear the word of Yahweh,
>And let your ears hear[139] the word of his mouth.
Teach your daughters how to wail,
>Teach[140] one another a lament.

21 [20] For death has climbed in through our windows.
>It has entered our castles,[141]
In order to cut off the children from the streets
>And the young men from the public squares.

22 [21] Say, "this is what Yahweh declares:

---

137. The LXX and the Syr. add the adj. κακῆς, "evil," to modify "their heart."
138. The LXX reads καὶ φθεγξάσθωσαν, "and let them speak out," for "let them come quickly."
139. Lit. "take."
140. Supplied from the previous line.
141. The LXX has εἰς τὴν γῆν, "into our land," where the MT has "into our castles."

'The corpses of men will lie like dung on the open field,
Like sheaves behind the reaper,
  Which no one gathers.'"

23 [22] Thus declares Yahweh:
"Do not let the wise man boast of his wisdom,
  Or the strong man boast of his strength,
  Or the rich man boast of his riches.

24 [23] But about this, let him who boasts boast:
  That he understands and knows me—
That I, Yahweh, exercise grace, justice, and do what is right in
  the earth;
  For in such I delight," declares Yahweh.

25 [24] "Behold, the days are coming," declares Yahweh,
  "When I will punish all who are circumcised only in the
    flesh:[142]

26 [25] Egypt, Judah, Edom, Ammon, Moab,
  And upon all those with shaven temples,
Who live in the desert;
  For all nations are uncircumcised[143]—
  And all the house of Israel is uncircumcised in heart."

COMMENTARY

9:2 [1] The speaker of vv. 2–3 [1–2] is probably God, as seen in vv. 3 [2],
6–7 [5–6], and 9 [8]. Yet, as in the previous section, it is not always possible to separate the words of God from those of the prophet, for what the
prophet speaks is the message that God has given to him in the first place.
Therefore, v. 2 [1] begins with God and the prophet expressing the wish
that they could flee away to some dwelling place in the desert in order
to escape from the people of Judah. The wish is certainly there ("O, that

---

142. Scholars have debated the meaning of the phrase "circumcised in the flesh." Some
have argued that it is referring to those "circumcised physically but not spiritually," while
others think it's referring to the fact that some of the people mentioned from the foreign
nations are only partially circumcised. See R. C. Steiner, "Incomplete Circumcision in Egypt
and Edom: Jeremiah (9:24–25) in the Light of Josephus and Jonckheere," *JBL* 118, no. 3 (1999):
497–526.

143. The LXX, the Syr., and the Tg. add σαρκί, "of flesh," to modify the pl. adj. עֲרֵלִים,
"uncircumcised."

I had"), but there is no word that suggests that such a retreat is found or that God and the prophet have actually abandoned their people. It is not as if God and the prophet wish to be hermits; it is just that a retreat some place far away from the Judahites would be preferable at this point to life with this people who refuse to listen to anything that is taught. They are still called "my people" in v. 2c[1c], but they still wish they could just plain abandon these rebels.

The Breakdown of Society (9:3-6 [2-5])

9:3 [2] The reasons for such a drastic wish are found in the list of the people's sins in vv. 2e-f, 3 [1e-f, 2]. There are few sins that these people have not indulged in, adultery and unfaithfulness being uppermost on the list. There is, however, nothing short of treason to the One they called Lord over all!

For example, they misuse their tongues in a backbiting manner, making their very words their weapons of choice. Both their tongues and their words were like bows with arrows that were bent on doing harm (cf. Jas 1:26; 3:1-12). In this case, however, the arrows are just plain lies that their tongues shoot out. They move from one evil to another, failing all the while to recall the reality of their marital relationship to Yahweh, an example of a lack of a real commitment to him. The fact is that "truth [does not] ... triumph in the land" (v. 3c[2c]). Here is a picture of a society that has lost its ability to function coherently and communally, for where there is no trust there is no longer a community.

9:4-5 [3-4] For these reasons, a warning goes out to all to be on their guard (v. 4 [3]); they are all acting like "Jacob" (v. 4c [3c]), the "deceiver" (Gen 25:26-33; Hos 12:3). There is a wordplay here on the word for "Jacob" and the word "to deceive" (יַעְקֹב). The impvs. ("beware," הִשָּׁמְרוּ; and "do not trust," אַל־תִּבְטָחוּ) are plural, which are, of course, addressed to the whole community. Each person deceives the other, and each lies to the other, for they "have taught their tongues to lie" (v. 5c[4c]). They have become so weary of spending all their energy on sinful activity that there is no strength to repent and do what was right! Could they not have picked a nobler cause than to devote themselves to constant evil?

9:6 [7] Verse 6 [5] switches its attention from the people to the prophet Jeremiah. Yahweh says to the prophet, "You (sg.) live in the midst of deception." The lifestyle of the people you serve is one of cheating and trickery; in fact, it is one that has no place for God. Their refusal to acknowledge God is clear but inexplicable, remembering all that God had done for them!

A Time for Divine Refining and Testing of Judah (9:7–9 [6–8])

9:7 [6] Verse 7 [6] begins with the word of judgment, "Therefore." Here the judgment will be put in the form of questions (v. 9 [8]). Yahweh is reluctant to act in judgment, but what else can he do for such impudent sinners as these? To remove the impurities from the nation, Yahweh will begin by refining and testing them (v. 7b [8b]). The imagery here is taken from the metal smelter, which also removes the impurities from ore, thus allowing the true quality to be ascertained/tested. The hopeful note is that there is something to be redeemed and recovered (as there is in the smelting of precious metals) from this process, even though it might be painful in the interim. Nevertheless, there is more than a hint of divine reluctance in v. 7c [6c]. But what else can God do? He has persistently sent warnings time and again over the years (7:24–26), but this was all to no effect. What means remain open to our Lord to bring these people face to face with their own sins?

9:8 [7] The sins of speech are at the heart of the concern of v. 8 [7] as they were in vv. 3–5 [2–4]. The tongue just cannot be trusted to avoid deliberate distortion. While they use their tongues for speaking in a civil way to their neighbors, deep down in their inner being they are doing little more than setting a trap for their neighbors. What appeared to be a word of friendship actually turns out to be a means of gaining an advantage over their neighbor in order to set him up for calamity.

9:9 [8] Jeremiah asks the same questions he had posed in 5:9, 29, but they bear repeating here once again: Is it not proper and right for Yahweh to punish this nation?[144] And should he not avenge himself on such a people

---

144. Mark Smith argues that the words in 9:9 "are the words of Yahweh and not Jeremiah. … For Yahweh, this identification of lover and enemy is the source of great lamenting, for the

as Judah (v. 9 [8])? The implied answer is "Yes" to both questions. For too long Judah has stored up trouble by their refusal to obey the commands and injunctions of the Lord.

Weeping over the Ruin of Town and Country (9:10–11 [9–10])

9:10–11 [9–10] All that has happened already and what is to come call for a lament and a dirge over the mountains and the wilderness. It is not just the prophet who weeps but God as well. The reason for the wailing and lamenting is that the mountains and the wilderness have all become heaps of ruins and uninhabitable. There are no more sounds of livestock or herds of animals, for all the birds and the animals have disappeared. This has resulted in a human and an ecological disaster. The "lament" (קִינָה) is not an expression of complaint, but it is a funeral or death song, crying out about the hopelessness of a situation for which there is no known earthly remedy. So severe is the coming disaster that there will be nothing left to sustain the birds of the air or the wildlife present. Jerusalem, the beautiful city of God, will become "the haunt of jackals" (v. 11 [10]), similar to the destiny of Babylon (51:37). These scavenging animals are just one more sign that only devastation and ruins remain in the once-beautiful city.

An Explanation for the Ruin (9:12–16 [11–15])

9:12 [11] As if to expand on vv. 10–11 [9–10], vv. 12–16 [11–15] state in prose form why all this tragedy has to be visited on Judah. Thus, the challenge is raised: What mortal would care to try to explain all of this disaster? Are any men in the professional class of wise men willing to step forward and explain this? Furthermore, has anyone received a word from the Lord who wishes to tell us what all of this means? "Why has the land been ruined?" (v. 12c). Speak up, if you will!

9:13 [12] Since no takers are apparent, God himself steps forward and explains it all. "It is because they have forsaken my law, which I set before them; they have not obeyed me or followed my law" (v. 13 [12]). The answer

---

one Yahweh loves, Yahweh must destroy." See M. S. Smith, "Jeremiah IX 9—A Divine Lament," *VT* 37, no. 1 (1987): 289–93.

to the problem is not all that complicated; it is just plain old rebellion wherein Judah refuses to obey what God has said.

9:14 [13] The problem is that the people have instead adopted an alternative way of living: they prefer to heed the direction of their own stubborn hearts, and they prefer to follow the Baal deities, which their fathers had taught them to observe and worship (v. 14 [13]). This Baal worship has another inducement: it involved sexual activity along with the worship. This is an inherited legacy that their fathers had taught them.

9:15 [14] God's introductory word of judgment is this: "Therefore (v. 15 [14]), this is what the Yahweh of Hosts, the God of Israel says ... " God will feed the Judeans with "wormwood" and "poisonous water." Wormwood (לְעֲנָה) is a small shrub in the aster family with multiple branches and hairy leaves bearing masses of small yellow flowers, often seen in southern Israel. It is mentioned seven times in the OT and twice in the NT (ἀψίνθιον, Rev 8:11 [2x]), and it has a reputation of having a bitter taste and poisonous effects. Scripture uses this shrub as a metaphor for the experience of suffering and bitter sorrow, and even cruelty (Lam 3:15, 19; Jer 23:15).

There are two species grown in Israel, one that has a camphor-like smell and is extremely bitter; the other is still used to keep maggots or moths away from woolen garments by placing the dried plants between the garments. Instead of the manna and the water God had graciously supplied to Israel as they crossed the wilderness (Exod 15:22–25), they will experience a whole new diet from the hand of God. It will be deadly!

9:16 [15] Once again, there is the threat of the nation's dispersal in exile (v. 16 [15]). The word for "scatter" (פּוּץ) is also used for water running in the streets (Prov 5:16), or of a farmer scattering seed on the land (Isa 28:25). God will scatter Judah among nations that they are not familiar with. In addition, the sword will come among them as well (v. 16 [15]).

Call for the Professional Mourners (9:17–22 [16–21])

9:17-20 [16-19] There is a call for more lamentation from those women who are specially known for wailing and lamenting. These professional women would make their hair a disheveled mess, bare their breasts, fling their arms all about, and give shrill cries for the dead. This note is a call for such women to get ready to act as their profession demands of them (v. 17 [16], cf. Amos 5:16, 17). All of this must be done quickly, for in the Near East funerals follow quickly as soon as a person dies. The women are called to take up a dirge over the nation Judah so that their eyes may run down with tears and their eyelids flow with water (v. 18 [17], cf. 14:17). The tragedy is that devastation has struck (in that coming event) and their land lies abandoned and their houses are now torn down according to what was seen here (v. 19 [18]). So great will be the destruction of Jerusalem and Judah that the number of professional women will just not be sufficient for the task; other women will be needed to join them!

9:21-22 [20-21] Even more graphically, death is depicted as the grim reaper who prowls about as a burglar would seek a window through which to slip into the house (v. 21 [20]). When that window is found, death climbs in the window. Death also cuts down the ordinary citizen, the officials of the city, the city's young men and its inhabitants.[145] No obstacle is too challenging for death. Human corpses will be found everywhere in that day, for they will drop like manure on the surface of the soil, and like newly cut grain that is left behind the reaper; obviously, few, if any, pick up what has fallen (v. 22 [21]).

Boasting and Being Circumcised (9:23–26 [22–25])

9:23-24 [22-23] Over against the dark picture of the previous section, no one should be under the delusion that such judgment will never happen to them. If someone thinks that because they are wise, or they are strong, or they are rich, they will escape all that is threatened, then think again. No one can boast in any of these assets, for all boasting is clearly out of the picture.

---

145. Cassuto connects this verse with a portion of the Ugaritic Baal cycle. He argues that "Baal feared that Mot would enter the window and kill his wives." However, it seems that Yamm and not Mot is the enemy named in the Baal cycle. See M. Smith, "Death in Jeremiah, IX, 20," *Ugarit-Forschungen* 19 (1987): 289–93.

But if anyone wants to boast, let him boast about the fact that he knows Yahweh, that he is the Lord.[146] He is the One who is able to show grace (חֶסֶד), justice, and doing what is right on the earth. These are the things that God delights in, for he signs, as it were, his name to such a statement as an attestation of his solemn declaration. The basis of all human living is having a proper perspective on who God is and what he has done. This is where a proper insight into understanding takes its beginning. It begins with his covenant name, Yahweh.

God's special kindness or grace is seen in his loving commitment to his people. God's "justice" (מִשְׁפָּט) covers the administration of his realm with standards of equity and truth, reflective of his character. Finally, God's "righteousness" (צְדָקָה) means that he always does what is right (Ps 145:17). The NT picks up this same thought from vv. 23–24 [22–23] in 1 Cor 1:31 and again in 2 Cor 10:17.

9:25 [24] But not only can God's people be deluded about their own personal strengths and gifts; they also can be deluded in the area of religious practices (vv. 25–26 [24–25]). They can think, as they mostly do, that outward signs of the covenant are the same as the real, internal essence. Already in Jeremiah we have seen how many think the mere possession of the ark (3:16), the temple (7:4), or the book of the law (8:8) is equal to a right relationship with God. Moses has already warned in Deut 10:16; 30:6 that circumcision of the flesh does not suffice as evidence of a real heart relationship with God. Therefore, Yahweh will punish those who are circumcised in the flesh only and not in their hearts (v. 25 [24]).

9:26 [25] Jeremiah produces a list of the nations that practice circumcision, including Egypt, Judah, Edom, Ammon, and Moab, along with other peoples as well, but Judah will be lined up just as these other pagan nations for judgment because what is merely external and perfunctory will not substitute for the real obedience from the heart. In fact, even if these and

---

146. O'Day argues that Paul uses Jer 9:22–23 in 1 Cor 1:26–31 when she writes, "Jeremiah's critique of wisdom, power, and wealth as false sources of identity that violate the covenant are re-imaged by Paul as a critique of wisdom, power, and wealth that impede God's saving acts in Jesus Christ." See G. R. O'Day, "Jeremiah 9:22–23 and 1 Corinthians 1:26–31: A Study of Intertextuality," *JBL* 109, no. 2 (1990): 259–67.

others were meticulous about not cropping the edges of their beards, or the sides of their head, as the law warned in Lev 19:27 and Deut 14:1, it still will not be equal to what God is looking for in real obedience. Pagan nations often cut their hair off, as forbidden here, to dedicate it to a pagan deity.

An uncircumcised heart is what Jeremiah and Yahweh warn against; they want circumcised hearts, not just fleshly circumcision or rote performance in the things of God.

My first teacher in the Old Testament was Dr. Samuel Schultz. Whenever he signed a Bible or a book, he invariably would add Jer 9:23-24. This text stands out in stark contrast to the judgment theme that surrounds these verses. The Apostle Paul used this same text in 1 Cor 1:26–31, "Let the one who boasts boast in the Lord." Therefore, neither the wise, the strong, or the rich have any reason to boast. Instead, if anyone has anything they wish to brag about, then let it be that the person understands and knows the Lord, who exercises love, justice, and righteousness.

A MOCKING HYMN TO IDOLS AND A DOXOLOGY
TO THE INCOMPARABLE GOD (10:1–25)

TRANSLATION

1 Hear what Yahweh has spoken concerning you, O house of Israel. **2** This is what Yahweh has said:

> "Do not learn[147] the way of the nations
>> And the signs of the sky,
> Do not be terrified,
>> Even though the nations are scared of them.
> **3** For the customs of the people are worthless![148]

---

147. The prep. אֶל, "concerning," could have been misread for the sign of the direct obj. אֵת.

148. The word הֶבֶל is translated "worthless" in this passage but it can also be translated "vanity, vapor, meaningless." H. M. Barstad argues that the word is a distortion of the Canaanite fertility god Hubal. See B. Becking, "Does Jeremiah X 3 Refer to a Canaanite Deity Called Hubal," VT 43, no. 4 (1993): 555-57. S. Cohen and V. A. Hurowitz argue that Jeremiah's taunt resembles earlier Akkadian language from "Verse Account of Nabonidus." This view suggests that "Jeremiah heckles from the sidelines in the language of the adversaries that they are all wrong, for any cult statue is worthless as a representation of the one true God

It's but wood chopped out of the forest,

 Made with a tool in the hands of a craftsman.

4 They adorn [the idol] with silver and with gold;

 They fasten it with nails and hammer so it will not wobble.

5 Like a scarecrow[149] in a melon patch, their idols cannot speak;

 They must be carried about because they cannot walk.

Do not fear them;

 They can do no harm, nor can they do any good."

6 There is no one like you, O Yahweh;

 You are great, and your name is powerfully great.[150]

7 Who would not fear you, O king of the nations?

 Yea, that is your due!

Among all the nations' wise ones,

 And in all their dominions,

 There is no one like you.

8 And as one they are unreceptive and foolish;

 Fleeting discipline is a wooden idol.

9 Hammered silver is brought from Tarshish

 And gold from Uphaz[151];

They are the work of the craftsmen

 And of the hands of the goldsmith;

Their clothing is violet and purple;

 They are all the work of skilled craftsmen.

10 But Yahweh is the true God,

 He is the living God, the eternal King.

 His wrath causes the earth to quake,

 And the nations cannot endure his fury."

---

who created the universe." See S. Cohen and V. A. Hurowitz, "חקות העמים הבל הוא (Jer 10:3) in Light of Akkadian *Parṣu* and *Zaqīqu* Referring to Cult Statues," *JQR* 89, nos. 3–4 (1999): 277–90.

149. The word תֹּמֶר, "scarecrow," is a **hapax legomenon**. The word does not appear in the LXX, and the Vg. and the Syr. translate it "palm-tree."

150. Vv. 6–8 and 10 are missing from the LXX. These missing verses deal with anti-idol polemics and are not found in the DSS fragments of 4QJer[b] either. Some scholars argue that the verses were inserted by a redactor. See J. Ben-Dov, "A Textual Problem and Its Form-Critical Solution: Jeremiah 10:1–16," *Textus* 20 (2000): 97–128.

151. The location "Uphaz" appears as "Ophir" in the Syr. and the Tg., and as "Mophaz" in the LXX.

11 Here is what you are to say to them:

> "May the gods who did not make the sky and the earth
>> Perish from under this sky."[152]

12 But God is the One who made the earth by his power,
> Founded the world by his wisdom
> And stretched out the heavens by his understanding.

13 When he utters his voice,[153]
> There is a tumult of waters in the heavens,
> And he makes a mist[154] rise from the ends of the earth.

He makes lightning for the rain,
> And he brings wind from his storehouses.

14 Everyone is stupid and without understanding,
> Every goldsmith is put to shame by his idols,

Because his images are a fraud;
> They have no breath in them.

15 They are worthless,
> A work of delusion;[155]

At the time of their punishment,
> They will perish.

16 He who is the portion of Jacob is like none of these,
> For he is the Maker of all things,

Including Israel, the tribe[156] of his inheritance,
> Yahweh of Hosts is his name.

17 Gather up your belongings from the land,

---

152. V. 11 is written in Aramaic. Since there is not another place in the Bible where the language switches (from Heb. to Aramaic, or vice versa) in a single verse, this leads some to believe that the verse "was added to the original text unit by association to the already present anti-idol polemics." See Ben-Dov, "Textual Problem and Its Form-Critical Solution." G. Reid, on the other hand, suggests that "its Aramaic rendering is crucial given its intended use as a polemical summary of the Hebrews' theology, designed as a *kerygmatic* challenge they are to deliver to their Babylonian captors proclaiming Yahweh as the true God. See G. Reid, "'Thus You Will Say to Them': A Cross-Cultural Confessional Polemic in Jeremiah 10.11," *JSOT* 31, no. 2 (2006): 221–38.

153. The phrase לְקוֹל תִּתּוֹ, "when he utters his voice," is missing in the LXX.

154. Or "clouds."

155. Rudman affirms that "the disrespect is towards God in his role as Creator, by the physical act of manufacturing an image." See D. Rudman, "Creation and Fall in Jeremiah X 12–16," *VT* 48, no. 1 (1998): 63–73.

156. The words "Israel" and "tribe" are missing from the LXX.

You who live under siege.

18 For this is what Yahweh says:

"Behold, I will hurl out those living in this land at this time,

    I will bring distress on them so that they may be captured."

19 Woe to me because of my wound!

    My injuries are so severe.

    But I said, truly, this is my sickness and I must bear it.

20 My tent is devastated; all its ropes are snapped.

    My sons are gone from me,[157] and they are no more;

No one is left to pitch my tent

    Or to set up my shelter.

21 For the shepherds are stupid,

    And they do not inquire of Yahweh;

Therefore they do not prosper

    And all their flock is scattered.

22 Listen! A rumor. It is coming—

    A great commotion out of the north country.

It will make the cities of Judah a desolation,

    A hiding place for jackals.

23 I know, Yahweh,

    That the way of a man is not in himself,

    That it is not in man who walks to direct his steps.

24 Rebuke me,[158] Yahweh, but in just measure,

    Not in your anger, lest you bring me to nothing!

25 Pour out your wrath on the nations that do not acknowledge you,

    On the peoples who do not call on your name;

For they have devoured Jacob;

    They have devoured him and consumed him

    And have laid waste his habitation.

---

157. The LXX adds καὶ τὰ πρόβατά μου, "and my sheep/flocks," after "My sons are gone from me."

158. The LXX has "rebuke us" where the MT has "rebuke me."

COMMENTARY

A Scarecrow in a Melon Patch versus an Incomparable God (10:1–16)

Verses 1–16 are a hymnic interlude that bears a satirical thrust that mocks Israel's trust in worthless idols vis-à-vis a God who exceeds all comparisons (vv. 6–7, 10, 12–13, 16).[159] It is written almost as if it were an antiphonal liturgy addressed mainly to the nations, for the theme of "the nations" provides the figure of speech known as **inclusio** in vv. 2, 25, thus embracing the entire chapter. Yet, the opening section is addressed to the "house of Israel," probably because the Jewish people were acting exactly as the pagan nations acted. Therefore, this section is a strong polemic against worshiping idols. Here the prophet is not addressing northern Israel but Judah as a representative of what is left of that nation Israel.

10:1–4 A radio preacher once received a question that went like this, "Bishop Johnson, should we or should we not put up Christmas trees at this season like everyone else is doing?" He responded, "Thank you for that important question. Now turn to Jeremiah 10:1–4; I am going to ask my assistant to read that Scripture." When the assistant was finished reading the text, Bishop Johnson said: "Do you hear how the text warns us: 'Do not learn the ways of the nations … for the customs of the peoples are worthless'? It says in verse 3 that 'they cut down a tree,' and that is what they are doing right now [at the end of November]. Why, I saw two truckloads of them coming into our city. Then they buy a tree and put it up in a big window of their house and, as in verse 4, 'they adorn it with silver and gold; they fasten it with hammer and nails so it will not totter.' That's why they put tinsel and gold balls on it. These are the customs of the people; they are false and worthless, so do not practice putting up a Christmas tree." This made for a fascinating guidance to his radio audience; the only problem was that he stopped at verse 4 and did not go on to speak of the idols of the people. This is a great example of allegorizing, a method of interpreting Scripture that takes away its authority and inspiration! Instead, the prophet Jeremiah was distinguishing Israel's God from the nations' idols in

---

159. Even though many scholars suggest that this passage does not originate with Jeremiah, "linguistic criteria clearly indicate … that Jeremiah must be considered its author." See M. Margaliot, "Jeremiah X 1–16: A Re-examination," *VT* 30 (1980): 295–308.

terms of the created order itself. These idols were the products of human hands, made from wood from the forests. The idols were silent, inactive, unable to move, or even able to make people afraid.

So what made these idols attractive to Israel and the nations? First, idolatry was the "in thing"; everyone was having an idol made for themselves. Public opinion has great force, so the customs of the people spoke for most people, for no one wanted to be thought of as being "out of it" or being "a square" by rejecting what custom taught. Not only was idolatry the custom of the day, it was also trendy and fashionable: "hammered silver [was] brought from Tarshish and gold from Uphaz," which Uphaz may well have been the same as "gold from Ophir," which was found on an ostracon as a shipping receipt found near Tel Aviv. Idolatry also had a certain type of aesthetics about it as well, for their idols were often "dressed in blue and purple" (v. 9). That, along with the silver and the gold, gave the idol an air of importance and intrinsic value.

It is interesting to note that in Jeremiah's day, the issue is not atheism but idolatry. But this is not to say that idolatry is no longer an issue for us in our day, for we give heed to the gods of naturalism, nationalism, consumerism, technology, and militarism. Even though those ancient and modern gods have seductive power, they lack life; they cannot do anything. There are all sorts of substitutes for the living God: money, power, sex, popularity, leisure, securities, and the like. That is why the chapter warns us to stay clear (that is, "Do not learn") of the idolatrous "ways of the nations" (v. 2).

10:5 These idols, ancient and modern, are about as real and helpful as a "scarecrow in a melon patch" (v. 5). Not only do they lack a brain; they must be carried about if they are going anywhere (v. 5), and they have no breath in them (v. 14). They make even the "wise men" in these nations look ridiculous and foolish (v. 8). How could what is manmade seem as real, legitimate, when it was just about as real as a gust of wind? So why is Israel being taken in by all this silly talk?

10:6–9 In direct contrast to all that is said about these idols is the One and only true, living God (vv. 6–7). "No one is like you, O Yahweh" (v. 6). Idols can be found all over the landscape, like scarecrows in a field, but only God is great, and his name is mightier and more powerful than any competitor ever raised against him. Besides the greatness of his person and his sovereignty in his rule over all, his wisdom remains without any equal as well (v. 7).

10:10 Yahweh is a God who is alive (v. 10). Moreover, he is the "eternal King" (v. 10b). Idols have a short shelf life, with no breath or vitality in them at all. Verses 11–16 are repeated in Jer 51:15–19 in a new setting, but the contrast between the idols and the living God of all creation is still basic to both texts. Idols are manufactured and cannot make anything; God is eternal and is alive forevermore.

10:11 While the identity of those who are being addressed here is not altogether clear, it seems that this verse is directed the exiles in Babylon to instruct them that these idols did not make the heavens and the earth (v. 11); instead, these mere scarecrows will surely perish. However, in contrast to these manufactured gods and goddesses, the true God is the maker of all things (v. 16). In fact, he also made Israel. Thus, in addition to making the heavens and the earth, God made for himself a people. Deut 32:9 teaches "Yahweh's portion is his people." When he claimed Israel as his "portion," he signaled that the people belonged to him just as the land of Israel belonged to him as well. The traditional term, "portion" (חֵלֶק), is a spiritual metaphor for Levi's "portion" in the land being Yahweh himself, rather than an assigned piece of real estate (Num 18:30). Just as Yahweh is Israel's "portion" (Pss 16:5; 73:26; 119:57; 142:5 [6]), so Israel is his "portion."

10:12–13 This Scripture announces in most certain terms that "God made the earth by his power; he founded the world by his wisdom and stretched out the heavens by his understanding" (v. 12). Yahweh can also put on a spectacle as well, for in the storm, he thunders, sends lightning, wind, and rain (v. 13).[160]

---

160. In light of a Ugaritic parallel, David Reimer suggests that "When he utters his voice" should instead be translated "In the clouds he gives forth thunder." See D. J. Reimer, "A Problem in the Hebrew Text of Jeremiah X 13, LI 16," *VT* 38 (1988): 348–54. R. Althann, on the other hand, suggests that this is an inverse const. chain that harmonizes well contextually and syntactically, and thus should not be amended. See R. Althann, "The Inverse Construct Chain and Jer 10:13, 51:16," *JNSL* 15 (1989): 7–13.

These cold images of gods and goddesses were icons of stupidity rather than divine wisdom. They were nothing more than shams, mere jokes, doll-like representations that were as dead as door nails, nonentities that were mere "puffs of wind" that have no substance and as such were paltry and fraudulent attempts by humans to do what everyone else was doing.

Clendenen sees the following **chiasm** as part of Jeremiah's discourse strategy:[161]

a Emptiness of pagan worship (vv. 3-5)[162]

  b None like Yahweh (vv. 6-7)

    c Brutish and empty idols (vv. 8-9)

      d Yahweh shakes the earth (v. 10)

        e Idols shall perish form earth and heaven (v. 11)

      d' Yahweh causes rumbling in heaven (vv. 12-13)

    c' Brutish and empty idol worship (vv. 14-15)

  b' Yahweh not like these (v. 16)

The Coming Exile: A Lament and an Intercession (10:17-25)

10:17 The Judahites are told to pack up their belongings, for they are about to leave the land of Israel for the land of Babylon (v. 17). The city is not only under siege, but it is almost at the point of capitulation. So take what few possessions will fit into a sheet that will serve for a bundle to carry it all and get ready, for it's time to get out of town. The thought could not be more jarring, for the prophet and Yahweh have just spoken of Israel's being God's "portion."

10:18-22 The justification for this exhortation to get ready to leave is a divine message from God: God will "sling" (like as stone from a catapult,

---

161. See E. R. Clendenen, "Discourse Strategies in Jeremiah 10:1-16," *JBL* 106, no. 3 (1987): 401-8.

162. Clendenen identifies "a" as not a part of the **chiasm**; it "is semantically and lexically parallel to strophes (c) and (c'), [and] serves to introduce the topic of the discourse" (Clendenen, "Discourse Strategies," 405).

cf. Judg 20:16) them out of the land and into Babylon (v. 18). This distress will come so that they will feel it. In the face of the onslaught, there is not much to be done by the people or the prophet other than to endure it. The imagery seems to be drawn from the realm of health, but it also has definite physical aspects. Their tents have been destroyed and the tent ropes snapped. Their children have disappeared because they probably have been killed. No one is left to help with the devastation after their homes have been decimated, for their sons had gone into battle and they too are no doubt captured or killed as well (vv. 20-22).

Some of this mess can be charged as the fault of the "shepherds" (that is, Israel's leaders; 3:15; 6:3; 23:1) who had been plain "stupid" and had not sought a word from Yahweh (v. 21). Because of their resistance to the will of Yahweh, the people and the nation had not prospered, and Yahweh's people ("flock") had been scattered. While the people are not let off the hook, the key factor in Judah's present state of affairs is the unwise actions of the religious and political leaders.

10:23-25 All of this leads to an intercessory prayer by Jeremiah (vv. 23-25), whose themes also reappear in the book of consolation (30:11, 16). The time of this prayer seems to be after the destruction of Jerusalem (v. 25b). The prophet's prayer begins like a wisdom saying on how God and man are related (v. 23a; Ps 37:23; Prov 16:9; 20:24). The prophet thinks that part of the judgment that has come on the people is due to outside influences.

On behalf of the people, Jeremiah prays that the Yahweh will correct him and the people (v. 24a; Ps 6:1), but his prayer is that that correction will not come with God's anger against sin, otherwise they all will be reduced to nothing. The words of v. 25 are taken from Ps 79:6-7. After Jeremiah has interceded for Judah, he now intercedes against Babylon and their allied nations. The reason for his prayer is specifically stated: These nations have wasted Judah and leveled their homes and destroyed their land. In doing so they have exceeded God's command and appointment in acting too harshly against God's people. Thus, they have earned the wrath of God.

There are several application points that can be drawn from this section. First, nothing compares to our living God; everything else is but a sham. Second, when people refuse to listen to God's way, they invent strategies that are bound to fail, as Judah's did. And, last, the prayer of Jeremiah, for

God to bring judgment on both Judah and on Babylon, is to be respected. God will fulfill that request, then and now.

REJECTING THE COVENANT
FROM GOD (11:1–13:27)

Even though it is notoriously difficult to outline Jeremiah and to follow the line of argument in the book as a whole, certain blocks of material seem to go together naturally. This can be said for chapters 11–20, where the material appears to be bracketed by "Cursed be the man" in 11:3 and "Cursed be the man" in 20:15 as a sort of **inclusio**. In between this bracketed material fall four major sections of material: 11:1–13:27; 14:1–15:9; 15:10–17:27; and 18:1–20:18.

The material in the larger picture of these ten chapters seems to be much more open to the life and feelings of Jeremiah than chapters 1–10 were. This is especially true of those passages typically referred to as the "confessions" of Jeremiah, found in 11:18–23; 12:1–6; 15:10–21; 17:14–18; and 18:18–23. Perhaps the prophet's own experiences are in some manner a foretaste of what the nation will experience for its intransigence and stubbornness to obey the covenant God has so graciously given to them.

This immediate section, located in chapters 11–13, focuses on the covenant: first the people's negative response to the covenant (11:1–17), and second, the people's attitude toward the covenant messenger (11:18–12:17), and the Lord's attitude to those covenant breakers' disobedience, which he expresses in parables (13:1–27). In this, the second major prose sermon in this book (see the first in 7:1–8:3), the citations and allusions to the book of Deuteronomy are often noted by commentators as strong evidence of literary dependence on Deuteronomy, but the references are of a general sort, and one must also note the presence of such distinctive vocabulary, as the words "conspiracy" in 11:9 and "forefathers" in 11:10.

A CONSPIRACY AGAINST THE COVENANT (11:1–17)

TRANSLATION

1 The word that came to Jeremiah from Yahweh: **2** "Listen to the terms[163] of this covenant and speak to the men of Judah and to those who live in Jerusalem. **3** You shall say to them, Thus says Yahweh the God of Israel, 'Cursed is the man who does not obey the terms of this covenant, **4** which I commanded your fathers in the day I brought them out from the land of Egypt, out of the iron-smelting furnace,' saying, 'Listen to my voice and do all that I command you. So you shall be my people and I will be your God, **5** that I may perform my oath, which I swore to your fathers, to give them a land flowing with milk and honey, as [it is]at this day.'" And I answered and said, "Amen, Yahweh!"

6 Yahweh said to me, "Proclaim all these words in the towns of Judah and in the streets of Jerusalem: 'Listen to the terms of this covenant and do them. **7** For I solemnly warned your fathers in the day I brought them up from the land of Egypt until today, warning them persistently, saying, "Obey me."' **8** But they did not listen or incline their ear, but every one walked in the stubbornness of his evil heart.[164] So I brought on them all the terms of this covenant, which I commanded them to do, but they did not keep."

9 Then Yahweh said to me, "There is a conspiracy among the people of Judah and those who live in the land. **10** They have turned back to the iniquities of their forefathers, who refused to hear my words. They have followed other gods to serve them.[165] Both the house of Israel and the house of Judah have broken the covenant that I made with their fathers. **11** Therefore, thus says Yahweh, 'Behold, I am bringing disaster on them that they cannot escape; though they cry out to me, I will not listen to them. **12** Then the cities of Judah and the inhabitants of Jerusalem will go and cry out to the gods to whom they burn incense, but they will not save them one bit in the time of their distress. **13** For your gods have become as many as your

---

163. Lit. "words."

164. Vv. 7 and 8, with the exception of the last two words of v. 8, are missing in the LXX.

165. The LXX adds ἰδού, "behold," before "They have followed other gods to serve them."

cities, O Judah; and as many as the streets of Jerusalem are the altars you have set up to shame,[166] altars to burn incense to Baal.'

14 "But as for you [Jeremiah], do not pray for this people, nor lift up a cry or prayer on their behalf, for I will not listen when they call on me in the time of their distress. **15** What [right] has my beloved[167] in my house when she has done evil deeds? Can vows[168] and sacrificial flesh avert your doom? Can you then rejoice? **16** Yahweh called your name [once] 'a leafy olive tree, beautiful with beautifully formed[169] fruit'; but with the roar of a mighty storm he will set it on fire, and its branches will be consumed. **17** Yahweh of Hosts, who planted you, has decreed disaster against you, because the house of Israel and the house of Judah have done evil and provoked me to anger by burning incense to Baal."

COMMENTARY

Jeremiah 11:1–17 is the second block of prose material in this book (after Jer 7:1–8:3). It summarizes what has been said thus far and introduces the next section of this book, chapters 11–20. It stresses the certainty of the judgment that is to follow. For the most part this section records laments from God, the prophet, and the people.

11:1–2 This section begins with the introductory formula in v. 1 that marks a new word from Yahweh, much as in 7:1; 18:1; and 30:1. The call is for the people of Judah and Jerusalem to heed the "terms/words" of the covenant. This covenant is the very one God gave to Moses while they were in Egypt, which was but a renewal of the earlier covenant made with the patriarchs, Judah's forefathers. Even though this is the first time Jeremiah uses the term *covenant* in his book, nothing major should be made of this fact, since "covenant" also appears later, in 14:21; 22:9; 31:31–34; 32:40; 33:20–26; 34:8–22; 50:5.

---

166. The expression לַבֹּשֶׁת מִזְבְּחוֹת, "shameful altars," is missing from the LXX.

167. The MT text is corrupt. BHS suggests emending the text to מֶה לִי דוֹדְיִךְ, "what to me are your baskets?" for "What [right] has my beloved?"

168. The LXX reading, εὐχαί, "prayers," makes more sense in context. Thus the MT's הָרַבִּים should be emended to הַנְּדָרִים (translated "vows" here).

169. The word תֹּאַר, "form," is missing in the LXX.

11:3 As Jeremiah gives the terms of the covenant, he reminds the people of Judah that not only are they to heed what is asked of them in this covenant but that these terms are administered under an oath of a curse if the people fail to obey and do what they had agreed to do. Not only did the kings of the ancient world impose a similar type of curse on those who failed to live up to their promised covenant obligations, but that same structure of curses and blessings prevailed in the Sinai Covenant in Lev 26:3–46 and Deut 28; 30:15–20. That curse was imposed in the presence of Yahweh himself.

11:4–5 This covenant is not between equal parties, however, for Yahweh had imposed these terms because he was the One who had rescued Israel from the land of Egypt in his grace, out of the iron furnace, which is about as real a picture of the suffering Israel had endured as one can get. Israel would have continued to endure such suffering had it not been for the mercy and grace of God that rescued them from Egypt.

On the other hand, the positive aspects of the covenant are to be theirs if they obey: Yahweh will be their God, and they will be his people (v. 4), which double promises made up two parts of the much-repeated tripartite formula for the promise-plan of God, recited throughout the entire Scripture about fifty times. If they obey, then Yahweh will be free to fulfill his oath by giving them a land flowing with milk and honey (v. 5). This proverbial use of milk and honey is a way of stating the bounty and fertility of the land, and it occurs repeatedly in the Pentateuch and the rest of the OT. Jeremiah gives the proper liturgical response for agreeing to the terms of the covenant: "Amen, Yahweh." This is how the people had also answered in Deut 27:15–26.

11:6–7 Whether Jeremiah usually gave his messages in the temple or he was limited to a peripatetic ministry cannot be stated definitively. But we can be sure that Jeremiah hammered home the terms of the covenant that the people of Judah had not only accepted at Sinai but renewed at Josiah's ceremony on the rediscovery of the book of the law. But there are no covenant blessings without covenant obedience. Here is where the trouble began. In Israel's long history she had repeatedly flouted and rejected the terms of the covenant, going all the way back to the days when God mercifully

brought them up out of the bondage of Egypt. Again and again Israel has
sinned against Yahweh and has been repeatedly warned to reverse their
direction and actions (v. 7). The word for "warn" appears three times in
the Heb. of v. 7, thus the cautions are clearly visible to all.

11:8 Despite a few times when there was some evidence of obedience now
and again, for the most part Israel has obdurately and steadfastly shown a
stubborn and unrepentant heart toward Yahweh (v. 8). What else can God
do than to bring the curses of the covenant on Judah and Israel? Therefore,
inevitably the curses have to be activated.

11:9-10 This is nothing less than a "conspiracy" among the people (v. 9), a
word usually employed in political contexts (for example, 1 Kgs 16:20) of a
hostile action against a government. But this conspiracy has been formed
with the inert, nonliving idols, which turn out to be nothings with no
brains, truth, or stability to them. The people have switched loyalties and
plotted treasonously against Yahweh.

11:11-13 In this same syncretistic brand of religious exploration of options
for alternative deities, when the people of Judah encountered a real crisis,
they would cry out to Yahweh in the wake of their impending judgment
and the disaster that awaited them (v. 11). But there is no use doing that, for
God will no longer listen to them, nor will he hear them (vv. 12, 14). There
is no use in Jeremiah's interceding on their behalf either, for if they are
going to go to other gods in their times of worship, they can just as well go
to these stupid idols in their time of need (vv. 12, 13). So great is their problem of infidelity that the number of their gods is the same as the number of
their towns, and the number of altars matches the number of the streets
of Jerusalem (v. 13)! Here is pluralism with a vengeance!

11:14 There is no turning back the coming judgment now (v. 14), for it is
too late to pray; in fact, it is too late for everything; the cup of iniquity has
been filled up to the brim. God will not even listen to the prophet's prayer
(cf. 7:16; 14:11; 15:1). That this prohibition is renewed seems to indicate that
Jeremiah continued to plead on behalf of the people of Judah. This prohibition is itself perhaps a symbolic action that time has expired for Judah

to show any signs of repentance. The end of the line has come on Judah. Judgment will arrive!

11:15 Except for the impending doom on the nation being a lot closer, the words of vv. 15-17 are very similar to those of 7:21-26. The text of v. 15 is badly transmitted, but the general idea seems to be the same for all commentators despite some garbling of the text.[170] The point is that Judah's worship has been compromised, even though she still pretends that all is well as she routinely goes through her empty rituals. But such offerings are ineffective in turning away the threatened judgment on this rebellious people. What the people get the most joy out of is carrying out their evil schemes.

11:16 In an endearing picture of faithfulness, Yahweh's former attitude toward his people was reflected in the imagery of a thriving olive tree that produced an excellent crop of olives. But those times are long past and are now over, and so it is necessary to face the roar of an approaching storm that already could be heard. The lightning of that storm will set on fire the branches of this olive tree broken off in the storm (v. 16). Accordingly, the lightning-struck olive tree is now but a shadow of what it once was.

11:17 This section closes in v. 17 with the note that Yahweh, who had planted that olive tree, is the One who also has decreed disaster on that same tree, for both the house of Israel and the house of Judah have wickedly perpetuated evil, and they have deliberately provoked Yahweh to anger, especially by burning incense to Baal. The curse of the covenant is very real, yet the people had brought this disaster on themselves. They knew this would be the outcome of their brazen acts of worship of Baal, the Canaanite god of fertility, dew, and rain. So why do they persist in going that route?

When God's people break the covenant he has made with them, they can expect the judgment to occur, as it did. The phrase "cursed is the man" in v. 3 begins every verse in Deut 27:15-26, with the people responding with

---

170. The original poem may have read as, "What right has my beloved in my house? She has done wickedness! Can fatlings and holy flesh avert from thee thy doom? 'A spreading olive-tree, beautiful in form' was thy name called. Fire was kindled against it, its branches were shattered!" See J. P. Hyatt, "The Original Text of Jeremiah 11:15-16," *JBL* 60, no. 1 (1941): 57-60.

"Amen" at the end of every verse, as Jeremiah does for them in Jer 11:5. The terms of this covenant go way back to the days when Israel was delivered from Egypt. But this is not the last time God warns Israel, for just as our Lord continues to warn us, he warned Israel over and over again (v. 7).

Alas, it is not just Israel that was so stubborn and disobedient; it is the whole human race. Tragically, the disaster God had warned might come has now indeed been set for sure. Will future generations of Jews and Gentiles learn anything from such warnings? A similar disaster awaits all of us if we continue to flout responding to the call and word of God.

REJECTING THE MESSENGER OF THE COVENANT (11:18–12:17)

TRANSLATION

18 So Yahweh declared to me[171] and I knew [their plot], for at that time he[172] showed me their [foul] deed. **19** I had been like a docile lamb led to the slaughter, not knowing it was against me they had hatched their plots: "Let us destroy the tree with its fruit,[173] let us cut him off from the land of the living, that his name be remembered no more." **20** But O Yahweh of hosts, who judges righteously, who tests the heart and mind, let me see your vengeance on them, for to you I have committed my cause.

21 Therefore, this is what Yahweh says concerning the men of Anathoth who are seeking your life and saying, "Do not prophesy in the name of Yahweh or you will die by our hand." **22** Therefore, this is what Yahweh of hosts says: "Behold, I will punish them. Their young men will die by the sword, their sons and their daughters will die by famine; **23** Not even a remnant will be left to them, because I will bring disaster on the men of Anathoth in the year of their punishment."

---

171. The LXX has the impv. γνώρισόν μοι, "make it known to me," where the MT has the hiphil pf. הוֹדִיעֵנִי, "he made it known to me."

172. Lit. "you showed me." The change in person from third to second is a common shift in poetry. It is translated as "he" to aid the English audience, who is not used to such sudden shifts while still referring to the same person. Scholars refer to this shift as a form of enallage. Cf. L. Zogbo, "Enallage: Shifting Persons in Old Testament Texts" (paper for United Bible Societies Triennial Translation Workshop, May 1994).

173. The LXX has δεῦτε καὶ ἐμβάλωμεν ξύλον εἰς τὸν ἄρτον αὐτου, "come and let us put wood in his bread," where the MT has "let us destroy the tree with its fruit."

12:1 You are in the right, O Yahweh,
  When I complain to you.
Yet I plead my case before you.
  Why does the way of the wicked prosper?
  Why do all those doing treachery thrive?
2 You have planted them, and they have taken root;
  They grow and bear fruit.
You are near on their lips,
  But are far from their hearts.
3 But you, O Yahweh, know me;
  You see me and test my thoughts about you.
Drag them off like sheep for the slaughter,
  And set them apart for the day of slaughter.
4 How long will the land be parched,
  And the grass in every field wither?
Because of the wickedness of those who live in it,
  The beasts and the birds are snatched away,
  Since the [people] are saying, "He will not see our latter
    end."
5 If you have raced with men on foot,
  And they have worn you out,
  How can you compete with horses?
And if in a safe country you fall down,[174]
  How will you do in the jungle of Jordan?
6 For even your brothers and the house of your father,
  Even they have betrayed you;
  Even they have cried out behind you.
Do not trust them,
  Even though they speak well of you.

---

174. The MT has "and if in a safe land you are so trusting," but there is an Arabic cognate to בּוֹטֵחַ that means "to fall down, lie prostrate." Thus, in context, it makes better sense to say, "And if in a safe country you fall down, how will you do in the jungle of Jordan?" See A. Ehrman, "A Note on בוטח in Jer. XII. 5," *JSS* 5, no. 2 (1960): 153. See also J. Sternberger, "Un oracle royale à la source d'un ajout rédactionnel aux 'confessions' de Jérémie: Hypothèses se rapportant aux 'confessions' de Jérémie XII et XV," *VT* 36, no. 4 (1986): 462–73.

7 I will[175] forsake my house,
　　I will abandon my inheritance;
I will give the one I love
　　Into the hands of her enemies.
8 My inheritance has become to me
　　Like a lion in the forest;
She roars at me;
　　Therefore I hate her.
9 Is not my inheritance to me like a speckled bird of prey?[176]
　　That other birds surround and attack?
Go, assemble all the wild beasts;
　　Bring them to dine.
10 Many shepherds have destroyed my vineyard
　　And trampled down my portion.
　　They have turned my portion into a desolate wilderness.
11 It will be made a wilderness,
　　parched and desolate before me;
The whole land will be laid waste,
　　Because no one gives it a thought.
12 Over the heights in the wilderness
　　Destroyers will[177] come;
For the sword devours
　　From one end of the land to the other;
　　No one will be safe.
13 They will sow wheat but reap thorns;[178]
　　They will wear themselves out but profit nothing.

---

175. The qatal (pf.) verbs are translated here with a fut. tense because they are read as prophetic pfs. It is also possible, though, to read them as past tense ("I forsook") or pres. pfs. ("I have forsaken").

176. The LXX has σπήλαιον, "cave," in place of the MT's עיט, "bird of prey."

177. Prophetic pf.

178. The LXX has impvs., "sow ... reap," where the MT has pf. verbs.

They shall be ashamed of their[179] harvest
Because of Yahweh's fierce anger.[180]

14 This is what Yahweh says: "As for all my wicked neighbors who seize the inheritance I gave to my people Israel to inherit: 'Behold, I will pluck them up from their lands, and the house of Judah I will pull from among them. **15** And after I have plucked them up, I will return and have compassion on them, and I bring back each to his own inheritance and each to his own country. **16** And it shall come to pass if they really learn the ways of my people, to swear by my name, "As Yahweh lives," even as they [once] taught my people to swear by Baal—then they will be established among my people. **17** But if any nation does not listen,[181] then I will totally uproot that nation and destroy it, declares Yahweh.'"

COMMENTARY

The Plot against Jeremiah from His
Hometown of Anathoth (11:18–23)

The timing of this plot against the prophet Jeremiah is not known, for it could easily be placed either around the time of Josiah's reformation in 621 BC or early in the reign of Jehoiakim. If it is the former, then Jeremiah might have been seen as a supporter of abolishing the idol shrines, with the temple being the only remaining authorized place of worship. This suppression of local shrines, when it came in Josiah's reign, may have cut deeply into the livelihoods of Jeremiah's relatives and neighbors at Anathoth, and this may partly explain their anger against him. But it seems it may fit better under the days of gloom in Jehoiakim's time. Whereas an assassination attempt on Jeremiah might have received swift recompense

---

179. Lit. "your harvest." The 2 m. pl. pronominal suf. is often emended to a 3 m. pl. to maintain consistency with the preceding verb "and they shall be ashamed" (וּבֹשׁוּ). Another option is to read the previous verb as a m. pl. impv. ("be ashamed!"), which requires no emendating of the verbal form as both parsings would look the same. With this reading, then, the 2 m. pl. pronominal suf. needs no emendation: "Be ashamed of your harvest!"

180. The LXX has αἰσχύνθητε ἀπὸ καυχήσεως ὑμῶν ἀπὸ ὀνειδισμοῦ ἔναντι κυρίου, "be ashamed of your boasting, because of reproach before the Lord," where the MT has וּבֹשׁוּ מִתְּבוּאֹתֵיכֶם מֵחֲרוֹן אַף־יְהוָה, "they shall be ashamed of their harvests because of Yahweh's fierce anger."

181. The LXX has ἐὰν δὲ μὴ ἐπιστρέψωσιν, "if they will not return/repent," where the MT has וְאִם לֹא יִשְׁמָעוּ, "if they will not listen."

in King Josiah's day, by King Jehoiakim's time a plot against the prophet might have been welcomed by the court and the judiciary of the land.

This is the first of the "confessions of Jeremiah," though it would be more accurate to call this a "lament." A lament is a mournful, sad response to some threat, disaster, sickness, or unusual attack on one's person or community. Oftentimes professionals, normally wailing women, would give expression to the grief by shrieking, beating on their breast, or just plain crying out loud in deep consternation. Technically, a lament takes literary form in poetic lines, setting forth a complaint or a response to a national calamity. Usually these poems follow a conventional form that embraces some or all of the following constituent forms:

1. an address,

2. the complaint,

3. the petition to God in prayer to lift the cause of the distress,

4. a statement of confidence, and

5. a praise response.

This lament form appears in at least one-third of the Psalms. There are both individual laments and communal laments, often with a 3+2 meter known as *qinah* or "lament" meter, which has a sort of limping sound, as if one shoe has been dropped but the second one never falls, and one is left suspended in time, awaiting the sound of completion, or the balancing equivalent of the first line in the second line.

Laments bemoan the hardship of the crisis being faced yet openly seek a divine intervention for the sake of change. Elmer Martens (302) identifies elements of lament in Jer 11–20:

Complaint	"They said, 'Let us cut him off'" (11:19)
	"Why do wicked prosper?" (12:1)
	"Everyone curses me" (15:10)
	"Why is my pain unending?" (15:18)
	"Lord, you have deceived me" (20:7)

Petition	"Let me see your vengeance on them" (11:20; 20:12)
	"Drag them to be butchered" (12:3)
	"Avenge me of my persecutors" (15:15)
	"Save me" (17:14, 18)
Statement of Innocence	"You test my thoughts" (12:3)
	"What passes my lips is open to you" (17:16)
	"I spoke on their behalf" (18:20)
Statement of Confidence	"You judge righteously" (11:20)
	"You are in the right" (12:1)
	"I will deliver you" (15:11)
	"Yahweh is with me" (20:11)
Praise	"Give praise to Yahweh" (20:13)

For Jeremiah, prayer was something like going into a divine court and addressing the presiding judge, who was able to test one's "kidneys and heart," which in our modern usage would be equal to "heart and mind." The prophet's prayer might be for vengeance, which seems at first to be out of sync with the saintly piety we would expect from such a prophet. But the Hebrew use of the word "vengeance" (נְקָמָה) calls for God's legitimate power and zeal for what is just, fair, and right. The prophet wants God to demonstrate that he is God in front of all the people.

11:18 Jeremiah learns of this plot against him by a revelation from God (v. 18).[182] Before God makes Jeremiah understand what is going on, Jeremiah

---

182. Gosse sees 11:19–12:6 as a conversion of Jeremiah from trusting in people to trusting in Yahweh. This reversal is shown through a couple of wordplays, on the verbs "to sacrifice," and "to trust." He sees this passage based on Pss 1; 10; 69; 79; 89; 7:10; and 44:22–24. See B. Gosse, "Le prophéte Jérémie en Jer 11, 18–12,6 dans le cadre du livre de Jérémie et en rapport avec Psautier," *ZAW* 118 (2006): 549–57.

is taken totally off guard by this plot and is for the moment blindsided by what his own relatives and neighbors back home are preparing for him. He is aware of some things, but he does not grasp the significance of these pieces of information until Yahweh reveals to him what they want to do.

11:19-21 So unsuspecting is Jeremiah ("I did not realize") that he is like a "gentle lamb" being set up for slaughter (v. 19), much as our Lord was "like a sheep before his shearers" in Isa 53:7. However, in our Lord's case the issue was nonresistance, but in Jeremiah's case the issue is one of being blindsided. But these conspirators are out to get Jeremiah's life (v. 21). They want to destroy the "tree" and its "fruit" (v. 19).

Who are these enemies of Jeremiah? They are men from his own home-town of Anathoth (v. 21; cf. 1:1), that is, fellow priests and relatives. But why are they so upset, even to the point of wanting to take his life? It is mainly because they do not like what he is saying and attributing to Yahweh: "Do not prophesy in the name of Yahweh, or you will die by our hands" (v. 21). Their motto, unlike the state of New Hampshire ("Live free or die"), was: "Live in silence or die!" A really tough congregation!

What a lesson in faithfulness for the minister of God; whether that congregation knows it or not, they stand or fall in accord with how faithfully the word has been preached and how well they have responded to that word. The men of Anathoth do not care to hear God's voice even though they themselves are a town of priests! But Jeremiah has been making unpopular comments about those who carried the word of God. For example, in Jer 5:31, he says: "The prophets prophesy lies, the priests rule by their own authority, and my people love it this way." In 6:13 he condemns the priests as a group by saying they are all greedy for gain and they, along with the false prophets, practice deceit. Such preaching will not endear oneself to a belligerent group of people such as the Judahites are at this time.

11:22-23 Yahweh's response comes in vv. 21-23. These Anathothian conspirators who tried to silence the preaching of Jeremiah, much as the priest Amaziah attempted to do at the city of Bethel, also tried to silence the prophet Amos (Amos 7:12-13), but divine judgment awaits them (v. 22). So thorough will the punishment be against the men of that city that it will affect their sons and daughters so that "not even a remnant would be left" (v. 23). Ezra 2:23 informs us that 128 men from the town of Anathoth returned at the end of the Babylonian exile, so there was mercy for some in that town. Jeremiah, however, has to endure hostility for all the days of his ministry, starting with those from his own family and neighbors back home.

The Second Confession (12:1–6)

Jeremiah 12:1–6 is usually linked with 11:18–23 and treated as one confession, though others separate it and make it a second confession. Whether it is two confessions or one, in this passage Jeremiah raises the traditional problem of theodicy, that is, the presence and persistence of evil. It could be that Jeremiah is still thinking about his own family and friends who have opposed him so stiffly and steadfastly. Nevertheless, the prophet begins his questioning with a declaration of his confidence in the integrity and faithfulness of Yahweh. On every occasion when he has brought a case in the past, God has given a sentence that was right.

12:1-2 Nevertheless, Jeremiah wants to have a word with Yahweh. So he asks: "Why does the way of the wicked prosper? Why do all the faithless live at ease?" (12:1d, e). If Yahweh is in total control, as he is, and everything the wicked do is within that sphere of control, as it also is, then God must be to blame for evil, otherwise he would do something about it! In fact, is it not true that Yahweh has "planted them" (v. 2a)? Did they not take root under his auspices (v. 2b)? So there is no reason to question God's sovereignty; but what about his sense of goodness? How can a good God allow wicked people to prosper, even if it is only for a little while? The effect is just the opposite of Ps 1, where it is the righteous man who is "like a tree planted by the streams of water, which yields its fruit in season." But in Ps 1 the wicked are like "chaff that the wind blows away." And has not the psalm writer Asaph raised the same objection in Ps 73:1–5, 12? The wicked have "no struggles ... they were free from burdens common to man; they were not plagued by human ills." But in Asaph's case it was not until he went into the house of God and considered the end of the wicked that he began to understand. And Jeremiah has heard that God will destroy the men of Anathoth, but perhaps he too feels that calamity should come sooner. Jeremiah wants relief right away!

12:3 "Drag them off" to be butchered like sheep (v. 3c–d), the prophet urges. Some object to the prophet's harsh sentiments and think such statements should not be in the sacred text. However, the martyr's prayer in Rev 6:10 presents a similar request: "How long, Sovereign Lord, holy and true, until you judge the inhabitants of the earth and avenge our blood?"

12:4 Even the land itself seems to join in the questioning of the goodness of God in v. 4, for it is drying up and is polluted because of Israel's infidelities. What is worse still is that the conspirators think that they can get away with killing Jeremiah, for God "will not see our ways." What a brazen attitude on the part of the impudent wicked: they think God covers his face and never sees all the wrong that goes on in the world. But God says just the reverse in Deut 32:20.

12:5–6 God's response to Jeremiah comes in vv. 5–6. What is the answer to why bad things happen to good people? Is it true that the wheels of divine justice sometimes seem to turn too slowly? Even though God does not always explain his workings in providence, in this case it seems he feels his prophet needs some cheering up, so he gives an explanation.

The answer of God comes in the form of two questions: Question 1—If what is relatively easy is too much for you, what are you going to do when things really get tough, as apparently they will in the future? Question 2— If you tripped in the land in which the landscape was safe and relatively easygoing, what are you going to do when the territory gets anything but safe and is jungle-like? So the point is, Jeremiah, stop your bellyaching; you haven't seen anything yet! The men on foot may be a metaphor for his relatives in Anathoth and the horses a similar metaphor for the priests in Jerusalem. But God's answer is not philosophical or apologetical, but pastoral and practical. In fact, the prophet is acting here like the hypothetical questioner about predestination who deserves a similar retort as that found in Rom 9:20: "Who are you, O man, to talk back to God?" He also shows a similarity to Job, whom God had to stop in his tracks with this question in Job 38:2–3, "Who is this who darkens my counsel with words without knowledge? Brace yourself like a man; I will question you, and you answer me."

God's word to those who have been harassed by those to whom they hoped they were ministering is this: do not let the little things prevent you from fulfilling your calling. The word of God is still more important than the trouble these little minds can bring your way. It is Yahweh who gives strength and power to the weak. That is why they soar like eagles, run and do not grow weary, walk and do not faint (Isa 40:28–31).

God Will Not Forsake His House (12:7–13)

12:7 Yahweh's challenge is for Jeremiah to view his own problems in light of those Yahweh himself is facing. The first three lines in v. 7 describe Yahweh's situation. These verbs are Heb. pf. verbs, which commonly refer to incidents in the past. However, here they function as prophetic pfs., in which the future actions are so certain that they are viewed as already complete.

Yahweh utters almost as if in exhaustion, "I will forsake my house," where "house" may refer either to the temple or the "people." But the three-fold build-up here begins probably with the temple, which was abandoned as "Yahweh's glory" left in 592 BC (Ezek 10:3, 18, 23). What follows in the second expression is "I will abandon my inheritance," where his "inheritance" is his people (as it is in 10:16, or the land in 2:7).[183] The third expression, "I will give the one I love into the hands of her enemies," is a prediction of delivering the people into the power of a conqueror.

12:8 In fact, the people have so changed in their behavior against Yahweh that they act more like a "lion" in its untamed ferocity against him (v. 8). Such persistent rebellion against God has caused him to "hate her [Judah]" (v. 8b). Gone is that closeness and love for Israel expressed so frequently in other contexts!

12:9 From the metaphor of a lion to a new metaphor of a "speckled bird of prey" (v. 9), God views the nation of Judah as a carrion eater, a wild bird

---

183. On the unusual comparison between a lion and an inheritance see K. Seybold, "Der Löwe von Jeremia XII 8: Bemerkungen zu einem prophetischen Gedicht," *VT* 36, no. 1 (1986): 93–104.

with a propensity to devour whatever it can.[184] Since the alienation is complete, Yahweh issues a call, to whomever, "to go and gather all the wild beats [and] bring them to devour" (v. 9b) the nation of Judah.

12:10–11 As Jeremiah continues with the Heb. pf. verb form in v. 10, the action is slated for the future. The "shepherds" may either be Judah's incapable leaders or the leaders of the nations invading them. These leaders not only will "trample down my field," declares Yahweh, but they "will turn my pleasant field into a desolate wasteland" (v. 10b). Since the land no longer enjoys the protection of Yahweh, it is now open game for destruction to the point where it will look more like a "desolate wasteland." There are six words in vv. 10–11 that use a s/sh sound (שְׁמָמָה, šĕmāmâ; שָׁמָה, śāmāh; לִשְׁמָמָה, (li)šmāmâ; שְׁמֵמָה, šĕmēmâ; נָשַׁמָּה, nāšammâ; שָׁם, śām), all of which emphasize the parched, desert-like aftermath of the invasions on the land (Mackay, 427). This happens in part because "there is no one who cares" (v. 11c).

12:12 The pf. form of the verbs continues in v. 12 for what is to take place in the future as the enemy sweeps in over the military outposts ("barren heights") as they act as the hand of judgment from Yahweh. "No one is safe" (v. 12c) when God moves in judgment against the wicked.

12:13 All agricultural efforts are wasted, as, for example, what will happen to the wheat crop. It will be planted, but the chief grain crop of Israel will either be looted by the invaders or destroyed by the same group. Despite how hard the people of Judah work, they will just wear themselves out (v. 13b); it will all be useless. With these types of outcomes from farming, the prophet urges them "to bear the shame of [their] harvest" (v. 13c). This was happening because of Yahweh's fierce anger against them. The two Pentateuchal texts of Lev 26 and Deut 28 warn of a whole series of consequences from Yahweh as a result of disobedience, but none of those statements goes as

---

184. Some scholars suggest that a better translation of the verse is, "Is my inheritance to me a hyena's cave? Are the birds of prey against it round about?" See John A. Emerton, "Notes on Jeremiah 12:9 and on Some Suggestions of J. D. Michaelis about the Hebrew Words *naḥā, æbrā, and jadă*," ZAW 79, no. 2 (1967): 225–28.

far as this text to say Yahweh will "abandon" them. However, despite such dire consequences, there always is a brighter future day for Israel, for God's promise is secure even if that generation does not participate in it.

The Promise of Paradise Regained (12:14–17)

After such a hard section, we are not prepared for what comes next. But Jeremiah often does this: he will shift suddenly from a slow four-wheel drive into the speedy overdrive of a racecar. One moment he is all judgment, and the next he is all rosy-tinted predictions of what God is going to do in the distant future.

12:14–17 Jeremiah again returns to the metaphors of "uprooting" (v. 14a, b) and "establishing/building" (v. 16). God's prophet gives four prophecies of a paradise that is regained and restored. They are:

1. The "wicked neighbors" of Israel will be uprooted from their lands (v. 14a).

2. The house of Judah will be rescued from exile (v. 14b).

3. God will show compassion on the wicked nations and bring them back to their own countries (v. 15).

4. Depending on their individual response, each nation will either be saved or destroyed (vv. 16–17).

God will punish those nations that "seized" his inheritance, for they too will be uprooted from their lands. Just as northern Israel, and now Judah, are subjects for deportation and loss of their lands, so the other nations will face the same prospect. In like manner, Judah will be subject to the same "uprooting" process, but Yahweh will nevertheless take compassion on them and bring them back to their land (v. 15). But this surprise is matched by an even greater one: God will bring back the wicked neighbors of Israel if they too learn the ways of the Lord and swear by his name alone and not by the names of gods such as Baal; then they too could be "my people" (vv. 16–17). But those nations that remained truculent will be completely destroyed and uprooted forever.

God's judgment will not be limited to the house of Judah (v. 7); he will judge the unrighteousness of the neighboring nations as well (vv. 14–17). The leaders of Judah wreck the vineyard of the Lord, but that is not how things will end. God will once again have compassion on them after he uproots both Judah and those nations. He will bring them back to their lands and then teach them the ways of the Lord. Those who fail to listen will be uprooted once more and destroyed. What a warning to all the nations on earth! God will act in judgment if we do not respond.

REJECTION OF THE PEOPLE OF THE COVENANT (13:1–27)

TRANSLATION

1 This is what Yahweh said to me: "Go and buy yourself a linen waistcloth and put it around your waist, but do not let it touch water."[185] **2** So I bought the waistcloth as Yahweh had directed and put it around my waist. **3** Then the word of Yahweh came to me a second time:[186] **4** "Take the waistcloth you bought and which you have on, and go to the Perath[187] and hide it there in the cleft of the rock." **5** So I went and hid it at Perath as Yahweh told me. **6** Then, many days later Yahweh said to me, "Go now to Perath and get the waistcloth I commanded you to hide there." **7** So I went to Perath and I dug up the waistcloth from the place where I had hidden it, but now it was ruined and completely useless.

8 Then the word of Yahweh came to me: **9** "This is what Yahweh says: In the same way I will ruin the pride of Judah and the great pride of Jerusalem. **10** These wicked people are refusing to listen to my words, and who, following their stubborn hearts,[188] have gone after other gods to serve and to worship them—becoming like this waistcloth—completely useless. **11** For just as the waistcloth clings around the waist of a man, so I have made the whole house of Israel and the whole house of Judah cling to me, declares Yahweh—that they might be my people, my renown, praise, and glory— and yet they have not listened."

---

185. Lit. "Do not cause it to go into the water."
186. The word שֵׁנִית, "a second time," is omitted in the LXX.
187. Possibly a reference to the Euphrates. See discussion below.
188. The LXX omits the phrase הַהֹלְכִים בִּשְׁרִרוּת לִבָּם, "who stubbornly follow their own heart."

12 Say to them this word, "This is what Yahweh the God of Israel says: 'Every wine jar should be filled with wine.' They will reply, 'Don't we know that every wine jar will be filled with wine?' **13** Tell them, 'Here is what Yahweh says, "I am going to fill all the inhabitants of this land—the kings who sit on David's throne, the priests, the prophets, and all the citizens of Jerusalem[189]—with drunkenness. **14** I will smash them one against the other, fathers and sons alike, declares Yahweh. I will allow no pity, no mercy, nor compassion to deter me from destroying them."'

> **15** Hear and pay attention! Do not be arrogant—
>> Because Yahweh has spoken.
> **16** Give glory to Yahweh your God
>> Before he brings darkness,[190]
> And before your feet stumble,
>> On the darkening mountains.
> You hope for light,[191]
>> But he will turn it into impenetrable gloom,
>> Changing it into thick darkness.
> **17** But if you will not listen,
>> In secret my soul will weep
>> Because of your pride;[192]
> My eyes will weep profusely,
>> Overflowing with tears,
>> Because the flock of Yahweh will be taken captive.
> **18** Tell the king and the queen mother:
> "Come down from your thrones;
>> Because your glorious crowns,
>> Will fall from your heads."

---

189. The LXX adds καὶ τὸν Ιουδαν, "and Judah," after "of Jerusalem."

190. Michel suggests that "shadow of death" is a better solution than "darkness." See W. L. Michel, "Ṣlmwt, 'Deep Darkness' or 'Shadow of Death'?," *Biblical Research* 29 (1984): 5-20. Stone suggests that in Heb. poetry death can refer to darkness, and darkness can refer to death. See A. Stone, "Does 'Shadow of Death' Mean 'Deep Darkness'?," *BR* 51 (2006): 53-57.

191. The LXX adds καὶ ἐκεῖ σκιὰ θανάτου, "and behold the shadow of death," before "You hope for light."

192. The *BHS* editors suggest emending this to גֹּלָה, "your captivity," instead of גַּוָה, "your pride." The Syr. has "your distress."

19 The Negev towns are closed off,
    There will be no one to open them.
All of Judah will be totally deported[193]—
    Deported entirely.
20 Lift up your eyes,
    And see those coming from the north.
Where is the flock that was given to you,
    Your beautiful flock?
21 What will you say,
    When he [Yahweh] appoints over you,
Those whom you taught,
    As your special allies?
Will not labor pains seize you,
    Like that of a woman giving birth?
22 And if you ask yourself,
    "Why have these things happened to me?"
It is because of your many sins
    That your skirts have been uncovered
    And your heels have suffered violence.
23 Can an Ethiopian change his skin,
    Or a leopard his spots?
Then you might also learn to do good,
    Who are accustomed to doing evil.
24 I will scatter you like the chaff,
    Driven by the desert wind.
25 This is your lot, your measured share,[194]
    From me—declares Yahweh,
Because you have forgotten me
    And trusted the lie.
26 I, even I, will put up your skirts,
    Over your face,
    That your shame might be seen.

---

193. Or "exiled."

194. The LXX has τοῦ ἀπειθεῖν ὑμᾶς, "your rebellion," in place of the MT's "your measured share."

27 Your adulteries and your lustful neighings,
And your shameless fornication,
I have seen your indecencies[195]
Upon the heights and in the fields.
Woe to you, O Jerusalem!
How much longer can this go on?

COMMENTARY

The Linen Waistcloth (13:1–11)

Whereas this nation, Judah, should have the closest spiritual relationship to Yahweh, she is depicted in this chapter as having one of the most corrupt relationships. In a desperate move to communicate the word of God, Jeremiah is instructed to employ one of his many symbolic actions to attract the attention and response of the nation of Judah. These symbols point beyond themselves and thus make the message of the prophet more vivid.

The linen waistcloth was the first of several symbolic actions used by Jeremiah to make his message more vivid and memorable in 13:1–11. The following texts are those that have traditionally been part of this classification:

- 13:1–11—The linen waistcloth

- 13:12–14—The smashing of the wine jars

- 16:1–9—The prohibiting of the prophet to marry and have children

- 18:1–11—The potter's house

- 19:1–15—The smashing of the clay jar

- 25:15–29—Forcing the nations to drink wine from the cup

- 25:27–28—Nations are to drink wine and get drunk

- 32:1–15—Buy a field in the prophet's hometown of Anathoth

---

195. Lit. "detestable thing/abomination."

- 43:8–13—Bury the large stones in pharaoh's pavement

- 51:59–64—Write all the disasters coming to Babylon and then throw it in the Euphrates River

These actions are called symbolic because they were meant to point beyond themselves to the reality they depicted in figurative form. Even though they graphically enhanced the word spoken by the prophet, it did not seem that the people responded any better to the symbolization of the coming judgment. Few could see what Jeremiah was calling them to see. It may be that these symbols had a type of delayed action inherent in them as the people in exile suddenly awakened retrospectively to the fact that what had taken place was much like the picture they had been given well in advance of these events. However, these actions were not to be understood as something that was magical or that the symbolic action directly or even indirectly caused the event to take place in some mysterious, magical, or psychic way. None of the acts influenced the future but were merely to enhance and dramatize the spoken word of the prophet for the listeners.

13:1–3 In this symbolic action of the linen waistcloth, the prophet is given a series of commands (vv. 3–4, 6). Because Jeremiah carries out each, the next command is given in the series. He is told first to buy a linen waistcloth. This is part of a male undergarment that usually was made either of linen or leather. It extended from the waist to the thighs and ordinarily was loosened at night for sleeping but sometimes was changed for use in the day. The poor owned but a few such garments, while the wealthy possessed a more extensive wardrobe.

In this case, the loincloth functions as a metaphor for the people of God. As such, Jeremiah is to buy this new change of linen underwear (loincloth) and put it on himself, but he is not to dip it in water (apparently assuring its newness). Linen, of course, was valuable, as it was used for special situations such when burial shrouds were called for.

13:4–5 Then Jeremiah is told to go to a river called Perah, the ordinary Heb. name for the Euphrates River. This would have included approximately some seven hundred miles round trip (taking about three to four months to complete the trip) on foot or by donkey. Therefore, many identify Perah with a town called Parah in the eastern part of Benjamin's territory, with the modern name Tell Fara, about six miles (ten kilometers) north of Jerusalem and three miles (five kilometers) northeast of Anathoth, where a spring still contributes to the water supply of Jerusalem. If this latter identity is correct, then this site may have been chosen because of the similarity of the name of that place to the Heb. name for the Euphrates. The River Euphrates would carry a further significance, for the people will be ruined in the very place where Jeremiah was to hide the loincloth. Accordingly, the prophet is instructed to put the linen loincloth in a "crevice in the rocks." The word "crevice" (נְקִיק) is used elsewhere only in Isa 7:19 and Jer 16:16 as a place where people seek refuge and safety. This could also be part of the imagery intended here as well, where a place of perceived safety provides no safety.

13:6–9 After an unspecified amount of time, Jeremiah is told to go back and retrieve the linen waistcloth. So he goes and digs it up (vv. 6–7) and finds that it is now ruined and completely useless. The meaning is clear: this is an allegory of the coming exile for Judah. Despite their former closeness to Yahweh, as close as the linen waistcloth is around its wearer's thighs, that relationship was now ruined. They are dirty and polluted, just as the loincloth is. God will ruin the pride of Judah (vv. 8–9).

13:10–11 More than their buildings, temple, palace, and homes are ruined; their pride will also be ruined. They have adamantly refused to listen to God's word and insisted on following the stubbornness of their own hearts (v. 10). Moreover, their seeking after other gods was as beneficial as this loincloth now is—both are useless. Previously God had bound the whole house of Israel and the whole house of Judah around his waist, but the people have not reciprocated that same desire for closeness to him (v. 11). So the loincloth has a double symbolism: it is a picture of the coming exile; it also is a picture of the way God will use the exile to remove their arrogance and pride.

But this word of judgment is not Yahweh's final word, for he still recalls that he had originally entered into an irrevocable covenant with them. As such, these people will receive an honorable name and renown because of their relationship to Yahweh. Despite the fact that the loincloth will be ruined, Yahweh's original purpose would not be abrogated. How faithful is Yahweh!

The Smashed Wine Jars (13:12–14)

13:12–13 A second symbolic action is used by the prophet to grab the attention and hopefully the positive response of the people of Judah. The brief prose speech appeals to a metaphor that is drawn, no doubt, from their everyday speech: "Every wine jar should [or: is meant to be] filled with wine" [not with other stuff] (v. 12). The meaning then is that the people are meant to be like these full wine jars:[196] filled with the blessings that come from a faithful relationship to Yahweh. However, instead of being filled with blessings, they are now filled with drunkenness, which in this case is the wrath of God (cf. 25:15–16, 27).

This symbolic action is related to the people (v. 12). At first the people feel what the prophet is telling them is a truism, for they interpret the image literally, without perceiving its deeper meaning as it relates to them. However, Yahweh will fill these jars not with wine of blessings, as one would ordinarily expect, but with the wine of drunkenness; they will receive the effects of their own sinful actions. In this case, Yahweh has not introduced something new into their lives, but judgment and drunkenness are the natural results of the way the people were going. Terence Fretheim (206) points out there is also a possible wordplay here as well, for the Heb. word for "jar" (נֶבֶל, *nebēl*) plays off the Heb. word for "fool" (נָבָל, *nābāl*). Accordingly, these foolish people are about to drink the wrath of God's wine.

13:14 The picture is one of crass confusion among all the people, lack of control and little or no coordination. The "kings" are no doubt those who came after King Josiah. In their drunken state they careened one into another, a man against his brother, and a father against his son. Society has lost its cohesiveness and direction. As a result, the curse of a broken covenant was falling upon the people (v. 14). The entire population in Judah was included,

---

196. There is some debate as to whether the translation should be "wine jar" or "wineskin," as the NIV has it. The Heb. word *nebēl* indicates an animal skin used to hold liquid, but since the verb "smash" is used with it (v. 14), it is probably a wine jar and not a wineskin. That is how it is also used in Jer 48:12; Isa 22:24; 30:14; and Lam 4:2.

for kings, priests, prophets, and all those living in Jerusalem were under this indictment (v. 13). Consequently, Yahweh had a threefold judgment: they will receive "no pity," no "mercy," and no "compassion" (v. 14b). God will not hold back or spare his judgment, he will not look with love on them, nor will he allow his emotion that comes from a deep bond to the people to affect the way he handles them: he will destroy them (v. 14c).

A Third Warning before the Exile (13:15-17)

13:15 Now for the third time, God warns the people not to be haughty or prideful, or literally "to be high" (גָּבַהּ, v. 15). This warning comes to those who think themselves to be so "high up" in their own eyes that they do not need to heed any divine warnings. In Greek thought this is called *hubris*, the sin of pride. The reason these same people must obey is that it is Yahweh who has spoken (v. 15c).

13:16 Instead of having proud, haughty ways, the prophet urges them to "Give glory to Yahweh [their] God" (v. 16), not in order to stop the judgment coming but to give them strength and hope for those difficult days they will be called on to endure. What is coming is likened to "darkness," perhaps what sometimes overtakes travelers running late before they reach their destination (v. 16b). "Darkness" is also used metaphorically of a time of deep suffering (Job 3:1-6; Ps 44:19), which is the image here.

A Royal Humiliation as a Fourth Warning (13:18-19)

13:18 The fourth warning comes to the king and his queen mother (גְּבִירָה), who are widely assumed to be King Jehoiachin and his mother, Nehusta, daughter of Elnathan, from Jerusalem (2 Kgs 24:8).[197] This eighteen-year-old son of King Josiah ruled for a mere three months (597 BC), then he was carted off to Babylon by Nebuchadnezzar. Because 2 Kgs 22:24-27 gives so much attention to Jehoiachin and his mother, they are the best candidates for the proud, unnamed king and his mother. Both are called on to cast themselves down and to humble themselves (שָׁפֵל, "to be/become low, be

---

197. Bowen suggests that a better translation of the word גְּבִירָה is "great lady" or "principal lady," since it could refer to the king's wife or grandmother, not just as his mother, as some translations suggest. See N. R. Bowen, "The Quest for the Historical Gĕbîrâ," *CBQ* 63, no. 4 (2001): 597–618.

leveled, be humiliated"), for very shortly they will lose their royal perks and status. Their royal crowns will fall from their heads (v. 18). If this refers to the golden diadem worn in front of the king's turban, then it is applied by extension to the queen mother, because she is connected to her royal son.

13:19 The villages in the Negev, the southern part of Judah, have already been taken, so some of the last lines of defense for Jerusalem are systematically being removed from the picture, and Jerusalem is set to be irretrievably captured in the very near future (v. 19). However, when it says that "all Judah will be carried into exile" (v. 19c–d), the language is a conscious exaggeration (hyperbole) to impress the seriousness of the conquest on all Judah; neither in 597 nor in 586 BC were all in Judah taken into captivity. The statement is more for effect than it is for exact demographic purposes.

The Fifth Warning (13:20–27)

13:20-21 The mother city of Jerusalem is addressed in this section. While the language shows that judgment is announced, it has the form at times of a lament. At the heart of this fifth warning is the question from the people: "Why have these things happened to me?" (v. 22). This "Why?" is the signal that we are in a lament form. Once again, the warning is sounded that the foe will come out of the north (v. 20b). Yahweh wants to know, "Where are the leaders of Jerusalem whom he has set over the flock of his people?" (v. 20c–d). Is no one in charge and able to help the flock?

13:22-23 God himself answers the question, however, and in this instance he will use sexual language (v. 22, cf. 5:19; 9:12–16). The women will be victimized in a time of war. The foe from the north will violate and humiliate their wives. Yahweh frames his answer in terms of a proverb that becomes here a rhetorical question: "Can an Ethiopian change his skin?" And if they still do not get the point, God asks another rhetorical question: "Or [can] a leopard change its spots?" (v. 23). The answer to both questions, of course, is "No!" And neither can Judah at this time and at this place change, given her hard-heartedness. The text is not saying that human sinfulness is inevitable! Neither is it saying that repentance is futile! Nor is it saying that human beings are just not capable of doing any good. But given the present circumstances, one could think that the above statements surely apply to this situation. Instead, it is that the nation itself has come to a point at which it cannot not separate itself from sin! Sin has bound them all as if by cords.

13:24–25 God moves to an agricultural metaphor in v. 24, threatening to "scatter" them "like chaff." Chaff references the husks that are left from the winnowed grain. Thus the nation of Judah will be blown about like these husks in a desert wind, which comes from the east (v. 24b). This will be the "portion" of Judah that Yahweh has "decreed" for them because they have "forgotten [him]" and "trusted false gods" (v. 25c-d).

13:26–27 The final two verses (vv. 26–27) return to the sexual language. Jerusalem will be treated like a harlot or a prostitute. The people's "adulteries," their "lustful neighings," and their "shameful fornications" (v. 27a), which were part of the Baal **cult** and associated with ritual sexual behavior, have been observed by Yahweh all over on Judah's hills and fields. The whole matter is so disgusting. It raises the question: "How much longer can this go on?" or, alternatively, "How long will [this nation] be unclean?" (v. 27d). Will the answer be the seventy years of exile? Time will tell!

Through these symbolic actions Yahweh, through Jeremiah, describes the seriousness of how Judah has broken the terms of the covenant she made with God. In fact, their actions are like a conspiracy against Yahweh and his word. Throughout the Israelites' rebellion, Yahweh was always in the right. But there is still the question of why on earth he allowed what had happened to Jeremiah go on so long. A partial answer is that Yahweh is patient and merciful. He continually gives people a chance to repent. He even calls for Judah's king and queen to humble themselves before God. Such repentance would draw favor from Yahweh and also serve as a model to the people and is their only chance left for a reversal of God's threatened judgment.

DOOM AND LAMENT (14:1–17:27)

This section is dominated by laments: some from the people, some from the prophet, and some from God. The point in these verses is that nothing can now stop the destruction of the nation Jeremiah has tried to get to repent. The whole country, false prophets, priests, officials, and the king himself are without any sign of repentance; they are hardened beyond any sign of changing. Therefore, the judgment of God must ensue.

DROUGHT AND DISASTER (14:1–15:9)

TRANSLATION

1 What Jeremiah received as the word of Yahweh concerning the drought:
  2 Judah mourns,
    Her gates languish;
  They wail for the land,
    And an outcry goes up for Jerusalem.
  3 Their nobles send their menials for water;
    They came to the cisterns,
    But found no water.
  They return with their jars empty,
    Dismayed and bewildered,
    They cover their heads.[198]
  4 The ground is cracked
    Because there is no rain in the land;
  The farmers are ashamed
    And cover their heads.
  5 Even the doe in the field
    Abandons the fawn she bears,
    Because there is no grass.
  6 Wild donkeys stand in the open spaces,
    Panting for air like jackals;[199]
  Their eyes fail,
    Because there is no pasture.
  7 Although our iniquities testify against us,
    Yahweh, do something for the sake of your name,
  For our backslidings are numerous,
    Against you have we sinned.

---

198. The LXX is missing the last part of the verse, בֹּשׁוּ וְהָכְלְמוּ וְחָפוּ רֹאשָׁם, "dismayed and bewildered, they cover their heads."

199. The expression כַּתַּנִּים, "like jackals," is missing in the LXX.

8 O hope of Israel,[200] its savior in time of trouble,
    Why are you like an alien[201] in the land,
    Like a traveler who stays only a night?
9 Why are you like a man taken by surprise,
    Like a soldier who cannot save?
Yet you, O Yahweh, are among us,
    We are called by your name;
    Do not leave us!
10 This is what Yahweh said about his people:
They greatly love to wander,
    They do not restrain their feet.
So Yahweh does not take pleasure in them,
    He will remember their iniquities,
    And punish their sins.[202]

11 Yahweh said to me, "Do not pray for the welfare of this people. **12** Though they fast, I will not hear their cry, and though they offer burnt offerings and grain offerings, I will not accept them. Instead, with sword, famine, and plague I will destroy them." **13** Then I said, "O Adonai Yahweh, the prophets keep telling them, 'You will not see the sword, or experience famine, for I will give you true peace[203] in this place.'"

14 Yahweh said to me, "The prophets are prophesying lies in my name. I have not sent them, nor did I command them or speak to them. They are prophesying false visions, divinations, idolatries, and delusions of their own minds." **15** Therefore, this is what Yahweh says about the prophets[204] who are prophesying in my name: "I did not send them, yet they are saying, 'Sword and famine will not come on this land'; these prophets will perish by sword and famine. **16** And the people to whom they have been prophesying will be hurled into the streets of Jerusalem because of the sword

---

200. Some mss and the LXX add κύριε, "Lord," before "of Israel."

201. The LXX has ὡς αὐτόχθων, "like a native," in place of the MT's וּכְאֹרֵחַ, "like an alien."

202. The LXX omits the last phrase, וַיִּפְקֹד חַטֹּאתָם, "and punish their sins."

203. The LXX, the Syr., and a few Heb. mss have ἀλήθειαν καὶ εἰρήνην, "peace and truth," in place of שְׁלוֹם אֱמֶת, "true peace."

204. The LXX adds ψευδῆ, "false," to modify "prophets."

and famine. There will be no one to bury them, or their wives, their sons, or their daughters. I will pour out upon them their wickedness."

17 You shall speak to them this word:
"Let my eyes with tears run down night and day,
　　And let them not cease,
For the virgin daughter of my people,
　　Has suffered a great wound,
　　A crushing blow."
18 If I go into the field,
　　Behold, those slain by the sword!
And if I enter the city,
　　Behold, the diseases of the famine!
For both prophet and priest
　　Wander through the land they do not know.
19 Have you totally rejected Judah?
　　Does your soul loathe Zion?
Why have you smitten us,
　　So there is no healing for us?
We hoped for peace, but no good came;
　　For a time of healing, but there is only terror.
20 We acknowledge our wickedness, O Yahweh,
　　The guilt of our fathers;
　　For we have sinned against you.
21 Do not spurn[205] us for your name's sake;
　　Do not dishonor your glorious throne;
Remember your covenant with us,
　　And do not break it.
22 Are there any among the false idols of the nations that can
　　bring rain?
　　Or can the heavens give showers?
Are you not he, O Yahweh our God?[206]
　　Therefore, our hope is in you,
　　for you have done all these things.

---

205. The LXX has the impv. κόπασον, "refrain," for the MT's juss. אַל־תִּנְאַץ, "do not spurn."
206. The LXX omits the expression יְהוָה אֱלֹהֵינוּ, "O Yahweh, our God."

15:1 Then Yahweh said to me:

"Though Moses and Samuel[207] stood before me, yet my heart would not turn towards this people. Send them out of my sight, and let them go!"

2 "And if they ask you, 'Where shall we go? You shall say to them, "Thus says Yahweh, 'Those for pestilence, to pestilence; and those for the sword, to the sword; those for famine, to famine; those for captivity, to captivity.'"'" **3** I will appoint four types of destroyers against them," declares Yahweh, "the sword to kill, the dogs to drag away, and the birds of the air and the beasts of the earth to devour and destroy. **4** And I will make them abhorrent to all the kingdoms of the earth because of what Manasseh, the son of Hezekiah, king of Judah, did in Jerusalem."

> **5** Who will have pity on you, O Jerusalem?
>> Or who will mourn for you?
>> Who will turn aside to ask[208] how you are?
> **6** It is you who rejected me, says Yahweh.
>> You keep on going backwards.
> So I have stretched out my hand against you and destroyed you—
>> I am tired of showing compassion.
> **7** I will winnow them with a winnowing fork,
>> In the city gates of their land.
> I will bring bereavement of children[209] and I will destroy my people,
>> For they have not changed their ways.[210]
> **8** I will make their widows more numerous
>> Than the sand of the sea.
> I will bring a destroyer at midday,
>> Against the mother of their young men.
> Suddenly I will bring down on them
>> Anguish and terror.

---

207. The LXX[A] and the Arabic version have "Aaron" in place of "Samuel."

208. The verb לִשְׁאֹל, "to ask/inquire," is absent in the LXX.

209. Piel of שָׁכֹל, referring specifically to the loss of an unborn child.

210. Where the MT has מִדַּרְכֵיהֶם לוֹא־שָׁבוּ, "they have not changed their ways," the LXX has διὰ τὰς κακίας αὐτῶν, "because of their iniquities."

9 She who bore seven has languished;
　　And breathed her last.
　He who bore seven has languished;
　　And breathed her last.
Her sun went down, while it was yet day;
　　She had been shamed and disgraced.
And the remnant of them I will give to the sword,
　　Before their enemies, declares Yahweh.

COMMENTARY

The Drought and Its Effects (14:1–6)

14:1 This section begins with an unusual formula ("what came as the word of Yahweh")—a formula repeated in Jer 46:1; 47:1; 49:34; and possibly in 1:2. That word that comes concerns a drought that is followed by a famine.

In Deut 28:23–24, God warned such disasters would be part of the covenant curses if the people walked in disobedience. Though such droughts were not infrequent in the land of Israel (cf. Ruth 1:1; 1 Kgs 17:1; 2 Kgs 8:1; Hag 1:10–11), they were rarely, if ever, looked on as a chance occurrence. Instead, these events were evidences of the hand of God and therefore regarded as a rebuke on sins. This drought indeed is severe, as Walter Brueggemann (136) describes it: "no water" (14:3), "no rain" (v. 4), "no grass" (v. 5), and "no herbage" (v. 6).

14:2 The description of this drought begins in v. 2 with a general statement of the extent of the drought, which is then explained in four pictures in vv. 2–6. The total effect is to show how intense the suffering was on the people and the land. In fact, the word for "languish/ mourn" (אָמַל) in v. 2 may be a deliberate play on a homonym for "be dried up." So both Judah and her cities are feeling the effects of this lack of water. There is physical exhaustion as well as emotional sapping of the people's strength.

The word "gates" is a **synecdoche**, where a part of the city (the gates) is put for the whole city as well as implying the activity that normally would be going on at those gates and in the city itself. But now, by way of personification, the "gates" function for the "cities" as a "wail" that has gone up because of the barren land. This cry "goes up," apparently as a reference to a prayer going up to God.

14:3 Even the upper class of people, who are normally able to get by during hard times, are affected by this drought (v. 3). So the civic dignitaries also feel the effects of this emergency, for when they go to the "cisterns," they too find no water. The unusual word for "cisterns" (גֵּבִים), rather than the usual word (בּוֹר), signifies something dug, so it could mean some are hastily digging holes, perhaps even in the dry river beds, hoping that they will fill with underground water. The point is that all means possible are being used to obtain any water they could find. But the results are discouraging, and the whole scene is just plain embarrassing. To show their distress, they cover their heads as a further gesture of grief (2 Sam 15:30; 19:5).

14:4-6 As a result, the ground cracks open because of the dry conditions. Even the "farmers" (v. 4) cover their heads as well. In addition to the effect the drought is having on the land, there is an effect also on the animals (v. 5). For instance, the "doe" is deserting her newborn "fawn" in the open "field" (v. 5), which is a strange place to leave that newborn fawn. Normally a doe would choose a wooded spot, but circumstances have turned everything into the most extreme conditions. Now the fawn will die without its mother. Even the type of animals that were somewhat used to such stringent conditions are pictured as sniffing the wind to see whether they can detect any moisture (v. 6). But these donkeys are likewise worn out and emaciated, coming close to the point of death (v. 6). Their eyes are glazed over as the pastures give out—and so do they.

A Penitential Lament and a Divine Response (14:7-10)

Most do not think that these verses are a real report of what the people actually said. That the prophet is told not to pray for the community (v. 11) may indicate that Jeremiah is the speaker of this penitential prayer, which he here offers vicariously on behalf of the people even though he has previously been told not to pray for this people (7:16). Even though the people have not uttered these words, the prophet knows this is the way of divine providence and healing.

14:7 The prayer, despite our inability to say who it is that offers this prayer, begins in v. 7 with a threefold repetition of a confession of the people's

"iniquities," "backslidings," and "sin." Jeremiah knows better than to petition God on the basis of some good that supposedly is still possibly resident in the people; instead, the petitioner asks on the basis of the powerful
name of God. The name of God stands for all that God is and all that he
has revealed himself to be. The "apostasy" of the people has, nevertheless,
been enormous (v. 7c).

14:8–9 In contrast to their apostasy, God is called the "Hope of Israel" (v. 8),
which is far from our weaker Western use and meaning of the noun *hope*
or our modern Western use of the verb *to hope*. Here, instead, it points to
an enduring expectation that is able to triumph over adverse conditions.
God alone can be called their "Savior in times of distress."

In the stereotypical interrogative of the lament forms in the Bible, the
prophet asks on behalf of Judah, "Why?" (vv. 8c, 9a). If Yahweh has promised to dwell in the midst of them in the famous tripartite formula of the
promise-doctrine (that is, "I will be your God, you shall be my people, and
I will dwell in the midst of you"), why now has God acted more like a resident alien, one who would move back and forth from his homeland and
stay only temporarily in Judah? Why is God more like a "traveler" who
stops off the road now and again but never stays for a permanent residence? Furthermore, why does it seem as if God has been taken by surprise, now acting like a soldier unable to save anyone (v. 9)? Though the
prophet speaks on behalf of the people, he poses questions that have an
edge to them and reflect, no doubt, what the prophet is hearing the people
accuse God of in their dire straits.

Has God forgotten that he is among us and that Judah bears his name
as well (v. 9c–d)? Please, God, do not abandon us now (v. 9e). Judah now
plays the card of her covenant bond to Yahweh, which declares that they
are the people of God, but this seems to come to the hearts and minds
of the people somewhat belatedly and without that note of sincerity or
heart-action that God looked for!

14:10 Yahweh's response to the prophet's (if he is the one who prayed
this request) vicarious prayer on behalf of the people comes in v. 10. He
addresses them not as "*my* people," as usual, but "*this* people," which shows
a division and some distance has now come between God and the people.

Yahweh announces to Jeremiah, "[This people] greatly love to wander [away from me]" (v. 10b). This is another reference to their "backsliding" and "apostasy" (v. 7). Moreover, they just "do not restrain their feet" (v. 10c). This is why Yahweh does not accept them, for he must now punish their sins if he is still to be their holy and just God (v. 10d–f).

Sword, Famine, and Plague, and Lies from the Prophets (14:11–16)

14:11 Once again, Jeremiah is told he is not to pray for the welfare of this people (v. 11, cf. 7:16; 11:14; 15:1). Since Yahweh will not listen to Israel's prayers, he will not listen to Jeremiah's prayers on behalf of the people. Some in Judah tried to force Yahweh to listen to their prayers by fasting or offering up burnt offerings or grain offerings, but meeting such formal ritual criteria will not serve as a substitute for a genuine turning back to God in full repentance and godly sorrow. Fasting was a period of time of abstinence from eating as an act of genuine repentance and sorrow, especially in times of personal or national crisis. It was often accompanied by other acts of humiliation, but in order for it to be of any value in the sight of God, it had to be accompanied by positive virtues (Isa 58:1–7). If there was no true obedience to God (6:20; 7:21–28; 11:25), the whole act was a waste of time.

There were three main types of fasting. A normal fast involves a total abstinence from food, for example, Jesus "ate nothing" in Luke 4:2, though he did not abstain from water. An absolute fast is exemplified in Acts 9:9, where the apostle Paul "did not eat or drink" for three days (cf. Ezra 10:6; Esth 4:16). A partial fast employs a restriction of diet, as in Dan 10:3, for physical benefits.

All religious fasting, which differs from fasting for other reasons (such as for dieting), is a deliberate laying aside of food for a particular period of time when one is seeking to know and follow the Lord in a deeper experience of his word.

14:12 At any rate, the people apparently are ready to go through any amount of rituals in the **cult** as a substitute for a genuine turning back to God in repentance. But such showy external rituals are rejected by God; he will not accept them (v. 12). God will "destroy them with sword, famine, and plague" (v. 12c). Each of these three judgments of God is set forth most distinctively by repeating the prep. "with" (-בְּ) with each judgment in Heb. The "sword" depicts the loss of life in battle; "famine" depicts not a natural drought but what comes about as a result of an enemy invasion as they destroy the crops and set up sieges; "plague" refers to an epidemic that results in multiple deaths. All of this trouble will come on the people for their failure to obey what they had promised in the covenant (Lev 26:25–26).

14:13 Instead of interceding for the people, Jeremiah raises another factor that may have contributed to the sin of Judah: the prophets are lying. These deceiving prophets have been telling them that they will not suffer the sword, famine, or plague (v. 13). With the word, "Ah/O Adonai Yahweh," the prophet introduces his complaint to Yahweh with a note of dismay. Yet, he deliberately uses the title "Adonai Yahweh," used almost exclusively in the Abrahamic and Davidic covenants (Gen 15:2, 8; 2 Sam 7:18, 19, 22, 28, 29). Thus we have dismay coupled with the greatest promise-plan ever given to mortals in the Abrahamic and Davidic covenants.

14:14–16 With the threefold denials of a sword, famine, and plague come a threefold divine evaluation of the prophecies of these charlatans: lying visions, worthless divination, and deception (v. 14). A divine judgment is pronounced on them in v. 15. First of all, these deceivers were not sent by God; they are speaking on their own. Second, they will not be spared any of the forthcoming judgments; they too will perish by the same sword and famine. Moreover, the people these false prophets have bamboozled will be cast into the streets with no one left to bury their corpses, or the corpses of their wives, sons, or daughters. They will get the calamity they have earned (v. 16).

God and People Lament (14:17–22)

14:17–18 Since those addressed are referred to as "virgin daughter" and "my people" (v. 17d), it seems to be that Judah is still considered the people of God. Thus, the divine lament introduced in vv. 17–18 is given to Jeremiah to pass on to the people. It is as if the people are given an insight into the inner life and thinking of God. God not only weeps over what is happening, but he weeps night and day over the crushing blow that Babylon is going to deliver to Judah (v. 17). Moreover, no matter where God looks, whether it be in the countryside or the cityscape, all he sees are those slain by the sword or who have been taken by the famine (v. 18). But one of the reasons for all the ravages of war and famine is that the prophet and the priests have done their own thing without any true knowledge of God or his word (v. 18e–f). They were hucksters who peddled wares that they knew would do only harm and destruction. The Heb. verb for the prophet and the priest "going about in a circuit" (סָחַר) was also used for traders who roamed about selling their wares.

14:19 To respond to God's lament, the people pose their own lament in vv. 19–22 in language similar to Lam 5:20–22. Here the Judahites use good-sounding religious vocabulary, but there is no heart or commitment behind the words. They begin their lament with questions:

1. Has God completely rejected them?

2. Does God find them loathsome?

3. Why has God struck them down so severely, with seemingly no healing available? (v. 19)

14:20–21 The people's lament moves from questioning God to a sort of forced threefold confession:

1. They acknowledge their own sin and the sins of their fathers.

2. They know they have sinned against God.

3. They ask God not to despise them for the very sake of his name (vv. 20–21).

In fact, they give altogether three reasons why Yahweh should act to alleviate their distress and not bring judgment on them:

1. It would involve the good name of God.

2. It would dishonor God's "glorious throne."

3. It would show a failure to remember the covenant God made with them (v. 21), which is the height of chutzpah in light of the fact that they had consistently broken the covenant!

14:22 Three rhetorical questions conclude this section in v. 22; the first two call for a negative answer. Do idols bring rain? Are the skies themselves (with their associated astral deities) the ones who decide to send rain? But then there is a third rhetorical question that calls for a positive answer: Is it not you, O Yahweh, who alone can do these things? Borrowing from the title they had bestowed on Yahweh in v. 8, "Hope of Israel," they return to this affirmation in v. 22d. But was this the "hope" that the false prophets have encouraged, or is it the biblical hope that is authentic to Scripture? They say this hope is in Yahweh, but with all the deceptive teaching, it is difficult to say for sure.

Four Kinds of Destruction from an Unrelenting God (15:1–9)

15:1 Despite the people's lament, God will not listen (14:10–12). Furthermore, even if the prayers of a Moses or Samuel were available for this people (v. 1), God's heart would not go out to this people. Moses' intercessions were known already in Exod 32:11–14, 30–34; Num 14:13–24; Deut 9:18–20, 25–29, as were Samuel's in 1 Sam 7:5–9; 8:1–22; 12:19–25. They had been able to engage God at the level of seeing the future changed or even reversed because of the intercessory prayers of these leaders. But that would not be true in this case, for the people have gone too far for too long. Now it is time to "send them away," "to let them go!" (v. 1e). These words are the same commands given to Pharaoh when Israel left Egypt; now they are being used against Israel herself!

15:2–4 If in such desperate circumstances the people ask, "Where can we go?" Jeremiah is told to give them four destinations that are available to them; they can go to "pestilence," "sword," "famine," or on to "captivity!" Judah is now a spiritual outcast, doomed to face a fourfold destruction: a "sword to kill," "dogs to drag away," "birds of the air and beasts of the earth to devour and destroy" (v. 3). God will use these four agents to wreak havoc on the people. Thus God will make Israel a "horror" to all the nations (v. 4). And the reign of the former King Manasseh is one of the primary instigators for all this trouble that is now coming on the whole nation of Judah (v. 4).

King Manasseh was the Davidic ruler in Judah for fifty-five years (696–641 BC)—the longest reign in Judah's history. He was the son and successor of good King Hezekiah, whose reign and the events of that reign were recorded in 2 Kgs 21:1–18 and 2 Chr 33:1–20. Manasseh was a mere twelve years old at his father's death. He is remembered most for his zealous promotion of idolatry in Jerusalem and probably provides the background for most of Jeremiah's vitriolic language against Judah's faithlessness to Yahweh.

Manasseh is especially named in 2 Kgs 21:1–20; 23:12, 26, and particularly 24:3 for the vileness of his acts. That last text reads: "Surely these things happened to Judah according to Yahweh's command, in order to remove the [people of Judah] from [God's] presence because of the sins of [King] Manasseh and all he had done, including the shedding of innocent blood. For he had filled Jerusalem with innocent blood, and Yahweh was not willing to forgive." These references to Manasseh and his vileness makes it clear that the fall of Jerusalem had been long in coming—in fact, more than a century.

15:5–7 Verse 6 says it all: Yahweh is weary of relenting; he can no longer show compassion on Judah. Given that, the rhetorical questions of v. 5 are in effect: "Who is going to mourn for you now? Who is going to ask how you are doing now?" In the past it had been God alone who had ameliorated the effects of their sin. But those days had come and are now gone. It is you, you have rejected me, God affirms, with emphasis on the pronoun "you" (v. 6). Now God will stretch out his hand over the people who have constantly been backsliding. God will toss them in the air as a farmer would use a wooden fork to toss in the air the grain after it was first crushed by a threshing sled so that the grain and the husk would be separated by making the husk airborne; this action allowed the heavy grain to fall in place as the chaff blew off to the side of the grain pile (v. 7).

15:8 There is an allusion to the Abrahamic covenant (v. 8a; Gen 22:17; 32:13), only here it is a reversal of the promise of proliferation and multiplication. Now the widows will be as numerous as the sands of the sea. The promise is not canceled in this text, but it is a sobering moment of threatened judgment, to say the least.

15:9 The mother who has given birth to seven, usually a full complement of sons from whom one could look forward to a secure provision for one's old age, she too grows faint (v. 9a). The sun sets on her days (v. 9b) as this metaphor for death climaxes her days instead. Rather than being recompensed, she too will be disgraced and humiliated (v. 9d). Even the "survivors" will still face the sword (v. 9e).

Things have gotten so serious that, in one of those rare moments in Scripture, Jeremiah is told that even if Moses and Samuel were to intercede in prayer on behalf of Judah, it would all be to no avail. Wickedness has risen to such a level that God refuses to accept any prayers on behalf of the Judahites. Instead, now God will make the people of Judah abhorrent to all the kingdoms of the earth.

Has our nation reached such a point of disgust to God? Have we exhausted all the avenues of grace and mercy from God? This is one scary word from God about how serious accumulated sin is and can become.

ANOTHER JEREMIAH CONFESSION (15:10–21)

TRANSLATION

> **10** Woe is me, my mother, that you bore me,
>> A man with whom the whole land strives and contends.
> I have not lent, nor have I borrowed,[211]
>> Yet everyone curses me.
> **11** Yahweh said, "Surely I will deliver you for a good [purpose];
>> Surely I will cause the enemy to entreat you in times of
>>> trouble and distress."
> **12** Can one break iron[212]—
>> Iron from the north—or bronze?
> **13** Your wealth and your treasures I will give as spoil without
>> price,
> For all your sins throughout all your territory.
> **14** I will enslave[213] you to your enemies,

---

211. The LXX adds ἡ ἰσχύς μου ἐξέλιπεν, "my strength has failed," before the end of the verse: כָּלֹה מְקַלְלוּנִי, "all of them curse me."

212. The LXX has εἰ γνωσθήσεται σίδηρος, "will iron be known?" where the MT has הֲיָרֹעַ בַּרְזֶל, "can one break iron?"

213. This translation follows a variant reading from the LXX (καταδουλώσω), where the MT וְהַעֲבַרְתִּי ("I will cause to cross over") was read as וְהַעֲבַדְתִּי, "I will cause to serve." This is

In a land that you do not know.
For my anger will kindle a fire,
That will burn against you.
15 O Yahweh, it is you who understands;
Remember me and visit me,
Avenge me of my persecutors.
You are long-suffering[214]—do not take me away;
Think[215] how I suffer reproach for your sake!
16 Your words were found and I ate them;
They were my joy and heart's delight,
For your name is called over me,
O Yahweh, God of Hosts.
17 I did not sit in the circle of merrymakers,
And I did not make merry [with them].[216]
Because your hand was on me, I sat alone,
For you have filled me with indignation.
18 Why is my pain unending,
And is my wound incurable,
Refusing healing?
Will you be to me a deceptive brook,
Like waters that unreliable?
19 Therefore, this is what Yahweh says:
"If you repent then I will restore you that you may stand before
me;
If you utter what is precious and not what is worthless,
You will be my mouth.
Let them turn to you,
But you must not turn to them.
20 I will make you for this people a wall,
A fortified wall of bronze.

---

caused by the change of of a ד (*dalet*) to a ר (*resh*).

214. The LXX reads μὴ εἰς μακροθυμίαν, "do not bear long with them," where the MT has "you are long-suffering."

215. Or "know."

216. The LXX has εὐλαβούμην, "I feared," where the MT has "I did not rejoice."

> They will fight against you,
> But they will not be able to overcome you,
> For I am with you, I will save you and deliver you, declares
>   Yahweh.
> **21** I will deliver you[217] from the hands of the wicked,
> And redeem you from the grasp of the adversary."

COMMENTARY

Jeremiah's Lament and Yahweh's Response (15:10–14)

15:10 It is not possible to say whether Jeremiah's mother is still alive at this time, but if she is, she would have been as distressed as her son Jeremiah over what he says. Jeremiah seems to lapse into a soliloquy in which he expresses his feelings of dejection and downright misery. Though his words are probably said to himself, obviously he also knows that he speaks these words in the presence of God. Despite his being called by God even from his mother's womb, in his deep despondency he wishes he had never been born (v. 10). He is one dejected servant of God!

He depicts himself as a man who stirs up contention and strife wherever he speaks. Instead of his speaking having its desired effect, the people turn on the prophet and fight against him. His message is meant to bring repentance and peace, but it has had the opposite effect. Besides all that, he has never lent or borrowed anything, which are two of the most frequent sources of strife and ill will. In short, Jeremiah has simply not engaged in those sorts of activities that engender quarrels. So why is it that no one speaks well of him, he wonders. He is not naturally a contentious person; it is the message he is given by God that has brought all the trouble over his head. Not only has he lost his friends over this mission; he has lost his own family (11:21–23).

15:11 God responds in vv. 11–14, though these words are most difficult textually to interpret. Most interpret these words as positive words from

---

217. The last part of v. 20 and the first part of v. 21, "declares Yahweh. I will deliver you," are absent in some LXX mss.

Yahweh. God promises that he will intervene and deal with those opposing him. It is almost as if God stops Jeremiah in the middle of his speech, before he goes too far. God's intervention will be for Jeremiah's "good," but what that good is is not specified exactly.[218] God continues with another asseveration: he will make Jeremiah's enemies plead with him to gain help from heaven (v. 11b–c). Therefore, when trouble comes, then Jeremiah will see how the tables will be turned; those same people will come to him for help and advice, which is exactly what happened (21:1; 37:3, 17; 38:14; 42:1–7).

15:12 This is followed by an enigmatic question: "Can a man break iron—iron from the north—or bronze?" (v. 12). "Bronze" in this question represents Jeremiah, while the first mention of "iron" represents the stubborn people, and the "iron from the north" represents Babylon. This word picture depicts the strength God will give Jeremiah in the face of the people's opposition. The stubborn Israelites with their iron will will not be able to break either Babylon's "iron" or Jeremiah's "bronze." This rhetorical question from God reassures Jeremiah of his God-given strength and his promise.[219]

15:13 God will also hand over as booty the people's wealth and the "treasures" they have kept locked up thus far and retained securely in the nation of Judah. But that will soon change. The divine reason for this outcome is given: "because of all your sins throughout the territory/borders" (v. 13c).

15:14 There are more judgments for those antagonizing Jeremiah: they will be sent off to a land they do not know (v. 14) and they will be enslaved to their enemies, the Babylonians. This change in venue will be sponsored by Yahweh's anger. There has been plenty of warning that this will be the outcome if no repentance has taken place in the nation.

---

218. Smith suggests "that Jeremiah was forced to ask himself and God the question: Why go on as God's prophet to Judah if Judah is rejected?" See G. V. Smith, "The Use of Quotations in Jeremiah XV 11–14," VT 29, no. 2 (April 1979): 229–31.

219. Smit identifies several war-related terms and metaphors in God's response to Jeremiah. See J. H. Smit, "War-related Terminology and Imagery in Jeremiah 15:10–21," OTE 11 (1998): 105–14.

Another Lament of Jeremiah and God's Response (15:15–21)

The previous dialogue between the prophet and God continues, in part as a response to what God has said in vv. 11–14. It begins again with a petition to God in v. 15a–b, which is followed by a protest, based on the prophet's long record of faithfulness (vv. 15c–17), then changing to a complaint (v. 18).

15:15 Jeremiah begins by noting that Yahweh knows him and his present circumstance (v. 15a), but like the psalmist (cf. Pss 17, 44, 88) and many of us today, he goes ahead and briefs Yahweh on what he already knows. His petition is that God will remember him in his oppressive circumstances and that he will visit him with a specific action: bringing retribution on the heads of those who are persecuting him (vv. 15d–16). The verb "to remember" (זָכַר) is not simply the action of calling something back to one's mind as a cerebral action but always had the overtone of accompanying that mental act with the appropriate physical action as well. What good will it do if God merely recalls what has taken place if there is no appropriate follow-through with a loving action in light of what has been remembered?

The prophet prays also for God not simply to "take him away" (v. 15d), which could mean either to spare his involvement as one of the exiles, or his own death. The expression of "take me" (v. 15d) is used of Enoch being "taken" to heaven (Gen 5:24) and of Elijah's transport to heaven (2 Kgs 2:1). Now the prophet seems to be arguing against what he said in v. 10: at one moment he wishes he had never been born; at the other he wants to continue in this life. Such is the state of his confused mind and soul.

15:16 Jeremiah supplies God with reasons why he should act on his behalf in vv. 15c–17. First, the prophet brings up the matter of his call (1:9); God is the one who put him in this situation in the first place (v. 16). While his call was a joy and a delight, the effects of his call have been anything but. Moreover, when he has been presented with the words of God, he does not reject them: he ingests and takes them into his very being (v. 16a). He is troubled, for he is taking heat from his enemies due to bearing God's name (v. 16c).

15:17 As further support of his protestation, the majority of his message is on the side of judgment; it is not merely along the lines of public celebration of a lot of good news (v. 17). His life is not one of partying with merrymakers; he instead "sat alone because [God's] hand was on [him]" (v. 17c). God's "hand" is here as the pressure of the content of the divine message he is to bring to the people.

15:18 Jeremiah proceeds to ask "Why?" questions of God (v. 18). "Pain" (כְּאֵב) here may refer to his mental anguish, and his "wounds" may here refer to the effects his troubles had on his whole life and outlook. From other passages in Jeremiah (8:18–9:1; 13:17; 14:17), Jeremiah participates in the pain and suffering of God. But still there is the question of "why?"

Because the prophet's suffering seems endless, he reproaches God full force (v. 18c–d). Will God act toward him like a "deceitful brook" (v. 18c)? Like waters that give out (v. 18d)? Has not God promised to be for him a "fountain of living waters" (2:13)? Where, then, is this promised relief? Everyone in Israel knew what it meant to come to a wadi (an occasional brook) that in the rainy season was filled with water but in the dry season was desiccated and contained no water.

15:19–20 Yahweh reacts to the prophet's lament in vv. 19–21. He begins with the word "therefore," which is used in judgment sections (v. 19a). Yahweh does not quibble with the prophet over the accuracy of his descriptions, but he does take on the prophet's attitude and challenge him directly. Basically, God says, "Let's get on with it."

But also, Jeremiah, Yahweh reminds him, you must face up to it: You too must repent of your attitudes if you are going to serve me. You must speak words that are "excellent, precious, costly" (יָקָר), not words that are "frivolous, worthless, foolish, insignificant" (זָלַל). Only then will Jeremiah continue to be God's "mouthpiece" or "spokesman" (v. 19e). So, repent, Jeremiah, just as you are calling on the people to repent.

Whatever you do, O prophet, do not capitulate to the people or downgrade your message so that you can win the acceptance of the people to yourself; let the people turn toward you, instead of your turning to them

(v. 19f). As Yahweh has promised in his call (1:18–19), Yahweh will make him a "fortified wall of bronze" to this people and will rescue him and be with him. They will not overcome Jeremiah; God will overcome them.

15:21 Yahweh promises he will "deliver [Jeremiah] from the hands of the wicked" (v. 21a) and "redeem [him] from the grasp of the adversary" (v. 21b). But Jeremiah's deliverance depends on his willingness to repent of his worthless and unworthy words that he had uttered against Yahweh.

Jeremiah prays to the Lord, and he begins by naming his complaints to God. With four verbs he calls for God to intervene on his behalf: "Remember me, ... care for me, ... avenge me, ... do not take me [from this earth?]." However, he also recalls God's word, which he received with joy and delight even though he sat isolated from others. But Jeremiah cannot understand why his prayers are being unanswered, for God's prophet is scared, lonely, hurt, angry, and now charging God for his state of mind and soul.

God's word to Jeremiah and to us is the same. There are two conditions God prescribes: We must return to God, and we must reject our doubts and reproaches against God. We must realize that God has prayed for us that our faith might not fail (Luke 22:31–32). God repeats what he told Jeremiah when he called him in Jer 1:8, 18–19. He will be with him and make him like a wall to his people as he rescues him and delivers him from their hands.

A CALL TO CELIBACY AND ISOLATION (16:1–21)

TRANSLATION

1 The word of Yahweh came to me:[220] **2** "You shall not take a wife,[221] nor shall you have sons or daughters in this place. **3** For this is what Yahweh says concerning sons and daughters born in this place, and concerning mothers who bore them and the fathers who begat them in this land. **4** They will die horrible deaths. They will not be lamented, nor will they be buried; they will be as dung on the surface of the ground. They will perish by the

---

220. The first verse is missing in the LXX.

221. The LXX adds λέγει κύριος ὁ θεὸς Ισραηλ, "says the Lord, the God of Israel," after "You shall not take a wife."

sword and by famine, and their dead bodies will be food for the birds of the air and for the beasts of the earth."

5 For this is what Yahweh says: "Do not enter the house of mourning, and do not show sympathy for them; because I have taken away my peace from this people, [my] steadfast love and mercy," says Yahweh.[222] **6** The high and the low will die in this land; they will not be buried or mourned. And no one will cut himself or make himself bald for them. **7** No one shall break bread[223] for the mourner, to comfort him for the dead; nor shall anyone give a cup of consolation to drink for his father of his mother. **8** You shall not go into the house of feasting to sit with them, to eat and drink. **9** For thus says Yahweh of Hosts, the God of Israel, "I will make to cease from this place, before your eyes and in your days, the sounds of joy and gladness, the voice of the bridegroom and the voice of the bride."

10 And when you tell this people all these words and they say to you, "For what reason has Yahweh pronounced all this great disaster against us? What is our iniquity? And what is the sin we have committed against Yahweh our God?" **11** Then you shall say to them, "Because your fathers have forsaken me, declares Yahweh, and have followed other gods and served and worshiped them. They have forsaken me and have not kept my law. **12** But you have behaved more wickedly than your fathers. Behold, every one of you follows his own stubborn evil will, refusing to listen to me; **13** So I will hurl you out of this land into a land that neither you nor your fathers have known, and there you will serve other gods day and night,[224] for I will not show you any favor."

14 "Therefore, behold, the time is coming, declares Yahweh, when it will no longer be said, 'As Yahweh lives who brought up the children of Israel out of the land of Egypt,' **15** But 'As Yahweh lives who brought up the children of Israel[225] out of the north country and out of all the countries where I have banished them.' For I will restore them to their own land, which I gave to their fathers.

---

222. The end of v. 5 and beginning of v. 6 are missing in the LXX.

223. The word לְהֶם should be read לֶחֶם, "bread," as the LXX, the Vg., and some Heb. mss.

224. The LXX omits יוֹמָם וָלַיְלָה, "day and night."

225. The LXX has τὸν οἶκον Ισραηλ, "the house of Israel," where the MT has אֶת־בְּנֵי יִשְׂרָאֵל, "the sons/children of Israel."

16 "Behold, I am sending for many fishermen, declares Yahweh, and they will catch them; and after that I will send for many hunters, and they will hunt them down on every mountain and every hill, and from the crevices of the rocks. **17** For my eyes are on all their ways; they are not hid from me,[226] nor is their iniquity concealed from my eyes. **18** First of all,[227] I will pay them back twice over for their wickedness and their sin, because they have polluted my land with the carcasses of their detestable idols and have filled my inheritance with their abominations."

> **19** Yahweh, my strength and my fortress,
>   My refuge in time of trouble.
> To you the nations will come
>   From the ends of the earth and say,
> "Nothing but lies have our fathers possessed,
>   Nothings, of no use at all!
> **20** Can a mortal make gods for himself?
>   [Nay!], they are no gods!
> **21** So look, I am going to teach them,
>   This time I am going to teach them,
> My power and my might;
>   Then they will know my name is Yahweh."

COMMENTARY

Do Not Marry and Have Children (16:1–4)

16:1-2 Since children were very important in this ancient Middle Eastern culture, the prohibition on Jeremiah against his marrying (v. 2) must have been startling news to him. But far from being an arbitrary restraint, this divine restriction on the prophet's life is designed to be a prophetic teaching-symbol for the whole nation. As such, Jeremiah does not simply proclaim God's word: he embodies that word and actually lives it out.

---

226. The LXX omits the expression לֹא נִסְתְּרוּ מִלְּפָנָי, "they are not hidden from me."

227. The adj. רִאשׁוֹנָה, "first," is missing in the LXX.

It is a matter of special interest that this prose passage, which some scholars insist on attributing to the work of some Deuteronomistic preachers in the exile, does not fit well as an address to the entire community, as those who say the prose section came from an influence of the book of Deuteronomy on the prophet argue. Surely it fits best as addressed to an individual. What good would it do to tell the whole community not to marry and have children, argues Jones (228–29), for they will go ahead and marry and have children regardless of the crisis.

Jeremiah is not forbidden to marry because of the present crisis, as was the case with Paul (1 Cor 7:26), but because his life is a symbol of his message. Elijah and Elisha lived the same type of single life as well. Jeremiah had been told in his call in 1:18 (cf. 5:20) that he will be "an "iron pillar" and a "bronze wall" to stand against the whole land. There is no doubt that this command of celibacy contributed further to his sense of loneliness and isolation, even though his celibacy would protect him in the future from the grief parents would suffer as they witnessed the horrible deaths of their children in the coming battle with Babylon.

16:3–4 Four groups of persons are enumerated in v. 3: sons, daughters, women who will be mothers, and men who will be fathers. The announcement of God in v. 4 makes it even more realistic: "They will die of deadly diseases." It will be a time of unprecedented trouble and catastrophe. Rather than their deaths being followed with mourning and burial, they will lie on the ground like trash or even as dung as their carcasses became food for the birds of heaven and the beasts of the earth. So overwhelmed will the survivors be that there will be too few or none who have strength enough to perform the customary funeral rites for the dead.

Do Not Participate in Funerals or Weddings (16:5–9)

16:5 When the judgment of God strikes, there will be no room for consoling those mourning for the dead (vv. 5–7) or rejoicing with those getting married (vv. 8–9). The first symbolic action of a life of celibacy is followed by this second symbolic action, which pertains to deaths that occur during Jeremiah's ministry, even before the predicted destruction of the land. The previous prohibition toward marriage in v. 2 used a negative generally attached to a permanent ban (לֹא), but in v. 5 a different negative (אַל) is used, which normally points to a specific prohibition that is temporary (that is, with no indication that it endures for a longer period of time). According to these distinctions of the Heb. negatives, Jeremiah is to remain unmarried all his life, but there might be times when he could enter a home for a funeral meal in some specified emergencies.[228]

The reason the prophet is restrained from attending funerals of his people is that he is to be a living warning that Yahweh no longer has sympathy for the people of Israel in that generation. Instead of "blessing" and "peace," signaling their well-being and favor from God, there is a spurious peace, for the covenant relationship has been broken.

16:6 Death in that day will be no respecter of whether one was highborn or low; neither one will be mourned. In fact, "no one will cut himself or shave his head for them" (v. 6), which in themselves were pagan practices associated with the **cult** of the dead and the Canaanite gods Mot and Baal. These practices are forbidden in Lev 19:28; 21:5; and Deut 14:1.[229] Yet despite this prohibition, they continued to be practiced widely in Israel (Jer 41:5; 47:5; 48:37; Isa 15:2–3; 22:12; Ezek 7:18; Amos 8:10; Mic 1:16).

Cutting or mutilating the body was expressly prohibited for Israelites, in contrast to the practices of her neighboring peoples. Moabites expressed their grief by shaving their heads, cutting off their beards, and slashing their hands and perhaps their backs as well (Jer 48:37).

The prophets of Baal, we are told, slashed their bodies and laid gashes on their backs in order to move Baal to sympathetic action (16:9), but this practice was also strongly disapproved of by God (Lev 19:27–8; 21:5; Deut 14:1–2). The **cult** of the dead was large in Canaanite society, and Israel is warned not to fall into the cultural pattern of their neighbors.

---

228. Extrabiblical evidence combined with Amos 6:7 attest that going to a house of mourning was a social custom in ancient Israel. See V. C. l. Maier and E. M. Dörrfuss, "'Um mit ihnen zu sitzen, zu essen und zu trinken' Am 6,7; Jer 16,5 und die Bedeutung von *marzeaḥ*," ZAW 111 (1999): 45–57.

229. These were customs performed by people belonging to pagan cults or done to ward off spirits of the dead. See T. Rata, "Notes on Leviticus 19:28," in *Holman Christian Study Bible* (Nashville: Broadman & Holman, 2010).

16:7-8 Life will take on tragic proportions. No one will offer food or drink at a funeral anymore, for comfort will have long since been exhausted. Whether this is clean food that was no longer used or food that came in the evening hours as the fast of the mourners was halted temporarily for that day cannot be determined here. But the prophet is clearly told to disassociate himself from all social events; whether it is a funeral or a marriage, he is not to be present.

16:9 In v. 9, the references to "your eyes" and "your days" are m. pl.; therefore, the injunction applies to the whole community. In the era of that generation, the sounds of happiness and communal times of gathering will "end" (v. 9). There will be no more joy left in town!

Three Questions from the People (16:10-13)

16:10 Jeremiah is warned that when he tells the people these things, they will immediately ask these three questions:

1. "Why has Yahweh threatened us with such horrible misfortune?"

2. "What is our crime?"

3. "What sin have we committed against Yahweh our God?"

Because the prophet has been drumming away in this land for all these years with explanations, these questions almost seem comical if not for the seriousness of the situation. Where have these people been for all the times Jeremiah has been pleading, warning, and exhorting them on these very topics? These folks are like the ones the prophet Malachi preached to in his book around 400 BC, for they too kept asking in effect, "Who, us? We did all these things? When did we do these things?" (six times in Mal 1:2, 6, 7, etc.). So insensitive and hardened are the people of Judah that it just is not getting through to them. Perhaps they figure that the poor spiritual conditions under King Manasseh had really turned around when young King Josiah had instituted his revival, so God can now call off his threatened judgment since the king and some his officials in the nation had repented.

16:11-13 There are three responses to their questions that the prophet is authorized to announce:

1. The former generation had forsaken God (v. 11).

2. Their own generation has acted more wickedly than the previous one (v. 12).

3. God's verdict is that they will most certainly be thrown out of their land (v. 13).

The former generation "forsook" Yahweh, "followed other gods," and "served and worshiped them" (v. 11), a clear allusion to the injunctions in the opening of the Decalogue. But if that is a sin from those in the past, the present generation is no better, but even worse (v. 12). By now they too have regressed from any positive effects left from Josiah's revival. The divine verdict is: "I will throw you out of the land" (v. 13). They will be driven into a land they have no personal knowledge of Babylon. No mercy will be shown to them. They will be captive exiles!

Restoration of Israel and the Nations (16:14–21)

16:14-15 A list of reasons is followed by the typical "Therefore" (v. 14), which normally signals an announcement of judgment. So abrupt does this section appear in this context that it has become commonplace to declare that vv. 14-15 are an interruption to Jeremiah's sermon, if not a misplacement of the text. But so dramatic are the words of God casting out his people from the land that it is necessary for those in exile to hear a qualification to that word of judgment. Their punishment does not set aside the previous harsh words of their exile, but it presumes a new confession (v. 15). Moreover, it shows that God's word of judgment is not his final word, but it is always followed by his word of restoration, thus the declaration that Yahweh will show no mercy, love, or favor (vv. 5, 13) is now shown to have temporal limits. There is mercy in the future!

Surprisingly, the divine pledge is that, whereas in former days oath taking had involved invoking the name of Yahweh God, who had brought Israel up out of the land of Egypt, the days are coming when that oath formula will be changed to a new reference: to Yahweh who restored the Israelites from the land of exile in the north and brought them back home again (vv. 14–15). A second exodus is planned by God even before Judah is carted off to Babylon for seventy years of captivity. God will be true to the promise he had made to Abraham, Isaac, and Jacob; Israel will be restored to their land once again in the coming days.

16:16 But who then are the "fishermen" and "hunters" (v. 16), and what work will they do? Augustine thought the apostles were the fishermen, for Jesus had said to them, "I will make you fishers of men" (Wenthe, 125). What were the hunters for? Augustine answered, because people wandered through the mountains of Donatism, Arianism, Plotinus, and Novatus, God needed these hunters.

However, the context of Jeremiah indicates that the fishermen represent the people of that day trapped in Babylon's dragnet, who were followed by similar hunters who caught up with the fugitives hiding in the rocks and crevices, thinking these were inaccessible hiding spots where they could not be found. But God's judgment will be carried with ruthless perfection and completion.

16:17–18 The reason for such thorough action is the constant scrutiny of God on all the ways of mortals (v. 17). God is the one who watches and sees all that goes on in the earth. Some worry that, as v. 18 claims that God "will repay them double," Israel will be asked to pay a price that is twice as severe as their sin, but the word "doubly" (מִשְׁנֶה) may also be correctly rendered as "equivalent,"[230] that is, what they bear as a punishment will be a carbon copy of what they have done wrong (Deut 15:18; Isa 40:2). The offense that God is speaking of is the one of defiling his land by means of idolatry. These idols are really "nothings" and "lifeless forms" of vapor that have spread all over the promised land.

16:19–21 Verses 19–21 are the first of a medley of poems through 17:13 rather than one continuous poem. The first poem addresses God as Jeremiah's "strength," his "fortress," and "refuge in a time of trouble" (v. 19a). He sees the "nations ... come from the ends of the earth" and confess that all the idols they had previously declared as gods are just homemade gods that

---

230. M. Kline, "Double Trouble," *JETS* 32 (1989): 176–77.

are nonfunctioning zeros (v. 18c, d). Mortals cannot make a god; they turn out to be no gods at all (v. 20). But God will teach Israel and the nations his "power" (lit. "hand") and "might" (v. 21). Then a worldwide revival ensues, for then they will all personally know me, announces Yahweh.

Judah's professed innocence as she asks what she has done wrong to result in the Lord declaring that he will throw them out of their land really is unnecessary. She knows what she has done, and it is stinking up the land to high heaven. Such wicked behavior by all the nations will be dealt with by the Lord himself. There is no use in our trying to say we never knew some of this stuff like idolatry was wrong. Where was Judah when the preached word from Jeremiah was being broadcast abroad? And where are we in our day when we try to state the same objection to God? Will it pass muster with him? I doubt it!

WHOM SHALL WE TRUST? (17:1–27)

TRANSLATION

1 Judah's sin is written with an iron stylus,
   With a diamond point it is engraved
On the tablets of their hearts
   And on the horns of their altars.
2 While their children remember
   Their altars and their Asherim,
Beside leafy trees on high hills,
   3 My mountain in the countryside.
Your wealth and all your treasures,
   I will give away as booty
As the price for your sin,
   [Committed] inside all your borders.
4 Through your own fault you will lose
   The inheritance I gave you.
I will make you serve your enemies
   In a land that you do not know.
For a fire is lit in my anger,[231]

---

231. Lit. "nose/nostrils."

Which will burn forever.[232]

5 Thus says Yahweh:[233]

"Cursed is the man,

    Who puts his trust in humanity,

And makes mortal flesh his strength,

    And whose heart turns away from Yahweh.

6 He will be like a juniper in the wilderness;

    He will not see prosperity when it comes.

He will dwell in the parched places of the desert

    In a salt land where no one lives.

7 Blessed is the man who trusts in Yahweh,

    Whose confidence is in Yahweh.

8 He will be like a tree planted near water

    That sends out its roots toward the stream.

It does not fear when the heat comes;

    Its leaves remain verdant.

In the year of drought it has no worries;

    It never fails to bear fruit.

9 The heart is of all things most crafty[234]

    And incurably sick.

Who can understand it?

10 I, Yahweh, search the heart,

    And examine the mind,

To reward a man according to his conduct,

    According to what his actions deserve.

11 Like a partridge that hatches eggs it did not lay,

    So is he who gains riches unjustly.

Midway in his life they will leave him;

    In the end he will prove to be a fool."

12 A glorious throne, exalted from the beginning,

    Is the place[235] of our sanctuary.

---

232. Vv. 1–4 are absent in the LXX.

233. The introductory formula כֹּה אָמַר יְהֹוָה, "thus says Yahweh," is missing in the LXX.

234. The LXX has βαθεῖα, "deep," instead of the MT's עָקֹב, "deceitful."

235. The LXX omits מֵרִאשׁוֹן מְקוֹם, "from the beginning (is) the place."

13 O Yahweh, the hope of Israel,
　　All who forsake you will be put to shame.
Those who turn away from you will be written in the dust,
　　Because they have forsaken Yahweh, the fountain of living
　　　　water.
14 Heal me, O Yahweh, and I will be healed;
　　Save me and I will be saved,
　　For you are the one I praise.
15 Behold, they keep saying to me,
　　"Where is the word of Yahweh?
　　Let it happen!"
16 I have not run away from being your shepherd;[236]
　　You know I have not desired the disastrous day.
　　The utterance of my lips lies before you.
17 Do not be a terror to me;
　　You are my refuge in the day of trouble.
18 Let those pursuing me be ashamed,
　　But keep me from shame;
Let them be terrified,
　　But keep me from terror.
Bring on them the day of evil.
　　Break them and break them again!

19 This is what Yahweh said to me: "Go and stand at the gate of the people, by which the kings of Judah go in and go out, and in all the other gates of Jerusalem, **20** and say to them, 'Hear the word of Yahweh, you kings of Judah and all you people of Judah, and everyone living in Jerusalem who enter by these gates! **21** This is what Yahweh says: "Take care of your lives, do not carry a load on the Sabbath day or bring it through the gates of Jerusalem. **22** Do not bring a load out of your houses on the Sabbath day, or do work of any kind, but keep the Sabbath day holy, as I commanded

---

236. The LXX has ἐγὼ δὲ οὐκ ἐκοπίασα κατακολουθῶν ὀπίσω σου, "I have not been weary of following you," where the MT has וַאֲנִי לֹא־אַצְתִּי מֵרֹעֶה אַחֲרֶיךָ, "I have not run away from being your shepherd."

your fathers— **23** who, however, did not listen or pay any attention;[237] they were stiff-necked and refused to listen or respond to discipline.

24 ""And now, if you are careful to obey me, declares Yahweh, and bring no load through the gates of this city on the Sabbath day, but keep the Sabbath day holy, by doing no work on it, **25** then there shall pass through the gates of this city kings who sit on David's throne, with their officials. They and their officials will come riding in chariots and on horses, they and their princes, together with the people of Judah, and those living in Jerusalem. And this city will be inhabited forever. **26** And people will come from the towns of Judah, and from and the villages around Jerusalem, from the land of Benjamin, from the Shephelah, the hill country, and the Negeb, bringing burnt offerings and sacrifices, cereal/grain offerings and incense, together with those bringing thank offerings to the house of Yahweh. **27** But if you will not obey me to keep holy the Sabbath day, by not carrying any load as you come through the gates of Jerusalem on the Sabbath day, then I will set an unquenchable fire in the gates of Jerusalem that will consume her fortified palaces."""

COMMENTARY

This chapter is famous for the wisdom poem found in vv. 5–8, which is so reminiscent of Ps 1. Both of these scriptures trace two basic paths a mortal can take in life: the way of the wicked or the way of the righteous. This is followed by vv. 9–11, which offers three wisdom sayings further elaborating on the need to be vigilant about a relationship with God. But it begins, first of all, with a message of judgment (vv. 1–4).

Judah's Sin and Resulting Judgment (17:1–4)

17:1 The contrast between what has just been said about the Gentile nations rejecting idolatry in the future (16:19–20) and now Judah's adamant and stubborn preoccupation with idolatry is so sharp that we as readers are stunned. Judah's sin has been indelibly engraved with an iron tool (v. 1), with a diamond or a flint point.[238] If there ever were a way of saying that

---

237. The LXX adds τοῖς πατράσιν ὑμῶν, "more than their fathers," after "did not listen or pay any attention."

238. Gosse suggests that the emphasis on the sin of Judah "wishes to underline the new covenant, which will give occasion for a forgiveness relating to the fall of Babylon." See B.

sin had left an indelible or permanent mark, then this must be the way to say it. Job 19:24 records a similar time in Job's life when something similar to this was called for, but in his case he cried out to God that he, or someone else, might take a stone and chisel out his complaint to God in the rock, and then fill the letters with lead so they could not be rubbed out or erased later by others.

The hard material that the inscription is set in is not in stone or written on gems but on the "tablets of their hearts" (v. 1c). But so hardened are the people's hearts that they have become impervious to God's pleas to repent or his calls for change. The divine charges are also written on "the horns of their altars" (v. 1d). These "horns" were stone projections at each of the four corners of the altar, where the blood of the sacrifice was smeared to indicate the propitiatory nature of the offering (Exod 27:2; 29:12; 30:1-3; Lev 4:7, 30, 34; 8:15; 16:18). But now with their sins chiseled into the rock of the four horns on the altar, Judah's sins cannot be rubbed out. Since the word for "altar" is in the pl., "altars," this could just as well be a reference to the pagan altars, which also had four corner horns to them. If so, then this could suggest that the altars had no atoning value and their sins were a matter of permanent record.

Archaeologist Gabriel Barkai made a sensational discovery in 1979 while excavating burial caves at Ketef Hinnom, on the hillside southwest of Jerusalem's city walls. There Barkai found two small rolled-up silver amulets or ornaments that appeared to be talismans. The amulets were inscribed with Hebrew letters, one with the benediction found in Num 6:24-26.[239] These inscriptions were incised with some sharp instrument that seems to have been reminiscent of the tool in Jer 17:1 and Job 19:24. The larger amulet exhibited fifty-one letters and the smaller forty-eight letters. Not only do they include the divine name "Yahweh," but also they represent the earliest biblical text (ca. seventh century BC) found so far with an almost identical textual reading to the biblical text we have today.

Gosse, "Jérémie 17, 1-5aa dans la rédaction massorétique du livre de Jérémie," *Estudios Bíblicos* 53 (1995): 165-80.

239. A. Yardeni, "Remarks on the Priestly Benediction on Two Ancient Amulets from Jerusalem," *VT* 41 (1991): 180. Also see P. J. Long, *Jeremiah: An Archaeological Companion* (Louisville: Westminster John Knox, 1993), 100-101.

This seems to counter the idea that diamonds were not known in this earlier period and that the Pentateuch did not exist until the postexilic period.

17:2 Verse 2 notes that the children of those who stand so adamantly against what God calls for will carry on the same false worship of God at these pagan altars and at the Asherah poles. These sacred poles appear to be trees, or wooden poles (Jer 2:27; Judg 6:25), that represented the goddess Asherah. Her poles were set up on the "high hills" and "beside leafy trees" and were associated with her alleged control over fertility and rain for crops. Asherah was the consort of Baal, as the two of them made up the center of Canaanite pagan religion (1 Kgs 15:13; 18:19; 2 Kgs 21:7; 23:4).

17:3-4 Judah has no one to blame but herself, for it is "through [their] own fault" (v. 4a), or by their own actions, that they will lose their heritage in the land God had promised to them. The people's "wealth" and "all [their] treasures" will become spoils for Babylon as Jerusalem falls and is devastated (v. 3b). This will be the "price" (v. 3d) for their sins. Judah will serve her enemies (v. 4c), for they have "lit a fire in [God's] nostrils" (v. 4e), which would "burn forever," that is, for a long, long time, an irreversible judgment that would fall on that generation.

Trust Those Who Are Like a Tree (17:5–11)

While in most cases in Scripture the blessings come before the curses, here they are reversed. This wisdom saying, as almost all commentators have noted, resembling Ps 1, comes on the heels of the discussion of the sins of Judah in vv. 1–4. Judah's sin singled out here is not particularly idolatry, but this time it is the sin of leaning on the strength of the arms of humanity to save or to deliver the nation (v. 5).

17:5 There are three distinct words for "man" in v. 5: גֶּבֶר, "strong man"; אָדָם, "mankind" (from the word אֲדָמָה, "ground"); and בָּשָׂר, "flesh." The words for "man" culminate when the man "makes his mortal flesh his strength [זְרֹעַ]." All three words for "man" are symbols of humanity's weak and mortal being. It is as if Jeremiah warns, beware of the self-made man, who puts his confidence in his mere humanity, or any mortal who trusts in public opinion, or human power, whether that power is military, economic, technical, or intellectual power. Worst of all, this man's "heart turns away from Yahweh" (v. 5e). There is the chief ailment of these mortals!

17:6 Such a person is best represented as a bush, perhaps a juniper bush that is planted in the desert wilderness. That man and bush are alike—both are dehydrated, desiccated, and destitute of any good (v. 6), for that bush fails to see any good, if and when it comes. Such men also had in the past pinned their false hopes on the armies of Egypt and their horses (Isa 31:3), or on the Queen of Heaven (Jer 44), but all such substitutes involved in any of these actions were also a waste of time and effort. What good are frauds in a real time of trouble?

17:7-8 On the other side of the coin is the man who trusts in Yahweh (v. 7). This person is "blessed" by Yahweh, for this person "trusts in Yahweh" (repeated twice in this verse). That person is "like a tree planted near the water," where a steady stream of nourishment can come up through the roots of that tree to bless the whole bush/tree. It has no fear when the heat comes, or when there is a drought, for its leaves remain verdant and green, and it never fails to bear fruit (v. 8). Here is the supreme promise with the best hope for individuals who will live through the desperate days ahead and the Babylonian exile; there is hope, but it is exclusively in Yahweh.

17:9 Verses 9-11 carry three wisdom sayings that call for the need to be constantly vigilant in Israel's relationship to Yahweh if they are to be like that tree planted by the waters. The first wisdom saying is a warning that "The heart is above all things most crafty" (v. 9).[240] The individual is represented here as the heart, which includes not just one's emotions but also the thoughts and will of that person. Such a heart is "deceptive," "devious," and "crafty." As such, it is "incurably sick" or "terminally ill." The constant struggle noted here is one where there is a battle going on to supplant the place that should be solely occupied by Yahweh. This craftiness is located

---

240. Novick suggests that "the verse speaks not of the heart's perversity but of its unfathomability." See T. Novick, "עקב הלב מכל ואנש הוא מי ידענו (Jeremiah 17:9)," *JBL* 123, no. 3 (Fall 2004): 531–35.

deep within the inner life of a person. So the question is this: "Who can understand it?" (v. 9c).

17:10 The second wisdom saying is the response of Yahweh in v. 10. His answer to the final question in v. 9 ("Who can understand [the heart of a person]?") is this: "I [Yahweh] search [that is, understand] the heart!" He is the One who searches the heart and examines the mind. The word rendered "mind" here literally means "kidneys" (כִּלְיָה), which is the seat of emotions/affections (cf. 11:20). This test is not to be understood legalistically, but relationally; what is tested here is the level of maturation in a person and the level of trust in one's relationship with God; what has it produced (v. 10c, d)? The test will result in a reward governed by the fruit produced by one's deeds (Matt 16:27; Rev 22:12).

17:11 The third wisdom saying is in v. 11 and is highlighted by the image of a partridge hen (or a "calling" bird), who hatches the eggs of other birds and raises the young as if they were her own. The general analogy that is made is that "so is he who gains riches (a **paronomasia**, עֹשֶׂה עֹשֶׁר, *ʿōśe ʿōšer*, "gain riches") unjustly. Midway in his life [his riches] will leave him; in the end he will prove to be a fool" (v. 11b–d). If a person enriches himself by means that are not fair, just, and right in the eyes of God, then he will have very little enjoyment of that wealth and ill-gotten gain; it will leave him prematurely, just like the partridge that sits on other birds' eggs but who is suddenly stripped of her expected family when the brood suddenly leaves with no thanks.[241]

The partridge makes its nest close to the ground and is therefore subject to attack by predators. The nest may also contain a large number of eggs, but not all of these eggs can be hatched because of the large number, so in like manner the rich may gather a great deal of wealth, but they too can just as quickly lose all they have worked for because of their greed and injustice in the way it was gained.

---

241. Sawyer suggests that here "the fool is compared to a brooding partridge, unaware of he dangers hanging over him and defenseless when disaster strikes." See J. F. A. Sawyer, "A Note on the Brooding Partridge in Jeremiah XVII 11," VT 28, no. 3 (July 1978): 324–29.

An Interlude of Praise (17:12–13)

17:12-13 A contrast is noted between the security that comes to those who know Yahweh versus the plight of those who turn away from Yahweh. God's throne is praised as a metaphor for God, with an emphasis on his rule and reign from that throne. One day Jerusalem will become the throne of God again (3:17). In the meantime, Yahweh himself will continue to be the hope of Israel (17:13a).

But for those who are turning away from Yahweh, they can expect little more than "shame" (v. 13b). They turn away from the "fountain of living waters" (v. 13d), which links this text back to the themes of vv. 5–8. Moreover, the cost for turning away from Yahweh is that they "will be written in the dust" (v. 13c); in place of having their names written in the divine "book of Life" (Pss 69:28; 87:6; 139:16), their names will be recorded "in the dust," a record that could easily be erased.

Where Is God's Judgment? (17:14–18)

This is the briefest of Jeremiah's many confessions, in which just one petition is addressed to God. There is no divine reply to this petition in this instance, however. Instead, the prophet presents himself as one who sincerely trusts in Yahweh and devoutly worships him. He, therefore, pleads for divine healing and deliverance.

Jeremiah calls for healing in the basic lament tradition of the Psalter. As in previous laments, Jeremiah protests his innocence; he does not think he deserves to be treated the way he has been regarded. Moreover, he has not shirked his duty by running away from it (v. 16a), nor has he desired that disastrous day to come on Judah.

17:14 The prophet is hurting, for his persecutors have been unremitting in making all sorts of charges against him. Nevertheless, he is still confident that when he calls for healing and deliverance, Yahweh will hear him and answer. The reason God will intervene is that Yahweh himself is "the One [he] praise[d]" (v. 14c).

17:15 The prophet is exasperated because the typical reaction from the people of Judah to his message is "Where is the word of Yahweh?" (v. 15b).

They take the mercy and long-suffering of God as evidence that he is not going to fulfill Jeremiah's judgment. They foolishly taunt Jeremiah, "Let it happen [or: be fulfilled]!" (v. 15c)—but they doubt it will be fulfilled! But as sure as one of the tests for a true prophet is that the word of the true prophet comes true (Deut 18:22), these sarcastic hecklers are toying with real disaster. This type of heckling might mean that this prophecy was given at the time of the 597 BC capture of Jerusalem, when its treasures were removed (2 Kgs 24:13), but this was by no means the end of things as yet—if only they knew and believed what was up ahead, they might have had the sense to turn back to God. But they listened to nothing and believed none of Jeremiah's words or warnings.

17:16 Jeremiah, on his part (וַאֲנִי, "but as for me"), has not "run away from being [God's] shepherd" (v. 16a). He knows his job is that of being a "shepherd" for the "flock" of the persons committed to his charge. He has indeed cared for them as a "shepherd should"; neither has he "desired the disastrous day," as some must have charged him with wishing (v. 16b), nor has he been the source of this prophecy, which came from God. He has no desire to wish ill on his people. What is more, "The utterance of [his] lips was before [God]" (v. 16c). Yahweh has heard all that he has spoken in the open to the people. So what is Judah's problem? What part of what he said do they not understand? Can't they hear? Shouldn't they repent and turn back to God before it is too late?

17:17 Jeremiah's request is that God might not be "a terror to [him]" (v. 17a), which God had warned, when he first called him, would only be true if he turned tail and was intimidated by the faces and words of his audience so that he toned down the message so it became more palatable (1:17). Instead, he claims God as his "refuge" (v. 17b) in a "day of trouble" (Pss 46:2; 91:9; 94:22).

17:18 Finally, in this brief "confession" of Jeremiah, he prays that those persecutors who are taunting him will soon realize their "shame" and "terror." Let them, not me, be broken, shattered, and faced with double destruction (v. 18).

The Meaning of the Sabbath (17:19-27)

Suddenly the prophet shifts into a prose style after using the poetic form in the previous verses. Frequently this section is dismissed by scholars as being a later insertion from late exilic times, for it seems to reflect the same theology as found in the postexilic book of Neh 13:15-22. But in fact, even Nehemiah had observed that Israel's forefathers had violated the Sabbath, just as they were doing in these later days (Neh 13:18). Moreover, the concerns about Sabbath keeping were expressed in the preexilic eighth-century prophets such as Amos (8:5) and Isaiah (58:13-14).

But why, asks Walter Brueggemann, would the whole future of Israel hang on Sabbath keeping, when there is so much emphasis in the prophets on idolatry (Brueggemann, 166-67)? How could it be that this one issue would be so determinative as a basis for bringing judgment? Would this not amount to the charge of legalism? Brueggemann answers wisely by noting that Sabbath keeping is not brought up here as an isolated matter but as one more indication of the people's adamant stubbornness (v. 23). In addition to this, Brueggemann goes on to show that the Sabbath was the most dramatic sign that Israel was honoring God's will. To violate the Sabbath was to violate God's will and distrust his gifts. However, Sabbath keeping is not the only sign of human faithfulness, yet Sabbath *breaking* is certainly a true sign of unfaithfulness (Brueggemann, 166-67).

17:19-20 Verse 19 begins with "This is what Yahweh said to me" (found only here and in 13:1; 25:15; and 27:2). The prophet is to go and stand in a prominent gate of the city, which was used by Judean kings (a gate of unknown location, unless it refers to a gate in the temple used by the kings and the people in general), and he is there to proclaim the word of Yahweh. He is to give his message in an area where the traffic is the heaviest but also one that addresses the royal class first of all with a promised blessing since the leaders were to be the exemplars to the rest of the people. This message is to be repeated at other gates as well (v. 19c).

17:21-23 The message is what had been taught in the Mosaic Decalogue, the fourth commandment: "Remember the Sabbath day by keeping it holy" (Exod 20:8); it had been set forth from the beginning in the creation narrative (Gen 2:2-3). The Sabbath was given as a sign of the covenant (Exod 31:13, 17), for it was a key indicator of the nation's spiritual commitment to Yahweh in first place. It would indicate whether the people put themselves, their economy, or something else first in their lives and lifestyle. There were two blatant breaches of this commandment detected as the people carried out their business: they carried loads on the Sabbath day, and they brought them through the gates of Jerusalem as they tried to work seven days, rather than six that had been set aside for business, in order to get ahead in the business world.

But Yahweh issues a strong caution: "Take care of your lives" (v. 21b). Infringing on the rights and prerogatives that belonged only to God is placing one's "soul" (נֶפֶשׁ) at risk. A change in this matter would require a change in an individual's lifestyle. Just as God had commanded their forefathers, so they too are now to obey (v. 22c). Unfortunately, these early fathers had paid no attention to God's command to keep this day as holy to Yahweh, but instead they too were stiff-necked and refused to listen or to respond to God's discipline (v. 23).

17:24-25 The Sabbath day is not to be viewed as a legalistic ritual that is impersonal and to be boringly observed in a routine way, but it is to be a source of spiritual blessing for those who exhibit personal loyalty to Yahweh (v. 24). But if there is a *royal* blessing promised in vv. 24-25, there also is a *civic* and external blessing in v. 25b—"This city will be inhabited forever." The only route by which the future of that generation can be assured is by covenantal obedience to God's commands.

17:26-27 But there also is a *national* blessing (v. 26), in which the whole population will come from every part of the land of Israel—the towns of Judah, the villages around Jerusalem, the land of Benjamin, the lowlands of the Shephelah, the hill country, and the Negev in the south—bringing sacrifices and offerings to Yahweh (v. 26). The sacrifices—offerings, sacrifices, grain/cereal offerings, incense, and thank offerings—all speak of a day when generosity and abundance will be evident as the people worship Yahweh. However, such times of blessing and revival have not yet arrived in this generation. Instead, three other works of God will be manifested:

1. God will set fire to the very gates where this command is given if there was no response.

2. This fire will consume the palaces and fortresses of Jerusalem.

3. This fire will not be quenched.

The choice is now up to the people.

Here is one more way Jeremiah indicates how autocratic and selfish the people have become: they refuse to acknowledge the day of rest that God built into the created order. True, in the list of days of feasting and days for festivals, our Lord had shown prophetically that the eighth day was also to be set aside as a new day of rest in honor of what our Lord would do in the future. But for the moment, Judah has run over God's command, as so many continue to do to this day. Sunday has now become the major and biggest day for shopping in the week. Doesn't anyone think that this excites the anger of God against those people and those nations who are so blatant in their reproach of him and his day for rest and worship?

AN OBJECT LESSON (18:1–20:18)

All the material in Jer 18-20 is closely linked together thematically around the prophet's visit to the potter's house in chapter 18 and the breaking of the potter's vessel in chapter 19. These chapters provide a sort of summary of Israel's deep involvement in sin and the resulting threatened judgment of God. But the prophet is to use this visit as an illustration from everyday life to see whether the truths he has been teaching can be caught any faster from his object lesson.

JEREMIAH AND THE POTTER (18:1–23)

TRANSLATION

1 The word that came to Jeremiah from Yahweh: **2** "Arise, Get going down to the house of the Potter, and there I will give you my message." **3** So I went down to the potter's house, and there I saw him busy working at the wheel. **4** When the vessel which he was making from clay was marred in his hands, he turned to make it again into another vessel as it seemed best in his eyes to make it.

5 Then the word of Yahweh came to me: **6** "Can I not do with you, O house of Israel, as this potter does?" declares Yahweh.[242] "Like clay in the hand of the potter, so are you in my hand, O house of Israel. **7** If at any time I announce that a nation or a kingdom is to be uprooted, torn down, and destroyed, **8** If that nation which I warned turns from its evil, then I will relent concerning the disaster I had planned to do to it.[243] **9** If at another time I announce that a nation or a kingdom will be built up and planted, **10** but if it does evil in my sight, and does not obey my voice, then I will relent of the good I had intended to do to it."

11 Now, therefore, say to the people of Judah and to those living in Jerusalem, This is what Yahweh says:[244] "I am forming against you a disaster and devising a plan against you. Turn now, each one of you, and reform your ways and your actions." **12** But they will reply,[245] "It's no use! We will follow our own plans; each one of us, as his own stubbornly wicked heart directs."

13 Therefore, this is what Yahweh says:

"Ask now among the nations, 'Who has ever heard anything like
      this?'
   An utterly horrible thing has been done by Virgin Israel.
14 Does the snow of Lebanon ever vanish from its rocky slopes?[246]
   Do its waters from afar ever dry up?
15 Yet my people have forgotten me;
   They burn incense to a fraud,
Which caused them to stumble[247] in their ways
   In the ancient paths,
And to walk on by-paths
   And on roads not built up.
16 Their land will be laid waste,

---

242. The expression נְאֻם־יְהוָה, "declares Yahweh," is absent in the LXX.

243. The expression אֲשֶׁר דִּבַּרְתִּי עָלָיו, "concerning which I have spoken," is missing both the LXX and the Syr.

244. The expression לֵאמֹר כֹּה אָמַר יְהוָה, "saying, thus says Yahweh," is missing in the LXX.

245. The LXX, Syr., and the Tg. read aor. καὶ εἶπαν, "and they said," where the MT reads an impf. with *waw*-conjunctive, וְאָמְרוּ, "and they will say."

246. The LXX reads μαστοί, "breasts," where the MT has שָׂדָי, "field."

247. The LXX reads καὶ ἀσθενήσουσιν, "and they weakened," where the MT has וַיַּכְשִׁלוּם, "they caused them to stumble."

An object of lasting scorn.

All who pass by will be appalled and shake their heads.

17 Like the wind from the east,

I will scatter them before the enemy,

I will show them[248] the back of my neck and not my face,

In the day of disaster."

18 Then they said, "Come, let us make plans against Jeremiah; for the teaching of the law by the priests will not be lost, nor will the counsel from the wise, nor the word from the prophets. So come, let us attack him with our tongues and pay no attention to what he says."

19 Listen to me, Yahweh,

And hear what my opponents are saying.[249]

20 Should good be repaid with bad?

Yet they have dug a pit for me.

Remember how I stood in your presence,

And spoke for their good advantage,

To turn away your wrath from them?

21 Therefore, give over their children to famine,

And hand them over to the sword.

Let their wives be childless and widowed,

Let their men be put to death,

Their young men be slain by the sword in battle.

22 Let a cry be heard from their houses,

When you suddenly bring marauders against them!

For they have dug a pit to capture me,

And have laid hidden traps for my feet.

23 But you know, O Yahweh,

All their plots to kill me.

Do not atone their crimes,

Do not blot out their sins from your face.

Let them be overthrown before you—

At the time of your anger deal with them.

---

248. The MT's qal אֶרְאֵם, "I will see them," should be read as hiphil "I will show them," like the LXX, the Vg., the Tg., and the Syr.

249. The LXX reads τῆς φωνῆς τοῦ δικαιώματός μου, "the voice of my righteousness/pleading," where the MT has לְקוֹל יְרִיבָי, "the voice of my opponents."

COMMENTARY

It is customary to divide this chapter into at least three units: vv. 1–12, 13–17, and 18–23. The book of Jeremiah is best known for vv. 1–12, with the symbolic action of the potter working on his potter's wheel and the message God gives to the prophet by means of this symbolism.

Visiting the Potter's House (18:1–12)

18:1-2 Once again, Jeremiah begins his message with the notice that what he has to say is from Yahweh. Urgently (*"Arise, Get going down"*) he is directed by Yahweh to head for the potter's house again, where God will give him a symbolic act as the basis for his next message. This command came to the prophet when he was on higher ground, as much of Israel was in general. But the place where the potter worked needed to be near water, for much water was used in making pottery, so he had to "go down" to some lower terrain.

18:3 As usual, Jeremiah is obedient to God's directives, so he goes down to the potter's house, where he finds the potter working on the wheel. The word "wheel" (אָבְנָיִם) is a dual form of "stone" (אֶבֶן), hence describing the two stones that made up his wheel. The potter can make both stones work in tandem by spinning the lower one with his foot; on the upper stone he throws down the clay to begin shaping the vessel. What sort of "pot" or "vessel" the potter was crafting this time is not mentioned, nor is it important to understand in order to grasp what is meant by the symbolic action used here.

18:4 The object-lesson-oracle God has intended occurs when the pot the potter is making is "spoiled/ ruined" (שָׁחַת). This exact verbal form is found elsewhere in the OT only in 13:7, where, in another object lesson, Jeremiah's once-new belt is found "useless" or "ruined" after it was hidden in the rocks near what some have thought to be the Euphrates River. It is important to note that the failure that developed in the clay pot is not a problem that originated with the potter—or by analogy in the object lesson, with God, who is the chief potter and Creator of the nation of Israel; the problem is with the clay: that is, the people! There may be grit in the clay, or perhaps the clay is too wet, or it is mixed with other intrusive elements.

The amazing thing is that the potter does not suddenly swipe the clay off the wheel with his hand, saying, "You can't get good clay anywhere these days," or something of that sort. No, he "turned [it]" (שׁוּב). Since "turning" sometimes refers to repentance in the OT, this word could serve here as a reminder of the need for repentance.

The pot the potter made was the one he wanted to come from his own hands and the one that would be "best" (יָשַׁר, "straight, upright") in his own eyes or opinion. This natural lesson provided the spiritual lesson, for vv. 5–12 go on to make what may have seemed to some to be a hidden teaching but actually is an open truth of the symbolic action.

18:5–10 Israel (mentioned twice in v. 6) is exactly like the clay in the potter's hands. God certainly is the "Potter" (יוֹצֵר, *yôṣēr*, a ptc. from the verb יָצַר, *yāṣar*, "to form, shape or mold"), and the same verb is used to describe his creating the world and also in his working with the nations. Moreover, the truth taught here is put in principial form already, for it is applied to any nation or any kingdom and not just to Israel or Judah. So God can do with Israel and the nations whatever he chooses, just as the potter can do as he chooses. This metaphor of the potter and the clay is used elsewhere in Scripture as well (Isa 45:9–10; 2 Cor 4:7).

In Scripture at large there is always a suppressed or an expressed "unless," or even a conditional "if," to all God's predictions, except those attached to his promised salvation in the Edenic protoevangelium of Gen 3:15, the Abrahamic covenant of Gen 12:1–3, the Davidic covenant of 2 Sam 7, the new covenant of Jer 31:31–34, the Noahic covenant with the seasons in Gen 8:21–22, and the promise of the new heavens and the new earth in Isa 65 and 66. All other promises or predictions of God's promised mercy depend on repentance, or judgment for failure to respond (for example, Lev 26:40–45; Ezek 18:5–29; Luke 13:3, 5; Rev 2:5, 16, 21–24; 3:3, 19–20), always directly teaching or implying that the blessing or the judgment will be called off if there is a reversal of the nation's actions resulting in sincere repentance. This passage is significant because it demonstrates that even when God gives a direct threat of judgment, even without mentioning explicitly any conditions, they are still implied from the whole teaching of Scripture and can be counted on to shape the outcome differently from the strong terms of the judgment deserved by the people. The reverse is also true in those cases where God has promised blessing to come to a nation or a people; those blessings will be withdrawn if God's people turned away from him.

It is the theology of this passage that makes the preaching of the prophets so real. This factor explains why the prophet Jonah was so reluctant to go and merely announce judgment on Nineveh, for if the people ever caught on and suddenly repented, then all bets on Nineveh's destruction were off, much to the chagrin of God's prophet, who sincerely wished for Nineveh's destruction after all the savage destruction he had seen them raise against Israel! Therefore, "If at any time" (רֶגַע, "a moment," cf. v. 7) in the past, present, or future, God announces doom or deliverance, should those receiving the message get careless and tend instead to rest on their laurels, or presume God will not stick to his threats, and there is no repentance, then this is a sure miscalculation of God and his word. Eli also learned this lesson the hard way as God had truly promised that "[his] house and [his] father's house would minister before [God] forever." But after his failure to act on God's word to him about the loose character of his sons, Yahweh declares: "Far be it from me! Those who honor me I will honor, but those who despise me will be ashamed" (1 Sam 2:30). Sometimes modern readers of the Bible mistakenly conclude that when things do not turn out the way that God had predicted through his prophets that God has lied or that he lacks the power to carry out his promise or his threats; however, these folks do not realize that what was spoken did come to pass, for that word is based on a holistic view of Scripture that sometimes involves unconditional promises for God and at other times conditional prophecies that call for a change on the part of the people.

18:11 The principles of the preceding life-analogy are now applied, for when Yahweh says in v. 11, "I am forming against you a disaster," the word "forming" or "shaping" is the same participial form of the verb use for the "potter" (יוֹצֵר), "one who forms, shapes, creates." Elsewhere in Jeremiah Yahweh is called the "fashioner" or "former" of everything (1:5; 10:16; 33:2; 51:19), or the One who breaks or destroys the pot (19:11).

Amazingly, there still is time to repent (v. 11c), if Judah turns away from her wicked ways and evil deeds; this, despite God havng been devising a plan against them. But there are no indications that Judah will turn back to Yahweh or repent.

18:12 Even more amazing is their awful reply: "It's no use!" (נוֹאָשׁ). The people of Judah defiantly take an obstinate posture and inform the prophet that no matter what he or Yahweh are going to say or do, they are not going to change their plans or the direction they are going in (v. 12). The fault, of course, is in the clay, but so what, they mock? Interestingly enough, there is even in this case an outright confession by the people that they have been stubborn and wicked as charged by God. This seems to be the only time in Jeremiah when the people describe themselves as having stubborn hearts. Instead, they are going to take their chances with what the false prophets were teaching.

Who Has Ever Heard Anything Like This? (18:13–17)

This section of poetry follows the prose section in vv. 1–12 and is intended to be the divine response to the stunning attitudes displayed in v. 12. This indicates that few if any in Judah believed the proposed divine judgment was going to come on the nation if they did not mend their ways and their actions. This is why v. 13 begins with the divine "Therefore," usually a signal of a coming judgment.

18:13 First, God asks a rhetorical question in v. 13: "Who has ever heard anything like this?" The question implies that no matter where you ask or search, you are never going to be able to find such impudence and arrogant stubbornness, even if you go to pagan nations. It is an altogether repulsive state of affairs: "Virgin Israel," the name that implied she was a covenant people of God, still living in Yahweh's land, in the household of her heavenly Father, dares to act and talk in such a shocking and defiant manner.[250] What do we think the assessment of the pagan nations would be as regards Judah and her actions and words to Yahweh? Since Judah has had such greater amount of teaching, one would think her answers and response would be more carefully framed!

---

250. Schmitt suggests that the expression "virgin of Israel" does not refer to the people of Israel collectively but rather to the capital cities, Samaria and Jerusalem. See J. J. Schmitt, "The Virgin of Israel: Referent and Use of the Phrase in Amos and Jeremiah," *CBQ* 53, no. 3 (July 1991): 365–87.

18:14 Two more rhetorical questions in v. 14 may help all to see how constant things were in the natural world compared to the inconstancy of Judah's faithfulness. "Does the snow of Lebanon ever vanish from its rocky slopes?" Why, the very name of "Lebanon" depicts the high mountains of that region as "white" and "snowy." It would be most unnatural for the snow and the water to disappear. But if that is so, would it not be just as unnatural for Israel to forget Yahweh, her lord?

That leads to a second question: "Do its waters from afar ever dry up?" To ask the question is to point to the unthinkable; just so unthinkable is Israel's brazen response to Yahweh. It is unnatural and totally uncalled for. Nature, then, is a lot more reliable and dependable than mortals made in the image of God. How could such vacillation be even contemplated for creatures made in God's image, who were beneficiaries of so great a covenant from God?

18:15 Judah acts as if she has totally forgotten who Yahweh is. Worse still, the people have taken up the practice of burning incense to outright "frauds," worthless idols that had caused them to stumble (v. 15). They no longer walk in the "ancient paths," but they have taken to walking on paths and trails that are off the main travel routes and going where there are no roads (v. 15d–f). They have made it hard for themselves when going God's way would have been loads easier. The old paths and tried roads of doctrine and teaching in Israel are now being substituted for outright fraudulent idolatry and false theology.[251]

18:16 The results of what the people are now bringing on themselves will be obvious to all who see the desolation of the land of Judah. In fact, it will make Judah an object of "lasting scorn" (v. 16). So appalled will all be who pass that way and observe what has happened that it will lead to pagans shaking their heads in astonishment.

---

251. For the metaphorical use of "way" see J. K. Aitken, "ΣΧΟΙΝΟΣ in the Septuagint," *VT* 50 (2000): 433–44.

18:17 This horrible state of affairs calls for another image from creation, the hot sirocco winds that come from the east (4:11; 13:24; 18:17; Hos 13:15), which is the direction from which Babylon will come. This dry, scorching wind that blew in off the desert would wreak havoc on the crops and all vegetation of the land. So will the invasion of Babylon have a similar effect. God will scatter Judah the way the sirocco wind scattered things.

Finally, God will show Judah his "back and not his face" (v. 17c). Previously, Israel had been described as turning their backs as a symbol of estrangement from God, but now Yahweh will turn his back on Judah, for this will take place in the "day of disaster." This will be like Hos 5:15, where Yahweh says he "will go back to [his] place until they admit their guilt."

"Let's Get Jeremiah" and the Prophet's Response (18:18–23)

18:18 The ringleaders of the anti-God movement in Judah now name Jeremiah as the real culprit for the first time (v. 18). There had been former plots to attack Jeremiah (11:18–23; 12:1–4; 15:10–21; 17:14–18), but now it seems as if the whole religious establishment is in one accord against him. "Come, let us make plans against Jeremiah," they enjoin one another (using a Heb. coh. expression of self-encouragement). Even though the speakers are not identified, the absence of kings and that the presence of priests, the wise, and the prophets are pointed out point to a religious clique that has had enough and wants Jeremiah to be gone and done with.

The three named groups involved in this personal coup claim the Torah, the wisdom writings, and the prophetic words of Scripture as their authority. But in so doing, this attack is not solely on Jeremiah; it is also an attack on God (v. 12). The plots on the life of the prophet Jeremiah (v. 18) have so coalesced that the enemies of the prophet are now also the enemies of God.

That they want Jeremiah dead is not directly stated, for their first line of attack will be to attack him with their tongues (v. 18d).[252] They will use slanderous speech and malicious and mendacious clap-trap to reduce him in the eyes of the public. They will conduct a massive propaganda

---

252. Foreman suggests that the conspiracy is actually to strike Jeremiah's tongue, since "cutting out an individual's tongue was a familiar form of punishment in the ANE." See B. A. Foreman, "Strike the Tongue: Silencing the Prophet in Jeremiah 18:18b," *VT* 59, no. 4 (2009): 653–57.

program that will discredit Jeremiah and lead to posting false charges against him. But the goal is to get the citizens of Jerusalem to "pay no attention to what he says" (v. 18e).

18:19 This sinister plot against Jeremiah leads the prophet to make another lament to God, or another of what are usually called the "confessions of Jeremiah." If his fellow citizens are not going to listen to him, then Jeremiah turns to Yahweh, who has called him in the first place, for Jeremiah knows that God that listen to him (v. 19). The reason God should act on Jeremiah's behalf is that he has surely heard what Jeremiah's accusers are saying (v. 19b). When God hears, the case has landed in the hands of the Judge of the whole universe. There is where justice will be served.

18:20 The prophet's question to God is direct: "Should good be repaid with bad?" (v. 20a). Here Jeremiah repeats what the psalmist asks in Pss 35:12; 38:20; 109:5. Moreover, the people have sought to entrap him by digging a pit for him (vv. 20b, 22; Ps 57:6; 119:85; 140:1-5), as if he is some sort of vicious beast. This metaphor is drawn from the life of hunters, who would dig a hole in the ground and cover it over with camouflage so that animals would fall into the pit and be slain (Ps 7:16). Jeremiah asks Yahweh, will all the good I have done on behalf of my opponents be rewarded with such evil?

He begs Yahweh to remember how he had stood in God's presence, like a servant must stand in the royal court in the presence of a king, waiting for his orders. The wrath Jeremiah announced to the people was not one of his ideas; he had delivered the very words from God, but now they are attributing the message solely to Jeremiah (v. 20c-e). In fact, Jeremiah's aim has been to avert the wrath of God by calling his fellow citizens to repentance and a return to Yahweh.

18:21-22 Whereas Jeremiah had interceded in prayer for the people previously, his outlook has now changed. With harsh words that began with an introductory "Therefore" (v. 21a), he calls for famine, sword, and pestilence on the people, the very same language God used earlier against Judah (14:12; 15:2). The promised disaster will come to four groups:

1. their children,

2. their wives,

3. their men, and

4. their young men (v. 21a–e).

Some commentators, such as Calvin (2:423), thought the prophet had been driven through his indignation to express imprecations that were not consistent with what Christ taught in other parts of Scripture (for example, about loving those who persecute us); these commentators contend that it would have been better if nothing like this had been said by Jeremiah. But to condemn Jeremiah is to condemn God. Not only is the prophet justified in being angry, but he has by now realized that all that could be done or said was now ended as far as this audience was concerned, for this people is not going to change. Instead, the prophet merely urges God to fulfill his own words.

18:23 The word "atone" (כַּפֵּר, v. 23c) is used only here in Jeremiah. This word does not mean "to cover" one's sins, as though one "covers up" something bad, which has too often wrongly been the explanation used by evangelicals. This is based on connecting the verbal root with its use in Gen 6–8, where the ark was "covered" and smeared with pitch. Instead the word means "to ransom or to atone for by a substitute." This verb is paralleled by the verb "to wipe" or "to blot out" their sins (מְחֵה) from God's face (v. 23d). Jeremiah is not saying that God's grace will merely overlook their sins and forgive them completely, since repentance does not seem to be forthcoming! Rather, what he is saying is that without any repentance and turning back to God, may Yahweh provide no escape from the consequences of their sin. In this case, they must be "overthrown" and dealt with according to the justice and anger of God.

When the passage about the potter and the clay is read, many almost automatically think of the words to the hymn written by Adelaide Pollard (1862–1934) called "Have Thine Own Way, Lord." While its message is memorable and fits this passage to a degree, the teaching should not be limited to the lesson that God is the sovereign potter and we are the clay as mortals, for, as we have seen, its teaching goes beyond this individualizing trend.

The clay in Jeremiah's teaching actually stands for the nation Judah and the nations of the earth. Nevertheless, the words point to valuable aspects of the teaching found here. Pollard's hymn goes this way:

> Have thine own way, Lord! Have thine own way!
> Thou art the potter; I am the clay.
> Mold me and make me after they will,
> While I am waiting, yielded and still.
> Have thine own way, Lord! Have thine own way!
> Hold o'er my being absolute sway!
> Fill with thy Spirit till all shall see
> Christ only, always, living in me!

While God is still calling, there is hope if we, our nation, and the other nations of the world turn around and reverse our direction and repent of all our sin individually and corporately. Notice that the Scripture already put this whole teaching in the form of a principle, for it does not address it solely to Israel or Judah. It is addressed to any nation. We must repent if we expect any kind of change to come from God.

THE SHATTERED JAR (19:1–20:6)

TRANSLATION

1 This is what Yahweh says,[253] "Go and buy a potter's earthenware jug. Take along some of the elders of[254] the people and some of the senior priests. **2** Go out to the Valley of Ben-Hinnom,[255] which is near the entrance of the Potsherd Gate, and there proclaim the words that I speak unto you." **3** Hear the word of Yahweh, O kings of Judah[256] and inhabitants of Jerusalem! "This is what Yahweh of Hosts, the God of Israel says, Lo, I am going to bring a calamity on this place that will make the ears of all who hear it ring— **4** because they have forsaken me, and profaned[257] this place by burning

---

253. The LXX adds πρός με, "to me," after "This is what Yahweh says."

254. The LXX omits וּמִזְּקְנֵי, "the elders of."

255. Instead of the MT's אֶל־גֵּיא בֶן־הִנֹּם, "to the Valley of Ben-Hinnom," the LXX has εἰς τὸ πολυάνδριον υἱῶν τῶν τέκνων αὐτῶν, "to the burial place of the sons of their children."

256. The LXX adds καὶ ἄνδρες Ιουδα, "and men of Juda," after "kings of Judah."

257. Lit. "to treat as foreign."

sacrifices in it to gods that neither they nor their fathers nor the kings of Judah ever knew, and they have filled this place with the blood of the innocent. **5** They have built the high places of Baal in order to burn their sons in the fire as burnt offerings to Baal—something I did not command or mention, nor did it come to my mind. **6** Therefore, behold the days are coming," says Yahweh, "when people will no longer call this place Topheth, or the Valley of Ben-Hinnom, but the Valley of Slaughter. **7** I will ruin the plans of Judah and Jerusalem in this place. I will cause them to fall by the sword before their foes, at the hand of those who seek their lives, and I will give their carcasses as food to the birds of the air and the beasts of the earth. **8** I will make this city such a horrible and shocking sight that all who pass by will shutter and scoff because of all its wounds. **9** I will make them eat the flesh of their own sons and the flesh of their daughters, and they will eat each other's flesh during the pressure of the siege to which their enemies and those who seek their lives will subject them."[258]

10 Then break the jar in the presence of the men who have come with you. **11** Say to them, "This is what Yahweh of Hosts has said, 'I will break this nation and this city just as this potter's jar is broken in pieces and cannot be repaired. They will bury again in Topheth until there is no room left. **12** This is what I will do to this place and to those who live here, says Yahweh. I will make this city like Topheth. **13** The houses in Jerusalem and the houses of the kings of Judah will be defiled—like the place of Topheth—all the houses where they burn incense on the roofs to all the starry heavens and poured out drink offerings to other gods.'"

14 Jeremiah then returned from Topheth, where Yahweh had sent him to prophesy, and he stood in the court of Yahweh's house and said to all the people, **15** This is what Yahweh of Hosts, the God of Israel, says, "Behold, I am going to bring on this city and the villages around it[259] every disaster I pronounced against them, because they were stiff-necked and would not listen to my words."

20:1 When the priest Pashhur, son of Immer, the chief overseer in the house of Yahweh, heard Jeremiah prophesying these things, **2** Pashhur

---

258. The LXX omits the last phrase וּמְבַקְשֵׁי נַפְשָׁם, "and the ones seeking their lives."

259. The LXX reads only καὶ ἐπὶ τὰς κώμας, "and its villages," instead of "on this city and the villages."

had Jeremiah the prophet beaten[260] and put in stocks at the upper gate of Benjamin[261] at Yahweh's temple. **3** The next day,[262] when Pashhur released Jeremiah from the stocks, Jeremiah said to him, "Yahweh did not call your name Pashhur, but 'Terror on all Sides/ All around.'[263] **4** For this is what Yahweh says, 'I will make you a terror to yourself and to all those loving you; with your own eyes you will see them fall by the sword of their enemies. I will hand all Judah over to the king of Babylon, who will exile them to Babylon or put them to the sword. **5** I will hand over to their enemies all the wealth of this city—all its products,[264] all its valuables, all the treasures of the kings of Judah. They will take it away as plunder and carry it off[265] to Babylon. **6** And you, Pashhur,[266] and all who live in your house, will go into exile to Babylon. There you will die and there you will be buried, you and all your friends, to whom you have prophesied lies.'"

COMMENTARY

Because Pashhur is described as the "chief officer" of the temple, whereas in 29:26 another person was named as holding this post, Zephaniah, son of Masseiah, this passage no doubt dates from an earlier period in the life of the prophet. Jeremiah 29 is dated to after the 597 BC invasion by Nebuchadnezzar, so most readers of this text place the events of chapter 19 in the middle of Jehoiakim's reign. At any rate, Jeremiah's treatment in 20:2 seems to be the precursor of his being formally banned from entering the temple precincts in 36:5. This suggests a date of around 605/604 BC.

Despite the fact that by now the populace seems to be growing tired of Jeremiah and his prophecies (cf. 18:18), he appears to have no trouble gathering a crowd of influential people to accompany him as he buys a clay jar from the potter and take it along to the Valley of Ben-Hinnom, near the entrance of the Potsherd Gate, to illustrate what he is going to say (v. 2).

---

260. The LXX simply has καὶ ἐπάταξεν αὐτόν, "he struck him," instead of וַיַּכֶּה פַּשְׁחוּר, "Pashhur struck him."

261. The LXX has οἴκου ἀποτεταγμένου τοῦ ὑπερῴου, "the upper house that was set apart," for MT's בְּשַׁעַר בִּנְיָמִן הָעֶלְיוֹן, "the upper Benjamin Gate."

262. The LXX omits the opening phrase וַיְהִי מִמָּחֳרָת, "the next day."

263. The LXX reads μέτοικον, "exile," in place of אִם־מָגוֹר מִסָּבִיב, "terror on every side."

264. The LXX omits "all its gains/products."

265. The LXX omits וּבְזָזוּם וּלְקָחוּם, "who will plunder and seize them."

266. The LXX omits Pashhur's name.

To be sure, the impact Jeremiah and Yahweh desire to have on this elite group involves another way to call for repentance and a change of heart from his audience. It is not a matter of magic, as if some type of supernatural powers are wielded by breaking the jar, by calling for a curse on one's enemies. Rather, this mode of teaching is used because of the effects it will have on those viewing the suddenness and completeness of the destruction of the clay pottery, which will be how the nation will suddenly be smashed as well. The spoken message together with the visual image will clarify whatever up to this point in his speaking may have been missed or is not yet understood.

Another change that has occurred between chapters 18 and 19 is that, in the symbolic action of chapter 18, the clay is still pliable and worthy of being reshaped by the potter, but by now the vessel has been completed and baked hard in the oven; that particular piece can only be smashed to pieces without being restored (19:10).

Jerusalem Will Be Broken in Pieces Like Shattered Pottery (19:1–9)

Another symbolic action is presented in Jer 19:1–15. It is closely tied to chapter 18, for it continues the pottery theme, though this time the potter's jar is broken beyond repair (vv. 10–11). Following this symbolic action, three announcements of judgment are introduced, which are followed by Jeremiah's prosecution by the priest Pashhur, son of Immer (2:1–6).

19:1 The earthenware jug (בַקְבֻּק, *baqbuq*; only here and in 1 Kgs 14:3) is made of clay, as evidenced in its capability of being broken, and ties in with the clay vessel in chapter 18. Specifically, this type of "jar" was four to ten inches high, with a narrow neck, a ring-burnished decanter type of vessel that functioned as a carafe. It had a heavy body with a handle attached to its neck and rim. Because of its narrow neck, it emitted a gurgling sound when water was poured from it. Thus, on the basis of the onomatopoeia (the use of a word whose sounds suggests its sense), the Heb. name for this jar (בַקְבֻּק, *baqbuq*) literally means "the gurgling vessel."[267] Note that later, in v. 7, the word "I will ruin" (בַּקֹּתִי, *baqqōtî*), is a wordplay on the name for

---

267. See the illustration in P. J. King, *Jeremiah: An Archaeological Companion* (Louisville: Westminster John Knox, 1993), 172.

the jar. For Jeremiah to smash this costly vessel typifies what will happen to Jerusalem. Yahweh will destroy the city and its environs in Judah.

19:2 The prophet is to take the jar and "go out to the valley of Ben-Hinnom, which is near the entrance of the Potsherd Gate [west side of Jerusalem]" (v. 2). The west side of Jerusalem is where all of the city's rubbish is dumped, but as for the actual location of the "Potsherd Gate," it is as yet unknown. The Jewish Tg. identifies it with the "Dung Gate," but while that gate is known from Neh 2:13; 3:13–14; 12:31, its location is also otherwise unknown as yet. Potsherds were broken pieces of pottery, so the connection with rubbish is easily understood.

19:3 The reason for the pl. form of "kings" in v. 3 is that kings from the times of Manasseh and Ahaz were part of what went on in this valley, and thus multiple kings contributed to the problem. In an attempt to get Judah's full attention, the prophet uses the full name of God: "Yahweh of Hosts, the God of Israel" (v. 3). There is no call for repentance or any offer of mercy or grace: the smashing of the jar (v. 10) will bring a certain finality to this prolonged invitation to the nation to turn back to God. Instead, the coming disaster is so certain that it will produce effects of a proverbial size: an involuntary physiological reaction to this shocking news. It will have an effect on all ears like that of the ringing of bells or sounding of the cymbals (v. 3d). Something momentous is about to happen!

The judgment was imminent; God is about to bring disaster (מֵבִיא, imminent fut. ptc.) on "this place" (v. 3c). The place mentioned is not as clear, for the phrase "this place" (הַמָּקוֹם הַזֶּה), when used in Scripture, usually means the sacred precincts, or even the city of Jerusalem, but the continued reference to "this place" in vv. 4 and 6 points in this case to the valley of Ben-Hinnom.

19:4 The reasons for this threatened judgment are once again given in v. 4. First, there has been a disregard for the covenant between God and Judah; they have just plain "forsaken" (עָזַב) Yahweh. Second, they have "profaned this place" (v. 4b). The Heb. word for "profaned" (נִכֵּר) means "to act or treat as something foreign"; therefore, they "profaned" the place by treating it as something not dedicated to Yahweh, making it unacceptable in Yahweh's eyes. Third, they had "burned sacrifices to a god that they did not know, neither they nor their fathers, nor the kings of Judah" (v. 4d). Fourth, "they [had] filled this place with the blood of the innocent" ones (v. 4e). Here again, everything depends on what "this place" means, for if it is taken to mean Jerusalem and the land of Judah as a whole, then the charge is against the way they have oppressed the poor and afflicted the widow and the orphan. But since child sacrifice is mentioned in the next verse (v. 5), then it is best to identify "this place" as the valley of Ben-Hinnom.

19:5 Usually the "high places" (v. 5a) were the sacred sites under a tree on a hill or an elevated spot in the land. The charge of vv. 5-6 repeats the charges leveled in 7:31-32. They were guilty of the disgusting practice of presenting their children to a foreign god, usually Molech, and having the child totally consumed in the fire, which was built within the false god's belly. The child would be presented on the outstretched arms of the molten deity, which was built so that the child would roll down the arms and into the mouth of this depiction of a foreign deity, where a fire had been built to consume the child! God had solemnly warned against Molech worship (Lev 18:21; 20:2-5; 2 Kgs 23:10). This form of disobedience was so outrageous and so inconceivable that God strictly commanded them to avoid such an abomination. The people of Judah have so greatly lost their way that now they are engaging in evil that was clearly out of the limits of what one could even imagine as evil, much less do!

19:6 All of this calls for divine sentencing in vv. 6-9. The day is soon to arrive when the Valley of Ben-Hinnom will no longer be known by that name, or even its other name, "Topheth," but it will be called "the Valley of Slaughter." As in 7:31, the name "Topheth" is an insult that disparages the place by associating it with shame (see "Excursus: Topheth"). In this chapter Topheth occurs a total of five times out of eight in the whole OT (vv. 6, 11-14). This frequency indicates that this was a major problem during Jeremiah's days. More trust was put in Topheth than in Yahweh.

19:7-9 God will punish Judah by "ruining" (see above for the word play on *baqbuq*) their "plans" or "counsel" (עֵצָה). Then the prophet again repeats his earlier threats that the casualties of war will be huge, and many carcasses will be left unburied (v. 7) as food for the birds of the air and the beasts of the earth (7:32–8:2; 14:16; 16:4). In fact, so overwhelming will be the devastation of the city that it will be talked about for years to come (v. 8). The curse described in v. 9 is gruesome, to say the least, yet it is almost a verbatim repetition of the covenantal curses in Deut 28:53, where the siege will be so severe that the people will take to eating their own children's flesh in order to stay alive (Deut 28:55, 57). Yahweh himself takes responsibility for this despicable act: "I will cause them to eat … " (הַאֲכַלְתִּים). How awful sin is: One day they are offering their children in the fires of Molech, the next they are eating their children! There are related images of this same type of scene in Isa 49:26 and Zech 11:9b.[268]

The Smashing of the Jar (19:10–13)

19:10–12 Now, in front of the delegation that went along with Jeremiah, God commands the prophet to break the jar into pieces (v. 10). While this is a symbolic action, it is not a pretend game or playacting; it is a serious word of the destruction that will fall on the nation if there is no turning back to God (v. 10).[269] Jeremiah is to follow this action with an explanation: God will "break this nation" (v. 11) and "this city" "just as this potter's jar is smashed and cannot be repaired." The Heb. word "to make whole, to heal" (לְהֵרָפֵה)[270] means "to be repaired" and brings to mind Deut 28:27, 35, where that text mentions the "incurable" nature of the covenant curse. The fact that this sin-sickness cannot be "cured" does not mean that there are no future possibilities for a restoration to God's favor again. This word of judgment is for the present generation; there will be no reversals for those who have failed to respond so frequently to the message currently being delivered, but the promises of God made to the patriarchs and others about his choice of the nation, his gift of the seed that will bring salvation, his gift of the land, and especially his gift of the gospel (that is, that in your seed all the nations of the earth will be blessed), are all irrevocable (Rom 11:29). The

---

268. See Josephus's account of the same problem, only at a much later date, in *J.W.* 6.201–13.

269. Gosse suggests that v. 8 must be read in connection with vv. 10–11. Furthermore, he sees a close relationship with chap. 36. See B. Gosse, "The Masoretic Redaction of Jeremiah: An Explanation," *JSOT* 77 (1998): 75–80.

270. The word is spelled here defectively with a final *heh* (ה) instead of a final *aleph* (א).

land of Judah and the population of that nation will become like Topheth, a place of death and defilement (vv. 11–12).[271]

19:13 As the chapter began, so now this section closes with the kings of Judah and the people of Jerusalem (vv. 3, 13). Here, however, the prophet gives us even greater reason to see why God is bringing such a judgment on these groups. On top of all the flat roofs in Jerusalem the people have burned incense to the gods and goddesses of the starry hosts of heaven, and there they have poured out drink offerings to other gods (v. 13). These were gods they did not even know previously, yet they receive the worship and service of these stupid persons.

The Temple Sermon (19:14–15)

19:14 After Jeremiah has completed all that God had told him to do in Topheth's valley, he returns to the Temple (v. 14) and gives a summary of the message he had given in the Hinnom Valley. Just as God had commanded him to go and prophesy in the temple in 7:1 and 26:1–2, so he must have been told to do so here, even though there is not an explicit command to that effect.

19:15 In v. 15 we are given a summary of the message of vv. 1–13, which effectively encapsulates the challenge of the first eighteen chapters of this book. Once again the prophet uses a full designation of God's name, and thus the divine authority stands behind what he says. Jerusalem and its suburbs are to experience the threatened disaster and every other disaster God has pronounced against them (v. 15b). All this could have been avoided if only Judah would have humbled herself (2 Chr 7:14) and turned back to Yahweh. But the people of Judah continue to be "stiff-necked and would not listen" (v. 15d).

---

271. Schiller suggests that Topheth was the original place of the prophet's symbolic action. See J. Schiller, "Jeremia und das Tofet: Bemerkungen zur grammatischen Interpretation von Jer 19,11–12," *ZAW* 123, no. 1 (2011): 108–12.

Terror on Every Side (20:1-6)

20:1 Pashhur, son of Immer (v. 1), is not one of the priestly elders in the temple, but he seems to be the head of something like the temple police. The name Pashhur, according to Philip King, is probably of Egyptian origin, meaning "son of Horus," an Egyptian god, but the name was fairly common, as attested by its use elsewhere in Scripture, including another of the same name that King Zedekiah sends to inquire of Yahweh (Jer 21:1-2), specifically Pashhur son of Malchiah.[272] Pashhur's contemporaries may have taken the meaning of his name from Aramiac sources to mean "joy all around," but this may reflect popular ways of regarding the name rather than strict etymology (popularization often carried the greater weight anyhow).

20:2 Pashhur, as "chief," takes it on himself to have Jeremiah "beaten" or "struck" (v. 2a) for what he said. There is no indication Pashhur had been in the elite group that accompanied Jeremiah to Topheth, but he probably heard his temple sermon (19:15), and that was enough for him. Since Jeremiah's message was not one of happiness and smooth sailing ahead, his words were greeted with hostility and anger.

Then Pashhur puts Jeremiah into "the stocks" (מַהְפֶּכֶת). The prophet is put into stocks that hold his hands, feet, and neck in a contorted position, causing him pain. This stock is at the "Upper Gate of Benjamin" (v. 2c), somewhere in the northeastern sector, in the direction of the tribe of Benjamin.

20:3-5 Pashhur releases Jeremiah the next day (v. 3), but by then he has suffered a good deal of humiliation and discomfort, not to mention his need to relieve himself. Jeremiah renames Pashhur as "Magor Missabib," "Terror on Every Side."[273] The literal Aramaic meaning of Pashhur's name is "fruitful all around";[274] thus Jeremiah successfully distorts his name from "Fruitful All around" to "Terror All Around," from something delightful to

---

272. This later Pashhur, son of Malchiah, and Gedaliah, son of Pashhur, together imprisoned Jeremiah in a cistern (Jer 38:1-6). Yet another Pashhur is found in Ezra 2:38. Also, in the ostraca found in the Arad sanctuary, there is the name of Pashhur as well. See King, *Jeremiah*, 58.

273. This name, "Terror on Every Side" appears four more times in Jeremiah (6:25; 20:10; 46:5; 49:25; cf. Psa 31:13).

274. Pashhur likely comes from the Aramaic "fruitful" (*pash*) and "surrounding" (*sehor*).

something terrible.[275] Pashhur will be an eyewitness to Yahweh's handing over Judah to the king of Babylon, who is here mentioned by name for the first time (v. 4). Previously, the foe was only mentioned as coming from the north (1:14), but that is the direction from which all trouble had to come, for no one could survive crossing the desert straight out of the east, or the south, as an attacking army. To this hostile army the wealth of Jerusalem and all its products will be turned over (v. 5).

20:6 If Pashhur thought that will not be too bad, v. 6 has even more damaging news for that man and his family. "All who [lived] in [his] house [would] go into exile to Babylon. There [Pashhur would] die and ... be buried" (v. 6), along with all his friends to whom he had "prophesied lies" (v. 6c). Pashhur had preached "lies" (בַּשֶּׁקֶר, "falsely"). He is one of those prophets who has spoken fair words about Judah's destiny, and he has claimed no harm would come their way (cf. 7:4, 8). A truly harrowing experience awaits the city in the days to come as they refuse to turn back to God.

It does not matter that Pashhur held a position of influence; the point is that he has taken Jeremiah as being in his own sphere of authority and beat him for proclaiming the word of the Lord. We should not look lightly on those who belittle or try to disgrace God's servants as they reject his word. Those who deny the inscripturated word of God in our day and mock those who try to faithfully teach are in for a rough time from the Lord of the word. They bring disgrace on the whole nation!

JEREMIAH'S FINAL LAMENT (20:7-18)

TRANSLATION

> **7** You deceived me, O Yahweh, and I let you deceive [me],
>   you overpowered me and prevailed.

---

275. Christensen argues that Jeremiah is saying that Pashhur's name is a false prophecy and that his opponent's name is "from every point of view." See D. L. Christensen, "'Terror on Every Side' in Jeremiah," *JBL* 92, no. 4 (1973): 498-502. Holladay argues that "the whole matter is intended by Jeremiah as an overturning of the tradition of God's renaming of Abram as Abraham and Jacob as Israel ... , wherein God promises both to bring fertility and to provide a land, Canaan, in which to sojourn." See W. L. Holladay, "Covenant with the Patriarchs Overturned: Jeremiah's Intention in 'Terror on Every Side' (Jer. 20:1-6)," *JBL* 91, no. 3 (September 1972): 305-20.

I have become the laughingstock all the time;
  All of them[276] make fun of me.
8 Whenever I speak, I cry out,[277]
  "Violence and destruction" is what I shout,
Because the word of Yahweh has brought me
  Insults and scorn all the day long.
9 But if I say, "I will not mention him,
  Or speak any more in his name,"
His word is in my heart[278] like a blazing fire,
  [A fire] shut up in my bones.
I am tired of holding it in;
  I cannot [contain it].
10 I hear many whispering,
  "Terror[279] on every side!
  Denounce him! Let's denounce him!"
Every man of peace
  Is waiting for me to stumble, saying,
"Perhaps he will be deceived;
  Then we will prevail over him
  And take our revenge on him."
11 But Yahweh is with me like a powerful warrior;
  So my pursuers will stumble[280] and not prevail.
They will be thoroughly disgraced, for they will not succeed;
  Their dishonor will never be forgotten.
12 O Yahweh of Hosts, you who examine the righteous,
  And probe the heart and the mind,
Let me see your vengeance on them,
  For I have committed my cause to you.
13 Sing to Yahweh!

---

276. The LXX has πᾶσαν ἡμέραν, "continually," where the MT has כֻּלֹּה, "everyone."

277. The LXX has ὅτι πικρῷ λόγῳ μου γελάσομαι, "for I will laugh because of my bitter speech," where the MT has כִּי־מִדֵּי אֲדַבֵּר אֶזְעָק, "for when I speak, I cry out."

278. The LXX omits בְּלִבִּי, "in my heart."

279. The LXX has συναθροιζομένων κυκλόθεν, "gathering round," for the MT's מָגוֹר, "terror."

280. The LXX reads very differently from the MT. Where the LXX has ἐδίωξαν καὶ νοῆσαι οὐκ ἠδύναντο, "they persecuted but they could not perceive," the MT has רֹדְפַי יִכָּשְׁלוּ, "my persecutors will stumble."

Give praise to Yahweh!
For he delivers the life of the needy,
From the hands of the wicked.

14 Cursed be the day I was born!
May the day my mother bore me not be blessed!

15 Cursed be the man who brought to my father the news, saying:
"It's a boy, you've got a son"
(How glad it made him).

16 May that man be like the towns,[281]
Yahweh overthrew without pity.
May he hear a cry for help in the morning,
A battle cry at noon.

17 For he did not kill me in the womb,
With my mother as my grave—
Her womb pregnant forever.

18 Why did I come forth from the womb,
To see trouble and grief,
And end my days in shame?

COMMENTARY

Jeremiah concludes his laments with two more so-called confessions (vv. 7-12, 14-18). Some worry about v. 13 being interruptive because it sounds the note of praise. However, often in laments there is the certainty of being heard by God, so praise language is also a natural overflow of the emotions.

This section is probably best placed on the eve of his public beating and humiliation in the stocks at the hand of Pashhur, the chief officer of the priests (vv. 1-6). The total lament of vv. 7-18 is best divided between v. 13 and v. 14. Verses 7-13 describe his first complaint, then this is followed by a lament for his whole life (vv. 14-18). Thus we move from a view of Jeremiah's public life in 20:1-6 now to a view of his private life (20:7-18). Despite the deep sorrow of his soul, he does not resort to a casting off of all restraint, such as indulging in alcohol or consorting with prostitutes or anything like that; instead, he goes to Yahweh.

---

281. The LXX adds ἐν θυμῷ, "in wrath," before "overthrew without pity."

Jeremiah's First Complaint (20:7–13)

The tone and content of his laments or confessions grow in intensity until we reach these final ones. Previous confessions can be seen in Jer 11:18–23; 12:1–6; 15:10–11, 15–21; 17:14–18; 18:19–23. Here in 20:7–13 it appears that Jeremiah is coming close to the breaking point.

20:7 In Jeremiah's complaint he accuses Yahweh of three things: "deceiving" (piel of פָּתָה), "overthrowing" (חָזַק), and "prevailing" (יָכֹל). The first accusation, the act of "deceiving," comes from a verb that is used elsewhere of a man enticing a woman into having sex with him, thus he "seduces" her in a rape.[282] This seems to be a strange rendering for this context, for how could God deceive or entice Jeremiah, when the nature of his mission was laid out for him in the very beginning (Jer 1)? Perhaps Jeremiah felt that he was "coerced into being a prophet" (cf. NET translation). Or perhaps Jeremiah is simply speaking out of intense emotion and saying what he feels even though he knows it is not reality.

20:8 The prophet continues to cry out about "violence and destruction" (v. 8), which he sounded so frequently that some must have called him "Old Two-Pointer," for his two points constantly were "violence and destruction."

20:9 Jeremiah then confesses his inability to stop speaking the word of God (v. 9). It is not as if this is something he could stop; he feels compelled to speak out on behalf of Yahweh. If the prophet thought that the solution to his problem was to not mention Yahweh's name or speak any longer about him, he was wrong, for he still feels a divine "must" to his speaking. He cannot keep the word of God bottled up inside himself, for God's word is inside his heart and mind like "a blazing fire" (v. 9c). It is no use pretending he could resign; he just cannot do it! The word of God sets a blaze going on the inside of his being that was beyond containment or holding back (v. 9e–f). Jeremiah is the only prophet to liken the word of God to

---

282. Snyman recommends that the exegete differentiate between the uses of *pth* and *ykl* in vv. 7 and 10. He suggests that "it seems better to distinguish between a divine (vv. 7–9) and a human (v. 10) side in the interpretation of this passage." S. D. Snyman, "A Note on PTH and YKL in Jeremiah XX 7–13," *VT* 48, no. 4 (1998): 559–63.

"fire" (5:14; 23:29). Surely this demonstrates that the message he brought was not of his own devising, but it was a word from God, no matter how difficult it was for his hearers to receive. God's word is an unquenchable and uncontainable fire in his bones; that is why it weighs so heavily on him and why he cannot hold it in.

20:10 There is another problem Jeremiah has to contend with: a "whispering campaign" (v. 10a). The people of Judah sarcastically repeat his message, but they turn around the new name Jeremiah had given to Pashhur, and now they use it to summarize the prophet's message: "Terror on every side" (v. 10b). Such actions of sinful people to God's faithful are not new; in Ps 31:13, David had complained:

> For I hear the slander of many;
> There is terror on every side;
> They conspire against me
> And plot to take my life.

This is precisely the experience of Jeremiah as well. There is a conspiracy against Jeremiah; they want "to get him." By turning around the name Jeremiah had given to Pashhur, "Terror on every side," they are rebuking Jeremiah for the alleged failure of his prophecies to come true—all Jeremiah can see, they yell, is terror here and terror there, and destruction will be the result! Therefore, these "fairweather friends" (lit. "every man of my peace") denounce him, hoping "perhaps he will be deceived" (v. 10f); then they can "prevail over him and take [their] revenge on him" (v. 10g–h). Poor Jeremiah is left to ask himself, "Why?" Where did this vengeful spirit come from? What has he done to attract it?

20:11 But who are these people in comparison to Yahweh, who has promised to be "with" this prophet, for is not God a powerful warrior (v. 11a)? If Yahweh can prevail over Jeremiah (v. 7), can he not also prevail over his opponents? The one work of God (v. 7) is the assurance of another work of God (v. 11). That means that the opposition will be "thoroughly disgraced" (v. 11c), with their dishonorable deeds never to be forgotten (v. 11d). In that case, theirs will be a disgrace in perpetuity.

20:12 This leads to a divine appeal in v. 12, for God is the one who examines the heart and mind; Jeremiah can rest his case with Yahweh. He will see that Jeremiah is innocent and the people are guilty. The examination and probing belong to Yahweh, and therefore the vengeance will not be misdirected or arbitrary; it will be just and fair.

20:13 Thus, just as happens in the individual laments in the Psalter, so the prophet's expected deliverance is the basis for his challenge to others to celebrate God's goodness with singing and praise to Yahweh (v. 13; cf. Pss 22:22–31; 34:3–9). Accordingly, this verse is not incongruous in this context. But what is strange is that, after representing the prophet's total confidence in Yahweh, the verses that follow are full of despair, dejection, and heartache.

Jeremiah's Accursed Day (20:14–18)

20:14 With a sudden but understandable switch in mood, Jeremiah crashes back to earth again (v. 14). Whether these words in vv. 14–18 were written right after he wrote vv. 7–13 or sometime later, the prophet's life is like a rollercoaster, one of going up to the heights, then down to the depths of despair. In words that are reminiscent of Job 3:3–12, Jeremiah wishes that he had never been born (v. 14a). It is impossible to calculate the agony of heart and spirit the prophet was going through. So he speaks, perhaps, by way of irony: the news about his birth, which should have been good news, he now he views as a curse. May the day his mother bore him be cursed as well (v. 14b).

20:15–17 He also curses the day a messenger brought the news to his father, saying: "It's a boy; you've got a son!" (v. 15b). That man is the one he now holds responsible for the starting the rejoicing in his family that never should have occurred. How could the birth of one like what Jeremiah has become have been the occasion for good news? What that messenger should have done was kill Jeremiah while he was still in the womb (v. 17a). Then Jeremiah's mother's womb could have been his grave (v. 17b). The prophet's heart and mind are too jumbled at this point to even imagine how this could ever have happened, or even whether such an act was right or wrong morally and biblically. His own despair is so all-consuming that that all he can think about right now is some quick way out of this mess! For the moment he has forgotten how Yahweh knew him "before [he] came out of the womb" (1:5)

20:18 Jeremiah is still not done with airing his grief and the toll his task has taken from him, for in words again reminiscent of Job (3:20–23), he asks plaintively: "Why did I ever come forth from the womb?" (v. 18a). His work, up to this point, can be summarized as "trouble and grief" (v. 18b).[283] But before we are too quick to condemn Jeremiah's lament as unsuitable for a servant of God, we need to realize the sheer stress, tension, and frustration he was under in serving for so long a period of time without any positive response or an encouragement of any sort from those he was called to serve. This sort of world, warped by sin and disobedience, calls for his offering up to God prayers and petitions accompanied by loud cries and tears to the only one who could save him from death, a case very similar to that of our Lord Jesus in Heb 5:7. However, the gloom of Jeremiah's despair falls short of the beautiful submission of Jesus, who said, "Your will be done" (Matt 26:42). This man is made of clay, but he nevertheless remains faithful to him who called him.

Jeremiah has had it; it is all getting to him, and he is beginning to lose it. This has happened to others in Scripture and in our day. For example, Elijah fled the country after Queen Jezebel threatened his life. He stops under a broom tree in the southern desert and cries to God: "I've had it; take my life, Lord." But if that is what he really wants, he should have stayed up north, where he just called down fire from heaven on the altar on Mount Carmel; Jezebel would have taken his life at no cost! But the Lord touches him twice and prepares not only sleep but also a hot meal for him. Then God tells him to go the the cave on Mount Sinai, where he is to emerge from that cave, for God is about to make all his "goodness" to "pass by." Jeremiah, Elijah, and we, in our depressed states, need to have whole new

---

283. Lundbom proposes that Jeremiah "blames Yahweh for not killing him in the womb." As far as the controlling theology, "we learn also that the ways of the Almighty are ultimately unknowable and inscrutable." See J. R. Lundbom, "The Double Curse in Jeremiah 20:14–18," *JBL* 104, no. 4 (1985): 589–600.

vision of the greatness, magnificence, and awesomeness of our God. So let God cause all "his goodness" to "pass by" in review.

DENOUNCING THE KINGS AND
THE PROPHETS (21:1-23:40)

From this point on in the book of Jeremiah, most of the messages are addressed to specific persons. We are now getting very close in time to the enactment of the threatened judgment on Jerusalem and the temple. It is beginning to look to at least some of the people that Jeremiah is on the right side of the argument after all, for the Babylonian king, Nebuchadnezzar, is already on the warpath, and Judah is just now being attacked.

After the devastating blow of having their king, Jehoiachin, exiled to Babylon, opinion in Jerusalem about their oppression is beginning to shift. King Zedekiah, who will later be exiled to Babylon, was Judah's final king (597-586 BC). At this point of Jeremiah Zedekiah is now in his ninth year of reign, and he had attempted to throw off the vassal status of his nation by stopping the required taxation demanded by Nebuchadnezzar, but such rebellion was not only against Babylon; it was also against the determined plan of God (52:3b).

Nebuchadnezzar had begun his siege of Jerusalem in 588 BC and would continue for eighteen months before it was all over for Judah (52:4-5). Thus Jeremiah, nearing some forty years in his ministry, is still alive and preaching even at this late day in Judah's history. It was this same Nebuchadnezzar who had appointed Zedekiah as king, even changing his name from Mattaniah to Zedekiah as another sign of the foreign king's control over Judah (2 Kgs 24:17). So Jeremiah turns out to be right: "a foe from the north" (1:1) does come—Nebuchadnezzar of Babylon—and he is just now attacking the city.

Often Jer 21:1-10 is separated from 21:11-23:8 and placed much later because in this section Nebuchadnezzar is already attacking Jerusalem.[284] Chapter 21, however, consists of three oracles: (1) to King Zedekiah (21:1-7), (2) to the people of Jerusalem (21:8-10), and (3) to the house of the king of

---

284. See W. McKane, "Jeremiah (20th and 21st Century Interpretation)," in *Hebrew Bible: History of Interpretation*, ed. J. H. Hayes (Nashville: Abingdon, 2004), 218-19.

Judah (21:11–14).[285] Wherever these oracles were attached originally, they were now tied together in this chapter. Their setting is best thought of as 588–587 BC, just after Zedekiah rebelled against the king of Babylon.

Some treat these four chapters as an appendix to the previous chapters in Jeremiah (Craigie, 283). These chapters do treat several Davidic kings and focus on the capital city of Jerusalem. But on the whole these chapters deliver one huge crushing blow to Israel's political and religious leadership.

INDICTING JUDAH'S LEADERSHIP (21:1–14)

TRANSLATION

1 The word that came to Jeremiah from Yahweh when King Zedekiah sent Pashhur son of Malkijah and the priest Zephaniah son of Maaseiah, saying: **2** "Inquire, please, of Yahweh for us: for Nebuchadnezzar,[286] king of Babylon, is attacking us. Perhaps Yahweh will perform miracles for us as in times past so that he will withdraw from us."

3 But Jeremiah said to them, "Here is what you are to tell Zedekiah,[287] **4** 'This is what Yahweh, the God of Israel,[288] says: "Look out, I am going to divert the weapons of war that are in your hands, which you are using to fight the king of Babylon and the Chaldeans who are outside the wall besieging you, and I will gather them inside this city. **5** And I myself will fight against you with an outstretched hand and a mighty arm in anger, and fury, and great wrath. **6** I will strike down those living in this city, both men and beasts; they shall die in a horrible plague. **7** After that," declares Yahweh, "I will hand over Zedekiah king of Judah, his officials and the people in this city who survive the plague, sword, and famine, to

---

285. Thelle argues that Jer 21 (along with Jer 37) "demonstrates the important prophetic functions of *both* consulting the deity in a situation of distress and delivering the divine response." See R. I. Thelle, "דרש את־יהוה: The Prophetic Act of Consulting YHWH in Jeremiah 21,2 and 37,7," *SJOT* 12 (1998): 249–56. McKane concludes that "chapter 21 is not a continuous, cohesive piece of literature" and that the editor wanted to represent 21:1–10 as "a three-stage sequence of events corresponding to Jer. 52:4–16." See W. McKane, "The Construction of Jeremiah Chapter XXI," *VT* 32 (1982): 59–73.

286. Nebuchadnezzar's name (נְבוּכַדְרֶאצַּר) is missing in the LXX.

287. The LXX adds βασιλέα Ιουδα, "king of Judah," after "Zedekiah."

288. The expression אֱלֹהֵי יִשְׂרָאֵל, "God of Israel," is missing in the LXX.

Nebuchadnezzar king of Babylon,[289] and to their enemies who seek their lives. He will put them to the sword. He will show no mercy, or pity, or compassion."'

8 "To this people you shall say, 'This is what Yahweh says: "Look! I am setting before you the way of life and the way of death. **9** Whoever stays in this city will die by the sword, famine, or plague.[290] But whoever goes out and surrenders to the Chaldeans who are besieging you will live. He will escape with his life. **10** For I have set my face/determined to do this city harm and not good," declares Yahweh. "It will be given into the hand of the King of Babylon, and he will destroy it with fire."''"

> **11** "To the royal house of Judah, say:
>
>   'Hear the word of Yahweh;
>
> **12** O house of David,
>
>   This is what Yahweh says:
>
> "Execute justice every morning;
>
>   Rescue the robbed from the hand of the oppressor
>
> Lest my wrath break out like fire,
>
>   And burn so that none can quench it,
>
>   Because of the evil you have done.[291]
>
> **13** Look! I am against you, who live above the valley,[292]
>
>   On a rocky[293] plateau, says Yahweh.
>
> You say, 'Who can descend upon us?[294]
>
>   Who can enter our safe place?'
>
> **14** I will punish you[295] as your deeds deserve," declares Yahweh,
>
>   "I will kindle a fire in your forests,
>
>   that will consume everything around you."''"

---

289. The phrase בְּיַד נְבוּכַדְרֶאצַּר מֶלֶךְ־בָּבֶל, "by the hand of Nebuchadnezzar king of Babylon," is missing in the LXX.

290. The LXX omits וּבַדֶּבֶר, "and by pestilence."

291. The LXX omits the phrase מִפְּנֵי רֹעַ מַעַלְלֵיהֶם, "because of the evil of their deeds."

292. Lit. "dwellers of the valley."

293. Like the Syr., the LXX has Σορ, "Sor" (Tyre), where the MT has צוּר, "rock."

294. The LXX reads τίς πτοήσει ἡμᾶς, "who shall alarm us," for MT's מִי־יֵחַת עָלֵינוּ, "who shall come down against us?"

295. The LXX omits וּפָקַדְתִּי, "And I will punish."

COMMENTARY

A Royal Request (21:1–2)

21:1 Zedekiah decides, though in a most belated way, to send messengers to the prophet Jeremiah to inquire how things are going to turn out—as if he had not heard Jeremiah's message over and over again prior to this time! The messengers are Pashhur son of Malkijah (not the same Pashhur of 20:1) and Zephaniah son of Maaseiah. This Pashhur (son of Malkijah) is a royal prince who owns the cistern into which Jeremiah is lowered as a prisoner for a time (38:6). Later, in the time of Nehemiah (Neh 11:12), one of Pashhur's descendants becomes a priest.

The other messenger, Zephaniah, will appear later in Jeremiah 29:25, 29; 37:3; 52:24. This Zephaniah was a very influential man in Jerusalem, for he was "next in rank" to the chief priest (52:24) and therefore was an overseer of the temple. Zephaniah was also later rebuked by the prophet Shemiah for not opposing Jeremiah's prophecy regarding the length of the exile (29:24–32). After Jerusalem falls in 587 BC Nebuchadnezzar executes him at Riblah (52:24–27).

21:2 Zedekiah, perhaps, is hoping that Yahweh will miraculously intervene on Judah's behalf once again, as he had so often worked in Israel's past. The deputation is told to deal kindly with Jeremiah, as they made the request, for they include the grace note of "please" (נָא, *nāʾ*). But apart from that brief word of kindness, the whole request is the height of delusion and really, in a way, offensive for a prophet who has been pouring out his heart to get the attention of such playmakers as the king and his officials. It makes a mockery out of all that Jeremiah has been saying for forty years; it is as if no one has been listening. No wonder this scripture goes on to bristle with divine irony as Yahweh says in effect, "You want me to fight for you by displaying my mighty arm and my miraculous deeds; I will do no such thing, for I am going to fight against you, that is what I am going to do!"

Yahweh's Response to King Zedekiah (21:3–7)

21:3 Zedekiah's scheme to send Pashhur son of Malkijah, from the political realm, and Zephaniah, from the religious realm, does not work. Usually Jeremiah has to inquire of Yahweh what answer he should give, but here he knows the answer instantaneously, for the answer should have been obvious after all those months and years of preaching; it is what he has been saying all along. Has he not preached on this very matter over and over again?

21:4 First (v. 4), Yahweh says he will gather all Judah's own weapons back in the center of Jerusalem itself, where instead of having those weapons help Judah to fight Babylon, they will be used against Judah. That means that Judah and her weapons will be in retreat and totally ineffective against Babylon. A similar phrase to the one recorded here ("turning [divert] ... weapons of war") was discovered in a thirteenth-century BC Hittite king's treaty, as well as another in a seventh-century Babylonian treaty. In both cases, as here in this verse, the deity is the subject of the phrase "to turn ... weapons." Thus, the phrase describes a full military retreat, in addition to all the other confusion and all the destruction was going on.

21:5 But things are even more critical than Zedekiah realizes. In v. 5 Yahweh shows the king how out of touch with reality he really is, for when the king uses the terminology of God's fighting for Israel at the time of the exodus, it demonstrates that he did not know that in this situation, in marked contrast with the former one, God himself will not fight for Judah; instead he will fight *against* Judah. The terms "outstretched hand" and "mighty arm" were often used of Yahweh's intervention on Israel's behalf at the exodus from Egypt (for example, Deut 4:34; 5:15; 7:19; 11:2–3; 26:8). But King Zedekiah is far off the mark in this situation, for he has presumptuously assumed that even after his adamant stand on disobeying Yahweh, he can still call out to God at the very last minute for divine help. The realization that the king cannot use God as a last-minute stopgap must fall on him like a ton of bricks. Worse still, v. 5 is the only time in the OT where Yahweh says, "I myself will fight against you," meaning against Israel. This pledge to oppose Zedekiah and the people of Judah ends in the triple threat that God's "anger, and fury, and great wrath" are aimed directly at Judah (v. 5b; cf. Deut 29:28). This time Israel will experience the mighty power of God not in deliverance, as at the exodus, but in his "great wrath."

21:6 The divine fatal blow will "strike down" "both men and beasts," who will "die of a horrible plague" (v. 6). This means that in addition to causing the Babylonians to triumph over them, God himself will "strike down" (hiphil of נָכָה) the population of Jerusalem with a deadly plague.

21:7 That is not all, for in v. 7, "after that," God promises for those who manage somehow to survive this first round of judgments, that he has an awful trilogy of woes still pending: "plague, sword, and famine." Among those who survive the first wave of destruction will be King Zedekiah, some of his officials, and some of the populace, but there is more to come. His officials are "his servants" (עֲבָדָיו), which probably includes his higher echelons of advisers. But Nebuchadnezzar will "kill/strike" (נָכָה) them with his sword. There is not the slightest hint of mercy, favor, or compassion. This will be dramatically carried out as Nebuchadnezzar takes Zedekiah, his sons, and his officials and puts them to death in front of Zedekiah's eyes, and then he will shackle all of them and will lead Zedekiah away as his prisoner.

A Message for the People (21:8–10)

21:8–9 While this may not have been part of the response to the king's inquiry of the prophet, it apparently comes at the same time as the response to the king. It sets before the people the way of life and the way of death, similar to the way Moses had set "life and death" before his people in Deut 30:15–20. However, in Moses's case life meant long life in the land and death meant exile; but now, if one chooses to stay in the land of Judah under these circumstances, one faces a horrible death. Surrendering to this Chaldean (that is, Babylonian) army means going into exile but still being alive to tell about it later on. In this latter case one's life will become the booty of war (v. 9c).

"The way of life" no longer will include remaining in the land and obeying Yahweh, for that generation in Israel passed that opportunity a long time ago. Life now consists of submission to Babylon. Previously the path of life involved obedience to the covenant requirements (Josh 24:15), but now it is all over; the time is up, and the people had made their decision. The phrase translated as "surrender to" in v. 9 (נָפַל עַל) literally means "to fall upon/to," and it can refer either of surrendering to an enemy or deserting to one's enemies. Either reading fits the context. There were "deserters" to Babylon, as recorded in 2 Kgs 25:11; Jer 37:14; 39:9; 52:15. Amazingly, those who were promised life in the land will now find the path to life in desertion or surrender because of their sin.

21:10 The reason desertion or surrender is the only path to life is that is what Yahweh has determined to do to Jerusalem. It is now God's irrevocable decision to destroy the city. It will be destroyed by fire. It will be handed over by God to the king of Babylon, who will serve as God's earthly agent to carry out his wrath in an unquenchable fire.

A Message for the Royal House (21:11–14)

21:11–12 It is possible that this is a message from God delivered to the king of Judah at an earlier time, but if so, how appropriate that a reminder of its veracity should come at this very moment with Nebuchadnezzar besieging the city. Anyway, vv. 11–12 are addressed to the "royal house of Judah" (v. 11a). More particularly, the "house of David" (v. 12a) is called on to lead out the way by "execut[ing] justice every morning" (v. 12c).

It is surprising, however, that David and his dynasty are mentioned only in this verse in Jeremiah; "house of David" appears only eight other times in all the prophets (Isa 7:2, 13; 22:22; Zech 12:7–8, 10, 12; 13:1). Second Samuel 8:15 had prescribed that David should be "doing what was just and right for all his people," thus this may be why the name "David" is used just as Jeremiah is calling those in his royal line to follow the same example.

The call for "justice" for the oppressed, the needy, and for the disenfranchised had been the oft-repeated call for leaders in Israel (Exod 22:25; 23:6; Deut 15:4, 11; 24:10–15). In those older passages God had warned that should his word be ignored, his anger and his wrath would burn like a fire that could not be put out. Now it is too late for the Judeans to start waking up to the truth of what God had said; it will happen if they refuse to heed it—and it is happening. The final straw, as it were, comes in the reign of Zedekiah. Apparently the courts usually convened in the mornings, before the day got too hot. But justice is not carried out at all by those who were the leaders. Here is another reason for the sacking of Jerusalem.

Zedekiah, as one in the line of David, should have "rescue[d]" and snatched back from disaster those who were being oppressed and "robbed," but here again there is little or no desire to seek out injustices that needed correcting or to rectify wrongs (v. 12d–e). The king and his officials failed to carry out one of their main tasks; therefore the fire of judgment, which God had promised, is sure to come (v. 12f–h).

21:13–14 In vv. 13–14 the subject changes from the king and leaders to all of Jerusalem (as indicated by the fem. verb). In this case the city, like its leaders was haughty, proud, and deceived. She counted herself unique as she embraced a false sense of security because she existed in the midst of a valley surrounded by the hills or the rocky plateau. Therefore she boasted, "Who can descend upon us?" "Who can enter our refuge?" In other words, she felt she was unconquerable and invincible should an attack come.

But such a strong sense of inviolability is not connected with a living faith and an obedience to Yahweh. Therefore, Yahweh will punish them, just as their deeds deserved. He will set their forests on fire, and it will consume everything. Payday must come someday, and that day has arrived.

"Now" is the time of salvation. For all too many of us that time will expire, as it did for King Zedekiah and for Judah. God has finally decided "I am against you, Jerusalem," and yet the irascible people cry out, "Who can come against us? Who can enter our refuge?" Answer: God can, and God will! And so it will happen to all the nations of the world that think they are above the observation of heaven and that no danger will overtake them. But it will, and the reason is that they have failed to believe in the Man of Promise who is coming, and they have flouted his word.

THE FAILURE OF THE LAST KINGS OF JUDAH (22:1–23:8)

TRANSLATION

1 This is what Yahweh says: "Go down to the palace of the king of Judah and proclaim this message there. **2** Say, 'Hear the word of Yahweh, O king of Judah, you who sit on David's throne—you, your officials,[296] and your people who come through these gates. **3** This is what Yahweh says: "Do what is just and right! Rescue the one who has been robbed from the clutches of

---

296. The LXX reads σὺ καὶ ὁ οἶκός σου, "you and your house," where the MT has אַתָּה וַעֲבָדֶיךָ, "you and your servants."

the oppressor![297] Do not wrong or maltreat the resident alien, the orphan, or the widow, or shed innocent blood in this place! **4** For if you really act to carry out these commands, then kings who sit on David's throne will come through the gates of this palace, riding in chariots and on horses, accompanied by their officials and their people. **5** But if you do not obey[298] these commands, declares Yahweh, I swear by myself that this palace will become a ruin."'''

6 For this is what Yahweh says concerning the palace of the kings of Judah:

"Like Gilead are you to me
Or Lebanon's crest;
I will surely make you a desert,
Like towns not inhabited.
7 I will commission against you wreckers,
Each with his tools;
They will fell your splendid cedars,
And throw them into the fire."

8 Then people from many nations will pass by this city and they will ask each other, "Why did Yahweh do such a thing to this great city?" **9** And the answer will be, "Because they forsook the covenant of Yahweh their God[299] and have worshiped and served other gods."

10 "Do not weep for the dead,[300] nor bemoan him;
Weep rather for him who is departing,
For he will never return, nor see his native land again."

11 For this is what Yahweh says about Shallum son of Josiah, king of Judah,[301] who succeeded his father Josiah on the throne: "He who has gone from this place will never come back again. **12** In the place to which they have deported him, there he will die. He will never see this land again."

---

297. The word עשׁוק is to be read "his oppressor," with the LXX, Syr., and the Tg.
298. The LXX reads μὴ ποιήσητε, "you will not do," where the MT has לֹא תשׁמעו, "you will not obey."
299. Several mss have "the God of their fathers" instead of "their God."
300. Possibly a reference to the death of their king.
301. The LXX omits מֶלֶךְ יְהוּדָה, "king of Judah."

13 "Woe to him who builds his house by unfairness,[302]
  Its upper rooms by injustice,
Who works his neighbor for nothing,
  Nor pays him for his labor.
14 He says, 'I will build myself[303] a great palace,
  With spacious upper rooms.'
So he widens its windows,
  Panels it with cedar,
  And paints it bright red.
15 Does that make you a king
  Because you compete in cedar?
Did not your father have food and drink?[304]
  He did what was right and fair,
  So all went well with him.
16 He defended the cause of the poor and the needy;
  And so all went well.
Isn't this what it means to know me?"
  Declares Yahweh.
17 "But your eyes and your heart are set only on dishonest gain,
  On shedding innocent blood, on oppression, and extortion."

18 Therefore, this is what Yahweh says about Jehoiakim son of Josiah king of Judah:[305] "They will not mourn for him. 'Alas my brother! Alas sisters!' They will not mourn for him: 'Alas my master! Alas his splendor!'[306] **19** [They will give him] a donkey's funeral!—dragged out and dumped outside the Jerusalem gate."

20 "Go up to Lebanon, and cry out!
  In Bashan, let your voice be heard!

---

302. Lit. "without righteousness."

303. The LXX reads ᾠκοδόμησας σεαυτῷ, "you have built for yourself" instead of "I will build myself."

304. The LXX is quite different from the MT. It has "because you are provoked with Achaz, your father," instead of "Did not your father have food and drink?"

305. The LXX adds οὐαὶ ἐπὶ τὸν ἄνδρα τοῦτον, "Woe unto this man," after "Jehoiakim son of Josiah king of Judah."

306. The LXX omits וְהוֹי הֹדֹה, "Alas, his splendor!"

Cry out from Abarim,

>For they have crushed to pieces all your allies.

21 I warned you when you felt secure,[307]

>But you said: 'I will not listen.'

This has been your way from your youth,

>For you have not heeded my voice.

22 All your shepherds the wind will drive away,

>And your allies will be taken for booty,

Then you will be ashamed and humiliated because of all

>your wickedness.[308]

23 You who live in Lebanon,

>Who are nestled down in cedar buildings,

How you will groan[309] when the pains come upon you,

>Pains like those of a woman in labor."

24 As I live—declares Yahweh—even if you, Coniah, son of Jehoiakim, king of Judah, were a signet ring on my right hand, yet I would snatch you off **25** and I would hand you over to those who seek your life, those you fear—to Nebuchadnezzar king of Babylon[310] and to the Chaldeans. **26** I will hurl you and the mother who bore you into another country, where neither of you were born, and there you shall both die. **27** You will never come back to the land to which you desperately long to return.

28 Is this man Coniah a despised, smashed pot,

>A utensil no one wants?

Why, then, is he and his children hurled, cast out,

>To a land that they do not know?

29 O land, land, land, hear the word of Yahweh,

---

307. The LXX reads ἐν τῇ παραπτώσει, "in your transgression," where the MT has בְּשַׁלְוֺתַיִךְ, "in your security/peace."

308. The LXX reads πάντων τῶν φιλούντων σε, "all your lovers," where the MT has רָעָתֵךְ, "all your evil."

309. The LXX reads καταστενάξεις, "you will groan," where the MT has נֵחַנְתְּ, "you will be pitied."

310. The expression וּבְיַד נְבוּכַדְרֶאצַּר מֶלֶךְ־בָּבֶל, "and into the hand of Nebuchadnezzar king of Babylon," is missing in the LXX.

30 This is what Yahweh says,[311]
"Write this man [as] childless,
   A man who will not prosper in his lifetime,
     For none of his offspring will prosper,
      None will sit on the throne of David
      Or rule in Judah again."

23:1 "Woe to the shepherds who are destroying and scattering my sheep!"[312] declares Yahweh.[313] **2** Therefore, this is what Yahweh, the God of Israel says concerning the shepherds who shepherd my people: "[because] you have scattered my flock and driven them away and not taken care of them, Look, I am going to punish you for the evil you have done," declares Yahweh. **3** I myself will gather what is left of my flock from all the countries where I have driven them, and I will bring them back to the pasture where they will be fruitful and multiply. **4** I will place over them shepherds who will shepherd them, and they will no longer be afraid or terrified, nor will any be missing,[314] declares Yahweh. **5** Behold, the days are coming, declares Yahweh, when I will raise up to David a righteous Branch, a king who will reign wisely and do what is just and fair[315] in the land. **6** In his days, Judah will be saved and Israel will live in safety. And this is the name by which he will be called, Yahweh our Righteousness.[316] **7** Therefore, see, the days are coming, declares Yahweh, when people will no longer say, 'As surely as Yahweh lives, who brought the Israelites[317] up out of Egypt,' **8** but rather [they will say], 'As surely as Yahweh lives who brought up the descendants of the house of Israel out of the land of the north and out of all the countries where he had driven them,' Then they will live[318] in their own land."

---

311. The introductory כֹּה אָמַר יְהוָה, "thus says Yahweh," is missing in the LXX.

312. Lit. "The sheep of my pasture."

313. The expression נְאֻם־יְהוָה, "declares Yahweh," is missing in the LXX.

314. The last verb, וְלֹא יִפָּקֵדוּ, "they will not be missing," is missing in the LXX.

315. Lit. "Righteous."

316. The LXX transliterates the Heb. צִדְקֵנוּ, "our righteousness," as Ιωσεδεκ, "Josedek."

317. The LXX reads τὸν οἶκον Ισραηλ, "house of Israel," where the MT has אֶת־בְּנֵי יִשְׂרָאֵל, "the children of Israel."

318. The LXX has the aor. καὶ ἀπεκατέστησεν αὐτούς, "and he has restored them," where the MT has the pf. with the waw-consec. וְיָשְׁבוּ, "and they will dwell."

COMMENTARY

This section records a number of messages for the last kings of Judah, including the three sons of King Josiah and their uncle Zedekiah. After the death of King Josiah, the people of Judah installed Jehoahaz as king, who was also known as Shallum in 609 BC. But he only ruled for three months before he was removed from his throne and exiled by Pharaoh Necho to Egypt, where he died at an unknown date.

Jehoiakim (also known as Eliakim) reigned then from 609 to 598 BC, but there is no known direct confrontation of this king with the prophet Jeremiah, even though his reign is mentioned in Jeremiah's superscription to his book (1:1). He was the older brother of Jehoahaz and twenty-five years old when Pharaoh Necho placed him on the throne. But when he later rebelled against Nebuchadnezzar, he was killed by him in 598 BC.

Jehoiachin (also known as Coniah), brother to both of the previously named kings, came to the throne of Judah when he was eighteen years old (2 Kgs 24:8–10) by the will of the people, yet Nebuchadnezzar deposed him and exiled him along with his family to Babylon after he too had ruled for only three months in 598 BC. Nebuchadnezzar then placed the uncle of these three boys on the throne, Zedekiah (also known as Mattaniah), who reigned from 598 to 587 BC, until Jerusalem was burnt to the ground by the Babylonians.

The oracles in this section are addressed to each of these four kings. Zedekiah is addressed first (22:1–9) and last (23:1–8), thereby making it a nice **inclusio**. Jehoahaz (Shallum) is addressed in 22:10–12, Jehoiakim (Eliakim) comes next in 22:13–19, and then Jehoiachin in 22:24–30.

Zedekiah: Why Was Jerusalem Destroyed? (22:1–9)

The focal point of this section comes in the question of v. 8: "Why did Yahweh do such a thing to this great city?" That is what all those who pass by want to know. Even though the "palace" of David's throne is mentioned in vv. 1, 4, the key concern is the city. And the short answer is given in v. 9, "Because they forsook the covenant of Yahweh their God, and have worshiped and served other gods."

22:1–2 Jeremiah is told to "go down" to the palace of the king, for he must have been in the temple, which is to the north of the king's palace in

Jerusalem and on higher ground. King Zedekiah is addressed as one who sat "on David's throne," which not only is an honor for those who were descendants of David, but also sets a standard of expectations for him. But the message to him is not given in private, for included in the addressees are his "officials" and his "people who c[a]me through these gates," which may not have been the whole nation, but mainly those in his royal household.

22:3 The message is a word from God in which he orders that the king carry out the basic covenant demands that were at the heart of his role as a Davidic king. He is to "Do what is just and right!" (v. 3). This involves more than seeing that social justice is maintained in the community; every aspect of life is to be lived in a way that shows Judah has a relationship to Yahweh. Living righteously before God is no small task. Zedekiah's job is to see that he and his people show this to be true in their lives.

Moreover, Zedekiah is also ordered to "rescue the one who has been robbed from the clutches of the oppressor!" (v. 3b). If the rich and powerful are robbing the weak and the poor, the king and his administration are duty-bound by God to come to the defense of these victims. The same command comes to the king with regard to the resident alien, the fatherless, and the widow; if Zedekiah does not come to their defense, then where on earth is justice to be found? There is even a curse in the law of Moses for those who prey on any of these three groups: the alien, the fatherless, and the widow (Deut 27:19). In addition to this, there is to be "no shed[ding of] innocent blood in this place" (v. 3d). God had seen what King Manasseh had done in his reign (2 Kgs 21:16), and that certainly was not to be done among them.

22:4–5 Verse 4 promises that if these commands are carried out by this administration, then royalty sitting on David's throne will continue to come through the gates of Jerusalem, riding on their chariots and horses along with all their officials. The land will be prosperous, and God will continue to bless them. But if Zedekiah and his ilk reject this call for justice and the doing of what is right, then v. 5 predicts that God himself will bring down this very same palace in a "ruin" (חָרְבָּה). Not only will the palace become a pile of rubble, but the regime and the dynasty itself will collapse. When

God swears an oath ("I swear by myself") to a future judgment, God himself stands behind this word; thus it will remain true for as long as God is God (Jer 11:5; 16:14–15; 44:26; 49:13; 51:14), which is forever!

22:6 The ruin of the palace is further described in v. 6 by means of a metaphor. Judah will be as "Gilead" to Yahweh and like "Lebanon." Just as Gilead is known for its livestock, pastures, and in general for its plenty, and Lebanon (northeast of Canaan) is known in the Transjordan for its tall and stately cedars, that is how Israel is to God. But with this judgment that will change. It will be as if Gilead and Lebanon were transformed from all that loveliness and stateliness to a desert-like existence with uninhabited towns! That would be quite a comedown to say the least, from riches to rags and even less!

22:7 Yahweh will "send" (lit. "sanctify;" קָדַשׁ) "destroyers" who will carry out this demolition (v. 7). Rather than helping Israel as he had in the past, Yahweh will institute a war in which Israel's enemies will act as his own emissaries. These destroyers will each have their own weapons and will "cut up your fine cedar beams" used in the construction of the palace and other key buildings in Jerusalem (v. 7).

22:8–9 So drastic and total is the destruction that is to come on Jerusalem that Gentile nations that pass by ask each other: "Why did Yahweh do such a thing to this great city?" (v. 8). Instinctively, the pagans know this is the result of the hand of God and not just some small setback that has befallen the people. Moses warns in Deut 29:24 that all the nations will ask this question after they see what has happened to Jerusalem. Jerusalem becomes an object of horror and a lesson to all the nations round about, for they too are subject and liable to the same happenings if they refuse the repeated calls of God. The answer to the nations' inquiry is found in v. 9; Judah has forsaken God's covenant and has gone off to worship other gods, even though they were warned long ago by Moses (Deut 29:25–26). How can a nation breach the first and greatest commandment in the Decalogue and still expect to go on existing (Exod 20:3; Deut 5:7)? Even pagans know this is not possible!

Concerning King Jehoahaz (Shallum) (22:10-12)

22:10 The poem of v. 10 is clarified in the prose oracle of vv. 11-12. The "dead [king]" they are not to weep for is good King Josiah, who had been killed trying to stop Pharaoh Necho from assisting the Assyrian army against the new rising power in the Near East—the nation of Babylon. This tragedy happened at the Megiddo pass in 609 BC, in the thirty-ninth year of King Josiah. God had promised that he would spare Josiah from seeing all the trouble that had to come on the nation due to the wicked actions of his grandfather, King Manasseh, and his father, Amon. Despite the interim of King Josiah's good reign, the people in general steadfastly refused to turn back to God as Josiah had done.

22:11-12 The people of Judah immediately placed Josiah's youngest and most popular son, King Jehoahaz, on the throne in place of his father. Jeremiah admonishes the people of Judah not to weep for their fallen king Josiah; they are to lament instead for King Shallum, that is, Jehoahaz (cf. 1 Chr 3:15), who is summoned to Riblah, where he is summarily deposed after he has reigned for a brief three months. Jehoahaz was exiled to Egypt, where he subsequently died (2 Kgs 23:30-34; 2 Chr 36:2-3). The point is that "he will never come back again" (v. 11c) to his native land. Pharaoh Necho replaced Shallum with his brother Jehioakim.

Concerning King Jehioakim (22:13-19)

King Jehoiakim is not identified until v. 18, but this whole segment is an indictment of his unjust practices (especially vv. 13-17), followed by an announcement of judgment over him (vv. 18-19). The section begins with "Woe" (הוֹי), which often is a warning in the prophets of the judgment that is to follow. This cry of judgment originated as a cry of lament, used when mourning a death. For example, in 1 Kgs 13:30, "woe!" is used six times as a means of mourning for the dead, as perhaps used at funerals of that day, and it appears another four times in Jer 22:18 in a similar role.

22:13-14 The focus of the indictment on Jehoiakim is on "his house" (= palace) (vv. 13, 21-22), which he apparently built with forced labor from his fellow citizens without paying them for their services. Therefore, in doing this he literally built injustice and oppression into the very structure of his palace, if not into the very structure of his government. This luxurious palace was built to be quite roomy, with spacious quarters, large windows, cedar paneling, and ostentatious painting in vermilion, a brilliant red. Jehoiakim's treatment of his workers contrasts vividly with the way Solomon used only foreigners as workmen when he built his palace (1 Kgs 5:13–18; 12:3–4; in his case, the workers were presumably well paid). Such practices as these were in direct violation of the charge given to the Davidic rulers in v. 3 and 21:12.

Verse 14 supplies some of the details of Jehoiakim's construction. It is described it as "a house of measurements" (בֵּית מִדּוֹת), that is, one of great size, and it had "spacious" rooms (מְרֻוָּחִים), which is a m. pl. pual ptc. following a f. pl. "upper rooms" (עֲלִיּוֹת). Most take the ptc. as in apposition to the "upper rooms," that is, rooms that are spacious. However, the word rendered "spacious" may be related either to "wind" (רוּחַ), hence "airy rooms," or "broad" (רָחָב), hence broad and spacious rooms. The large "windows" (חַלּוֹנָי) are possibly a dual form and therefore would be "double windows." Of course, the cedar paneling signals a royal residence, and the "red" or "vermilion" paint was a bright red pigment that came from a metal oxide used for painting walls, but not for dyeing fabric.

The mound of Ramat Rahel is located on a prominent hill (818 meters above sea level) about halfway between the old city of Jerusalem and Bethlehem. Archaeologist Y. Aharoni, who excavated this site in the 1950s and 1960s, identified five stratums of occupation, beginning with the Iron Age, especially the end of that age in 608–597 BC.[319] Aharoni identified this site with Beth-Haccherem, an identification many other scholars share. In Jeremiah's day, fire signals were sent up from Beth-Haccherem (Jer 6:1) to warn Jerusalem of an approaching enemy. The Mishnah, as well as the Genesis Apocryphon[320] and the Copper Scroll[321] of the DSS, place Beth-Haccherem very close to Jerusalem. These sources are in harmony with the excavations of this site, which suggests this was the ancient royal citadel and palace described in this passage.

---

319. Y. Aharoni, "Ramat Rahel," in *The New Encyclopedia of Archaeological Excavations in the Holy Land*, ed. Ephraim Stern (New York: Simon & Schuster, 1993), 4:1261–67.

320. 1QapGen ar, XXII.14.

321. 3Q15, X.5.

The site was fortified with a masonry casemate wall, which enclosed a large courtyard, a stone house, and a palace. Near Eastern potentates usually financed such extravagant public works from their heavy taxation procedures or from their military campaigns, but King Jehoiakim had neither of these resources available to him, so he carried out his visions of grandeur by making his countrymen work for nothing in the construction of this palace.

The window balustrades found in the excavations seem to match those described in Jer 22:14b. These window balustrades consist of a row of colonettes decorated with palmettes topped by capitals joined to one another in the proto-Aeolic style. The colonettes and capitals are made of limestone and even bear the remains of red or vermilion paint! Fragments of these windows, which probably adorned the upper story of the western façade, were found in the heap of debris in the northwestern corner of the citadel.[322]

22:15–17 To drive this matter home, Jeremiah asks some pointed questions in vv. 15–16. Does Jehoiakim think that living in cedar is what constitutes his being a king? Did his father, King Josiah, exhibit this type of lifestyle? Rather, his father did what was right and just, and that is why all "went well with him" (v. 15c). Isn't it a fact that his father defended the cause of the poor and the needy, and is that not another reason why "all went well" with him (v. 16a)? Were not the practices of his father exactly what it meant to know Yahweh (v. 16b)? Therefore, it is not the splendor or size of one's palace that determines who is a king, or who is outstanding in God's eyes; it is rather the practice of justice and doing what is right and just in the eyes of God that shows who really knows God in a personal way. The king above all others should exhibit by his lifestyle what it means to know Yahweh and to live in a manner pleasing to him. Alas, Jehoiakim was consumed with greed, murder, and oppression, just as the former King Manasseh, who was similarly rebuked primarily for his idolatry (15:4).

22:18 The ever-present "therefore" of judgment speeches appears in v. 18. The verdict of Yahweh against Jehoiakim comes because he cares so little

---

322. Aharoni, "Ramat Raḥel," 4:1261–67.

for the well-being of his own people. His death will be markedly different from his father's death; in fact, none of the traditional sounds of mourning ("Alas, my brother! Alas, my sister!") will accompany his death—which amounts to the ultimate insult for a person of his stature. The LXX is so offended by the words "Alas, my sister" that it omits them altogether, but these words may be nothing more than a routine expression of grief used on other occasions as well as a stereotypical formula.

22:19 Jehoiakim will have "a donkey's funeral," in which the carcass is literally dragged out of the city to be left for scavengers (v. 19). Once while visiting the city of Kiriath Jearim in Israel, I saw a dead donkey thrown on top of a city dumpster, left to be carted away in the trash and garbage. The image was an unforgettable one, to say the least, as the flies, maggots, and smell filled both the carcass and the air! That unpleasant image (and smell!) is Jehoiakim's fate.

However, 2 Kgs 24:6 says that "Jehoiakim rested/slept with his fathers," which is usually interpreted as meaning he died peacefully and was buried properly with his ancestors. How does this affect the faithful fulfillment of this judgment oracle against this king? The perceived discrepancy exists only if we assume that the clause in 2 Kgs 24:6 means that Jehoiakim had a peaceful death and was subsequently buried. But that supposition cannot be sustained in light of the description of King Ahab's death in 1 Kgs 22:34–40. King Ahab died disguised as a common Israelite (1 Kgs 2:32) and bled out in a chariot. Ahab did not die peacefully or with dignity, but his body was eventually buried. This allows for the fulfillment of Jer 22:19, while 2 Kgs 24:6 could indicate that what was left of his body was later buried in some fashion. According to the Jewish historian Josephus, Nebuchadnezzar had Jehoiakim's body thrown outside the wall[323] of the city, but the Bible does not report that event, even though it does repeat a similar dire prediction that his body would be thrown out on the ground in Jer 36:30. So Jehoiakim did come to an ignominious end, to say the least.

---

323. *Ant.* 10.6.3.

Judgment on Jerusalem (22:20-23)

22:20-22 God's speech is addressed in the f. sg. to "Daughter Zion," for she has remained resolutely against responding to Jeremiah's appeals ever since he began his ministry (v. 21). The whole land of Israel is represented in this text: "Lebanon" in the northwest, "Bashan" in the northeast, and Abarim in the southeast, as it now cries out for help, "for they have crushed to pieces all your allies" (v. 20d). Here are the ultimate depths of betrayal, for when one depends on foreign allies rather than on Yahweh, there is no help available in times of trouble. During the days of Judah's peaceful and quiet security, it was easy to refuse to listen to the voice of God. But because they have spurned Yahweh, God will scatter the foreign rulers that have pledged to help Judah. This will produce groans in Judah similar to those of a woman bearing a child (v. 23). The people will be utterly "ashamed and humiliated because of all [their] wickedness" (v. 22).

22:23 "Daughter Zion" is still addressed in v. 23, but here she is addressed as "Lebanon" and as those "who are nestled in cedar buildings," a remark that aimed at the upper classes in Jerusalem, who also built homes paneled with cedar, but cared little about the poor and the disenfranchised. But all that comfort and ease will soon stop, and pain and suffering will be the new future for Jerusalem.

Concerning King Jehoiachin (22:24-30)

22:24-27 Jehoiachin's reign lasted only three months and ten days (2 Chr 26:9), as it ended with the capture of Jerusalem on March 16, 597 BC. This king was only eighteen years old (2 Kgs 24:8; 2 Chr 26:9) when King Nebuchadnezzar took him, his mother, and the royal court into exile and installed in his place as the new king his twenty-one-year-old uncle Zedekiah instead (2 Kgs 24:6-15). Perhaps due to the brevity of his reign, his name is omitted from the list in Jer 1:2-3, along with the name of Jehoahaz (that is, Shallum), yet both are featured in this chapter, while Jehoiachin appears eight more times in Jeremiah (24:1; 27:20; 28:2; 29:2; 37:1; 52:31, 33-34).

Jehoiachin's name appears in five variant forms in Heb., giving three English variants in translation: his throne name no doubt was "Jehoiachin" (52:31, 33), presumably from his original name, "Jeconiah" (24:1; 27:20; 28:4;

29:2), which in a shortened form is "Coniah" (22:28; 37:1). His name seems to mean "Yahweh will establish."

Two messages are given to Jehoiachin, the first in prose (22:24–27) and the second in poetry (vv. 28–30). Jehoiachin is taken to Babylon in exile, never to return. He was released from his Babylonian prison on April 2, 561 BC (52:31), but there is no word on how long he lived after that in Babylon. A Babylonian ration tablet was found near the Ishtar Gate with the name of Ya'ukin inscribed on it, indicating Jehoiachin's presence in the exile. It is clear, however, despite Jehoiachin's mere one-hundred-day reign, that he had during that brief time managed to offend God very deeply, even though we have no information on what that might have been.

Regardless, he is told that even if he "were a signet ring on [God's] right hand," God would "still snatch you off." A signet ring had the seal of its owner inscribed inside a circle, which acted as the signature of the king or a person of means. It was used as a stamp on official documents, which gave those letters full authority of the person who signed them. Thus, Zerubbabel, as a member of the Davidic line of rulers, is announced as a "signet ring" in Hag 2:23 (cf. Gen 41:42; Esth 3:10). Even if Jehoiachin were a "signet ring" on God's right hand, God would "hurl" him and his government into a country that was not his own (v. 26).

22:28–30 The second message from Yahweh reinforces vv. 24–27 with a poetic rendition of the same judgment. Jehoiachin is likened to a "pot" (עֶצֶב). This describes a vessel of inferior quality and therefore serves as a sarcastic reference to his inabilities as a leader. In a passionate threefold repetition and address to the "land" (v. 29), God calls to both the land and the people in it who had any hopes left for Jehoiachin's coming back to rule some day in the future. His message is: that is an empty hope!

What is more, even though Jehoiachin had seven descendants, according to 1 Chr 3:16–17, this king is to be recorded as being "childless," for none of his sons will sit on the "throne of David" (v. 30). Instead, they are made "eunuchs" in the palace of Babylon (Isa 39:7). Verses 29–30 function almost as an obituary for the house and line of David. But how can they do so in light of the eternal promises of God? Will the promised Davidic kingdom now come to an end? How can David's line survive if "none" of Jehoiachin's offspring will ever sit on that throne?

However, Jeremiah continues and in 23:5 gives the promise that "the days are coming ... when I will raise up to David a righteous Branch, a king who will reign wisely and do what is just and fair in the land." The answer, then, is that when Jeremiah says that "none" of Jehoiachin's descendants will sit on the throne of David (22:30), he refers only to Jehoiachin's immediate offspring. However, the family line of David continues, and that promised rightful king did later come in the Messiah. In the meantime, a grandson of Jehoiachin named Zerubbabel is appointed to govern Judah after the time of the exile.

Return to the Land under the Righteous Branch (23:1-8)

23:1-2 From 20:1 to 22:30 Jeremiah's words focus on sinning leaders. Therefore, one would expect that the next prophetic statement will be about the last king (at least for those days) of Judah, King Zedekiah, which is exactly what happens in this text. Jeremiah 23:1 begins with another "Woe!" The leaders, here called "shepherds," are cited for "destroying and scattering the sheep" (23:1). Because they have scattered the people of God, his sheep, they too will be scattered, and so they are sent off to Egypt and Babylon.

23:3-4 But there is another day coming: a day when God himself "will gather what is left of [his] flock" and he "will bring them back to the pastures where they will be fruitful and multiply" (v. 3). It will be a day when they no longer will be afraid, and none will be missing (v. 4). Sadly enough, it will only be a "remnant," but once they come back into the land, God will grant them men such as Zerubbabel, Joshua, Ezra, and Nehemiah, harbingers of even more godly leaders to come.

23:5-8 The real hope for the future is the messianic prophecy of vv. 5-8. Once again the prophet announces, "The days are coming ... when [God] will raise up to David a righteous Branch [צֶמַח, "branch/shoot"]; a king."[324] Five times this messianic name ("branch") appears in the prophets. The

---

324. Wiebe shows how the expression "righteous branch" is of a "kin with other Semitic titles designating a royal figure." See J. M. Wiebe, "The Form of the 'Announcement of a Royal Savior' and the Interpretation of Jeremiah 23:5-6," *Studia Biblica et Theologica* 15 (1987): 3-22.

early church regularly used to give four major pictures of the Messiah in the Gospels. The four titles were:

Messianic Title	Prophets Reference	Gospel	Aspect
"David, a righteous Branch, a king"	Jer 23:5; 33:15	Matthew	kingly
"My Servant the Branch"	Zech 3:8	Mark	servant
"the man, whose name is Branch"	Zech 6:12	Luke	human
"The Branch of Yahweh"	Isa 4:2	John	divine

Branch became a technical term for the Messiah. He would be the coming King who would do everything the previous Davidic kings had neglected to do. As new life sprouts from the roots of a fallen tree, so Jesus the Messiah would bring new life to the fallen dynasty.

The name by which he would be called is "Yahweh our Righteousness" (יְהוָה צִדְקֵנוּ).[325] Interestingly enough, this messianic title is a reversal of the name of the last king of Judah, Zedekiah, meaning "My righteous One is Yahweh" or "Yahweh who secures my vindication." But since Zedekiah sinned against Yahweh (2 Kgs 24:19), his name stands in stark contrast to the One whom God would send as his Messiah.

Because the coming of the Messiah will be attended by a great restoration of both "Judah" and "Israel" back to their land (v. 6) as one people (after being split apart since 931 BC), Yahweh God will be renowned for his physical deliverance of his people; this time, however, it will not be from Egypt but from "the north" and "all the countries where he had banished

---

325. McCord posits that the phrase "Yahweh our righteousness" is a name for Jesus Christ. See H. McCord, "The Meaning of YHWH Tsidhkenu ('The Lord our Righteousness') in Jeremiah 23:6 and 33:16," *Restoration Quarterly* 6, no. 3 (1962): 114–21.

them" (v. 8). Such a reunion and reunification of the northern ten tribes with the two southern tribes in Israel has not yet taken place, but it too will be part of the days that are coming in connection with the whole complex of events associated with Messiah's arrival.

In Jer 22:24-30 we have one of the great messianic predictions in the Bible. God will remove the "signet ring," which identified Jehoiachin's royal office with authority, and will hand him over to Nebuchadnezzar, king of Babylon. Moreover, Jehoiachin will be regarded as "childless," despite his seven sons. These will be made eunuchs, while the ancient promise of God made to David will be transferred to another of David's sons, not through the line of Solomon but his son Nathan. None of his children will ever sit on David's throne, but God has in the meantime provided other sons of David so that his promise will not be wrecked by this clown Jehoiachin.

The promise of God to Abraham (Gen 12:2-3; 15:16) and David (2 Sam 7:11-19) will not fail, for if it did, God would be guilty of lying and showing he is unable to maintain what he promised so long ago. However, thanks be to God, such an alternative never happened, and it was never necessary to replace Israel with the church in order for the promises to be fulfilled.

TRUE AND FALSE PROPHETS (23:9-40)

TRANSLATION

9 To the prophets:
My mind is shattered within me;
   All my bones tremble.
I am like a drunken[326] man,
   Like a man overcome by wine,
Because of Yahweh—
   Because of his holy words.[327]
10 For the land is full of adulterers;[328]
   Because of a curse the land lies parched,

---

326. The LXX has συντετριμμένος, "broken," where the MT has שִׁכּוֹר, "drunken."

327. The LXX reads καὶ ἀπὸ προσώπου εὐπρεπείας δόξης αὐτοῦ, "because the beauty of his glory," where the MT has וּמִפְּנֵי דִּבְרֵי קָדְשׁוֹ, "because of his holy words."

328. The opening phrase כִּי מְנָאֲפִים מָלְאָה הָאָרֶץ, "for the land is full of adulterers," is missing in the LXX.

And the pastures in the desert are withered.
The course [of the population] is an evil one,
    And [the use of] their power is not what is right.
11 Both prophet and priest are godless;
    In my house I have found their wickedness,
    Declares Yahweh.
12 Therefore their path will turn for them,
    Like slippery places in the darkness
    On which they will be pushed down and fall,
For I will bring disaster on them,
    In the year of their punishment—declares Yahweh.
13 Among Samaria's prophets I saw a stupid sight:
They prophesied by Baal
    And led Israel, my people, astray.
14 But among Jerusalem's prophets,
    I have seen a horrible thing:
    Adultery and living in deceit.
They strengthen the hands of the wicked,
    So that no one turns from his wickedness.
They are all like Sodom to me,
    And its residents like Gomorrah.
15 Therefore, this is what Yahweh of Hosts said about the prophets:
"I am going to give them wormwood to eat,
    And poison to drink;
For it is from Jerusalem's prophets,
    That ungodliness has gone out to the whole country."
16 This is what Yahweh of Hosts said:
"Do not listen to the words the prophets are prophesying to you;[329]
    They are filling you with empty prophecy,[330]
They speak from their [own] minds,
    Not from the mouth of Yahweh—
17 [They] keep on saying to the scorners of Yahweh's word,

---

329. The LXX omits the phrase הַנִּבְּאִים לָכֶם, "the ones who prophesy to you."
330. Lit. "vain hopes."

'You will have peace';
And to all those following their stubborn wills,
    They say, 'No harm will come to you.'"
18 But who [of them] has stood in the council of Yahweh,
    And seen and heard his word?[331]
    Who has listened to his message and heard?
19 Look, the storm of Yahweh will be unleashed in wrath,
    A whirlwind storm;
    Upon the head of the wicked it will swirl.
20 Yahweh's anger will not subside
    Until he fully accomplishes the purposes of his heart.
At the end of the days,
    you will understand it clearly.
21 "I did not send these prophets,
    But [off] they ran.
I did not speak to them,
    Yet they have prophesied.
22 Yet if they had had a place on my council,
    They would have let my people hear my word.
They would have turned them from their evil ways
    And from the corruption of their deeds.
23 Am I just a God who is nearby,"
    Declares Yahweh,
    "And not a God who is far away?"
24 "Can anyone hide in secret places,
    And I not see him?" Yahweh asks.
Am I not the One who fills
    Heaven and earth?" declares Yahweh.[332]

25 I have heard what they have said—the prophets who prophesy lies in my name. They say, "I had a dream! I had a dream!" **26** How long is this to go on? Is it in the minds of the prophets who prophesy lies, who are

---

331. The LXX reads καὶ εἶδεν τὸν λόγον αὐτου, "and seen his word," in place of the MT's וְיִשְׁמַע אֶת־דְּבָרוֹ, "and heard his word."

332. The expression נְאֻם־יְהוָה, "declares Yahweh," is missing in the LXX.

prophets of their own delusions— **27** is it their intention to use the dreams they relate to one another to make my people forget my name,[333] just as their fathers forgot my name because of Baal? **28** The prophet who has a dream, let him tell his dream; but he who has my word, let him faithfully speak my word. What has straw to do with wheat? **29** Is not my word like fire, declares Yahweh, like a hammer that breaks in pieces the rock?

30 Therefore, declares Yahweh, I am against the prophets who keep stealing my words from one another. **31** Believe me, I am opposed to the prophets who wag their tongues[334] and make declarations [allegedly from Yahweh], declares Yahweh. **32** Believe me, I am against those who prophesy fraudulent dreams, declares Yahweh, and who, by repeating them, mislead my people with their reckless claims. I myself never sent them or appointed them. They certainly do not benefit this people, declares Yahweh.

33 If these people, a prophet or a priest, should ask you, "What is the burden of Yahweh?" Say to them, "You are the burden![335] and I will abandon you," declares Yahweh.

34 As for the prophet, the priest, or anyone else who claims, "[This is the] the burden of Yahweh," I will punish that man and his household. **35** This is what each of you keeps saying to one another, among yourselves, "What answer did Yahweh give? Or, what did Yahweh say?" **36**[336] But you must not mention[337] the burden of Yahweh again, because every man's own word becomes his burden and so you distort the words of the Living God, Yahweh of Hosts, our God. **37** This is what you shall say to the prophet, "What answer did Yahweh give you?" Or, "What did Yahweh say?" **38** And

---

333. The LXX has τοῦ ἐπιλαθέσθαι τοῦ νόμου μου, "to forget my law," where the MT has לְהַשְׁכִּיחַ אֶת־עַמִּי שְׁמִי, "to make my people forget my name." The Syr. has "to cause my people to err in my name."

334. Where the MT has הַלֹּקְחִים לְשׁוֹנָם, "who take up their tongues," the LXX has ἐκβάλλοντας προφητείας γλώσσης, "who cast out prophecies of the tongue." The Tg. has "who prophesy according to the good pleasure of their heart."

335. It is better to follow the LXX and Vg. here. The MT reads אֶת־מַה־מַשָּׂא, "What burden?" (cf. NIV). The LXX reads ὑμεῖς ἐστε τὸ λῆμμα, "you are the burden." The LXX appears to have read the Heb. direct obj. marker and "what?" as אַתֶּם, which regroups the consonants and deletes the heh (ה). With this reading the problem disappears, and it makes excellent sense in this context.

336. The end of v. 36 and the beginning of v. 37 are missing in the LXX.

337. Lit. "remember."

if you say, "the burden of Yahweh"[338]—then this is what Yahweh has said: "Because you use this expression, 'the burden of Yahweh,' though I did not send you to say, 'the burden of Yahweh,' **39** believe me, I will therefore surely[339] forget you and cast you out of my presence along with the city I gave you and your fathers. **40** I will bring on you everlasting disgrace— everlasting humiliation that will not be forgotten."

COMMENTARY

From the preceding sections one gains the impression that Jeremiah's problems are mainly with the political leaders, but blame is to be shared with the religious leaders as well. But, whereas the names of the leaders of state are given previously, no names are given for any religious leaders in this section. Who among those who go by the name of "prophet" actually speaks the word of God? What criteria does a person in Judah use to determine who is telling the truth from God?—for it surely seems as if the majority of the prophets are against Jeremiah and his jeremiads.

Yahweh's Denunciation of the False Prophets (23:9–15)

23:9-10 Jeremiah begins his lament noting how disturbed his mental state is rather than merely speaking of his emotional state; thus he is more extremely disturbed in his mind and shocked rationally than he is heart-broken in our sense of the term. The reason is that the land was full of adulterers, with an overwhelming amount of upsetting evidence of corrupt behavior in the land.

23:11-12 What is worse is that both the prophets and the priests indulge in the same immorality, even as they practice it also in the very temple of God (v. 11). A description of such immoral practices carried out in the temple is documented in 2 Kgs 21:5 and Ezek 8:6–18. It is remarkable that neither this text nor the OT in general uses the term "false prophet." But that did not mean that there are no tests for determining whether a prophet is genuine or not, for Deut 18:15–22 and 13:1–9 give five such tests for a true prophet. They are:

---

338. The LXX omits וְאִם־מַשָּׂא יְהוָה תֹּאמֵרוּ, "if you say, the burden of Yahweh."
339. The LXX omits the emphatic "surely" expressed in the Heb. as finite verb + inf. abs.

1. The true prophet has to be an Israelite (Deut 18:18).

2. The true prophet has to speak in the name of Yahweh (Deut 18:20).

3. The true prophet has to predict the near as well as the distant future (Deut 18:21-22).

4. The true prophet has to perform signs and wonders with his prophecy (Deut 13:1-3).

5. The true prophet has to conform to the previously revealed word of Yahweh (Deut 13:6-9).[340]

For those who proved false, the treacherous nature of their predictions would become evident by the slippery paths formed by their flattery and smooth words as well as the darkness that would come along with the judgment of God (v. 12) due to a lack of repentance.

23:13–15 This denunciation is followed by another judgment speech in vv. 13-14, with the sentencing coming in v. 15. The sin of the northern prophets from Samaria (v. 13) is that they prophesied in the name of Baal (7:15; 1 Kgs 18:16-40). The scandal of the prophets from Judah or Jerusalem (v. 14) is even worse, for they espoused adultery and pagan worship, and they lived a lifestyle filled with lies, all of which is reminiscent of the wickedness of Sodom and Gomorrah. Even as they claimed to be prophets of Yahweh (and not, as the northern prophets claimed to be, prophets who spoke in the name of Baal), their actions and words ran directly counter to how God had instructed them to live and teach in his word. Instead, "they strengthened the hands of wicked, so that no one turn[ed] from his wickedness" (v. 14d). Their lives and teaching lessons are no moral guide by which to live or act!

---

340. W. C. Kaiser Jr., "False Prophet," and "Prophet, Prophetess, Prophecy," in *The Evangelical Dictionary of Biblical Theology*, ed. W. Elwell (Grand Rapids: Baker, 1996), 242-43; 641-47.

The Characteristics of False Propheticism (23:16–24)

23:16–22 In light of such treacherous teaching and living from those who are supposed to be the model of uprightness and truth, Jeremiah gives an exhortation from Yahweh (vv. 16–20). Stop listening to these provocateurs of empty and foggy hopes (v. 16b). Their talk is completely insubstantial (הֶבֶל), and there is no reality or truth behind their speeches. Instead, they talk out of their own thinking and not from a revelation given by God (v. 16d). The problem is not with the mode of their prophetic reception, for dreams are often used by God, but with its source; it comes from a human origin and not from a divine revelation. Nevertheless, these false prophets "keep on saying to the scorners of Yahweh's word, '[Yahweh says,] "You will have peace"'" (v. 17a–b) and "no harm will come to you" (v. 17d). This is nothing less than evidence of a "stubbornness of will [or heart]" on the part of the prophets and the people (v. 17c).

But the question of the hour is this: Who has been part of the council of God to hear and see what God has to say (v. 18)? Only Jeremiah can say that he has stood in the council of God and heard God's word about the coming judgment, which will break out on Judah like a storm (vv. 19–20).[341] The competing prophets are on their own, for none of them has had the privilege of having a place at the table of God's council.

The image of the storm (v. 19) is reminiscent of theophanies that depict God as a warrior who moves in judgment against the wicked (Hab 3:1–19). Elsewhere, Jeremiah used the storm imagery frequently (4:11–12; 13:24; 18:17; 25:32), for, as Lord of all, God has mastery and lordship over even the storms.

The council of God is portrayed in Scripture as a gathering of divine beings, presided over by Yahweh, concerning earthly affairs (cf. 1 Kgs 22:19–23; Job 1–2; 15:8; Ps 82; Isa 6:1–8). They appear to act as a consultative group. Surprisingly enough, the true prophets of God seem to participate at times in this group in order to obtain Yahweh's word, which they were to bring back to earth.

---

341. Even though critical scholars suggest that the expression is a postexilic addition, Lipinski argues that Jer 23:16–22 is an early, orderly literary unit that fits in the oracles against the false prophets. See E. Lipiński, "באחרית הימים Dans les Textes Préexiliques," VT 20, no. 4 (1970): 445–50.

Yahweh is not presented as being in heaven alone, but as One who has a relationship with others in a social context in the council. Some have proposed analogies with Mesopotamian or Canaanite myths of a divine council, in which there are meetings of the pantheon of gods, but the monotheism of the Scriptures argues against the helpfulness of this analogy.

Angels are depicted as presenting themselves before God (Job 1:6; 2:1). Satan even appears to be an infrequent attender (Job 1:9–11; 2:4–5), yet he is not a permanent member of the council. Revelation 4:6b–8 pictures angelic beings as among those who perpetually stand around God's throne.

23:23-24 Verses 23–24 ask three rhetorical questions. The answer to the first question is that God is both near and far off. The answer to the second question is that no one can hide from God, for God fills both heaven and earth. This answer is remarkable, for God is everywhere; no one can hide from him. The false prophets thought they made God close by as a result of their speaking, but God's revelation is "far" from them. They also may think that they can escape and hide from God during the time of judgment, but that too is not true, for God will find their hiding place no matter where it might be.[342]

Who Has the Actual Burden of Yahweh? (23:25–40)

23:25-28 With pride these false prophets announce, "I had a dream! I had a dream!" even though they only have lies (v. 25). God wants to know from them: "How long will this [nonsense] go on?" (v. 26). Their prophecies come from their own hearts and minds, not from Yahweh or from any dreams he has sent. Do these charlatans think that they can get God's people to forget his name by giving these dreams one to another (v. 27), as had happened among some of their fathers? This of course is not a polemic against

---

342. The LXX has the indic. "I am a God at hand … and not a God far off," where the MT has the interrogative "Am I a God at hand … and not a God far off?" Lemke argues that the MT reflects the prophet's thought and message. He states that Jeremiah's affirmation should be "understood not in terms of some general theological assertion concerning God's omniscience or transcendence, but in terms of the more polemic context of Jeremiah's struggle with other prophets of his day and the dominant theological perspectives which they represent." See W. E. Lemke, "The Near and Distant God: A Study of Jer 23:23–24 in Its Biblical Theological Context," *JBL* 100, no. 4 (1981): 541–55.

dreams, for what is attacked, once again, is not the vehicle of revelation but the alleged source.

23:29-32 The real word of God is more like "fire" and the blows of a "hammer" in judgment than the tepid and vacuous words of these false prophets. Fire is used by Jeremiah as the symbol of destruction (21:14; 43:12, etc.) but also of God's anger (4:4; 17:4; 21:12, etc.); it surely is not some romantic idea of peace and security. Therefore God is most definitely against these false prophets who plagiarize their words from each other and claim their words came from their own revelation (vv. 30-31).[343] Three times Yahweh repeats that he is against these prophets (vv. 30, 31, 32). These prophets wag their tongues in all sorts of reckless declarations that have the sound of authentic revelations, but they are so false "they certainly do not benefit this people" (v. 32d).[344]

23:33-40 The final section (vv. 33-40) focuses on the "burden" (מַשָּׂא) of Yahweh. While some have rendered "burden"[345] as "oracle," regardless these prophecies consist exclusively of threats, and the term usually is followed not by the gen. of the speaker (that is, "the oracle of Jeremiah"), but by the gen. of the obj., such as "the burden/oracle of Babylon, of Moab, etc."[346] Apparently, as part of the mockery of Jeremiah's message, the question keeps coming to him in mock sincerity, "What is the burden of Yahweh?" Jeremiah is told to reply: "You are the burden! and I will abandon you" (v. 33).

For those prophets and priests who persist in announcing what they perceive to be the burden of Yahweh, God will punish them and their households (vv. 34-35). Since every false prophet thinks his burden is the

343. Werblowsky suggests that the false prophets were looking at each other "as a source of inspiration." See R. J. Zwi Werblowsky, "Stealing the Word," VT 6, no. 1 (January 1956): 105-6.

344. De Hoop argues that the use suggests a basic meaning of "to deceive." See R. de Hoop, "The Meaning of *phz* in Classical Hebrew," ZAH 10 (1997): 16-26.

345. This word appears twenty-seven times; all except two (Prov 30:1; 31:1) occur in prophetic contexts.

346. See W. C. Kaiser, "'Massa,' II. A Burden," in *Theological Wordbook of the Old Testament*, ed. R. L. Harris, G. L. Archer Jr., and B. K. Waltke (Chicago: Moody Press, 1980), 2:601-2.

divine burden, the whole concept of the burden of Yahweh must not be announced anymore. Every false prophet's burden is evidence against him, for in this way they all continue to distort the words of the living God (v. 36).

God will totally forget those who persist in claiming they are speaking on his behalf (note the pun on נָשָׂא, *nāśā*ʾ, "to lift up" [hence "burden"] and נָשָׁה, *nāšâ*, "to forget"; v. 39). Instead, God will bring on them everlasting disgrace and their "everlasting humiliation that will not be forgotten" (v. 40). These false prophets did not expose Judah's sins and so they did not ward off the coming captivity.

Teaching and preaching the genuine word of God cannot be artificially replicated out of one's own mind. God's real word is like a "hammer that breaks a rock in pieces." God's word is not only like a hammer but also like a "fire" and like real "grain," as opposed to chaff, which the wind can easily blow away.

Three times over in vv. 30–32, God declares he is against such false prophets, for their plagarizing his word by stealing what he had said in other contexts and uselessly wagging their tongues, claiming it was the declaration of the Lord as they fill their speeches with their own dreams. Such teachers and proclaimers of what they claim is the word of God will earn from God his everlasting contempt, and the shame they accumulate will never be forgotten by the Lord, whom we all must face in that final day.

GOOD AND BAD FIGS (24:1–10)

This chapter takes us into the reign of the last king of Judah, Zedekiah. Its contents go beyond the first deportation of 597 BC and represent the period between this deportation in 597 BC and the final destruction of Jerusalem in 587 BC, as 24:1 indicates. This section tells in an autobiographical style how the message came to the prophet Jeremiah.

TRANSLATION

1 Yahweh showed me—and there, arranged in front of the temple of Yahweh were two baskets of figs. (It happened after King Nebuchadnezzar of Babylon had deported from Jerusalem King Jeconiah ben Jehoiakim of Judah, along with the princes of Judah, the craftsmen, and the

metalworkers,[347] and taken them to Babylon.) **2** In one basket the figs were very good, like first ripe figs. In the other basket the figs were extremely bad, so bad that they were inedible. **3** Then Yahweh said to me, "What do you see, Jeremiah?" I answered, "Figs. The good figs are very good and the bad figs are very bad, so bad as to be inedible."

4 Then the word of Yahweh came to me: **5** "This is what Yahweh, the God of Israel says: 'Like those good figs so I will regard as good the exiles of Judah, whom I sent away from this place to the land of the Chaldeans for their good. **6** I will look out for them for their good and restore them to this land; I will build them up and not tear them down, I will plant them and not uproot them. **7** I will give to them[348] a heart to know me, that I am Yahweh. They will be my people, and I will be their God, for they will return to me with all their heart. **8** But like figs that are too rotten to eat—indeed this is what Yahweh has said—so I will treat Zedekiah king of Judah and his princes and the survivors from Jerusalem, whether they remain in this land or live in Egypt. **9** I will make them an object of horror and an offense[349] to all the kingdoms of the earth, and a reproach, a byword, a taunt, and a curse in all the places where I will scatter them.[350] **10** I will send on them the sword, famine, and plague, until they have died off the land, which I gave them and their fathers.'"[351]

COMMENTARY

The Vision (24:1–3)

24:1–3 God "showed" (הִרְאַנִי) Jeremiah a vision (as he had shown Amos in 7:1, 4, 7; 8:1), whereby he announced the future of two groups among the people of Israel. Chapter 25 will announce the future of Babylon and all

---

347. The LXX adds καὶ τοὺς δεσμώτας καὶ τοὺς πλουσίους, "and the prisoners and the rich," after "and the metalworkers."

348. Walton argues that the first words in vv. 7 and 9 (וְנָתַתִּי and וּנְתַתִּים) are part of a wordplay, just like the ones present in 1:11–15. If so, "the wordplay would not negate the force of the interpretation based on analogy, but would add another dimension to the relationship between display and the oracle." See J. H. Walton, "Vision Narrative Wordplay and Jeremiah XXIV," *VT* 39, no. 4 (October 1989): 508–9.

349. The LXX omits לְרָעָה, "for evil."

350. The *BHS* editor suggests that the phrase "in all the places where I will scatter them" (בְּכָל־הַמְּקֹמוֹת אֲשֶׁר־אַדִּיחֵם שָׁם) is an addition from Deut 28:37.

351. The LXX omits וְלַאֲבוֹתֵיהֶם, "and to their fathers."

the other nations, but in chapter 24 Yahweh focuses on Judah. Jeremiah is not told to announce this word to any special audience; the vision seems more for the prophet's own enlightenment. This report is coming some twelve years after the death of good King Josiah, in the days of Zedekiah, who will prove to be Judah's last king. King Jehoiachin, Josiah's grandson, has already been taken as a prisoner of King Nebuchadnezzar, along with a number of the key skilled craftsmen of Judah, including the golden vessels from the temple (2 Kgs 24:13).

It is easy to see how many in Judah were perhaps thinking that with the removal of King Jehoiachin, the temple's golden vessels, and the skilled workers of the nation, that now the worst is over and the Babylonians will think that this is a tough-enough lesson for God to impose on the land of Judah! No, they conjecture, things will calm down, and Jeremiah's predictions of the extent of the coming destruction will not take place—or so they hope. Things will normalize very soon, for the worse just has to be past already.[352]

The vision the prophet receives is of two baskets of figs (*ficus carica*). Figs appear in the Bible some sixty times, usually representing peace and security, as when the people of the Bible sit down under their own fig tree. These two baskets of figs, however, are placed in front of the temple. The very good figs probably point to the early crop of figs, which came in June, whereas the second crop of figs came in August–September. The bad figs were rotten and inedible, thus dividing the groups to be described into two separate categories.

This vision comes to the prophet now some thirty years into his ministry. When asked what he has seen, he answers correctly, just as he had been complimented on seeing correctly in his first vision in Jer 1:12 (cf. 1:11, 13)—"You have seen correctly."

---

352. Stipp erroneously suggests that Jeremiah's vision is "redrawn Judean history" in which the exile is not a tool of judgment but of salvation. See H.-J. Stipp, "Jeremia 24: Geschichtsbild und Historischer Ort," *JNSL* 25, no. 1 (1999): 151–83.

The Good Figs (24:4-7)

24:4-7 As Jeremiah describes what he has seen of these two baskets of figs, the assumption among the people would be that those who have already been exiled were the bad figs in God's sight, but those who remain in the land constitute the good figs. But that is not the case at all. Now, after thirty years of ministry, Jeremiah finally has some good news about "building" or "planting" that had been promised in Jer 1:10 as he was called. But the good news is for those who have already been exiled to Babylon with King Jehoiachin; they are the ones likened to good figs (v. 5).

God will set his eyes to "watch over" them for good (v. 6; cf. Amos 9:4), and ultimately he will bring them back home to their land in Judah (v. 6b), as he had pledged to the patriarchs and as later confirmed in the Sinaitic covenant and in the promises made to David. Why our Lord uses figs here instead of some other fruit is not clear, but these suggestions can be made: 1) There were two fig harvests each year, which would lend itself to the discussion of a second wave of exiles, or 2) ripe figs can be quite delectable, whereas rotten figs are inedible and noxious.

The point is that the negative oracles against King Jehoiachin are directed more against him (see 22:24-30 and 52:31-34), but this judgment against him personally will not remove from Judah and Israel the promises God had given to Abraham and David. This promise seems to anticipate the promises of 31:31-34 and 32:37-41.

God will "give them a [new] heart to know [him]" (v. 7). This is an amazing announcement, given what Jeremiah has said about the people's stubborn hearts already in 3:17 and 5:23. Even though these earlier exiles are addressed as "good figs" (though no less guilty than others who will be exiled later), they still need a new heart and a new will. A new work from God is needed among even these called good figs, for this too is not a minor issue. Therefore, both a specific place to live in the land and a new heart are needed. The people who experience this are not people from another nation; no, they are the same people of Israel. Thus, there is continuity beyond the threatened disaster. There will be continuity in the matter of the land and continuity in the old rotten hearts that might now have a desire to know God because of his gift of a new heart.

How then is the old heart linked to the new (v. 7)? It does not seem to be conditioned on the nation's turning back to God with their whole heart, for if that were the case, why then are they *given* a new heart? The promises of God are based on his unchanging character. However, at the same time, these persons are not passive mortals; they are called on to "return" to the land and to work that land as it once had been worked.

The Bad/Rotten Figs (24:8–10)

24:8–10 As for the inedible or rotten figs, King Zedekiah is the chief figure in this group, which also includes those who remained in the land after the exile in 597 BC and those who had gone to live in Egypt with King Jehoahaz (that is, Shallum; v. 8, cf. 2 Kgs 23:34). They will be treated the same way that one would handle rotten figs: they will be thrown away. Their future is described in 29:16–19. God will make them a horror or an evil thing to all the nations in all the places where they will be scattered (v. 9). They will become, in one of the rarest litanies of such a collection of words of judgment, a "reproach," a "byword," "an object of ridicule," and the objects of "cursing" in all of the diaspora (v. 9b). The problem for many is that they remain unrepentant.

But this only highlights one of the chief blessings of the covenant: it is to know the living God. Jeremiah had taught in 9:23–24 that it was not the wise man who gloried in his wisdom, or the rich man who gloried in his riches, but if there was anything to glory in, it was that a mortal with a new heart could actually know and understand God. God gets the most pleasure when people have knowledge of Yahweh: "I desire: the knowledge of God more than burnt offerings," says God in Hos 6:6. This is why the promise of the good figs is the best of all possible announcements. "I will give them a heart to know me, that I am Yahweh" (Jer 24:7a). Such is the evidence of the grace of God as it overcomes all obstacles that can be thrown against it.

The figs are placed at the entrance to the temple of Yahweh: one basket of good figs and the other of bad, inedible figs. Jeremiah is told that the good figs represent those who will be exiled from the land of Israel to Babylon, which is exactly what happened in 597 BC. They are those who possess skills as craftsmen and are the leaders of the nation. God will watch over them and eventually bring them back to the land of Israel. He will be their God, and they will be his people, for they will return to God with all their heart and soul.

The bad figs, however, represent those who, like King Zedekiah, are left in the land or have already been taken to Egypt. They will become abhorrent to the Lord and the basis for ridicule on the nation.

THE SEVENTY YEARS OF BABYLONIAN CAPTIVITY (25:1–14)

The twenty-fifth chapter of Jeremiah is most complex because of the differences between the Heb. and the Septuagint (LXX) text.[353] The most obvious difference is that the LXX places the messages against the nations, chapters 46 through 51 in the MT text, immediately after 25:13a. For many, this is primary evidence that the material here has undergone some type of revision. It is just as likely, though, that the problem originated with the LXX and not the Heb. text. The Heb. text as it exists in our English translations is divided into three parts:

1. a summary prose message of Jeremiah (vv. 1–14),

2. a narrative about a symbolic action (vv. 15–29), and

3. an announcement of judgment against the nations (vv. 30–38).

TRANSLATION

1 The message for all the people of Judah that Jeremiah received in the fourth year of King Jehoiakim son of Josiah king of Judah (which was the first year of Nebuchadnezzar, king of Babylon),[354] **2** which Jeremiah the prophet[355] spoke to all the people of Judah and to all those living in Jerusalem: **3** "From the thirteenth year of Josiah, son of Amon king of Judah until this very day—twenty-three years—the word of Yahweh has come

---

353. Aejmelaeus argues that the shorter text of the LXX should be preferred. See A. Aejmelaeus, "Jeremiah at the Turning-Point of History: The Function of Jer. XXV 1–14 in the Book of Jeremiah," VT 52, no. 4 (2002): 459–82. Christiansen, on the other hand, argues for the integrity of the MT, with both traditions having treated it as canonical. See D. L. Christensen, "In Quest of the Book of Jeremiah: A Study of Jeremiah 25 in Relation to Jeremiah 46–51," JETS 33, no. 2 (1990): 145–53.

354. The phrase הִיא הַשָּׁנָה הָרִאשֹׁנִית לִנְבוּכַדְרֶאצַּר מֶלֶךְ בָּבֶל, "that was the first year of Nebuchadnezzar king of Babylon," is missing in the LXX.

355. The phrase יִרְמְיָהוּ הַנָּבִיא, "Jeremiah, the prophet," is missing in the LXX.

to me[356] and I have spoken unto you again and again, but you have not listened.[357] **4** And although Yahweh has sent all his servants[358] the prophets to you[359] again and again, you have not listened or paid any attention, **5** Saying, 'Turn now, each of you, from your evil ways and your evil practices and you can stay in the land, which Yahweh gave to you[360] and to your fathers forever and ever. **6** Do not follow other gods to serve and to worship them. Do not provoke me to anger with what your hands have made. Then I will not harm you.[361] **7** But you did not listen to me,'[362] declares Yahweh, 'and you have provoked me with what your hands have made, and you have brought harm to yourselves.'

8 "Therefore, thus says Yahweh of Hosts, 'Because you have not listened to my words,[363] **9** Look out, I am going to send all the peoples of the north,[364] and my servant, Nebuchadnezzar, king of Babylon,' declares Yahweh,[365] 'and I will bring them against this land and its inhabitants and against all the other surrounding nations. I will devote them to destruction and make them an object of horror, scorn, and an everlasting ruin.[366] **10** I will banish from them the sound of jubilation, the sound of joy, the voice of the bridegroom, the voice of the bride, the sound of the hand-mill[367] and the light

---

356. The phrase הָיָה דְבַר־יְהוָה אֵלַי, "the word of Yahweh was/came to me," is missing in the LXX.

357. The phrase וְלֹא שְׁמַעְתֶּם, "but you have not listened," is missing in the LXX.

358. The LXX reads τοὺς δούλους μου, "my servants," where the MT has עֲבָדָיו, "his servants."

359. The LXX reads καὶ ἀπέστελλον πρὸς ὑμᾶς, "and I sent to you," making Yahweh the speaker, instead of "Yahweh has sent to you."

360. The LXX reads ἐπιτηδευμάτων ὑμῶν, "I gave to you," where the MT has נָתַן יְהוָה לָכֶם, "Yahweh has given to you."

361. The LXX reads τοῦ κακῶσαι ὑμᾶς, "to do you harm," where the MT has וְלֹא אָרַע לָכֶם, "then I will do you no harm."

362. The LXX has only the beginning phrase, καὶ οὐκ ἠκούσατέ μου, "But you have not listened to me"; it is missing the rest of the verse.

363. The LXX reads οὐκ ἐπιστεύσατε τοῖς λόγοις μου, "you have not believed my words," where the MT has לֹא־שְׁמַעְתֶּם אֶת־דְּבָרָי, "you have not obeyed my words."

364. The LXX has τὴν πατριὰν ἀπὸ βορρᾶ, "a family from the north," where the MT has אֶת־כָּל־מִשְׁפְּחוֹת צָפוֹן, "all the tribes of the north."

365. The expression נְאֻם־יְהוָה וְאֶל־נְבוּכַדְרֶאצַּר מֶלֶךְ־בָּבֶל עַבְדִּי, "declares Yahweh, and for Nebuchadnezzar the king of Babylon, my servant," is missing in the LXX.

366. The LXX reading is καὶ εἰς ὀνειδισμὸν αἰώνιον, "and an everlasting reproach," where the MT has וּלְחָרְבוֹת עוֹלָם, "and an everlasting ruin/desolation."

367. The LXX has ὀσμὴν μύρου, "the scent of myrrh," where the MT has קוֹל רֵחַיִם, "the sound of hand-mill/millstones."

of the lamp. **11** This whole country will become a desolate wasteland and these nations will serve the king of Babylon[368] seventy years.'

12 "'But when the seventy years are fulfilled, I will punish the king of Babylon[369] and his nation, the land of the Babylonians, for their guilt,' declares Yahweh, 'and will make it desolate forever. **13** I will bring upon that land all the things I have spoken against it, all that are written in this book and prophesied by Jeremiah against all the nations. **14** They themselves will be enslaved by many nations and great kings; I will repay them according to their deeds and the work of their hands.'"

COMMENTARY

Disregarded Warnings (25:1–7)

25:1 This word comes to Jeremiah in 604 BC, that eventful fourth year of King Jehoiakim (25:1).[370] This is also the first year of Nebuchadnezzar's reign (25:1). In the previous three years Jehoiakim had been a vassal to Pharaoh of Egypt (2 Kgs 23:34–36), but when Nebuchadnezzar defeated the Egyptians at Carchemish in May 605 BC (Jer 46:2–12), it was a foregone conclusion that Jehoiakim would now need to be beholden to Babylon and not to Egypt any longer. It is important to note that it was a common practice for scribes to take the dates given in another country that used a differing system of counting the years and translate them into their own system. For example, Dan 1:1 uses the accession year method of calculating (wherein the year of accession was not counted until one began with the start of a new year, to count the time that a ruler was on the throne), so Daniel reads: "In the third year of King Jehoiakim of Judah, King Nebuchadnezzar of Babylon came to Jerusalem and besieged it." Jeremiah, however, uses the Palestinian-Jewish non-accession year method (wherein the year of accession was the first year, even if the ruler only reigned one day of that year), so what Daniel calls the "third" year is recorded by Jeremiah as the "fourth" year (Jer 25:1, 9; 46:2). Daniel writes from a Babylonian perspective, while Jeremiah writes from the Judahite perspective.

---

368. The LXX is missing the reference to the king of Babylon.

369. The expression עַל־מֶלֶךְ־בָּבֶל, "the king of Babylon," is missing in the LXX.

370. Also note three other references to this same fourth year in 36:1; 45:1; 46:2.

The threatened judgment is huge, for no less than twenty-nine times is the word "all" (כֹּל) used in this chapter. This is but another way to point to the comprehensive nature of the coming judgment. But somewhere near the end of Jehoiakim's fourth year or at the beginning of his fifth year, Jeremiah will be restricted from that time forward from addressing all the people of Judah as he does on this occasion (36:1–5)—especially address-ing them from the temple courts. In fact, this expression, "all the people of Judah," is found only here and in 26:18. This "all" includes both groups of figs in the previous chapter, good and bad.

25:2–3 Even though Jeremiah has now been ministering to the people for twenty-three years (v. 3), the people of Judah have been persistently unre-sponsive to his message. When one wonders how this prophet could have had the stamina to continue under such intense pressure, the answer must be this: his message does not originate in his own person, but from Yahweh. Naturally, the disinterest shown by the people of Judah must weigh heavily on Jeremiah; nevertheless, he is obedient to the call of God. These twen-ty-three years began in 627 BC and include nineteen under King Josiah and now four under King Jehoiakim, as well as the three months of King Jehoahaz's reign.

However, now that Nebuchadnezzar has ascended to the throne, Jeremiah's dire predictions about a "foe from the north" (1:14) must have a more realistic sound even to those who have hardened their hearts against Jeremiah's warnings from Yahweh. The prophet's ministry from the thir-teenth year of King Josiah (1:2) until this twenty-third year (627–604 BC) is a record of faithfulness and consistent calling for the people to return.

25:4–6 Jeremiah was not the only prophet God sent to Judah, for there are other contemporary prophets such as Uriah, Huldah, Zephaniah, and Habakkuk, and in Babylon itself there is Ezekiel, in addition to a long line of prophets who preceded them. Nevertheless, there is a continuity in the message of the prophets: "Turn now, each of you, from your evil ways and your evil practices" (v. 5). No single word is more characteristic of the message of the sixteen writing prophets in the OT than this word "turn" (שׁוּב). The call is for a reversal in their general lifestyle ("way"; דֶּרֶךְ) and from the general consensus of what "practices" (מַעֲלָל) were acceptable and unacceptable. In Judah's case, both their lifestyle and their practices are "evil."

But if they "turn" in repentance to Yahweh, then they will be allowed to "dwell" in the land, which also involves a deliberate wordplay of the Heb. words "turn" (שׁוּב, *šûb*) and "dwell" (יָשַׁב, *yāšab*). If the people repent of their sin, they will be allowed to dwell/stay in their land "forever and ever" (v. 5; עוֹלָם, "forever"; cf. v. 9). Judah and Israel will be given possession of the land as promised in the Abrahamic Covenant without a limit on the time.

25:7 However, the people outrageously rebel against God's word by substituting pagan worship in place of serving Yahweh. They deliberately flout what God has instructed them, thus "provok[ing]" (כָּעַס) God to anger. The way for the people to avoid "harm" (רַע) is to repent and turn from their wicked ways. Amazingly, however, the people refuse to listen to Yahweh, for it is clear from v. 7 that when they refuse to hear and obey what the prophets said, they are refusing to listen to Yahweh himself ("you did not listen to me, declares Yahweh"). In so doing they bring "harm" to themselves (v. 7).

Seventy Years of Captivity (25:8–14)

A divine sentence is therefore given against Judah: they will go to Babylon and be in subjection to it for seventy years. This will be the case until Babylon is swept away as a nation (vv. 12–14).

25:8–9 That the people of Judah continue to exhibit a lack of response to the warnings that have been issued by Yahweh leads to the judgment that must now come. Verse 9 begins literally with "Behold me summoning," which is rendered, "Look out, I am going to send all the peoples of the north and my servant Nebuchadnezzar, king of Babylon." Here Jeremiah affirms for the first time that the threatened conquerors will not only come from the north, but they will originate in Babylon. This assumes that Pashhur's action in debarring Jeremiah from prophesying in the temple in 20:4, 6 comes after this address.

But what must have been especially galling to Judahites is that Jeremiah called the conqueror Nebuchadnezzar "my [God's] servant" (v. 9; also see 27:6; 43:10). So shocked were the Gk. translators of this text (LXX) that they omit this reference to "my servant."[371] But this is not unusual, for has not God, through the prophet Isaiah, called Cyrus the Persian king "my shepherd," even God's "anointed" one (Isa 44:28; 45:1)? Surely, as sovereign over all, God can even call the wind his servant (Ps 104:4), Balaam's donkey his servant (Num 22:21–33), and the nations of Assyria the rod of his anger and his servant (Isa 10:5), and now a foreign king will act as his servant. Nevertheless, the whole idea of Babylon being God's servant must have sounded treasonous to the people.

Nebuchadnezzar, under the direction of God, will be brought not only against the land of Judah, but also against the surrounding nations. God will utterly destroy (חָרַם) them. This term is used earlier in the Heb. Bible to describe the complete destruction of the Canaanites, whose iniquity had by then completely filled up the entire cup of wrath (Gen 15:16; Deut 20:17–18; Josh 6:18). God will make an involuntary offering of the people and their towns, who are thus put under a ban and dedicated to destruction.

25:10–11 Since his people have broken the covenant, they will receive the curses of that same covenant. The pagan nations living as if Yahweh is not God over all will suffer many of the same inflictions. The joys and jubilations of everyday life will cease and be replaced with Judah and the nations becoming "objects of horror," scorn, and "everlasting ruin[s]" (vv. 9–10). Five times the word "sound/voice" (קוֹל) reappears in v. 10, as if it were sounding like a drum beat at a funeral dirge. All mirth, joy, and sounds of the bride and bridegroom, not to mention a churning of the millstones in the morning and the light of the lamp in the evenings, will also be silenced.[372] The whole country will become a "desolate wasteland" (v. 11), and the nations will also serve the king of Babylon (v. 11b). This will

---

371. Lemke suggests that the designation of Nebuchadnezzar as the servant of Yahweh "owes its existence to an accidental error in the textual transmission of the book which bears the Prophet's name." See W. E. Lemke, "Nebuchadrezzar, My Servant," *CBQ* 28, no. 1 (1966): 45–50.

372. Grossberg suggests that the expression אוֹר נֵר "is to be understood both as 'light of the lamp' and 'tilled land.'" See D. Grossberg, "Pivotal Polysemy in Jeremiah 25:10–11," *VT* 36, no. 4 (1986): 481–85. In light of archaeological evidence, Lamaire sees similarity between that language of Jeremiah and Neo-Assyrian oath language found in the eighth and ninth centuries BC. See A. Lemaire, "Jérémie XXV 10B et la stèle araméenne de Bukân," *VT* 47, no. 4 (1997): 543–45.

be the prospect for the next seventy years (v. 11b), until the Babylonian Empire falls in 539 BC.

25:12-14 When the seventy years are completed (v. 12), however, God will punish the king of Babylon as well. God will treat Nebuchadnezzar as he had treated his captives. All that Yahweh had spoken against Babylon will be fulfilled (v. 13). That nation will be repaid according to its deeds and actions (v. 14b). Thus, God's justice is retributive but not arbitrary. All misconduct while Babylon acts as God's servant is reviewable and subject to retribution.

There is an ongoing debate as to how we are to understand the "seventy years" (25:11; 29:10). Should they be regarded as literal years, metaphorical years, or a literary convention? Seventy is used as the conventional number of years for one's life in Ps 90:10 (Craigie, 366). Some point to an inscription from the reign of King Esarhaddon of Assyria, which mentions a seventy-year period of subjugation for Babylon. But the biblical usage does not seem to fit this conventional type of usage, for it is repeated in too many other biblical contexts with strong chronological overtones (2 Chr 36:21; Dan 9:2; Zech 1:12; 7:53).

Others connect it with the amount of time that the land of Israel had to remain in rest for the years of her infidelity. Still others have figured that the seventy years started with the destruction of the temple in 586/7 BC and concluded with the temple being rebuilt in 515/6 BC. This, however, does not fit the **terminus ad quem** that ends with the destruction of Babylon.

These years can also be seen as a general approximation for the nearly seventy years that went from 605/604 BC, when this announcement was given, to 539 BC, when Cyrus of Persia conquered Babylon and permitted the exiles to return home (Ezra 1:1–4, cf. Zech 1:12). Some sixty-six years had expired, making the number seventy a good approximation (cf. Craigie, 366; Huey, 226). The best solution seems to be starting the seventy years earlier by extending it back to 597 BC, when Jerusalem first fell into Babylonian hands. Seventy years is linked with a period of retribution for the people's neglect of observance of the law of the Sabbath year (2 Chr 36:21), so we take the seventy years to be more of a literal designation than one that is metaphorical or conventional.

Nebuchadnezzar is called God's "servant" despite how horrifying it sounds to the people of God. God is Lord and Sovereign over all. Elsewhere King Cyrus of Persia is called God's shepherd (Isa 44:28) and his anointed one (Isa 45:1). God can use his own people and the events of his own making, but he can do more. He can also use people who are not part of his family, or events that he merely permits but does not direct.

THE CUP OF GOD'S WRATH (25:15–38)

This section focuses on the "cup of God's wrath," which is a fairly common metaphor throughout the OT. It is used as a positive metaphor in Pss 16:5, 7; 23:5; 116:13; Hab 23:16; Ezek 23:32; Isa 51:17-21, yet it can also be used as a symbol of God's judgment that causes him to take action against those who have sinned against him (Pss 48:26; 49:12; 51:7; 11:6; 75:9; Lam 4:21; Ezek 23:31-34; Hab 2:16). This same metaphor is carried over into the New Testament in Mark 10:38; Luke 22:42; John 18:11; Rev 14:10; 16:19; 17:4; 18:8.

While some have attempted to find the background for this imagery in certain rites of ratifying an international treaty, as an act of malediction in the case of any treaty breaking, or even in the drinking of the cup of ordeal in Num 5:11-31, it is best to see the cup in a metaphorical sense as an image coming directly from the hand of Yahweh.

TRANSLATION

15 For this is what Yahweh, the God of Israel says to me, "Take from my hand this cup filled with the wine of my wrath[373] and make all the nations to whom I send you drink it. **16** They will drink and stagger[374] and go mad because of the sword I will send among them."

17 So I took the cup from Yahweh's hand and made all the nations to which Yahweh sent me drink it: **18** Jerusalem and all the cities of Judah, together with its rulers and nobles—making them a desolation, a horrible and shocking sight, a curse, as they now in fact are;[375] **19** Pharaoh king

---

373. The LXX reads τοῦ οἴνου τοῦ ἀκράτου, "unmixed wine," where the MT has הַיַּיִן הַחֵמָה, "wine of wrath."

374. The LXX reads καὶ πίονται καὶ ἐξεμοῦνται, "and they will drink and vomit," where the MT has וְשָׁתוּ וְהִתְגֹּעֲשׁוּ, "and they will drink and stagger."

375. The LXX omits וְלִקְלָלָה כַּיּוֹם הַזֶּה, "and a curse, as as they now in fact are."

of Egypt, his attendants, his officials, and all his people, **20** together with all the foreign people there; all the kings of the land of Uz;[376] all the kings of the land of the Philistines, that is those of Ashkelon, Gaza, Ekron, and the people left at Ashdod; **21** Edom, Moab, and the Ammonites; **22** all the kings of Tyre and Sidon; all the kings of the coastlands[377] beyond the sea; **23** Dedan, Teman, Buz,[378] and all the people with shaven hairline; **24** that is, all the kings of Arabia,[379] and all the kings of foreign people who live in the desert; **25** all the kings of Zimri, all the kings of Elam, all the kings of the Medes; **26** all the kings of the north, near and far, one after another— all the kingdoms on the face of the earth. And after all of them, the king of Sheshach will drink it too.[380]

27 Then say to them, 'This is what Yahweh of Hosts, the God of Israel says: 'Drink and get drunk and vomit, and fall to rise no more, because the sword I am sending among you.'" **28** But if they refuse to take the cup from your hand and drink, tell them "This is what Yahweh of Hosts says: You must drink it! **29** For look here! On the city which bears my name I am beginning to bring disaster, and will you go unpunished, for I am calling down a sword upon all who live on earth, declares Yahweh of Hosts."[381]

30 As for you, you are to prophesy all these things to them. Say to them: Yahweh will roar from on high; from his holy dwelling[382] he will thunder and roar mightily against his land. He will shout like those treading grapes, shout against all the inhabitants of the earth. **31** The tumult will resound to the ends of the earth, for Yahweh has indicted the nations, he will bring judgment on all flesh; the wicked he will give up to the sword—declares Yahweh.

32 This is what Yahweh of Hosts says: "Look out! Disaster is proceeding from nation to nation; a mighty storm is building up from the ends of the

---

376. The LXX omits וְאֵת כָּל־מַלְכֵי אֶרֶץ הָעוּץ, "and all the kings of the land of Uz."

377. The LXX omits הָאִי, "of the coastlands."

378. The LXX has Ρως, "Ros," where the MT has בּוּז, "Buz."

379. The LXX omits וְאֵת כָּל־מַלְכֵי עֲרָב, "and all the kings of Arabia."

380. The LXX omits וּמֶלֶךְ שֵׁשַׁךְ יִשְׁתֶּה אַחֲרֵיהֶם, "and after all of them, the king of Sheshach will drink it too."

381. The LXX omits נְאֻם יְהוָה צְבָאוֹת, "declares Yahweh of hosts."

382. The LXX omits וּמִמְּעוֹן, "from the dwelling of."

earth. **33** At that time,[383] those slain by Yahweh will be everywhere—from one end of the earth to the other. They will not be mourned or gathered up[384] or buried, but will be like dung lying on the ground. **34** Howl, you shepherds! Cry out! Roll in the dust, you leaders of the flock. For the time of your slaughter has come;[385] you will fall and be shattered like fine pottery.[386] **35** The shepherds will have nowhere to flee, the leaders of the flock no place to escape. **36** Hear the cry of the shepherds, the wailing of the leaders of the flock, for Yahweh is destroying their pasture. **37** The peaceful meadows will be laid waste because of the fierce anger of Yahweh. **38** Like a lion he will leave his lair, and their land will become a shambles before the sword[387] of the oppressor and because of Yahweh's fierce anger."[388]

COMMENTARY

The Wine of Yahweh's Wrath (25:15–29)

25:15–16 Verse 15 begins with "for" (כִּי), which points back to v. 11, as it describes in detail what will happen to the nations listed here. Thus the prophet is given both a cup of wine for the nations to drink as well as the word from Yahweh. In fact, the two actions are linked, for making the nations partake from this cup of wrath means that simultaneously the nations also hear the word from Yahweh. Moreover, as the nations begin to drink from that cup, it induces a sort of madness as they stagger in their drunkenness and vomit.[389] It is clear that Yahweh will be "sending" (ptc.) the invading Babylonians to carry out this work against Judah and the nations. It is not as if Jeremiah will now go on a trip to each nation's capital city, or even offer this cup to the embassies of the ambassadors from those nations living in Jerusalem, but it might well be that as the prophet

---

383. The LXX reads ἐν ἡμέρᾳ κυρίου, "on the day of Yahweh," where the MT has בַּיּוֹם הַהוּא, "on that day."

384. The LXX omits לֹא יִסָּפְדוּ וְלֹא יֵאָסְפוּ, "they will not be mourned or gathered up."

385. The LXX omits וּתְפוֹצוֹתִיכֶם, "and your dispersion."

386. The LXX reads ὥσπερ οἱ κριοὶ οἱ ἐκλεκτοί, "like choice rams," where the MT has כִּכְלִי חֶמְדָּה, "like a choice vessel."

387. The LXX adds τῆς μεγάλης, "great," to modify τῆς μαχαίρας, "sword."

388. The LXX omits וּמִפְּנֵי חֲרוֹן אַפּוֹ, "and because of his fierce anger."

389. The LXX renders the word to "stagger" (גָּעַשׁ, gāʿaš) as "vomit" (ἐξεμέω).

speaks against each nation, he may extend a cup in his hand symbolically in the direction of each country as he gave God's indictment against them.

25:17-29 Jerusalem and its towns in Judah, along with their kings, officials, and leaders, will be turned into a source of ruin, horror, scorn, and a curse, terms that had already been announced in vv. 9 and 11. The clause "as they are today" (v. 18c), cannot refer to conditions after 605/604 BC but must refer more to the state of affairs in Jerusalem and the Judean countryside after 587 BC. Accordingly, it is best to see what began in 605/604 BC as finally consummated in 587 BC and part of a later addition to this prophecy.

The indictment of the nations begins in the south with Pharaoh of Egypt, his leaders, and people (v. 19), and moves northward. Approximately half of the nations listed in vv. 19-26 are the subjects of special messages in chapters 46-51, and this may be the reason why the LXX inserts these chapters immediately after chapter 25. From Egypt in northeastern Africa, Jeremiah moves geographically to Uz, which seems to be in the Negev of Israel, as Yahweh moves to the cities of the Philistines along the coast of Canaan, then to the countries of Transjordania (Edom, Moab, and Ammon), then back to the northern coast of Phoenicia and on to the islands of the Mediterranean, such as Cyprus. This geographical tour goes south once again into northern Arabia (Dedan, Tema, and Buz) and past Mesopotamia with Babylon, which he skips for the moment, into southwestern Iran/Persia (Elam and Media). This all is summarized as "all the kings of the earth," meaning apparently all those of that day. The cup of God's wrath cannot be held back from any of these nations, for if Judah is guilty and must experience judgment, then these others nations are just as certain to be guilty and ready for judgment as well.

Babylon is finally mentioned in v. 26b; however, it appears in cryptic fashion in a figure of speech knows as an *atbash* cryptogram. The word used here is "Sheshach" (v. 26b; 51:41). In this cryptogram, the alphabet is divided in half so that the letters corresponding to the word "Sheshach" are read from the opposite half of the alphabet in reverse order. "Sheshach" yields "B(a)b(e)l." God will use the "hosts" or "armies" of Babylon as his instrument of bringing judgment and justice before finally judging Babylon too.

The Storm of God's Judgment (25:30-38)

25:30-31 The judgment discussed in the previous section is now reiterated. Verses 30-31 set the stage with judgment beginning at the house of Gog in Jerusalem, but ultimately the roar of God's thunder will be heard and realized around the earth. In fact, that storm of his wrath will build to hurricane proportions (vv. 31-32). But this stormy judgment of God will finally focus on the people's shepherds and leaders who, more than others, have been responsible for the ruin that is now coming on the nations.

The "sword" announced in vv. 31 and 38 is the sword of Babylon, which will be the instrument God will use to discipline Judah and the nations that have chosen to disregard his call for justice and repentance. Just as the prophets Amos (1:2) and Joel (4:16) have chosen the imagery of a lion and its roar as it is in its leaping attack, so Jeremiah uses that same figure in v. 30. His roar is directed at first against the "pasture" (נָוֶה) of his land Judah, where his holy dwelling resided. God's attack will begin with a "shout," or a war cry, but a shout different from the joyous noise at the time of harvest as those who work the winepress tread on the grapes and cry out in rhythm (v. 30e). Rather, in this case the shout and noise will come from the armies gathered together in conquest, resulting also in the cries of alarm from their victims.

25:32-38 This disaster continues to spread from Judah to all the surrounding nations as well. Verse 33 has "at that time" or "on that day" (בַּיּוֹם הַהוּא; both have an eschatological note about them), and they seem to be a harbinger of the final judgment of God on planet Earth. So many will die in the battles on that day that it will not be possible to bury them all as the corpses will lie exposed on the ground where they fell in battle.

As a result of this tragedy, the kings, nobles, officers, shepherds, and leaders will not be able to escape the ensuing destruction, which perhaps has already begun. Instead, these leaders are instructed to cry aloud and roll in the dust, for their "time of slaughter" (v. 34; טִבְחָה, cf. 11:19, the usual word for butchering an animal) has come. Here is a real case of sarcasm, for whereas sheep were the usual victims for sacrifice, now the shepherds are being offered up.

There is no doubt that this presents a strong image as it depicts Yahweh slaying his people (v. 33) and others for sacrifice. However, what God *permits* may also be *attributed directly* to him, since the Hebrew Bible does not always pause to note secondary causes, as we in our culture are so prone to do so. But a text such as 27:8 does in a more detailed fashion point to the exact explanation we have given here, for it says "I have completed its destruction by his [Nebuchadnezzar's] hand." In fact this very same context uses the name of Babylon with the very same language attributed to God: "The slain of all the earth have fallen because of Babylon." Moreover, it is important to note that even though God is the one who slays (v. 33; חָלָל), in Jer 9:1 God weeps for those same "slain of [his] poor people." The God who "slays" persons (through the sword and hands of conquerors) is the same God who mourns over the slain and calls others to join him in his lamentations (9:17). The point, however, is that if God has used a pagan king like Nebuchadnezzar, and later Cyrus, does this not alert us to ask whether and how God could still use similar pagan leaders of nations in our own day to be the agents and instruments of his judgment when any people decide to turn away from him and act with injustice and unrighteously against his ordinances?

Verse 38 returns again (cf. v. 30) to the image of God as a "lion" (כְּפִיר) who has left his lair to prowl, for the land is now desolate because of the fierce anger of Yahweh.

When the roar of God sounds, as it did in Joel 3:16 and Amos 1:2, the judgment of God has already begun on Judah and the nations, who likewise opposed Yahweh. God is the One who brings charges against every nation that deserves it. And as for the leaders or shepherds of the people of Judah, they too will face the wrath of God for the delinquent way they have led them.

Leadership carries with it awesome measures of accountability to God. Leaders are not to act as if they are gods or owners of the countries they rule or ones they capture—they are not all-powerful; they are mortals. Hitler will face God's judgment for the autocratic way he ruled and destroyed millions of lives. But so too will all other presidents, kings, generals, and judges have to face God for what they did or failed to do during their reigns or times of leadership, no matter how large or how small their sphere of influence and governance was.

INCREASING UNBELIEF AND OPPOSITION (26:1–29:32)

C hapter 25 can be seen as a hinge chapter, for it concludes Jer 1-24 with a message against all the nations, just as chapters 26-45 again conclude with messages against the nations in 46-51, along with an historical appendix in chapter 52. In fact, the Gk. Septuagint includes the prophecies to the nations (placed in the Heb. in Jer 46-51) instead right after the first half of 25:13.

However, from a topical point of view, it might be best to keep chapters 26-29 together, for these chapters are made up exclusively of narrative material except for the one piece of poetry quoted from Mic 3:12 in Jer 26:18. Add to this that chapters 30-33 are traditionally called "the book of consolation" and are mainly in poetic form. In this case, then, Jer 36 would act as the concluding text, much as the way Jer 25:1-14 acts for the first half of Jeremiah's book. Moreover, both 26:3 and 36:3 have as their setting the precincts of the temple.

THE TEMPLE ADDRESS AND JEREMIAH'S ARREST AND TRIAL (26:1-24)

Chapter 26 is generally regarded as recalling Jeremiah's temple message already described in 7:1-15, which is now seen here in an abbreviated form of the same incident. There is no doubt that many of the same words used in chapter 7 and following reappear in this chapter, for example:

- "Reform your ways and your actions" (26:13; 7:3, 5),

- "Follow/walk in my law" (26:4; 9:12),

- "This house will be like Shiloh" (26:6, 9; 7:12–14), and

- "because of the evil they have done" (26:3, 7:9–10).

But if both chapters 7 and 26 are dual records of the same event, chapter 7 does not go on to record the consequences of that message, as chapter 26 does. In this chapter Jeremiah goes on trial for his life for speaking so boldly about the destruction of the temple and the city of Jerusalem as the price for Judah's national disobedience.

TRANSLATION

1 In the beginning of the reign of Jehoiakim, son of Josiah, king of Judah, this word came from Yahweh, saying,[1] **2** "Here is what Yahweh has said: Stand in the court of Yahweh's house and address all the city-people of Judah who come to worship in Yahweh's house, saying to them everything that I have ordered you to say. Do not omit a word! **3** Perhaps they will listen and turn each from his evil way. Then I will relent and not bring on them the disaster I was planning because of the evil they had done. **4** Say to them: 'Here is what Yahweh said: "If you will not listen to me, and conduct yourselves according my law, which I have set before you, **5** [and if] you do not listen to the words of my servants the prophets, whom I sent to you again and again (though you have not listened [to them either]), **6** Then I will make this house like Shiloh and this city[2] a curse word to all the nations on earth."'"

7 Now the priests, the prophets, and all the people heard Jeremiah utter these words in Yahweh's house. **8** When Jeremiah had finished saying all that Yahweh had ordered[3] him to say, the priests, the prophets, and all the people seized him, crying out, "You deserve to die!" **9** "Why do you prophesy in Yahweh's name, saying that this house will be like Shiloh and this city will be desolate and devoid of its inhabitants?" And all the people crowded around Jeremiah in Yahweh's house.

---

1. The Syr. and the Tg. add "to Jeremiah" after "saying."
2. The expression וְאֶת־הָעִיר הַזֹּאתָה, "this city," is missing in the LXX.
3. The LXX, Syr., and Tg. add the pronominal suf. "him" to "ordered."

10 When the officials of[4] Judah heard these things, they went up from the royal palace to the house of Yahweh and they took their seats at the entrance of the New Gate of Yahweh's house. **11** Then the priests and the prophets said to the officials and all the people, "A sentence of death for this man!" for he has prophesied against this city as you have heard with your own ears.

12 Then Jeremiah said to all[5] the officials and all the people: "It was Yahweh who sent me to prophesy against this house and this city all the things you have heard. **13** Now reform your ways and your actions and obey Yahweh your God. Then Yahweh will relent and not bring disaster he has pronounced against you. **14** As for me, I am in your power. Do with me whatever you think is good and right. **15** Nevertheless, be very sure you realize that if you do put me to death, you will bring the guilt of innocent blood on yourselves and on this city and on inhabitants in it. For in truth Yahweh did send me to you to speak these words in your hearing."

16 Then the officials and all the people said to the priests and the prophets, "This man should not be sentenced to death for it is in the name of Yahweh our God he has spoken to us!" **17** Some of the elders of the land stood up and addressed the whole assembled crowd, saying: **18** "Micah of Moresheth used to prophesy[6] in the days of Hezekiah, king of Judah; he said to all the people of Judah, 'This is what Yahweh of Hosts says: "Zion will be ploughed like a field, Jerusalem will become a heap of rubble, and the temple hill a mound covered with thickets."'[7] **19** Did Hezekiah king of Judah or anyone else in Judah put him to death? Did not Hezekiah fear Yahweh and seek his favor? And did not Yahweh relent, so that he did not bring the disaster he pronounced against them? We are about to bring a terrible disaster on ourselves."

20 There was indeed another man, Uriah son of Shemaiah, from Kiriath-jearim, who proclaimed prophecies in the name of Yahweh. He prophesied against this city[8] and against this land, just as Jeremiah has

---

4. The LXX[Q], Syr., Tg., and Vg. add "house of."

5. The LXX omits "all" [of the officials].

6. The LXX omits the ptc. נִבָּא, "prophesying."

7. The LXX reads εἰς ἄλσος δρυμοῦ, "a grove of trees," where the MT has לְבָמוֹת יָעַר, "wooded height."

8. The LXX omits עַל־הָעִיר הַזֹּאת, "against this city."

done. **21** And when King Jehoiakim and all his officers and all his princes,[9] heard what he said, the king sought to kill him. But Uriah heard of it and fled to Egypt in fear.[10] **22** King Jehoiakim, however, sent Elnathan son of Achbor with a company of men[11] to Egypt. **23** These men extradited Uriah from Egypt and brought him to King Jehoiakim, who had him executed with a sword and his body thrown into a burial place for the common people.[12]

24 However, because Ahikam son of Shaphan lent his support to Jeremiah, he was not handed over to the people to be put to death.

COMMENTARY

The Temple Sermon (26:1–6)

26:1-3 In this one and only instance in this book, the prophet is told not to hold back any of his words (26:2c). The reason Jeremiah is to give his prophesying his best efforts is there is still a chance that some of the people might repent of their evil deeds, and thereby they would avert the impending danger (v. 3). God will, if the people repent and turn back to him, relent and change his threatened judgment on them. This did not mean that God is fickle and inconstant in his own mind as to what he would or should do; rather, it is that all his threatened judgments, whether directly or only implied, always come with a suppressed "unless" or on the condition that "you repent." The goal of all prophetic preaching is to get the people to turn around and abandon their evil ways and put their full trust in Yahweh. It is not as if God does not finally know what he is going to do, or, as some who call themselves open theists argue, that God left some future things open and outside his knowledge. According to that viewpoint, in these cases that involve the future God actually does not know what would or will happen. Instead, Scripture asserts God's omniscience, that is, he knows all that will, as well as what might, happen in the past, present, and future (cf. 1 Sam 23).

---

9. The LXX omits וְכָל־גִּבּוֹרָיו, "and all his warriors."

10. The LXX omits the phrase וַיִּרָא וַיִּבְרַח, "he was afraid and fled."

11. The LXX omits אֶלְנָתָן בֶּן־עַכְבּוֹר וַאֲנָשִׁים אִתּוֹ, "Elnathan the son of Achbor and others with him."

12. The LXX has υἱῶν λαοῦ αὐτοῦ, "of the sons of his people," at the end of the verse.

26:4-6 What has the people of Judah so stirred up is that Jeremiah claims that if there is no repentance, then God will make the house of Yahweh and the city of Jerusalem exactly like the now-destroyed place in Shiloh where the tabernacle of God had been located at first before it was destroyed and leveled by the Philistines in 1050 BC (7:12; Ps 78:60–61). However, does not God promise in Ps 132:13–14 that Yahweh had "chosen Zion for his dwelling … for ever and ever"? Do not the sons of Korah sing in Ps 48:1–2,

> Great is Yahweh, and greatly to be praised,
> In the city of our God,
> In the mountain of his holiness.
> Beautiful its situation,
> The joy of the whole earth:
> Is mount Zion on the sides of the north,
> The city of the Great King.

It is downright treasonous, the people argued, for Jeremiah to speak the way he has, for this city and its temple are inviolable—at least they are inviolable in their way of thinking. They have a special promise of God's protection on them; therefore, for any prophet, be he Jeremiah or Uriah, to declare otherwise is tantamount to speaking blasphemy and sedition against God himself.

Anyway, Jeremiah's message has not changed: he still is complaining that God has sent his prophets over and over again (v. 5), urging the populace to repent in order to avoid some disaster he claims God is going to bring on them if there is no change in the direction of the people. If there is no change coming from the people, then both the city of Jerusalem and their temple will be totaled in a complete destruction, and the Jewish people will become a mere curse word among the nations (v. 6).

Jeremiah Faces a Death Sentence (26:7-16)

26:7-9 Here follows one of the most detailed accounts that we have in the OT of a trial. Even though we are only given a synopsis of the charges brought against Jeremiah, there is no doubt that this is an emotionally charged event. It is also amazing that those who lead in bringing the charges are the priests, the [false] prophets, and the general populace. Jeremiah is given an opportunity for a rebuttal, but when he has had his say, the pent-up fury of the crowd spontaneously erupts against him as they all seize him, saying, "This man deserves to die!" The case is not about theology but about saving and maintaining the **cult** and the tradition of the temple and the sacred city of Jerusalem. Perhaps they reason: What do you mean, we have to repent? What were all the reforms that King Josiah so recently introduced? Isn't that enough? Don't those events count for anything? The point is wrapped up in their key question: "Why do you prophesy in Yahweh's name that this house will be like Shiloh and this city will be desolate and without inhabitants?" (v. 9).[13] This is no request for an answer; it is a summary of their complaints against him.

26:10-16 The court session is described in vv. 10-16. The whole party, with all the dignitaries, goes up the hill from the palace grounds to the "New Gate in Yahweh's house" (v. 10), for the temple is on the highest ground in Jerusalem. There the officials, the priests, and the false prophets take their seats as the antagonists begin to rehearse their charges against Jeremiah. There is not much to hear that is new, for they all have heard what Jeremiah is saying with their own ears (v. 11).

Jeremiah once again makes his case before the people, as he has many a time in the temple. It is Yahweh who has sent him and told him to call for repentance or the city and the temple will be destroyed. This message must make an impression on some of the officials, for some very probably have heard similar things in Josiah's reform movement, during those years when they served under Josiah. Jeremiah's speech brings many of these things back to their memory. The prophet concludes by saying, "I am in your power. Do with me whatever you think is good and right. Nevertheless, be very sure you realize that if you do put me to death, you will bring the guilt of innocent blood on yourselves and on this city. For in truth Yahweh did send me to you to speak these words in your hearing" (vv. 14-15). Suddenly the trial takes a turn that is exactly the opposite of what the religious leaders and government officials hope for (v. 16): the consensus now is, "This man should not have a death sentence" (v. 16).

---

13. See D. U. Rottzoll, "Die *KH 'MR* ... -Legitimationsformel," *VT* 39, no. 3 (1989): 323–40.

The Precedent of Micah the Prophet (26:17–19)

The verdict of acquittal seems to have been given, but the speech for the defense is now provided to explain why there is such a sudden reversal and also to persuade the people that it is the right decision. Moreover, it is included here in Scripture as a further vindication of Jeremiah and his charges against the people. But it cannot be clearer that, in sharp contrast to King Jehoiakim (and his people), who has been conspicuously quiet or even absent (or behind the scenes) all through these proceedings yet very much in control, does not similarly humble himself, nor does the nation as a whole, as they did in Hezekiah's day (715–687 BC; 2 Kgs 19).

26:17–18 Some of the elders, perhaps now suddenly awakened in their consciences, step forward and remind the people, religious leaders, and officials that Micah the prophet from Moreseth, around 715 BC, had also prophesied that "Zion would be ploughed like a field, and Jerusalem would become a heap of rubble, with the temple hill overgrown with thickets" (Mic 3:12). The town of Moresheth was some twenty-five miles southwest of Jerusalem, so he, like the other prophets mentioned here in these narratives, did not come from the capital city of Jerusalem. This is the only direct quote from another prophet in the OT prophets, even though there are numerous allusions to the writings of the other prophets. In fact, the elders may have a copy of this same prophecy.

26:19 However, in Micah's case King Hezekiah reacted correctly with a prayer recorded in 2 Kgs 19:14–19 and, as a result, the threatened prophecy did not take place (v. 19). True, Hezekiah's prayer did not mention Micah, but as a matter of fact, Yahweh did deliver the people from the Assyrians. Now that should have been a model of humility for Jehoiakim, but he is surely much different from Hezekiah.

The Martyrdom of Uriah the Prophet (26:20–24)

26:20–23 When it comes time for Jeremiah and Baruch to record this previous incident in Scripture, Yahweh directs them to put alongside it the case of Uriah son of Shemaiah, from Kiriath-jearim, as a counterpoint to the life of Micah. Kiriath-jearim, nine miles west and north of Jerusalem (originally a Gibeonite city, Josh 9:17), was where the ark of the covenant had been housed for those years that followed the destruction of the city of Shiloh (1 Sam 7:1–2). So here too is another outsider who was a prophet from outside the city to the people in the city of Jerusalem.

Uriah had also prophesied against the city of Jerusalem and the temple (v. 20) during the time of King Jehoiakim. When Uriah learned that King Jehoiakim was unhappy with his prophecies and that he had sought to put him to death, he fled to Egypt in fear of his life. Is this evidence of a lack of courage or of some other defect in his life? We are unable to say for sure. However, the king sent Elnathan to capture him and to bring him back to Jerusalem. Elnathan was the father of Nehushta, the mother of King Jehoiakim (2 Kgs 24:8). This may indicate that Jehoiakim's mother, Nehushta, had her hands in this matter as well. Elnathan served as one of the government officials in his maternal grandfather's government.

26:24 Verse 24 offers a note on how Jeremiah has done in light of the tragic outcome of Uriah's life. The point is that Jeremiah did not meet the same end because of the protection of Ahikam, son of Shaphan, who supported him. This same Ahikam must have been a rather influential figure in Jerusalem, for six members of his family were known to be active during the reigns of the last five kings of Judah. For example, his father Shaphan had been a scribal secretary to King Josiah (2 Kgs 22:12, 14; 2 Chr 34:20), if the name refers to the same man. Moreover, he and his father had served as members of the high-ranking delegation that King Josiah had sent to the prophetess Huldah after the scroll of the law was found in the temple. Three of Shaphan's sons were also named: Ahikam, Elasah, and Gemariah. Elasah also served as one of Zedekiah's messengers to Nebuchadnezzar as well as serving as the messenger who carried Jeremiah's letter to the exiles in Babylon (29:3). Ahikam does not appear to have been part of Jehoiakim's government cabinet, as his brother Gemariah was, but Ahikam's son, Gedaliah, appears to have been chief minister in King Zedekiah's cabinet and later was named by the Babylonians as the governor of Judah under the Babylonians after the fall of Jerusalem and the destruction of the temple (39:14; 40:5). In general, this family seems to favor the prophet Jeremiah.

Whether their attitude comes from the remaining influence of Josiah's reign and those who surrounded him is unknown. It is this same Gemariah who puts a room at Baruch's disposal (36:10, 25) and who also tries with all in his power to prevent King Jehoiakim from cutting up and throwing Jeremiah's scroll into the fire. One more generation is also active in protecting and favoring Jeremiah— Gemariah's son, Micaiah. He is the first person who hears Baruch read the scroll and reports the same to the officials (36:11). Given all this family lineage with their high standing in the community, it is no wonder then that they favor Jeremiah.

The temple gate message, also recorded in Jer 7, is a pivotal point in Jeremiah's ministry. He almost is sentenced to death by the officials of the land. But Jeremiah stands steadfast in the word he has received from the Lord. He argues vigorously that it is God who has ordered him to speak against the temple, so the officials pull back their indictment against him— that is, the charge of blasphemy against the house of God! In fact, some of the elders of the land, perhaps suddenly remembering their days of revival under King Josiah, recall with the help of God the ministry of Micah of Moresheth in the days of King Hezekiah. He had also offered some tough words about Jerusalem being plowed up like a field and left a pile of rubble, but the people repented, and that judgment did not come immediately. So accusers had better be careful, for if they plan to carry through on what they have said in the beginning, they may well bring disaster on their own heads. How careful we must be of speaking against God's servants!

And so it is for those who today are clamping down on laypersons and pastors for speaking out against new laws that demand opposing the word of God. They are in grave danger of pulling their houses down on their own heads. It will do no good for Jeremiah, as it did not pay the prophet Uriah, or for us, to flee to another country after delivering the word of God, for King Jehoiakim sent assassins after him in Egypt, and he lost his life there. Our trust must be in God. But woe to those who go after God's servants when they have spoken his word and his will. They are headed for real trouble with God.

God has placed his servants, like Ahikam, strategically in positions where he can use them, as he did in rescuing Jeremiah. Thanks be to God.

THE YOKE OF SUBMISSION
TO BABYLON (27:1-22)

Jeremiah 27 is linked with Jer 28 with the words "In the fifth month of the same year." In both of these chapters, Jeremiah performs a symbolic act similar to the "linen belt" in 13:1-14, the provision that he is not to marry in 16:1-13, the visit to the potter's house in 18:1-12, the smashed clay pot in 19:1-15, and the two baskets of figs in 24:1-10.

Another feature that binds these two chapters together is Jeremiah's opposition to King Zedekiah's attempt to stir up a rebellion against the rule of the Babylonians. Judah's only hope, Jeremiah keeps saying, is to submit to the Babylonians; Judah must reject the voices of the false prophets who are advising just the opposite of what Jeremiah teaches. These false prophets teach nothing but lies (27:10, 14, 16), and the people of Judah must not listen to them (27:9, 14, 16, 17).

The text in chapters 27-29 is much shorter in the LXX, which omits 27:1, 7, 13, 17, and 20, but the LXX also adds isolated words and phrases in 27:15, 16 that are not found in the MT. These additions do not add new ideas to the text; rather, they draw out the significance of what is implied in the context, for example, by calling these prophets "*false* prophets."[14]

Finally, one other unique feature in these chapters is the shortened form of names. Names that incorporate "Yahweh" as part of the name are normally spelled with a longer "-yahu," but in this chapter they are shortened to "-ya." For example, only in these chapters is Jeremiah's own name spelled in a shortened form (יִרְמְיָה, *Yirmeya*) instead of the way it is spelled everywhere else (יִרְמְיָהוּ, *Yirmeyahu*). The spelling changes could lead to the conclusion that a different hand wrote this section, which was then modified by a Judean redactor, but that suggestion seems to be without any other verification than the facts we have just traced. It tells a clear enough story and continues the book as it is quite nicely.

---

14. See E. Tov, "Exegetical Notes on the Hebrew *Vorlage* of the LXX of Jeremiah 27 (34)," *ZAW* 91, no. 1 (1979): 73-93.

TRANSLATION

1[15] Early in the reign of Zedekiah son of Josiah king of Judah, this word came to Jeremiah from Yahweh saying: **2** "This is what Yahweh said to me,[16] 'Make yourself a yoke and fetters and put them on your neck. **3** Then send word to the kings of Edom, Moab, Ammon, Tyre, and Sidon through their ambassadors who have come to Jerusalem to Zedekiah king of Judah.[17] **4** Give them a message for their masters and say, "This is what Yahweh of Hosts, the God of Israel, has said, and this is what you shall tell your masters: **5** 'It is I, who by my great power and outstretched arm, have made the earth with the men and the animals that are in it.[18] I give it to anyone I please. **6** And now it is I who have delivered these countries[19] into the hand of Nebuchadnezzar, king of Babylon, my servant.[20] Indeed, I have even given him the wild beasts to be his subjects. **7**[21] All the nations will be subject to him and his son and his grandson until the time for his country comes when he will be in servitude to many nations and great kings. **8** As for the nation or kingdom that will not serve Nebuchadnezzar, king of Babylon,[22] or bow its neck under his yoke, I will punish that nation with sword, famine, and plague,' declares Yahweh, 'until I destroy it by his hand.' **9** As for all of you, 'Do not listen to your prophets, your diviners, your dreamers, your soothsayers, your sorcerers, who keep telling you, "Do not submit to the king of Babylon." **10** For it is a lie that they are prophesying to you, which will only serve to remove you far from your land; for I will scatter you and you will perish.[23] **11** But the nation that brings its neck under the yoke of the king of Babylon and will serve him, I will let that nation remain in its own land to till it and to live there, declares Yahweh.'"'"

---

15. The entire verse is missing in the LXX.

16. The prep. plus pronominal suf. אֵלַי, "to me," is absent in the LXX.

17. The LXX adds εἰς ἀπάντησιν αὐτῶν, "to meet them."

18. The phrase אֶת־הָאָדָם וְאֶת־הַבְּהֵמָה אֲשֶׁר עַל־פְּנֵי הָאָרֶץ, "with the men and animals that are on the earth," is missing in the LXX.

19. The LXX has τὴν γῆν, "the earth," where the MT has אֶת־כָּל־הָאֲרָצוֹת הָאֵלֶּה, "all these lands."

20. The LXX has δουλεύειν αὐτῷ, "to serve him," where the MT has עַבְדִּי, "my servant."

21. The entire verse is missing in the LXX.

22. The phrase לֹא־יַעַבְדוּ אֹתוֹ אֶת־נְבוּכַדְנֶאצַּר מֶלֶךְ־בָּבֶל וְאֵת אֲשֶׁר, "not serve this Nebuchadnezzar king of Babylon," is missing in the LXX.

23. The phrase וְהִדַּחְתִּי אֶתְכֶם וַאֲבַדְתֶּם, "for I will scatter you and you will perish" is missing in the LXX.

12 To Zedekiah, king of Judah, I spoke the same message, saying: "Bring your neck under the yoke of the king of Babylon,[24] and be subject to him and to his people that you may live. **13**[25] Why will you and your people die by the sword, famine, and plague with which Yahweh has threatened any nation that will not serve the king of Babylon? **14** Do not listen to the talk of the prophets who keep saying to you, 'Do not submit to the king of Babylon,' for they are prophesying lies. **15** No, I did not send them!—declares Yahweh. But they keep on prophesying lies in my name. Therefore, I will scatter you and you will perish, you and the prophets who have been prophesying to you."

16 Then to the priests and to all these people I spoke these words: "This is what Yahweh has said: 'Do not listen to the talk of your prophets who keep giving to you this prophecy: "Look, all the vessels of the house of Yahweh will be returned from Babylon very soon,"[26] for they are prophesying a lie to you.[27] **17**[28] Do not listen to them. Serve the king of Babylon, and you will live. Why should this city become a ruin? **18** If they really are prophets and have the word of Yahweh in them, let them make intercession, please, with Yahweh of Hosts that the furnishings left in the house of Yahweh and in the palace of the king of Judah and in Jerusalem not be taken to Babylon.[29] **19** For this is what Yahweh of Hosts has said about the pillars and concerning the sea, the stands, and concerning the rest of the furnishings that are left in the city,[30] **20**[31] which Nebuchadnezzar king of Babylon did not take away when he carried Jehoiachin king of Judah into exile from Jerusalem to Babylon, along with all the nobles of Judah and Jerusalem— **21** Yes, this is what Yahweh of Hosts, the God of Israel, says about the things that are left in the house of Yahweh and in the palace of the king of Judah and in Jerusalem: **22** "They will be taken to Babylon and

---

24. The expression בְּעֹל מֶלֶךְ־בָּבֶל, "under the yoke of the king of Babylon," is missing in the LXX. The LXX does not make sense with the omission.

25. The whole verse is missing in the LXX.

26. The LXX omits עַתָּה מְהֵרָה, "very soon."

27. The LXX adds οὐκ ἀπέστειλα αὐτούς, "I did not send them."

28. Verse 17 is missing in the LXX.

29. The last part of the verse is missing in the LXX.

30. The expressions צְבָאוֹת אֶל־הָעַמֻּדִים וְעַל־הַיָּם וְעַל־הַמְּכֹנוֹת, "of hosts, concerning the pillars, the sea, the stands," and הַנּוֹתָרִים בָּעִיר הַזֹּאת, "that are left in this city," are missing.

31. The last part of v. 20, the entire v. 21, and the first word of v. 22 are missing in the LXX.

there they will remain until the day I come for them, declares Yahweh. Then I will bring them back and restore them to this place.""'"

COMMENTARY

Yahweh's Message to the Nations (27:1–11)

27:1 The majority of the Heb. mss read 27:1 as "in the beginning of the reign of Jehoiakim," but this is clearly a textual copying error for "Zedekiah," who is the king mentioned in vv. 3 and 12. Furthermore, the reading of "Jehoiakim" in this text is at odds with the link in 28:1, which in speaking of the fourth year of the reign of Zedekiah reads "in the same year" (28:1). The LXX is of no help here, for it omits 27:1 altogether, yet the correct reading of Zedekiah does appear in at least three Heb. mss and in the Syr. version.

27:2 While v. 1 is recorded in the third person, talking about Jeremiah, in vv. 2, 12, 16 Jeremiah takes up the narrative in the first person. Once again he is given a symbolic sign to act out for his message. This time he is told to make a "yoke," such as oxen wore when they were plowing the fields. The yoke was a wooden bow that was usually placed around the necks of a pair of oxen, secured below the neck with by leather straps. A wooden shaft was then attached to the crossbar, which hung down and passed between the team of oxen back to pull the cart or the plough it was pulling. The yoke then became a wonderful metaphor for submission and servitude.

27:3 Jeremiah is told to make such a yoke and then to wear it (v. 2) as an object lesson for the envoys or ambassadors who are in Jerusalem representing their countries (vv. 3–6). One can imagine how silly Jeremiah must have appeared as he tried to maneuver this clumsy crossbar through the crowds of the city. Jeremiah's point is to make sure these envoys graphically remembered this message for the kings who had sent them to Jerusalem. They must understand that they too must submit to Nebuchadnezzar king of Babylon just as Judah must submit. The kingdoms represented included Edom, Moab, Ammon, Tyre, and Sidon (v. 3). Of course, it is too early to think of such institutions as permanent foreign embassies in foreign capitals, but these envoys, we are directly told, have been sent to discuss some current political situation. If our guess about the timing of this

unofficial conclave here is correct, then this event must have fallen sometime between the years of 596 and 594 BC, for the Babylonian Chronicles
show that these years were troubling ones for Nebuchadnezzar, with internal unrest taking place in Babylon from December 595 to January 594 BC.
Somehow, word of this hiatus of Nebuchadnezzar's attention from his
empire must have reached the ears of the smaller states at the western
fringe of Babylon's empire, so they may have come to Jerusalem to see
whether these developments can be turned to their advantage. But nothing
ever came of this enclave; in fact, Zedekiah even personally went to Babylon
in his fourth year (51:59), after Nebuchadnezzar had gotten word that some
type of possible rebellion may have been under way as a possible threat
against him; Zedekiah's visit must have been to reassure Nebuchadnezzar
of Judah's loyalty.

27:4–11 Jeremiah has a word for each of these messengers from the kings of
these smaller western states: Don't even think of revolting! Yahweh, Lord of
the armies of heaven and earth as well as the Creator of the earth itself, has
by his great power and irresistible might not only made the earth together
with the people in it, and the animals on that earth (v. 5), but he has also
warned that it is he who has decreed that all the countries will be handed
over to Nebuchadnezzar. In fact, even the wild animals have been made
subject to Nebuchadnezzar as well (v. 6c). So the coalition should just drop
any plans about any possible sedition against Babylon. This Babylonian
domination will last not just as long as Nebuchadnezzar lives but for the
duration of the reigns of his son and grandson as well (v. 7).[32] Jeremiah
issues a warning to all these kings of the smaller western states: "As for
any nation or kingdom that will not serve Nebuchadnezzar, ... [Yahweh]

---

32. Nebuchadnezzar was succeeded by his son Amel-Marduk (also called Evil-Merodach;
562–560 BC), who after reigning for two years was murdered and succeeded by Nergal-
Sharezer (also called Neriglissar) in 560–556 BC. Neriglisssar was an army general and a
brother-in-law. He was followed by Labasi-Marduk, who reigned for just a few months
in 556 BC before he too was murdered. The neo-Babylonian empire was coming to an end
under Nabonidus (555–539 BC), who ruled along with his son Belshazzar. Some have argued
that Belshazzar was in fact Nebuchadnezzar's grandson (see P. J. Achtemeier, *Harper's Bible
Dictionary* [San Francisco: Harper & Row, 1985], 102), for he married Nebuchadnezzar's daughter Nitocris, but this is far from being firmly established. The point of the passage, however,
is not the exact succession but the length of the Babylonian rule.

w[ould] punish that nation with sword, famine, and plague" (v. 8). These were the typical effects of invading armies on conquered nations (v. 8; 14:12–18; 15:2; 21:7–9; 24:10).

Yahweh's Message to King Zedekiah (27:12–15)

27:12 Zedekiah receives the same warning that Yahweh has given to Jeremiah for all the nations (v. 12). Zedekiah, as well as the people of Judah, have to "bow under the yoke" of Nebuchadnezzar (lit. "to make enter, or lower their necks," הָבִיאוּ אֶת־צַוְּארֵיכֶם). That is the only way the king and the people of Judah are going to live (v. 12c). If they submit, they will live.

27:13–14 The cost of disobedience, however, is very high, for the warning and results of challenging this directive (v. 13) are the same for the king and people of Judah as for the nations in v. 8. It is clear, however, that there are many other prophets in Judah who are giving the opposite advice. But Jeremiah repeatedly warns: "Do not listen [to them]" (v. 14), for they are telling you nothing but "lies" (vv. 10, 14). In giving this same warning to the nations, Jeremiah has to speak harshly about trusting "diviners, interpreters of dreams, mediums, and sorcerers" (v. 9), even though some of this same sort of thing is undoubtedly going on in Judah. The more serious problem in Judah comes from these "*shalom* prophets" who always predict "peace" no matter what.

27:15 The main problem with these peaceniks is that God had not sent them (v. 15). The people who trust the words of these peace prophets, along with these prophets themselves, will be scattered all over the earth and will perish (v. 15). Examples of such bitter results for such false prophets can be seen in the cases of Hananiah in 28:15–16 and Shemiah in 29:31–32.

Yahweh's Message to the Priests and People (27:16–22)

The message addressed to the priests and people does not change from the warning that was given to the nations or the one given to the king of Judah and his people. The false prophets have predicted, "Look, all the vessels of the house of Yahweh will be returned from Babylon very soon" (v. 16). But that, too, is a lie.

The LXX text of vv. 16–22 omits the elements of hope and gives a much gloomier view of what is about to happen. Critical scholars argue for their version of the text both ways: some saying the LXX is shorter due to the abbreviating tendencies of the Gk. translators, with others criticizing the Masoretic text as expansionistic. Neither can prove with certainty their point of view.

27:16-18 The point is that the peace prophets are indulging, as usual, in lies (v. 16c). Once again, Jeremiah has to warn: "Do not listen to them" (v. 17), as he warned the nations in v. 9. Instead, "serve the king of Babylon and you will live" (v. 17). If the peace prophets think they have the word of Yahweh, and that God has said that the furnishings from the temple are coming back home (v. 18), then let them; instead of offering such wild speculations, plead with Yahweh that those furnishings that are left in the temple and in the palace of the king of Judah will not also be carried off to Babylon (v. 18).

27:19-21 The reason Jeremiah urges that these false prophets and the people should intercede with Yahweh is that all that is left in the city is going to be taken by the king of Babylon, including the "pillars" of Jakin and Boaz, which Solomon had made for the front porch of the temple (1 Kgs 7:15-22; 2 Chr 3:15-17); the "sea," which was the large basin used by the priests for their own washing (1 Kgs 7:23-26; 2 Chr 4:4-5); the "moveable stands," which refers to the ten bronze stands on wheels that supported the basins used for rinsing the sacrifices (1 Kgs 7:27-37; 2 Chr 4:6); and the other furnishings that had been left from the first sack of the temple in 597 BC. But if there was no repentance, then all of these furnishings would be lost to Babylon along with "the nobles of Judah and Jerusalem" (v. 20c).

27:22 How long will all these furnishings be left in Babylon? Verse 22 states that they will remain there "until the day I come for them." This pronouncement must have been an awful blow to the peaceniks. However, that is what happened in 586 BC—off to Babylon it all went (Jer 52:17-23; 2 Kgs 25:13-17; 2 Chr 36:7, 10, 18). However, God will restore these items in this timing, which he apparently did in the events that took place under the return of Ezra from Babylon (Ezra 1:7-11). He brought these articles back to the land of Judah.

God called Jeremiah to be a "prophet to the nations" (Jer 1:5), so that is what he does as he sends word through the various envoys who have come to Jerusalem from Edom, Moab, Ammon, Tyre, and Sidon. In 27:1–11 Jeremiah instructs these envoys that the same Lord who made the earth, people, and animals on that earth is the one who now is counseling these nations to submit to Nebuchadnezzar, for any attempts to fight him are fruitless. God has ordained that all these nations should serve this Babylonian king. If some wish to resist him, then God will punish them with sword, famine, or plague.

God is in charge of all of history, and obedience is required from all. Judah will fall under the same indictment as the rest of the nations. The false prophets had a less harsh message than Jeremiah's, though, and the false prophets of our day are just as busy trying to contravene the word from God. What they prophesy is nothing but lies. All that the people in that time were so proud of in the temple and the palace would go off to Babylon. In our time, God can and will take all the stuff in our nation, churches, and homes away from us because we trust in that stuff more than we trust in our Lord. It will be gone if we do not turn in repentance and faith in him.

JEREMIAH'S CONFRONTATION
WITH HANANIAH (28:1–17)

Apparently Jeremiah is still wearing the yoke he had put on in the previous chapter when this clash between himself and the false prophet named Hananiah took place. As in previous sections of this part of the book of Jeremiah, the LXX and the MT diverge quite widely in this chapter. The LXX is quite terse and more condensed, while the MT is more expanded.

TRANSLATION

1 In the fifth month of the same fourth year of the reign of Zedekiah,[33] king of Judah, the prophet Hananiah son of Azzur, who was from Gibeon, said to me, in the house of Yahweh in the presence of the priests and all the people, **2** "This is what Yahweh of Hosts, the God of Israel says, 'I will break the yoke of the king of Babylon. **3** Within two years I will bring back

---

33. The LXX reads ἐν τῷ τετάρτῳ ἔτει Σεδεκια, "in the fourth year of Zedekiah," where the MT has בַּשָּׁנָה הַהִיא בְּרֵאשִׁית מַמְלֶכֶת צִדְקִיָּה, "In that year, at the beginning of the reign of Zedekiah."

to this place all the furnishings of Yahweh's house that Nebuchadnezzar king of Babylon removed from here and took to Babylon.[34] **4** I will bring back to this place Jeconiah [Jehoiachin] son of Jehoiakim[35] king of Judah and all the other exiles of Judah who went to Babylon, declares Yahweh,[36] for I will break the yoke of the king of Babylon.'"

5 Then Jeremiah the prophet replied to the prophet Hananiah the prophet in the presence of the priests and all the people who were standing in the house of Yahweh.[37] **6** Jeremiah the prophet said, "Amen! May Yahweh do so. May Yahweh fulfill the words you have prophesied by bringing the furnishings of Yahweh's house and all the exiles back to this place from Babylon. **7** Nevertheless, listen to what I am going to say[38] in your hearing and in the hearing of all the people. **8** The prophets who were of old, before my time and before yours, prophesied against many countries and great kingdoms of war, of famine, and plague.[39] **9** [But] the prophet who prophesies peace will be recognized as one truly sent by Yahweh only if his prediction comes true."

10 Then the prophet Hananiah took the crossbar off the neck of Jeremiah the prophet and broke it. **11** And Hananiah said before all the people, "This is what Yahweh says: 'In the same way I will break the yoke of Nebuchadnezzar[40] king of Babylon off the neck of all the nations within two years.'"[41] At this the prophet Jeremiah went on his way.

12 Sometime later after the prophet Hananiah had broken the crossbar off the neck of Jeremiah the prophet, the word of the Yahweh came to Jeremiah as follows: **13** "Go and tell Hananiah, 'This is what Yahweh has

---

34. The last half of the verse is missing in the LXX.

35. The phrase בֶּן־יְהוֹיָקִים מֶלֶךְ־יְהוּדָה, "the son of Jehoiakim, king of Judah," is missing in the LXX.

36. The LXX omits the phrase הַבָּאִים בָּבֶלָה אֲנִי מֵשִׁיב אֶל־הַמָּקוֹם הַזֶּה נְאֻם־יְהוָה, "I am bringing back to this place all the exiles who went to Babylon, declares Yahweh."

37. The LXX reverses the order and has Jeremiah addressing the people, then the priests. Renkema suggests that the LXX's "priests-people" is to be preferred since the same order appears in v. 1. Also, he suggests that the verb "to stand" means "to serve, to officiate," so these people and the priests were servants at the temple. Furthermore, he suggests that "the 'corrected' MT version of Jer. xxviii 5 lacks the notion of an adjudicating priestly presence." See J. Renkema, "A Note on Jeremiah XXVIII 5," VT 47, no. 2 (April 1997): 253–55.

38. The LXX has λόγον κυρίου, "the word of Lord," where the MT has הַדָּבָר הַזֶּה, "this word."

39. The LXX omits the last two words, וּלְרָעָה וּלְדֶבֶר, "of famine, and of plague."

40. The LXX omits Nebuchadnezzar's name.

41. The LXX omits the phrase בְּעוֹד שְׁנָתַיִם יָמִים, "within two years."

said: "You have broken the wooden crossbars, but in their place make cross-bars of iron!" **14** For this is what Yahweh of Hosts, the God of Israel says: 'I will put an iron yoke on the necks of all these nations to make them serve Nebuchadnezzar[42] king of Babylon, and they will serve him. Indeed, I have even given to him the wild beasts well.'"[43] **15** The Jeremiah the prophet said to Hananiah the prophet, "Listen, Hananiah! Yahweh did not send you, yet you have persuaded this people to believe a lie! **16** Therefore, this is what Yahweh has said, 'I am going to send you right off the face of the earth. This very year you are going to die, because you have preached rebellion against Yahweh.'"[44] **17** Hananiah the prophet[45] did die in that same year, in the seventh month.

COMMENTARY

Hananiah's False Hope (28:1–4)

28:1 Chapter 28 opens with a reference to "in the same year" (28:1, cf. 27:1), which links chapters 27 and 28 not only in time but also in content with the narrative about the yoke still continuing as well as the debate over whether the smaller western nations should submit to Nebuchadnezzar or risk staging a revolt.

Into this fray comes a prophet named Hananiah (whose name means "Yahweh has been gracious") from the town of Gibeon, which was about six miles northwest of Jerusalem, where one of the most important high places was located before the temple was built (cf. 1 Kgs 3:3–15; 1 Chr 16:39; 2 Chr 1:3). Hananiah initiates the conversation by addressing Jeremiah, for Hananiah "said to me [that is, to Jeremiah] in the presence of the priests and all the people" (v. 1).[46] Since Hananiah comes from Gibeon of the tribe of Benjamin, he probably had a similar upbringing as Jeremiah.

---

42. The LXX omits Nebuchadnezzar's name.

43. The LXX omits the phrase וְעֲבָדֻהוּ וְגַם אֶת־חַיַּת הַשָּׂדֶה נָתַתִּי לוֹ, "and they shall serve him, for I have given him even the beasts of the field."

44. The LXX omits the phrase כִּי־סָרָה דִבַּרְתָּ אֶל־יְהוָה, "because you have preached rebellion against Yahweh."

45. The LXX omits חֲנַנְיָה הַנָּבִיא בַּשָּׁנָה הַהִיא, "in the same year, the prophet Hanniah."

46. Di Pede suggests that the LXX incorrectly defuses the tension between the true and false prophet. The following chapters show that Jeremiah is the true prophet since the exile

28:2-4 Hananiah uses the proper messenger formula ("Thus says Yahweh"); he claims that what he says is said in the name of Yahweh and from him, and he too uses symbolic actions. The only problem is that what he says will happen does not: none of the furnishings come back home to Jerusalem; none of the captives come back home; and the exile does not end within two years! Hananiah has a truth problem—a big one! This lack of truth casts major doubts on his alleged source.

Jeremiah, however, is told to continue (27:2; 28:10) to wear this yoke on his neck as a sign for Judah and the nations who had come to Jerusalem, who were trying to decide what they could do together against the Babylonian hegemony. Jeremiah's message is simple and straightforward: submit to the king of Babylon, and then you will continue to live on your own countries. But Hananiah's message is much more popular: Within two years God is going to break the yoke from the necks of Zedekiah king of Judah and from all the kings that had sent envoys to Jerusalem (28:3). So if the confrontation is not a direct rebuttal to Jeremiah's submission to Nebuchadnezzar, then it is somewhat less direct and is over the matter of timing—within two years. Even so, if it were only over a matter of timing, which is most doubtful, God has already specified a much longer time than two years; it will be for "seventy years" (25:11; 27:7). Therein lies the problem for Hananiah.

Jeremiah's Cautious Acceptance of Hananiah's Message (28:5-9)

Jeremiah treats Hananiah kindly at first, for he says "Amen" (v. 6) when he first hears the prediction of Hananiah. He goes even further; he prays, "May Yahweh fulfill what you just said and may all the furnishings of the temple and the exiles return to this land." However, Jeremiah still has a nagging problem. If one argues on the basis of tradition, is it not true that in the history of prophecy the vast majority of the prophets have usually preached about war, famine, and plague as the means God will use to get the people to repent and to turn from their wicked ways? That is what Jeremiah has done for the nation of Judah and the nations round about it (14:12; 27:8). But there is another issue as well: whenever the prophets

---

will last a long time. See E. Di Pede, "La manière de raconter et l'enjeu du récit: Jérémie présente Ananias en Jer 28,1 TM et 35,1," *BibInt* 16, no. 3 (2008): 294-301.

of former days preached peace and well-being as "*shalom* prophets," as Hananiah had done, is it not true that they were legitimated only if their predictions came to pass (v. 9; Deut 18:22)? Consequently, simply judging things on the face of it all, it seems as if Hananiah has the harder road to walk than Jeremiah, given the content of their messages. Hananiah has to produce proof that what he says is happening.

Hananiah Symbolically Breaks the Wooden Crossbar (28:10–11)

Hananiah's only response is a dramatic symbolic action of his own, in which he tears the crossbar from Jeremiah's neck and proceeds to break it in pieces (v. 10) as he announces once more that the hegemony of Babylon will be broken in the same way he has just now broken this yoke. But that cannot substitute for the action of God. Hananiah no doubt thinks he is nullifying Jeremiah's symbolic act of wearing the yoke on his neck. In doing so Hananiah uses the messenger formula that ordinarily was used by Yahweh's true prophets. Jeremiah is at first stunned by this sudden switch in messages, for Yahweh has not told him anything about this change, and he has not seen any real change in the repentance of the nation or of their turning back to Yahweh. So Jeremiah simply "went on his way" (v. 11c).

Jeremiah Replaces the Wooden Crossbar with an Iron One (28:12–17)

28:12–14 "Shortly after this" (v. 12), however, Yahweh tells Jeremiah to make another yoke, but this time he is to make it out of iron (v. 13), which human beings are incapable of breaking. Jeremiah again confronts Hananiah and restates his former prophecy about how Nebuchadnezzar will come and take Judah, its king, Zedekiah, and the other nations with him into exile (v. 14), where they will serve the Babylonian king. Hananiah's prophecies are not only wasting the time of day; nothing he says is even close to the truth.

28:15–17 Moreover, Jeremiah has a personal word for Hananiah from Yahweh: The content of his message is nothing but "lies" (v. 15). Furthermore, he has also poisoned others by convincing his compatriots of the truthfulness of his lies (v. 15). Therefore, Yahweh is about to remove this charlatan from the earth in this very year. If the people want to judge whose words are true, then watch for the near fulfillment of their prophecies as a gauge to determine the validity of the distant prophecies (Deut 18:22). Hananiah is one of those lying prophets the prophet Jeremiah has warned the people against in 27:9–10, 14–15, 16–18. Therefore, Hananiah is liable to death (Deut 18:20; 13:1–11).

Hananiah does die in the seventh month of that year (Jer 28:17), within two months of Jeremiah's prediction (see 28:1). There is no indication how he died; it merely says he died. That is the proof that Hananiah was a false prophet.

Jeremiah continues to wear the yoke he put on in 27:2. The Lord and his prophet are so desirous that Judah understand the message that they use a visualization of the truth by having Jeremiah wear a wooden piece used by a team of oxen to pull a plow or wagon together. This symbol aims to impress God's people with this graphic picture of their political submission to the Babylonian king. I am sure Jeremiah felt silly as he tried to maneuver in the shopping plazas or markets of that day so as to avoid hitting others with the yoke. Many must have asked: "Who is that?"

But the false prophet Hananiah intervenes and publicly breaks up the yoke with the popular words: "We will be rid of that yoke from Babylon within two years." What a climax to all that embarrassment on Jeremiah's part! Has God neglected to tell Jeremiah about this change in divine plans?

But later God sends his word to Jeremiah. "Make a yoke out of iron; Hananiah will not be able to break this one." The yoke of Babylon was still on, but this time it pointed especially to Hananiah. Moreover, you, Hananiah, have not been sent by God, neither are the words you say from God. You have instead preached rebellion against God. In fact, you, young as you are, are going to die this very year. Two months later Hananiah died.

Do not play around with God's word, for it is an act of rebellion that attempts to mess with God. Today we have religious authorities who make pronouncements that are directly counter to what God has taught about marriage, sexual morality, the distinction of the genders, and all other sorts of forms of rebellion against God and his word. Guess how some of that stuff will end!

JEREMIAH'S CORRESPONDENCE
WITH THE EXILES (29:1-32)

Rumors of what the false prophets back home had predicted have now reached the exiles in Babylon and given them false hope for an early release and return to their homeland. This prompts Jeremiah to send a letter to the exiles that addresses much of what is addressed in chapters 26-28. Chapter 29 records three letters[47] from Jeremiah to correct these false hopes, as well as a reference of one letter from Shemaiah.[48]

The first letter (29:1-23) is apparently sent following the deportation of the exiles in 597 BC (2 Kgs 24:10-16) to help them prepare for a rather long stay. It is surprising that no mention is made of the Judean king and queen, who had been carried away in that earlier deportation. Jeremiah then writes a second letter (29:24-28) to counter the teachings of the false prophet Shemaiah. Then a third letter comes from Jeremiah (29:29-32) warning the people one more time about the fallout that will come from the insubstantial hopes of these false prophets.

TRANSLATION

1 This is the text of the letter Jeremiah the prophet sent from Jerusalem to the surviving[49] elders among the exiles and to the priests, the prophets, and all the other people whom Nebuchadnezzar had carried into exile from Jerusalem to Babylon.[50] **2** (This was after King Jeconiah, the queen mother,

---

47. Some identify the last two letters as one letter (Keown, 66). Dijkstra suggests that "the form and content of Jer. xxix 24-32 can be explained … if we suppose it to be an almost unchanged copy of a letter to Shemaiah written by Jeremiah's secretary, a letter to Shemaiah himself in addition to the letter which he had to send to the exiles." See M. Dijkstra, "Prophecy by Letter (Jeremiah XXIX 24-32), VT 33, no. 3 (1983): 319-22. Büsing argues that chapter 29 is a compilation of three different sources that are logically placed here. See G. Büsing, "Ein alternativer Ausgangspunkt zur Interpretation von Jer 29," ZAW 104, no. 3 (1992): 402-8.

48. There is another letter, called "The Letter of Jeremiah," that is alleged to have come from Jeremiah and been sent to the exiles. While not a part of the Protestant canon, it is included in the deuterocanonical books. This letter is found in the sixth chapter of the book of Baruch, which in all likelihood originated in the fourth century BC. It mimics the style of Jeremiah's original letters, castigating the worthlessness of idol worship and majoring on themes that are found in Jer 10:1-16.

49. The LXX omits the word יֶתֶר, "surviving," which modifies "elders."

50. The LXX omits the last phrase of the verse, אֲשֶׁר הֶגְלָה נְבוּכַדְנֶאצַּר מִירוּשָׁלַ͏ִם בָּבֶלָה, "whom Nebuchadnezzar had taken into exile from Jerusalem to Babylon."

the palace officials, the princes of Judah and Jerusalem,[51] and the craftsmen and metalworkers had gone into exile from Jerusalem.) **3** He entrusted the letter to Elasah son of Shaphan and to Gemariah son of Hilkiah, whom Zedekiah king of Judah had sent to King Nebuchadnezzar[52] in Babylon. It said:

4 "This is what Yahweh of Hosts, the God of Israel, has said to all the exiles whom I have deported from Jerusalem to Babylon: **5** 'Build houses and settle down. Plant gardens and eat their produce. **6** Marry and beget sons and daughters; take wives for your sons and give your daughters as wives, so they may beget sons and daughters[53] and increase there and not decrease. **7** Also seek the peace of the city[54] to which I have deported you, and make intercession on its behalf to Yahweh, for on its welfare your own [welfare] depends.' **8** Yes, this is what Yahweh of Hosts, the God of Israel, has said: 'Do not let those prophets of yours who are in your midst, or your diviners, deceive you. Do not listen to the dreams which you cause to be dreamed.[55] **9** It is a lie they are prophesying to you in my name! I did not send them,'" declares Yahweh.

10 For this is what Yahweh has said: "When seventy years are completed for Babylon, I will come to you and fulfill my gracious promise to bring you back to this place. **11** Surely I know the plans that I[56] have for you,' declares Yahweh, 'plans to prosper you and not to harm you, plans to give you hope and a future.' **12** When you call on me, and come, and pray to me, I will hear you.[57] **13** When you search for me, you will find me. Yes, when you seek for me with all your heart. **14** And I will be found by you,"[58] declares Yahweh, "and I will bring you back from captivity. I will gather you from

---

51. The LXX has only καὶ παντὸς ἐλευθέρου, "and all the nobles," where the MT has שָׂרֵי יְהוּדָה וִירוּשָׁלַָם, "the officials of Judah and Jerusalem."

52. Nebuchadnezzar's name is omitted in the LXX.

53. The expression וְתֵלַדְנָה בָּנִים וּבָנוֹת, "that they may bear sons and daughters," is missing in the LXX.

54. The LXX reads τῆς γῆς, "the land/country," where the MT has הָעִיר, "the city."

55. The LXX[26] reads "they are dreaming" where the MT has אַתֶּם מַחְלְמִים, "you are dreaming." In context, the LXX[26] makes better sense.

56. The LXX omits אֶת־הַמַּחֲשָׁבֹת אֲשֶׁר אָנֹכִי יָדַעְתִּי, "I know the plans that I ... " This could be an unintentional scribal error.

57. The LXX omits the last phrase וְשָׁמַעְתִּי אֲלֵיכֶם, "and I will listen to you."

58. The LXX reads καὶ ἐπιφανοῦμαι ὑμῖν, "And I will be seen by you," where the MT has וְנִמְצֵאתִי, "and I will be found by you." The rest of the verse is missing in the LXX.

all the nations and places where I have banished you," declares Yahweh, "and I will bring you back to the place from which I carried you into exile."

15 Now, because you say, Yahweh has raised up prophets for us in Babylon,[59] **16** but this is what Yahweh says about the king who sits on David's throne and all the people who remain in this city, your compatriots who did not go with you into exile. **17** Yes, this is what Yahweh of Hosts says: "I will send the sword, famine, and plague against them and I will make them like poor figs that are so bad they cannot be eaten. **18** I will pursue them with the sword, famine, and plague and will make them abhorrent to all the kingdoms of the earth and an object of cursing and horror, of scorn and reproach, among all the nations where I drive them **19** as a recompense for the fact that they have not listened to my words," declares Yahweh, "'words' that I sent to them again and again by my servants the prophets, but you did not listen," declares Yahweh. **20** Therefore, hear the word of Yahweh, all you exiles whom I have sent away from Jerusalem to Babylon. **21** This is what Yahweh of Hosts, the God of Israel, says about Ahab son of Kolaiah[60] and Zedekiah son of Maaseiah, who are prophesying in my name a lie to you.[61] "Look, I am going to hand them over to Nebuchadnezzar, king of Babylon, who will execute them in front of your eyes, **22** And a curse word will be derived[62] from them which will be used by all the exiles from Judah in Babylon: 'May Yahweh make you like Zedekiah and like Ahab, who the king of Babylon roasted in the fire.' **23** Inasmuch as they have done outrageous things in Israel, for they have committed adultery with their neighbors' wives and in my name they have spoken a lie,[63] which I did not command them to do. I know it and [I am] a witness to it," declares Yahweh.

24 To Shemaiah the Nehelamite you shall say: **25** "This is what Yahweh of Hosts, the God of Israel, has said:[64] 'Because you have sent letters in your

---

59. Verses 16–20 are missing in the LXX.

60. The const. בֶּן־קוֹלָיָה, "son of Kolaiah," is absent in the LXX.

61. The phrase בֶּן־מַעֲשֵׂיָה הַנִּבְּאִים לָכֶם בִּשְׁמִי שָׁקֶר, "son of Maaseiah, who are prophesying in my name a lie," is missing in the LXX.

62. Lit. "will be taken" (qal pass. ptc.).

63. The word שָׁקֶר, "lie," is missing in the LXX.

64. The first part of the verse, כֹּה־אָמַר יְהוָה צְבָאוֹת אֱלֹהֵי יִשְׂרָאֵל לֵאמֹר, "thus says Yahweh of hosts, the God of Israel, saying," is missing in the LXX.

own name to all the people in Jerusalem, to Zephaniah son of Maaseiah the priest, and to all the priests [in which you have said]:[65] **26** "Yahweh has appointed you priest in place of the priest Jehoiada to be overseer in the house of Yahweh to put any insane[66] man who acts as if he is a prophet in stocks and iron collar. **27** So why then have you not reprimanded Jeremiah from Anathoth who poses as a prophet among you? **28** Why, he has even sent [a message] to us in Babylon[67] saying: 'It's going to be a long time! Build houses and settle down. Plant gardens, and eat their produce.'"

29 Then Zephaniah the priest read this letter to Jeremiah the prophet. **30** So the word of Yahweh came to Jeremiah: **31** "Send to all the exiles[68] and tell them, 'This is what Yahweh has said about Shemaiah the Nehelamite: "Because Shemaiah has prophesied to you, even though I did not send him, and has led you to believe a lie, **32** therefore this is what Yahweh says: 'I will surely punish Shemaiah the Nehelamite and his descendants. He will have no one left among this people, nor will he see the good things I will do for my people, declares Yahweh, because he preached rebellion against me.'"[69]

COMMENTARY

The First Letter from Jeremiah (29:1–23)

29:1–2 This first letter is addressed to all the exiles including the "surviving elders … and … the priests, and the prophets, and all the other people [who were exiled]" (v. 1). The description of the elders as "surviving" is difficult to understand; it could refer to those who had made the journey to Babylon without tragedy befalling them. But others beside the elders had faced just as difficult a time, so why single out the elders as "surviving"? This phrase likely refers to internal difficulties that developed in Babylon, wherein some who caused problems were executed by Nebuchadnezzar. If some of the elders were involved in such disturbances, then they too suffered even though they were leaders in the community.

---

65. The LXX omits סְפָרִים, "letters," and וְאֶל כָּל־הַכֹּהֲנִים לֵאמֹר, "and to all the priests, saying."
66. Or "crazy;" lit. "madman."
67. The LXX[VCal] adds διὰ τοῦ μηνός τούτου, "in the course of this month."
68. Some LXX mss omit הַגּוֹלָה, "exiles."
69. The LXX omits the last part of the verse נְאֻם־יְהוָה כִּי־סָרָה דִבֶּר עַל־יְהוָה, "says Yahweh because he preached rebellion against Yahweh."

The problem of the false prophets has not gone away, for some of these same false prophets are among those who have gone into exile in Babylon. All their prattle about the demise of Nebuchadnezzar's reign and the imminent restoration of the people and temple furnishings to Jerusalem has a dampening effect on the purpose God had intended for the exiles. Instead of repentance and a renewed understanding of their relationship to Yahweh, they are filled with false hope about a quick end to this tragedy. They still do not get it.

29:3 This letter is delivered by Elasah, son of Shaphan and Gemariah, son of Hilkiah. Some think it is highly likely that Elasah was the brother of Ahikam (26:24) and of Gemariah (36:10) (Huey, 251; Keown, 70). Such a connection is possible, but the Gemariah in this passage (26:3) is a different Gamariah ("son of Hilkiah" as opposed to "son of Shaphan" in 36:10). The Gamariah of this passage may be a son or grandson of Hilkiah the priest who discovered the book of the law during the reign of Josiah (2 Kgs 22:8–10), but not the same as Jeremiah's father (1:1). Elasah's father was Shaphan, who had been a prestigious member of Josiah's court (Jer 26:24).

It is a matter of interest that Jeremiah is able to send a message through diplomatic couriers to Babylon, which again may show the residual favor he still retains with the conquering government. Since there is no salutary opening line, as was customary in such letters, we may assume that what we have in this chapter is a summary of the substance of the letters rather than a complete verbatim transcript of what was said. This letter is sent in the fourth year of Zedekiah (28:1), so it may be another part of the efforts of the Judeans to assure Babylon of their loyalty.

29:4 The question the exiles were facing is, how can they have a relationship with Yahweh now that they no longer have access to the temple and its sacrifices? The answer to this inquiry, of course, is to be found in the clear assertions by Jeremiah that Yahweh is sovereign over the country in which they now are exiled. His plans for them and for his ongoing purpose in the world are not suddenly abandoned or seriously modified.

29:5-7 It is a revolutionary message: these exiles must now build houses in this new land of their captivity, settle down, and plant gardens so they can eat from their produce (v. 5). Moreover, they are to marry, produce sons and daughters, find wives for their sons, and give their daughters in marriage, so they too can have sons and daughters and increase in their numbers and not decrease the population (v. 6). This sounds very similar to the command God gives in the creation of the universe (Gen 1:28), and to what happened while Israel was in Egypt for four hundred years (Exod 1:7; cf. Deut 26:5).[70] Even though they are in a pagan country and city, they are to intentionally seek ways to promote the peace and general welfare there, for as they promote the interests and prospects of that pagan city and nation, they are ultimately benefiting themselves and the plan of Yahweh, who brought them to this place. This is more than mere prudential or pragmatic talk, for in doing so the people of Judah demonstrate they are once again the means by which God will bless all the nations of the earth. This advice is very similar to that which the apostle Paul gives in 1 Tim 2:1–4. In that context Paul mandates that prayers be made for all kings and for all who are in authority to the end that all who live in that realm might live peaceable and quiet lives with all godliness and holiness. Moreover, in acting in this way, the aim is that all might be saved and come to acknowledge the truth.

29:8–10 Running contrary to this advice, however, are the lies advanced by false prophets, diviners, and other charlatans among them. These schemers opt for a quick fix and an early return home, which of course pleases the populace. But Jeremiah is not at all vague in his pronouncements, for Yahweh has announced that the exile will last for "seventy years" (29:10). At the end of that time, after approximately two or three generations, their sons and daughters, who also will have had children, will be among those who will return to the place from which they came.

29:11 Yahweh will fulfill his "gracious promise" to them, for his plans for them are plans of peace, prosperity, and well-being. They are plans for a

---

70. Berlin suggests that the four common elements found in Jer 29:5–7 and Deut 20:5–10 could be literary allusions and could point to Jeremiah's "rhetorical cleverness." These elements are: build houses, plant vineyards, marry wives, and the well-being of the city. See A. Berlin, "Jeremiah 29:5–7: A Deuteronomic Allusion," *HAR* 8 (1984): 3–11.

future filled with hope and not hurt against them. The judgment of the exile will not be God's final word!

29:12–19 God's offer is for the exiles to pray to him (v. 12), for when they seek him with all their heart and soul, he will surely be found by them (vv. 12–14). Yahweh has never forgotten about his promise to the patriarchs and to David (Gen 12:2–3; 15:1–6; 2 Sam 7:1–25). There will be a restoration of the people of Israel to their land, but in the meantime, neither the king, nor the city, nor the temple will be spared the required judgment that has built up as a result of their sin (v. 16–17). This judgment will involve the customary Jeremianic triad of the sword, famine, and plague (v. 18). That the people who have been given such great promises, and who have been warned by prophet after prophet and time after time, still harden their hearts and show no sign of turning to God is almost unbelievable.

29:20–23 Two false prophets who are not mentioned elsewhere, Ahab son of Kolaiah and Zedekiah son of Maaseiah, are likely among those prophets who are peddling an optimistic message of a quick return from Babylon (v. 21). Actually, the text does not explain exactly what they said, but it is severe enough that they were summarily handed over to Nebuchadnezzar, who executes them in front of all by roasting them in the fire (vv. 21–22). So startling is their sentence of judgment that their names become a byword that is used as a curse word among the exiles (v. 22). Some of what they did is hinted at in the text, for Yahweh himself is a witness to their committing adultery with their neighbors' wives and their using God's name and reputation to distribute their lies.[71]

Letters 2 and 3: Jeremiah's Controversy with Shemaiah (29:24–32)

29:24–28 Even in the midst of the Babylonian exile, there still are those who oppose the prophet Jeremiah (v. 24), for God has to give a direct warning to Shemaiah the Nehelamite, who is sending letters in his own name to all those back in Jerusalem. He also addresses his verbal campaign to some of the leaders, such as Zephaniah son of Maaseiah, the priest, and to

---

71. Dahood suggests that the text is poetic due to the unusual word order. See M. Dahood, "Word and Witness: A Note on Jeremiah 29:23," VT 27, no. 4 (1977): 483.

other priests as well (v. 25). He too uses the prophetic formula of "Thus says Yahweh" (v. 25a). In his letter he wants to know why Zephaniah, who is not the high priest but an overseer in the temple (similar to the job Pashhur had held when he had put Jeremiah in stocks and neck-collar earlier; Jer 20),[72] has not rebuked Jeremiah. So the question is: why has Zephaniah not put Jeremiah, who was by all accounts out of control and acting like a "madman," into stocks and neck-irons? (v. 26). "Madman" (מְשֻׁגָּע) is the derogatory term applied to a prophet someone wants to discredit (2 Kgs 9:11; Hos 9:7). In the opinion of Shemaiah, Jeremiah has to be brought under control, and the best person to do that is the overseer of the temple. He wants this prophet from Anathoth to be reprimanded (v. 27). Shemaiah thinks the letter to the exiles have received from Jeremiah in Babylon is outrageous; something should be done about it.

29:29–32 Instead of taking action, Zephaniah reads this letter to Jeremiah (v. 29). As a result, Jeremiah sends another letter, his third letter, to the exiles (vv. 30–31). He labels Shemaiah's charges a "lie" and prophesies on orders from God that that the false prophet will not have one of his descendants left among all the Israelites; in fact, none of his relatives will live to see the good God is going to do for the exiles. He has preached not just against Jeremiah; he has taken on God himself and is in rebellion against God (v. 32).

Finally this long section against false prophets comes to an end, but on what a sobering note! God's people cannot lightly toss off what God has spoken through his true prophets; his words will come to pass and be fulfilled. His plan will not suffer any deviations or subtractions; he will fulfill it all, just as he fulfilled his judgments against those who opposed him in Jeremiah's day.

It is bad enough to have your message refuted and declared absolutely not to be from God. But when the opposition begins to call the servant of God "crazy," that is harder to take. That is what Jeremiah has to put up with. But God is his strength and his portion, so he will not be afraid—and neither should we.

---

72. Pashhur may have been followed by an unknown Jehoiada, and he in turn is now followed by Zephaniah.

Many today think that laypersons or clergy who announce that we must turn back to God in repentance, or that we and our nation are in harm's way, are likewise crazy and out of our minds. But God has said that we must not be suddenly persuaded to say what the masses wish to hear. God's word remains true even when others do not like it!

THE RESTORATION OF
ISRAEL AND JUDAH TO
THE LAND (30:1–33:26)

E ven though Jeremiah is often called "the weeping prophet" (cf. 9:1), he is remembered for his repetition of the two big repeated points in his messages, that is, "violence and destruction" (1:10b). Yet even these two points do not summarize his whole mission, for God has also given him, as part of his mission, the command "to build and to plant" (1:10c). The positive part of his mission finds its most prominent display in chapters 30–33, which are traditionally called "the book of consolation," a section filled with an enormous hope and a remarkable future in the grace of God.

This is not to say that Jeremiah offers no hope or comfort earlier in his ministry, for what is recorded in the earlier portions of his book proves that conclusion incorrect; indeed, such a view would deliberately need to overlook 3:14–18; 16:14–15; 23:3–8; 24:4–7; and 29:10–14, 32. Even though such words of comfort and divine grace are offered by Jeremiah from time to time throughout his ministry, his main message is to warn Judah of an impending disaster if they do not turn back to God and repent of their sins. The note of judgment is never a subordinate note; it is his main theme despite the clear instances when he offered the hope and comfort of God to his fellow citizens.

The task of locating an occasion in the life of the prophet or in Judah's history for these four chapters has generally led in one of two directions. The first approach says that it was necessary for calm to have settled over Judah before hope could be offered. Such days of calm have been identified as the days after Jerusalem had fallen and Gedaliah had been installed by Babylon as governor in the town of Mizpah. Before such an event it would have been unimaginable to have the words of hope as are found in chapters 30 through 33. This interpretation is hampered by chapter 32 dating its messages to the latter part of Zedekiah's reign, which is prior to Gedaliah's governership (32:1). Moreover, Jeremiah's purpose in buying part of the family parcel in Anathoth is before Babylon had captured and burnt the city of Jerusalem (32:7).

A second approach for identifying a time when these chapters could have been given to Jeremiah goes in the other direction and opts for placing this material in the early days of Jeremiah's ministry, because chapters 30-31 include the northern kingdom in their message of hope; for example, his use of "Ephraim" in 31:6, 9, 18. Therefore, the thought is that these chapters came during reign of Jehoiakim or in the early part of Zedekiah's rule.

A third option, and the one supported here, is that it is best to locate these four chapters in the time of Jeremiah's imprisonment in the closing hours of the city of Jerusalem, just before it was taken by the Babylonians in 586 BC. Is this not the reason Yahweh told the prophet to put this section in *writing*? For the scholars who argue that the exile had not yet taken place, how could the prophet now write of days beyond this crisis? The answer is found in the God who knows all; he is the One who can communicate such a message to him.

In many ways the heart of OT theology as well as the central message of Jeremiah is found in the teaching of the "new covenant" (31:31-34). Set almost in the center of the "book of consolation/comfort" (chaps. 30-33), Jeremiah's message in these sections rises to the same lofty peaks as does Isaiah's message in Isa 40-66. Especially significant are the *six* **strophes** found in chapters 30-31, as first itemized as such by Charles Briggs in 1889.[1] They are:

1. 30:1-11: The Day of Jacob's Trouble

2. 30:12-31:6: The Healing of Israel's Incurable Wound

3. 31:7-14: God's Firstborn Restored to the Land

4. 31:15-22: Rachel Weeping for Her Children

---

1. This outline is suggested by C. A. Briggs, *Messianic Prophecy* (New York: Scribners, 1889), 246-47. Also in G. H. Cramer, "The Messianic Hope of Jeremiah," *BSac* 115, no. 459 (1958): 237-46.

5. 31:23–34: The New Covenant

6. 31:35–40: The Inviolable Covenant Given to Israel

THE DAY OF JACOB'S TROUBLE (30:1–11)

TRANSLATION

1 The word that came to Jeremiah from Yahweh: **2** "This is what Yahweh, the God of Israel has said: Write down everything I have said to you in a book. **3** For look! The days are coming, Yahweh declares, when I will reverse the captivity of my people, Israel and Judah, and I will restore them to the land which I gave to their fathers and they will possess it."

> **4** These are the words that Yahweh spoke concerning Israel and
> Judah:
> **5** Yes, this is what Yahweh has said:
> A cry of terror we hear,
>> terror and not peace.
> 6 Ask now and see—
>> Can a male bear children?
> Why, then, do I see a strong man,
>> With his hands on his loins,
> Like a woman in labor?[2]
>> Every face is turned sickly pale.
> **7** Wow![3] For that day will be awful!
>> There will be none like it.
> It will be the time of trouble for Jacob,
>> But he will be saved from it.

8 On that day, declares Yahweh of Hosts, I will break the [oppressor's] yoke from off your neck and I will tear off your bonds; and foreigners will no longer enslave [Jacob].[4] **9** Instead, they will serve Yahweh their God and David their king whom I will raise up for them.

---

2. The LXX omits כְּיוֹלֵדָה, "like a woman in labor."

3. The LXX reads ἐγενήθη, "they will be," where the MT has the interjection הוֹי, "Alas!" or "Wow!"

4. The LXX has αὐτοί, "them," where the MT has "him."

10 So, then, do not be afraid, O Jacob my servant, declares Yahweh, nor be dismayed, O Israel.

> For look! From a distant place I will save you,
>> Your offspring from the land of their captivity.
> Jacob will return to rest,
>> And no one will make him afraid.
> **11** For I am with you and will save you, declares Yahweh.
>> Though I completely destroy all the nations,
>> Among whom I have scattered you,
> Nevertheless, I will not completely destroy you;
>> I will chastise you, but with justice,
>> I will not let you go completely unpunished.[5]

COMMENTARY

Restoring the Fortunes of Israel and Judah (30:1–3)

30:1-2 Normally the prophet delivered his proclamations orally to the people, but that the prophet is told to write the message God was giving him (v. 2) may indicate that Jeremiah is in prison and therefore cannot announce these words in public, as he usually did in the temple. It may also be that chapters 32 and 33, which are in prose, are have been dictated by the prophet to his secretary Baruch. The prophet is to write the words in a "scroll" (later in history these scrolls will be replaced by what we call a "book"). The theme of these next chapters is this: "The days are coming ... when I will reverse the captivity of my people, Israel and Judah, and I will restore them to the land which I gave to their fathers and they will possess it" (v. 3). This work of divine restoration of the nation will affect both the northern and southern kingdoms. This promise to "reverse/return the captivity" (שַׁבְתִּי אֶת־שְׁבוּת) marks off the coming work of God to restore the people to their land.

30:3 It is important to note that this theme of the restoration of Israel will be the dominant topic of the book of consolation/comfort. Five times in

---

5. Verses 10 and 11 are missing in the LXX.

this book a formula will announce a time that is coming: "For look, the days are coming!" (30:3; 31:27, 31, 38; 33:14). It is also noteworthy that both the northern and the southern parts of Israel are included in this promise of restoration.

"The days are coming" is the prophet's expression or formula for the "day of Yahweh" (17:16–18; cf. Isa 2:12–21; Amos 5:18–20; Zeph 1:14–18). This expression usually points to the distant future. Many scholars want to locate the concept of the day of Yahweh as first appearing in Amos 5:18:

> Woe to you who long
>   for the day of the LORD!
> Why do you long for the day of the LORD?
>   That day will be darkness, not light.
> It will be as though a man fled from a lion
>   only to meet a bear,
> As though he entered his house
>   and rested his hand on the wall
>   only to have a snake bite him. (Amos 5:18–19)

However, Amos was written in the mid-eighth century BC, and both Joel and Obadiah, who use this phrase, may have been written before Amos. Moreover, large parts of Joel are repeated in many of the other prophetic books, so it is possible that Joel is the prophetic origin of this concept in the eighth century BC. However, there may be an even earlier root for this idea of the "day of Yahweh." Moses writes in Exod 32:34 about a "day of [God's] visitation."

> Now go, lead the people to the [place] I spoke of to you.
> Behold, my angel will go before you.
> And *in the day of my visitation,*
> I will punish their sin upon them.

So the word "day" is not one day only, when God's activity would stand out as supreme in comparison with all other times God would act, both in judgment for those deserving it and in deliverance for those who had trusted fully in him. It is the whole period of time that embraces God's final judgment and his final deliverance and restoration of his people to the land.

In addition to the expression "the day of Yahweh," there are other parallel phrases such as: "in the latter days," "that day," or "the days are coming." In some OT contexts, any one of these expressions might mean some subsequent or indefinite time when the universal reign of God could be expected as Yahweh shows himself victorious over all challengers. Thus any one of these terms often embraces two ages: "this age," and "the age to come." These two ages appear together in the NT some thirty times. "This age" covers the time from creation up to and including at least the present time, while "the age to come" had already overlapped "this age" in Heb 1:1 with the first coming of Jesus to earth. But the "age to come" will especially and mostly be located in the time of the latter days, when the eschatological times are in evidence.[6]

Free to Serve God and David Their King (30:4–11)

This section is made up of a number of literary forms, including:

1. an announcement of judgment (vv. 4–7),

2. a word of promise and rescue (vv. 8–9), and

3. a declaration of assurance (vv. 10–11).

30:4 Verse 4 continues to address this prophecy to both "Israel and Judah." We must go back to Jer 13:11 to find the last time "Israel" and "Judah" are mentioned together, but this reference is not the final one, for the two nations will appear together in 31:27, 31; 32:30, 32; 33:14; 36:2; 50:4, 20, 33; 51:5.

30:5 The word of judgment begins with "A cry of terror we hear, terror and not peace" (v. 5). The cries, motivated by fear and anxiety, are so strong that as yet the source of the cries cannot be determined. But one thing is for sure, and that is that there is no peace, which can only be had when the people have entered into a right relationship with God. Only when war is absent can there be peace. So for those who cry out to God and Jeremiah, the instruction from on high is "Ask now and see" (pl. verbs referring to all Israel; v. 6). Has no one thought about how God waits for the prayer of

---

6. For more detail, see W. C. Kaiser Jr., *Preaching and Teaching the Last Things: Old Testament Eschatology for the Life of the Church* (Grand Rapids: Baker Academic, 2011), xiii –xvi, 77–88.

his children? Why do folks complain to others with no or little attempt to go first to God for relief?

30:6 This is followed by a question that is filled with irony! "Can a male bear children?" (v. 6). The answer to that question is pretty obvious! Well, if that is so obvious, then why do we see real "strong men" holding their loins and stomachs as if they are women in labor delivering babies? Something has happened that is so unnatural and so abnormal that the agony of these men is so excruciating that "every face is turned sickly pale" (v. 6f). The word used here to describe the pallor on the faces of all mortals (יֵרָקוֹן) is normally rendered "yellowness" and associated with a disease found in grain, like a blight. But what is ordinarily applied to plants is now applied to people who have become "jaundiced" (Brown, 373n7).

30:7 "Wow!" exclaims the prophet, "that day will be awful!" (v. 7a). It exceeds the awesomeness of previous days because of the insertion of divine wrath in this final day of judgment (Hos 1:11 [2:2]; Zeph 1:14). "There will be none like it" (v. 7b). Why is that so? Because "it will be the time of trouble for Jacob" (v. 7c). What day and what time is this passage speaking about?

The range of opinions is extremely large here, for some merely identify this time of Jacob's trouble as the sixth century BC, during the days of the last kings of Judah. Others locate its reference in a future period known as the time of the "great tribulation" (also called the seventieth week in Dan 9), with little to no reference in this passage to the historic times of Jeremiah. In particular, dispensational authors are good examples of this last view; they claim these sufferings will hit Israel and Judah after the church has been "raptured" at the beginning of the seven years of tribulation spoken of in Dan 9. However, Jeremiah gives no hint that this is what he has in mind. In fact, there are few or almost no references in these verses to any sufferings on the part of Israel and Judah from the Babylonians or anyone else! As Michael Brown points out, there is instead a series of blessings found in this section known as the time of "Jacob's trouble." They include:

- v. 3, the return from exile,

- v. 8, the breaking of the yoke of the oppressor,

- v. 9, serving Yahweh and the messianic king,

- vv. 10–11, words of comfort and security, and

- v. 16, punishment of Judah's enemies and healing of her own wounds (Brown, 370).

30:8-9 Thus, despite what otherwise could be seen as one of the darkest days for the nation, she will emerge from all of her troubles triumphantly, heirs of the grace of God. In the very midst of this time of trouble, Yahweh declares that he will surely deliver his people by breaking the oppressor's neck, and he will remove the yoke from Judah, much as Hananiah had falsely and prematurely removed the "yoke" from Jeremiah's neck (Jer 28). When that day comes, no longer will Israel be enslaved; instead she will be free, for instead of serving the king of Babylon, she will serve Yahweh as her God and David her king, a ruler whom God will raise up for them in that final day. In this text (v. 9), Messiah is called "David," an identity also found in Hos 3:5; Amos 9:11; Ezek 34:23-24; 37:24-25 (cf. Jer 30:21; 23:5-6; 33:14-26). Therefore, the appearance of a new King David is connected with the "tearing off of [the] bonds [of] ... foreigners" (v. 8). Jeremiah has already mentioned the "righteous Branch" (23:5) as the coming Messiah's title. It is also important to note that serving Yahweh as Lord is not in opposition to serving this "king," whom God will "raise up for them" (v. 9). The Davidic king that God will raise up is the Messiah, King of kings and Lord of lords!

30:10-11 The upshot of God's promise of assurance to the people was "Do not be afraid ... nor be dismayed" (v. 10). This particular word is for those who fit the description of "Jacob my servant" (v. 10); both "Jacob" and "Israel" are mentioned here as the covenantal people of God. For those who walk faithfully with Yahweh and are his servants, there is hope in the midst of the crises and catastrophes that will befall the nations, both in the days of the sixth century BC and the distant future. They will not go unpunished (v. 11f), but neither will they be completely destroyed (v. 11b), and they will return to rest and will have no reason to fear (v. 10).

This poetic assurance of deliverance in vv. 10–11 is virtually repeated in Jer 46:27-28, where the context concerns the burden of Yahweh against the nations. If the Heb. particle "for" (כִּי) is treated asseveratively (that is, "surely"), as the NIV does, then both Israel and Judah are promised that God will *surely* save them from "a distant place" (v. 10). Wherever that place is, in whatever country and in whatever condition they exist, Yahweh will bring them back in "peace and security," so that "no one would make [Jacob] afraid" anymore (v. 11). This theme is emphasized in Jeremiah; Yahweh will not make an end to Israel (cf. 4:27; 5:10, 18). Yes, there will be divine chastisement, but he will not completely destroy Israel (v. 11; cf. 10:23–25; 31:18). All other nations may be completely destroyed by God, but this will not be true of Israel.

God astonishingly promises to bring back both the northern ten tribes of Israel and Judah and Benjamin from the Babylonian captivity. He furthermore promises to be with them! Now, this is not done as a particular favor to the Jewish people but rather as a sign so the whole world can see that he is God indeed. Though Israel and Judah will be judged for their sin, yet God will not completely destroy them, for he has his ancient word to Abraham, Isaac, Jacob, and David on the line. He cannot lie to them or to the world. A day will come when Israel and Judah will serve the Lord and David their king. What a magnificent Lord!

HEALING ISRAEL'S INCURABLE WOUND (30:12–31:6)

This second section of the book of consolation is a further description of an incurable wound or hurt Israel received, as well as an examination of what caused it. Israel's sickness has both internal and external aspects to it. An astounding number of metaphors are introduced to show how desperate Israel's case is. For instance, no court will take her case, no medicine will bring a cure, no physician can heal the wound, no lovers are left to come to her aid—all of which leaves no help from any natural source, be it human or physical, to rescue her in her condition.

TRANSLATION

12 Yes, this is what Yahweh has said:

"Your particular hurt is incurable,[7]
   your wound beyond healing,
13 There is no one to plead your case,
   No salve for your sore,
   No healing for you.
14 All your lovers have forgotten you;
   They do not seek you,
When I inflicted on you an enemy's blow
   With a cruel chastisement,
   Because your guilt is so great and your sins are so
      numerous.
15[8] Why cry out over your wound,
   Your incurable pain?
Because your guilt is so great
   And your sins so numerous,
   I have done these things to you.
16 Therefore, all who devour you will be devoured;
   All your enemies will go into exile;[9]
Your despoilers will be for spoil;
   All who loot you I will give for loot.
17 Yes, I will restore you to health,
   And heal your wounds,"[10] declares Yahweh,
"Because you are called an outcast, Zion,[11]
   For whom no one cares."
18 This is what Yahweh has said:

---

7. The LXX reads ἀνέστησα σύντριμμα, "I have brought destruction," where the MT has אֲנוּשׁ לְשִׁבְרֵךְ, "your hurt is incurable."

8. Verse 15 is missing in the LXX.

9. The LXX has κρέας αὐτῶν πᾶν ἔδονται, "shall eat all their own flesh," where the MT has בְּלָם בַּשְּׁבִי יֵלֵכוּ, "they shall go into captivity." Dahood proposes a revocalization that "uncovers a clever word play on *kol* and *kōlīm*. Thus, the first two lines should read, 'Therefore all who devoured you shall be devoured, and all your adversaries consumed.'" See M. Dahood, "The Word-Pair 'ĀKAL || KĀLĀH in Jeremiah XXX 16," VT 27, no. 4 (1977): 482.

10. The LXX reads ἀπὸ πληγῆς ὀδυνηρᾶς, "from your grievous wound," where the MT has only מִמַּכּוֹתַיִךְ, "from your wounds."

11. The LXX has θήρευμα ὑμῶν, "your prey," for the MT's צִיּוֹן, "Zion." Jacobson suggests that "*ṣiyyôn hî* needs to be read also as *ṣāyôn hî* (see Isa. Xxv 5, xxxii 2). Thus, "'this is Zion' on the one hand, but 'this is a wasteland' on the other." See H. Jacobson, "Jeremiah XXX 17: היא ציון," VT 54, no. 3 (2004): 398–99.

"Look, I am going to restore the fortunes of the tents of[12] Jacob,
And take pity on his dwellings.
The town will be built on its tell/mound,[13]
And the stronghold will stand where it should.
19 From them will come thanksgiving
And the sound of rejoicing.
I will increase their number,
And they will not be diminished;
I will exalt them,
And they will not be disdained.[14]
20 Their children will be as [many] as they used to be;[15]
Their assembly will be established under me;
I will punish all who oppress them.
21 Their prince will be one of their own;
Their ruler will arise from among them;
I will bring him near,
And he will come close to me.[16]
For who is he who will devote himself to be close to me?
declares Yahweh.
22[17] Then you shall be my people,
And I will be your God."
23 Look, a storm of Yahweh will burst out in wrath.
A heavy gale is swirling
Upon the heads of the wicked.
24 The burning anger of Yahweh will not turn back
Until he completes the purposes of his heart.

---

12. The const. אָהֳלֵי, "tents of," is missing in the LXX.

13. The LXX has καὶ αἰχμαλωσίαν αὐτοῦ, "and on his prisoners," where the MT has וּמִשְׁכְּנֹתָיו, "and on his dwellings."

14. The last part of the verse, וְהִכְבַּדְתִּים וְלֹא יִצְעָרוּ, "and I will honor them, and they will not be insignificant," is missing in the LXX.

15. The LXX has καὶ εἰσελεύσονται, "and they shall go in," where the MT has וְהָיוּ, "and they shall be."

16. The LXX has καὶ συνάξω αὐτοὺς καὶ ἀποστρέψουσιν πρός με, "and I will gather them, and they will return to me," where the MT has וְהִקְרַבְתִּיו וְנִגַּשׁ, "I will make him draw near, and he will approach me."

17. The entire verse is missing in the LXX.

In the days to come you will understand this.

31:1 In that day, declares Yahweh, I will be the God of all the families[18] of Israel, and they shall be my people.

2 This is what Yahweh has said:
The people[19] who survive[20] the sword,
  Will find[21] favor[22] in the desert;
  I will give rest to Israel.
3 From long ago Yahweh appeared to [us],[23] [saying]:
I have loved you with an everlasting love;[24]
  Therefore I have drawn you [to me] with grace.[25]
4 Once more, I will build you up,
  And you will be rebuilt, O Virgin Israel.
Again you will take up your tambourines,
  And you will go out with merrymaking dancers.[26]
5 Once again I will plant vineyards on the hills of Samaria.
  The planters will eat the crops and rejoice.[27]
6 Yes, the time is coming when the watchmen,
  Will cry out[28] on the hills of Ephraim:
  Come, let us go up to Zion, to Yahweh our God."

---

18. The LXX has the sg. τῷ γένει, "to the family," where the MT has "to all families."

19. The LXX and α´ have μετὰ, "with," where the MT has עַם, "people."

20. The word שָׂרִיד, "survivor," appears four times in Jeremiah (31:2; 42:17; 44:14, and 47:4), the first time in the context of salvation and the last three in the context of judgment. See K. D. Mulzac, "ŚRD as a Remnant Term in the Context of Judgment in the Book of Jeremiah," *Asia Adventist Seminary Studies* 7 (2004): 39–58.

21. The LXX has εὗρον, "I found," where the MT has מָצָא, "he found."

22. The LXX has θερμόν, "warm," where the MT has חֵן, "favor."

23. The LXX has αὐτῷ, "to him," where the MT has לִי, "to me."

24. The LXX precedes the noun "everlasting love" with the prep. εἰς, "in."

25. Feuillet prefers the LXX and the Vg. translation of the last part of the verse, "therefore, I have drawn you with compassion." The author cites John 6:44 as proof. See A. Feuillet, "Note sur la Traduction de Jer 31:3c," *VT* 12, no. 1 (1962): 122–24.

26. The LXX has μετὰ συναγωγῆς, "with a congregation," where the MT has בִּמְחוֹל, "in a dance."

27. The LXX has the impv. καὶ αἰνέσατε, "and praise," where the MT has וְחִלְּלוּ, "they will enjoy."

28. The LXX has κλήσεως ἀπολογουμένων, "a call of those who plead," where the MT has קָרְאוּ נֹצְרִים, "watchmen will cry out."

COMMENTARY

An Incurable Wound (30:12–17)

At the heart of this section is the imagery of Israel's need for healing from all her pain and hurt. These verses are not loath to set out the reality of how hopeless and seemingly incurable Israel's suffering is (vv. 12–14a), nor is the message hesitant to say what has brought all of this about (vv. 14b–15). There can be no doubt that the nation of Judah is in real trauma over what she is experiencing. Interestingly enough, neither Israel nor Judah is directly mentioned in this section; however, Zion is mentioned in v. 17.

30:12 The suffering experienced by this nation should not be spoken of in figurative or spiritual terms, for it is real—in fact, it is all too real! God is the One who has wounded and smitten this nation; their affliction has come from his hand. The only way the people can ever get back to health is by turning to Yahweh and repenting of their sin. Moreover, Jeremiah calls the wound "incurable," a description of God's punishment for sin found elsewhere in Ps 38:3–11; Isa 1:5–6; Neh 3:19. If any recovery is to be felt, God will need to intervene (Isa 53:4–5; 57:15–19; Hos 6:1).

30:13 Jeremiah, along with the prophets of the Hebrew Bible, calls for a "healing" (רָפָא) as the best route to full recovery and restoration. The prophets use the verbal form of this Heb. root some twenty-nine times and the nominal form another nine times, for a total of thirty-eight occurrences. Jeremiah alone uses almost half of those: thirteen verbal forms and five nominal forms for a total of eighteen times in his book. Just as the wounds from the bitter Assyrians and the hostile Babylonians are anything but figurative, so the healing needed from Yahweh is just as real.

30:13–14 In addition to noting that there is no cure for Israel's condition, no one is prepared to plead her case in court, or to seek out her welfare, or to care for her (vv. 13–14). In fact, God has struck them as if they were the enemy. Israel has to be punished because her guilt is so great and her sins so numerous (v. 14), a fact repeated here for emphasis.

30:15 This raises a question that at first does not seem fair: "Why do you cry out over your wound?" (v. 15). This verb, to "cry out" (זָעַק), is sometimes used for addressing God with prayer full of agony. They are crying out to God because of the affliction he is instigating, causing the pain and hurt; is it not redundant to cry out in agony to the one causing the agony? God's answer is so important because it shows that their agony does not come from the affliction itself; he repeats from the previous verse: it is "because [their] guilt is so great and [their] sins are so numerous" (vv. 14, 15).

30:16 Verse 16 begins with a "therefore," which generally signals the word of judgment. But in this case, instead of giving the expected consequence of their sins, the divine word from on high shifts to some surprising words of hope: "All who devour you will be devoured; all your enemies will go into exile" (v. 16a–b). Even though no identity is given for these nations, they will themselves be devoured as they are trying to devour Israel. Indeed, God has divinely appointed them to this action of smiting Israel and Judah, but that does not mean they are left to do as they please and there is no accountability for them. Once they overstep the boundaries God had set for them, they become liable to punishment from God.

30:17 "Yes," affirms Yahweh, "I will restore you [Judah] to health and heal your wounds" (v. 17). What a major reversal in the action of God! Here the compassionate love of God takes over. God sees his people Israel as "an outcast … for whom no one cares" (v. 17c, d). Those who thought Yahweh was incapable of defending his people were wrong. On the contrary, Yahweh will intervene in a salvific way in order to further his own plan and purposes both for this nation and for the nations of the world.

Jacob, the Restored People (30:18–22)

30:18 The healing of these wounds that were thought to be incurable is now equated with "restoring the fortunes" (שָׁב שְׁבוּת, šāb šĕbût; see "Excursus: Shub Shebut" and 29:14). Instead of war and the suffering that comes with it, the picture is one of peacefulness as neighbors go from one tent or house to another as a result of the compassion that Yahweh had brought to the land and its people (v. 18). Cities and fortified places that had been destroyed are now to be rebuilt on their original tells, where they had once stood (v. 18d–e). All the dwellings in the land will break out in "songs of thanksgiving" as the restored congregation lifts up their voices in rejoicing (v. 19).

30:19 Moreover, God will add to their numbers instead of decreasing them (v. 19c–d). God himself will see that they are honored and not treated contemptuously of disdainfully (v. 19e–f). That is precisely what was promised in the covenant God had made with them centuries ago (Deut 28:13).

30:20–22 The people will thrive and enjoy the kind of population growth seen in olden days (v. 20). Furthermore, all who dare to oppress this nation will have to face God himself (v. 20c). God will raise up the promised "leader" and "ruler" from among their own people (cf. Deut 17:15). It is noticeable that the text seems to avoid mentioning the title of "king" or the man "David," but this may have been done purposely, so as not to tie this coming leader so closely to the failures of Judah's past kings. God will bring this leader "near" him, and he will allow him to "come close to [God]" (v. 21c). Surely these words are messianic, for the Messiah will be a "priest-king." His kingdom will rule over all nations and all peoples, and they will be given access to him just as the messianic priest-king will be given access to God.

This raises another question: "who is he who will devote himself to be close to me?" (v. 21d). It is the height of hubris to approach God without being invited. It is just as improper and brashly out of place to dare to take on oneself the task of ruling over God's people. This is not a task that one should volunteer for. Nevertheless, the restored people of God may recall the formula for the promise-plan of God: "you shall be my people and I will be your God" (v. 22), a theme repeated throughout both Testaments almost fifty times.

A Storm for the Wicked and a Rest for God's People (30:23–31:6)

30:23–24 Verses 23–24 are a repetition of 23:19–20, with two changes: "And" does not introduce the clause "a driving wind ...," and the verb describing the action of the storm is adjusted to fit the text from "whirlwind" to "driving wind." God promises that his burning wrath will not turn back from the wicked until he has fully completed the purposes he has in his heart

(v. 24). Now, if all of this seems mysterious or incomprehensible, the readers of this scroll are assured that "In days to come [they] will understand this" (v. 24d).[29] It is not as if everything is hidden, or is without any sense, but for the present we are all called to walk by faith in those parts of this plan that seem to be beyond our ability to completely figure out.

31:1 Jeremiah 31:1 is sometimes placed as the last verse of the previous chapter, for it is a transitional verse and repeats the content of 30:22. But the six verses it introduces in chapter 31 are addressed to "all the families of Israel," and has as a result the reunification of all of that nation as its object, which nation had been divided since 931 BC.

31:2 But a new start comes in v. 2, for what follows some have declared to be one of the most explicit declarations found in all of Scripture of the all-encompassing love of God for his people. Brown claims that this text in Jeremiah is "the OT equivalent to Romans 11:26" (Brown, 380). Thus, the weeping prophet from Anathoth, who time after time announces "violence and destruction" to the unrepentant people, is now seen in the opposite light, giving one word after another of tender love and comfort to a people one would easily judge to be the least deserving of such grace and kindness. But that is what is happening in this text. The perceived incurable wound makes way for the peaks of grace and mercy that culminate in the repetition of God's ancient promise and the renewal of the covenant, called the new covenant.

Verse 2 addressed "the people who survive the sword." But who are those people? Are they those who were delivered from Egypt long ago? Or is this a future reference to the exiles who will come back from Babylon? It is difficult to determine which of these two allusions Jeremiah is making in this text. Even the pf. form[30] does not tell us.

---

29. Willis suggest that the expression "in the days to come" refers to an immediate future that "must come within the lifetime of his hearers." See J. Willis, "The Expression *be' acharith hayyamin* in the Old Testament," *ResQ* 22, nos. 1–2 (1979): 54–71. Lipiński argues that the text is preexilic, just like Gen 49:1 and Num 24:14; he also argues for an eschatological reading. See E. Lipiński, "באחרית הימים Dans les Textes Préexiliques," *VT* 20, no. 4 (1970): 445–50.

30. The pf. verbal form is often rendered into English as past tense; unless it is a prophetic pf., and then it is rendered as a fut. tense.

The "rest" that Yahweh will give (v. 2b) is usually related to Israel's entry into the land of Canaan (Exod 33:14; Josh 1:13; Deut 28:65). It seems, then, that the "favor [Israel would find] in the desert" (v. 2) in the future will be similar to what the exiles from Egypt and Babylon found as they had to cross the desert wastelands to get to Canaan in the first place at different times in the past. The physical and spiritual lessons are very much alike. But what was common to times past will also be true in the days to come: Yahweh will be faithful, and he will reverse the covenantal curse into times of great blessing.

31:3 Israel is reminded that Yahweh had "from long ago ... appeared" (v. 3), or as others render it "out of a distant place," meaning the exile. Even more important is the divine declaration: "I have loved you with an everlasting love; ... I have drawn you with grace [or loving- kindness]" (v. 3b). Here is the only use of the word "to love" (אָהֵב) in the book of Jeremiah with Yahweh as its subject. Of course, Deuteronomy has many such uses of Yahweh's "love" (Deut 4:37; 7:8, 12, 13; 10:14, 15). What is significant is that despite all of Judah's rebellion and wandering away from Yahweh, the offer of God's forgiveness and fellowship with himself is still open. The call to return home to a loving Heavenly Father is perpetually open and available even to the most reprobate of sinners. God will "draw" (or: "extend," "prolong") Israel with his love and grace.

31:4 After Yahweh shows Jeremiah what his love will mean for the future of the people, he now in v. 4 shows them what it will mean as he restores the land. In brief, the whole structure of society will be "built" up again. He addresses the people as "O Virgin Israel" (v. 4b). This form of address is found in v. 21 as well as in 8:13. In light of vv. 5–6, this is best understood as a reference to northern Israel.

A picture of unabated joy and rejoicing is described in v. 4. Tambourines are used by the merrymakers to express their joy. The tambourines were made with a circular frame, over which was stretched a membrane of skin, and they were held in one hand and beaten with the other hand. Later tambourines show pieces of metal hanging on them that jangled as they were shaken, much like modern tambourines, which include metal jingles.

31:5-6 Verse 5 gives another picture of the restoration by using a "plant" to point to the revival of the fruitfulness of the land. The farmers will plant vineyards on the terraced hillsides and will enjoy the fruit from these vines. Even the "watchmen" will call out from the hills of Ephraim an invitation to come to Zion to worship Yahweh their God (v. 6). That will be a different day, for those in the north will advise all to go to Jerusalem in the south. This is another note of a reunified nation. It is a whole new role for Samaria's "watchmen," who traditionally looked out for foxes and intruders into the vineyards.

Yes, a storm is in store for the wicked—indeed, the fierce anger of God. Meanwhile, God will restore his people to their land. This will include rebuilt houses, planted vineyards, and joyful dances, for God will ransom Jacob.

The love of God is greater than all of our sin. We need to be thankful for the model of what God will do in Israel, for that is what the rest of the believing Gentile world is rooted in. The olive tree's roots and trunk are established by Yahweh, allowing Gentiles to be grafted in by faith (Rom 11:17-24). Finally Israel herself will be regrafted into the olive tree from which she had been lopped off.

GOD'S FIRSTBORN RESTORED
TO THE LAND (31:7-14)

It is difficult to identify who is addressed in this section, but since the nations are mentioned in v. 10, it could be that Yahweh is calling for all the peoples, from all the nations, to join in praising and rejoicing in the return of Israel and Judah to their land.

TRANSLATION

> **7** Yes, this is what Yahweh has said:
> "Sing with joy[31] for Jacob!
>> Shout for the first of the nations!
> Make [it] heard! Praise! And say,

---

31. The word שִׂמְחָה, "joy," is absent in the LXX.

'Yahweh has saved[32] his[33] people,[34]

The remnant of Israel.'

8 Look, I am bringing them from the land of the north,

And I am gathering them from the remotest part of the earth;

Among them will be the blind, the lame,[35]

With pregnant mothers, and women in labor;

Together they will return here; a great throng.

9 They will come[36] with weeping;

They will pray[37] as I bring them back;

I will lead them beside streams of water

On a path too smooth for stumbling;

For I am Israel's Father,

And Ephraim is my Firstborn."

10 O nations! Hear the word of Yahweh!

Proclaim it in distant shores! Say:

"He who scattered Israel will gather them,

He will guard his flock like a shepherd."

11 Yes, Yahweh has ransomed Jacob

And redeemed him from the hand of those stronger than he.

12 They will come and rejoice on Zion's height[38]

And thrill to the goodness of Yahweh,

The grain,[39] the new wine, and the olive oil,

The sheep and the cattle.

---

32. The LXX has the aor. ἔσωσεν, "saved," where the MT has the impv. הוֹשַׁע, "save."

33. The LXX has τὸν λαὸν αὐτοῦ, "his people," where the MT has עַמְּךָ, "your people."

34. The translation of this line follows the LXX. The MT reads, "Yahweh save your people!"

35. The LXX has ἐν ἑορτῇ φασεχ, "to the Passover feast," where the MT has בָּם עִוֵּר וּפִסֵּחַ, "with the blind and lame."

36. The LXX has ἐξῆλθον, "they went forth," where the MT has "they will come."

37. The LXX has καὶ ἐν παρακλήσει, "and with consolations," where the MT has וּבְתַחֲנוּנִים, "and with prayers."

38. The LXX has ἐν τῷ ὄρει, "in the mountain," where the MT has בְמְרוֹם, "on the height."

39. The LXX has "to a land of grain" where the MT has "because of the grain."

They will be like a well-watered garden,[40]
    Never to languish again.
13 Then maidens will dance[41] and be glad,[42]
    Young men and old as well.
I will turn their mourning into gladness;
    I will give them comfort[43] and joy instead of sorrow.[44]
14 I will give the priests[45] their fill of fat things,[46]
    While my people are satisfied with my bounty,
    Declares Yahweh.

COMMENTARY

The Homecoming of Israel (31:7–9)

31:7 Verse 7 begins with a כִּי, "for," which often suggests continuity with the previous section, but in this case it acts as an asseverative emphasizing the clause; that is, "There's more here to say!" God is going to act so marvelously in that future day by ransoming and redeeming Israel that it will be cause for all nations to break out in a mighty chorus of praise to the name of God! Moreover, it is significant that Yahweh calls the nations of the world to rejoice on behalf of Jacob. This is in direct contrast to many scolding words to the nations on previous occasions. Add to all of this the even more impressive fact that the nations join in a prayer to God to save his people Israel (v. 7)! Five impvs. lead off this section with these exhortations: "Sing with joy," "Shout," "Make it heard," "Praise," and "Say."

Surely this speaks of how important the redemption of Israel is to the program and plan of God. This is similar to the apostle Paul's writing that Israel's redemption in that final day will mean "life from the dead" for many (Rom 11:15). However, in the end day God will bring Israel from the "land

---

40. The LXX has ὥσπερ ξύλον ἔγκαρπον, "like a fruit tree," where the MT has עַל־דָּגָן, "a well-watered garden."

41. The LXX has ἐν συναγωγῇ νεανίσκων, "in the assembly of youth," where the MT has בְּמָחוֹל וּבַחֻרִים, "maidens will dance."

42. The LXX has χαρήσονται, "they will rejoice," where the MT has יַחְדָּו, "together."

43. The word וְנִחַמְתִּים, "and I will comfort them," is absent in the LXX.

44. The LXX has μεγαλυνῶ, "I will enlarge," where the MT has מִיגוֹנָם, "from sorrow."

45. The LXX adds the phrase υἱῶν Λευι, "sons of Levi," after "priests."

46. The word דָּשֶׁן, "fat thing(s)," is absent in the LXX.

of the north" and gather them "from the remotest part of the earth" (v. 8). This can hardly be fulfilled by a mere return from the Babylonian exile, for that will not be from the "remotest part of the earth"! This promise is so frequent in Scripture it is hard to imagine how so many have substituted a replacement theology for Israel and said that the church now replaces Israel as the recipient of the divine promises made in the OT. (See this same language echoed in many of the passages in the prophet Isaiah, such as 35:3–10; 40:3–5; 41:17–19; 42:16; 43:5–6; 48:20; 49:9–13).

31:8 The picture of those returning includes even the challenged and physically disadvantaged, including the blind, the lame, pregnant mothers, and women in labor (v. 8). What an enormous contrast between Yahweh's gentle care of these persons and the brutality of the enemy forces that invaded Israel and Judah. The point is clear: "a great throng" "will return here" (v. 8d).

31:9 This enormous throng will come back home "weeping" and "pray[ing]" (v. 9). The tears are indications of both happiness and sadness, for despite all of the waywardness of the nation of Israel, God has led them beside "streams of water" on "a path too smooth for stumbling" (9c, d). He has done all of this because he is Israel's "Father" (v. 9e). This title for God as "Father" is not common in the OT, but it does appear in 3:19; 31:9; Deut 32:6; Isa 63:16; 64:8. Israel is God's "son"; in fact, "Ephraim" is his "firstborn son." The word "firstborn" here does not refer to the chronological order of birth, but instead it refers to "first in rank," "first in preeminence." "Ephraim" was actually the second son of Joseph; he was raised above Manasseh, Joseph's oldest son, to a place of preeminence. It is for this reason that the Arian heresy (which argued that Jesus was the firstborn in the sense that he was not eternal but was the first to be created of all of God's creation) was rebuked; instead Jesus is "first" in rank and first in preeminence, for he too is eternal, just as God the Father. But it is also true in another sense that Israel is God's "firstborn son" and as such is the object of divine special care and protection (Exod 4:22; Deut 32:6; cf. 2 Sam 7:14; Hos 11:1) like the One who was first in rank and first in priority and preeminence.

Zion's Future Happiness (31:10-14)

31:10 Whereas in the past the nations have had to listen to the awful news about coming disasters, now they are invited to hear the good news about God's child Israel (v. 10). Just as the nations have been witnesses of what God has done already, now they must be witnesses of what he will do as he brings Israel back into their land. It is this word that the nations will announce to the most distant shores and coastlands; they must tell the peoples of the world that the God who scattered Israel is the same one who will now in that future day gather them from all over the globe (v. 10). Israel has seen lots of "shepherds" in the past: some who invaded her land (6:3); some from her own people, who cared not a whit for them (10:21; 13:20; 23:2-3); but God is the only good "shepherd" who will one day gather his flock (Ezek 34:15) and care for and watch over his "firstborn."

30:11 More reasons are given why the nations should pay close attention to Yahweh's deliverance of Jacob: Yahweh will "ransom" (פָּדָה) his people, and he will "redeem (גָּאַל) them from the hand of those stronger than he [Jacob]" (v. 11). These two verbs often describe the work of God in the past when Israel was delivered from Egypt (Exod 6:5; 15:13; Deut 7:8; 9:26). This setting of the people free will be the exclusive work of God and his intervention with power and might.

30:12 The very "goodness of Yahweh" (v. 12) will be seen in the way he blesses the people with "grain," "new wine," "olive oil," and "the sheep and the cattle." Whereas the land had been unproductive, now it will be like a "well-watered garden." Never again will the fields languish, for God will introduce a new day altogether. Goodbye to all sources of all kinds of threats to the joy of working in the fields.

30:13-14 All of this experience of the goodness of God will lead to unbounded joy and rejoicing for all that God is doing. It will not be left to the young people to do the dancing and showing their gladness over the works of God, for now the old people will join in the dancing and rejoicing as well. (v. 13). The transformation of the people and the land will lead to a transformation in worship as well. This emphasis is hinted at in v. 14, as the priests are also given the choice portion of the sacrifices that are offered to God. They too will enjoy the bounty of God.

The happiness of the Jewish people contined to increase as they experienced the bounty of the Lord. How glad are you when you survey all that God has done for you in the past and what he has promised he will yet do in the future? God can, can't he, turn sadness and sorrow into gladness? Haven't we all experienced a bounty from the lavish hand of God? Have we thanked him yet for all he has done in Israel and through them what he is going to do for us as well?

RACHEL WEEPING FOR HER CHILDREN (31:15–22)

Once again there is a sharp change from scenes of joy to descriptions of sadness and discomfort. The sounds of joy just mentioned in the previous section have now given way to the sound of weeping as Rachel, Jacob's wife and the mother of Joseph and Benjamin, weeps as she dies in childbirth with Benjamin (cf. Gen 35:16–18). Her two sons represent a northern and a southern tribe, as demonstrated after the kingdom of Israel was divided in two in 931 BC.

TRANSLATION

15 This is what Yahweh has said:
"A voice in Ramah is heard,
  Mourning and bitter weeping.
Rachel weeping for her sons,
  For her sons, refusing to be comforted,
  Because they are no more."
16 This is what Yahweh has said:[47]
"Stop your sobs of weeping,
  Your eyes from tears!
For there is a reward for your labor, declares Yahweh,
  They will return from the land of the enemy.

---

47. The phrase נְאֻם־יְהוָה, "a declaration of Yahweh," is absent in the LXX.

17 There is hope for your future, declares Yahweh,[48]

   Your sons will return to their own borders.[49]

18 I have heard it, I have heard it—

   Ephraim's remorse,

'You chastised me and I got chastised,

   Like an untrained calf;

Restore me so I can come back,

   Because you are Yahweh my God.

19 After I turned away,[50] I repented,

   After I wised up,[51]

I slapped my thigh,

   I am ashamed,[52] yes, humiliated,

   For I bear the disgrace of my youth.'

20 Is [it because] Ephraim is a dear son to me,

   The child in whom I delight?[53]

Though[54] I often speak against him, I still remember him.

   My heart yearns for him;

   I have great compassion for him, declares Yahweh.

21 Erect road signs[55] for yourself,

   Put up guideposts for yourself.

Set your mind on the highway,[56]

   On the road you have come.

---

48. The phrase וְיֵשׁ־תִּקְוָה לְאַחֲרִיתֵךְ נְאֻם־יְהוָה, "There is hope for your future, declares Yahweh," is absent in the LXX.

49. Ossom-Batsa makes a compelling case that the "turn/return" motif is used to refer to divine forgiveness and human conversion. "Yahweh's actual forgiveness of Israel is manifested only when Israel confesses her sin and becomes committed to living a new covenantal relationship." See G. Ossom-Batsa, "The Theological Significance of the Root *ŠWB* in Jeremiah," *Andrews University Seminary Studies* 39, no. 2 (2001): 223–32.

50. The LXX has αἰχμαλωσίας μου, "my captivity," where the MT has שׁוּבִי, "I turned away."

51. Lit. "after I was taught."

52. The LXX has ἐστέναξα ἐφ᾽ ἡμέρας αἰσχύνης, "I groaned for the day of shame," where the MT has סָפַקְתִּי עַל־יָרֵךְ בֹּשְׁתִּי, "I slapped my thigh, I am ashamed."

53. The LXX and Syr. omit the interrogative.

54. The LXX and Syr. omit the conj. אִם.

55. **21** The LXX has Σιων, "Zion," where the MT has צִיֻּנִים, "road signs."

56. The LXX has εἰς τοὺς ὤμους, "to the shoulder," where the MT has לִמְסִלָּה, "to the highway."

> Come back, O Virgin Israel,
>> Come back to these[57] towns of yours.
> **22** How long will you waver,
>> Backsliding daughter?
> For Yahweh has created a new thing on earth:
>> A woman will surround a man!"

COMMENTARY

Rachel's Weeping (31:15–17)

After speaking so excitedly about the future, Yahweh switches the time reference from the distant future to a time when there was deep wailing and weeping over the loss of Rachel's children (Gen 35:18). The depth of sorrow cannot be expressed more intensely than the vocabulary used here. This story about Rachel is filled with even more tragedy when the whole life of this woman is brought back to memory. Remember how deeply she longed to have children (Gen 30:1); then Joseph was born, and later Rachel died while giving birth to Benjamin.

31:15 Ramah was a town in the tribe of Benjamin located on the border between northern Israel and southern Judah, some five or more miles north of Jerusalem. Rachel was the favorite wife of Jacob who bore to him Joseph, the father of the two large northern tribes of Manasseh and Ephraim. The northern ten tribes have already been deported out of northern Israel by the Assyrians in 722 BC. In order to dramatize the trauma of this event, Rachel is depicted here as weeping disconsolately for her children, represented by her son's sons, Manasseh and Ephraim. Rachel refused to be consoled, because "her children are no more" (v. 15). They have been removed for the land of Israel.

Ramah was where the northern tribes were assembled to begin their trek into exile. The traditional site of Rachel's tomb, however, is at Ramat Rachel, a short distance north of Bethlehem. This site is based on an understanding of Gen 35:16 that implies that Rachel died and was buried close to "Ephrath," an older name for Bethlehem. However, another option is

---

57. The LXX has πενθοῦσα, "mourning," where the MT has אֵלֶּה, "these."

to interpret the rare term "distant" (כִּבְרַת) not as "a little distance" (NKJV) but as "still some distance" (NIV) from Ephrata. First Samuel 10:2 tells us that Rachel's tomb is located in the otherwise-unknown town of Zelzah. So the exact site remains unknown.

All this is further complicated by the allusion to this passage in Matt 2:16–18, which sees the fulfillment of this verse in Herod's vile act of slaughtering all the children in Bethlehem in order to kill the child and where the wise men learn that it is the birthplace of the one who is to be king of the Jews. Some believe that this event directly fulfills Jeremiah's prediction; others see the destruction of the people of Samaria by the Assyrians (and the later destruction of Judeans by Babylon, who used the same assembly point in Ramah, Jer 40:1–4) as a type of a massacre of the infants in these earlier events, which also laid the basis for Herod, who became king of the Jews and who wished to destroy any competitor who would replace him. Thus, he also massacred the infants of Bethlehem. This would make Herod's action an analogous one that has the same resulting grief that came to Rachel in the first place. The exiles will weep as Rachel had once wept for her children as they passed her gravesite on their way to exile.

31:16–17 Yahweh enjoins Rachel to end her weeping and her stream of tears, for (31:16) a reward awaits Rachel and her children, which is this: "they will return from the land of the enemy" (v. 16d). So positive is this message that it is stated once again: "There is hope for [the] future" (v. 17). Instead of lamentation there is real "hope" (תִּקְוָה) and a blessed future as Israel returns once again to her own "borders."

Ephraim's Repentance (31:18–20)

31:18–19 In place of the sound of weeping, another sound is heard: the sound of a repentant Ephraim (v. 18). Finally, the lesson that God has attempted to teach prior to this disaster is beginning to sink in as the people react to the rough treatment of the exile. They are depicted here as moaning in their grief (v. 18a) and experiencing discipline from the hand of God, similar to the training that an "unruly calf" goes through as it resists being hooked up with a yoke and plow. This picture is very similar to the one the prophet Hosea uses in 4:16—"The Israelites are stubborn, like a stubborn heifer."

Ephraim is now ready for the work of God, for she pleads: "Restore me, and I will return, because you are Yahweh my God" (v. 18d, e). Now at the end of themselves, Ephraim realizes they are helpless to restore themselves: they need divine help. Spiritual renewal must come from God alone. In v. 19, Ephraim recalls another reason why the northern nation now calls for God to intervene on their behalf: they have wandered away from God, but now that they understand, they repent and "slapped [their] thighs" (v. 19d). This slapping/beating on one's thighs was a well-known expression of grief in the ancient Near East, as Ezek 21:12 notes ("And then he groaned and smote of both his thighs ... and so in sorrow spoke"). Clearly, Ephraim is quite overwhelmed by the pain that resulted in this grief. This is followed by shame and humiliation; how could such a nation as theirs be so overrun and taken into captivity? All the sins of their earlier days ("youth," v. 19f) come back to them. The whole experience is beyond their ability to fully describe their suffering.

31:20 One would think this earlier experience of the deportation of northern Israel would have affected Judah and made her wiser, but it has not had that effect at all. Verse 20 raises some questions for Judah. Has not Ephraim been God's "dear son"? Isn't that son the "child in whom he took delight"? Yes, it has been necessary to speak against Ephraim repeatedly, just as it has been necessary to speak against Judah, but yet Yahweh "still remember[ed] him" (v. 20d). In fact, rather than producing a detached and impersonal response in God for all Ephraim's past failures, God still "yearn[ed] for him" (v. 20e), for Yahweh had "great compassion for him" (v. 20f). God's emotions are stirred for Ephraim just as much as he had claimed in Hos 11:8–9.

> How can I give you up, Ephraim?
> How can I hand you over, Israel?
> How can I treat you like Adamah?
> How can I make you like Zeboiim?
> I will not carry out my fierce anger,
> Nor will I turn and devastate Ephraim.
> For I am God, and not man—
> The Holy one among you.

God Creates a New Thing (31:21-22)

31:21 There is a sudden change from the masc. references to "Ephraim" as "son" to the fem. references to "Virgin Israel." These two separate metaphors for Israel's relationship to God as son and as bride are used throughout the OT to describe various facets of their relationship. Here, the switch to "Virgin Israel" depicts their backsliding, which is often related to adultery.

The command is for the deportees to set up "road signs" (צִיּוּן, *tsîyyûn*; which sounds like "Zion") or stones that will be left to mark the road travelers should take through such desolate places. These stones ("stone pillars" or "heaps of stones"; Feinberg, 570) are also called "guideposts" (תַּמְרוּר, *tamrûr*; v. 21), a word that has a similar sound to the Heb. word for "bitterness" (מְרָה, *mārāh*). Could this be a little hint along the way that God will "turn their captivity" into a release, and they indeed will one day "return to [their] towns" (v. 21f)? So take notice of this route, for one day the people will retrace their steps and return home. "Virgin/Maiden Israel" is the form of address that is also used in 14:17; 31:4.

31:22 The question, though, remains: how long will this "unfaithful daughter" wander? (v. 22). The word for "wander" (תִּתְחַמָּקִין) is a Heb. reflexive verb that means to "dillydally" or "to turn this way and that" as they aimlessly go along. Such has been all too true of the habit of life, but all of that is going to change. Yahweh is going to "create" (בָּרָא) a new thing on earth" (v. 22c). This verb "to create" is used exclusively of God as the subject and never with any agency of material in its forty-five usages; that is, created out of nothing. It is used of the original creation in Gen 1:1 and of the new heaven and new earth (Isa 65:16–18).

What does the expression "A female will surround a man" (v. 22d) mean? The word for "female" or "woman" is without any special significance (נְקֵבָה, cf. Gen 1:27) and the term for "man" refers to a strong man (גֶּבֶר, cf. Gen 30:6), and the word to "surround" (סָבַב) means "to go around," "to surround." Each of these words has a straightforward meaning that does not aid in solving the mystery about what they mean together.

The early church saw this as a prophecy of the virgin birth, but that cannot be affirmed exegetically. Calvin (4:113) tried to relate this passage back to 30:6, where the Israelites are likened to women without strength. The new thing, then, would be that God will suddenly equip his formerly weak people (compared to women) into a mighty force for himself against their enemies (the strong men). Another line of interpretation identifies the woman with the people of God and the "strong man" with Yahweh himself. Thus, whereas in the past Yahweh previously surrounded his weak people, in this new situation God will reform Israel so that they will "surround" and willingly "embrace" Yahweh as never before (cf. Lange, 269). But using "strong man" to describe Yahweh would be most unusual, though he is referred to from time to time as "powerful," using the cognate adj. (גָּבוֹר). One other attempt to interpret this conundrum contrasts Rachel's past, in which she was deprived of her offspring, with her now being enabled by God to "enfold" a man (that is, a son) as a sign of God's blessed gift that new life will come to the land. Yahweh will open up the way in the future for his new thing that he will create. This text has not been completely resolved here, but it does have parts of the answer, and the complete fulfillment might have to wait until history reveals all the nuances of meaning that are in this text.[58]

The Jewish people, especially the tribe of Ephraim, are told to set up markers and guideposts so that after their trial of exile was over, they can find their way back home to the land God will have given to them in due time. Surely God will do a "new thing," but what that "new thing" is cannot be determined as yet, in spite of all our best efforts to identify it. However, when God does bring this "new thing" into being, it will be obvious to all and will result in praise and glory to God. Are we willing to trust our Lord in this matter, especially after he has disclosed so many details about what

---

58. Finley examines the use of the verb "to create" and breaks it down as follows: the physical construction, the sociological construction, the ethical construction, the spiritual construction, the construction of praise, and the performance dimension. He suggests that this verse fits in the last dimension, as only Yahweh will be able to make a woman so strong that "she can provide protection even for a man." See T. J. Finley, "Dimensions of the Hebrew Word for 'Create' (בְּרָא)," BSac 148, no. 592 (1991): 409–23. Holladay similarly suggests that Jeremiah is in effect saying, "You have traditionally been addressed with a tender, feminine reference—virgin, daughter—and this feminine reference finally turned nightmarish as God's punishment on his people has turned the warriors to women. Never fear: stop acting like a silly female, out there in the wilderness: God has withdrawn the curse, he is about to revise creation, he will reverse the sex-roles so that the female has priority, initiative, dominance over the male. Your warriors have become female? Look: the female will surmount the warrior! Take heart; come home." See W. L. Holladay, "Jer. XXXI 22B Reconsidered: 'The Woman Encompasses the Man,'" VT 16, no. 2 (1966): 236–39. See also J. B. Kipper, "Ein übersehenes Fragment Aquilas in Jr 38(31),22b," Bib 66, no. 4 (1985): 580–81.

will happen in that future day? It will involve "a woman surrounding a man," but all the attempts to say who or what that is are only conjecture. Some things, I suppose, must await their future happening or an explanation when we see our Lord.

THE NEW COVENANT (31:23–34)

After addressing Ephraim in the previous section, the focus now returns to Judah and Israel. Jeremiah uses the third person to refer to the people, and the first person points to Yahweh. Here in this section, Israel and Judah have returned from their exile, and their ancient fortunes are now restored to them again. The city is restored; so is the temple with its worship. It is a time of peace, and it also a time of unusual spiritual blessing.

TRANSLATION

23 This is what Yahweh of Hosts, the God of Israel, has said: "When I bring back from captivity, the people in the land of Judah and in its towns will once again use these words: 'Yahweh bless you, O righteous dwelling, O holy mountain!'[59] **24** They will live in it—Judah and all his towns—together, farmers and those who move about with their flocks, **25** for I will refresh the weary and satisfy the faint. **26** At this I awoke and I looked, for my sleep had been pleasant to me.

27 "Look, the days are coming"—declares Yahweh—"when I will sow the house of Israel and the house of Judah with the seed [of both] men and beasts. **28** And just as I kept watch over them to uproot and tear down, to overthrow, destroy,[60] and bring disaster, so I will watch over them to build and to plant," declares Yahweh.

> **29** "In those days they will no longer say,
> 'The fathers ate sour grapes;
>   And the children's teeth are set on edge.'[61]

---

59. The LXX has εὐλογημένος κύριος ἐπὶ δίκαιον ὄρος, "blessed be the Lord on his righteous holy mountain," where the MT has יְבָרֶכְךָ יְהוָה נְוֵה־צֶדֶק הַר, "Yahweh bless you, O righteous dwelling, O holy mountain."

60. The LXX omits לִנְתוֹשׁ, "to uproot," וְלַהֲרֹס, "to overthrow," and וּלְהַאֲבִיד, "to destroy."

61. The meaning of the verb קהה is uncertain. See Rata, *Covenant Motif in Jeremiah's Book of Comfort*, 41.

30 "But rather, everyone will die for his own sin; whoever eats sour grapes—his own teeth will be set on edge."

31 "Look, the days are coming"—declares Yahweh—"when I will make a new covenant with the house of Israel and the house of Judah: **32** Not like the covenant I made with their fathers when I took them by the hand to bring them out of the land of Egypt, which covenant of mine they broke, though I was their Lord[62]—declares Yahweh. **33** Rather, this is the covenant I will make with the house of Israel after that period"—Yahweh's word: "I will put my Torah within them, and on their hearts I will write it: I will be their God and they shall be my people. **34** And no longer will each person need to teach his neighbor, and each his brother, saying, 'Know Yahweh.' For they shall all know me, from the least of them to the greatest"—declares Yahweh; "for I will forgive their iniquity, and their sin I will remember no more."

COMMENTARY

The Nation Reestablished (31:23-30)

31:23 As the focus returns to Judah, the plan of God returns again to "restoring the fortunes of the nation" (31:23; 29:14; see "Excursus: Shub Shebut"). God will indeed restore the fortunes of the nation as a direct reversal of the days of sword, famine, and exile. *God will also "bless"* the people, the land, and their dwellings. This is the fourth and final time in this book that this word of blessing appears (31:23c). Instead of the land and the people living under a curse, they will in that coming day receive God's blessing and favor; they will be called an abode of righteousness as well as a holy mountain (v. 23d). That is, Israel and Judah will become, in that day, a place where what is "right" and "just" abide. The "holy mountain" (v. 23) is a reference to Zion, Mount Moriah, where the temple stood.

31:24 A new picture of perfect contentment is presented in v. 24 as all the people of Judah live happily together, including farmers and shepherds. It is not as if the upper class or the city dwellers are favored, but all are

---

62. The LXX has ἠμέλησα, "I neglected," where the MT has בְּעַלְתִּי, "I was (their) Lord."

content, even those who represent the agricultural and shepherding segments of society.

31:25 In that day there will be enough water so that all can be saturated or refreshed and so that the weary and the faint will also find relief (v. 25). This provision will come from the hand of Yahweh himself. There will no longer be those who are drained of physical strength or who are faint from some type of insufficiency. God will be the source of every need and he will fulfill it.

31:26 Verse 26 is most unusual, for there are no other parallels to it in the book of Jeremiah: "At this I awoke and looked around. My sleep had been pleasant to me." This suggests that the words just given in vv. 23-25 were received in a dream. It is no wonder that Jeremiah's sleep is so pleasant, for the words of hope are most encouraging to him; they depict a whole new day and way of life.

31:27-28 The phrase that introduced the book of comfort (30:3) is now repeated: "The days are coming" (v. 27); these same words are reiterated in a number of the sections that follow (vv. 27, 31, 38: 33:14). But on this occasion, this formula about the future is used to halt a proverb that must be making the rounds among the captives: "The fathers have eaten sour grapes, and the children's teeth are set on edge" (v. 29). It is a convenient way to shift the blame from oneself to one's fathers.[63]

But before this issue is taken on, Yahweh declares that the human population, as well as the animal count, will increase due to the "planting" work of God (v. 27b). God's salvific work for mortals will be matched by his care for the whole created order. God himself will be "watching" over them, as he promised in his call to Jeremiah (1:11-12), for "uprooting," tearing down," "overthrowing," "destroying," and "bringing disaster," as well as "watching" over the nation of Israel "to build" and "to plant" (v. 28; cf. 1:14, 16). The same God who had brought judgment can and will bring deliverance as well.

---

63. Becking posits that this is a wisdom saying that "should not be interpreted as a sign of the rise of individualism, but as a feature of a symbol system that stresses personal responsibility." See B. Becking, "Sour Fruit and Blunt Teeth: The Metaphorical Meaning of the MĀŠĀL in Jeremiah 31,29," *SJOT* 17, no. 1 (2003): 7-21.

If judgment was the theme in the past due to Israel's persistence in sinning, God's work in the future will be one of "building" and "restoration"!

31:29-30 But what about the proverb that dangles over the heads of the community? This text affirms that "In those days," which are the coming days of blessing, the cycle of sin and judgment will be interrupted and broken by the intrusive work of Yahweh (v. 29). The sloganeers who have taken a fatalistic and determinist stance of blaming the fathers for causing their problems will be out of vogue, for now this complaint will be outmoded. Instead, every person will be responsible for his own sin (v. 30). Forget about any reference to "sour grapes"; sinners will receive immediate retribution for their own sin, for this is what Moses teaches in Deut 24:16 (cf. Ezek 18). The point is this: the sins of the former generations will not shape the future of those who return to the land of Israel. God's grace will set a whole new pattern for his people in that day.

The New Covenant (31:31-34)

With this text we have reached the apex of biblical theology for both Testaments.[64] It is the longest OT text quoted in the NT, Heb 8:8-12, and it is repeated in Heb 9:15-22 and 10:16-17. It also appears in Luke 22:20; 1 Cor 11:25; 2 Cor 3:5-14.

31:31-32 This is the only place in the OT where this is called a *"new covenant,"* yet the same covenant is referred to by similar terms, including seven times as an "everlasting covenant" (Jer 32:40; 50:5; Isa 24:5; 55:3; 61:8; Ezek 16:60; 37:26), a "new heart and a new spirit" (Ezek 11:19; 18:31; 36:26; Jer 32:39 LXX),[65] a "covenant of peace" (Isa 54:10: Ezek 34:25; 37:26), and "a

---

64. For an in-depth treatment of 31:31-34 see Rata, *Covenant Motif in Jeremiah's Book of Comfort*, 29-54.

65. The LXX translates the word "covenant" as διαθήκη, a word "that appears in the New Testament both in the gospels in Christ's institution of the new covenant and in Hebrews when the author of Hebrews argues for the superiority of the new covenant." See Rata, *Covenant Motif in Jeremiah's Book of Comfort*, 41.

covenant" or "my covenant" (Isa 42:6; 49:8; Hos 2:18–20), making a total of some sixteen or seventeen passages.[66]

Whereas the Abrahamic and Davidic covenants were made with those men as representatives of all who should believe in the promised Seed that is to come, the "new covenant" is made with all the "house of Israel and the whole house of Judah" (v. 31). The word *new*, however, must not lead us to separate this covenant from the content of the Abrahamic or Davidic covenants. There are at least two reasons why this is so:

1. The Heb. word for "new" (חָדָשׁ) functions for the concept of brand new and a renewal of the old.

2. Almost three-fourths of the contents of the new covenant are but a repetition of what was in the earlier covenants.[67]

This new covenant is contrasted with the Sinaitic or Mosaic Covenant (v. 32), "which covenant of mine," says Yahweh, the people "broke" (v. 32e). The fault with the old covenant was not with the covenant but with the people.

The structure of the new covenant is best analyzed by B. W. Anderson.[68] He points out that the Heb. expression "declaration of Yahweh" (נְאֻם־יְהוָה) appears four times: twice in the first section, indicating its beginning (v. 31a) and its conclusion (v. 32b), and twice in the second section, again marking its beginning (v. 33a) and its end (v. 34b). In this second section there are two climactic כִּי clauses ("for," "because," or "indeed").

31:33–34 Within this promise-plan of God there are the features of inwardness, fellowship, individualism, and forgiveness. It is important to notice

---

66. See W. C. Kaiser Jr., "The Old Promise and the New Covenant: Jeremiah 31:31–34," *JETS* 15 (1972): 11–23.

67. The LXX translates the word חֲדָשָׁה as καινήν, which "refers to something that is new in nature, better than the old or superior in value or attraction. The Hebrew, however, must serve both ideas: new in time and renewed in nature." See Kaiser, "Old Promise and the New Covenant," 17.

68. B. W. Anderson, "The New Covenant and the Old," in *The Old Testament and Christian Faith*, ed. B. W. Anderson (New York: Harper & Row, 1963), 230n11.

the four times that Yahweh declares his "I will" in this text (vv. 31b, 33c, 33d, 34c).

1. "I will make a new covenant with the house of Israel and the house of Judah,"

2. "I will put my Torah in their minds,"

3. "I will be their God," and

4. "I will forgive their iniquities."

The initiative and the responsibility for carrying out this covenant is altogether with Yahweh and not with the people of Israel.

What, then, is new about this covenant, and when will it come into force? It will not be the content of the New Covenant that is different, but the way that content is learned. No longer will there be a need to teach everyone, for it will be imprinted on their hearts. Moreover, later Christian participation in the new covenant will be grounded in its Jewish roots and divine promises. This covenant does not envisage a change in the partners to the covenant.[69] Nor will a supersessionist reading now be in vogue, since it is called "new," and the name "new covenant" is used in the Christian Eucharist, and the apostles are included as apostles of this new covenant. Instead, the new covenant applies to the Gentile believing community in the same way that Israel was called to be a light to the nations and a priestly nation to the world (Gen 12:3). Yahweh does not make any kind of a covenant with the church; instead, the church reaps the benefits of the Abrahamic-Davidic-new covenants as she too participates in the roots and the trunk of the one olive tree rooted in the promises of God to the patriarchs of Israel (Rom 9–11). The church has no grounding and no vitality except through the promises made to Israel. Israel has been hardened in part until the full number of the Gentiles comes in, but then Jewish people will turn to their Messiah in such vast numbers that it will be said that "all Israel" will be saved (Rom 11:25b–27).

---

69. The law written on stone can be broken, the law written on parchment can burned, but if the law is written on the heart "external limitations and vulnerability ... will be eliminated." See, Keown, Scalise, and Smothers, *Jeremiah 26–52*, 134.

In this new covenant God's law will be put within the hearts of his people (v. 33). And the knowledge of God will so be so pervasive that the need for continual instruction in that knowledge will be unnecessary (v. 34). Everyone, regardless of class, status, or gender, be they commoner, king, peasant, child, or adult, will know Yahweh. Yahweh will "forgive (סָלַח, v. 34). God is the exclusive subject of the verb; he will forgive their sin and remember them no more. "The forgiveness of sin was a key part in Israel's survival thus far, but it seems that faithfulness to the new covenant is a 'gift of divine mercy, not a human achievement.'"[70]

Our Lord told Jeremiah he would be "watching" over the house of Israel and the house of Judah, not only to bring judgment on them when needed but also to build and plant them in the land. Here at the peak of Jeremiah's prophecies, the Lord announces that things will not be like the days in which the Jewish people "broke [his] covenant"; he will now put his Torah on the hearts of his people and henceforward they will be his people. Just as the Lord "cut/made a covenant" with Abraham in Gen 15:1-6, he will this time "cut a new covenant" with Israel. What a magnificent promise that continued the promise-plan of God from Abraham and David! Now God will write his Torah on all of our hearts rather than on stone!

THE INVIOLABLE COVENANT (31:35-40)

This sixfold section ends with a pledge that the provisions of the new covenant will be permanent and as enduring as the sun, moon, and stars. This section is reminiscent of the type of hymns that appear in the book of Psalms. It is a most joyful part of the Scriptures.

TRANSLATION

35[71] This is what Yahweh has said: "He who appoints the sun to shine by day, who decrees[72] the moon and the stars to illumine the night, who stirs up[73] the sea so that its waves roar—Yahweh of Hosts is his name. **36** If

---

70. See Rata, *Covenant Motif in Jeremiah's Book of Comfort*, 44, and Keown, Scalise, and Smothers, *Jeremiah 26-52*, 135.

71. The verse order in the LXX varies from that of the MT. Verses 35 and 36 are located between vv. 37 and 38.

72. The word חֻקֹּת, "a decree," is absent in the LXX.

73. The LXX has καὶ κραυγήν, "and a roaring," where the MT has רֹגַע, "he stirs up."

these decrees should vanish from before me—declares Yahweh—then the descendants of Israel might cease from being a nation before me all the days." **37** This is what Yahweh has said:[74] "If the heavens above can be measured,[75] or the foundations of the earth below can be ascertained,[76] then I might reject the descendants of Israel because of all[77] they have done," declares Yahweh.

38 Look, the days are coming"[78]—declares Yahweh—"when Yahweh's city will be rebuilt from the Tower of Hananel to the Corner Gate.[79] **39** The measuring line will stretch from there[80] straight to[81] the hill of Gareb and then turn to Goah.[82] **40** The whole valley where dead bodies and ashes[83] were thrown, and all the cemeteries[84] above the brook Kidron as far as the corner of the Horse Gate to the east, shall be holy to Yahweh. It will never again be torn down or destroyed."

COMMENTARY

Yahweh's Irrevocable Commitment to Israel (31:35–37)

31:35 The old promise made years ago with Abraham, Isaac, and Jacob, as well as David, is declared by Yahweh to be of permanent force and reliability. God's gracious plan of restoring Israel to her land is said to be as certain,

---

74. The phrase כֹּה אָמַר יְהוָה, "This is what Yahweh has said," is absent in the LXX.

75. The LXX has ὑψωθῇ, "it could be raised," where the MT has יִמַּדּוּ, "they (can) be measured."

76. The LXX has ταπεινωθῇ, "it could be sunk," where the MT has וְיֵחָקְרוּ, "they (can) be ascertained."

77. The LXX lacks כָּל, "all."

78. *BHS* suggests בָּאִי, "coming," was lost due to haplogr. because of its similarity to נאם, "utterance."

79. The LXX adds ἕως, "as far as," before "Corner Gate," which *BHS* takes to indicate that the prep. לְ, "to," was lost in the MT due to haplogr. because the previous word ends with לְ.

80. The LXX has αὐτῶν, "of them," where the MT has a 3 sg. suf. "it."

81. Some Heb. mss, the LXX, and Tg. have עַד / ἕως, "as far as," in place of עַל, "on."

82. The versions vary in how they translate גֹּעָתָה, "Goah." The LXX has κύκλῳ ἐξ ἐκλεκτῶν λίθων, "a wall of choice stones"; α´ and σ´ have Γαβαθα, "Gabatha," which is a place in Jerusalem; and, the Syr. has *lbrjkt'gl'*, "to the pool of precious stones" (Keown, 126).

83. The phrase וְכָל־הָעֵמֶק הַפְּגָרִים וְהַדֶּשֶׁן, "The whole valley where dead bodies and ashes," is absent in the LXX.

84. The **Qere** has הַשְּׁדֵמוֹת, "the terraces," where the **Kethiv** has הַשְּׁרֵמוֹת, which is translated here as "cemeteries."

sure, and durable as his appointment of the stars to shine, and his decree
for the moon to also shine (v. 35). Just as God committed himself way back
in creation in the fixed orders of creation, in the same way he will continue
to keep his word to the descendants of Israel.

31:36 In order to dramatize how permanent and enduring God's promise
is to his people Israel, he states two impossible conditions with two "if"
clauses in vv. 36 and 37. The placement of vv. 35-37 right after vv. 31-34
seems to anticipate on God's part that the Gentile church might get the
wrong idea that since a new covenant is announced, then there must be a
new people—the church; however, supersessionism is nipped in the bud
by saying that God plans on continuing to operate on an unchanging basis
just as he had announced from the beginning. God's promise to Israel will
be as durable as Yahweh's power and might can be seen in the fixed order
of day and night. God regards both the natural order of creation and the
spiritual order of the promise-plan as belonging to the "fixed decrees."

31:37 None of the promises in this plan depend on others, for God alone
stands behind their guarantee. Some wonder, "But what about Israel's continued propensity to sin? Will that not ultimately make God divest himself
of Israel and bequeath his promise to the Gentile believers?" But that idea
is wrong, for v. 37 scraps that notion by saying that it could come to pass
"only if the heavens above could be measured and the foundations of the
earth below could be searched out." So, for all those who keep on guessing
as to whether God will ever abandon his people Israel, the answer is clear:
it will never happen! Remember, only Yahweh passed between the pieces
when the covenant was made with Abraham (Gen 15:1-5); this covenant is
unconditional and unilateral in its provisions. God alone obligated himself;
Abraham slept through the whole event!

The Final Rebuilding of Jerusalem (31:38-40)

31:38 Jeremiah looks forward to a time in the distant future when not only
will Jerusalem be restored, but the city will be rededicated to Yahweh.
This city will be rebuilt, but even more significant is that it will never
be destroyed again. It will be rebuilt not just for Israel, but, interestingly

enough, the text says it "will be rebuilt for me"; this is the declaration of Yahweh (vv. 38, 40).

While the main component of the new covenant is spiritual, "part of the restoration will also entail the physical rebuilding of Jerusalem."[85] The rebuilding of the city of Jerusalem will begin at the "Tower of Hananel," which is probably a reference to the eastern part of the northern wall of Jerusalem, north of the temple, where the Babylonian armies are thought to have broken through to enter the city. The northern part of the city was the most vulnerable side of the whole layout, since there was no steep valley to protect it, as there was on the other sides of the city. The Corner Gate was also on the north side of the city, at the northwestern corner.

31:39 From these two points, a straight line is stretched out to mark out how the wall would run in that future day. Neither Gareb nor Goah are readily identified as yet, but it seems to run in a counterclockwise direction, going down the west side and around to the east side. The Valley of Dead Bodies seems to be an allusion to the Hinnom Valley on the west and southwest corner of the city where babies had been previously offered to Molech and Baal (v. 40). The Kidron Valley was on the southeast and east side of Jerusalem, as was the Horse Gate, near the northern end of the Kidron Valley.

31:40 The whole city in that coming day of the end times "will be holy to Yahweh; the city will never again be uprooted or demolished" (v. 40). These last two verbs come from Jeremiah's call chapter (1:10). Regarding the holiness of Jerusalem, Schmid affirms that "the holiness of the city of Jerusalem in 31:38-40 is compared to the holiness of the land in 31:23-25."[86] What a grand hope and what an encouraging conclusion to generations of struggle with sin in Israel!

Just how enduring is the promise-plan of God? Will he not need to scrap it in the event that those he gave it to become so adamant and headstrong that they consistently refuse to accept him or his gift? Has Israel

---

85. Rata, *Covenant Motif in Jeremiah's Book of Comfort*, 49.

86. "Die Heiligkeit der Stadt Jerusalem in 31:38-40 ist derjenigen des Landes in 31:23-25." K. Schmid, *Buchgestalten des Jeremiabuches*, 179.

forfeited, or will she ever, her share in the promises made in the covenant to Abraham and David?

Surprisingly enough, the answer to that very good question is: Never! Never once will God retract and go back on what he promised Abraham, Isaac, Jacob, and David. Why, it can only happen if the sun by day and the moon by night vanish from the sky; then the "renewed covenant" God has made with his people Israel and Judah will be nullified and withdrawn from operation. However, in the event that both sun and moon continue to appear in the skies (as it seems they are), then count on the veracity and faithfulness of God. This is not about humans remaining faithful; no, it is about God keeping his word of promise!

PURCHASING A FIELD IN ANATHOTH (32:1–44)

Chapters 32–33 represent the second part of the book of consolation (chaps. 30–33), and it also signals a switch from the poetry format used in the previous two chapters to a prose literary form in these latter two chapters. The deportation of the people was close at hand, so it was important for Yahweh to dramatically indicate that there would indeed be a return to the land. This would be illustrated by Yahweh's command to his prophet Jeremiah that he was to purchase a field in his hometown of Anathoth, but he was also to take particularly strong measures to preserve the documents of this legal transaction. Even though Jeremiah carried out these instructions from Yahweh, he was more than puzzled by what this meant in light of what he and the nation were now facing. It is for this reason that his honest prayer of bewilderment (vv. 17–25) and Yahweh's response (vv. 26–44) are recorded in this passage.

TRANSLATION

1 This is the word that came to Jeremiah from Yahweh in the tenth year of Zedekiah, king of Judah,[87] which was the eighteenth year of Nebuchadnezzar.[88] **2** The king of Babylon's army was besieging Jerusalem, and Jeremiah the prophet was imprisoned in the court of the guard, in the palace of the king of Judah, **3** where Zedekiah the king of Judah had

---

87. The word יְהוּדָה, "(of) Judah," is absent in the LXX.
88. The LXX adds βασιλεῖ Βαβυλῶνος, "king of Babylon," after "Nebuchadnezzar."

confined him, saying: "Why do you prophesy as you do? You say: 'This is what Yahweh says: "Look! I am about to hand this city over to the king of Babylon and he will take it. **4** Zedekiah the king of Judah will not escape the clutches of the Chaldeans, but will most surely be handed over to the king of Babylon, and he will speak with him face to face and see him with his own eyes. **5** He will take Zedekiah to Babylon, where he will remain[89] until I deal with him, declares Yahweh. If you fight the Chaldeans you will have no success.""'[90]

6[91] Jeremiah said, "The word of Yahweh came to me: **7** 'Get ready! Hanamel son of Shallum, your uncle, is going to come to you and say, "Purchase my field at Anathoth, for you have a kinsman's right to redeem/purchase it."' **8** Then, just as Yahweh had said,[92] Hanamel, my cousin, came to me in the court of the guard and said to me, 'Please purchase my field[93] at Anathoth, in the territory of Benjamin, for the right of possession and redemption is yours, buy it for yourself.'[94] Then I knew that this was Yahweh's word; **9** So I bought the field at Anathoth[95] from my cousin Hanamel and weighted out for him seventeen shekels of silver. **10** So I wrote on a scroll and I sealed it and had [men] witness it, and I weighed out the silver on scales. **11** Then I took the deed of purchase—the sealed copy containing the contract and the conditions,[96] along with the open copy— **12** and I gave the deed of purchase to Baruch son of Neriah, the son[97] of Mahseiah in the presence of my cousin Hanamel, and in the presence

---

89. The LXX mss ^A, C, min^ have ἀποθανεῖται, "it will die," where the MT has יִהְיֶה, "he will be" (i.e., remain).

90. The portion עַד־פָּקְדִי אֹתוֹ נְאֻם־יְהוָה כִּי תִלָּחֲמוּ אֶת־הַכַּשְׂדִּים לֹא תַצְלִיחוּ, "until I deal with him, declares Yahweh. If you fight the Chaldeans you will have no success," is absent in the LXX.

91. The LXX version of this verse is καὶ λόγος κυρίου ἐγενήθη πρὸς Ιερεμιαν λέγων, "And the word of Yahweh came to Jeremiah, saying."

92. The phrase כִּדְבַר יְהוָה, "just as Yahweh had said," is absent in the LXX.

93. The LXX places the phrase "in the territory of Benjamin" after "my field."

94. The LXX has καὶ σὺ πρεσβύτερος, "you are an elder," where the MT has וּלְךָ הַגְּאֻלָּה קְנֵה־לָּךְ, "and redemption is yours, buy it for yourself."

95. The phrase אֲשֶׁר בַּעֲנָתוֹת, "at Anathoth," is absent in the LXX.

96. The phrase הַמִּצְוָה וְהַחֻקִּים, "the contract and the conditions," is absent from the LXX.

97. The editors of *BHS* suggest prefixing the word דֹּד, "uncle," with the word בֶּן, "son," to match some Heb. mss, the LXX, Syr., Tg. See also v. 8.

of the witnesses[98] who had signed[99] the deed of purchase, and in the presence of all the Judeans who were sitting in the court of the guard. **13** In their presence I gave Baruch these instructions: **14** This is what Yahweh of Hosts,[100] the God of Israel says: 'Take these documents[101]—the deed of purchase—the sealed copy and the open one—and put them in an earthenware jar, so that they may last a long time.' **15** For this is what Yahweh of Hosts, the God of Israel, says: 'Houses, fields, and vineyards will once again be bought in this land.'"

16 "After I had given the deed of purchase to Baruch son of Neriah, I prayed saying: **17** 'Ah, Adonai Yahweh, truly, you have made the heavens and the earth by your great power and outstretched arm. Nothing is too hard[102] for you! **18** You show grace to thousands, while repaying the iniquity of the fathers [and placing it] into the laps of their children after them. O great and mighty God, whose name is Yahweh of Hosts, **19** great is your purpose and numerous are your deeds. Your eyes are open to all the ways of the sons of men; you reward each person according to his conduct and according to the fruit of his deeds.[103] **20** You performed miraculous deeds and wonders in the land of Egypt, and unto this day, both among Israel and among humanity, gaining renown for yourself that is yours today. **21** You brought your people Israel from the land of Egypt with miracles and wonders, with a strong hand, an outstretched arm, and with great terror. **22** You gave them this land you had sworn to their fathers to give them,[104] a land flowing with milk and honey. **23** They came in and took possession of it, but they did not listen to your voice or follow your law; all which I commanded them to do,[105] but they did not do [it]. So you brought all this disaster on them. **24** Look! The siege ramps[106] are going up to take the city. Through the sword, starvation, and disease, the city is delivered

---

98. The LXX has τῶν ἑστηκότων, "the ones standing," where the MT has הָעֵדִים, "witnesses."

99. Several mss, α´, σ´, Syr., and Tg. have הַכְּתוּבִים, "the ones who are written," where the MT has "the ones who had written [signed]."

100. The phrase אֱלֹהֵי יִשְׂרָאֵל, "the God of Israel," is absent in the LXX.

101. The phrase אֶת־הַסְּפָרִים הָאֵלֶּה, "these documents," is absent in the LXX.

102. The LXX has ἀποκρυβῇ, "it is hidden," where the MT has יִפָּלֵא, "it is hard."

103. The phrase וְכִפְרִי מַעֲלָלָיו, "fruit of his deeds," is absent in the LXX.

104. The phrase לָתֵת לָהֶם, "to give them," is absent in the LXX.

105. The phrase לַעֲשׂוֹת, "to do," is absent in the LXX.

106. The LXX has ὄχλος, "crowds," where the MT has הַסֹּלְלוֹת, "the siege ramps."

to the Chaldeans who are attacking it. What you said has happened, as you now see it.[107] **25** Yet you say to me, Adonai Yahweh,[108] "Purchase for yourself the field with silver, and have the transaction witnessed—when the city is delivered over to the Chaldeans.""[109]

26 Then the word of Yahweh came to Jeremiah,[110] saying: **27** "Look! I am Yahweh, the God of all flesh. Is anything too hard[111] for me?"[112] **28** Therefore, this is what Yahweh says: "Pay attention![113] I am going to hand over this city to the Chaldeans and to Nebuchadnezzar[114] the king of the Babylonians, who will capture it. **29** The Chaldeans who are attacking this city will come in and set this city on fire and they will burn it [down], with the houses on whose rooftops they made offerings to Baal, and made drink-offering libations to other gods in order to provoke me to anger. **30** For the sons of Israel and the sons of Judah alike have done nothing but evil in my sight from their youth. Indeed! The people of Israel have done nothing but provoke me by the things they have done, declares Yahweh.[115] **31** For from the day this city was built until the present, it has aroused my anger and wrath so that I must remove it from my sight **32** because of all the wickedness which the people of Israel and of Judah have done in order to provoke me—they, their kings, their officials, their priests and their prophets, the men of Judah and the citizens of Jerusalem [must be removed]. **33** They

---

107. The phrase וְהִנְּךָ רֹאֶה, "and behold you see (it)," is absent in the LXX.

108. The phrase אֲדֹנָי יְהוִה, "Adonai Yahweh," is absent in the LXX.

109. The LXX adds the phrase καὶ ἔγραψα βιβλίον καὶ ἐσφραγισάμην, "and I wrote a book and sealed it."

110. The LXX has πρός με, "to me," where the MT has אֶל־יִרְמְיָהוּ, "to Jeremiah."

111. The LXX has κρυβήσεται, "it will be hidden," where the MT has יִפָּלֵא, "it is hard." Compare 32:17.

112. Fretheim argues that "Jeremiah understands the purchase of land, not as a sign of *future* restoration but as a sign that God will now bring a halt to the judgment in progress and move directly to restore Israel's fortunes." See T. E. Fretheim, "Is Anything Too Hard for God? (Jeremiah 32:27)," *CBQ* 66 (2004): 231–36.

113. The word הִנְנִי, "pay attention [lit. behold me]," is absent in the LXX, and the LXX has δοθεῖσα παραδοθήσεται, "it will indeed be given," where the MT has the sg. ptc. נֹתֵן, "giving."

114. The phrase הַכַּשְׂדִּים וּבְיַד נְבוּכַדְרֶאצַּר, "the Chaldeans and to Nebuchadnezzar," is absent in the LXX.

115. The phrase כִּי בְנֵי־יִשְׂרָאֵל אַךְ מַכְעִסִים אֹתִי בְּמַעֲשֵׂה יְדֵיהֶם נְאֻם־יְהוָה, "The people of Israel have done nothing but provoke me by the things they have done, declares Yahweh," is absent in the LXX.

have turned their backs to me and not their faces, though I taught[116] them over and over again, they would not listen or respond to [my] discipline. **34** Instead, they set up their detestable idols in the house that is called by my name and [thus] defiled it. **35** They built high places for Baal in the Valley of Ben Hinnom to sacrifice their sons and their daughters to Molech, a thing I did not command, nor did it enter my mind, that they should do this abomination and so make Judah sin."[117]

36 "Now, therefore,[118] this is what Yahweh, the God of Israel, has said concerning this city of which you say,[119] 'Through sword, starvation, and disease[120] it is delivered up to the king of Babylon.' **37** Look! I am going to gather them from all the countries[121] where I have driven them in my anger and great indignation. I will bring them back to this place and let them live in safety. **38** They will be my people and I will be their God. **39** I will give them singleness of mind and action,[122] for their own good and the good of their children after them. **40** And I will make with them an everlasting covenant: I will not stop doing good to them;[123] I will put the fear of me in their hearts so that so that they may never turn away from me. **41** I will rejoice in doing them[124] good and will assuredly plant them in this land with all my heart and with all my soul. **42** This is what Yahweh has said: 'As I have brought all this great calamity on this people, so I will bring on them all the good things that I have promised[125] them. **43** Fields shall be bought in this land, of which you say, "It is deserted, empty of men and beasts, delivered into the hands of the Chaldeans." **44** Fields will be bought for silver and deeds will be signed and sealed and witnessed in the

---

116. The MT has the inf. abs. "teach" and lacks a finite verb. The editors of BHS suggest emending the text to וָאֲלַמֵּד, "and I taught," as found in the LXX (ἐδίδαξα, "I taught"), Syr., and Vg.

117. The LXX adds βασιλεῖ, "king."

118. The word לָכֵן, "therefore," is absent in the LXX.

119. The MT has the pl. אַתֶּם אֹמְרִים, "you say." The LXX has the sg. σὺ λέγεις, "you say."

120. The LXX has καὶ ἐν ἀποστολῇ, "and through banishment," where the MT has וּבַדֶּבֶר, "and through disease."

121. The LXX has the sg. τῆς γῆς, "the land," where the MT has the pl. הָאֲרָצוֹת, "the lands."

122. The LXX has ὁδὸν ἑτέραν καὶ καρδίαν ἑτέραν, "another way and another heart," where the MT has לֵב אֶחָד וְדֶרֶךְ אֶחָד, "singleness of mind and action [lit. one heart and one way]."

123. The phrase לְהֵיטִיבִי אוֹתָם, "doing good to them," is absent in the LXX.

124. The LXX has καὶ ἐπισκέψομαι, "and I will visit," where the MT has וְשַׂשְׂתִּי, "and I will rejoice."

125. Lit. "I am speaking" (ptc.).

territory of Benjamin, in the environs of Jerusalem, and in the towns of Judah, the towns of the hill country, of the Shephelah and the Negeb, for I will restore their fortunes,'" declares Yahweh.

The Poor Prospects for an Unbelieving King (32:1–5)

32:1 This chapter is a separate message from the new covenant given in chapter 31, for instead of the chapter beginning with a bright outlook, it is cast against the certain onslaught of the Babylonian army and the capture of King Zedekiah of Judah. The dating in v. 1 gives the year in which the word of Yahweh came as being the tenth year of Zedekiah and the eighteenth year of Nebuchadnezzar. Such dual dating already diminishes the kingship of Zedekiah, for the master of the land is now more in line with Nebuchadnezzar than with the Davidic king in Judah (cf. 25:1). This is a major change since the earlier days of the Abrahamic and Davidic covenants. Second Kings 25:1 informs us that the siege began in the tenth month of Zedekiah's ninth year, or to be more specific in terms of our calendar, on the fifteenth of January, 588 BC. It will last until the ninth of Tammuz (2 Kgs 25:3), which for us would be July 18, 586 BC, and the city was finally destroyed on the seventh of Ab (2 Kgs 25:8), that is, August 14, 586 BC. This means the siege lasted for some two and a half years.

32:2 It would appear that for most of the time of the siege of Jerusalem Jeremiah was imprisoned in the courtyard of the guard in the royal palace. The Babylonians, who were also known as the Chaldeans, lifted the siege temporarily during part of this time as an Egyptian invasion from the south appeared to be imminent (37:5–11). That temporary letup in the siege may have come one year after the beginning of this attack on Jerusalem, a time when Jeremiah tried to take advantage of this let up in hostilities by trying to go north two or three miles to Anathoth to see the field he had purchased, but he is stopped in his attempt by his own people of Judah, who fear he is actually going to desert to the Babylonian foe. Instead, he is arrested and incarcerated once again and placed in arrest in Jonathan's house (37:16); later on, by Zedekiah's orders, he is moved to the courtyard of the guard in the palace (37:21).

32:3 Surely King Zedekiah, much as the rest of Judah, has heard the words of Jeremiah so frequently that he has memorized them already (vv. 3–5). This may well be the telltale sign that neither the king nor the people can any longer shake the growing impression that the prophet's words are coming true—their truthfulness is beginning to haunt them! So Zedekiah wants to know (once again): "Why do you prophesy as you do?" (v. 3). The only simple answer, of course, is because it is true; it is what God has revealed to him; it is what is going to happen in this city of Jerusalem, barring any revival or sudden turning back to God.

32:4–5 In addition to repeating what Jeremiah prophesied about the city and the land of Judah, Zedekiah also knows the king of Babylon will take Zedekiah into exile, where God will deal with Zedekiah. The king of Judah will personally meet Nebuchadnezzar, and he will see him with his own eyes. It will be no use to fight him, for God has already given the battle over to the Chaldeans. Zedekiah is finished as a ruler of Judah, and so are the Judeans!

Jeremiah Purchases Some Family Property in Anathoth (32:6–15)

32:6–7 God's command to purchase a family plot in Anathoth is another example of the symbolic acts found in this book (13:1–4; 16:1–13; 19:1–15). Long ago, in the days of Abraham, God had the patriarch purchase land in Canaan (Gen 23) as a burial plot for Sarah, for it, too, was a sign that God would one day give the land to the people of Israel. What makes this command difficult for Jeremiah to act on is that there is almost total certainty that Nebuchadnezzar will soon enter the city and all will be lost to the Babylonians. So what is the use of investing in land?

Back in Jer 12:6, where we last heard anything about Jeremiah's relatives, relationships between the relatives and this prophet were not going well at all; in fact, the relatives from Anathoth were trying to find a way to kill him, for they must have assumed that he had lost his mind by prophesying the way he had. He is an embarrassment to them. In the meantime, due to his prophetic calling, Jeremiah has been required by Yahweh to remove himself from all family weddings and funerals (16:5–9), so it is a surprise when an appeal comes from his family to bail them out of their trouble by purchasing land in his hometown of Anathoth.

The law calls for a kinsman to redeem any land that is likely to pass out of the control of the family (Lev 25:25). It appears that this is what drives the family to ask Jeremiah to purchase the ancestral property. Is this is a sign that an unrecorded reconciliation with the family has taken place in the meantime, or, instead, does this indicate that Jeremiah's family is desperate and has no other options but to come to him and, as it were, eat humble pie and beg Jeremiah to rescue them in their financial plight? It is not clear either whether Jeremiah is the first one approached in the family. All we know is that it is now Jeremiah's "right" (מִשְׁפַּט) "to redeem" (גָּאַל) the field as a "kinsman redeemer" (vv. 6–7).

32:8 Jeremiah's cousin Hanamel is the messenger who carries this request for the family. Just as Yahweh predicted, Hanamel comes into the court of guard of the palace (v. 8), where he makes his formal proposal to Jeremiah to "possess" and "redeem" this land in the territory of Benjamin, some two or so miles north of Jerusalem. It not clear what sort of land Jeremiah is purchasing for a priestly family, for priestly families generally were not allowed to own land (Num 18:20–24). Some suggest that some Levitical cities, of which Anathoth might be one, had pasturelands attached to them for raising sheep, goats, and cattle (Lev 25:34; Num 35:5). Or perhaps this property had come to the priestly family through marriage.

32:9 Jeremiah buys the property for seventeen shekels (v. 9). Since a shekel was about 0.4 ounces of silver, Jeremiah paid almost seven ounces of silver (coinage had not yet been in common usage in Israel), which at our current $30 an ounce for silver would mean he paid around $210 for this land. Since we do not know how large a plot of land this was, we cannot tell whether this is a high or low price. However, given the present state of affairs, with the Babylonians no doubt camped on or near that very same piece of land just north of Jerusalem, it probably was available at a very low price! The purchase price is then weighed out on scales, which the current practice demanded.

32:10–11 This transaction is carefully recorded, witnessed, and sealed (vv. 10–11), with one copy of the deed of purchase sealed for future reference and the other copy unsealed.[126] Archaeological light has been cast on what would happen here from finds in Elephantine, Egypt. A deed of purchase would be written twice on one piece of papyrus with a space between the two copies to allow the papyrus to be torn into two. One copy would then be rolled up, tied with a cord, and sealed with clay seals (called bulla) so that it could not be tampered with, leaving the open copy to be consulted if needed. Only if questions arose about the legitimacy of the deed would the sealed copy be opened, but usually only in court proceedings.

32:12 Jeremiah gives the sealed deed to Baruch son of Neriah, his amanuensis, in the presence of his cousin Hanamel and those who witnessed the transaction (v. 12). It is significant that a bulla was found in Israel reading: "Berekhyahu son of Neriah the scribe."[127] This is almost certainly the same Baruch mentioned here—only in this case it is the longer form of his name. Another seal also was found reading "Berekhyahu son of Neriyahu son of Mahseiah," again using the longer form of the same names seen in this narrative.

32:13–15 The instructions given by the prophet to Baruch come from Yahweh himself (v. 14). Baruch is to take both documents and place them in an earthenware jar, which was no doubt sealed with pitch, as evidenced from examples from Elephantine and Qumran's DSS. This is to protect the contents, for they are to last a long time, since "houses, fields and vineyards will once again be bought in this land" (v. 15), declares Yahweh. Therefore, Jeremiah's purchase will have very long-range implications for the exiled Judeans coming back into the land at some distant time in the future. The picture of the present distress will not prevail, for the dislocation of Israel and Judah will one day come to an end as Yahweh relocates them in the very land they had left.

---

126. Peters argues that the second part of the verse, which is not in the LXX, was added later as "the law and the statutes." See J. P. Peters, "Notes on Some Difficult Passages in the Old Testament," *JBL* 11, no. 1 (1892): 38–52.

127. Y. Shiloh and D. Tarler, "Bullae from the City of David: A Hoard of Seal Impressions from the Israelite Period," *BA* 49, no. 4 (1986): 204.

Jeremiah's Prayer (32:16–25)

32:16 Jeremiah's response to the events of vv. 6–15, and the promise of the word of God (vv. 14–15), is found in his prayer. This is the only time in this book where the prophet prays for personal guidance. This outpouring in prayer is no mere signal that the transaction is now over; instead, it is an outpouring of his heart after what seems an implausible call to obedience in the light of impossible circumstances of an impending conquest of the land. Jeremiah will teach in 33:3, "Call on me [says Yahweh], and I will answer you and tell you great and unsearchable things you do not know." Thus Jeremiah prays, and accordingly God answers him.

32:17-19 His prayer begins with a sigh, "Ah, Adonai Yahweh" (vv. 17, 25), similar to his sigh when he was called to be a prophet (1:6). The name used for God is most significant, for while it is used in Isaiah and Ezekiel to indicate God's supremacy, it is the vast majority of the time the distinctive term for God in his covenant-making activity. For example, it is found in the Abrahamic covenant (Gen 15:2, 8) and in the Davidic covenant (2 Sam 7:18, 19 [2x], 20, 22, 28, 29). This name therefore is a reminder of those covenants and the name of God that stands behind them.

The prophet begins his prayer with thanksgiving to such a great sovereign God. God made the universe (v. 17b) by his great power and with his outstretched arm, thereby showing that neither creation nor the promise just made about the return of Israel to the land is too difficult or too hard (פָּלֵא, "to be miraculous, hard, difficult") for him (cf. Gen 18:14; Judg 13:18; Isa 9:6; Zech 8:6). All this is not beyond God's capabilities or powers. Rather, God shows his "love, grace, mercy" (חֶסֶד) to thousands (v. 18), but he will repay (שָׁלֵם, piel stem) or "impose a penalty" for the father's sins into the laps of the children who follow them. The promised love/grace of God comes from Exod 34:6–7 and God's promised judgment on all sins. God's judgment is not brought on children without their deserving it, for this is seen in that children repeat the sins of their fathers. But where a son departed from his father's sins and instead followed Yahweh, he is not punished for his father's sins (Deut 24:16). God is a great and mighty God, Yahweh of the armies in heaven and on earth! His purposes are likewise marvelous, and his deeds for humanity are beyond numbering (v. 19).

32:20-25 Jeremiah thanks Yahweh for his goodness (vv. 20-23a), as evidenced in the power he displayed in the exodus, which was still visible up to that very day (v. 20); that is where his renown was gained as well. In fact, Yahweh brought Israel into Canaan, a land flowing with milk and honey—verses that reflect Deuteronomy 26:8-9. Thus, Yahweh has kept his word about the land (v. 23a).

A cry of distress goes up in the prophet's prayer (v. 23b-24) as Chaldean siege ramps are being built up against the city of Jerusalem. Yes, what God has warned is now beginning to happen (v. 24c). The city will surely be invaded very soon. Nevertheless, God commanded Jeremiah to purchase the property in Anathoth with his own silver and have that transaction witnessed (v. 25), even when the city is about to be lost to the Babylonians.

Yahweh's Response in Judgment (32:26-35)

32:26-29 Yahweh answers Jeremiah's prayer in the form of a question: "Look, I am Yahweh, the God of all flesh. Is anything too hard for me?" (v. 27). Yahweh begins by repeating to Jeremiah the prophet's identical affirmation about his Lord. Yahweh actually repeats the very same verb that Jeremiah had used in v. 17 (פֶּלֶא). Nothing is outside the realm of possibilities for God, for he remains the omnipotent One. He is the God of all humanity (בָּשָׂר, "flesh"; v. 27), so all persons, all nations, and all actions are under his control and authority—including the Babylonians. Thus, judgment will come to Jerusalem; it will be utterly destroyed and crushed (v. 29).

32:30-32 God states his case against the people of Judah (vv. 30-31). The record of both northern Israel and the southern two tribes of Judah is one of continued evil since their earliest days (vv. 30, 31). They provoked Yahweh by burning incense on their rooftops and making drink offerings to other gods (v. 29). The city has to be burnt down for such atrocities. What is true of the evil done by the general population of Israel and Judah is also true of their kings, officials, priests, and prophets (v. 32). Every part of society has been affected by evil, and there are few left to act as a remnant. No wonder Yahweh says he is "provoked" three times in four verses (vv. 29, 30, 32).

32:33-35 All this perpetual evil came to a head earlier under the abominable rule of King Manasseh (2 Kgs 21:2-7). Even though King Josiah, Manasseh's grandson, had purged the temple and had introduced a revival of some sort (2 Kgs 23:4-12), which stayed the judged for the time being, Judah had quickly reverted to its evil former self as the high places went up for Baal in the Valley of Ben-Hinnom and fiery sacrifices of their sons and daughters were enacted in live immolation for the god Molech (v. 35; see comments on Molech at 49:1). God never commanded any such vile perversion; indeed, neither has it even ever entered God's mind (v. 35c). Payday for Judah's sin now has to come.

Yahweh's Seven Wonderful Promises (32:36-44)

32:36 In the second part of Yahweh's answer to Jeremiah's prayer (vv. 36-44), Yahweh demonstrates that despite all such evil and wickedness on Israel's part, and her deserving the hand of God's judgment, yet "nothing is too 'wonderful' for him," for just as surely as judgment must come (v. 36), so must the everlasting promises of God likewise come to pass as well (v. 37).

32:37 First of all, God is going to bring the captives home to Israel from all the countries where he has driven them in his anger and enormous indignation (v. 37). This promise will fulfill the ancient word given to the patriarchs and to David; Israel will be restored to their land after a worldwide dispersion of the Jewish people (v. 37b). Currently, as this commentary is being written, some 6.5 million Jewish people have returned to Israel. This represents almost one-half of the total Jewish population of the world and an increase from a mere 650,000 Jews in the land when Israel was given the status of statehood on May 14, 1948. Second, God will cause them to live in safety (v. 37c, cf. 23:6). That has rarely if ever been achieved in Israel, but when God restores them to the land, he will accompany their return with a pledge of safety from all harm and threats of invasion and conquest.

32:38 Third, Yahweh repeats two parts of the tripartite formula of the promise-plan of God: "They will be my people and I will be their God" (v. 38). These words are also part of the contents of the new covenant (31:33d), even if they are in reverse order, which is probably to emphasize that it is the people who are the focus of God's action here.

32:39 Fourth, God now promises a harmony among the people of God wherein they will have "one heart and one way," that is, "a singleness of heart and action" (v. 39). Rata notes, "the restoration that Yahweh will bring will have an eternal component to it, but it has as its main focus the human heart which represented the center of their emotion, will, and reason."[128] This is a promise of moral integrity and the absence of their long history of ambivalence and panting after other gods, a whole new lifestyle for this nation. Now they will have an undivided heart; one that will fear God (Psa 86:11). Only by fearing God will they enjoy what is for their own good and the good of their children after them (32:39b).

32:40 Fifth, God will make an "everlasting covenant" with them (v. 40). This is another term for the "new covenant" that is found at least a half dozen times in the OT (50:5; Isa 55:3; 61:8; Ezek 16:60; 37:26).[129] The promise God gave in the covenants made with the patriarchs and with David is meant to be perpetually binding and relevant. In spite of Israel and Judah's resolute sinfulness, God will not be deterred from keeping his promise—he will conclude history by doing good to the people of Israel and Judah. He will do this by putting the fear of himself in their hearts so that they will never turn away from him (v. 40b). Schmid puts the eternal nature of the covenant in the context of the whole book of comfort: "This 'new' covenant (31:31–34)—as one continues to read in Jeremiah 32–33—is subsequently established as the 'eternal' covenant (32:37–41). ... The Israel of 31:31–34 began a salubrious new future, which the Israel of 32:37–41 subsequently establishes forever."[130]

32:41 Sixth, God will "rejoice in doing them good" (v. 41). It will be a pleasure for God to be able to constantly do good for his people now that they

---

128. Rata, *Covenant Motif in Jeremiah's Book of Comfort*, 66.

129. Rom-Shiloni sees the passage as of exilic **provenance** and excludes Jeremiah from being the author. He argues that "under the prophet's name they wrote independent prophecies, some of which put forth a conception of the exile that the prophet himself would have opposed." See D. Rom-Shiloni, "The Prophecy for 'Everlasting Covenant' (Jeremiah XXXII 36–41): An Exilic Addition or a Deuteronomistic Redaction?," *VT* 53, no. 2 (2003): 201–23.

130. "Dieser "neue" Bund (31,31–34), liest man in Jer 32–33 weiter, wird nachfolgend als "ewiger" Bund (32,37–41) festgeschrieben. ... Die Israel 31,31–34 eröffnete heilvolle, neue Zukunft festig 32,37–41 nachfolgend auf ewig" (Schmid, *Buchgestalten des Jeremiabuches*, 72).

have been blessed with a new heart and a new spirit. The joy motif is not new (31:4, 7, 12, 13), "but now it is Yahweh who will be rejoicing over the people's restoration."[131]

Finally, in the seventh place, God will "assuredly plant them in this land" (v. 41b), for he now promises this in one of the most unique and unusual expressions ever used of God—"with all [his] heart and soul" (v. 41c). Such expressions are used previously in Scripture by mortals, but here God states resolutely, "I really mean this, for I am telling you this as I pledge it with everything that is in my being."

32:42-44 This section ends in vv. 42-44 with a summary of promises and judgments just made. The future restoration is just as certain as past judgment (v. 42).[132] Once more, promises Yahweh (v. 43), fields will be bought in this land, just as Jeremiah has just purchased a field against that coming day of Yahweh. Deeds will be signed, sealed, and witnessed once more in all the territory of Benjamin and Judah, because this Babylonian incursion, or any future ones, will not pronounce the end of the story; history will go on to the finish mark that God had set for it. He will restore the fortunes of Israel and Judah as he had previously promised. Rata notes,

> The extent of the restoration is shown in the mention of three specific geographic locations and three general, topographic designations. The three geographic locations are "in the territory of Benjamin" (בְּאֶרֶץ בִּנְיָמִן) where Jeremiah bought his field, "in the environs of Jerusalem" (וּבִסְבִיבֵי יְרוּשָׁלַ‍ִם), and "in the towns of Judah" (בְּעָרֵי יְהוּדָה), the place where Jeremiah and most of his audience resided. The topographic designations along with the specific geographic locations mentioned point to the extent of the restoration, namely, that the restoration will be all-encompassing. Just as the judgment affected everyone and everything, in the same manner, the restoration will be comprehensive. The restoration formula, "for I will restore their fortunes" (כִּי־אָשִׁיב אֶת־שְׁבוּתָם), which also occurs at the

---

131. Rata, *Covenant Motif in Jeremiah's Book of Comfort*, 67.
132. Ibid.

conclusion of the Book of Comfort in 33:11 and 33:26, concludes the promise of restoration.[133]

The seven promises gathered here set forth some of the most majestic aspects of what God is going to do for his people Israel. All attempts to spiritualize these blessings fall far short of the actions, words, and certainties of this text. Only those who want to unseat and displace Israel from God's word of promise stumble and trip over these straightforward words.

These promises, however, were not meant for Israel's bragging rights but are meant to prove that God will be faithful to his promise-plan as he had offered it to Abraham and David. Thanks be to God for his gifts, which include in them the blessings that will come from the root and trunk of the olive tree (Rom 9–11).

A CONCLUDING WORD OF BLESSING
AND PROSPERITY (33:1–26)

This chapter brings the book of consolation to a tremendous climax, as it focuses in on the work of God through his Davidic Messiah and the restoration that he will bring to the land.

TRANSLATION

1 The word of Yahweh came to Jeremiah a second time, while he was still confined in the courtyard of the guard, saying: **2** "This is what Yahweh[134] has said: 'He who made [the earth], who formed it and established it— Yahweh is his name. **3** Call on me, and I will answer you and declare to you great and unsearchable things[135] you do not know. **4** For this is what Yahweh, the God of Israel, has said about the houses of this city and about the houses of Judah's kings,[136] which have been torn down to be used against

---

133. Ibid., 68.

134. The word יְהוָה, "Yahweh," is absent in some Heb. mss, the LXX, Syr., and Vg.

135. A few Heb. mss, the oriental **Kethiv** tradition, and Tg. have וּנְצֻרוֹת, "and guarded things," where the MT has וּבְצֻרֹת, "and unsearchable things."

136. The LXX has the sg. βασιλέως, "king," where the MT has the pl. מַלְכֵי, "kings."

the siege ramps and the sword.[137] 5 [In the][138] fight with the Chaldeans[139] the [city] will be filled with the corpses of men I will slay in my anger and in my wrath. I will hide my face from this city[140] because of all its wickedness. 6 Look! I am going to bring healing and a cure to it; I will heal them [that is, my people] and reveal to them abundance[141] of peace and truth. 7 I will bring back the captives of Judah and the captives of Israel[142] and I will rebuild them as before. 8 I will cleanse them from all their sin that they have committed against me and I will forgive all their sins of rebellion against me. 9 And she [Jerusalem] will bring me renown, joy,[143] praise, honor, before all nations on earth that hear all the good things I do for her.[144] And they will fear and tremble at all the bountiful good things that I provide for her.'"[145]

10 This is what Yahweh has said: "Once more it will be heard in this place of which you say, 'It's an empty waste, without men or beasts—in the cities of Judah and in the streets of Jerusalem that are now deserted and inhabited by neither men nor animals'— 11 Sounds of joy and gladness, the voice of bridegroom and bride, the voices of men bringing thank-offerings[146] to the house of Yahweh, saying, 'Give thanks to Yahweh of Hosts, for Yahweh is good; his grace endures forever. For I will restore the fortunes of the land as they were before,'" declares Yahweh.

12 This is what Yahweh of Hosts has said: "Once more in this place, now desolate and without men or beasts—and in all of its towns, [there will again be] pasture for shepherds to rest their flocks. 13 In the towns of the hill country, in the towns of the Shephelah, and in the towns of the

---

137. The LXX has καὶ προμαχῶνας, "and fortifications," where the MT has "and against the sword."

138. The word בָּאִים, "coming," is absent in the LXX.

139. Some mss have אֶל, "against," instead of the sign of the acc. אֵת.

140. The LXX has ἀπ᾽ αὐτῶν, "from them," where the MT has מֵהָעִיר הַזֹּאת, "this city."

141. Where the MT has עֲתֶרֶת, "abundance," the LXX has καὶ ποιήσω, "and I will make"; LXX⁻ᴮ ¹⁰⁶ has εἰσακούειν, "to hear"; and, the Syr. has šbjl', "paths of" (Keown, 166).

142. Some LXX mss have Ιερουσαλημ, "Jerusalem," where the MT has יִשְׂרָאֵל, "Israel."

143. The LXX has εἰς εὐφροσύνην, "for joy," where the MT has לִי לְשֵׁם שָׂשׂוֹן, "to me a name of joy."

144. Other Heb. mss and versions have לָהֶם, "for them," where the MT has לָהּ, "for her."

145. The word אֹתָם, "them," is absent in the LXX. The editors of BHS suggest emending it to אתה, "her," to conform to לָהּ, "for her," at the end of the verse.

146. The LXX and θ′ have δῶρα, "gift," where the MT has תוֹדָה, "thank-offerings."

Negeb, in the land of Benjamin, in the environs of Jerusalem, and in the towns of Judah, flocks will again pass under the hand of the tally-keeper,"[147] declares Yahweh.

14[148] "Look! The days are coming," declares Yahweh, "when I will fulfill the good promise[149] I made to the house of Israel and to the house of Judah. **15** In those days, at that time, I will make sprout to David a righteous Branch,[150] who will execute justice and righteousness in the land. **16** In those days, Judah will be saved and Jerusalem will live in safety. This is the name[151] by which he will be called:[152] 'Yahweh our Righteousness.'"[153] **17** For this is what Yahweh has said: "David will not lack a man to sit on the throne of the house of Israel, **18** nor will the Levitical priests lack a successor to stand before me to offer burnt offerings, to present sacrifices, and to make sacrifices continually." **19** The word of Yahweh came to Jeremiah, saying: **20** "This is what Yahweh has said: 'If you can break[154] my covenant with the day and my covenant with night, so that day and night no longer come at their appointed time, **21** then my covenant with David my servant and my covenant with the Levites, who are priests ministering before me, can be invalidated, so that no descendant of his should sit as king on his throne. **22** Just as the heavenly hosts is innumerable, so I will multiply the seed of David servant, and the Levites who minister to me.'"[155]

23 The word of Yahweh came to Jeremiah, saying: **24** "Have you not noticed what these people have been saying: 'The two families which

---

147. The Tg. interprets the phrase תַּעֲבֹרְנָה הַצֹּאן עַל־יְדֵי מוֹנֶה, "flocks will again pass under the hand of the tally-keeper," as *jtnhwn 'm' lptgmj mšjḥ'*, "a people will join itself to the words of a messiah."

148. The LXX omits vv. 14–26.

149. Lit. "word."

150. LXX[OL] and θ´ have "rising," which the editors of BHS see as a translation of צֶמַח, "Branch," in the MT.

151. A few Heb. mss and Syr. add שְׁמוֹ, "his name." The editors of BHS suggest inserting הַשֵּׁם, "the name," as in LXX[OL], θ´, and Vg., or שְׁמָהּ, "her name," as in Tg.

152. A few mss, Syr., and Vg. have יִקְרָאוּהוּ, "he will be called," where the MT has יִקְרָא־לָהּ, "she will be called."

153. A few Heb. mss, LXX[OL], and θ´ have the adj. צַדִּיק, "righteous," instead of צְדָקָה, "(of) righteousness," as in the MT. Multiple Heb. mss add וּמֶלֶךְ מֶלֶךְ וְהִשְׂכִּיל. "a king who will reign wisely," as in 23:5.

154. LXX[L], Tg., and Syr. have the pass. διασκεδασθήσεται, "it will be broken," where the MT has the act. תָּפֵרוּ, "you break." Also in v. 21.

155. Many Heb. mss lack the final word אֹתִי, "(to) me."

Yahweh chose he has now rejected'[156]—and my people they are spurning, considering them to be a nation no more?" **25** This is what Yahweh has said: "If my covenant with day and night does not stand, [and if] I did not establish the heavens and the earth, **26** Then will I also reject the seed of Jacob and David my servant, so that his line/seed will not be a source for rulers over the line of Abraham, Isaac, and Jacob. Most assuredly, I will restore[157] their fortunes and show compassion on them."

COMMENTARY

An Awful Judgment Is Coming (33:1-5)

33:1-3 The book of consolation (30:1-33:26) comes to a climax in this passage. It is filled with messianic promises and stresses the restoration of Jerusalem and Judah. There is no attached notice of anger or any stern warnings about the need for rebuking Judah for her sin. Instead, Yahweh identifies himself to Jeremiah as the One who "made the earth, formed it and established it" (v. 2). Three participial phrases are used for "making," "forming," and "establishing" the earth, all three of which speak of how the same God who wielded his powerful word in bringing the universe into being in the first place is also the God who now is available for rebuilding and restoring that same world, as is particularly illustrated in Jerusalem and Judah. The concluding phrase, "Yahweh is his name," acts much like the way a signature guarantees the legitimacy and authority of the God who has spoken.

This is the "second time" (v. 1) that the word of Yahweh comes to the prophet, just as God's word came to Jeremiah twice on the day he was called into the ministry (1:10-13). Once again, Jeremiah is invited to "call on [Yahweh]," for he will indeed answer him and show him "great and unsearchable (or "inaccessible," בְצֻרוֹת) things [that he did] not know" (v. 3). This is a grand invitation from God to inquire of what God alone can provide. What is inaccessible from a human perspective will be available to

---

156. LXX[L], θ´, and Syr. read the 1 sg. "before me" where the MT has the 3 pl. לִפְנֵיהֶם, "before them."

157. Many mss and the **Qere** have the hiphil verb אָשִׁיב, "I will restore," where the **Kethiv** has the qal verb אָשׁוּב, "I will return."

the prophet. The verb "to call" (קְרָא) is a sg. impv., thus it is directed to Jeremiah alone. But the sg. is also used at times for the people at large or as a whole, thus it is possible that the people of God in general are thereby also invited to call on Yahweh and to seek his assistance and knowledge about things beyond human ability to sort out or to define.

33:4–5 Before the full message of hope can be announced in v. 6, there is a reminder that houses and royal palaces will be torn down because these materials will need to be employed in putting up the defenses against the Babylonians. On an even grimmer note, these very same houses that have to be torn down are the very places that will be filled with the corpses of those whom Yahweh will slay in his anger and in his great wrath (v. 5). Even though the Babylonians are the primary agents, Yahweh himself clearly takes responsibility for this great massacre. During this time, Yahweh's face will be hidden from this city and country due to the sin of the people.

Health and Healing Will Come (33:6–13)

33:6–7 Abruptly, a major transition is made in v. 6 from the horrors of the judgments just briefly described in vv. 1–5. The metaphors of "healing" and a "cure" are introduced and applied first of all to the city of Jerusalem and then to its houses. But there is also a larger sense in which these metaphors are answers to the earlier cries in this book for healing that comes from God (8:15, 22; 15:18; 17:14; 30:13). That is why the talk about healing and a cure is followed in v. 6b by an "abundance or peace and truth." Another metaphor, found in v. 7, was of "rebuild[ing]." The city and its destroyed homes will be rebuilt as God brings back both Judah and Israel from their captivities (v. 7).

33:8 Israel and Judah need more than a mere economic or social boost; there is an even deeper need for spiritual renewal (v. 8). This will be in keeping with the promises made in the new covenant (24:7; 31:31–34; 32:37–41). God's healing will bring healing, purification, and forgiveness for all sins. The noun "iniquity" (עָוֺן), the verb "to sin," (חָטָא), and the verb "to rebel" (פָּשַׁע) are all objects of God's forgiveness. God will "cleanse" Judah and Israel from all their sin.

33:9 As a result of being forgiven and cleansed, the once-cursed city of Jerusalem, now in its "healed" and "rebuilt" status, will bring Yahweh "renown," "joy," "praise," and "honor" (v. 9). When the nations finally see what God has done to this once-devastated city, they will "tremble in awe" and be amazed at the "bountiful good things [God will have] provided for [Jerusalem]" (v. 9b). The nations will acknowledge that Yahweh has indeed done great things for his people and given them a wonderful salvation.

33:10–13 Whereas it has been noted that this city and country were deserted and uninhabited by humans or beasts, now it will be once a place where shepherds graze their flocks (v. 12) and where the sounds of joy and laughter break out (v. 11).[158] There will also be the voices of the bride and bridegroom and the voices of the committed bringing their thank-offerings to Yahweh. God will indeed restore the fortunes of the captives, that is, bring Israel and Judah back to their land (vv. 10–11).

God's speech in v. 12 begins with "once more," which points to a restoration of former blessings of land, people, and animals. The geography of the land is ticked off in routine manner so that there may be no question about what land God is talking about: it was the land of the "hill country," the one that had "the western foothills, a southern Negeb, a territory belonging to Benjamin, with villages surrounding Jerusalem and towns in Judah (v. 13). There, not only will shepherds pasture their sheep, but "flocks will again pass under the hand of the tally-keeper" (v. 13b). This theme surely points to a special individualized care given by the shepherd to his flock and one that signals the same tenderness God will show that nation of Israel, as well as to all who belong to God's flock (cf. Luke 15:3–7; John 10:1–18). Gone are the days of chaos and catastrophe; now loving care for individuals and order have arrived from on high to replace the topsy-turvy world of the past.

---

158. The MT has "bring a thank-offering" where the LXX has "bring gifts"; the Vg. follows the LXX. See Wolfram Herrmann, "Zu Jer 33,11," *BN* 123 (2004): 41–44.

David's Righteous Branch (33:14–16)

33:14 Even though vv. 14–16 are missing from the LXX, the context now takes a very straightforward messianic approach.[159] This section begins in v. 14 with the familiar eschatological note of "'Look! The days are coming,' declares Yahweh." This formula appears in 30:3; 31:27, 31 and here in the book of consolation. This promise is described as a "good promise" (v. 14) because it will not only bring goodness and graciousness to the people, but it also comes from the hand of a good and gracious covenant-making God.

33:15 What is promised is this: in a future day of blessing, God will "make sprout to David a righteous Branch, who will execute justice and righteousness in the land" (v. 15). This is similar to what is promised in Jer 23:5. In yet one more metaphor, God will make a "shoot/sprout" or "branch out" from the Davidic tree, his promised David dynasty (v. 15). This Coming One, it can be counted on, will execute "justice and righteousness in the land" (v. 15b). This will be the rule and reign of no one less than Messiah himself.

33:16 What is more, "in those days" (v. 16a) Judah will experience deliverance, and the result will be that Israel and Judah will be able from then on to live in "safety" (v. 16b). Once more, so important is this pledge that Yahweh signs his name to this declaration: "Yahweh Our Righteousness" (v. 16c).[160] The meaning of this title is no small deal: the new and final messianic King will be the very embodiment of the righteousness that will be found in his people as they are finally restored and returned to their land as a cleansed, purified, forgiven, and redeemed people.

---

159. Rata notes that 33:14–26 "is the longest passage of Jeremiah missing in the LXX." See T. Rata, *Covenant Motif in Jeremiah's Book of Consolation*, 82. Grothe presents clear and strong arguments for the textual genuineness of the MT. See J. F. Grothe, "An Argument for the Textual Genuineness of Jeremiah 33:14–26," *Concordia Journal* 7 (1981): 188–91. For a treatment of the relationship between 23:1–8 and 33:14–26 see J. N. Mavinga, "Jeremiah's Royal Book: A Twofold Aspect Applied to the Royal Oracle (23:1–8; 33:14–26)," *Journal for Semitics* 18 (2009): 105–30.

160. Wessels proposes that 33:15–16 is not a widening of the perspective presented in 23:5–6, but rather 33:15–16 should be "linked to the conflict between the disenfranchised Levites and the Zadokites who displaced them." See W. J. Wessels, "Jeremiah 33:15–16 as a Reinterpretation of Jeremiah 23:5–6," *Hervormde Teologiese Studies* 47 (1991): 231–46.

A Perpetual Promise to David and the Levites (33:17–26)

33:17 Despite the ominous outlook for the future of the Davidic line of kings in Judah, what with King Jehoiachin already in exile and King Zedekiah about to go into exile, God gives a strong affirmation of the future of his promise of the royal line to David's descendants (v. 17)! To promise that "David will not lack a man to sit on the throne of the house of Israel" (v. 17b) seems to be a stretch in the face of the inevitable events at that time, but that is the promise of God. God long ago made it clear that he will do exactly what he promises, as seen for example in 2 Sam 7:16. Some of David's descendants might not participate in all the benefits of the promise, but they have to transmit those blessings on even if they themselves never enter into the joys of that promise because of their lack of faith and belief in God's Man of Promise, the Messiah. The promise of perpetual kingship that was promised to David's son Solomon continues through the new covenant.[161]

Text	MT
Jer 33:17	לֹא־יִכָּרֵת לְדָוִד אִישׁ יֹשֵׁב עַל־כִּסֵּא בֵית־יִשְׂרָאֵל
1 Kgs 2:4	לֹא־יִכָּרֵת לְךָ אִישׁ מֵעַל כִּסֵּא יִשְׂרָאֵל

33:18 This promise of perpetuity and permanence is not offered just to David's dynasty; similar terms are offered to the Levitical priests (v. 18).[162] It is surprising to remember the promise to the Levitical priests, since Jeremiah was very critical of the priesthood of his day—as he also was of the Davidic line of kings. But just as Yahweh has made provisions for the Davidic king, despite the failures of many in that line, so he will make provisions for the priestly stock, despite a corresponding lack in their line as well. They too will not "lack a successor to stand before [Yahweh] to offer burnt offerings, to present sacrifices, and to make sacrifices continually" (v. 18). God does not promise a perpetual priesthood (cf. Deut 18:1–18), yet a

---

161. See Rata, *Covenant Motif in Jeremiah's Book of Comfort*, 83.

162. Snaith suggests that the offering referred to here is "the grain-offering which accompanied every whole-offering (Num. xvi 1–16), of which only a token handful went on to the altar and was consumed in smoke." See N. H. Snaith, "Jeremiah XXXIII 18," *VT* 21, no. 5 (1971): 620–22.

"perpetual covenant" is promised to the priests of the house of Aaron within that Levitical family (Num 25:10–13; cf. Exod 29:9; 40:15). Could this be what is in Jeremiah's mind here? Note, however, the "Levitical priests" are also given a future role in Ezek 40:46; 43:9; 44:15; 48:11. In fact, an "Aaronic gene" has been discovered recently as a result of the genome project, giving some idea as to how this might be identified and used in the future to determine who in Israel was from a Levitical line.[163] There is more here than currently we mortals are able to figure out, for it seems at points to run counter to the idea in the book of Hebrews that Christ has offered himself as the final sacrifice once for all so that future sacrifices will no longer be needed. Is this language, then, using older liturgies to make the future understandable to those in Jeremiah's time? This is one suggestion as to how we are to understand such contrasting ideas.

33:19–26 Verses 19–22 ground the covenantal promises made to David and the Levites in God's promise to Noah, when he made a "covenant with day and ... night" (v. 20). God bound himself to that Noahic covenant, just as he likewise did in the promises made to David and in that promise to the Aaronic priesthood. Just as "David [is called] 'my Servant,'" the Levitical priests are "ministering before [him]."[164] People have once again been saying that the two kingdoms of Israel and Judah are rejected and despised, so these two nations can now be forgotten as constituting a part of the family of nations. However, God's response is that that would only be true if his covenant with day and night and the fixed laws of heaven and earth could be revoked or had been abandoned for one reason or another (vv. 25–26). But since it is obvious that day and night are still around, and so are the fixed laws of heaven and earth, it would be better if those who hold that opinion cease and desist from their rumor-mongering. God will keep his promises—count on it!

Both the royal and priestly families of Israel will flourish under the hand of God. Both will enjoy numerous progeny and the blessing of God. This will happen because God will see to it that the line of David will never

163. See D. M. Behar et al., "Multiple Origins of Ashkenazi Levites: Y Chromosome Evidence for Both Near Eastern and European Ancestries," *American Journal of Human Genetics* 73 (2003): 768–79.

164. See Rata, *Covenant Motif*, 84.

lack a man to sit on the throne of David, and in a similar way there will not be a lack with the covenant made with the priesthood. These promises could only be broken, once again, if God could retract the covenant he had made with Noah in Gen 9:8-17, which was a covenant that the day and the night should appear on schedule each day. In the meantime, the Lord will make the seed of David and the descendants of Levi as numerous as the stars in the heavens and the sand on the seashore.

THE CALL FOR FAITHFULNESS
(34:1–36:32)

After the stunning heights of promise and blessing announced in the four chapters of the book of consolation (Jer 30–33), the narrative in the book of Jeremiah returns to chronicling the abysmal failures of the people of Judah as they exhibit a continual amount of unfaithfulness for the next three chapters. These three chapters (34–36) do not follow a chronological order, for they begin with a message to the final king of Judah, Zedekiah, who can be paraded forth as a prime example of complete moral disintegration as the leader of the people. Chapter 34 illustrates how the people are just as guilty before God, for they too release those they were holding in slavery only to go back on their word and place them in bondage again. It was a case of "like leaders, like people."

Over against such bad examples of unfaithfulness, the conduct of the Rechabites is given in chapter 35 as a prime illustration of faithfulness over the centuries even to a human pledge. This is nothing but amazing when compared to how poorly Judah kept a divine pledge.

Finally, in chapter 36 we go back in history to the times of King Jehoiakim, who showed a total lack of respect for the word of God as he took his infamous penknife and cut up each section of the scroll containing the word of God and tossed each cut-off piece into the fireplace that was keeping him warm in his winter palace. Instead of responding to that word, he brazenly and systematically destroyed it after it was read to him. He, like the people he led, utterly rejected that word of God.

THE SIEGE OF JERUSALEM BEGINS (34:1–22)

Nebuchadnezzar's tactic was to make an incursion into the land by capturing other Judean cities that might come to the defense of Jerusalem before he put the squeeze on the capital city. It appears that Zedekiah himself had prompted this Babylonian response when he rebelled against Nebuchadnezzar in 589 BC. The siege of the capital began in 588 BC, perhaps around January of that year. Both Jer 37:5–8 and external sources indicate that later, sometime around late winter of 588 or spring 587 BC, Pharaoh Hophrah marched out of Egypt to come to Zedekiah's aid.[1] This distracted Nebuchadnezzar's forces as they faced this challenge, leading them to lift the siege temporarily.

In order to highlight the unfaithfulness of the people, along with their king, an incident that occurred during these chaotic days of the siege (perhaps in its earlier days) is recorded in 34:8–22. The people cut a covenant before God to let all the indentured fellow Hebrews go free in an order of emancipation. This is more than an offhand agreement or something said in passing; rather, it is a covenant entered into with the usual solemn sanctions over which God had the oversight (v. 15). However, when the promise of Egyptian help appeared, they reneged and took back all those they had set free (vv. 15–16).

TRANSLATION

1 The word that came to Jeremiah from Yahweh, while Nebuchadnezzar, king of Babylon, and his entire army, and all the kingdoms and peoples of the land he ruled,[2] were attacking Jerusalem and all its towns,[3] saying: **2** "This is what Yahweh, the God of Israel, has said: 'Go to Zedekiah king of Judah and tell him, "This is what Yahweh has said, 'Look here, I am going to hand[4] this city over to the king of Babylon, and he will burn it [down] with fire.[5] **3** You will not escape from his clutches, but you will certainly

1. COS, §3.42B.

2. The LXX has καὶ πᾶσα ἡ γῆ ἀρχῆς αὐτου, "and all the country of his domain," where the MT has וְכָל־מַמְלְכוֹת אֶרֶץ מֶמְשֶׁלֶת יָדוֹ וְכָל־הָעַמִּים, "and all the kingdoms and peoples of the land he ruled."

3. The LXX has τὰς πόλεις Ιουδα, "the cities of Judah," where the MT has עָרֶיהָ, "towns."

4. The LXX has παραδόσει παραδοθήσεται, "it shall certainly be delivered," where the MT has הִנְנִי נֹתֵן, "look here, [I am] going to hand." A similar issue is found in 32:28.

5. The LXX adds the phrase καὶ συλλήμψεται αὐτήν, "and he will take it."

be captured and handed over to him. You will see the king of Babylon with your own eyes, and he will speak to you face to face.⁶ And to Babylon you will go!'"' **4** Only heed the word of Yahweh, O Zedekiah king of Judah. This is what Yahweh has said concerning you:

"'You will not die by the sword.⁷ **5** You shall die peacefully. As your forebears, the previous kings who came before you, had burning [funeral] ceremonies,⁸ so the same will be done in your honor and [they will] lament,⁹ "Alas, O master!"¹⁰ For I myself make this promise,' declares Yahweh."

6 So Jeremiah, the prophet, repeated all these words to Zedekiah king of Judah, in Jerusalem, **7** while the army of the king of Babylon was attacking Jerusalem and all¹¹ the other cities of Judah that remained,¹² namely, Lachish and Azekah, for they were the only fortified cities left in Judah.

8 The word that came to Jeremiah from Yahweh after King Zedekiah had made a covenant with all¹³ the people in Jerusalem¹⁴ to make a proclamation of liberty.¹⁵ **9** Everyone was to free¹⁶ his Hebrew slaves, both male and female; no one was to hold a fellow Jew in bondage. **10** All the officials and all the people who entered into this covenant agreed to free their male and female slaves and no longer hold them in bondage as they complied¹⁷ and set them free.¹⁸ **11** Later, however, they changed their minds, and took

---

6. The phrase וּפִיהוּ אֶת־פִּיךָ יְדַבֵּר, "he will speak to you face to face," is absent in the LXX.

7. The phrase לֹא תָמוּת בֶּחָרֶב, "you will not die by the sword," is absent in the LXX.

8. Many Heb. mss, LXX, αʹ, Tg., and Vg. agree. Many Heb. mss, Tg.ᴹˢ read וּבְמִשְׂרְפוֹת, "and with a burning," where the MT has וּכְמִשְׂרְפוֹת, "and like a burning." The LXX has ὡς ἔκλαυσαν, "as they wept," which the editors of BHS suggest is probably a free translation.

9. The LXX has κλαύσονται, "they will weep," where the MT has יִשְׂרְפוּ, "they will burn."

10. The phrase יִשְׂרְפוּ־לָךְ וְהוֹי אָדוֹן, "they will burn for you, alas, O master," is absent in the Syr. The editors of BHS suggest this is the result of homoioarcton.

11. The word כָּל, "all," is absent in the LXX.

12. The word הַנּוֹתָרוֹת, "(that) remained," is absent in the LXX.

13. The word כָּל, "all," is absent in the LXX.

14. The phrase אֲשֶׁר בִּירוּשָׁלַם, "who are in Jerusalem," is absent in the LXX.

15. Or "emancipation." The word לָהֶם, "to them," is absent in the LXX and Syr.

16. Lit. "send away."

17. The LXX has καὶ ἐπεστράφησαν, "and they returned," where the MT has וַיִּשְׁמְעוּ, "and they obeyed."

18. The phrase חָפְשִׁים לְבִלְתִּי עֲבָד־בָּם עוֹד וַיִּשְׁמְעוּ וַיְשַׁלֵּחוּ, "free … and no longer hold them in bondage as they complied and set them free/sent them away," is absent in the LXX.

back the slaves, male and female, whom they had set free,[19] and forced them to become to become slaves again.

12 Then the word of Yahweh[20] came to Jeremiah, saying: **13** "This is what Yahweh, the God of Israel says: 'I [too] made a covenant with your forefathers when I brought them out of the house of bondage in Egypt, saying: **14** "Every seven[21] years each of you shall set free [any] fellow Hebrew who has sold himself to you. After he has served you for six years, you must set him free." But your fathers did not listen to me or pay any attention. **15** Recently you repented[22] and you did what was right in my eyes by proclaiming freedom to your countrymen. You[23] even made a covenant before me in the house that bears my name. **16** But you have turned around and profaned my name. Each of you has taken back the male and female slaves you had set free to go where they wished, and you have forced them to become[24] your male and female slaves again.'"

17 Therefore, this is what Yahweh has said: "You have not obeyed me; you have not proclaimed freedom each to his brother and each to his neighbor. Look out! I am going to proclaim your freedom, declares Yahweh—[it will be a] freedom to [fall by] the sword, plague, and famine! I will make you something that will horrify all the kingdoms of the earth. **18** I will hand over the men who have transgressed my covenant, who did not keep the terms of the covenant which they made in my presence, when they cut the young bull in two and passed between its pieces.[25] **19** The leaders of Judah and Jerusalem,[26] the high officials, the priests and all the people of the land

---

19. The sentence וַיָּשׁוּבוּ אַחֲרֵי־כֵן וַיָּשִׁבוּ אֶת־הָעֲבָדִים וְאֶת־הַשְּׁפָחוֹת אֲשֶׁר שִׁלְּחוּ חָפְשִׁים, "Later, however, they changed their minds, and took back the slaves, male and female, whom they had set free/sent away," is absent in the LXX.

20. The phrase מֵאֵת יְהוָה, "from Yahweh," is absent in the LXX, Syr., and Tg.[Ed.]

21. The LXX has ἕξ, "six," where the MT has שֶׁבַע, "seven."

22. The LXX has the 3 pl. ἐπέστρεψαν, "they repented," where the MT has וַתָּשֻׁבוּ, "(and) you repented.

23. The emphatic pronoun אַתֶּם, "you," is absent in the LXX.

24. The phrase וַתִּכְבְּשׁוּ אֹתָם לִהְיוֹת, "and you have forced them to become," is absent in the LXX.

25. The LXX has ἐποίησαν ἐργάζεσθαι αὐτῷ, "which they made to serve it," where the MT has כָּרְתוּ לִשְׁנַיִם וַיַּעַבְרוּ בֵּין בְּתָרָיו, "they cut in two and passed between its pieces."

26. The phrase וְשָׂרֵי יְרוּשָׁלַם, "and the leaders of Jerusalem," is absent in the LXX.

who walked between the pieces of the young bull,²⁷ **20** I will hand them over to their enemies who are seeking their lives.²⁸ Their carcasses will be food for the [carrion] birds and the wild beasts. **21** I will hand²⁹ over Zedekiah king of Judah and his officials to their enemies who seek their lives,³⁰ to the army of the king of Babylon, which has withdrawn from you. **22** Look out! I am going to give the order, declares Yahweh, and I will bring them back to this city. They will attack it, take it, and burn it down. And I will make the cities of Judah desolate so that no one can live there."

COMMENTARY

A Warning to King Zedekiah (34:1–7)

34:1-2 The Judean king Zedekiah is the object of several warnings by Jeremiah (21:1-7; 37:3-10, 17-21; 38:14-28). Some regard the warning found in this passage as the earliest of those warnings.³¹ In this divine declaration, however, an even more ominous note is struck in that the Babylonian attack will not simply be on Jerusalem but against "all" of Israel's cities (v. 1). Furthermore, it is not just Nebuchadnezzar and his army who will be involved in the attack on Judah, but "all the kingdoms of the earth" (v. 1). Surely there is hyperbole here, yet there is a sense in which the whole world of that day is engaged against Judah, for Nebuchadnezzar's empire stretched over much of the known world of that day. However, even in this situation it is the word of Yahweh that initiates what is said and what is to come. It was not unusual for empire leaders in that day to require military personnel to come from all the vassal peoples they had under their command and allegiance. Some have noted that Jer 35:1 mentions Aramaean

---

27. The LXX has καὶ τὸν λαόν, "and the people," where the MT has וְכֹל עַם הָאָרֶץ הָעֹבְרִים בֵּין בִּתְרֵי הָעֵגֶל, "and all the people of the land who walked between the pieces of the young bull."

28. The phrase וּבְיַד מְבַקְשֵׁי נַפְשָׁם, "and in the hand of the ones seeking their lives," is absent in the LXX. See also 34:21.a–a.

29. The LXX has καὶ δύναμις, "and power," where the MT has וּבְיַד חַיִל, "and the hand of power."

30. The phrase וּבְיַד מְבַקְשֵׁי נַפְשָׁם, "and in the hand of the ones seeking their lives," is absent in the LXX. See also 34:20.a–a.

31. Lipiński argues that vv. 1-7 are a combination of poetry and prose, with vv. 1-2a, 4ab, and 6-8 being prose. See E. Lipiński, "Prose ou Poésie en Jér 34:1-7," VT 24, no. 1 (1974): 112-13.

armies in this Babylonian force, and Psa 137:7 seems to point to Edomite involvement also.

All of this only adds to the hopelessness and desperate nature of what Zedekiah and Judah are facing. What is striking in this passage, however, is that the city is condemned to being burned down (v. 2b; cf. 21:10; 52:13).

34:3-5 Amazingly, in spite of all the dire predictions against Zedekiah, he is given some hope about his death and burial—always an important concern in those days. Even though no conditions are directly stated or mentioned, the command to "hear/listen" in v. 4 suggests that Yahweh is offering a promise to honor him in his death as a Davidic king if he surrenders to Nebuchadnezzar. Surely, this promise is an offer that is in strong contrast to the fate King Jehoiakim suffered (22:18-19). But Zedekiah is taking no chances on any promises of hope, so Zedekiah later dies in prison (52:10-11); he must have turned down this conditional prophecy. He had his eyes put out as he was led away in fetters to Babylon. Had Zedekiah counted too much on Egypt's intervention, so that he thought he had other options open to him than the ones offered by Yahweh? It is hard to say.

34:6-7 As Jerusalem is being attacked, other Judean cities are attempting to hold out against this Babylonian king. With the capital of Jerusalem surrounded, it is in no shape to offer assistance to any other city. Thus, it comes down to two remaining fortified cities: Lachish and Azekah (v. 7). Lachish incorporated a much larger area than Jerusalem and was less than thirty miles southwest of the capital, while Azekah was not quite twenty miles south of Jerusalem and some ten miles or so north of Lachish. Excavations at Lachish have produced, among other things, twenty-one pottery sherds (known as ostraca) that contain notes written on them from officers of some of the various parts of the Judean army under the oversight of the commander of Lachish. In Ostracon IV an outpost leader complains that he can no longer see signal fires from Azekah, presumably because it has already been captured.[32]

---

32. *ANET*, 292-93.

Broken Covenants (34:8–22)

34:8 The word of Yahweh comes to Jeremiah after King Zedekiah has "cut a covenant" (v. 8) with all the persons living in Jerusalem that everyone should proclaim "freedom" for all those fellow Hebrews who have been held by them as debt slaves. This expression is also used, for example, in Gen 15:7-21 to describe a ceremony that was used to solemnize the agreement being made between two parties.[33] The key verb in this expression comes from the Hebrew word "to cut" (כָּרַת), indicating that the use of sacrificial animals and the passing between them by the parties involved was central to this ceremony.

The procedure for this covenant making involved the selection of several sacrificial animals along with a couple of small birds (which were not to be divided because of their small size). The larger animals were then cut in half and placed opposite each other so that an aisle was formed between the arranged pieces. The party or parties to this agreement then walked between the slaughtered animals as each invoked on oneself a fate that was similar to the beasts that now lay slaughtered. Those walking down this newly formed aisle said: "May God/the gods, in whose name(s) I make this agreement, see to it that I suffer the same fate as these animals if I do not keep the terms of this agreement." In the case of Abraham in Gen 15:7-21, only God walked between the pieces, thus it is a unilateral and unconditional covenant in which only God obligated himself, while Abraham was in a deep sleep on the side.

Similar ceremonies were common in the ancient Near East. Such an event not only solemnized the agreement but also called down a curse on the head of any who chose to violate what had just been agreed to. An eighth-century BC example of the imprecatory part of covenant making can be seen in the Sefire inscription of Bar-Ga'yah and Mati`el, which says in part: "[Just as] this calf is cut in two, so may Mati`el be cut in two and may his nobles by cut in two."[34] Other examples can be found in Hittite sources and Alalakh.

---

33. See G. F. Hasel, "The Meaning of the Animal Rite in Genesis 15," *JSOT* 19 (1981): 61–78; and A. S. Kapelrud, "The Interpretation of Jeremiah 34,18 ff.," *JSOT* 22 (1982): 138–41.

34. *ANET*, 660 (Selfire I A).

Here, the action is initiated by Zedekiah, for though he often appears as a weak man during his reign, every once in a while he shows he has some good intentions about him. It may be that in light of the dire circumstances the king and people of Jerusalem face that he reasons that a royal command for the release of all those who are working off their debts might be a means of obtaining divine favor.

34:9 The law of God is clear that such "Hebrew slaves" (v. 9) could only be bound for six years (Exod 21:1–4; Deut 15:12); when the six years are up, they have to be released and all debts forgiven. The use of the word "Hebrew" (עִבְרִי) is unusual, for it is rarely used as a term of self-designation. Moreover, it seems to be used mainly in contexts where the Hebrews as subjected to oppression (cf. Exod 21:2; Deut 15:12).[35]

The expression "to proclaim freedom/release" (דְּרוֹר ... לִקְרֹא) is found in Lev 25:10 and here in vv. 8, 15, 17.[36] The Torah speaks of releasing slaves in the Jubilee Year, but the release mentioned here is not the one that came in the fiftieth year, as Lev 25:8–17 mentions, but the release mentioned in Exod 21:2 and Deut 15:12, which occurred every six years. What finally motivates Zedekiah to press for this emancipation is not known, but it is either to gain favor with Yahweh or to enlarge his fighting force to defend the capital city. It might have been both.

34:10 The officials and the people twice are said to have "agreed" (שָׁמַע, lit. "to hear," "to obey") to Zedekiah's order, meaning they thereby enter into the covenant Zedekiah has made (v. 10). Therefore, all slaves are released, even those who have not served their full six years of service. It is important to note that it was impossible to use one's land as equity or collateral in obtaining a loan, therefore the sole means of getting a loan or getting out of debt was to sell one's labor to another as collateral on the loan.

---

35. For an analysis of the relationship between Jer 38:8–14 and the Pentateuch see S. Chavel, "'Let My People Go!' Emancipation, Revelation, and Scribal Activity in Jeremiah 34.8–14," *JSOT* 76 (1997): 71–95.

36. As an interesting side note, Lev 25:10 is inscribed on the American Liberty Bell in Philadelphia.

When the people "repent" and release their slaves, God approves of the actions, as he clearly declares that what they have done is right in his sight (v. 15). The covenant they made to release those who had been in bondage, moreover, was made in "the house that bears [God's] name," so it is not to be thought of as being trivial in any sense of the term (v. 15).

34:11 This obedience, however, is of short endurance, for the slaveholders "turned around" (vv. 11, 16) from their recent "repentance" (שׁוּב, v. 15) and "took back" (וַיָּשִׁבוּ, hiphil of שׁוּב, vv. 11, 16) their slaves, another of Jeremiah's many wordplays. Apparently the respite in the Chaldean siege invokes the prospect of better and more normal days ahead for the citizens of Jerusalem, so things can revert to where they had been in terms of slavery of their fellow Jews.

34:12–18 This reversal in their actions brings Yahweh into the picture, for he now reminds them of the covenant he had cut with their forefathers when he brought them up out of the land of Egypt (v. 13). The whole nation had been slaves in the land of Egypt (Exod 13:3, 14; 20:2; Deut 6:12), therefore you would think that the Jewish people would pay more careful attention as to how they treat their fellow Jews who have fallen on hard times and become bondservants to them. In v. 14 it is especially noted that the words used here are very similar to those of Deut 15:12, which closely follows an emphasis on a fellow covenant member of Judah "selling himself" into slavery. This selling of one's self into debt slavery places an emphasis on an economic predicament that has befallen another Hebrew. This form of bond-service, however, is never allowed to last beyond six years (Exod 21:2–6; Deut 15:12–17). The Heb. expression in v. 14 is difficult, for it literally reads, "at the end of seven years" (מִקֵּץ שֶׁבַע שָׁנִים), but this can be interpreted as a Heb. time expression that counts both the partial first and the final years in such situations. God is not pleased with this reversal of positions by the officials and the people, for this covenant was made "before [him]" (v. 18). The use of God's name in the covenant-making ceremony is not to be taken as some empty ritual form, for God will see to it that the oath pronounced will be brought down on their own heads. God cannot be toyed with or mocked, for God will treat them as they treated the young bull calf cut it in half (v. 18c).[37] Such reversal of actions is a profaning of God's name (v. 16).

34:19-21 The result of such unfaithfulness to the covenant is God's "handing them over" (lit. "give in the hand of") to their enemies who are seeking their lives (v. 20). Even King Zedekiah and his officials will be handed over (v. 21). The curse for such disobedience is that they will have their dead carcasses left out on the open field, where the carrion birds and scavenging animals will consume their flesh—a curse often found in ancient treaties and Scripture (for example, Deut 28:26).

34:22 One final wordplay appears in v. 22. First, the people "turned back in repentance" (שׁוּב, v. 15) and freed their slaves; but they "turned around" (שׁוּב) again and reneged on their releasing them to freedom (v. 11) as they forced them to "return" (שׁוּב, v. 11); accordingly, Yahweh commanded the armies of Babylon to "return" as he "brought them back" (hiphil of שׁוּב) to Jerusalem (v. 22). It is clear that there is no faithfulness among this people at all.

Even while King Nebuchadnezzar is taking one Judean town after another and has Jerusalem under siege, God still sends a word by the hand of Jeremiah to the Judean king Zedekiah. Zedekiah is told to surrender to the Babylonian king if he wants to survive, for the doom of Jerusalem has already been determined by God.

Word has also come from God that all slaves are to be given their freedom; no one is to hold a fellow Jew in slavery any longer. Even though the Judeans made a covenant to this effect, they suddenly change their minds and take their slaves back into slavery again. This angers God, and he reminds them that according to the covenant he had made with the people, fellow Jewish slaves are to be released every seventh year. Now that the Judeans have turned back on their release for those enslaved, God has a new freedom for those owners: they will be "free ... to fall by the sword, plague, and famine."

---

37. Patrick Miller sees sin, punishment, and judgment expressed in three ways: repetition of the key verb and its obj.: *qārā' děrôr*, indirect correspondence, and repetition and wordplay. See P. D. Miller, "Sin and Judgment in Jeremiah 34:17–19," *JBL* 103, no. 4 (1984): 611–13.

Giving one's word is not a matter to be taken lightly, for God in heaven will hold us accountable to that word. In a day when truth telling is at an all-time low, this is a reminder to remember that God in heavens sees what is going on, and he will not fail to do what is right on behalf of those who have been hurt by our lying actions and words. Psalm 120 focuses on truth telling and its importance for those who listen to the word of God.

THE FIDELITY OF THE RECHABITES (35:1–19)

Following the rebuke of King Zedekiah for his failure to lead the people in justice, this chapter presents an example of a good leader and those who follow. If the previous chapter is an illustration of the inconstancy of leaders and people, chapter 35 is an illustration, by way of contrast, of how constant and obedient a people can be to a leader who requires strict separation from the surrounding culture and how faithfully the Rechabites adhered to that command even after their leader died.

Jeremiah steps back ten or more years before that event of chapter 34, to the reign of King Jehoiakim (609–598 BC). Since the army of the Arameans is mentioned (v. 11), this passage probably takes place in the latter part of Jehoiakim's reign, according to 2 Kgs 24:2. Jehoiakim has just revolted against Nebuchadnezzar, the Babylonian king, but Nebuchadnezzar is unable to bring his army at that time to deal with this Judean situation. Instead, he has the Arameans send in marauding parties to harass the land of Judah until Nebuchadnezzar can get free to come himself.

TRANSLATION

1 The word that came to Jeremiah from Yahweh in the days of Jehoiakim son of Josiah king of Judah, saying: **2** "Go to the members of the Rechabite community and speak with them, and bring them to Yahweh's house, to one of the chambers [there], and give them wine to drink." **3** So I got Jaazaniah son of Jeremiah,[38] son of Habazziniah, and his brothers and all his sons— the entire Rechabite community.[39] **4** I brought them to Yahweh's house to the room of the sons of Hanan, son of Igdaliah,[40] the man of God, which

---

38. The LXX has Ιερεμιν, "Jeremin," where the MT has יִרְמְיָהוּ, "Jeremiah."

39. H. Migsch, "Zur Interpretation von *We'et Kāl-bêt Hārekābîm* in Jeremia XXXV 3," VT 51, no. 3 (2001): 385–89.

40. The LXX has Γοδολιου, "of Godolias," where the MT has יִגְדַּלְיָהוּ, "Igdaliah."

was next to the room of the officials, above the room of Maaseiah son of Shallum, the keeper of the door. **5** Then I placed before the members of the Rechabite family pitchers full[41] of wine, and cups, and I said to them, "Drink some wine."

6 But they replied, "We do not drink wine, because our ancestor, Jonadab son of Rechab, commanded us, 'You shall drink no wine, neither you nor your sons forever. **7** You must not build houses, but you must always live in tents, in order that you may live a long time where you dwell as aliens.' **8** And we have obeyed the command of Jonadab, son of Rechab, our ancestor, in everything, drinking no wine as long as we live—neither we, nor our wives, nor our sons and daughters, **9** and building no houses to live in. We have no vineyards, no fields, and no seed. **10** We have continued to live in tents and have fully obeyed everything our forefather Jonadab commanded us. **11** But when Nebuchadnezzar, king of Babylon, invaded the land, then we said, 'Come, let us go to Jerusalem, out of the way of the armies of the Chaldeans and the armies of the Arameans.'[42] So we are living in Jerusalem."

12 Then the word of Yahweh came to Jeremiah,[43] saying: **13** "This is what Yahweh of Hosts, the God of Israel says: 'Go and say to the men of Judah and the inhabitants of Jerusalem: Will you never accept correction and listen to what I say, declares Yahweh? **14** Jonadab, son of Rechab, ordered his sons never to drink wine and this command has been kept.[44] They do not drink wine to this day, because they obey their forefather's command,[45] but I have spoken to you persistently, yet you have not obeyed me. **15** I have sent to you all my servants the prophets persistently [and repeatedly]. They said, "Turn please each of you from your wicked acts and reform your practices! Do not follow other gods to serve them. Then you shall live in the land I have given to you and your fathers." But you neither paid attention nor listened to me. **16** Yes, the descendants of Jonadab, son of Rechab,

---

41. The LXX has κεράμιον, "a jar," where the MT has גְּבִעִים מְלֵאִים, "pitchers full."

42. The LXX has τῶν Ἀσσυρίων, "of the Assyrians," where the MT has אֲרָם, "Arameans."

43. The LXX has πρός με, "to me," where the MT has אֶל־יִרְמְיָהוּ, "to Jeremiah."

44. The LXX has ἔστησαν ῥῆμα υἱοί, "the sons kept the word," where the MT has הוּקַם אֶת־דִּבְרֵי, "he kept the words."

45. The LXX omits עַד־הַיּוֹם הַזֶּה כִּי שָׁמְעוּ אֶת מִצְוַת אֲבִיהֶם, "to this day, because they obey their forefather's command."

have kept all the commandments which their ancestor gave them; but this people have not listened to me.'" **17** Therefore, this is what Yahweh of Hosts, the God of Israel, has said: "Look out! I am going to bring on Judah and on everyone living in Jerusalem every disaster I pronounced against them, because when I spoke to them, they did not listen, or when I called them, they did not answer."[46] **18** Then Jeremiah said to the Rechabite community, "This is what Yahweh of Hosts, the God of Israel, has said:[47] "Because you have obeyed the commandments of your ancestor Jonadab, abiding by all his instructions and doing everything he ordered you to do,[48] **19** therefore, this is what Yahweh of Hosts, the God of Israel has said:[49] Jonadab son of Rechab shall never lack a man to stand before me.[50]

COMMENTARY

An Invitation to the Rechabites (35:1–11)

35:1–4 Sometime during King Jehoiakim's eleven-year reign (609–598 BC), Jeremiah is instructed to invite a strange clan called the Rechabites to come into the temple, or more accurately, into one of the side rooms belonging to "Hanan, son of Igdaliah."[51] This room is alongside of the room "of the officials," who in this case are the court officials and not the priestly officials, since the temple is just adjacent to the palace. This room is also just over the room of "Maaseiah son of Shallum the doorkeeper" (v. 4). This suggests the room chosen for the Rechabites is on an upper floor of those rooms attached to the outside of the temple. This Maaseiah may be the

---

46. The LXX omits יַעַן דִּבַּרְתִּי אֲלֵיהֶם וְלֹא שָׁמֵעוּ וָאֶקְרָא לָהֶם וְלֹא עָנוּ, "because when I spoke to them, they did not listen, or when I called them, they did not answer."

47. The LXX has διὰ τοῦτο οὕτως εἶπεν κύριος, "because of this Yahweh said," where the MT has וּלְבֵית הָרֵכָבִים אָמַר יִרְמְיָהוּ כֹּה־אָמַר יְהוָה צְבָאוֹת אֱלֹהֵי יִשְׂרָאֵל, "Then Jeremiah said to the Rechabite community, 'This is what Yahweh of Hosts, the God of Israel, has said.'"

48. The LXX has ἐπειδὴ ἤκουσαν υἱοὶ Ιωναδαβ υἱοῦ Ρηχαβ τὴν ἐντολὴν τοῦ πατρὸς αὐτῶν ποιεῖν καθότι ἐνετείλατο αὐτοῖς ὁ πατὴρ αὐτῶν, "because the sons of Jonadab the son of Rechab have obeyed the command of their father, to do as their father commanded them," where the MT has שְׁמַעְתֶּם עַל־מִצְוַת יְהוֹנָדָב אֲבִיכֶם וַתִּשְׁמְרוּ אֶת־כָּל־מִצְוֹתָיו וַתַּעֲשׂוּ כְּכֹל אֲשֶׁר־צִוָּה אֶתְכֶם, "because you have obeyed the commandments of your ancestor Jonadab, abiding by all his instructions and doing everything he ordered you to do."

49. The LXX omits לָכֵן כֹּה אָמַר יְהוָה צְבָאוֹת אֱלֹהֵי יִשְׂרָאֵל, "therefore, this is what Yahweh of Hosts, the God of Israel has said."

50. The LXX adds the phrase τῆς γῆς, "of the earth."

51. Igdaliah is a longer form of "Gedaliah."

father of the priest Zephaniah (21:1). His title of "doorkeeper" makes him third in rank after the high priest.

The people group called the Rechabites descended from J(eh)onadab, son of Rechab. Jonadab or Jehonadab supported Jehu when he overthrew the dynasty of Ahab in northern Israel (2 Kgs 10:15–27) and was invited to join King Jehu in his chariot on his way to burn down the place of worship of all the Baal prophets. The Rechabites were related to the Kenites, the Midianite tribe from whom Moses's father-in-law, Jethro, descended (1 Chr 2:55). These Kenites attached themselves to the Israelites when they entered the land around the time of Joshua's conquest of Canaan. They were made up of two groups: one settled in the north, in the tribe of Naphtali (Judg 4:11, 17; 5:24), and the other selected the southern borders of Judah (1 Sam 15:6; 27:10; 30:29).

This was not a large community, for apparently they were all able to fit into one side room in the temple of Yahweh. They were, however, radical supporters of Yahweh, especially in the face of the Baalism espoused by the Omride dynasty in northern Israel. They adhered to a simple lifestyle as nomads and eschewed civilization because they felt it led to apostasy.

The Bible does not commend them for their nomadic or ascetic rules but rather for their faithfulness to keep a promise made to a human ancestor centuries ago. Their rules included the following:

1. abstention from intoxicating drinks, such as wine,

2. tent-dwelling rather than building established houses, and

3. a disdain for all forms of agricultural life, such as the growing of grapes or planting of seeds, which would require a settled life and waiting for the grapes to mature or the seed to grow.

One proposal argues that the Rechabites were likely a guild of metalworkers who wanted to keep the secrets of their trade to themselves.[52] Thus, in order to avoid any leaks of such secrets, they took a severe anticultural stand. However, all attempts to connect the Rechabites with craftsmen, especially as chariot makers, are dependent on the slim association of the three Hebrew consonants r-k-b (רכב) with the Hebrew word

---

52. F. S. Frick, "The Rechabites Reconsidered," *JBL* 90, no. 3 (1971): 284–85.

"chariot" ([Heb]רֶכֶב, *rekeb*); but no information exists to substantiate this connection.

The Rechabites had been forced temporarily to abandon some aspects of their lifestyle and nomadic way of living due to the Babylonian invasion into the land. As a result, they may have given up living in tents for the time as they flooded into Jerusalem. They may have been forced to sleep in the streets or in any space where they could spread out a tent in Jerusalem.

Jeremiah is not sneaking a bunch of vagrant refugees into the temple grounds. Rather, the location, next to the doorkeepers (of which there may have been three), is key, since the doorkeepers guard the three principal entrances to the temple. This event takes place in an area monitored to make sure that everyone who comes into this area is eligible to be there and that they keep the rules of ritual purity required for entrance into these sacred grounds.[53] Thus, the whole experiment is out in the open, for the lesson here is intended for all Judah and its officials to grasp.

35:5 There Jeremiah sets bowls full of wine along with individual drinking cups as he invites the men of Rechab to drink the wine. These guests are now put on the spot, for since they are guests of such a significant prophet as Jeremiah, and since are apparently were God-fearing worshipers of Yahweh, should they continue to observe their old rules and traditions, or should they bend these rules for the sake of showing appreciation for the prophet's hospitality?

35:6–11 The Rechabites are quick to respond negatively to Jeremiah's offer, for this is a principle they have adhered to for centuries (v. 6). Their eponymous ancestor Rechab ordered them not to drink wine "forever" (עַד־עוֹלָם). In addition to this, he had them commit to a nomadic lifestyle, which meant they are never to build houses or plant vineyards or sow seed. With such a simple lifestyle, the result promised is that they will live long in the land. It is not possible to determine whether the prohibition on wine is an anti-Baal stance, but drunkenness was a regular companion feature with Baal worship. It is impossible to say why Rechab demanded this abstinence; it

---

53. These guards also supervised the collection of gifts (2 Kgs 12:9).

may have been simply because grapes take several years before they produce, and this would contradict their nomadic lifestyle.

An Obedience to Be Compared (35:12–17)

35:12–14 Yahweh now issues another command to his prophet Jeremiah, to
go to the men of Judah and Jerusalem and use this exemplary pattern of
obedience to see whether it might stir up a similar obedience in the hearts
and lives of Jehoiakim's people (v. 12). In other words, the Rechabites are
not only an object lesson for Judah, but their ability to remain constant and
faithful condemns Judah and King Jehoiakim for their lack of constancy,
obedience, and faithfulness. So the question is this: Will the people of Judah
and Jerusalem learn a lesson from the Rechabites and obey Yahweh's commands for them to repent and turn from their wicked ways (v. 13)? To argue
that such obedience is humanly impossible flies right in the face of what
these tent-dwelling aliens have been able to demonstrate. These descendants of Jonadab, son of Rechab, have faithfully observed a command for
well over 250 years in the days of the reign of Ahab (v. 14).[54]

It might be tempting to argue that when these Rechabites claim they
have kept "all" (v. 18) the precepts Jonadab issued, they spoil the lesson
Yahweh has Jeremiah give the Judean people. For now that they have come
into Jerusalem in this time of war, they are presumably living in houses
in the capital city. While one could argue that circumstances in life often
demand occasional adjustments to what is the ideal, the main part of the
lesson still stands. It should be noted, though, that the command is that
they are not to build any houses, which they do not. Whether they were
able to live in their tents, if any open parcels of land were open in Jerusalem,
is not known.

35:15–17 Over and over again Yahweh has sent his servants, the prophets,
urging the people to "obey," "listen," and "heed" (vv. 10, 13, 14, 15, 16, 17, 18)
his call for a change of direction and a repentance of their sins (v. 15). The
citizens of Judah must turn from their wicked ways, reform their actions,

---

54. For two interpretations of Jer 35:14a see H. Migsch, "Die Interpretation von Jeremia
35,14a und die Vulgatalesart," *BN* 111 (2002): 28–33.

and refuse to follow any other gods (v. 15b). Then they will live in the land God has given to them. But since the people refuse to obey, God is going to bring a disaster (v. 17). Yahweh has spoken repeatedly and persistently, but no one listens and no one answers his call (v. 17c).

Faithfulness Rewarded (35:18–19)

35:18–19 In contrast to the trouble that awaits Judah, Jeremiah announces to the Rechabites (perhaps while they are still in the room attached to the temple, where Jeremiah has them meet) a divine blessing on them for the days to come (v. 18). Because they obeyed their human father so completely ("all" appears twice in v. 18), God issues his "therefore" (v. 19). Usually such a "therefore" introduces a word of judgment and condemnation, not a promise, but here it introduces a word of promise.

The promise is that "Jonadab son of Rechab shall never lack a man to stand before me" (v. 19). The expression to "stand before me" pictures a servant waiting to do the bidding of his master, usually in priestly or kingly service to God (cf. 15:1; 33:17–18). Later rabbinic traditions attribute various temple functions to the descendants of Jonadab. There is mention made of a Machijah son of Rechab who was said to be the ruler of a district called Beth-hakkerem ("house of the vineyard"). He is also mentioned as the one who repaired the Dung Gate in Jerusalem (Neh 3:14), but how this matches up with the former way of life of the Rechabites is difficult to assess.

The Rechabites are credited with being faithful to the command of their ancestor a whopping seven times (vv. 6, 8, 10, 14 [2x], 16, 18), with three of those times as part of the word of God. Never once in this whole example is it said that the Rechabites were faithful to Yahweh or to the Torah of Moses. Nor does God rebuke them for the absence of any comment toward these ends. This, however, may be done deliberately: it makes the point of contrast between Judah and the sons of Rechab all the sharper; if they can be faithful to a mere mortal's words, how much more should Israel listen to the words of the living God?

This is not a direct or an implicit endorsement of the Rechabite way of life. God is not saying that if the people of Judah and Israel had taken up a simpler style of life and removed themselves from such things as building houses, planting vineyards, or sowing seed, as well as abstaining from wine, they too would receive a blessing from God. The call of Yahweh and the prophet is to reverse the direction they are going and to repent of their sins; that is the form of obedience God is seeking from them.

This chapter does not make the case for teetotaling in place of using wine or even alcohol. Rather, it makes the case that obedience, even if it is only obedience to a human command, is possible. If Judah thinks it is too hard to be faithful to what God has instructed them, then how come these people have remained faithful to the commands of a great-great-great-grandfather whose commands were merely about terrestrial things and not about heavenly things? Obedience is no substitute for faith in the living God, but it is the fruit and demonstration that real faith is present. Surely it is also possible to observe God's instruction, for the faithfulness of these people to a terrestrial command shows it is more than possible to be obedient to a heavenly command.

KING JEHOIAKIM BURNS
JEREMIAH'S SCROLLS (36:1–32)

The narrative in this chapter is set in the fourth year of King Jehoiakim (605 BC), the very year that Nebuchadnezzar king of Babylon defeated the Egyptians at Carchemish. By 604 BC this king of the Babylonian empire was threatening Judah as the Babylonian armies were now in the vicinity of Jerusalem. Judah's King Jehoiakim, however, seems unperturbed by all that is happening around him.

The public reading of the scroll (v. 9) occurs in the ninth month of the fifth year of Jehoiakim (December 604 BC). It was about the same time that Babylon conquered Ashkelon, a mere fifty miles away from Jerusalem. This was part of a six-month campaign by Nebuchadnezzar from October 605 BC to March 604 BC. Just when it seemed that Assyria, as the former potential foe "from the north," had been defeated, Babylon arose to be an even more implacable opponent for the people of Judah.

There are similarities between chapters 36 and 26. Both are set in the reign of Jehoiakim, and in both chapters the prophet Jeremiah is threatened, thus providing for the structure of the book as an **inclusio** between chapters 26–36. Another option is to interpret chapter 36 as a "bridge chapter" that introduces chapters 37–45.

TRANSLATION

1 It was in the fourth year of Jehoiakim son of Josiah, king of Judah, that this word came to Jeremiah from Yahweh: **2** "Get yourself a scroll and write on it all the words I have spoken to you concerning Israel,[55] Judah, and all the [other] nations from the time I began speaking to you in the reign of Josiah until now. **3** Perhaps if the citizens of Judah hear of all the evil that I plan to do to them, each of them will turn from his wicked way, and then I can forgive their wickedness and their sin." **4** So Jeremiah called Baruch son of Neriah, and Baruch, at Jeremiah's dictation, wrote in a scroll-book all the words of Yahweh which [Jeremiah] spoke to him.

5 Then Jeremiah told Baruch, "I am barred: I cannot enter the house of Yahweh. **6** So you yourself must go[56] and, there in Yahweh's house in the hearing of the people, on a fast day, read the words of Yahweh from the scroll that you have written at my dictation.[57] Read them in the hearing of all the people of Judah who will be coming from their towns. **7** Perhaps they will bring their petition before Yahweh and each will turn from his wicked way; for great is the anger and wrath which Yahweh has spoken against this people." **8** And Baruch the son of Neriah did everything Jeremiah the prophet told him to do; at the house of Yahweh he read the words of Yahweh.

9 Now it was in the ninth month of the fifth[58] year of Jehoiakim son of Josiah king of Judah, that all the people in Jerusalem and all the people who had come to Jerusalem from the towns of Judah[59] observed a fast to Yahweh. **10** Baruch read from the scroll all the words of Jeremiah in Yahweh's house in the hearing of all the people, in the chamber of Gemariah son of Shaphan the secretary of state, which was in the upper court, at the New Gate.

11 When Micaiah son of Gemariah, son of Shaphan, heard all the words of Yahweh from the scroll, **12** He went down to the room of the secretary

---

55. The LXX has Ιερουσαλημ, "Jerusalem," where the MT has יִשְׂרָאֵל, "Israel."

56. The phrase וּבָאתָ אַתָּה, "so you yourself must go," is absent in the LXX.

57. The LXX has τούτῳ, "this," where the MT has אֲשֶׁר־כָּתַבְתָּ מִפִּי אֶת־דִּבְרֵי יְהוָה, "which you have written at my dictation."

58. The LXX has τῷ ὀγδόῳ, "the eighth," where the MT has הַחֲמִשִׁית, "the fifth."

59. The LXX has καὶ οἶκος Ιουδα, "and the house of Judah," where the MT has וְכָל־הָעָם הַבָּאִים מֵעָרֵי יְהוּדָה בִּירוּשָׁלָם, "and all the people who had come to Jerusalem from the towns of Judah."

where all the princes were seated [in session]: Elishama the secretary, Delaiah son of Shemaiah,[60] Elnathan[61] son of Achbor, Gemariah son of Shaphan, Zedekiah son of Hananiah, and all the officials. **13** And Micaiah told them everything he had heard when Baruch read from the scroll in the hearing of the people.

14 Then all the princes sent Jehudi son of Nethaniah son of Shelemiah son of Cushi to Baruch, saying: "The scroll from which you have read in the hearing of the people—bring it with you and come!" So Baruch son of Neriah went[62] to them with the scroll in his hand. **15** And they said to him, "Sit down,[63] please, and read it in our hearing." So Baruch read it to them. **16** When they heard all these words, they were perturbed and they said to Baruch[64] and to each other, "We will certainly have to report all these words to the king." **17** Then they questioned Baruch, "Tell us, please, how[65] did you come to write all these words at his dictation?"[66] **18** Baruch replied, "He[67] dictated all these words to me and I wrote them in ink[68] on the scroll." **19** Then the princes said: "Go and hide, you and Jeremiah! Do not let anyone know where you are!" **20** After they deposited the scroll in the room of Elishama, the secretary of state, they went to the king in the courtyard and reported in his hearing the whole affair.[69]

21 The king sent Jehudi to get the scroll, so Jehudi brought it from the room of Elishama, the secretary of state, and read it to the king and to all the officials standing beside him. **22** Now the king was seated in the

---

60. The LXX has Σελεμιου, "Selemiah," and LXXˢ has Σεδεκιου, "Sedekiah," where the MT has שְׁמַעְיָהוּ, "Shemaiah."

61. LXX* has Ιωναθαν ("Jonathan"), LXXᴬ has Ναθαν ("Nathan"), and LXXᴸ has Ελδαθαν ("Eldathan") where the MT has וְאֶלְנָתָן, "(and) Elnathan."

62. The LXX has καὶ κατέβη, "and he went down," where the MT has וַיָּבֹא, "and he went."

63. The LXX has πάλιν, "again," where the MT has שֵׁב, "sit down."

64. The phrase אֶל־בָּרוּךְ, "to Baruch," is absent in the LXX.

65. The LXX has πόθεν, "whence(?)," where the MT has אֵיךְ, "how(?)."

66. The word מִפִּיו, "from his dictation (lit. "from his mouth")," is absent in the LXX.

67. The LXX adds Ιερεμιας, "Jeremiah," to clarify "he."

68. The word בַּדְּיוֹ, "with ink," is absent in the LXX.

69. Many Heb. mss, LXXᴬ, ᴼ, ᴸ, ᶜ, Syr., and Tg. add "these."

winter house in the ninth month[70] with a fire[71] burning[72] in the brazier in front of him. **23** Whenever Jehudi had read three or four columns of the scroll, the king would cut them off with a penknife and toss them into the fire in the brazier until the entire scroll was consumed in the fire which was in the brazier. **24** Yet they were not afraid, nor did they rend their garments—neither the king nor any of his courtiers[73] who heard all these words. **25** Even though Elnathan, Delaiah,[74] and Gemariah begged the king not to burn the scroll, he would not listen to them.[75] **26** Instead, the king commanded Jerahmeel, son of the king, Seriah son of Azriel and Shelemiah son of Abdeel[76] to arrest Baruch the scribe and Jeremiah the prophet. But Yahweh had hidden them.[77]

27 After the king had burned the scroll and the words[78] that Baruch had written at Jeremiah's dictation, the word of Yahweh came to Jeremiah, saying: **28** "Go back and take for yourself another scroll, and write on it all the former words that were on the original scroll, which Jehoiakim, king of Judah, burned up. **29** As for Jehoiakim, king of Judah,[79] you shall say, 'This is what Yahweh has said: "You personally burned that scroll and said: 'Why did you write on it that the king of Babylon would surely come and destroy this land and exterminate from it both men and animals?'" **30** Therefore, this is what Yahweh has said concerning Jehoiakim, king of Judah: 'No descendant of his will sit on David's throne! His corpse shall be flung out to the heat by day and the frost by night. **31** I will punish him and his seed and his servants for their iniquity;[80] I will bring on them and those living in Jerusalem and on the men of Judah, all the evil I threatened them, but

---

70. The phrase בַּחֹדֶשׁ הַתְּשִׁיעִי, "in the ninth month," is absent in the LXX.

71. The LXX, Syr., and Tg. read וְאֵשׁ, "fire," where the MT has וְאֶת־, "and [sign of the acc.]."

72. The word מְבֹעָרֶת, "burning," is absent in the LXX.

73. The LXX has καὶ οἱ παῖδες αὐτοῦ, "and his servants/children," where the MT has וְכָל־עֲבָדָיו, "and all his servants."

74. The LXX has καὶ Γοδολιας, "and Gedaliah," where the MT has וּדְלָיָהוּ, "and Delaiah."

75. The clause וְלֹא שָׁמַע אֲלֵיהֶם, "and he would not listen to them," is absent in the LXX.

76. The words וְאֶת־שְׁלֶמְיָהוּ בֶּן־עַבְדְּאֵל, "Shelemiah son of Abdeel," are absent from the LXX.

77. The LXX has καὶ κατεκρύβησαν, "they were hidden," where the MT has וַיַּסְתִּרֵם יְהוָה, "but Yahweh had hidden them."

78. The LXX adds the word πάντας, "all."

79. The LXX is lacking עַל־יְהוֹיָקִים מֶלֶךְ־יְהוּדָה, "as for Jehoiakim, king of Judah."

80. The phrase אֶת־עֲוֹנָם, "their iniquity," is absent in the LXX.

which they refused to hear.'" **32** So Jeremiah[81] took another scroll and gave it to Baruch, son of Neriah,[82] the scribe, who wrote on it at Jeremiah's dictation everything that was in the scroll that Jehoiakim king of Judah had burned in the fire. And in addition to that, he added many words similar to them.

COMMENTARY

The Writing of the Scroll (36:1–4)

36:1–2 Jeremiah is instructed to get a scroll document (מְגִלַּת־סֵפֶר) and record all the words he has received from Yahweh about Israel, Judah, and the other nations (v. 2) from the beginning of his ministry, which was in the thirteenth year of Josiah's reign (627 BC), until the present (605/604 BC)—twenty-three years. It has always been a temptation for scholars to speculate how much of the present book of Jeremiah this would have included. The original scroll's content may have been limited to merely chapters 1–6, or it could continue on through chapter 20, or it could have continued all the way to 25:13a. A scroll of some twenty-four chapters would have been about twelve to fifteen columns of text.

That Jeremiah is told to write all that Yahweh has spoken to him in the past (v. 2) raises the question as to how these messages have been preserved up to that point. Has the prophet memorized them, or has he made notes on what he has been told without writing out these messages in full? There is no question that Jeremiah is literate and able to write, despite what some think, for when he is told to write in 30:1–2, there is no mention of a scribe, nor is a scribe mentioned when he is told to write in 51:60.

36:3 The word "perhaps" in v. 3 signals the same ray of hope that 26:3 sets forth. God has continued to hold out the offer of deliverance if they repent. The same hope is expressed in v. 7. Here is another example of a conditional prophecy, whose dire effects can be reversed if the people repent of their sins and change their ways. God does not want the disasters to come on

---

81. The LXX has καὶ Βαρουχ, "and Baruch," where the MT has וְיִרְמְיָהוּ, "and Jeremiah."

82. The sentence וַיִּתְּנָה אֶל־בָּרוּךְ בֶּן־נֵרִיָּהוּ הַסֹּפֵר, "and he gave it to Baruch, son of Neriah, the scribe," is absent in the LXX.

Judah; instead, his desire is for the people to repent so that he can forgive them and call a halt to judgment.

36:4 Jeremiah does what he is instructed to do, for he calls Baruch the son of Neriah to be his scribe.[83] As Jeremiah dictates the words, Baruch records them on the scroll. The term to "dictate," as used throughout this chapter, is literally "from the mouth of" God himself. God gives the message to the prophet, which the prophet in turn dictates to Baruch, which he then writes down.

The Reading of the Scroll to the People (36:5–10)

36:5–9 Jeremiah cannot read his own words to his people, for he is "barred" (עָצֻר, or "restrained, restricted") from going into the temple (v. 5). This does not mean necessarily that the prophet is imprisoned, for how can he and Baruch be told to "go and hide" (v. 19)? It is more probable that he has been prohibited from going into the temple and speaking there as a result of his infamous "temple gate message" (vv. 7, 26) or as a consequence of Pashhur's action (20:2). In this way the prophet is also able to distance himself from his messages, which then take on an independent life as God's word to his people. Therefore, the prophet orders Baruch to go to the temple and there read "the words of Yahweh from the scroll" (v. 6). He is to go there on a day of fasting (v. 6b). This is indeed a shrewd strategy, for public fasts were proclaimed during times of war, famine, or physical threat to the community. The people would appear at the house of God wearing sackcloth with ashes sprinkled on their heads as a sign of public lamentation.

This "fast" of v. 9 is not the fast for the Day of Atonement, for that occurred in October. The "ninth month of the fifth year of Jehoiakim" (v. 9) would be November-December 604 BC. Whether this is a long or short interval since God gave the instruction to commit these words to writing is not immediately discernible, but it is significant that the Babylonian army marched down the coast of Israel and captured Ashkelon right about at this time. Although it is impossible to say what occasion prompts the fast, it

---

83. Hoffman erroneously suggests that this chapter did not originate with Jeremiah, nor was it written down by Baruch. See Y. Hoffman, "Aetiology, Redaction and Historicity in Jeremiah XXXVI," *VT* 46, no. 2 (1996): 179–89.

might be associated with the political and hostile threat of Babylon, since the Babylonian troops are in the vicinity. This may have triggered the call for an emergency day of fasting, which becomes the appropriate moment for Baruch to read Jeremiah's scroll. If the enemy is that close at hand, and in the land of Israel, then surely all hopes that Jerusalem will avoid being included in similar hostile advances very soon are by now almost a foregone conclusion. Reality is beginning to set in for some in Judah! As the crowds are milling about in Jerusalem, no doubt talking about rumors of war and the impending hostilities, this presents a most opportune time to publically proclaim the words of Jeremiah as he received them from God.

The words of the scroll are to be read (lit. "in the ears of all Judah," vv. 6, 10, 13, 14, 15 [2x], 20, 21 [2x]), so the message is anything but private or a secret; it is to be a public proclamation for the king, his officials, and the whole nation. The emphasis on its being read in their own hearing cannot be missed in this passage. There is always the hope that as a result of hearing this word ("perhaps" 3, 7), the listeners will humbly fall prostrate before Yahweh and will each turn from their wicked ways. God's anger and wrath against the people are indeed enormous (v. 7c). So Baruch goes and does as he was instructed by Jeremiah.

36:10 Baruch reads from the scroll in the upper courtyard of the room of Gemariah. As an upper room, it would have stood above the outer courtyard where all the people were standing (1 Kgs 7:12; cf. 1 Kgs 6:36), and the "New Gate" (Jer 36:10c) must be the same as the Benjamin Gate. Thus Baruch reads either from a window or from the doorway to this room.

The Gemariah mentioned here is a different person from the man by the same name in 29:3, for this was a common name in that day. This Gemariah is the brother of Ahikam, whose family generally favored Jeremiah. His father is Shaphan, who is a royal secretary and who has already played a key role in the discovery and promulgation of the "book of the law" found in the temple during the reign of Josiah (2 Kgs 22:8–10), when he also played an instrumental role in the public reading of that document. Micaiah is the grandson of Shaphan (Jer 36:11) who, on hearing the reading of the scroll from Jeremiah, brings the news to the officials in the palace. One of those governmental officials is Elnathan, the father of Nehushta, the mother of King Jehoiakim (2 Kgs 24:8). He is the official that Jehoiakim sent to Egypt to retrieve the prophet Uriah, who fled to Egypt to escape being killed; Elnathan was to bring him back to Jerusalem for execution (2 Kgs 26:22–23). He also is one of those who urges the king not to burn the scroll. Jehudi acts as a key messenger but is otherwise unknown, and neither are any members of his family known either.

The Reading of the Scroll to the Officials (36:11–20)

36:11–13 After the first reading of the scroll, done in public in the house of God, Micaiah, grandson of Shaphan, the secretary of state, whose family, as we have noted, is supportive of Jeremiah, reports what he heard to the officials in the Judean government; the officials also appear to be generally sympathetic to the prophet, at least at first. These civil servants are gathered in the chambers of Elishama, a royal secretary (vv. 11–13). We are not informed any further on who Delaiah or Zedekiah are, other than that they too are present at this meeting. Elishama may be the grandfather of the assassin of Gedaliah (41:1); if so, then he is connected to the royal family (2 Kgs 25:25). There is a seal inscription from this general time period with the impression "Elishama, servant of the king."

36:14–15 The officials are struck by what is reported to them, but they do not know what to do about it. So they send a messenger, Jehudi, to Baruch to have the scroll brought to them (v. 14). Jehudi appears to be a gentilic name meaning "Jew" or "Judean" (though he is given a most impressive and somewhat expansive genealogy of three generations; v. 14). Baruch obliges them and comes into their presence, and they offer him a seat in their midst, from which he is invited to read the scroll in their hearing (v. 15).

36:16–17 The reaction of the officials is one of alarm and fright, as they look at one another as if to ask what they should do about this whole situation (v. 16). It is clear that King Jehoiakim must be informed about what they have just heard. But before they go to the king, it is absolutely necessary that they learn who is responsible for these words, so they ask Baruch, "Tell us, please, how did you come to write all these words? Did he [Jeremiah] dictate them?" (v. 17). They have to know whether Baruch has done this on his own initiative, or perhaps these are a collection of old messages from the prophet. Surely, there is little that is new in this scroll, for Jeremiah has been saying the same things for some twenty-three years of his ministry.

36:18-20 Baruch states what must be obvious to all of them by now: "he dictated all these words to me, and I wrote them in ink on the scroll" (v. 18). The officials do not react in a hostile or angry manner; instead, they urge Baruch to go and hide, both him and Jeremiah. They are not to let anyone know where they are hiding (v. 19). Thereupon, the officials leave the scroll in Elishama's room and go to report all of these events to the king (v. 20).

The Reading of the Scroll to King Jehoiakim (36:21–26)

36:21-22 Jehoiakim's response on hearing the report from his officials is to immediately send Jehudi to bring the scroll from Elishama's room (v. 21). When he returns with the scroll, the king demands that Jehudi read it to him; in the presence of his officers, it might have seemed more elegant for an attendant to read it rather than have the king himself repeat these words, which he no doubt already regards as inflammatory. This reading of the scroll takes place in the winter palace apartment, where a fire is burning in the brazier. This room might have a southern exposure to capture the warming effects of the sun and is possibly located on the first floor of what often was a two-story building, with a hallow in the floor, where the brazier, made of metal or ceramic, acted as a hearth or a firepot.

36:23 Whenever Jehudi finished reading several sections, the king "cut them off" (קָרַע, "to tear, rend") with a "penknife" (תַּעַר, "razor," "scribes' knife"), three or four "columns" (דְּלָת, lit. "doors"), showing little or no regard for what has been written as he impudently "toss[ed] them into the fire" (v. 23).[84] Perhaps Jeremiah intends another play on words here, for the word for "tear" or "cut off (קָרַע) is similar to the word for "read" (קָרָא). Surely this is an altogether different reaction to the reading of God's word from the response his father, King Josiah, gave when the newly discovered book of the law was read to him. Josiah "tore" his robes in grief (2 Kgs 22:11),

---

84. R. L. Hicks, "Delet and Megillāh: A Fresh Approach to Jeremiah xxxvi," *VT* 33, no. 1 (1983): 46–66.

but his son Jehoiakim maliciously tears the word of God instead and throws it into the fire. Does he think that by doing so he will magically get rid of the power and authority of that divine word?

36:24-25 Some of Jehoiakim's officials, with Elnathan, Delaiah, and Gemariah taking the lead, beg the king not to burn the scroll (v. 25), whereas the king's other attendants, apparently following the king's lead, show no fear when they hear these words read to them, nor do they rend or tear their clothes (v. 24). Thus, there is a division among the leaders about the respect that should be shown to this word of God.

36:26 Rather than repenting of his sin and leading the nation in following suit, Jehoiakim sends Jerahmeel, called "a son of the king," to go and arrest Baruch and Jeremiah (v. 26).[85] The reference to his being a son may indicate that he is a member of the royal family; a familial relation would be simply "his son." There is evidence from Egypt that this may have been a title for an official. At any rate, he is one of three members of a delegation that is to find and arrest the prophet and his scribe. The other two men are Seriah son of Azriel and Shelemiah son of Abdeel (v. 26). It is not enough for Jehoiakim to destroy the scroll; he must also destroy and silence those who wrote it. This troika is unsuccessful, for "Yahweh had hidden [Jeremiah and Baruch]" (v. 26c).

The Writing of Another Scroll (36:27–32)

36:27-28 Sometime after Jehoiakim burns the scroll (though we are unable to say how much time intervenes), God orders the prophet and his scribe to get another scroll and write on it "all the former words that were on the original scroll" (v. 28). Jehoiakim should have known better; destroying the word of God is not equal to eradicating the word of God itself, just as killing a prophet such as Uriah would not eliminate the word of God either. Yahweh expressed the hope that the message of the scroll would bring repentance (vv. 3, 7), but instead it has brought a determination to get rid of that divine word instead.

---

85. The name "Jerahmeel" is also known to us from a clay bulla from this time period that was found with the inscription "belonging to Jerahmeel, son of the king."

36:29 It is unlikely that Jeremiah is personally and directly to confront Jehoiakim with his brazen act of burning the scroll and failing to respond in repentance (v. 29), but he is to get that same word from God by some means. This king is still asking the prophet: "How could you prophesy such things?" (v. 29). How can Jeremiah predict that the king of Babylon will come and destroy Judah, its men, and its animals (v. 29c)?

36:30–31 The judgment of God will fall on the king, his descendants, and his officials (v. 31). This shows that those in authority are held by God to be just as accountable for their actions as the king. Yahweh's announcement of judgment is first of all that none of his offspring will occupy the throne of David (v. 30b). Jehoiachin does rule, but it is only for three months (22:30), after which he is taken into captivity in Babylon and never returned. He is followed by his Uncle Zedekiah, who also ends up in Babylon. A second judgment is that Jehoiakim will not receive a proper burial; his corpse will be left exposed to the heat of the day and the frost by night. 2 Kings 24:5–6 seems to suggest that he might have at first received a proper burial, but nothing of the events surrounding his death actually appear in the text. The historian Josephus[86] adds that after Jerusalem was captured in 597 BC, Jehoiakim's corpse was exhumed and exposed to the elements as a reprisal for his rebellion.[87]

36:32 Jeremiah and Baruch go to work on another scroll and write on it all that was on the scroll the king burned in the fire, along with many other words added to it (v. 32). As Jeremiah was promised in his call from Yahweh, "They will fight against you, but they will not overcome you" (1:19). Nor will anyone be able to overcome the word of God, whether by fire, murder, or rebellion! God's word will endure and triumph.

It is difficult for Jeremiah to learn that a good part of his life's work has just gone up in smoke as the obstreperous king Jehoiakim decides to dispose of all his hard work with the stroke of his penknife. It dismisses as plainly as one could all of Jeremiah's efforts of recalling all God had told him in the past and Baruch's hard work of putting it down in writing. Who

---

86. *Ant.* 10.6.3.

87. This has not been confirmed by external sources.

does Jehoiakim think he is? Has he forgotten it was God who placed him in the position in which he now sits?

For many in our own day, leaders in the executive, judiciary, and legislative branches of the American government have all too often forgotten that it was God who raised them up and allowed them to lead those under them, only to see so many in recent years speak or act as if God is now dead and they are the proper survivors! But God is still watching!

THE SIEGE, FALL, AND AFTERMATH IN JERUSALEM (37:1–45:5)

Eighteen years have elapsed between the events recorded in chapter 36 and what follows in chapters 37–45. In this long prose section (only 38:22b is in poetry), the final days of Jeremiah are recorded before Jerusalem falls, along with the events that came about as a result of that fall.[1] The great words of hope featured so prominently in chapters 30–33 now fall into the background as judgment becomes the dominant theme. Some would like to entitle this section as the "Baruch narrative," but the prophet Jeremiah is very much part of the narrative as well, even though he is not mentioned at all in 39:1–10; 40:7–41:15. The material is generally arranged in a chronological order, with chapter 45 devoted entirely to Baruch's own jeremiad about serving as the prophet's secretary only to see his life's work go up in smoke while his brother serves as an officer in the government. Chapters 37–39 treat events that lead up to the fall of Jerusalem.

---

1. For a literary analysis of chapters 37–45 see T. M. Willis, "'They Did Not Listen to the Voice of Yahweh': A Literary Analysis of Jeremiah 37–45," *ResQ* 42 (2000): 65–84.

THE CHARGE AGAINST A DESERTING
PROPHET PUT IN A PIT (37:1-21)

TRANSLATION

1 Zedekiah son of Josiah was made king[2] by Nebuchadnezzar king of Babylon. He reigned in place of Coniah [Jehoiachin] son of[3] Jehoiakim. **2** Neither he, his attendants, nor the people of the land paid any attention to the words of Yahweh spoken through Jeremiah the prophet. **3** King Zedekiah sent Jehucal, son of Shelemiah, and Zephaniah, son of Maaseiah, the priest, unto Jeremiah the prophet, saying: "Please pray to Yahweh our God for us." **4** Now Jeremiah moved[4] freely among the people,[5] for they had not yet put him in prison. **5** Pharaoh's army had marched out of Egypt, and when the Chaldeans, who were besieging Jerusalem[6] heard the report about them, they withdrew from Jerusalem.

6 Then the word of Yahweh came to Jeremiah the prophet, saying: **7** "This is what Yahweh, the God of Israel, has said, 'Tell the king of Judah, who sent you[7] to inquire of me,[8] "Look out! Pharaoh's army, which has marched out to support you, will go back to its own land, to Egypt."' **8** The Chaldeans will return and attack this city; they will take it and burn it down. **9** This is what Yahweh has said: 'Do not deceive yourselves, thinking, the Chaldeans will completely leave us, for they will not! **10** Even if[9] you were to defeat the entire Chaldean army that is attacking you and only wounded men were left in their tents,[10] they would get up and put this city to the torch.'"

11 Now when the Chaldean army had withdrawn from Jerusalem at the approach of Pharaoh's army, **12** Jeremiah started to leave the city to go

---

2. The word מֶלֶךְ, "king," is absent in the LXX.

3. The phrase כָּנְיָהוּ בֶּן־, "Coniah son of," is absent in the LXX.

4. Some mss (and the LXX) read וַיֵּצֵא, "and he went out," whereas the MT reads יֹצֵא וּ, "and he was going out."

5. The LXX has τῆς πόλεως, "the city," where the MT has הָעָם, "the people."

6. The phrase הַצָּרִים עַל־יְרוּשָׁלַם, "who were besieging Jerusalem," is absent in the LXX.

7. The LXX has the 2 sg. ἐρεῖς, "you will say," where the MT has the 2 pl. תֹאמְרוּ, "you will say."

8. The LXX has πρὸς σέ, "to you," where the MT has אֶתְכֶם אֵלַי, "you to … me."

9. The LXX has καὶ ἐάν, "and if," where the MT has כִּי אִם, "even if."

10. The LXX has ἐν τῷ τόπῳ αὐτοῦ, "in his place," where the MT has בְּאָהֳלוֹ, "in his tent."

to the land[11] of Benjamin to receive his share of the property among the people there.[12] **13** But when he reached the Benjamite Gate, the captain of the guard, whose name was Irijah,[13] son of Shelemiah, son of Hananiah, arrested him, saying, "You are defecting to the Chaldeans." **14** Jeremiah replied, "It's a lie! I am not deserting to the Chaldeans." But Irijah[14] would not listen to him. He arrested Jeremiah and brought him to the officials. **15** The princes, enraged at Jeremiah, had him beaten[15] and imprisoned[16] in the house of Jonathan, the secretary of state, for they had made that [place] into a prison.[17] **16** Jeremiah was, indeed,[18] put in one of the vaults[19] in [that] prison house, and Jeremiah was left there for some time.

17 Then King Zedekiah sent for him and had him brought[20] to the palace, where he questioned him secretly, "Is there any word from Yahweh?" Jeremiah replied, "There is! You will be handed over to the king of Babylon." **18** Then Jeremiah said to King Zedekiah, "What sin have I committed against you or your servants or your people, that you have put[21] me in prison? **19** Where[22] are your prophets who prophesied to you saying, 'The king of Babylon will not attack you or this land'? **20** But now, please listen to me, my lord the king. Do not send me back to the house of Jonathan the

---

11. Ms evidence from the Cairo Geniza shows לְאֶרֶץ, "to the land," and a few Heb. mss have אֶל־אֶרֶץ, "unto the land," where the MT has אֶרֶץ, "land."

12. The phrase לַחֲלִק מִשָּׁם, "to receive his share of the property ... there," has various representations in the versions. LXX has τοῦ ἀγοράσαι ἐκεῖθεν, "to buy there"; LXX[26] has τοῦ παροικεῖσαι ἐκεῖθεν, "to dwell there"; LXX[239] has τοῦ ἀποδρᾶσαι ἐκεῖθεν, "to flee there"; α´ and θ´ have τοῦ μερισθῆναι ἐκεῖ(θεν), "to be divided there"; σ´ has μερισασθαι ἐκεῖθεν, "to divide there"; the Vg. (with the Syr. and Tg.) reads et divideret ibi possessionem, "and share the portion there."

13. The LXX has ἄνθρωπος παρ᾽ ᾧ κατέλυεν Σαρουιας, "a man with whom he lodged Saruia," where the MT has בַּעַל פְּקִדֻת וּשְׁמוֹ יִרְאִיָּה, "the captain of the guard, whose name was Irijah." The Syr. has nrj', "Neriah," where the MT has יִרְאִיָּה, "Irijah."

14. The LXX has יְרִאִיָּה, "Saruia," and the Syr. has nrj', "Neriah," as in 13.a-a, 13.b.

15. The sebir suggests emending to the hiphil impf. וַיַּכּוּ, "and they beat," where the MT has the hiphil pf. וְהִכֻּהוּ, "and they beat."

16. The sebir suggests emending to the qal impf. וַיִּתְּנֻ, "and they put," where the MT has the qal pf. וְנָתְנֻ, "and they put."

17. The phrase בֵּית הָאֵסוּר, "prison," is absent in the LXX.

18. The LXX has καὶ ἦλθεν, "and he came," where the MT has כִּי בָא, "indeed he went."

19. The LXX has χερεθ, "Chereth," and LXX[o] has ανιωθ, "Anioth," where the MT has הַחֲנֻיּוֹת, "the cells."

20. The LXX has καὶ ἐκάλεσεν αὐτόν, "and he called him," where the MT has וַיִּקָּחֵהוּ, "and he received him."

21. The LXX has the sg. σὺ δίδως, "you put," where the MT has the pl. נְתַתֶּם, "you put."

22. The **Kethiv** has וְאַיּוֹ, "and where is he (?)," and the **Qere** has וְאַיֵּה, "and where."

secretary, or I will die there." **21** So King Zedekiah gave orders for Jeremiah to be placed in the court of the guard and given a loaf of bread daily from the street of the bakers until the bread in the city was gone. So Jeremiah remained in the court of the guard.

COMMENTARY

A Delegation from King Zedekiah (37:1–5)

37:1 The chapter begins with a notice of a change in the royal succession. Nebuchadnezzar has deposed "Coniah" (an abbreviated form for "Jehoiachin") after a three-month reign, and in his place he has installed Zedekiah, Jehoiachin's uncle (v. 1). Second Chronicles 36:10 refers to Zedekiah as Jehoiachin's "brother" (אח). There is no disparity between these two books, though, since this term is frequently used in Scripture in a much wider sense of a "kinsman." Zedekiah is twenty-one years of age when he is appointed king, but many within the land of Judah still regard Jehoiachin as the real king, whom they hope will soon be reinstated as the actual king after he is hopefully released from Babylon. But Zedekiah's troubles go beyond that, for there seems to be a strong pro-Egyptian party among his advisers who urge Zedekiah to revolt against the Babylonian vassal treaty imposed on Zedekiah by Nebuchadnezzar. Zedekiah had taken an oath of allegiance to this Babylonian overlord in the name of Yahweh (2 Chr 36:13), which means that any breach of this treaty is not only a revolt against this foreign power but also a breach of his oath before Yahweh.

37:2 Poor Zedekiah, he is torn and pulled in every direction. But rather than this political action giving him the opportunity to show the strength he finds in Yahweh, it only reveals some obvious character flaws. He shows that he was a weak man who vacillates terribly—over almost every decision he has to make. The only area in which he shows any decisiveness is in his refusal to listen to the word of God; he and his officials are united in their strong opposition to God's revelation through God's prophet Jeremiah.

Surprisingly enough, however, Zedekiah just cannot get away from what Jeremiah says, even though he refuses to act on any of the prophet's invitations. He acts like one who inwardly half-believes what this prophet says, yet he never can quite bring himself to the point of acting on those truths. Is he afraid to act because of the pressure of his cabinet? Or is he such a double-minded person that it would not matter who, or what, is being taught; he just cannot make up his mind which way to go on anything.

37:3 It is for this reason that he sends yet again another delegation (21:1) to the prophet to ask him to "Please pray to Yahweh [their] God for [them]" (v. 3), for this is the second time he has made such a request. Included in this delegation are two of the king's officials: Jehucal, who elsewhere shows signs of hostility to the prophet (38:1), and Zephaniah, the priest, who tends to be more receptive to the prophet. Perhaps Zedekiah is hoping for the same kind of miraculous deliverance that came during Hezekiah's reign in 701 BC, when the Assyrian siege against Jerusalem was suddenly and dramatically lifted as 185,000 of the enemy's army died in one night (2 Kgs 19:37). The only difference is that Zedekiah is hopeful that Yahweh will endorse policies of his government officials (Mackay, 2:337) instead of having a willingness to listen to God's call for repentance.

37:4-5 In the meantime, Jeremiah moves freely among the people, "for he had not yet been put in prison" (v. 4).[23] But it is also during this time that the recently installed Pharaoh Hophra (589-570 BC) moves his troops out of Egypt and is now coming into Israel, presumably at the request of the pro-Egyptian party in Zedekiah's government. Indeed, Zedekiah had already rebelled against Babylon in 589 BC in a new alliance with Egypt. Some point to a Lachish Ostracon II that seems to indicate that the Judean army officers sent to Egypt for military assistance, apparently based on this alliance. This military move is enough to make the Babylonians lift the siege they had put on Jerusalem, but this is short-lived, for the Egyptians refuse to engage the Babylonians, and so the siege recommences in rather short order.

---

23. Even though the word pair "to go out and to come in" is used sometimes in a military and/or political sense, here it just means "to cross the threshold of a city gate." Van Lingen erroneously concludes that Jer 37:4 is postexilic. See A. van Lingen, "*BWʾ-YṢʾ* ("To Go Out and to Come In") as a Military Term," *VT* 42 (1992): 59–66.

The Babylonians Continue the Siege (37:6-10)

37:6-8 One can only imagine the euphoria and unbridled joy that comes to Jerusalem over the lifting of the Babylonian siege (v. 5). However, Yahweh gives a response for Jeremiah to give to the two emissaries who formed the royal delegation to inquire of the prophet what they can expect for the city in the future. The prophet gives this word, which they are to transmit to Zedekiah: "Pharaoh's army ... will go back to its own land, to Egypt" (v. 7).[24] Moreover, the Babylonians will return and recommence their siege. They will attack this city, take it over, and burn it down (v. 8). This judgment must ring in the people's ears with a bit of poetic justice, for their previous king, Jehoiakim, had burned the scroll in the fire (36:25-32), so Nebuchadnezzar accordingly will burn the city of Jerusalem in the fire as well (37:8, 10; 38:17-18, 23).

37:9 Things are serious by now. The people and its leaders must stop deceiving themselves (v. 9). The popular thought of the day that the Babylonians are surely going to leave Judah alone and go home is not at all true. It is Yahweh's firm decree that judgment must come, for there has not even been a hint of any repentance. The judgment against this nation is sealed.

37:10 What is more, Yahweh adds in v. 10, "Even if you were to defeat the entire Chaldean army that is attacking you and only wounded [Babylonian army] men were left in their tents, they would get up and put this city to the torch." That is one strong affirmation, but it surely makes its point that there is to be no way out of the predicament that Judah has dug itself into. There is no use in seeking help from some outside source or hoping for some type of miraculous intervention: the scene is set, and it is set for destruction. That is that!

---

24. Thelle argues that Jeremiah 37 (along with Jeremiah 21) "demonstrates the important prophetic functions of *both* consulting the deity in a situation of distress and delivering the divine response." See R. I. Thelle, "דרש את־יהוה: The Prophetic Act of Consulting YHWH in Jeremiah 21,2 and 37,7," *SJOT* 12 (1998): 249-56.

Jeremiah Accused of Defecting to the Enemy (37:11–19)

37:11-13 The siege is lifted for approximately three months (ca. January–March 587 BC). Perhaps a number of Judeans use this time period to abandon the city of Jerusalem, for why should anyone stay there if the Babylonians will return? Jeremiah also takes this opportunity to travel the short two or three miles north to Anathoth to investigate the property that will come up later on in 32:7 (v. 12), but when he gets to the Benjamite Gate he is stopped by a captain of the guard named Irijah. He is then charged with trying to desert to the Babylonians and is arrested on this charge (v. 13). What makes Irijah's case for Jeremiah's alleged desertion seem most probable is that he has been urging the people to submit to the enemy (21:8–10; 38:2), which a number have already done (38:19; 52:15). His actions are, in the view of the government, destroying the morale and strength of resistance among the people.

37:14-16 Despite what seems to be an open-and-shut case, Jeremiah tries to deny that this is what he intends to do (v. 14). It is a "lie," Jeremiah asserts, to charge him with such motivations, but it does no good; Irijah will not listen to him. He arrests Jeremiah and brings him to the officials (v. 14b). The officials do not believe Jeremiah either; instead, the whole affair angers them (v. 15); there will be no prophetic immunity for this prophet. As a consequence, they have the prophet beaten and imprisoned in the house of Jonathan, the secretary of state, whose house they subsequently convert into a prison (v. 15b). In a dungeon-like section of the house, Jeremiah is thrown, and he remains there for a long time (v. 16).

Jeremiah's Imprisonment (37:17–21)

The Babylonian army returns to reestablish their siege on Jerusalem. Meanwhile, Jeremiah remains incarcerated after he has been beaten and deposited in what appeared to be a hewn-out pit, likely out of rock, plastered on its bottom and sides so that it can retain whatever runoff water could be caught from the roofs of the houses or from the groundwater running off the land in the rainy season.

37:17 Zedekiah, once more showing how torn he is internally, sends for Jeremiah to come to him privately, where he secretly questions him as to whether there is a word from Yahweh (v. 17). This may signal that things have steadily grown worse in the city and Zedekiah is at a loss as to which way to turn. Jeremiah plainly and directly tells him that "Yes, you [Zedekiah] will be turned over to the king of Babylon" (v. 17b). There is no beating around the bush; the prophet says what God said in terse and emphatic terms! Given that nothing has changed in Zedekiah's response to God, nothing has changed in God's response either!

37:18–19 Since the prophet has the attention and ear of the king, he takes the opportunity to ask why he is being held as he is (v. 18). Where has he erred, sinned, or been wrong in what he said? Anyway, where are the king's favorite prophets, who were so sure that the king of Babylon would not attack Judah (v. 19)? Shouldn't they be held responsible for their false prophecies? Since Zedekiah is responsible for all that has gone on in his realm, what is his explanation for the way Jeremiah has been treated? Surely it would be more logical to put those false prophets in jail than the one who predicted what was right about God's word and the future?

37:20–21 Jeremiah makes the plea: "Do not send me back to the house of Jonathan the secretary, or I will die there" (v. 20). Zedekiah softens a little in his attitude toward Jeremiah, for he commands that he be placed in the courtyard of the guard and given bread from the Baker's Street as long as the supply lasts (v. 21). That in itself is enough to let us know that the conditions of the siege have worsened and intensified to the point where it will not be long before they will run out of all food. In fact, the round, flat loaves of bread did run out on the day the city wall was breached (52:6).

Not only is King Zedekiah double-minded, but he tries to play both sides of the debate by asking Jeremiah privately whether there is any word from Yahweh. Why does he want to know, especially since he never responds to a word from God anyway?

Jeremiah gives him God's answer plain and simple: "You will be handed over to the king of Babylon." That apparently is not the answer the king was hoping for. But it does bring up the point: How many times, when God's word puts us on the hot seat like this, do we fudge and beat around the bush when God has spoken clearly? Our fearfulness does not bring about a careful presentation of the word of God to a hungry and needy generation.

JEREMIAH RESCUED FROM THE
MUDDY CISTERN (38:1–28A)

Because the events of chapter 38 are so similar to those of chapter 37, it could be a doublet, in which the same events are told in two different [often contradictory] ways. But there is no need for this suggestion, for Jeremiah experiences enough such rough situations that he could probably have filled a few more chapters. Moreover, chapter 37 includes an arrest, which is missing from chapter 38, and in chapter 37 he himself was able to negotiate with the king better confinement conditions, whereas in chapter 38 it is Ebed-Melech who effects Jeremiah's release.

TRANSLATION

1 Shephatiah son of Mattan, Gedaliah son of Pashhur, Jehucal son of Shelemiah, and Pashhur son of Malkijah[25] heard the things Jeremiah had been saying to the people, including, **2** "This is what Yahweh has said, 'Whoever stays in this city will die by the sword, famine, or plague, but whoever goes over to the Chaldeans will live. He will escape with his life; he will live. **3** This is what Yahweh has said: "This city will certainly be handed over to the army of the king of Babylon, who will capture it."'" **4** Then the officials said to the king, "This man should be put to death inasmuch as he is weakening the morale[26] of the soldiers who were left in this city, as well as of all the people, by saying such things to them. Indeed, this dude does not desire the welfare of this people, but their harm." **5** The King Zedekiah answered, "All right, he is in your hands; the king can do nothing to oppose you."[27] **6** So they took Jeremiah[28] and cast him into the cistern of Malkijah, the son of the king, lowering Jeremiah by ropes[29] into the cistern. It had no water in it, but only mud, and Jeremiah sank[30] down in the mud. **7** But Ebed-Melech, an Ethiopian, a eunuch/official[31] in the royal palace, heard that they had put Jeremiah in the cistern. While the king was sitting in

---

25. The phrase וּפַשְׁחוּר בֶּן־מַלְכִּיָּה, "and Pashhur, son of Malkijah," is absent in the LXX.
26. Lit. "hands."
27. The LXX has "to them" where the MT has אֶתְכֶם דָּבָר, "a thing against you."
28. The phrase וַיִּקְחוּ אֶת־יִרְמְיָהוּ, "so they took Jeremiah," is absent in the LXX.
29. The word בַּחֲבָלִים, "by ropes," is absent in the LXX.
30. The LXX has καὶ ἦν, "and he was," where the MT has וַיִּטְבַּע, "he sank."
31. The phrase אִישׁ סָרִיס, "eunuch/official," is absent in the LXX.

the Benjamite Gate, **8** Ebed-Melech went out of the palace and spoke to the king as follows: **9** "My lord, the king,[32] these men have acted wickedly in all that they have done to Jeremiah the prophet. They have thrown him into a cistern where he will starve to death[33] when there is no longer any bread in the city." **10** Then the king ordered Ebed-Melech the Ethiopian, "Take thirty men from here with you and lift Jeremiah the prophet out of the cistern before he dies." **11** So Ebed-Melech took the men with him and went to the palace, to the room under the treasury. He took from there some old rags,[34] worn-out clothes, and he let them down with ropes[35] to Jeremiah in the cistern. **12** And Ebed-Melech the Ethiopian said to Jeremiah, "Put these old rags and worn-out clothes under your armpits[36] as protection against the ropes." And Jeremiah did so. **13** Then they pulled him up with the ropes and lifted him out of the cistern. And Jeremiah remained in the courtyard of the guard.

14 Then King Zedekiah sent for Jeremiah the prophet[37] and had him brought to the third entrance of the temple of Yahweh. And the king said to Jeremiah, "I am going to ask you something. Do not hide anything from me." **15** Jeremiah said to Zedekiah, "If I were to tell you, would you not simply execute me? And if I were to advise you, you would not listen to me." **16** But King Zedekiah swore to Jeremiah in secret,[38] "As Yahweh lives, who[39] has given us breath, I will neither kill you nor hand you over to those seeking your life."[40] **17** Then Jeremiah said to Zedekiah, "This is what

---

32. The phrase אֲדֹנִי הַמֶּלֶךְ, "my lord, the king," is absent in the LXX.

33. The LXX has ἐπονηρεύσω ἃ ἐποίησας τοῦ ἀποκτεῖναι τὸν ἄνθρωπον τοῦτον, "you have acted wickedly in what you have done to kill this man," where the MT has הֵרֵעוּ הָאֲנָשִׁים הָאֵלֶּה אֵת כָּל־אֲשֶׁר עָשׂוּ לְיִרְמְיָהוּ הַנָּבִיא אֵת אֲשֶׁר־הִשְׁלִיכוּ אֶל־הַבּוֹר וַיָּמָת תַּחְתָּיו, "these men have acted wickedly in all that they have done to Jeremiah the prophet. They have thrown him into a cistern where he will starve to death."

34. The word בְּלוֹי, "rags," is absent in the LXX.

35. The word בַּחֲבָלִים, "with ropes," is absent in the LXX.

36. The LXX has ταῦτα θὲς ὑποκάτω τῶν σχοινίων, "put these under the ropes," where the MT has עֶבֶד־מֶלֶךְ הַכּוּשִׁי אֶל־יִרְמְיָהוּ שִׂים נָא בְּלוֹאֵי הַסְּחָבוֹת וְהַמְּלָחִים תַּחַת אַצִּלוֹת יָדֶיךָ, "Ebed-Melech the Ethiopian ... to Jeremiah, 'Put these old rags and worn-out clothes under your armpits.'"

37. The LXX has καὶ ἐκάλεσεν αὐτόν, "and he called him," where the MT has וַיִּקַּח אֶת־יִרְמְיָהוּ הַנָּבִיא, "and he brought Jeremiah the prophet."

38. The word בַּסֵּתֶר, "in secret," is absent in the LXX.

39. The **Qere** and many Heb. mss and versions lack the sign of the acc., אֵת.

40. The phrase אֲשֶׁר מְבַקְשִׁים אֶת־נַפְשֶׁךָ, "those seeking your life," is absent in the LXX.

Yahweh, God[41] of Hosts, the God of Israel, has said: 'If you will surrender/go out to the officers of the king of Babylon, your life will be spared, and this city will not be burned down with fire; you and your family will live. **18** But if you will not surrender/give up to the officers[42] of the king of Babylon, this city will be handed over to the Chaldeans and they will burn it down with fire; you yourself will not escape from their hands.'"[43] **19** But King Zedekiah said to Jeremiah, "I am afraid of the Jews who have deserted to the Chaldeans, lest I be handed over to them and they deal with me roughly." **20** Jeremiah answered, "They will not hand you over. Obey, I beg you, the voice of Yahweh in what I am telling you. It will be well with you and your life will be spared. **21** But if you refuse to surrender, this is the word/vision that Yahweh has let me see: **22** All the women left in the palace of the king of Judah will be brought out to the officials of the king of Babylon—the women[44] are saying:

> "They misled you and overcame you,
>> Those good friends of yours;
> Now your feet are sunk in mire,
>> They have left you and are gone!

23 "All[45] your wives and your children will be brought out to the Chaldeans, and you yourself will not escape from their clutches, but will be captured by the king of Babylon, and this city will be burned[46] down with fire."[47] **24** The Zedekiah said to Jeremiah, "Do not let anyone know about this conversation and you will not die. **25** And if the officials hear that I have spoken with you, and should come to you and say to you, 'Tell us, now, what you said to the king, and what the king said to you.[48] Do not

---

41. Cairo Geniza evidence lacks אֱלֹהֵי, "God."

42. Cairo Geniza evidence lacks שָׂרֵי, "officers."

43. The word מִיָּדָם, "from their hand," is absent in the LXX.

44. Lit. "they" (fem. sg.).

45. The word כָּל־, "all," is absent in the LXX.

46. A few Heb. mss and the LXX read the pass. תִּשָּׂרֵף, "it will be burned," where the MT has תִּשְׂרֹף, "it will burn."

47. The word בָּאֵשׁ, "with fire," is absent in the LXX.

48. The LXX reverses the order of the questions: מַה־דִּבַּרְתָּ אֶל־הַמֶּלֶךְ, "what did you say to the king?" and וּמַה־דִּבֶּר אֵלֶיךָ הַמֶּלֶךְ, "what did the king say to you?" The Syr. matches the order

hide it from us, or we will kill you,' **26** Then say to them, 'I was pleading with the king not to send me back to Jonathan's house to die there.'" **27** All the officials did come to Jeremiah and questioned him, but he told them exactly what the king had ordered[49] him to say. So they said no more to him, for no one had heard what had been said.[50] **28** And Jeremiah remained in the courtyard of the guard until the day Jerusalem was captured.

COMMENTARY

Jeremiah Is Cast into a Cistern (38:1–13)

38:1 It is assumed that since Jeremiah is still in the courtyard of the guard that this story takes up chronologically where 37:21 left off. Jeremiah, however, still seems to be able to get his message out to the people, for that is what the delegation in v. 1 reports. Some argue that the prophet was not able to speak to the people directly, so they translate the verb in v. 1 as a pluperfect: "had heard" Jeremiah say. But this fails to notice the presence of "all the Jews sitting in the courtyard of the guard" (32:12); his incarceration may not be as inhibiting as it might at first seem. Surely Jeremiah is no longer giving public sermons as he once had, yet the message is somehow still being made known to a public that must at least remain very curious, if not a bit anxious about the real truth about what is to take place given the presence of Nebuchadnezzar's army in the land. Jeremiah's presence in the courtyard of the guard gives plenty of notice to the officials in the government that the consequences for not obeying the call to repent and turn from their wicked ways are very real and imminent; the city lies in the path of certain destruction.

Of the four men mentioned in v. 1, Shaphatiah and Gedaliah are not known to us from other texts, but Jehucal and Pashhur are (37:3; 21:1). These men seem to be part of the pro-Egyptian party in Judah, which is no doubt tearing Zedekiah's cabinet apart in its conflicting advice.

---

in the MT.

49. Some Heb. mss, the LXX, Syr., Tg.[Ed], and Vg. read וּצִוּהוּ, "they ordered," instead of צִוָּה, "he ordered."

50. The LXX has λόγος κυρίου, "the word of the Lord," where the MT has הַדָּבָר, "the word."

38:2–3 The message of Jeremiah in vv. 2–3 and following includes nothing that is new. Moreover, given what has already taken place in Judah, based on Jeremiah's words, there ought to be no doubt left about the truthfulness of what Jeremiah is predicting. Whoever stays in the city, instead of deserting to the Babylonians, will face sword, famine, or plague; but if they desert the city and surrender to the Babylonians, they will escape and have their lives as their booty (v. 2b).

38:4 This is all the officials can take; in their estimation Jeremiah deserves the death penalty. He is a first-class traitor, guilty of treason, and a promoter of internal strife (v. 4)—a Babylonian sympathizer. However, Jeremiah's message is not born out of a personal vendetta against anyone or anything in the Judean government; it is not because he lacks any patriotism, nor does he fear for his own safety. He is first and last a spokesperson for Yahweh. He also wants his own people to respond to the call of God and to repent, for that is the only way they can get out of the circumstances they now are in. But the officials see him as "weakening the morale of the soldiers who were left in this city" (v. 4b)—he is destroying the morale of the people. This same charge is found in one of the Lachish Ostraca, Ostracon VI.[51] Since the prophet is unnamed in the ostracon, it is impossible to say for sure, but it well could be a reference to Jeremiah. Jeremiah spent forty years of his life trying to promote the welfare of the nation and the city (v. 4b). But the leaders who oppose him are leading the country into a situation where the capital city will be burned to the ground (v. 17c).

38:5 Zedekiah acquiesces to the demands of his officials; given their demands along with a charge of treason against the prophet, it seems as if his hands are tied. But it is clear that they have the upper hand in that government; they are the strong ones, and he obviously is the weak one. And they know it too! This is a remarkable reversal for one who claims to be king.

38:6 As a result, Jeremiah's four opponents seize him and cast him down by means of ropes into a waterless pit, a muddy cistern belonging to Malchiah,

---

51. *ANET*, 293.

the royal prince (v. 6).[52] This cistern, if it was similar to others, was carved out of limestone bedrock and formed into the shape of a pitcher. It silences the prophet, preventing him from getting his words out into the public hearing. Thus, Jeremiah sinks into the mud, without food or water, and is left to experience a slow death. His situation is about as dire and nasty as anything that his opponents could think up for him, short of death itself.

38:7-9 It is most ironical that an Ethiopian official in the royal palace has more trust in God's word given by Jeremiah than the king, his officers, and the people, who have so often seen the hand of God operating for them in the past and thus have an even greater reason for trusting in God (vv. 7-8). But here is one courageous man; he sees something that he counts as wrong and acts on it without any further advice or consultation. When he hears that Jeremiah was cast into a cistern, he immediately goes to the Benjamite Gate, where he knows the king will be sitting, adjudicating cases of mis-carriage of justice from among his people. Amazingly, however, the king himself is guilty of a massive miscarriage of justice, so why didn't he clean up his own mess with Jeremiah before going to straighten out other rup-tures of justice found elsewhere in his kingdom?

38:10 The king gives Ebed-melech immediate authority to correct the sit-uation by taking with him a force of "thirty men" (v. 10). Does the king expect resistance from those who threw Jeremiah in the pit? It is not clear. Some complain that "thirty men" would have attracted too much attention, so REV, NRSV read (with only one Heb. ms) "three men." Of course, not all thirty men are needed to pull Jeremiah out of the cistern, but if there is any trouble, they will indeed be needed.

38:11-13 Ebed-melech goes to the "room under the treasury," where he knows there are some old rags and worn-out clothes that he can have Jeremiah place in his armpits so the rope will not bruise his skin as they pull him out (v. 11). These they used to extricate Jeremiah from his terrible confinement (vv. 12-13).

---

52. See this same title of "the king's son" in 36:26, where it means one who has an official position, not necessarily a familial relationship.

The Final Interview with Zedekiah (38:14–28a)

38:14 The location of this third entrance to the temple of Yahweh is unknown, but if this is the same covered walkway used exclusively by royalty from the palace to the temple as mentioned in 2 Kgs 16:18, then it provides a secure place for Zedekiah to talk to Jeremiah. Everything the king did has to be done in a clandestine fashion, for no trust is left between anyone. It is a court filled with intrigue and one divided with opinions on what course of action they should follow, for the king is decidedly unable to make up his mind on any course of action (vv. 24–27).

The king has a question, which he apparently never gets around to asking specifically, for we never hear what that question is. But the king insists on having a straight answer from the prophet, with nothing held back in secret (v. 14). It is not hard to guess, however, what is on the king's mind: he wants to know from Jeremiah what is going to happen. What does Yahweh think of Judah? How will the siege end? Will the city be destroyed? What will happen to Zedekiah and his family? Why would the king want to hear the answers to these questions, if that is what is on the king's mind? Has he not heard what Jeremiah has been saying for forty years? Nothing has changed in God's plan!

38:15–16 First, however, Jeremiah wants some assurances, for if he repeats what God has said, will not the king and his cabinet charge him once again with treason and sapping the people of their morale (v. 15)? Zedekiah takes a secret oath that he will neither kill Jeremiah, nor will he hand him over to his detractors (v. 16). It is interesting that Zedekiah gives Jeremiah the very same assurances that he refused from God. If Jeremiah can trust the human word of the king, why can the king not trust a divine word from God?

38:17–18 Jeremiah draws a clear picture as to what is going to happen: God promises that if Zedekiah surrenders to the officers of Nebuchadnezzar, his life will be spared and those of his family (v. 17). This is the firm promise of God. But if he persists in resisting the Babylonians and declines to surrender to them, then Zedekiah will be handed over to the enemy, and Jerusalem will be taken and burnt to the ground with fire (v. 18).

38:19 Zedekiah hesitates still, despite the firm promise of the God of Israel (v. 19), for he fearfully worries that the Jews who have already gone over to the Babylonians will be given authority to take out their frustration on their former king, and they will deal harshly with him (v. 19b). He must worry about those who come from the leading circles in Jerusalem who had fled after their pro-Egyptian advice had been rejected. They will just plain take it out on me, Zedekiah incorrectly reasons.

38:20 Jeremiah assured him that that alternative is out of the question, for it will not happen, according to the promise of God (v. 20).[53] The one thing needed from Zedekiah is his obedience to Yahweh. If he will trust and obey, things will go well for him, and his life will be spared (v. 20b). But Zedekiah is too much of a realist to trust the promise of God, so he rejects the counsel of the prophet and takes his own course of action, which is to do nothing, just let things run their course.

38:21-23 Given that the king is refusing to surrender, as he is divinely advised, here is what he can expect: the women who are the king's wives will be left for his successor; in this case they will be handed over to the Babylonian officials (v. 22). Accordingly, the women will lament in a *qinah* meter poem, which has a 3:2 beat, leaving an empty or hollow, open-ended blank, or missing word, at the end of each line. Their wretched fortune of these wives is to set forth a taunting derision about Zedekiah's indecisiveness (v. 22c). The first line of their song is taken from Obad 7. In singsong fashion, they mockingly give their condolences to Zedekiah. This king has allowed himself to be tricked by his "trusted friends," so-called men of peace (שְׁלוֹם), but they end up deserting him with his feet stuck in the mud. Now, instead of the prophet's feet being stuck in the mud of the cistern, it is Zedekiah's turn, without an Ebed-Melech to rescue him. The outcome is now set for sure. How close this discussion is to the end of the siege is not known, but it cannot be very many days or weeks off (v. 23).

---

53. Ginsbury concludes that the ptc. דֹּבֵר is used "in the context of revelation to refer to God or do Divine messengers (angels) who through their communications are in constant contact with men." See P. N. Ginsbury, "*DOVÉR and M'DABER*," JBQ 33 (2005): 40–46.

38:24-28a This is not the message Zedekiah was hoping for. However, before this conversation ends, the king has to get a pledge from Jeremiah that he will not disclose what transpired between them (v. 24). If the pro-Egyptian party finds out what was said, the king will be helpless to protect Jeremiah's life; they will bring further charges against him. Zedekiah's suspicions are not far from being wrong, for that is exactly what the officials do (vv. 25-26). Jeremiah is to answer them that he was pleading with the king not to send him back to Jonathan's house, where he had been before (v. 26), which is the language of his earlier plea (37:20). At least the king is smart enough to realize how his courtiers will react and what moves they will make (v. 27). Satisfied, the officials leave and say no more about the matter. Jeremiah remains in the courtyard of the guard until the very day the city is breached and the Babylonians capture it as Jeremiah has been predicting. However, there is little joy in the prophet being correct, for now he and the people must suffer the loss of everything except their God.

The only way God can change what he has said is if men and women change and repent before him. But when mortals stick to their guns and refuse to budge in any kind of repentance, failing to follow the model of the Ninevites in the prophet Jonah's day, then the judgment of God will surely follow, for Judah and for any other nation, just as certainly as night follows day.

A BRIEF ACCOUNT OF THE FALL
OF JERUSALEM (38:28B-39:18)

The climactic point in the book of Jeremiah has now been reached in chapter 39. This brief narrative concisely records the fall of Jerusalem (39:1-10), the prophet Jeremiah's release from his confinement (vv. 11-14), and a promise to Ebed-Melech (vv. 15-18) for his rescuing Jeremiah from the cistern.

Verses 4-13 are not found in the Septuagint. Moreover, vv. 1-2 and 4-10 are often judged to have been taken from 52:4-16, with v. 3 being the only verse in vv. 1-10 that has no parallel in 52:4-16. Also see 2 Kgs 25:1-12. But many of these so-called instances of textual corruption have to do with the way transitional material and incidental information is presented in cultures other than our own. As J. A. Thompson observes:

Part of the problem for modern commentators is that they do not always understand the methods of the ancient compilers, who had their own ways of handling parentheses, of adding explanatory sentences, and of interrupting the flow of an argument. Some of our attempts to unravel an ancient editor's work would seem quite unnecessary to him. (Thompson, 645)

TRANSLATION

38:28b This is how Jerusalem was taken.[54]

39:1 In the ninth year[55] of Zedekiah king of Judah, in the tenth month,[56] Nebuchadnezzar king of Babylon came against Jerusalem with his whole army and laid siege to it. **2** And on the ninth[57] day of the fourth[58] month of Zedekiah's eleventh year, the city [wall] was breached. **3** Then all the officials of the king of Babylon came and took seats in the Middle Gate: Nergal-Sharezer[59] of Samgar; Nebo-Sarsekim, a chief officer; Nergal-Sharezer, a high official; and all the other officials of the king of Babylon. **4**[60] And when Zedekiah king of Judah and all the soldiers saw them, they fled, leaving[61] the city by night by the way of the king's garden, through the gate between the two walls, and headed towards the Arabah. **5** But the Babylonian army pursued them and overtook Zedekiah in the desert [near] Jericho.[62] They captured him and took him to Nebuchadnezzar king of Babylon at Riblah in the land of Hamath, where he pronounced sentence on him. **6** The king of Babylon executed Zedekiah's sons there in Riblah before his eyes. The

54. A few mss have וַיְהִי, "and it came to be," where the MT has וְהָיָה, "and it was." The phrase is absent in a few mss and Syr. The phrase כַּאֲשֶׁר נִלְכְּדָה יְרוּשָׁלָם, "how Jerusalem was taken," is absent in a few Heb. mss, the LXX, and Syr.

55. LXX[B, S 106.410] have τῷ μηνί, "in the month," where the MT has בַּשָּׁנָה, "in the year."

56. The phrase בַּחֹדֶשׁ הָעֲשִׂרִי, "in the tenth month," is absent in LXX[B, S 106.410].

57. The Vg. has quinta, "fifth," where the MT has בְּתִשְׁעָה, "on the ninth."

58. A few Heb. mss have הַחֲמִישׁ, "the fifth," where the MT has הָרְבִיעִי, "the fourth."

59. Many Heb. mss lack the maqqef and have שראצר, "Sarezer," and some also lack the maqqef and have שראצר, "Sharezer," where the MT has שַׂר־אֶצֶר, "Sar-ezer."

60. The LXX omits vv. 4–13. The editors of BHS suggest the omission is due to homoioteleuton.

61. Some Heb. mss, θ´, Syr., and Vg. read וַיֵּצְאוּ, "and they went out," where the MT has וַיֵּצֵא, "and he went out."

62. A few Heb. mss and Syr. add מעליו נפצו וכל־חילו, "and his whole army was scattered from him," after "Jericho."

king of Babylon also executed all the nobles of Judah. **7** Then he put out Zedekiah's eyes and bound him with bronze shackles to take him to Babylon. **8** The Chaldeans burned down the royal palace and the houses[63] of the people, and they tore down the walls of Jerusalem. **9** Nebuzaradan, captain of the imperial guard, carried into exile at Babylon the rest of the people who remained in the city, along with those who had deserted to him and the rest of the people. **10** But Nebuzaradan the captain of the guard left behind in the land of Judah some of the poor people, who owned nothing; and at that time he gave them vineyards and fields.[64]

11 Now Nebuchadnezzar king of Babylon had given these orders about Jeremiah through[65] Nebuzaradan captain of the imperial guard: **12** "Find him, look after him; don't harm[66] him but[67] do for him whatever he asks." **13** So Nebuzaradan, captain of the guard; Nebushazban, a chief officer; Nergal-Sharezer,[68] a high official; and all the other chiefs of the king of Babylon **14** sent and had Jeremiah taken out of the courtyard of the guard. They turned him over to Gedaliah, son of Ahikam, son of Shaphan, to take him back to his home.[69] So he remained in the midst of his own people.

15 While Jeremiah was confined[70] in the courtyard of the guard, the word of Yahweh came to him, saying, **16** "Go and tell Ebed-Melech the Ethiopian, 'This is what Yahweh of Hosts, the God of Israel says: "Look out! I am going to bring[71] to pass my words against this city for harm, not for good. In that day they will be fulfilled [right] before your eyes.[72] **17** But I will rescue you in that day, declares Yahweh; you will not be handed over to the men of whom you are afraid. **18** I will certainly save you. You will

---

63. Syr. has the pl. "houses" where the MT has the sg. בַּיִת, "house." The editors of BHS suggest reading as בָּתֵּי, "houses," or adding וְאֶת־בֵּית־יְהוָה, "[the house] of Yahweh and the houses [of the people]" (cf. Jer 52:13; 2 Kgs 25:9).

64. LXX^{O, L} and θ′ (with the Vg.) have καὶ ὑδρεύματα, "and cisterns," where the MT has וִיגֵבִים, "and fields."

65. The word בְּיַד, "through" (lit. "by the hand"), is absent in σ′, Syr., and Vg.

66. The Leningrad Codex has a daghesh forte in the ר of רָע, "bad."

67. The word אִם, "if," is absent in the **Qere** and many Heb. mss.

68. Cairo Geniza and many Heb. mss lack the maqqef and have שראצר, "Sarezer," where the MT has שַׂר־אֶצֶר, "Sar-ezer." See also 39:3.a–a.

69. The phrase אֶל־הַבָּיִת, "to the house," is absent in the LXX.

70. The phrase בִּהְיֹתוֹ עָצוּר, "he was confined," is absent in the LXX.

71. The **Qere** has מֵבִיא, "bringing," where the **Kethiv** has מֵבִי (translation uncertain).

72. The LXX omits וְהָיוּ לְפָנֶיךָ בַּיּוֹם הַהוּא, "In that day they will be fulfilled before your eyes."

not fall by the sword, but will escape with your life, because you trust in me, declares Yahweh.""""

COMMENTARY

The Fall of Jerusalem (38:28b–39:10)

38:28b–39:2 After a thirty-month siege that began on January 15, 588 BC, it all ends on July 18, 586 BC; Jeremiah's predictions have come true. The city of Jerusalem is starved, broken, and dispirited; it only remains for the walls to be "broken through" (v. 2). Some fighting might continue to go on, but the situation is now hopeless and irretrievable.[73]

39:3 Nebuchadnezzar's officials come into the city, perhaps some weeks later, and take their seats in the "Middle Gate" (v. 3).[74] Where this gate was located is uncertain, but some suppose it might have been in a wall separating the upper city (where the temple and palace were) from the lower part of the city.[75] Meanwhile, Nebuchadnezzar remains farther north at Riblah (v. 5). The names and titles of the invading officials have given opportunities for some confusion; the Septuagint, for example, has some six personal names: Nergal-Sharezer, Samgar-Nebo, Sarsechim, Rabsaris, Nergal-Sharezer, and Rabmag. Nergal-Sharezer's name appears twice, but that repetition is not a great problem, for the name is a common one in Babylon. However, the three, rather than the six, names as rendered in the NIV seem to be supported from Babylonian sources: that is, Nergal-Sharezer, meaning "May [the god] Nergal protect the king," as indicated in Babylonian sources, was ruler over a district in Babylon known as Samgar or Akkadian Sin-magir. He seems to have been Nebuchadnezzar's son-in-law and also later is identified with Neriglissar, the one who became ruler in Babylon in 560 BC after Nebuchadnezzar's son Amel-Marduk was removed from his reign. The second official was Nebo-Sarsekim, whose military rank is given as "chief officer." The third official was Nergal-Sharezer, whose

---

73. See E. Di Pede, "Le récit de la prise de Jérusalem (Jr 46 LXX et 39 TM): son importance dans le récit et son impact sur le lecteur," *Biblische Zeitschrift* 52, no. 1 (2006): 90–99.

74. Feigin conjectures that vv. 4–13 are an interpolation. See S. Feigin, "The Babylonian Officials in Jeremiah 39:3, 13," *JBL* 45, nos. 1–2 (1926): 149–55.

75. See S. Voth, "Jeremiah," *ZIBBC* 4:323.

title is unclear (רַב־מָג, *rab-māg*); the Heb. meaning is not yet attested from external sources. These are the men responsible for erecting a new administration in Jerusalem.

39:4 Once again King Zedekiah cannot make up his mind as to what he should do. But when he finally sees the soldiers of the enemy's force in the upper city (v. 4), he non-heroically decides it is time to flee the city. This is his final act of cowardice; he abandons the city, leaving the people he has governed for eleven years to fend for themselves as he sneaks off to the south, away from the direction of the Babylonian attack. He leaves the city at night by way of the "king's garden," which may have been on the southeastern slope of the city, where the Hinnom and the Kidron Valleys come together. Since we are unaware of a gate "between the two walls," this description may fit the point where the two walls came together around the upper city and the lower city. The truth, though, is that we do not know where it was. If this unknown gate was toward the east side of Jerusalem, then Zedekiah's plan is to go toward the Dead Sea and the Gulf of Aqabah, going down toward the Arabah. Perhaps he hopes to find asylum in Moab or Ammon, or something like it along the way, but he never makes it.

39:5 He and his men, who fled with him, are pursued by the Babylonian army and are all captured in the plains of Jericho. This is what Jeremiah had predicted (38:18–23). Zedekiah and his entourage are taken to Riblah in Hamath (v. 5), where Nebuchadnezzar waits for them. Riblah is an Aramean city located on a large plain close to the Orontes River in Syria. Thus, Nebuchadnezzar is not personally present when Jerusalem falls, but he has set up his headquarters at Riblah, located in a strategic area for north-south communication in the Syria-Israel corridor.

39:6–7 With typical ruthlessness for those times, Nebuchadnezzar executes all of Zedekiah's sons right in front of him, along with his nobles (v. 6). Then he blinds Zedekiah and binds him with bronze shackles and carts him off to Babylon (v. 7). Zedekiah has earned such treachery from the Babylonian king, for despite Nebuchadnezzar having "put him on the throne, whose oath he despised and whose treaty he broke" (Ezek 17:16), Zedekiah rebelled against him and held out for two and a half years during the siege. Zedekiah could have been treated much more kindly if he had surrendered to the hostile army when Jeremiah had advised him to do so, for King Jehoiachin before him had voluntarily surrendered and had been treated in a most hospitable way by the Babylonians (52:31–34), but Zedekiah could not make up his mind which way to go. What must be going through Zedekiah's mind as he is marched off to Babylon, now blind and with the last image in his mind that of own sons slaughtered right in from of him? Are any of the prophet's words still ringing in his brain? Why had he resisted the offer of God time and time again?

39:8–9 But the tragedy does not just affect the king and his officers; the city of God is set ablaze, along with the palace of the king and houses of the people (v. 8).[76] In 52:13 this same expression includes the "house of Yahweh" as well as the palace and the homes of the people. Now that the walls have been breached, both survivors and defectors are exiled to Babylon by Nebuzaradan (v. 9).[77] He is called the "captain/commander of the imperial guard." His name means "[The god] Nabu has given offspring."

39:10 Instead of leaving the area of Judah vacant, Nebuzaradan leaves behind in the land some of the poorest people of that land, who up to this point in time have owned nothing. But he now gives them vineyards and fields. Hopefully, these newly gifted poor people will be sufficiently grateful that they will not engage in intrigues or revolts against Babylon and instead will act as a buffer between the newly acquired lands of Babylon and the military threats from Egypt. To these who had owned nothing, new opportunities are given, but for the moment, this is not a land of promise, as it had been described when Israel left Egypt for the promised land so long ago.

---

76. Müller erroneously suggests that "the house of the people" refers to a place of political decision making; furthermore, he suggests that Jer 39:4–13 dates from a later time when the synagogue was a religious institution. See H.-P. Müller, "Das »Haus des Volkes« von Jer 39,8," ZAW 114, no. 4 (2002): 611–17.

77. For an analysis of the root *ytr* see K. Mulzac, "*YTR* as a Remnant Term in the Book of Jeremiah," *Journal of the Adventist Theological Society* 19, nos. 1–2 (2008): 3–17.

The Treatment of the Prophet Jeremiah (39:11–14)

All that remains to be asked after this tremendous calamity are these two questions: Whatever happens to the prophet Jeremiah? Is anything ever done for the Ethiopian Ebed-Melech? Verses 11–14 address the first question, and vv. 15–18 answer the second question. The prophet Jeremiah, who has faced such horrendous opposition all forty years of his ministry in Judah, is now treated royally by the conquerors of Jerusalem. How does Nebuchadnezzar learn of Jeremiah and his prophecies? Is he informed by some of those whom he is taking into exile? Do they tell him that all that has happened to the nation of Judah was predicted all along by this prophet Jeremiah? Has he also heard that this prophet urged that the king surrender to the king of Babylon, but that Zedekiah had refused to do so?

39:11–14 However it came about, Nebuchadnezzar gives very clear orders through his commander of the imperial guard, Nebuzaradan: Jeremiah is to be given the most detailed care and oversight; he is to have anything he requests (vv. 11–12). In v. 14 Nebuzaradan finds Jeremiah in the courtyard of the guard, but in 40:1 Nebuzadan finds him among the captives assembled at Ramah, bound in chains, about to be carried off to Babylon. Ramah was about five miles north of Jerusalem. How can these two accounts be reconciled?

The best solution seems to be that Jeremiah was released twice. His first release from the courtyard of the guard came as orders from the highest command, Nebuchadnezzar himself. But in the confusion and commotion of the capture of the city of Jerusalem, he is taken back into detention again and moved to Ramah with the other captives going into exile. But when he is recognized by the Babylonians, they again release him from his chains and give him a choice. What makes this suggestion more plausible is that when he chooses to stay in the land, he is told by Nebuzaradan to "Go back to Gedaliah" (whose name means, "Yahweh is great"), the newly appointed governor of the land of Judah (40:5), to whom he had originally gone to be with after his first release (39:14). This is not the same Gedaliah mentioned in 38:1, for this is the first mention of this one whom the Babylonians have left in charge as governor. His father had given protection to Jeremiah in Jehoiakim's reign (26:24), and he was a third-generation descendant of a line that goes back to the days of King Josiah. We have found a seal impression at Lachish with this inscription: "Belonging to Gedaliah, over the house." If the person named on this inscription is the same individual, then he also held a high position in the time of Zedekiah's reign. Gedaliah takes Jeremiah "back to his home" (v. 14), which probably meant to the governor's residence in Mizpah, not the prophet's hometown in Anathoth (cf. 40:6).

A Divine Promise to Ebed-Melech (39:15–18)

39:15–18 God sends word to Jeremiah while he is still confined in the courtyard of the guard (v. 15) that he is go and tell this Ethiopian who rescued him from the pit into which he had been cast, "I will surely save you in that day" (v. 17) when the enemy breaches the walls of Jerusalem. Some argue that the placement of this message is a dislocation of the text, for this word arrived from God prior to the enemy's breaking through the walls of the city. While the chronology of this observation is true, it is placed at this point in the text to show a remarkable contrast between what happened to Zedekiah and what happened to this foreigner who nevertheless was a man of faith who trusted in Yahweh (v. 18b). It is assumed that Ebed-Melech has easy access to the courtyard where Jeremiah is being confined, so he is able to receive this message.

God does fulfill the words he had spoken against Jerusalem, that it will experience great hurt and harm, not prosperity, as many had imagined due to the ancient promise of God. That promise repeated in the covenants, however, is only for those who repent and turn away from their sin. It is in no way to be treated as a good-luck charm or a talisman to overcome all their sin, regardless of how Judah acted or responded to their Lord. Thus, the man who is willing to do what was right and who risked his life to rescue the prophet of God is rewarded with the gift of his life and deliverance from the hands of the enemy. So Jeremiah remains with his people.

The Lord circles back in his revelation to give Jeremiah a word for the Cushite Ebed-Melech, who rescued him from the pit. Ebed-Melech will be saved from the edge of the sword and will escape with his life because he trusted in the Lord. Here certainly is a clear indication that God was saving Gentiles during Old Testament times. It also clearly indicates that God sees what is happening on earth, and he can and will reward or judge as necessary.

GEDALIAH THE GOVERNOR (40:1–41:18)

Chapters 40 and 41 describe what takes place after Jerusalem falls and how the Babylonians make Gedaliah the new governor of Judah. It seems that the Babylonian victory over Judah settles very little among some of the Jewish people who are left, for the various parties continued to battle on in their antagonism against whatever is done in the land of Judah. There seems to be little agreement about anything except they do not want to follow Yahweh.

Nebuchadnezzar appointed Gedaliah as governor of Judah in 586 BC, but that may have been another problem, for his name is linked some dozen or more times with the name of the prophet Jeremiah (also see 2 Kgs 25:22–26). That may have been the kiss of death for this leader, for there are signs already that he is not going to last very long in this role.

TRANSLATION

1[78] The word that came to Jeremiah from Yahweh, after Nebuzaradan, the captain/commander of the guard, had released him at Ramah. He had found him [Jeremiah] bound[79] in chains among all the captives from Jerusalem and Judah who were being carried into exile to Babylon. **2** When the commander of the guard found Jeremiah,[80] he said to him, "Yahweh your God has decreed this disaster on this place. **3** Now Yahweh has brought[81] it to pass; he has done just what he said[82] he would do. All this happened[83] because you people sinned against Yahweh and did not obey him.[84] **4** And now, there! I am freeing you from the chains on your wrists.[85] Come with me to Babylon, if you like, and I will look after you. But if it does not suit you to come with me to Babylon, then don't! See, the whole land lies before

---

78. The order of the text has been confused. The editors of *BHS* suggest moving 39:11–12; 40:2a, 1b, and 1aβ after 6a and deleting 1aα.

79. The phrase וְהוּא־אָסוּר, "he was bound," is absent in the LXX.

80. The editors of *BHS* question whether the ל prep. attached to לְיִרְמְיָהוּ, "Jeremiah," is correct.

81. The word וַיָּבֵא, "he has brought," is absent in the LXX.

82. The phrase כַּאֲשֶׁר דִּבֶּר, "as he said," is absent in the LXX.

83. וְהָיָה לָכֶם דְּבָר הַזֶּה, "and this happened to you," is absent in the LXX.

84. The **Qere** has הַדָּבָר, "the thing," where the **Kethiv** has דָּבָר, "a thing."

85. Many mss, LXX, Syr., and Vg. read יָדֶיךָ, "your hands," where the MT has יָדֶךָ, "your hand."

you; go wherever you please."[86] **5** However, before Jeremiah turned to go,[87] Nebuzaradan added, "Go back to Gedaliah son of Ahikam, the son of Shaphan, whom the king of Babylon has appointed over the towns[88] of Judah, and live with him among the people, or go anywhere else you please." Then the captain of the guard gave him provisions and a present,[89] and he sent him away. **6** So Jeremiah went to Gedaliah, son of Ahikam, at Mizpah, and lived with him among the people who were left in the land.

7 When all the army officers and their men who were still in the field heard that the king of Babylon had appointed Gedaliah, son of Ahikam, as governor over the land and put him in charge of the men, women, and children who were the poorest in the land, and who had not been carried into exile[90] to Babylon, **8** they came to Gedaliah at Mizpah—Ishmael son of Nethaniah, Johanan and Jonathan[91] the sons[92] of Kareah, Seraiah son of Tanhumeth, the sons of Ephai[93] the Netophathite, and Jaazaniah[94] the son of Maacathite and their men. **9** And Gedaliah, son of Ahikam, the son of Shaphan, gave his oath to them and their men. "Do not be afraid to serve[95] the Chaldeans," he said. "Stay in the land and serve the king of Babylon, and it will go well with you. **10** I myself will stay at Mizpah[96] to represent you before the Chaldeans as they come to us. As for you, you have only to harvest the wine, summer fruits, and the olive oil, and put them in

---

86. The LXX omits "but if it does not suit you to come with me to Babylon, then don't! See, the whole land lies before you; go wherever you please."

87. The phrase וְעוֹדֶנּוּ לֹא־יָשׁוּב וְשֻׁבָה, "and he was still not turning turn!," is corrupt. The editors of *BHS* suggest emending the text to בְּעֵינֶיךָ לָשֶׁבֶת שֻׁבָה, "in your eyes to return, return."

88. The LXX has ἐν γῇ, "over the land," where the MT has בְּעָרֵי, "over the towns."

89. The LXX lacks "provisions and" where the MT has אֲרֻחָה וּמַשְׂאֵת, "provisions and a present."

90. The LXX has καὶ γυναῖκας αὐτῶν οὓς οὐκ ἀπῴκισεν, "and their wives whom he did not remove," where the MT has וְנָשִׁים וָטַף וּמִדַּלַּת הָאָרֶץ מֵאֲשֶׁר לֹא־הָגְלוּ, "(and) women, and children who were the poorest in the land, and who had not been carried into exile."

91. The word וְיוֹנָתָן, "and Jonathan," is absent in many Heb. mss, the LXX, and Tg.

92. Many Heb. mss, the LXX, and Tg.[f. Ms] have "son of" where the MT has בְּנֵי, "sons of."

93. Syr. and Tg. follow the **Qere**, which has עֵיפַי, "Ephai." The LXX and Vg. follow the **Kethiv**, which has עוֹפַי, "Ophay."

94. A few mss and 2 Kings 2:53 have וְיַאֲזַנְיָהוּ, "and Jaazaniah," where the MT has וִיזַנְיָהוּ, "and Jezaniah."

95. The LXX has τῶν παίδων, "of the servants," and 2 Kgs 25:24 has "of the servants" where the MT of Jer 40:9 has מֵעֲבוֹד, "to serve."

96. The LXX adds the phrase ἐναντίον ὑμῶν, "before you," before "at Mizpah."

your storage jars and live in your towns[97] which you now occupy." **11** When all the Jews in Moab, Ammon, Edom, and all the other countries[98] heard that the king of Babylon had left a remnant in Judah, and had appointed Gedaliah son of Ahikam, the son of Shaphan, as governor over them, **12** all the Jews came back to the land of Judah, to Gedaliah at Mizpah, from all the countries where they had been scattered,[99] and they came to the land of Judah, to Gedaliah at Mizpah. And they brought an abundance of wine and summer fruit.

13 Johanan son of Kareah and all the army officers still in the field came to Gedaliah at Mizpah. **14** They said to him, "Don't you actually know that Baalis king of Ammon has sent Ishmael son of Nethaniah[100] to assassinate you?" But Gedaliah son of Ahikam[101] would not believe them. **15** Then Johanan son of Kareah[102] made a secret proposal to Gedaliah there at Mizpah: "Please let me go and kill Ishmael son of Nethaniah,[103] and no one will know it. Why should he murder you and cause all the Jews gathered around you to be scattered, and the remnant of Judah to perish?" **16** But Gedaliah, son of Ahikam,[104] said to Johanan son of Kareah,[105] "You shall do[106] no such thing! What you are saying about Ishmael is a lie!"

41:1 So it came to pass in the seventh month Ishmael, son of Nethaniah, the son of Elishama,[107] who was of royal descent, came to Gedaliah, son of Ahikam, at Mizpah, who had been one of the king's officers,[108] accompanied by ten men, as they were eating there a meal together, **2** Ishmael, son of Nethaniah, and the ten men who were with him, got up and struck down

---

97. The LXX has ἐν ταῖς πόλεσιν, "in the towns," where the MT has בְּעָרֵיכֶם, "in your towns."

98. The LXX has the sg. τῇ γῇ, "the land," where the MT has the pl. הָאֲרָצֹות, "the lands."

99. The LXX omits שָׁם נִדְּחוּ־אֲשֶׁר מִכָּל־הַמְּקֹמֹות הַיְּהוּדִים וַיָּשֻׁבוּ כָל־, "all the Jews came back to the land of Judah ... from all the countries where they had been scattered."

100. The phrase בֶּן־נְתַנְיָה, "son of Nethaniah," is absent in the LXX.

101. The phrase בֶּן־אֲחִיקָם, "son of Ahikam," is absent in the LXX.

102. The phrase בֶּן־קָרֵחַ, "son of Kareah," is absent in the LXX.

103. The phrase בֶּן־נְתַנְיָה, "son of Nethaniah," is absent in the LXX.

104. The phrase בֶּן־אֲחִיקָם, "son of Ahikam," is absent in the LXX.

105. The phrase בֶּן־קָרֵחַ, "son of Kareah," is absent in the LXX.

106. The **Kethiv** has תַּעַשׂ, "do!" and the **Qere** has תַּעֲשֵׂה, "do!"

107. The LXX has Ελασα, "Elasa," and Syr. has 'šm'jl, "Ishmael," where the MT has אֱלִישָׁמָע, "Elishama."

108. The phrase וְרַבֵּי הַמֶּלֶךְ, "and (who had been) one of the king's officers," is absent in the LXX and 2 Kgs 25:25.

Gedaliah, son of Ahikam, the son of Shaphan, with the sword, killing[109] the one[110] the king of Babylon had appointed as governor over the land. **3** Also Ishmael killed all the Jews who were there with Gedaliah[111] at Mizpah, as well as the Chaldean soldiers who happened to be there—[these] Ishmael slew!

4 It came to pass on the day after Gedaliah's murder, while no one knew[112] of it yet, **5** eighty men arrived from Shechem, from Shiloh,[113] and from Samariah, with their beards shaved off, their clothing torn, and covered with cuts/slashes, bringing with them cereal offerings and incense to present to the house of Yahweh. **6** Ishmael, son of Nethaniah, went out from Mizpah to meet them, weeping as he went.[114] When he reached them,[115] he said, "Come to [greet] Gedaliah son Ahikam." **7** But as soon as they had entered into the midst of the city, Ishmael, son of Nethaniah, and the men who were with him,[116] massacred them[117] and threw them[118] into a cistern. **8** But ten men among them[119] said to Ishmael, "Don't kill us! For we have wheat and barley, oil and honey, hidden in a field," so he spared them and did not kill them along with their companions. **9** Now the cistern into which Ishmael had thrown all the corpses of the men[120] he had killed along with Gedaliah was a large one;[121] it was the one King Asa had made as part of his defense against Baasha king of Israel. Ishmael filled it with the slain.

---

109. LXX[O, L], Syr., Tg.[Ed], and Vg. have the pl. "they killed" where the MT has the sg. וַיָּ֫מָת, "he killed."

110. The LXX omits אֹת֑וֹ בֶּן־אֲחִיקָ֜ם וַיָּ֣מֶת בַּחֶ֗רֶב בֶּן־שָׁפָ֜ן, "son of Ahikam, the son of Shaphan, with the sword, killing him."

111. The phrase אֶת־גְּדַלְיָ֑הוּ, "Gedaliah," is absent in the LXX.

112. The phrase וְאִ֖ישׁ לֹ֥א יָדָֽע, "and no one knew," is absent in the Syr.

113. The LXX has καὶ ἀπὸ Σαλημ, "and from Salem," and LXX[A], α΄, and σ΄ have Σαλωμ, "Salom," where the MT has מִשִּׁל֔וֹ, "from Shiloh."

114. The LXX has αὐτοὶ ἐπορεύοντο καὶ ἔκλαιον, "he was going and weeping," where the MT has הֹלֵ֥ךְ הָלֹ֖ךְ וּבֹכֶ֑ה, "weeping as he went."

115. The phrase וַיְהִ֖י כִּפְגֹ֣שׁ אֹתָ֑ם, "when he reached them," is absent in the LXX.

116. The LXX omits ה֗וּא וְהָאֲנָשִׁ֛ים אֲשֶׁר־אִתּֽוֹ, "he and the men who were with him."

117. The Syr. adds w'rmj 'nwn, "and he cast them," as do LXX[C, L]; cf. v. 9.

118. The word תּ֣וֹ, "the midst," is absent in the LXX.

119. The LXX has ἐκεῖ, "there," where the MT has בָ֑ם, "among them."

120. The phrase פִּגְרֵ֣י הָאֲנָשִׁ֔ים, "corpses of the men," is absent in the LXX.

121. The LXX has φρέαρ μέγα, "great cistern," where the MT has בְּיַד־גְּדַלְיָ֔הוּ, "by the hand of Gedaliah."

10 Ishmael made prisoners[122] of all the rest[123] of the people of Mizpah, including the daughters of the king, along with all the others who were left there,[124] over whom Nebuzaradan[125] commander/captain of the guard had appointed Gedaliah, son of Ahikam. Ishmael took them captive[126] and set out to cross over to the Ammonites. **11** When Johanan, son of Kareah, and all the army officers who were with him heard about all the evil Ishmael, son of Nethaniah, had done, **12** they took all their men[127] and marched out to engage Ishmael, son of Nethaniah, in battle; and they caught up with him at the great pool in Gibeon. **13** When all the people who were with Ishmael saw Johanan, son of Kareah,[128] and all the army officers with him, they were glad.[129] **14** All the people Ishmael had taken captive at Mizpah turned[130] and went[131] over to Johanan, son of Kareah.[132] **15** But Ishmael, son of Nethaniah, and eight of his men escaped from Johanan[133] and fled to Ammonites.

16 Then Johanan, son of Kareah,[134] and all the army officers who were with him, led [back] to Mizpah all the survivors whom he had recovered from Ishmael, son of Nethaniah,[135] after he had assassinated Gedaliah son

---

122. The LXX has καὶ ἀπέστρεψεν, "and he took back," where the MT has וַיִּשְׁבְּ, "and he made prisoners."

123. The LXX lacks וְאֶת־כָּל־הָעָם הַנִּשְׁאָרִים בַּמִּצְפָּה, "(along) with all the others who were left there."

124. The Syr. lacks אֶת־בְּנוֹת הַמֶּלֶךְ וְאֶת־כָּל־הָעָם הַנִּשְׁאָרִים בַּמִּצְפָּה, "(including) the daughters of the king, (along) with all the others who were left there."

125. The word נְבוּזַרְאֲדָן, "Nebuzaradan," is absent in the LXX.

126. A few Heb. mss and LXX[O, L] read וַיַּשְׁכֵּם, "and he rose early," where the MT has וַיִּשְׁבֵּם, "and he took them captive."

127. The LXX has τὸ στρατόπεδον αὐτῶν, "their army," where the MT has הָאֲנָשִׁים, "the men."

128. The phrase בֶּן־קָרֵחַ, "son of Kareah," is absent in the LXX.

129. The word וַיִּשְׂמְחוּ, "and they were glad," is absent in the LXX.

130. The LXX omits וַיָּסֹבּוּ כָּל־הָעָם אֲשֶׁר־שָׁבָה יִשְׁמָעֵאל מִן־הַמִּצְפָּה, "and all the people Ishmael had taken captive at Mizpah turned."

131. The word וַיֵּלְכוּ, "and they went," is absent in the LXX.

132. The phrase בֶּן־קָרֵחַ, "son of Kareah," is absent in the LXX.

133. The phrase מִפְּנֵי יוֹחָנָן, "from Johanan," is absent in the LXX.

134. The phrase בֶּן־קָרֵחַ, "son of Kareah," is absent in the LXX.

135. The phrase בֶּן־נְתַנְיָה, "son of Nethaniah," is absent in the LXX.

of Ahikam:[136] the soldiers,[137] women, children,[138] and court officials he had brought from Gibeon. **17** And they went on, stopping at Geruth[139] Kimham[140] near Bethlehem on their way to Egypt, **18** to escape the Chaldeans, for they were afraid of them because Ishmael, son of Nethaniah,[141] had killed Gedaliah, son of Ahikam,[142] whom the king of Babylon had appointed over the land.

COMMENTARY

Jeremiah Set Free Again (40:1–6)

40:1 The text begins with the statement that a word came to Jeremiah from Yahweh, but there is no explicit statement of what that word is (v. 1). Some have sought to reconstruct what that word might have been from the words of Nebuzaradan, which Jeremiah might have said from Yahweh (vv. 2–5b), but this suggestion is flawed in that it calls for a severe rearrangement of the text. It is better to take this introductory sentence as a heading, or as a superscription, similar to the one that appears in 1:1–3. As such, then, it would serve as a title for the section that continues up to 45:5.

A second problem faced in this text has already been treated in 39:11–14. Presumably, Nebuzaradan already freed Jeremiah from the courtyard of the guard in Jerusalem (39:11–14), but somehow in the confusion of all the things going on with regard to the captivity of the city, Jeremiah must have been mistakenly again chained by some of the other Babylonian soldiers. When word of this mixup apparently reaches Nebuzaradan, he finds Jeremiah at Ramah and sets him free again (v. 2). The assembly point for the

---

136. The LXX omits בֶּן־נְתַנְיָה מִן־הַמִּצְפָּה אַחַר הִכָּה אֶת־גְּדַלְיָה בֶּן־אֲחִיקָם, "to Mizpah ... son of Nethaniah, after he had assassinated Gedaliah son of Ahikam."

137. A few Heb. mss have גִּבּוֹרִים, "strong," where the MT has גְּבָרִים, "men." Cf. LXX, Tg., and Vg.

138. The LXX has καὶ τὰ λοιπά, "and the rest," where the MT has וְטַף, "and children."

139. The editors of BHS consider בְּגֵרוּת, "at Geruth," to be doubtful and suggest the meaning *in diversorio* ("in an inn") to match σ´, Tg., and Vg. The LXX and θ´ have the proper noun Γαβηρωθ ("Gaberoth"), α´ has ἐν τοῖς φραγμοῖς ("in the walls"), and Syr. has *b'dr'* ("on the threshing floor").

140. Many Heb. mss follow the **Qere** and read כְּמְהָם, "Kimham" (cf. 2 Sam 19:38). The editors of BHS see the **Kethiv** כְּמוֹהֶם, "Kimoham," as doubtful.

141. The phrase בֶּן־נְתַנְיָה, "son of Nethaniah," is absent in the LXX.

142. The phrase בֶּן־אֲחִיקָם, "son of Ahikam," is absent in the LXX.

captives at Ramah was about five miles north of the destroyed Jerusalem. Nebuzaradan gives Jeremiah "provisions and a present and [then] let[s] him go" (v. 5c). There is no indication what these provisions included or what that present was, but it shows that he wanted him to have these things as a kind gesture on behalf of the Babylonian government.

40:2–6 There still is the slight possibility that the word of Yahweh announced in v. 1 was not intended to be a superscription for chapters 40–45 but is a word given through Jeremiah to captain Nebuzaradan from Yahweh. Such a revelation to non-Judeans, or even to non-believers, is not unknown in Scripture, for that is precisely what happens to Pharaoh Necho in 2 Chr 35:22. Necho rebukes King Josiah for trying to stop him in his mission to go to Carchemish, which he claims is being carried out "at God's command," to which the text gives its assent. Therefore, it should not be thought to be a strange matter when so-called outsiders also show an understanding that "God had decreed this disaster to this place" (v. 2b) and that Yahweh has now done exactly what he said he would do (v. 3). Nebuzaradan's advice is that Jeremiah should "go back to Gedaliah ... and live with him among your people" (v. 5b–c). Not only is Yahweh able to use pagan rulers for his own purposes, but he is able to make Israel to be a "light to the nations," even when the people of Israel are rebellious and being punished by God. Nebuzaradan surely has a good knowledge of what the prophet has been prophesying over the years, for he is able in this text to present a rather good synopsis of what the prophet's message has included.

Gedaliah Appointed as Governor of Judah (40:7–12)

40:7 Jeremiah drops out of any further mention in this text until chapter 42. It is not clear why no mention is made of him during this time. Where is he? In the meantime, all the army officers of Judah hear about the appointment of Gedaliah as governor by Nebuchadnezzar (these are apparently those who were in the field when Jerusalem was taken), so they come to Mizpah, the center of operations now that Jerusalem has been destroyed. The land has suffered a huge amount of confusion and disorientation. However, the Babylonians do not want to leave the land vacant, for that would be an open invitation to others, such as Egypt, to move into that vacuum and take the land over, so the poorest people are left in the land and given a distribution of the vineyards and fields.

40:8-10 Among the soldiers who come to Mizpah are Ishmael, who according to 41:1 is a grandson of Elishama, of royal descent; Johana and Jonathan; Seraiah; the sons of Ephai and Jaazaniah; along with their men (v. 8). An agate seal was found in a tomb at Mizpah containing the inscription "belonging to Jaazaniah the servant of the king," which may be from the very same man mentioned here in this context. To all these men, Gedaliah swears an oath, thereby reassuring them that he is for them and will represent them all to the king of Babylon (vv. 9–10). There is no reason for them to be afraid; they should just settle down and serve the king of Babylon. They would do well to gather in the wine from the grape harvest, the summer fruits of the dates and figs, and the olive oil, and put them in storage jars for the months ahead (v. 10c).

40:11-12 If Jerusalem fell in the fourth month and was torched in the fifth month, then this (the seventh month, presuming it is still the same year) is about the time (September–October) when the summer fruits would have been ripening. Now with a decreased population, there will be more than enough from that summer's harvest to go around. Accordingly, when all the Jews who scattered to Moab, Ammon, Edom, and all the other countries round about hear that the king of Babylon has left Gedaliah, son of Ahikam, the son of Shaphan, in charge as governor, they too come back from all over (vv. 11–12). The harvest that year is one of great abundance of wine and summer fruit (v. 12b).

Gedaliah Assassinated (40:13–41:3)

40:13-14 One of the leaders of the troops in the field who had returned to Mizpah earlier, Johanan, son of Kareah, asks whether Gedaliah has heard about a conspiracy to murder him (v. 13). In fact, Johanan reports that this plot is being hatched by Baalis, the king in the nearby country of Ammon (v. 14).[143] Apparently, Baalis wants to damage whatever hold the Babylonians

---

143. Becking argues that "the element *b'l* does not refer to the Canaanite deity Baal, but the element is used appellatively and refers to the national deity of the Ammonites: Milkom."

continue to exert over Judah and his own land, so he encourages Ishmael, a member of the Davidic line (41:1), to assassinate Gedaliah, who is viewed as a traitor carrying out the wishes of the conquering Babylonians. When Johanan tells Gedaliah about this conspiracy, he refuses to believe it. But Gedaliah is not wise or prescient enough to realize that some of the former opposition to the pro-Babylonian policies is still very much alive and is insistent on having its own way. If this governor, whom they view as a stooge for the Babylonians, were to be killed, then the remnant in the land will be jeopardized, and this will upset some of the conqueror's plans—or so the thinking must be.

40:15-16 Johanan wants secret permission from Gedaliah to take a preemptive strike on Ishmael's life (v. 15). Ishmael may be smarting because he should have been named governor, rather than Gedaliah, for he was in the line of David, not Gedaliah. But Gedaliah will not grant that permission to Johanan; he thinks the whole report is a "lie" (v. 16). Gedaliah cannot see how someone with Davidic background and previous experience in the Judean government, such as Ishmael has, could be linked up with so dastardly a deed. So Johanan is prevented from carrying out his proposed secret mission.

41:1-3 Since there is no indication that any additional time elapses between the breach of the walls of Jerusalem and the assassination of Gedaliah, or even what particular year this is, we assume that the "seventh month" (41:1), that is, Tishri/September-October is a mere two months after the city was set to the torch, in early August of 586 BC. Moreover, Zech 7:5 and 8:19 later commemorate the fourth month (the walls of Jerusalem entered), fifth month (Jerusalem set on fire), and the seventh months (the murder of Gedaliah) as times of fasting. Gedaliah's death is the only one to be remembered in this way in Israel.

See B. Becking, "Baalis, the King of the Ammonites: An Epigraphical Note on Jeremiah 40:14," *Journal of Semitic Studies* 38, no. 1 (Spring 1993): 15-24. See also L. G. Herr, "Is the Spelling of 'Baalis' in Jeremiah 40:14 a Mutilation?," *AUSS* 23, no. 2 (Summer 1985): 187-91; and "The Servant of Baalis," *BA* 48, no. 3 (September 1985): 169-72.

Ishmael son of Nethaniah, son of Elishama, who was from the royal line of David, also is one of the officers of King Zedekiah (41:1). He comes to Mizpah with ten other men, and they are offered hospitality by Gedaliah around a common meal. However, during the meal Ishmael gets up and strikes down Gedaliah and kills him (v. 2). His action seems to be born out of both jealousy over who should be the leader of Judah and the desire to destabilize Judah on behalf of the Ammonites, who must also have their eyes fixed on obtaining a piece of the land of Judah as well. Ishmael does not stop with that action; he goes on to murder all the Jews who are with Gedaliah at Mizpah, including the Babylonian soldiers left there as a garrison with the governor (v. 3).

Ishmael's Insurrection (41:4–10)

41:4–5 All of Ishmael's anti-Babylonian actions run directly counter to what Jeremiah has been advocating at the insistence of Yahweh—Judah should submit to Babylon. It is extremely doubtful in light of these fast-moving events that Babylon will merely stand by and allow this type of challenge to their dominion go on without any kind of a military response.

But Ishmael still has not had enough; he wants to make an even greater impression of destabilization on the country, if not Babylon itself. Thus, before word gets out about his killings in Mizpah, eighty men came to Mizpah, intent on making offerings to Yahweh, from the northern cities of Shechem, Shiloh, and Samaria (v. 5). These northerners may be a sign that a new day is in the offing for north-south relationships, but this is not what Ishmael is hoping to see at this time.

That these eighty men came with "shaved beards," "torn clothes," and "cut/gashed bodies" might indicate that they are engaged in a sort of lamentation ritual (v. 5). However, though cutting oneself does signal mourning, it is a heathen signal, and furthermore is prohibited by Israel's Torah (Deut 14:1). These were symptoms of the syncretistic practices in the land that have so frequently blended Yahweh worship with pagan adulation. These are the very issues that the prophet Jeremiah has been decrying all during his ministry, for the people were trying to serve all the idol Baals as well as Yahweh—both at the same time. They come with gift/cereal offerings and incense apparently to offer in the temple of God (v. 5), which by now is burnt to the ground by the fires of the Babylonians.

41:6-9 Craftily, Ishmael, in an outrageous act of duplicity, goes out to meet the eighty men (how is he tipped off as to their coming?), pretending to be grief-stricken over the temple's destruction and the city's demise. This is convincing enough to fool this entourage as he leads them instead to see Gedaliah, but, as he knows, Gedaliah has already been murdered (v. 6). When they come into the city, Ishmael must have a trap set up so that he and his ten men are able to take on these eighty men (v. 7). Ten of the eighty are quick enough to see what is happening as they began to bargain for their lives by saying that they have hidden in a field wheat, barley, oil, and honey (v. 8). Even the proud Ishmael is not able to resist that deal, since those commodities must still be in short supply in those days, so he spares their lives (v. 8c). Meanwhile, the other seventy bodies of that party are thrown into the same pit where Gedaliah's corpse is already lying (v. 9). This cistern/pit is the one the Judean King Asa (913-873 BC) built to defend Judah against a northern invasion by King Baasha (900-877 BC; cf. 1 Kgs 15:16-24; 2 Chr 16:6). This cistern has not been found as yet; Mizpah, meaning "watchtower," may be Nabi Samwil, five miles northwest of Jerusalem, but that site has not yet been excavated. Another possible site in Benjamite territory, Tell en-Nasbeh, eight miles on the road north of Jerusalem, has been excavated, but no cistern of this size has been found there.

41:10 Still hungry for a larger conquest, Ishmael takes all the remaining people in Mizpah as hostages, including the king's daughters (a general description of women born to the royal family, but not necessarily Zedekiah's daughters). It is amazing that there is no mention of Jeremiah or Baruch during all this commotion, but then there is no mention of Johanan in these events either (cf. 2 Kgs 25:23). Ishmael sets out intending to cross over to the Ammonites, who were the sponsors of this insurrection (v. 10c), but that plan comes to a sudden halt.

Recovery of the Hostages and Flight to Egypt (41:11-18)

41:11-12 Somehow Johanan hears what Ishmael has done, so he and the army officers who are with him set out to locate and fight Ishmael (vv. 11, 12a). They catch up with him at the great pool of Gibeon, where David's men and Ishbosheth's supporters encountered each other (v. 12b; cf. 2 Sam 2:13). This site, also known as el-Jib, still displays a large cistern of some eighty feet deep, with steps circling its walls to allow access to the water supply in the cistern. Gibeon is some six miles northwest of Jerusalem, which seems to argue for Nabi-Samwil as the site for Mizpah, for Ishmael is heading south in order to get ready to cross over eastward to Ammon in Transjordania.

41:13–18 When the captives see Johanan and his army, they made a quick but joyful retreat to join Johanan and completely abandon Ishmael (v. 13). However, in the confusion, Ishmael gets away, but not without a loss, for his ten men are now reduced to eight, presumably as a result of the skirmish that takes place between Ishmael's men and Johanan's men (v. 15). Nevertheless, Ishmael has done quite a bit of damage already, as he has really upset the Babylonian plans for a replacement government and the occupation of the land by the poor people.[144]

It appears that Johanan at first leads those he has rescued back to Mizpah—the soldiers, women, young children, and court officials from Gibeon. They do not stay in Mizpah, however, for they fear that Babylonian reprisals will surely follow this turn of events. So this little troop trudges off to get out of the sphere of the Babylonian dominance and possible reprisals. They stop at "Geruth Kimham," six miles southwest of Bethlehem. Geruth means "lodging place," so this stopping place may have been the "lodging place of Chimham" (this site is unidentified as yet); Chimham may be the same person as the son of Barzillai who received land near Bethlehem from King David (v. 17; cf. 2 Sam 19:37). The key objective at this point is to get out of the reach of the Babylonians. Ishmael's savage deed has frightened all of them, for they have no idea what the Babylonians will do, but all are sure the Babylonians will not be pleased in the least.

It seems as if the Egyptian party finally gets its way, for the remnant of the poor people of the land plan to go to Egypt. They fear what the Babylonians might do as a result of the killings that are happening. But none of those in this group show any fear of the Lord. Like us sometimes, they are facing a crisis but still think they can do what is necessary using their own wits. For them, there is no need to call on God—at least not yet!

---

144. Regarding the unusual alliance with the Ammonites, see R. Hobson, "Jeremiah 41 and the Ammonite Alliance," *Journal of Hebrew Scriptures* 10 (2010): article 7.

REJECTING JEREMIAH'S ADVICE TO
STAY IN THE LAND (42:1–43:7)

A most bewildered and intimidated band of survivors of the Mizpah massacre continues to move south toward Egypt and hopefully out of the reach
of the Babylonian army's revenge, which is certain to come. As they travel
along, suddenly we learn that Jeremiah is among this small band. What has
he been saying or doing in response to all that has been happening during
these days? Is he in agreement with Johanan's directions? What does he
think about the assassination of Gedaliah and the massacre of the seventy
men who came to sacrifice? We have no record of any reaction on his part.

This group finally asks whether Jeremiah will inquire of Yahweh as to
what they should do (42:1–6). Ten days later Yahweh responds to the prayer
of Jeremiah and indicates that if they remain in the land, he, Yahweh, will
deliver them (vv. 7–18). But such a request seems to be too much of a test
for their faith. They steadfastly refuse to accede to Yahweh's directions,
even though they promised with an oath (!) that they would do whatever
God asked! Jeremiah urges them to trust Yahweh, but they refuse to do so
(42:19–22). All of this is just further confirmation that the judgment that
has come on the people is more than deserved, because even after the city
of Jerusalem has fallen and the temple of God burnt to the ground, just as
Jeremiah predicted, they still do not get it. Their rebellion against the word
of God is deep-seated and adamant. The facts are not going to confuse them!

TRANSLATION

1 Then all the military leaders, especially Johanan, son of Kareah,[145] and
Jezaniah,[146] son of Hoshiah,[147] and all the people from the least to the greatest approached **2** Jeremiah the prophet and said to him, "Please hear our
petition and pray on our behalf[148] to Yahweh your God for this entire remnant[149]—for as you can now see, though we once were many, now we are

---

145. The phrase בֶּן־קָרֵחַ, "son of Kareah," is absent in the LXX.

146. The LXX has καὶ Αζαριας, "and Azariah," where the MT has וְיִזַנְיָה, "and Jezaniah."
Compare 40:8 and 43:2.

147. The LXX has Μαασαιου, "Maasaiah," where the MT has הוֹשַׁעְיָה, "Hoshiah," here and
in 43:2. The editors of BHS are unsure about which reading is correct.

148. The word בַּעֲדֵנוּ, "on our behalf," is absent in the LXX.

149. The phrase בְּעַד כָּל־הַשְּׁאֵרִית הַזֹּאת, "for this entire remnant," is absent in the Syr.

but a few— **3** that Yahweh your God[150] would tell us the way in which we should go and the thing we should do." **4** Jeremiah the prophet[151] said, "I have heard you. I will certainly pray to Yahweh your God[152] as you have asked. And whatever answer Yahweh gives you,[153] I will let you know and I will hold back nothing from you." **5** Then they said to Jeremiah, "May Yahweh be a true and faithful witness against us if we do not do exactly what Yahweh your God[154] sends you to tell us to do; **6** whether it is favorable or unfavorable, we[155] will obey Yahweh our God, to whom we are sending you, so that it will go well with us, for we will obey Yahweh our God.

7 Ten days later the word of Yahweh came to Jeremiah. **8** So he called together Johanan, son of Kareah,[156] and all[157] the army officers who were with him[158] and all the people from the least to the greatest, **9** and he said to them, "This is what Yahweh the God of Israel, to whom you sent me to present your petition,[159] has said, **10** 'If you stay[160] in this land, I will build you up and not tear you down; I will plant you and not uproot you, for I am grieved over the disaster I have afflicted on you. **11** Do not be afraid of the king of Babylon, whom you now fear. Do not be afraid of him, declares Yahweh, for I am with you and will save you and deliver you from his grasp. **12** I will show you compassion so that he will have compassion[161] on you and will restore[162] you to your land. **13** However, if you say, "We will not stay

---

150. A few Heb. mss and Syr. have אֱלֹהֵינוּ, "our God," where the MT has אֱלֹהֶיךָ, "your God."

151. The word הַנָּבִיא, "the prophet," is absent in the LXX.

152. The LXX has θεὸν ἡμῶν, "our God," where the MT has אֱלֹהֵיכֶם, "your God."

153. The word אֶתְכֶם, "to you," is absent in the LXX.

154. The word אֱלֹהֶיךָ, "your God," is absent in the LXX.

155. The **Qere** has the usual form אֲנַחְנוּ, "we," and **Kethiv** has the postbiblical form אֲנוּ, "we." This is the only such occurrence in Biblical Heb. (Holladay 1989, 274n6a).

156. The phrase בֶּן־קָרֵחַ, "son of Kareah," is absent in the LXX.

157. The word כָּל־, "all," is absent in the LXX.

158. The LXX omits the phrase אֲשֶׁר אִתּוֹ, "who were with him."

159. The LXX omits אֱלֹהֵי יִשְׂרָאֵל אֲשֶׁר שְׁלַחְתֶּם אֹתִי אֵלָיו לְהַפִּיל תְּחִנַּתְכֶם לְפָנָיו, "the God of Israel, to whom you sent me to present your petition."

160. The LXX, Tg., and Vg. read יָשׁוֹב, "stay," the inf. abs. of יָשַׁב, where the MT has שׁוֹב, "return," the inf. abs. of שׁוּב.

161. The LXX, Syr., and Vg. have the 1 sg. "and I will have compassion" where the MT has the 3 sg. וְרִחַם, "and he will have compassion."

162. The LXX has καὶ ἐπιστρέψω, "and I will restore," where the MT has וְהֵשִׁיב, "and he will restore." α´, Syr., and Vg. have καὶ καθίσω ὑμᾶς, "and I will make you sit."

in this land," and so disobey the voice of Yahweh your God,[163] **14** and say, "No,[164] we will go to the land of Egypt, where we will not see war or hear the trumpet blast, or be hungry for bread, and we will stay there," **15** then, therefore, hear the word of Yahweh, O remnant of Judah.[165] This is what Yahweh of Hosts, the God of Israel,[166] says, "If you have really made up your minds to go[167] to Egypt, and you go to settle there, **16** then the sword you fear will overtake you there and the famine you dread will follow you into Egypt and there you will die. **17** Yes, all those who have made up their minds to go[168] to Egypt to settle there[169] will die by the sword, famine, and plague;[170] not one of them will survive[171] or escape the disaster I will bring on them. **18** For this is what Yahweh of Hosts, the God of Israel,[172] has said: 'Just as my anger[173] and wrath have been poured out on those who lived in Jerusalem, so will my wrath be poured out on you when you go to Egypt. You will become an object of cursing and horror, a curse-word and a disgrace; you will never see this place again.'"'"

19 "O remnant of Judah, Yahweh has told you, 'Do not go to Egypt.' Be sure of this:[174] 'I witness against you today[175] **20** that you have made a fatal mistake[176] when you sent me unto Yahweh your God[177] and said: "Intercede to Yahweh our God[178] on our behalf; tell us[179] everything Yahweh our God

---

163. The word אֱלֹהֵיכֶם, "your God," is absent in the Lxx.
164. The phrase לֵאמֹר לֹא, "say, No," is absent in the Lxx.
165. The phrase שְׁאֵרִית יְהוּדָה, "O remnant of Judah," is absent in the Lxx.
166. The phrase צְבָאוֹת אֱלֹהֵי יִשְׂרָאֵל, "of Hosts, the God of Israel," is absent in the Lxx.
167. The word לָבֹא, "to go," is absent in the Lxx.
168. The word לָבוֹא, "to go," is absent in the Lxx.
169. The Lxx adds the phrase καὶ πάντες οἱ ἀλλογενεῖς, "and all the foreigners," after "all those who have made up their minds to go to Egypt to settle there."
170. The word וּבַדֶּבֶר, "and (by) plague/disease," is absent in the Lxx.
171. The word שָׂרִיד, "survive (lit. a survivor)," is absent in the Lxx.
172. The Lxx lacks the phrase צְבָאוֹת אֱלֹהֵי יִשְׂרָאֵל, "of Hosts, the God of Israel."
173. The word אַפִּי, "my anger," and the following conj. are absent in the Lxx.
174. The Lxx adds καὶ νῦν, "and now," before "Be sure of this."
175. The phrase כִּי־הַעִידֹתִי בָכֶם הַיּוֹם, "I witness against you today," is absent in the Lxx.
176. *BHS* states that the **Kethiv** הִתְעֵתֶם is a scribal error and that the *Qere* הִתְעֵיתֶם, "you have made a mistake," should be followed. The Lxx has ἐπονηρεύσασθε, "you have done evil."
177. The phrase אֶל־יְהוָה אֱלֹהֵיכֶם, "unto Yahweh your God," is absent in the Lxx.
178. The word אֱלֹהֵינוּ, "our God," is absent in the Lxx.
179. The phrase כֵּן הַגֶּד־לָנוּ, "(thus) tell us," is absent in the Lxx.

says, we will do [it].” **21** I have told you today,[180] but you have altogether disregarded the voice of Yahweh your God in all[181] he has sent me to tell you. **22** So now, make no mistake about it,[182] you shall die by the sword, starvation, and disease[183] in the place where you are pleased to go and sojourn.’”

43:1[184] When Jeremiah finished repeating to all the people all the words of Yahweh their God[185]—everything Yahweh their God had sent him to tell them, **2** Azariah, son of Hoshaiah, and Johanan, son of Kareah, and all insolent[186] men said to Jeremiah,[187] “You are lying![188] Yahweh our God[189] has not sent you to say, ‘You must not go to Egypt to sojourn there.’ **3** Baruch, son of Neriah, is inciting you against us, to hand us over to the Chaldeans, so that they may kill us or carry us off into exile to Babylon.”

4 But neither Johanan, son of Kareah,[190] nor any of the army officers, nor any of the people, would listen to the voice of Yahweh and remain in the land of Judah. **5** Instead, Johanan, son of Kareah,[191] and all the army officers, took all the remnant of Judah, who had come back to live in the land of Judah[192] from all the nations where[193] they had been scattered— **6** the strong men,[194] the women and children, and the king’s daughters— [in short] every person Nebuzaradan, the commander of the guard[195] had left

---

180. The phrase וָאַגִּד לָכֶם הַיּוֹם, “I have told you today,” is absent in the LXX.

181. The phrase אֱלֹהֵיכֶם וּלְכֹל, “your God in all,” is absent in the LXX. Some Heb. mss, LXX[L], Tg.[Ms], and the Vg. lack the conj. “and” where the MT has וּלְכֹל, “and in all.”

182. The phrase יָדֹעַ תֵּדְעוּ כִּי, “make no mistake about it” (lit. “you will certainly know that”), is absent in the LXX.

183. The word וּבַדֶּבֶר, “and (by) plague/disease,” is absent in the LXX.

184. Jeremiah 43 in the MT appears in chap. 50 of the LXX. Cook argues that, in light of the DSS, the LXX “probably represents a Hebrew text that is older than the Vorlage of the MT.” See J. Cook, “The Difference in the Order of the Books of the Hebrew and Greek Versions of Jeremiah—Jeremiah 43 (50): A Case Study,” OTE 7 (1994): 175–92.

185. The word אֱלֹהֵיהֶם, “their God,” is absent in the LXX.

186. The word הַזֵּדִים, “insolent,” is absent in the LXX.

187. The LXX adds λέγοντες, “saying,” after “to Jeremiah.”

188. The phrase אַתָּה מְדַבֵּר, “you are speaking,” is absent in the LXX.

189. The LXX has πρὸς ἡμᾶς, “to us” (= אֵלֵינוּ), where the MT has אֱלֹהֵינוּ, “our God.”

190. The phrase בֶּן־קָרֵחַ, “son of Kareah,” is absent in the LXX.

191. The phrase בֶּן־קָרֵחַ, “son of Kareah,” is absent in the LXX.

192. The word יְהוּדָה, “of Judah,” is absent in the LXX.

193. The phrase מִכָּל־הַגּוֹיִם אֲשֶׁר, “from all the nations where,” is absent in the LXX.

194. The LXX has τοὺς δυνατοὺς ἄνδρας, “the strong men” (=גִּבּוֹרִים), where the MT has הַגְּבָרִים, “the men.”

195. The phrase רַב־טַבָּחִים, “the commander of the guard,” is absent in the LXX.

with Gedaliah, son of Ahikam, son of Shaphan,[196] including Jeremiah the prophet and Baruch, son of Neriah. **7** So they entered the land of[197] Egypt, for they did not obey the voice of Yahweh, and they came to Tahpanhes.

COMMENTARY

Requesting Guidance from Yahweh (42:1-6)

It is often asked, as has already been noted, where is Jeremiah during all that takes place in Mizpah? Some have suggested that he was living in Geruth Kimham (41:12), since that is where Johanan and his men stopped on their way to Egypt. If that supposition is correct, then that is what saves his life when Gedaliah is assassinated along with the others in Mizpah. But that is only a guess.

42:1-4 All at once, the army officers, Johanan and Jezaniah (40:8; = Azariah?), along with all the survivors from the land of Judah, approach the prophet with apparent humility and professed earnestness, requesting that he petition Yahweh his God (vv. 2-3, 5) for directions as to where they should go and what they should do. This seems, on the face of the request, to be somewhat redundant, since they are already on their way to Egypt. They have expressed their certainties that surely the Babylonians will kill them as a reprisal for what Ishmael had perpetrated in the land of Judah at Mizpah.

42:5-6 Nevertheless, they pledge that regardless of whether the directions from Yahweh are favorable, they will do everything *Jeremiah's* God (!) tells him they are to do (v. 5). How they could promise such a way on an oath is unimaginable, given their past record for obedience, unless they are almost certain in themselves that Yahweh will give a full endorsement of the path they already are on. They even note that Yahweh is their "true and faithful witness" (v. 5a), presumably both for and against them, so how can Jeremiah doubt their sincerity or intentions?

---

196. The phrase בֶּן־שָׁפָן, "son of Shaphan," is absent in the LXX.
197. The word אֶרֶץ, "the land of," is absent in the LXX.

The Answer Comes (42:7–22)

42:7–10 Jeremiah receives the divine answer to his inquiry ten days later (v. 7). Does Yahweh provide this time interval so that the people can harden in their own ways and arguments? But now the test will come; have this people changed at all in light of the catastrophic events that have taken place? Jeremiah is clear that the source of his message is none other than the Lord (v. 9).[198] The prophet begins his answer with God's offer of blessing if they stay in the land (v. 10); they will experience God's help in "building" and "planting'" and they will not experience the "tearing down or uprooting," if they obey, as was mentioned in Jeremiah's call chapter (1:10). Yahweh even goes on to mention how painful and how grieved (even to the point of "relenting" [נחֵם]) he is that he had to inflict disaster on them because of their disobedience (v. 10b). The remnant should not "be afraid," for God will be with them, just as Yahweh promised Jeremiah in his call chapter (1:9, 18). Yahweh himself will save them and rescue them from Nebuchadnezzar's power.

42:11–12 So God promises that there will be no need to fear the king of Babylon (v. 11, cf. 40:9). God will be with them. Moreover, just as Yahweh will now show compassion (נחַם) on them, so the king of Babylon will follow suit and show a similar compassion on them if they obey (v. 12).

Despite such broad and wonderful promises from God on high, these refugees impudently (and contrary to everything they so earnestly promised), deliberately retort to him (when he gives the word that they should not go down to Egypt): "You are lying!" (43:2). Even when the positive effects of their staying in the land are laid out for them (vv. 10–12), along with the negative effects of leaving the land (vv. 13–17), it all has no effect whatsoever on any of the military officers, leaders, or people. These people are just plain bent on doing what is wrong and going their own way— regardless of what they said earlier.

---

198. Jeremiah portrays Yahweh as a God of mercy who desires all people to display mercy to others. See W. Brueggemann, "At the Mercy of Babylon: A Subversive Rereading of the Empire," *JBL* 110, no. 1 (Spring 1991): 3–22.

42:13–18 The remnant has already exhibited an attitude of unwillingness to hear or do what Yahweh says. The prophet warns them that if they persist ("continued to say," v. 13), then they will surely face exactly what they are hoping to avoid by going there in the first place (vv. 13–16). The sword, famine, and plague will follow them right down to Egypt (v. 17).

42:19–22 Verses 19–22 repeat the order to halt their intention of going to Egypt, for it will only end up in judgment. But since they have already chosen to reject Jeremiah's counsel, they have made a "fatal mistake" (v. 20). All the prayer and urging by the prophet amounts to nothing in the minds of the remnant.

Divine Guidance Is Rejected (43:1–7)

43:1 After Jeremiah finishes recounting the word the remnant requested he seek from Yahweh (v. 1), his listeners are in no mood to heed anything he said. It all runs directly counter to what they have decided they will do anyhow. Despite their request that God give them directions in this desperate moment, they virtually decided in advance they would go to Egypt, despite this prayer request made of God.

43:2 This refusal to listen is prompted by Azariah and Johanan and "all the arrogant men" (v. 2). They are insolent and arrogant because they judged their opinions as better than those the prophet brought from God, and because they feel they should assume rights and authority over this group that has not been given to them. The word of Jeremiah from God is easily tossed off as some other opinion that is obviously less realistic and less accurate than their own. They simply declare his message to be a "lie" (v. 2). What these new leaders have learned from the events of the fall of the city and the end of the Davidic line in their day is of no benefit to them. Should these leaders not pause in their accusation of Jeremiah that he is a "liar," when all his previous predictions have come true? What about their own pledges to do whatever Jeremiah finds out that God commands them to do?

43:3 Instead, Azariah, Johanan, and their men try to rationalize that they themselves outright lied, only this time they have in effect accused God by saying that Jeremiah gave this word because he is under pressure to say so from his scribe, Baruch. Is this a tipoff that they are accustomed to their own prophets acting under the influence of others in those days? The only one they can think to accuse is Baruch, who up to this point has played a very minor role in all this history. So the newly concocted story is that Jeremiah's scribe, Baruch, son of Neriah, "enticed" (סות, sût) the prophet to say they should stay in the land of Judah so that the remnant can be handed over to the Babylonians to kill them or take them into exile to Babylon (v. 3). The spin they put on the story has some background to it; Jeremiah is by now probably very elderly, and Baruch had access to the previous government. Furthermore, had not Jeremiah advocated that Judah should submit to Babylon, and apparently both Jeremiah and Baruch were absent from Mizpah when Gedaliah was assassinated? But Baruch is a man of integrity, for he risked his life to be Jeremiah's amanuensis. He refused to bow to pressure before this, so this charge only shows how desperate these men are to present some kind of cover for their own actions. Baruch is the only available person they can think of to accredit this alleged word from God—that is, according to their view.

43:4-6 Regardless of what story these renegades invent for themselves, the verdict for their disobedience will soon evidence itself from God. They insist that Jeremiah and Baruch go with them into Egypt. So they impose their will on these men along with the survivors who are left from the tragic events of those days (vv. 4–6). They also, along with the men, women, children, and the "king's daughters" (v. 6), which represents the group placed under the control of the new governor, Gedaliah, are taken with the prophet and his scribe into Egypt. Why they want a prophet whose word they reject as being a "lie" to come along with them is not easily understood. Are he and Baruch there as hostages? Or are they there as some kind of lucky charm or as a type of insurance that God will not bring the predicted disaster on them if these two men are part of their group? In complete disobedience to Yahweh, they all enter Egypt and came to Tahpanhes. Tahpanhes was a border town on the northern frontier, part of the northeastern delta, also known by its Gk. name Daphne. It is here they stop, supposedly to decide what they are going to do next.

When the remnant pauses and seems to ask Jeremiah in sincere humility whether he will seek guidance from the Lord about whether they should go to Egypt, the Lord waits ten days before he answers. But when the answer is contrary to what they apparently hoped it would be, Azariah accuses Jeremiah of lying. He brashly argues that God has not sent him. However, Jeremiah's track record is exceedingly good. You would think that this point would have counted strongly in favor of him. Had Jeremiah not accurately predicted the destruction of Jerusalem and the temple? But Jeremiah and Baruch are forced to go to Egypt knowing God is not in this venture. What crass scorners of the word of God! Yes, and there are also contemporary scorners of the word of God. Guess what is in store for our nation and the nations of the world that follow a similar line of disobedience?

A FINAL SYMBOLIC ACT BY JEREMIAH (43:8-13)

It is surprising how slow mortals are to learn that God cannot be mocked, fooled, or trifled with. Even though divine guidance was not promised to this group, the flight to Egypt continues as the survivors take refuge there. But as promised, Nebuchadnezzar, whom they had feared, comes right to the place where they finally land.

TRANSLATION

8 In Tahpanhes the word of Yahweh came to Jeremiah, saying: **9** "Take some large stones and bury them in clay[199] in the brick pavement[200] at the entrance of Pharaoh's house in Tahpanhes, while the Jews are watching. **10** Then you shall say to them,[201] 'This is what Yahweh of Hosts, the God of Israel,[202] has said: "Look, I am going to send and bring Nebuchadnezzar, king of Babylon, my servant,[203] and I will set up[204] his throne over these stones I have hidden[205] here; he will spread out his royal canopy over them.

---

199. α´ and θ´ have ἐν τῷ κρυφίῳ, "in secret," where the MT has בַּמֶּלֶט, "in the clay."

200. The phrase בַּמֶּלֶט בַּמַּלְבֵּן אֲשֶׁר, "in clay in the brick pavement (which is)," is absent in the LXX.

201. The word אֲלֵיהֶם, "to them," is absent in the LXX.

202. The phrase צְבָאוֹת אֱלֹהֵי יִשְׂרָאֵל, "of Hosts, the God of Israel," is absent in the LXX.

203. The word עַבְדִּי, "my servant," is absent in the LXX.

204. The LXX has καὶ θήσει, "and he will set up," where the MT has וְשַׂמְתִּי, "I will set up."

205. The LXX has κατέκρυψας, "you have hidden," where the MT has טָמַנְתִּי, "I have hidden."

11 He will come and smite the land of Egypt, bringing death to those destined for death, captivity for those destined for captivity, and the sword to those destined for the sword. **12** He will set fire[206] to the temples of Egypt's gods;[207] he will burn their temples and carry their gods captive. He will pick clean[208] the land of Egypt like a shepherd delousing[209] his clothing, and then he will depart from there in peace. **13** He will shatter in pieces the sacred pillars of Beth-Shemesh—the one in the land of Egypt[210]—and the temple of Egypt's gods[211] he will burn to the ground.""'"

COMMENTARY

Traditionally, this event is attributed to 582 BC, about four years after the flight of the remnant to Egypt, but the truth of the matter is that no one knows how much time has elapsed since the remnant of Jews arrived in Egypt from Judah. In many ways this text seems to be in preparation for the message directed against Egypt in 46:13-26.

43:8-9 Jeremiah receives a word from Yahweh while he is in Tahpanhes, Egypt, to perform another one of his symbolic acts. He is to do it in front of all the Jews/Judeans who fled to Egypt for their lives (vv. 8-9). While Tahpanhes was not the capital of Egypt (Sais was), archaeologist Sir Flinders Petrie in the 1880s found remains of a government building with a pavement similar to the one described here. There also is a reference in the Elephantine papyri to a house belonging to Pharaoh in Tahpanhes, possibly used as an administrative center. Thus, even though not the capital, the pharaoh had a house in the city, the site of this symbolic act.

The prophet is told to take some large stones and to bury them "in clay in the brick pavement at the entrance to Pharaoh's palace in Tahpanhes" (v. 9). Some have worried about how unlikely it is that such an action would

---

206. The LXX, Syr., and Vg. have the third person "and he will set fire" where the MT has וְהִצַּתִּי, "and I will set fire."

207. The LXX has θεῶν αὐτῶν, "their gods," where the MT has אֱלֹהֵי מִצְרַיִם, "the gods of Egypt."

208. The LXX has φθειριεῖ, "he will delouse," where the MT has וְעָטָה, "he will pick clean."

209. The LXX has φθειρίζει, "he delouses," where the MT has יַעְטֶה, "he picks clean."

210. The LXX has τοὺς ἐν Ὠν, "the one in On," where the MT has אֲשֶׁר בְּאֶרֶץ מִצְרַיִם, "the one in the land of Egypt."

211. The LXX has τὰς οἰκίας αὐτῶν, "their houses," where the MT has בָּתֵּי אֱלֹהֵי־מִצְרַיִם, "the houses of the gods of Egypt."

be permitted on government grounds in front of a government building, so they suggest that perhaps the whole action was mimed rather than actually performed. Others argue that the clay was used as mortar rather than the material into which the stones were embedded. But whichever form was used, the point of this action is clear: Egypt is not going to provide the safe haven these refugees think it is going to supply.

43:10 Verses 10–13 supply the explanation of this symbolic action. Yahweh himself explains that Nebuchadnezzar, who is, surprisingly, called "my servant" (v. 10), will come and "set his throne over these stones" that Jeremiah buries there, and Nebuchadnezzar will also "spread out his royal canopy" above them, or this could possibly refer to spreading his "carpet" over it (v. 10c). In any case, the very monarch the Judeans fled from is the same one who will set his throne up on the very same spot that Jeremiah symbolically marks out in front of Pharaoh's center in Tahpanhes.

43:11 So God's judgment is marked out (v. 11), even though the Judean community is not specified. But it is doubtful that any could miss the point: what they hope to escape, God has now brought directly to them. Egypt will be involved as well, but it does not appear that the whole nation is conquered at that time. They can expect death, captivity, and the sword (v. 11). The prospect is not happy! What are the naysayers to Jeremiah's word of guidance some four years ago thinking now? Do they think now at last they should have listened to the word from God? Perhaps the Judean refugees think that they have buried and hidden themselves in Egypt (perhaps symbolized by the large hidden stones) so they will not be discovered by Nebuchadnezzar, God, or anyone else.

43:12 The verbs in v. 12 are most interesting, for the first verb in Heb. has God as the subject who sets fire to the temples of the gods of Egypt (וְהִצַּתִּי, "and I will set on fire"), but then the king of Babylon will burn down the temples and carry off the idols/gods into captivity (וּשְׂרָפָם, "he will burn them"). It is not unusual to see God and human agency working together to accomplish a divine purpose.

The simile in v. 12c is much more difficult, for at first blush it seems to say that Nebuchadnezzar will wrap himself (עָטָה) with Egypt just as easily as a shepherd wraps a garment around himself as he moves on. The metaphor of the "shepherd" functioning as a concept for a "ruler," of course, is well known in the ancient Near East. However, there is a second, if less elegant, interpretation that draws on an alternative meaning, "to delouse." In that case the illustration is of Nebuchadnezzar picking the Egyptians off himself as easily as a shepherd searches his garments for evidence of lice, which he can just as easily pick off and be done with them. The text goes on to say (v. 12d) that Nebuchadnezzar "will depart from there in peace."

43:13 As a final act of insult (v. 13), the king of Babylon will smash the obelisks (tall, four-sided, granite pillars, with a pyramidal top, to commemorate major victories) at the site of "temple of the sun," that is, the site of On, or Heliopolis, which in this context is called by its Heb. name of Beth-Shemesh, for some reason that is not readily apparent. If this is the correct identification, it refers to the temple of the sun god, named Amon-Re, in Heliopolis, which was lined with two rows of these obelisks. Only one obelisk remains on site in Egypt, for the rest of these obelisks have been carted off to Alexandria, Rome, Istanbul, London, and New York. The Pharaoh of this time was Amasis.

While this prophecy does not claim that Babylon ever conquered Egypt, there is a fragmentary description from Babylon of a campaign that Nebuchadnezzar conducted against in Egypt in his thirty-seventh year (568/567 BC). But this does not seem to be more than a raid, rather than an attempt to subjugate the country. Moreover, Pharaoh Amasis submitted to Babylonian control, which seems to fit with the word at the end of v. 12 that this Babylonian monarch "left in peace." There may have also been an earlier invasion around 582 BC, but firm evidence so far is lacking.

God has one more symbolic action for the rebels who have gone down into Egypt. While they (or we) fled from God's will, he can still carry out his plan. So while the Jews in Egypt are watching, God instructs Jeremiah to take some rather large stones and bury them under the tile and brick pavement in Tahpanhes, Egypt. Then the prophet of God is to say that Nebuchadnezzar will come into Egypt—the one from whom they thought they were fleeing and safely removed from—and will set up his throne for judging rebels like them right on top of the tiles where those stones were buried. That is what happened.

We cannot hide from God or his plan no matter how detailed our human plans seem to be. That must have stunned these rebels when they finally realized how wrong they had been!

REJECTING A REVIVALIST'S
VIEW OF HISTORY (44:1–30)

This is the final message Jeremiah uttered. It is one of the strangest and saddest in the whole Bible. The chapter is a strong attestation to the truthfulness of a statement of Hegel: "What experience and history teaches is this ... that people and governments never have learned anything from history, or acted on principles deduced from it."[212]

Jeremiah 44 seems to be a deliberate repudiation of the work and the effects of the revival that had come under King Josiah in 621 BC. But now, perhaps some six years after the fall of Jerusalem (580 BC), the old ways of looking at history, with its previous connections with righteousness, morality, and worship, are still surprisingly declared defunct by this generation. What is more, the nation's previous times of prosperity are now attributed to the goddess Queen of Heaven, perhaps the same as Ishtar or Asherah.[213] The populace howls and moans that when sacrifices to the Queen of Heaven stopped, that is when they began to lose money and the economy changed. The chutzpah and audacity of this group of survivors knows no boundaries. They totally reject all that good King Josiah stood for and what the revival that he had been part of symbolized.

TRANSLATION

1 The word that came to Jeremiah for all the Jews living in the land of [Lower] Egypt, that is, those in Migdol, Tahpanhes, and Memphis,[214] and in Pathros:[215] **2** "This is what Yahweh of Hosts,[216] the God of Israel, has said: 'You yourselves have seen the great calamity I brought on Jerusalem and

---

212. G. W. Friedrich Hegel, *The Philosophy of History* (1837), introduction, np.

213. See "Excursus: The Queen of Heaven." Cohn suggests that "it is reasonable to speculate that the 'Queen of Heaven' mentioned in Jer 7:18; 44:17, 18, 19, 25" may be identified with the goddess Anat. See H. Cohn, "Is the 'Queen of Heaven' in Jeremiah the Goddess Anat?," *JBQ* 32, no. 1 (2004): 55–57.

214. The word וּבְנֹף, "and in Memphis," is absent in the LXX.

215. That is, "Upper Egypt."

216. The word צְבָאוֹת, "of Hosts," is absent in the LXX.

on all[217] the towns of Judah. There they lie today[218] in ruins and uninhabited 3 because of the evil that they did in order to provoke me by going to offer[219] sacrifice to other gods, whom neither they nor their fathers[220] knew. 4 Again and again I sent unto them my servants[221] the prophets, begging [them], "Please do not do this abominable thing that I hate!" 5 But they did not listen[222] or incline their ears; they did not turn from their wickedness or stop burning incense to other gods. 6 So my fierce anger was poured out on them, and it blazed against the towns of Judah and the streets of Jerusalem, leaving them a desolate and ruinous waste as it is to this day.'"

7 And now, this is what Yahweh, God[223] of Hosts, the God of Israel,[224] has said: "Why do you bring such great disaster on yourselves by cutting off from Judah the men and women, the children and infants, so as to leave no remnant for yourselves? 8 Why provoke me by the work[225] of your [own] hands have made, making sacrifices to other gods here in the land of Egypt where you have come to sojourn? You will cut off respect for yourselves and make yourselves an object of cursing and reproach among all[226] the nations on earth. 9 Have you forgotten the wickedness[227] which your fathers, the kings of Judah, and their wives, as well as you yourselves and your wives,[228] committed in the land of Judah and in the streets of Jerusalem? 10 To this day they have not humbled themselves[229] or shown fear/reverence[230] [of

217. The word -כָּל, "all," is absent in the LXX.

218. The phrase הַיּוֹם הַזֶּה, "today," is absent in the LXX.

219. The word לַעֲבֹד, "to serve," is absent in the LXX.

220. The phrase הֵמָּה אַתֶּם וַאֲבֹתֵיכֶם, "neither they, you, nor their fathers," is absent in the LXX.

221. The word -כָּל, "all," is absent in the LXX.

222. The LXX has οὐκ ἤκουσάν μου, "they did not listen to me," where the MT has וְלֹא שָׁמְעוּ, "they did not listen."

223. The word אֱלֹהֵי, "[the] God [of]," is absent in the LXX.

224. The phrase אֱלֹהֵי יִשְׂרָאֵל, "the God of Israel," is absent in the LXX.

225. The Cairo Geniza, many mss, and the Syr. have בְּמַעֲשֵׂה, "work," where the MT has בְּמַעֲשֵׂי, "works."

226. A few mss have לְכֹל, "to all," where the MT has בְּכֹל, "among all."

227. The phrase וְאֶת רָעֹתְכֶם, "and your wickedness," is absent in the LXX and Syr.

228. The phrase וְאֶת רָעֹת נְשֵׁיכֶם, "and the wickedness of your wives," is absent in the LXX.

229. The LXX has ἐπαύσαντο, "they have ceased," where the MT has דֻכְּאוּ, "they have been humbled" (lit. "they have been crushed/contrite"). The editors of BHS consider the MT reading to be doubtful and suggest reading the word as נִכְאוּ, "they have been humbled."

230. The phrase וְלֹא יָרְאוּ, "and they have not feared," is absent in the LXX.

me], nor have they followed my law and my statutes[231] which I set before you[232] and before your fathers."[233]

11 Therefore, this is what Yahweh of Hosts, the God of Israel has said: "Look, I am determined[234] to bring disaster on you and to destroy all Judah. **12** I will take away[235] the remnant of Judah[236] who were determined to go to Egypt to settle.[237] There in Egypt[238] they will all perish. They will fall by the sword or perish from starvation,[239] both small and great. They will become an object of cursing and horror, a curse-word and a disgrace. **13** I will punish those who live in Egypt with the sword, famine, and plague,[240] as I punished Jerusalem. **14** None of the remnant of Judah who have gone to[241] live[242] in Egypt will escape or survive to return to the land of Judah, to which they long to return and live; none will return except a few fugitives."

15 Then all the men, who knew that their wives were burning incense to other gods, together with all the women who were standing by[243]—a great crowd in all—answered Jeremiah. **16** "As for what you have just said to us in the name of Yahweh, we are not going to listen to you, **17** for we will most assuredly do everything we said we would. We will offer sacrifice to the Queen[244] of Heaven and will pour out drink offerings to her just as we and our fathers, our kings, and our officials used to do in the towns of Judah

---

231. The LXX has τῶν προσταγμάτων μου, "in my ordinances," where the MT has בְּתוֹרָתִי וּבְחֻקֹּתַי, "in my law and in my statutes."

232. The word לִפְנֵיכֶם, "before you," is absent in the LXX.

233. The LXX has τῶν πατέρων αὐτῶν, "their fathers," where the MT has אֲבוֹתֵיכֶם, "your fathers."

234. The LXX has a briefer version of this verse: διὰ τοῦτο οὕτως εἶπεν κύριος ἰδοὺ ἐγὼ ἐφίστημι τὸ πρόσωπόν μου, "Therefore, thus says the Lord, 'Behold, I set my face.'"

235. The word וְלָקַחְתִּי, "I will take," is absent in the LXX.

236. The word יְהוּדָה, "of Judah," is absent in the LXX.

237. The LXX has τοὺς ἐν Αἰγύπτῳ, "the ones in the land of Egypt," where the MT has אֲשֶׁר־שָׂמוּ פְנֵיהֶם לָבוֹא אֶרֶץ־מִצְרַיִם, "who were determined to go to Egypt to settle there."

238. The phrase בְּאֶרֶץ מִצְרַיִם, "in the land of Egypt," is absent in the LXX.

239. The second occurrence in this verse of the phrase בַּחֶרֶב וּבָרָעָב, "by the sword or by starvation," is absent in the LXX.

240. The LXX has θανάτῳ, "by death," where the MT has וּבַדֶּבֶר, "by plague."

241. The word שָׁם, "there," is absent in the LXX.

242. The word לָשֶׁבֶת, "to live," is absent in the LXX and Syr.

243. The word הָעֹמְדוֹת, "standing by," is absent in the LXX.

244. Many Heb. mss have למלאכת, "for the service of," where the MT has לִמְלֶכֶת, "Queen." The LXX (βασιλίσσῃ, "Queen"), Vg. (*Reginae*, "Queen"), and 7:18 (לִמְלֶכֶת, "to the Queen") support the reading in the MT.

and in the streets of Jerusalem; for then we had plenty to eat and we were well off and experienced no harm. **18** But ever since we stopped burning incense to the Queen[245] of Heaven and pouring out drink offerings to her,[246] we have had nothing and have been perishing by sword and famine. **19** And the women added,[247] 'We will go on sacrificing to the Queen[248] of Heaven and pouring out libations to her. Were we making cakes in her image[249] without our husbands knowing it and pouring out drink offerings to her?'"

20 Then Jeremiah said to all the people, the men, the women, and all those who were answering him in this way: **21** "The incense you, your fathers, your kings and your officials, and the people of the land[250] burned in the towns of Judah and the streets of Jerusalem—did you think that Yahweh did not notice it or that it would never come to his mind? **22** No, it was because Yahweh could no longer put up with your wicked actions and the detestable things which you did that your land has become an object of cursing and a desolate waste without inhabitants,[251] as it is today. **23** Because you have burned incense and have sinned against Yahweh and have not obeyed the voice of Yahweh or followed his law or his decrees or his testimonies, this present disaster has come upon you as you now see."[252]

24 Then Jeremiah said to all the people, particularly the women: "Hear the word of Yahweh all Judah, who are in the land of Egypt![253] **25** This is what Yahweh of Hosts,[254] the God of Israel, says: 'You and your wives[255] have spoken by your mouths and fulfilled with your hands the actions you

---

245. See note on 17.

246. The phrase וְהַסֵּךְ־לָהּ נְסָכִים, "and pouring out drink offerings to her," is absent in the LXX.

247. The LXX[L] supplies the phrase καὶ αἱ γυναῖκες εἶπον, "and the women said," at the beginning of the verse, and the Syr. is similar.

248. See note on 17.

249. The word לְהַעֲצִבָה, "in her image," is absent in the LXX and Syr.

250. The word אֹתָם, "them," is absent in the LXX.

251. The phrase מֵאֵין יוֹשֵׁב, "without inhabitant," is absent in the LXX.

252. The phrase כַּיּוֹם הַזֶּה, "as it is this day," is absent in the LXX.

253. The phrase כָּל־יְהוּדָה אֲשֶׁר בְּאֶרֶץ מִצְרָיִם, "all Judah, who are in the land of Egypt," is absent in the LXX.

254. The word צְבָאוֹת, "of Hosts," is absent in the LXX.

255. The LXX has ὑμεῖς γυναῖκες, "you women," where the MT has אַתֶּם וּנְשֵׁיכֶם, "you and your wives." The editors of BHS suggest emending the MT to אַתֶּנָה הַנָּשִׁים, "you women," which would fit better with the following fem. verb וַתְּדַבֵּרְנָה, "and you have spoken."

promised: "We will certainly perform the vows we made to burn incense and pour out drink offerings to the Queen[256] of Heaven." Go ahead, then, do what you promised! Keep your vows![257] **26** But, hear the word of Yahweh, all from Judah living in Egypt, "Look out! I swear by my great name, declares Yahweh, that never again shall my name be invoked, 'as Adonai Yahweh lives,' by the mouth of any one from Judah living anywhere in all of Egypt. **27** Look out! I am watching over them for harm, not for good. All the Jews in the land of Egypt will perish by the sword and famine until they are all destroyed. **28** The survivors of the sword who return from the land of Egypt[258] to the land of Judah will be very few. Then the whole[259] remnant of Judah who came to sojourn in Egypt will know whose word will stand—mine or theirs![260] **29** This will be sign to you, declares Yahweh,[261] that I will punish you in this place, so that my threats against you will definitely stand.[262] **30** This is what Yahweh says: 'I am going to hand over Pharaoh[263] Hophra, king of Egypt, to his enemies, to those who seek his life, just as I handed over Zedekiah, king of Judah, to Nebuchadnezzar, king of Babylon, to his enemies who sought his life.'"'"

COMMENTARY

The Danger of Misunderstanding God's Previous Judgments (44:1–6)

The eternal promise and plan of God is declared "irrevocable" by the apostle Paul in Rom 11:29, but that is no guarantee that every person or every generation will participate in that promise God made to Israel, for that will only come by belief and trust in the coming Man of Promise, the Messiah. And it is just as easy for our generation to place our confidence in the alleged fact

---

256. See note on v. 17.

257. A few Heb. mss have נִסְכֵּיכֶם, "your drink offerings," where the MT has נִדְרֵיכֶם, "your vows."

258. The phrase מִן־אֶרֶץ מִצְרַיִם, "from the land of Egypt," is absent in the LXX.

259. The word כָּל־, "whole," is absent in the LXX.

260. The phrase מִמֶּנִּי וּמֵהֶם, "mine or theirs," is absent in the LXX.

261. The phrase נְאֻם־יְהוָה, "declares Yahweh," is absent in the LXX.

262. The LXX omits בַּמָּקוֹם הַזֶּה לְמַעַן תֵּדְעוּ כִּי קוֹם יָקוּמוּ דְבָרַי עֲלֵיכֶם, "in this place, so that my word against you will definitely stand." It is likely an example of homoioteleuton, in which the scribe was confused over the two occurrences of עֲלֵיכֶם, "against you," in this verse (Keown, 262).

263. The word פַּרְעֹה, "Pharaoh," is absent in the LXX.

that we are the church, the people of God. Judah, much like later generations, began to think that they were invincible; no evil could touch them!
They were the people of God. God had promised them the land. It would
all soon be rectified, and they would be restored—or so they thought.

44:1 But Yahweh calls those who have gone to Egypt in direct opposition
to his directives to think carefully about what they have done. Here they
are living in Lower Egypt in the delta region of Migdol, Tahpanhes, and
Memphis, with some in Upper Egypt or Pathros. Migdol and Tahpanhes
both were border towns in the eastern part of the Nile River delta, whereas
Memphis was at the head of the delta, some fourteen miles south of modern
Cairo. Memphis also was at one time the capital of Lower Egypt. The land
of Pathros, meaning in Egyptian, "the southern land," was in Upper Egypt,
which stretched from south of Memphis all the way down the Nile River
Valley for some three hundred miles to Aswan. Later in the Persian period,
a group of legal documents and letters from Elephantine, in southern Egypt
at the first cataract on the Nile River, would record the presence of a Jewish
community at that time who were said to worship Yahu (Yahweh?).[264]

44:2 Verse 2 begins by reminding the Judeans that they have personally
witnessed the "great disaster" (רָעָה) that Yahweh brought on Judah. This
word, "disaster, evil," occurs no less than fourteen times in this chapter
(vv. 2–3, 5, 7, 9 [5x in the pl.], 11, 17, 23, 27, 29). How can they or anyone dispute that what was threatened and predicted by Jeremiah actually came
to pass? Judah was destroyed, ransacked, and reduced to an uninhabited
place. Does that not show he is really an accredited prophet of God?

44:3 The sins of those former days that occasioned such devastation were
the worship of other gods, an insult to the exclusive loyalty and worship
they owe to the one and only true, living God. So why do these Judeans persist in "burning incense" (קָטֵר) to gods that neither they nor their fathers
ever previously knew (v. 3)?

---

264. See A. Kurt, *The Persian Empire: A Corpus of Sources from the Achaemenid Period* (New
York: Routledge, 2013), 857.

44:4 God has been slow to bring his judgments on this nation, for "again and again," Yahweh affirms, "I sent unto them my servants the prophets, begging [them], 'Please do not do this abominable thing that I hate!'" (v. 4). This disaster has not come all of a sudden, but repeatedly prophet after prophet came with divine warning that if this persisted, judgment would come. Even more pathetic is the plaintive nature of an appeal to Judah (אַל־נָא), "begging" them, which is the only time this expression appears in the Bible and attributed to God. God absolutely "hated" such "abominable" practices (v. 4).

44:5-6 Nevertheless, despite such long-suffering and slowness to final action, along with pleading and begging from the God of the universe with his creatures, they did not "repent" or "turn" (שׁוּב, v. 5) back to him. The "fire" of God's wrath had burned the towns of Judah and the streets of Jerusalem into a "ruinous waste" (v. 6), so why isn't anyone paying attention?

The Danger of Provoking God to Anger (44:7-19)

44:7-10 The rehearsal of all these facts is not intended by God to be a dry history lesson about the grand old days of the past; it is meant for the present survivors of that calamity as a hard reason why they should repent and to turn back to Yahweh in faith. So the obvious question now is this: Why do they bring [another] great disaster on themselves by "cutting off" (כָּרַת) those left in the remnant so that no one survives (v. 7)? Are these people so listless that they have already forgotten what took place in Judah, where he used the "disaster/evil" (רָעָה in vv. 5, 9)? Special attention is paid to the wives of the kings and the wives of the listeners, for there still is no evidence that the people have become "crushed/broken/contrite/humbled" (דְּכָא, v. 10) by the events they suffered. One would think they would be overwhelmed by now with the evil they have done.

44:11-14 Verse 11 begins with "therefore," for Yahweh is now "determined," or in the literal/idiomatic form, "I have set my face" against "all Judah," to "destroy" them (also vv. 7, 8). All those Judeans who went to Egypt in disregard of the word they allegedly sought with such furor through Jeremiah are proven to be first-class, incurable rebels. Just as Yahweh had punished

Jerusalem with the "sword, famine, and plague," so he will punish all of the Jewish people who fled to Egypt (v. 13). None will escape, and none of those refugees will return to Judah, "except a few fugitives" (v. 14).

44:15–16 Two groups of defiant and obstinate people outright reject and spurn the message from Yahweh given by Jeremiah: the men whose wives burn incense to the Queen of Heaven and all the women who are present, that is, all the people who went to Egypt (v. 15). Pointedly, they acknowledge that Jeremiah has gotten his message from Yahweh, but as for this word from above, they say, "We are not going to listen to you" (v. 16). That is that! There is no room for negotiating and none for repentance.

44:17–19 Their reason is most curious: "Ever since we stopped burning incense to the Queen of Heaven … we have had nothing and have been perishing by sword and famine" (v. 18). How about that for a view of revival? If King Josiah had not started this nonsense about repentance and revival, we would be far better off and living in a much better set of circumstances. It is not Yahweh who blessed them in the past; no, it was the Queen of Heaven.[265] She is the source of all our blessings! So the women lead the revolt. Anyway, they announce: "our husbands know about our burning incense to her and our pouring out libations to her" (cf. vv. 15, 19).[266] Thus, the whole community is involved, as Jer 7:18 noted earlier: the children gathered the wood for the sacrifices to this goddess, the men lit the fires, and the women kneaded cakes of bread for her. Once again, history is showing that the hand that rocks the cradle has an enormous influence on the lives of her children, if not on history itself. Moreover, their conception of prosperity is also disclosed: it means they have "plenty to eat," "were well off," and "experienced no harm" in those days when her worship was at a high point (v. 17). These are crass views indeed, filled with great defiance against God himself, sure to provoke the judgment of God.

---

265. See "Excursus: The Queen of Heaven."

266. Edelman suggests that *qiṭṭēr* is better translated as "burn the food offerings." See D. Edelman, "The Meaning of *QIṬṬĒR*," *VT* 35, no. 4 (1985): 395–404.

The Danger of Misunderstanding the Mercy of God (44:20–30)

44:20–21 What is Jeremiah to do? Surely this is a twisted defense of idolatry and an open contesting of all the former blessings that God sent as gifts. Now all that was good in those former days is being attributed to dead, deaf, and dumb idols. All that is left is for the prophet to ask is this: Do they think Yahweh himself has not noticed all this idolatrous worship? Or do they think that God does not even bring it to his mind (v. 20)? In fact, isn't this idolatry one of the reasons Jerusalem burnt to the ground in the first place (v. 21)? The involvement of all the survivors shows no exceptions. One and all are just plain rebels. Surely this shows that the judgment of God is more than justified; it had to come, for these folks are adamant in their stubborn sassiness.

44:25–28 Seeing the people are bent on destroying themselves, Jeremiah urges sarcastically, "Go ahead, then, do what you promised! Keep your vows!" to the Queen of Heaven (v. 25). (Apparently they have forgotten about any former vows to Yahweh!) But Yahweh swears by his great name that never again will any of that group ever invoke his name or the oath, "As Adonai Yahweh lives" (v. 26). They will all be destroyed in the land of Egypt, for God will be "watching" over them (שֹׁקֵד, v. 27), as he promised in the call chapter to Jeremiah that he would be "watching" over them (1:12); nothing will escape his notice, for very few of them will survive.

The great question, however, is this: Whose word will stand the test of time and real events of history—Yahweh's or the people's (v. 28b)? The proof will come from history itself and the ruins of a people who refused to obey God in order to work out their own safety, which they are shown to be unable to effect in the end!

44:29–30 God has one final sign for his prophet to give to this hardhearted bunch of rebels: In Egypt itself God will hand over Pharaoh Hophra's life just as Nebuchadnezzar had taken Zedekiah's life (vv. 29–30). Hophra is also known as Apries in Gk. and reigned from February 589 to 568 BC. Hophra was assassinated in a military coup led by Amasis (also known as Ahmose), who then succeeded him in the year 568 BC, the same courtier whom Hophra had sent to take charge of the Egyptian forces as they suppressed a revolt in Libya. But instead the army made this courtier king, and he shared rule with Hophra for a few years and eventually was part of his death in 568 BC (46:17).

Seldom have hearers of the word of God been so insolent and downright defiant as these refugees from Judah living in Egypt are to Jeremiah's message. What is even more tragic is that they know this is the word of the Lord, yet that in no way makes them regard it any more seriously. The wives will just continue in their idolatrous practices, for their husbands are fully aware of what they are doing. These wives argue, in effect, that they are under their husband's umbrella, so what is the problem with Jeremiah and the Lord?

BARUCH SEEKS THINGS FOR HIMSELF (45:1–5)

Pity parties are not fun to be around, but when it involves one of God's servants, it is even more pathetic. So it is that chapter 45 switches from telling us about Jeremiah's ministry to focus for a moment on his scribe, Baruch, the son of Neriah. This event is usually dated to about 605 BC, before the fall of Jerusalem, in the fourth year of King Jehoiakim, son of Josiah, king of Judah.

TRANSLATION

1 The word that Jeremiah the prophet spoke to Baruch, son of Neriah, in the fourth year of Jehoiakim, son of Josiah, king of Judah, after Baruch had written on a scroll these words from the lips of Jeremiah: **2** "This is what Yahweh, the God of Israel,[267] has said to you, Baruch: **3** 'You have said: "Woe is me!" for Yahweh has added sorrow to my pain. I am worn out[268] with my sighing, and find no rest.' **4** Thus you shall say to him: 'This is what Yahweh has said: "Look! What I have built I am about to tear down, and what I have planted I am about to uproot throughout the land.[269] **5** And

---

267. The phrase אֱלֹהֵי יִשְׂרָאֵל, "the God of Israel," is absent in the LXX.

268. The LXX has ἐκοιμήθην, "I go to sleep," where the MT has יָגַעְתִּי, "I am worn out."

269. The phrase וְאֶת־כָּל־הָאָרֶץ לִי הִיא, "and the whole land is mine," is absent in the LXX.

you—you expect great things for yourself? Do not seek [them], for, look! I am about to bring disaster on all flesh, declares Yahweh; I will give to you your life as a prize/booty wherever you go."'"

COMMENTARY

A Word to Baruch (45:1)

45:1 Yahweh gives a very personal word to Jeremiah to transmit to his scribe Baruch, son of Neriah. This chapter records the only words we hear from Baruch in this book, but he is the faithful amanuensis who wrote "these words" (v. 1) in a scroll—presumably the entire prophecy of Jeremiah up to the fourth year of King Jehoiakim. Whether this word came "after" (NIV) Baruch had finished the scroll or "when" (NJPS) he was writing it cannot be determined exactly. Perhaps this complaint of Baruch came after he had completed the first scroll that was unceremoniously cut up by King Jehoiakim and as he was being called on to do a second writing of the same material all over again. Baruch's brother Seraiah has a more honorable and prestigious job, for he is a member of Zedekiah's court (51:59). Perhaps that is what is irking Baruch. Add to that, his life's work on an earlier scroll has just gone up in flames. No wonder, then, that a chapter of the Bible singles him out for a special word from Yahweh. That the names of his father Neriah and his grandfather Mahseiah (32:12) are given may indicate that he comes from an educated family of the upper class.

Baruch's Complaint (45:2–3)

45:2–3 Baruch's complaint begins with the wail "Woe is me!" Jeremiah, at times, says the same thing (10:19; 15:10). This scribe contends that Yahweh has let him experience affliction by adding sorrow to his life (v. 3) to the point where he is "worn out with groaning and finding no rest" (v. 3b). After all, he too has seen all the evil and wickedness that is going on in his nation. He knows that God's payday has to come soon and will happen to his country! The act of writing all this down makes these facts all the more real and lamentable. Furthermore, he even has to read these same words out loud in the temple (36:4–8), a job he apparently does not cherish either. It indeed has been hard for both Jeremiah and Baruch; there is no denying that. But these are difficult times, and the people are in no mood to accept God's true words. These men bear the immediate brunt of the rejection that comes so frequently with Yahweh's announcements.

God's Response to Baruch (45:4–5)

45:4 God's word to the complaining scribe is in effect this: You think you have troubles? You haven't seen anything yet. Look at what I as the God of Israel must endure: I have to turn upside down everything that has taken me several millennia to build (v. 4a) in my purpose and plan for this nation and for the families of the earth. I have to uproot the vine of Israel that I carefully planted and have nourished to this point (v. 4b). It is not only the promise of the land but the whole promise-plan of God that has to be undone for the moment.

So now, says Yahweh, you, little you! You want to tell me that you have problems! Are you kidding? Your problem is that you have a surge of jealousy about your brother Seraiah's prestige, who has a big government job while you are just a low-paid, lowly scribe for a prophet who is not highly regarded and is the laughingstock of the nation. So what's your problem? Do you have a high-and-mighty image of what you should be and the success that should greet you that you are now too big for this scribe's job? Is that your problem? Is my call on your life too low a call? Am I a less highly regarded figure than some in the government or the like?

45:5 Do not seek great things for yourself (v. 5). Revise your personal ambitions for yourself and for the kingdom of God. I will give you the same gift I gave to Ebed-Melech (39:15–18): "I will let you escape with your life" (v. 5b). Then you will be able to go wherever you wish.

Paul the apostle taught in 1 Tim 6:6 that "godliness with contentment is great gain." Moreover, he taught in Phil 4:11 that he had "learned to be content whatever the circumstances," whether he had much or little. Baruch has to learn the same lessons. He must compare his work to the progress his brother is making as a successful worker in the government of the land, and here he is seeing his work of recording Jeremiah's preaching go up in flames. Baruch and all of us in the same boat with him need to think about Ps 131, for we ought not to concern ourselves about things too wonderful for us. We need to quiet our souls like a weaned child and put our hope only in the Lord.

God shows Baruch that he has worked all these centuries with his people Israel, but he is now bringing disaster on them. God will, however, grant Baruch his life as a consolation prize when all others who have left Judah will lose their lives for their disobedience.

PROPHECIES AGAINST NINE NATIONS (46:1–51:64)

Jeremiah was called from the very beginning of his ministry to be a prophet to all the nations (1:5, 10), so it is not surprising that he also has messages from Yahweh that pertain to other nations. That calling also matches the teaching that Yahweh is Lord not just over Israel and Judah, but over all the peoples and nations of the world. Thus, God's messengers, his servants the prophets, routinely have the task of announcing his message to the nations at large as well as to Israel and Judah. His alone is the right, power, and authority to set events in motion and to judge, when necessary, the nations (10:6–7; 46:28; 48:15; 51:57).

There is a debate whether these prophecies originate with Jeremiah or someone else. The reason for making this suggestion of a non-Jeremian authorship is, how could Jeremiah have urged submission to Babylon, which he did, and then turn around and announce judgment on Babylon? But this is not a great theological issue, for while Babylon was called by Yahweh to be the instrument of his judgment on Judah, as Assyria was also called in Isa 10:15, Babylon is simultaneously responsible for her actions and will be required by the judge of the whole earth to give an answer for how she acts in carrying out that divine commission.

Chapters 46–51 are clearly a separate section of this book of Jeremiah. It is widely recognized that the material in chapters 37–45 stands together and appears to be in chronological sequence in the Masoretic Text (MT), but the Septuagint (LXX) exhibits some variations from the MT. In the LXX version of Jeremiah, these prophecies are placed after 25:13a, but in a somewhat different order from the Heb. text. A good number of commentators believe the Septuagint's placement of these passages after 25:13a is where these chapters were originally located.[1] The order of the nine nations in the Masoretic Text, however, exhibits a more logical progression; it begins with Egypt, the second-greatest superpower of the day, and then moves from the southwest (where Egypt is located) to the northeast to finish with Babylon, the greatest superpower of that day. Moreover, the MT chapter 45 on Baruch appears in the LXX as 51:31–35, which further supports his role in writing both of these texts. An even more interesting question is this: Were these prophecies against the nations included in the first scroll or the second one that Jeremiah wrote (chap. 36)?

The Order of the Oracles against the Nations		
	MT Texts and Order	**LXX Texts and Order**
Egypt	46:2–28 (1)	26:2–28 (2)
Philistia	47:1–7 (2)	29:1–7 (4)
Moab	48:1–47 (3)	31:1–44 (9)
Ammon	49:1–6 (4)	30:17–21 (6)
Edom	49:7–22 (5)	30:1–16 (5)
Damascus	49:23–27 (6)	30:29–33 (8)
Kedar	49:28–33 (7)	30:23–28 (7)
Elam	49:34–39 (8)	25:14–20 (1)
Babylon	50:1–51:64 (9)	27:1–28:64 (3)

TWO ORACLES AGAINST EGYPT (46:1–28)

No nation has been more intimately connected with Israel and her past than Egypt. She is mentioned well over seven hundred times in the Bible, 125 times alone in the formula: "I am Yahweh your God who brought you

1. For a summary of views regarding the placement of the oracles against the nations see M. A. Taylor, "Jeremiah 45: The Problem of Placement," *JSOT* (1987): 79–98; B. Gosse, "Jérémie xlv et la place du recueil d'oracles contre les nations dans le livre de Jérémie" *VT* 40 (1990): 145–51; and E. Di Pede, "Jérusalem, Ebed-Melek et Baruch: Enquête narrative sur le déplacement chronologique de Jr 45," *RB* 111 (2004): 61–77.

up out of the land of Egypt, the house of bondage." The specific historical event that the first oracle (vv. 2–12) refers to is the defeat of Pharaoh
Necho (609–595 BC) at Carchemish (located on the border between Syria
and Turkey) at the hands of Nebuchadnezzar, soon to be king of Babylon.
It is the "fourth year of Jehoiakim, king of Judah," that is, 605 BC.

In the second oracle against Egypt (v. 13–24), it is more difficult to determine the precise time, for we lack too many pieces of evidence. One suggestion is that it is 604 BC, for just as Nebuchadnezzar had the Egyptians
on the run, after the Battle of Carchemish, he suddenly got word that his
father the king had died, and so he had to break off the chase. However, he
returned to the area a year later and captured Ashkelon, a Philistine city,
and he may have pressed the battle against Egypt again at this time. But
that there is a new introduction in v. 13 argues against that supposition.

Another major battle came late in 601 BC, but in that contest the two
sides fought to a standstill, so a Babylonian victory does not seem to fit the
bill here. Josephus, the Jewish historian, records a 582/581 BC campaign
against Egypt by Babylon,[2] but the Babylonian Chronicle for this period has
not yet been found, if it exists. Nebuchadnezzar is alleged to have brought
into submission Ammon and Moab, and attacked Egypt and murdered and
set up another king beside Pharaoh Hophra, but we know that Hophra
reigned from 589 to 570 BC, so this evidence does not appear to work here.
The best guess for placing this material is the year 568 BC, or at least the
text anticipates events connected with that year.

TRANSLATION

1[3] This is what came as the word of Yahweh to Jeremiah the prophet concerning the nations.[4] **2** About Egypt, concerning the army of Pharaoh
Necho,[5] king of Egypt, who was defeated at Carchemish on the Euphrates
River by Nebuchadnezzar, king of Babylon, in the fourth year of Jehoiakim,
son of Josiah, king of Judah.

---

2. *Ant.* 10.9.7.

3. This verse is absent in the LXX.

4. Many mss and LXX[O, L] add ־כָּל, "all," before "the nations."

5. The Syr. has *ḥgjr'*, "the lame one," and Tg. has חגיר, "lame" (Heb.: נְכֵה), where the MT
has נְכוֹ, "Necho."

3 Prepare your shields, large and small!
   Forward to the battle.
4 Harness the horses,
   Mount the steeds!
   Take your positions with helmets [on]!
   Polish[6] your spears,
   Put on your armor.[7]
5 What do I see?[8]
   They are terrified,
   They are retreating,
   Their warriors are beaten down,
   They flee pell-mell,
   Without looking back.
   Terror is on every side,
   Declares Yahweh.
6 No flight for the swift,
   No escape for the man of valor;
   Up north on the banks of the Euphrates,[9]
   They stagger and fall.
7 Who is this who rises like the Nile,
   Like rivers reeling to and fro?
8 [It's] Egypt[10] that rises like the Nile,
   Like rivers surging in a flood.
   He says: "I will rise up and cover the land,
   Destroying the cities and their people."[11]
9 Go up, you horses!
   Drive madly, you charioteers!

---

6. The LXX has προβάλετε, "put out," where the MT has מִרְקוּ, "polish."

7. Many Heb. mss have the alternate spelling השרינת, "the armor," where the MT has הַסִּרְיֹנֹת, "the armor."

8. The word רָאִיתִי, "I see," is absent in the LXX, rendering the question "Why do they fear ... ?"

9. The word נְהַר־, "river," is absent in the LXX.

10. The LXX has ὕδατα Αἰγύπτου, "waters of Egypt," where the MT only has מִצְרַיִם, "Egypt."

11. The LXX is lacking וְ עִיר, "the city and," from the phrase עִיר וְיֹשְׁבֵי, "the city and inhabitants," in the MT.

March out,[12] you soldiers!
Men of Cush and Put, who bear shields,
Men of Lydia, who wield the bow.
10 But that day is the day of Adonai Yahweh of Hosts,[13]
A day of vengeance, to be avenged of his foes.
The sword[14] will devour till it is satisfied,
Till it has been saturated with their blood.
For Adonai Yahweh of Hosts will offer sacrifice,
In the northern land, by the River Euphrates.
11 Go up to Gilead and bring back balm,
O Virgin Daughter Egypt!
In vain you heap up remedies,
There is no healing for you.
12 The nations have heard your outcry,[15]
Your wailing has filled the land.
For soldier will stumble over soldier;
Together they will fall down.

13 This is the word that Yahweh spoke unto[16] Jeremiah the prophet[17] concerning the coming of Nebuchadnezzar, king of Babylon, to attack the land of Egypt.

14 "Announce this in Egypt![18]
Proclaim it in Migdol;
Proclaim it in Memphis and Tahpanhes![19]

---

12. The LXX has the impv. ἐξέλθατε, "you go out," where the MT has the impf. וְיֵצְאוּ, "march out" (lit. "they will go out").

13. The LXX has κυρίῳ τῷ θεῷ ἡμῶν, "the Lord our God," where the MT has לַאדֹנָי יְהוִה צְבָאוֹת, "(of) Adonai Yahweh of Hosts."

14. The editors of BHS state that the word חֶרֶב, "sword," should be read as חַרְבּוֹ, "his sword," with the suf. וֹ, "his," lost due to haplogr. Cf. the LXX, which has ἡ μάχαιρα κυρίου, "the sword of the Lord."

15. The LXX has φωνήν σου, "your voice" (Heb.: קוֹלֵךְ), where the MT has קְלוֹנֵךְ, "your shame" (translated here as "your outcry").

16. The LXX has ἐν χειρί, "by the hand of," where the MT has אֶל, "unto."

17. The word הַנָּבִיא, "the prophet," is absent in the LXX.

18. The phrase בְּמִצְרַיִם וְהַשְׁמִיעוּ, "in Egypt and proclaim," is absent in the LXX.

19. The word וּבְתַחְפַּנְחֵס, "and Tahpanhes," is absent in the LXX.

Say: 'Take your positions and be prepared!

For the sword has devoured all around you.'[20]

15 Why are your warriors cut down?[21]

They cannot stand [their ground],

Because Yahweh will drive [them] out.

16 The multitude will stumble[22] and fall.

Then one man said to another,[23]

'Get up, Let us go back to our people,

To the land of our birth,

Away from the dreadful[24] sword.'

17 There they exclaim,[25] 'Pharaoh[26] king of Egypt,

Is a "[Loud] noise,"

He has missed his chance.'[27]

18 'As surely as I live,' says the King,

Whose name is Yahweh of Hosts:[28]

'One will come who is like Tabor among the mountains,

Like Carmel by the sea.

19 Pack your belongings for exile,

Inhabitants of fair Egypt!

For Memphis will be laid waste,

In ruins without inhabitant.

---

20. The LXX has τὴν σμίλακά σου, "your yew tree" (Heb.: סְבְכֵךְ), where the MT has סְבִיבֶיךָ, "all around you."

21. The LXX has διὰ τί ἔφυγεν ὁ Ἆπις ὁ μόσχος ὁ ἐκλεκτός σου, "Why does Apis, your chosen calf, flee?" where the MT has מַדּוּעַ נִסְחַף אַבִּירֶיךָ, "Why are your warriors cut down?"

22. The LXX has καὶ τὸ πλῆθός σου ἠσθένησεν, "and your multitude was weak," where the MT has הִרְבָּה כּוֹשֵׁל, "the multitude will stumble."

23. The LXX has καὶ ἔπεσεν καὶ ἕκαστος πρὸς τὸν πλησίον αὐτοῦ ἐλάλει, "and he fell and each one said to his neighbor," where the MT says נָפַל אִישׁ אֶל־רֵעֵהוּ וַיֹּאמְרוּ, "a man has fallen against his neighbor and they said." The current translation follows the LXX.

24. The LXX has Ἑλληνικῆς, "Greek," and α΄ and θ΄ have τοῦ περιστερᾶς, "of the dove," where the MT has הַיּוֹנָה, "the dreadful/oppressing."

25. The LXX has the impv. καλέσατε τὸ ὄνομα Φαραω, "Call the name of Pharaoh," where the MT has קָרְאוּ שָׁם פַּרְעֹה, "There they exclaim, 'Pharaoh ... '"

26. The LXX inserts the name Νεχαω, "Necho," after Pharaoh.

27. The LXX has Σαων-εσβι-εμωηδ, which is a transliteration of the Heb. phrase in the MT: שָׁאוֹן הֶעֱבִיר הַמּוֹעֵד, "[loud] noise, he has missed his chance" (Keown, 284n17b-b)

28. The LXX has λέγει κύριος ὁ θεός, "says the Lord God," where the MT has נְאֻם־הַמֶּלֶךְ יְהוָה צְבָאוֹת שְׁמוֹ, "says the King, whose name is Yahweh of Hosts."

20 Egypt is a beautiful[29] heifer,

But a gadfly is coming[30] from the north.

21 Also the mercenaries in her midst

Were like fatted calves;[31]

They too turned and fled together,

They did not stand their ground,

For the day of disaster had come upon them,

The time of their punishment.

22 Hear her [Egypt] hiss like a snake,[32]

When the army[33] approaches,

And the axes come upon her,[34]

Like men chopping wood.

23 They will cut down[35] her forest,' declares Yahweh,

'Impenetrable though it be;

For they are more numerous than locusts,

That cannot be counted.

24 The Daughter of Egypt is shamed,

Handed over to the clutches of the north.'"

25 Yahweh of Hosts, the God of Israel, has said, "Look! I am going to bring punishment on Amon god of Thebes, on Pharaoh, on Egypt and her gods and her kings and on those who are trusting in him.[36] **26**[37] I will hand them over to those who are seeking their lives, to Nebuchadnezzar king of

---

29. Many Heb. mss have the alternate spelling יפיפיה where the MT has יְפֵה־פִיָּה, "beautiful."

30. Many Heb. mss have בָּא בָהּ, "he is coming against her," where the MT has בָּא בָא, "he is coming, he is coming."

31. The LXX adds the phrase τρεφόμενοι ἐν αὐτῇ, "fed in her," after "fatted calves."

32. The LXX has ὡς ὄφεως συρίζοντος, "just as a serpent hisses"; the Syr. has 'jk ḥwj' dršp, "just like a serpent creeping"; and the Vg. has quasi aeris sonabit, "like the sound of brass," where the MT has קוֹלָהּ כַּנָּחָשׁ יֵלֵךְ, "her sound is like a serpent going."

33. The LXX has ἐν ἄμμῳ, "in sand," where the MT has בְחַיִל, "when the army."

34. Many mss have לְךָ, "upon you," where the MT has לָהּ, "upon her."

35. LXX^L and the Syr. have the impv. "cut down," and the LXX has ἐκκόψουσιν, "they will cut down," where the MT has כָּרְתוּ, "they cut down."

36. The LXX version of this verse is ἰδοὺ ἐγὼ ἐκδικῶ τὸν Αμων τὸν υἱὸν αὐτῆς ἐπὶ Φαραω καὶ ἐπὶ τοὺς πεποιθότας ἐπ' αὐτῷ, "Behold, I will avenge Amon her son upon Pharaoh and upon those trusting in him."

37. This verse is absent in the LXX.

Babylon and his officers, after which Egypt will dwell as in former times,"
declares Yahweh.

> **27** "As for you, fear not, O Jacob my servant,
>> Do not be dismayed, O Israel.
> For see! From a distant place I will save you,
>> Your offspring from the land of exile.
> Then Jacob will once more find rest,
>> No one will make him afraid.
> **28** So you, O Jacob, my servant, fear not," declares Yahweh,
>> "For I am with you.
> Even though I make a full end of all nations,
>> Among whom I have scattered you,
>> But of you I will not make a complete end;
> I will chastise you but with justice,
>> But I will not let you go entirely unpunished."

COMMENTARY

Egypt's Defeat at Carchemish (46:1–12)

46:1 Verse 1 is the title for all nine oracles against the foreign nations in
chapters 46–51.[38] Since this same title does not occur in the LXX, this verse
could have been added, so goes the argument, when these chapters were
relocated from what some considered to be their original setting after 25:13.
Such oracles of judgment appear in most prophetic books; for example:
Isa 13–23; Ezek 25–32; Amos 1–2; and most of the books of Obadiah, Jonah,
and Nahum. So it is not unusual for foreign nations to be included in the
oversight and watchful eye of Yahweh. It is true, of course, that this section of Jeremiah includes a wide variety of literary styles, but there is no
rule that says that either the prophet or Yahweh is limited to one special
literary style. While Jeremiah does not usually single out particular sins
that these nations have committed, nevertheless it is clear that their disregard for the God of all creation still holds them accountable.

---

38. J. P. van der Westhuizen, "A Stylistic-Exegetical Analysis of Jeremiah 46:1–12," *JBQ*
20 (1991–92): 84–95.

46:2 The Battle of Carchemish is a pivotal point in the history of the ancient Near East, for in this battle Babylon clearly establishes her supremacy over Egypt, which will be marginalized as a second-rate power from this point on, leaving the position of number-one power in the Near East to Babylon. This is the same Pharaoh Necho who killed King Josiah of Judah in a battle at Megiddo three years earlier, in 609 BC, as the thirty-nine-year-old righteous king of Judah attempted to stop Necho as he moved with his army toward Mesopotamia.

It is because the Assyrian power collapsed that Egypt began to awake from her previously fairly passive non-involvement in foreign policies to a now-greater interest in what is going on in Syria and Israel. Thus, for about the next four years, the Egyptians are based at Carchemish, as they extend their sovereign hand out over Syria and Israel until Nebuchadnezzar comes in 605 BC to challenge Egypt's presence and power in this part of the Near East. He is called "king of Babylon" (v. 2) in this text, but he actually is only the crown prince at this time, so it is included here by way of anticipating what will take place shortly after these events (by way of speaking proleptically).[39] Nebuchadnezzar thoroughly routs the Egyptians and might have chased them all the way back to Egypt had not news arrived suddenly that his father has unexpectedly died and he needs to get back to Babylon to assume the throne. But Egypt's dominion in this area has been broken to such a degree that a poem in vv. 3–6 mocks Egypt's former vaunted might and power.

46:3 Although Egypt is finally identified in the second **stanza** of this poem (vv. 7–12), the sole historical reference in the poem is to the "Euphrates River" (v. 6). The poem has an abrupt marshaling of staccato-like sharp commands that order the army to line up and move out in a disciplined way (v. 3). Two types of shields are alluded to in v. 3: a small round shield, usually held in the left hand and used to protect one's head, and the larger oval or rectangular shield, used to fend off projectiles coming at the body.

---

39. C. J. Sharp, "'Take Another Scroll and Write': A Study of the LXX and the MT of Jeremiah's Oracles against Egypt and Babylon," *VT* 47 (1997): 487–516.

46:4 Orders are given to get both the chariot forces and the foot soldiers ready for conflict (v. 4). It is time to put on the armor (v. 4e) and the leather helmets (v. 4c), which were usually hot and uncomfortable, so they were left off until battle commenced. The spears are to be polished, for that will made them look all the more threatening and awesome in the reflected sunlight (v. 4d).

46:5-6 Suddenly, Yahweh himself interrupts: "What's this I see?" (v. 5). What follows are six abrupt clauses: The Egyptians are completely terrified; they are running away in retreat instead of running into the battle; their warriors are beaten down; they are running pell-mell all over the place; they are not even looking back to see what is happening on the battle field; and "terror is on every side" (מָגוֹר מִסָּבִיב), which is the phrase used in Jeremiah to depict panic (6:25; 20:3, 4, 10; 49:29). This is nothing but an absolute rout of Egypt in the face of a surprisingly strong Babylon. The army is now in a hopeless situation as her strongest and best warriors are cut down by Babylon. Even the route of fleeing is not all that easy (v. 6), for both the swift of foot and the strong men are not finding an escape. The language seems to be borrowed from Amos 2:14-15. The source of this slaughter is from "up north on the banks of the Euphrates" (v. 6b); Egypt's men are stumbling and falling down dead.

46:7-9 In the second **stanza** of this poem (vv. 7-12), God speaks even more ironically. Who do these armies think they are, anyway? Their arrogant claims "rise up" like their own Nile River (v. 8) at flood stage. They make such grandiose claims that one would think their powers are as extensive over the earth as the flood waters of the Nile is as it overflows its banks year after year. In fact, there is more than a play on the words "go up" (vv. 4, 7, 8 [2x], 9, 11 [2x]); they are a signal that one of the great problems here is a prideful, self-exalting, boastful ambition that refuses to humble oneself under the mighty hand of God, much as seen in the tradition of Lucifer (Isa 14:13-14). Egypt's pride is seen even before the battle starts. Once again, the call to begin the battle goes out in v. 9, urging the horses and the charioteers to "go up" as they dash around madly, driving like madmen. The allies of Egypt—Cush, which is probably Ethiopia; with Put and the Ludim, which are probably Libya and perhaps Lydia—are likewise called to engage in the battle.

46:10 Suddenly there is a shift in v. 10 as "the day belonging to Adonai Yahweh of Hosts" is introduced. This is declared by God to be a time of vengeance on his foes. Despite the urgent appeals of the Egyptian army commanders and the reinforcements of v. 9, disaster is now a certainty for Egypt. The sword of the enemy will continue to devour until "it has been saturated with blood" (v. 10c). But this battle is no mere international clashing of opposing troops; it is a "sacrifice" by Adonai Yahweh (a name usually reserved only for its use in covenantal promises; Gen 15:2, 8; 2 Sam 7:18, 19 [2x], 20, 22, 28, 29, used here along with a metaphor for God's slaughtering these armies in judgment).

46:11 What can the helpless Egyptians do? God addresses Egypt as his "Virgin Daughter," which in itself is remarkable (v. 11; see also vv. 19, 24). Judah and Israel are not the only people who are called God's special people; he is concerned about all the peoples of the world, including the Egyptians.

The Egyptians are urged to go up to Gilead (v. 11; see 8:22) to bring back "balm" for their injuries. But that will also be difficult, for Gilead is northeast of the Sea of Galilee; Egypt dominated that area for the years 609-605 BC, but now it is under Babylonian control. As a result, there are no healing remedies (v. 11c); there is no "healing" (lit. "to go up"; presumably the words "coming up" are meant to indicate the growth of new skin to cover wounds). All attempts to remedy these military defeats will be useless.

46:12 Finally, the nations are brought into the shame and ignominy of the situation. Whether the four verbs, all of which are Heb. pf. tenses, should be rendered as English past tenses or, as the NIV renders them, prophetic pfs. in the fut. tense depends on whether the text views the defeat as impending or as a taunt of what already has happened. This first poem ends much like the last line of v. 6, with warriors stumbling and falling all over the place.

Nebuchadnezzar's Invasion of Egypt (46:13-24)

46:13-15 Prior to the Babylonian invasion, messengers or some type of heralds are to let Egypt, Migdol, Memphis, and Tahpanhes know what is going to happen (v. 14; cf. 44:1 for Migdol, and on the other cities see 2:16). Being close to the border, these Egyptian cities would feel the rages of war first. But then, just as in the first poem, an abrupt question intrudes: "Why are your warriors cut down/laid low?" (v. 15). The call is announced once again: "Take your positions and be prepared" (v. 14c). Those who are living around Judah have already felt the sting of Nebuchadnezzar's troops.

The LXX, the NRSV, and the REB divide the word "warrior" into two parts and translate Jer 46:15a, "Why has Apis fled? Why did your bull not stand?" If this is the correct rendering, it has some backing in that the verbs that follow are in the sg. form. In Egypt, the bull was a symbol of fertility and was often connected with the afterlife. Memphis was well known for the Apis bull, which was connected to the god Ptah, who was responsible for creation. Apis was also connected to another god of fertility and the afterlife, Osiris. Jeremiah may be mockingly questioning the alleged powers of Apis, as did Herodotus, who notes that the Persian leader Cambyses desecrated the Apis Bull in 525 BC when he defeated Memphis.

46:16-17 Verse 16 has the Egyptian troops stumbling and falling over one another as they try in their panic to get out of one another's way. Those who were hired on as mercenaries have had enough, for now they are saying to one another, "Let's go back to our own homes, instead of retreating back to the Egyptian delta" (v. 16c-d). They tend to blame this whole debacle on Pharaoh, who talks big but has no action to match his talk (v. 17). Pharaoh Hophra has certainly missed his great chance (v. 17c) to achieve what he wanted in this part of the world.

46:18 In all of these confusions and military movements, Yahweh, the real "king" (v. 18a), has given his word with an oath—that an unidentified party will come, rising up just like Tabor rises up from the mountains and Carmel likewise majestically stands some seventeen hundred feet high overall, but lower on the Mediterranean Sea (v. 18c-d). Tabor is located in the Esdraelon Valley and is clearly seen all over that area (1,843 feet high) because it is so isolated from the other mountains. But if these mountains dominate the landscapes where they are located, the coming conqueror will more than dominate Pharaoh, who typically in Egyptian art is depicted as standing much taller than all his subjects.

46:19–21 So get ready, Egypt; pack your belongings, for you are going into exile (v. 19). Memphis will be devastated and destroyed to the degree that not one inhabitant can dwell there (v. 19c–d). A series of images or metaphors now follows as Egypt and Babylon are variously described in sarcastic ways: as a "heifer," "fatted calves," "gadfly," "snake," "woodchoppers," and "locusts" (vv. 20–24). Babylon is the "gadfly" that will nip or bite Egypt, while the hired mercenaries will be like "fatted calves." These pampered troops will not help Egypt, however, when the real crisis comes, for they are out of there as soon as the battle looks as if it is going to turn against them. They turn on their heels and flee as fast as they can, refusing to stand their ground (v. 21).

46:22–24 Egypt is naturally depicted as a coiled serpent, which serpent traditionally appeared on Pharaoh's headdress. But forget about all of the terror that a hissing serpent is supposed to represent, for now Pharaoh and his army are fleeing away as fast as they can. The reference to the men chopping down trees reflects the practice of armies cutting down trees to prepare for a siegeworks to be raised against an embattled, locked-down city (v. 22). So great will be the number of the enemy that they will be as thick as "locusts" (v. 23c). The inhabitants of the land of Egypt will be handed over to the people from the north (v. 24), which is of course Babylon.

The Future of Egypt (46:25–26)

46:25–26 In what appears to be a sort of supplementary oracle against Egypt, God identifies who he means by this northern conqueror who is to come: it is Nebuchadnezzar, king of Babylon. Yes, there will be punishment for Egypt's having gone after Amon, god of Thebes, but judgment will not be the last divine word, nor will God say that Egypt will be decimated forever; no, "Egypt would be inhabited as in former times" (v. 26c).

The city of "Thebes," which is the name the Greeks gave to it, was the same city the Egyptians called "Waset" and the Hebrews called "No."[40] It was the center for the worship of the god Amon. Thebes was the most important city in Egypt and was located on the Nile River, 438 miles south of the Mediterranean Sea. In Egyptian texts Thebes is called "the city of Amon," who was referred to as the "Hidden One." He was said to manifest himself in the wind. Later he was somehow fused with Re, the sun god, and they were said to be one deity: Amon-Re. The famous temple of Karnak at Thebes is dedicated to Amon-Re, who was made the head of the Egyptian pantheon at the start of the New Kingdom (c. 1550 BC).

The theme of the absolute power of Yahweh is continued in these verses, for God will "hand over" the Egyptians to the king of Babylon and his officers (v. 26). Nevertheless, that will not signal an end to Egypt, for once again, as in other prophecies, such as Isa 19, Egypt will be inhabited as it had been in olden days (v. 26c). Therefore, Egypt is judged by Yahweh for their worship of Amon and their enmity against the people of God, but that word is also to show that such false deities are unable to stand in the face of the incomparability of Yahweh. Egypt will not be totally destroyed.

The Assurance Given to Jacob (46:27–28)

46:27–28 These two verses are almost identical to 30:10–11 and similar to other texts found in the prophet Isaiah (41:8–14; 43:1–5; 44:1–2). Isaiah calls Israel the "servant of Yahweh," and so does Jeremiah. Since Yahweh speaks of "all the nations" (v. 28b), this serves as an opportunity to note that God has not forgotten about "Jacob, his servant." Even though God will destroy all the nations among whom he has scattered Israel and Judah, he will not totally destroy them (v. 28b–c). That is why Israel is to "have no fear," for "no one will be able to make them afraid," given the promises of God. God will reestablish the people as he promised he would back in Abraham's day.

For all too many centuries the Christian church has wrongly decreed that God is finished with Israel because of its rejection of its Messiah. This has led to a theology in which all the promises (not the curses, however) made to Israel have now been given to the believing Gentiles worldwide. Unfortunately, there has also been a buildup of the hatred of the

---

40. There is no relation here to the English word *no*.

Jewish people all through history that eventually resulted tragically in the Holocaust, in which six million Jews were put to death.

But in this text God promises that even though he will completely destroy some Gentile nations, he will not completely destroy the Jewish people because he made a promise to Abraham, Isaac, Jacob, and David. He will never go back on his word, or he would die like the animals that had been cut apart when he made the covenant with Abraham!

AN ORACLE CONCERNING THE
PHILISTINES (47:1-7)

The superscription (v. 1) to this chapter mentions an attack on the Philistine cities of Tyre, Sidon, and of Gaza by an Egyptian pharaoh, who is unnamed. The LXX version of this passage leaves out the reference to Gaza (that is, the coastland of Caphtor), concerning itself only with the destruction of Tyre and Sidon. It is not clear when this destruction happened and under what circumstances.

TRANSLATION

1 This is the word of Yahweh that came to Jeremiah the prophet concerning the Philistines,[41] before Pharaoh attacked Gaza.

    2 This is what Yahweh has said:
"Look! The waters are rising up north;
    They will become an overflowing torrent.
They will overflow the land and everything in it,
    The towns and those living in them,
The people will cry out,
    All who live in the land will howl.
3 At the sound of the galloping hoofs of his steeds,
    At the roar of his chariots,
    And the rumble of their wheels,
Fathers will not look back [to help] their children,
    Their hands will hang limp.
4 For the day has come to destroy

---

41. The LXX version of this verse only has ἐπὶ τοὺς ἀλλοφύλους, "concerning the foreigners."

All the Philistines,[42]

And to cut off all survivors

   Who could help Tyre and Sidon.

For Yahweh will destroy the Philistines,[43]

   The remnant from the coasts of Caphtor.[44]

5 Baldness has come upon Gaza,

   Struck dumb[45] is Ashkelon.

O remnant in the valley,[46]

   How long will you gash yourself?

6 Ah![47] Sword of Yahweh,

   Will you never be still?

Return to[48] your sheath;

   Cease and be still![49]

7 How can it rest,

   When Yahweh has given it orders?

Against Ashkelon and the seacoast—

   There he assigned it."[50]

COMMENTARY

The Superscription (47:1)

47:1 Some connect Pharaoh's attack in v. 1 with the Egyptian attack conducted by Pharaoh Necho II in 609 BC when King Josiah was killed at Megiddo while trying to stop him. However, such a connection is uncertain, for nothing is known from external records.[51] Moreover, the reference

---

42. The LXX has τοὺς ἀλλοφύλους, "the foreigners," where the MT has פְּלִשְׁתִּים, "Philistines."

43. The phrase אֶת־פְּלִשְׁתִּים, "the Philistines," is absent in the LXX.

44. The LXX has τῶν νήσων, "the island," where the MT has אִי כַּפְתּוֹר, "the coasts of Caphtor."

45. The LXX has ἀπερρίφη, "thrown down," where the MT has נִדְמְתָה, "struck dumb."

46. The LXX has Ενακιμ, "Anakim," where the MT has עִמְקָם, "valley."

47. The word הוֹי, "ah!" is absent in the LXX.

48. Many Heb. mss and editions have אֶל, "to," where the Codex Leningradensis has אַל, "not."

49. The LXX has ἐπάρθητι, "be lifted up," where the MT has וְדֹמִּי, "be still."

50. The LXX has ἐπὶ τὰς καταλοίπους ἐπεγερθῆναι, "to awake upon the remaining ones," where the MT has שָׁם יְעָדָהּ, "there he has appointed it."

51. For a detailed analysis why Necho is the Pharaoh mentioned here see H. J. Katzenstein, "'Before Pharaoh Conquered Gaza' (Jeremiah 47:1)," VT 33, no. 2 (1983): 249–51.

to "the waters are rising up north" (v. 2) suggests an invasion from Nebuchadnezzar of the Babylonians, perhaps after he had won his victory at Carchemish and finally had time to follow it up after being crowned king. Such a Babylonian invasion seems to be supported, at least in the later texts in vv. 5, 7, by the destruction of the Philistine city of Ashkelon, which is north of Gaza.

Philistia was made up of the famous coastal pentapolis of Gath, Ekron, Ashdod, Ashkelon, and Gaza, known today as the Gaza Strip. Gaza lay in the southwestern part of Canaan, where the plain was the widest and the land was fertile. The Philistines settled there at least by the end of the thirteenth century BC, and they may have used it as a place to farm their crops in the summer. Verse 4, along with Amos 9:7 and Deut 2:23, says the Philistines came from "Caphtor," which most equate to the island of Crete.[52] Archaeological documents from Mari, Ugarit, and Egypt also mention Caphtor as the place of their origin, while a few scholars hold out for Cappadocia in Asia Minor (Turkey) as the location for Caphtor.[53]

Judgment on Philistia (47:2–7)

47:2 Babylon did attack nearby Ashkelon in 604 BC, one year after Nebuchadnezzar had defeated Pharaoh Necho II in 605 BC. Accordingly, the Babylonian armies advanced against Israel and her neighbors and consolidated their control over that region. The invaders are likened to a river rising up to flood stage and overwhelming its banks, much as both the Nile and the Euphrates Rivers did in Egypt and Babylonia. Necho II attacked Gaza on his retreat back home, likely because of the thrashing that he had received at the hands of the Babylonians at Carchemish in 605 BC. This may have been in a desperate effort to assist the Assyrians. At any rate, Gaza lay on the main road between Egypt and the road leading up the coast to the lands in Mesopotamia.

These "waters rising from the north" may remind Jeremiah of the symbol he was given in his call, in which he saw a boiling pot "tilting away

---

52. P. J. Achtemeier, *Harper's Bible Dictionary* (San Francisco: Harper & Row, 1985), 194.

53. See K. A. Kitchen, "The Philistines," in *Peoples of Old Testament Times*, ed. D. J. Wiseman (London: Oxford University Press, 1973), 53–72. Also see E. E. Hindson. *The Philistines and the Old Testament* (Grand Rapids: Baker Book House, 1971).

from the north" (1:13). This again points to Babylon as the main problem in Philistia. In fact, in one of the vassal treaties of Esarhaddon, king of Assyria (681–669 BC), he too threatened his vassal country with the words: "May a flood, an irresistible deluge, rise from the bowels of the earth and devastate you."[54] The metaphor apparently was used often in such contexts.

47:3 The impression these invaders make on the Philistines is unmistakable, for as the troops swarm over them like the banks of an overflowing river, an outcry and a howl goes up from all over the land. The sound of the galloping horses with the grind of their chariot wheels is enough to set a person's mind to distraction (vv. 2–3). Even fathers do not have the time or the luxury of looking back over their fleeing bodies to see what is happening to their own children (v. 4d–e).

47:4 Verse 4 announces the "day" that is about to come from Yahweh, as it had for Egypt (v. 46:10), to "destroy all the Philistines" (v. 4a–b). That time has been designated by Yahweh, and the power of the Philistines will be overthrown (v. 4e–f). All help that is expected to come from Tyre and Sidon (the two seaports further north up the coast in Phoenicia) is cut off (v. 4c–d). Many assume there was a treaty between Philistia and Judah, but no documented support for this has yet been found. Tyre was the principal seaport on the Phoenician coast, with part of its people on the mainland and part on an island half a mile off shore. Sidon was some twenty-five miles farther north of Tyre and often served as the capital of Phoenicia, possessing two harbors protected by a few small islands and a breakwater.

47:5 Gaza (v. 5) was in a fertile plain separated from the Mediterranean Sea by sand dunes for two and a half miles. As a result of the Babylonian attack, "baldness had come over Gaza," a gesture of deep grief and desperate feelings of despair. Likewise, Ashkelon is hit so hard that they are "struck dumb" (v. 5b). The silence here could also be a euphemism for a complete destruction of the city: no one is left to talk! Ashkelon is one of the largest archaeological sites in Israel, covering 150 acres. It is located

---

54. *ANET*, 222.

some twelve miles north of Gaza, ten miles south of Ashdod, again on the coastal highway.

So how long will they go on "gashing" themselves? Here is another symbol of mourning, but one that was strictly forbidden among the Jewish people (Deut 14:1) though often practiced among the nations surrounding Israel (5:7; 7:29; 16:6; 41:5). In their distress they fall back on their pagan practices instead turning to Yahweh.

47:6 The chapter ends not with a focus on Pharaoh but on this foe from the north; however, it is Yahweh's sword (v. 6) that is behind it all. So relentless is the attack that the people plead, "Will you[r sword] never be still?" (v. 6b). In other words, isn't this enough already? The cry to God is for the sword to "return to its sheath, cease and be still" (v. 6c–d).

47:7 The response to their plea is: "How can it rest?" (v. 7a). Isn't it acting out of respect for the commands given to it by Yahweh against Ashkelon and the seacoast (v. 7b–c)?

Our Lord is sovereign over all the nations of the world, and thus they can expect similar treatment when they too flout and reject his word and morality. God is Lord over all, not just the Jewish people. The ancient land of Philistia, located in the area of what is now known as the Gaza Strip, is still being watched by our Lord as it is given time to respond to him and to avoid what those who preceded the current inhabitants of the land experienced.

AN ORACLE CONCERNING MOAB (48:1–47)

For a small country, Moab receives a disproportionately long oracle. This oracle also shares almost a dozen similar phrases with Isa 15–16, in addition to other prophetic books that address the nation Moab as well: for example, Amos 2:1–3; Zeph 2:8–11; Ezek 25:8–11. Only the nation of Babylon receives a larger section than Moab. The reason for the extensive amount of material on Moab as opposed to other non-Babylonian nations is not clear to us today.

Moab is cited for a number of failures from a divine point of view:

1. She trusted in her own wealth and power (v. 7).

2. She expressed real satisfaction in her own treasures (v. 11).

3. She was very proud and exceedingly arrogant (vv. 14, 26, 29–30, 42).

4. She defied Yahweh (v. 26).

5. She ridiculed Israel during her times of suffering (v. 27).

Twenty Moabite cities are singled out for mention in this oracle, beginning with the towns in the north, and then, as if following an army moving south, the southern cities follow in line. We are dependent on the Mesha Stele, which dates to c. 835 BC, and its commemoration of the Moabite victory over an Israelite king, whom we guess to be King Jehoram, for the historical background of Moab from an outside source; otherwise almost all we know about this nation is from Scripture.[55] But despite this unusual amount of specificity, there is almost nothing in this chapter about the history of Moab; geography takes on more prominence than history in this context.

This chapter has a number of textual difficulties (such as vv. 9, 15, 32), and there is a division among scholars as to how much is poetry and how much is prose. Does chapter 48 also reflect earlier oracles against Moab, such as found in Num 22 and 24 as well as Isa 15–16? Moreover, the material is hard to outline, but Fretheim has suggested the following five sections (Fretheim, 596):

1. Moabite response to Babylonian invasion (vv. 1–10)

2. The imminent destruction of Moab (vv. 11–17)

3. A taunt against destroyed Moab (vv. 29–39)

4. Woe oracles against Moab (vv. 40–46)

5. The promise of restoration (v. 47)

TRANSLATION

1 Concerning Moab:

---

55. *COS*, §2.23.

This is what Yahweh of Hosts, the God of Israel[56] says:
"Woe to Nebo, for it will be ravaged![57]
  Kiriathaim will be disgraced[58] and captured,
  The stronghold will be humbled and shattered.
2 Moab will be praised no more.
  In Heshbon[59] they plotted her downfall:
Come, let us put an end to that nation!
  You too, O madmen, will be silenced,[60]
  The sword will follow you.
3 A voice screaming from Horonaim!
  Havoc and devastation!
4 Moab will be broken in pieces,
  Her little ones will cry out![61]
5 For they go up the hill to Luhith,
  Weeping bitterly as they go:
On down the slope to Horonaim
  As anguished[62] cries over the destruction are heard.
6 Flee! Run for your lives;
  Become like a juniper tree[63] in the desert.
7 Yes, because you trust in your deeds and treasures,[64]
  You too will be taken captive.
And Chemosh will go into exile,
  Together with his priests and his officials as well.

---

56. The phrase צְבָאוֹת אֱלֹהֵי יִשְׂרָאֵל, "of Hosts, the God of Israel," is absent in the LXX.

57. The pf. verbs in this oracle are translated here as prophetic pfs.

58. The word הֹבִישָׁה, "be disgraced," is absent in the LXX.

59. The LXX has οὐκ ἔστιν ἔτι ἰατρεία Μωαβ ἀγαυρίαμα ἐν Εσεβων, "There is still no healing for Moab or praise in Heshbon," where the MT has אֵין עוֹד תְּהִלַּת מוֹאָב בְּחֶשְׁבּוֹן, "Moab will be praised no more. In Heshbon … "

60. The LXX has παῦσιν παύσεται, "she will completely cease," where the MT has מַדְמֵן תִּדֹּמִּי, "Madmen you will be silent."

61. The LXX has ἀναγγείλατε εἰς Ζογορα, "proclaim it in Zogora," where the MT has הִשְׁמִיעוּ זְעָקָה צְעוֹרֶיהָ, "her little ones will cry out."

62. The word צָרֵי, "anguished," is absent in the LXX.

63. The LXX has ὥσπερ ὄνος ἄγριος, "just like a wild donkey," where the MT has כַּעֲרוֹעֵר, "like a juniper tree."

64. The LXX has ἐν ὀχυρώμασίν σου, "in your fortress," where the MT has בְּמַעֲשַׂיִךְ וּבְאוֹצְרוֹתַיִךְ, "in your deeds and treasures."

8 The destroyer[65] will come against every city,
    And not one town will escape.[66]
The valley will be destroyed,
    And the plateau will be wrecked,
    As Yahweh has said.
9 Give salt[67] for Moab;
    For she will be laid waste.[68]
Her cities will become desolate,
    With no one to live in them.
10 Cursed be one who does the work of Yahweh negligently!
    And cursed[69] be the one who holds back his sword from
        shedding blood!
11 Moab has been at rest from his youth,
    He has settled on his lees [that is, of his wine],[70]
Never poured from vessel to vessel,
    Never deported,
So his taste remains in him,
    And his aroma is unchanged.

12 Therefore, behold days are coming, declares Yahweh, when I will send men who will tilt/pour the vessels and pour [them] out. They will empty[71] her jars and smash her jugs.[72] **13** Then Moab will be ashamed of Chemosh, as the house of Israel was ashamed when they trusted in Bethel.

    14 How can you say, 'We are heroes,
        Men valiant in battle'?
    15 Moab will be destroyed and his towns invaded,

---

65. The LXX has ὄλεθρος, "destruction," where the MT has שֹׁדֵד, "the destroyer."

66. The LXX has σωθῇ, "it will be saved," where the MT has תִּמָּלֵט, "it will escape."

67. Meaning of צִיץ is uncertain. The LXX has σημεῖα, "signs," where the MT has צִיץ.

68. The LXX has ἀφῇ ἀναφθήσεται, "will be set on fire," where the MT has נָצֹא תֵצֵא, "fly away."

69. The second occurrence of וְאָרוּר, "cursed," is absent in the LXX.

70. The LXX has καὶ πεποιθὼς ἦν ἐπὶ τῇ δόξῃ αὐτοῦ, "and he trusts in his glory," where the MT has וְשֹׁקֵט הוּא אֶל־שְׁמָרָיו, "he has settled on his lees."

71. The LXX has λεπτυνοῦσιν, "break in pieces," where the MT has יָרִיקוּ, "they will empty."

72. The LXX has καὶ τὰ κέρατα αὐτοῦ, "and his horns," where the MT has וְנִבְלֵיהֶם, "and their jugs."

His choicest young men will go down in slaughter,
Declares the King, whose name is Yahweh of Hosts.[73]

16 Moab's disaster[74] is close at hand,
His calamity will come quickly.

17 Mourn for him, all you who live around him,
All who know his fame.
Say, 'How broken is the mighty scepter,
How broken is the glorious staff.'

18 Come down from your glory,
And sit on parched ground,[75]
O inhabitants[76] of the Daughter of Dibon!
For Moab's destroyer has come up against you,
And ruined [your] fortified cities.

19 Stand by the road and watch,
You who live in Aroer.
Ask the man fleeing and the woman escaping,
'What has happened?'

20 Moab is ashamed, yes, shattered;
Howl and cry out![77]
Announce by the Arnon that Moab is destroyed.

21 Judgment has come to the plateau:
On Holon, on Jahzah and Mephaath,
22 On Dibon, Nebo, and Beth Diblathaim,
23 to Kiriathaim, Beth Gamul and Beth Meon,
24 to Kerioth and Bozrah—to all the towns of the land of
Moab, far and near.

25 Moab's horn is cut off;

---

73. The LXX omits וֹמְשׁ תוֹאָבְצ הָוהְי ךְֶלֶמַּה־םֻאְנ, "declares the King, whose name is Yahweh of Hosts."

74. The LXX has ἡμέρα, "day," where the MT has דיֵא, "disaster."

75. Lit. "thirst."

76. Many Heb. mss, versions, and the **Qere** have the impv. יִבְשׁוּ, "and sit," where the MT has the ptc. יֵבְשׁי, "sitters/inhabitants."

77. Some Heb. mss, Syr., Tg., and Vg. follow the **Qere** with the m. pl. impvs. וּקַעְזוּ וּליִליֵה, "howl/wail and cry out," where the Codex Leningradensis has the f. sg. impvs. יִקַעְזוּ יִליִליֵה, "howl/wail and cry out." The LXX has the sg. impvs. ὀλόλυξον καὶ κέκραξον, "wail and cry out."

His arm is broken, declares Yahweh.[78]

26 Make him drunk,

For he has made himself great.

Let Moab expel his vomit[79]

And become a laughingstock.

27 Was not Israel a laughingstock to you?

Was he caught among thieves[80]

That you shake your head[81] with disdain

Whenever you spoke of him?[82]

28 Abandon the towns and dwell among the rocks,

You who live in Moab.

Be like a dove that nests

On the sides[83] of the edge of a ravine.

29 We have heard of Moab's pride—

Exceeding arrogance,

And conceit,[84] pride, arrogance

And haughtiness of heart.

30 I, myself, know of his insolence,"[85] declares Yahweh,

"His boasts accomplish nothing,[86]

And his deeds are false!

31 Therefore, I will wail[87] over Moab,

I will moan for the men of[88] Kir Hareseth.

---

78. The phrase נְאֻם יְהוָה, "declares Yahweh," is absent in the LXX.

79. The LXX has ἐν χειρὶ αὐτοῦ, "in his hand," where the MT has בְּקִיאוֹ, "in his vomit."

80. The LXX has ἐν κλοπαῖς σου, "among your thefts," where the MT has בְּגַנָּבִים, "among thieves."

81. The LXX has ἐπολέμεις "you wage war," where the MT has תִּתְנוֹדָד, "you shake *your head*."

82. The phrase מִדֵּי דְבָרֶיךָ, "whenever you spoke of him," is absent in the LXX.

83. The LXX has ἐν πέτραις, "in the rocks," where the MT has בְּעֶבְרֵי, "on the sides."

84. The word גֹּבְהוֹ, "conceit," is absent in the LXX.

85. The LXX has ἔργα αὐτοῦ, "his works," where the MT has עֶבְרָתוֹ, "his insolence," apparently misreading עֶבְרָתוֹ as עֲבֹדָתוֹ.

86. The LXX has οὐχὶ τὸ ἱκανὸν αὐτοῦ, "is it not enough for him?" where the MT has וְלֹא־כֵן בַּדָּיו, "his boasts accomplish nothing."

87. The LXX has αὐχμοῦ, "of a drought," where the MT has יֶהְגֶּה, "he will mourn."

88. The parallel verse in Isa 16:7 has לַאֲשִׁישֵׁי, "for the raisin cakes of," where Jeremiah has אֶל־אַנְשֵׁי, "for the men of."

32 I weep for you, as Jazer weeps,[89]
O vines of Sibmah!
Your tendrils reached to the sea,[90]
To Jazer they reached.
On your summer fruit and your vintage,[91]
The spoiler[92] has fallen.
33 Joy and gladness are gone from the orchards[93]
And the fields of Moab.
I have stopped[94] the flow of wine from the presses;
No one treads them with shouts [of joy].
Although there are shouts, they are not shouts [of joy].

34 The sound of their cry rises from Heshbon to Elealeh and Jahaz,[95] from Zoar as far as Horonaim and Eglath-Shelishiyah; for even the waters of Nimrim are dried up. **35** I will put a stop to those making offerings on high places[96] and burning incense to their gods," declares Yahweh. **36** "Therefore, my heart wails for Moab like a flute for the men of Kir Hareseth because the wealth[97] they acquired is gone.

37 Yes, every head is shaved,
And every beard is cut off;
On every hand are gashes,
On every waist[98] is sackcloth.

---

89. The LXX has ὡς κλαυθμόν, "as the weeping," and the parallel in Isa 16:9 has בִּבְכִי, "with the weeping," where the MT of Jeremiah has מִבְּכִי, "more than the weeping."

90. The second occurrence of the word יָם, "sea," is absent in two Heb. mss and the LXX. The current translation follows the LXX.

91. Isa 16:9 has קְצִירֵךְ, "your harvest," where the MT of Jeremiah has בְּצִירֵךְ, "your vintage."

92. Isa 16:9 has הֵידָד, "shouting," where Jeremiah has שֹׁדֵד, "the spoiler."

93. The word מִכַּרְמֶל, "orchard," is absent in the LXX.

94. The LXX has πρωί, "in the morning," where the MT has הִשְׁבַּתִּי, "I have stopped."

95. The LXX has αἱ πόλεις αὐτῶν, "their cities," where the MT has עַד־יַהַץ, "as far as Jahaz."

96. The LXX has βωμόν, "an altar," where the MT has בָּמָה, "a high place."

97. The Syr. has bjšt', "evil," where the MT has יִתְרַת, "wealth."

98. Multiple Heb. mss, with the LXX, Tg.f. Ms, and Vg., add כָּל, "every," reading "on every waist."

38 On all the roofs in Moab and in the public squares, there is nothing but mourning, for I have broken Moab like a jar that no one wants," declares Yahweh. **39** "How shattered he is![99] How they wail![100] How Moab turns his back in shame! So Moab becomes the laughingstock and an object of horror to all those around her."

40 Yes, this is what Yahweh has said:
"Look, like an eagle he swoops down,
    Spreading his wings over Moab.[101]
41 The towns are captured,
    The strongholds seized.[102]
In that day the hearts of Moab's warriors
    Will be like the heart of a woman in labor.[103]
42 Moab will be destroyed as a nation,
    Because he defied Yahweh.
43 Terror, pit, and snare await you,
    O people of Moab," declares Yahweh.
44 "Whoever flees[104] from terror,[105]
    Will fall into a pit,
Whoever climbs out of the pit,
    Will be caught in a trap,
For I will bring upon Moab
    The year of their vengeance," declares Yahweh.

---

99. The LXX has πῶς κατήλλαξεν, "how they changed," where the MT has אֵיךְ חַתָּה, "how shattered he is."

100. The word הֵילִילוּ, "(how) they wail," is absent in the LXX.

101. The LXX omits הִנֵּה כַנֶּשֶׁר יִדְאֶה וּפָרַשׂ כְּנָפָיו אֶל־מוֹאָב, "look, like an eagle he swoops down, spreading his wings over Moab."

102. The **Qere** of the eastern tradition has נִתְפָּשׂוּ, "they are seized," where the MT has נִתְפָּשָׂה, "it is seized."

103. The LXX omits וְהָיָה לֵב גִּבּוֹרֵי מוֹאָב בַּיּוֹם הַהוּא כְּלֵב אִשָּׁה מְצֵרָה, "in that day the hearts of Moab's warriors will be like the heart of a woman in labor."

104. The **Kethiv** of the eastern tradition, versions, and Isa 24:18 follow the **Qere** and have הַנָּס, "they will cause to flee," where the MT of Jeremiah has הַנִּיס, "the one who flees."

105. Isa 24:18, with the Syr. following, has מִקּוֹל, "from the sound (of terror)," where the MT has מִפְּנֵי, "from the face (of terror)."

45[106] "In[107] the shadow of Heshbon the fugitives stand helpless;[108]

For a fire has gone out[109] from Heshbon,

A blaze from the midst[110] of Sihon,

It burns the foreheads of Moab,

The skulls of the noisy boasters.

46 Woe to you, Moab!

The people of Chemosh are destroyed;[111]

For your sons are taken into exile,

And your daughters into captivity.

47 Yet I will restore the fortunes of Moab,

In days to come," declares Yahweh.

Thus ends the judgment on Moab.

COMMENTARY

Babylon's Invasion of Moab (48:1–10)

With a cry of "Woe," the tone is set for the sobbing, mourning, and wailing that will break out as death and destruction attend the advances of the (as yet unidentified) army in Moab. Moab was Judah's neighbor to the east of the Dead Sea, located on a plateau that rose to about three thousand feet above sea level. It was bounded on the north by the Arnon River (Wadi el-Mojib) and on the south by the Zered River (Wadi el-Hesa). It extended eastward to the Syrian-Arabian desert, and its western boundary was the narrow plain that lay alongside the Dead Sea.

---

106. Verses 45–47 are absent in the LXX.

107. The phrase בְּצֵל חֶשְׁבּוֹן עָמְדוּ מִכֹּחַ נָסִים, "in the shadow of Heshbon the fugitives stand helpless," is absent in the Syr.

108. θ´ has ἀπὸ παγίδος, "from the trap" (מִפַּח), where the MT has מִכֹּחַ, "helpless."

109. A few Heb. mss and the parallel in Num 21:28 have the fem. יָצְאָה, "it came," where the MT of Jeremiah has the masc. יָצָא, "it came."

110. A few Heb. mss have מבית, "from the house," and Num 21:28, with θ´ and the Syr. following, has מִקִּרְיַת, "from the city," where the MT has מִבֵּין, "from the midst."

111. Num 21:28, with θ´, Syr., and Vg., has אָבַדְתָּ, "you have destroyed," where the MT of Jeremiah has אָבַד, "he is destroyed."

48:1 Nebo (v. 1) was the mountain from which Moses viewed the promised land God said he would give to Israel (Deut 32:49; 34:1). In this context, however, it seems to refer to a nearby town, Khirbet Muhaiyat, lying in the territory north of the Arnon River, which was associated with Mt. Nebo, a town three miles northwest of Medeba and five miles southwest of Heshbon. The town's name seems to bear traces of a Babylonian origin, perhaps the Babylonian deity named Nabu.

The Mesha Stele, a Moabite inscription carved on black basalt stone by King Mesha in approximately the mid-ninth century BC, mentions the town of Nebo coming under the Moabites. Interestingly enough, Nebo had a type of Yahweh worship when Mesha captured it for Moab. The town had its most prosperous times in Iron I and II (1200–586 BC).

The cities of Moab were rather extensively ruined in Nebuchadnezzar's 582 BC campaign. Kiriathaim was the city King Mesha claimed to have built, about six miles west of Medeba, if it is the site of Khirbet el Qureiya. What happened to Nebo and Kiriathaim is but a foretaste of what will happen to the rest of Moab. But this raises the recurring problem of how to translate the Heb. prophetic pfs. Is the action so certain that it is seen as already having occurred, or is all of the action still pending and ready to take place in the future? If the action has indeed already occurred, then is Moab by now desolate? It's possible to interpret v. 8 as showing that the action is still to come.

48:2 Verse 2 warns that "Moab will be praised no more," which may be another signal that Moab is a country filled with self-praise (see v. 29). Heshbon was the former capital of the Amorite king Sihon (Num 21:26; Deut 2:24), and that is where the enemy "plotted" (חָשַׁב, ḥāšab; a possible wordplay on חֶשְׁבּוֹן, Heshbon) Moab's downfall (v. 2b). This site has not been firmly identified; neither is the identity of the "Madmen" known.

48:3–7 Horonaim (v. 3) is also mentioned in the Mesha Stele and in Isa 15:5, but its location is still unknown. Its dual form suggests an upper and lower city, but that is the only clue as to any possible identity. Moab is sure to be broken (v. 4), as even her "little ones" cry out (v. 4b). Like most of these places mentioned here, Luhith (v. 5) has not yet been located. All that is known is that the people will ascend to Luhith, escapees weeping bitterly over the harm, destruction, and murder they are seeing all around them (v. 5b–d). They are urged to "flee and run for their lives" (v. 6), for they will need to depend on a juniper tree/bush for minimal nourishment. Their previous trust in their deeds and treasures (v. 7a) will be of little or no help now, as will their trust in their god Chemosh.

Chemosh is mentioned eight times in the OT. In Judg 11:24 Chemosh is associated with the Ammonite worship, but previously, in Num 21:29, the Moabites call their god Chemosh as well. Chemosh appears twelve times on the Mesha Stele.[112] He also is featured in the Kerak Inscription[113] and the Dibon Inscription, and he is noted as one who is worshiped at Ebla and Ugarit. He is depicted as a god of war in a stele found at Shihan. In the Mesha stone Chemosh's name is compounded with "Ashtar." Solomon built a high place for Chemosh, but 1 Kgs 11:7, 33 describes Chemosh as the "abomination of Moab."

48:8–9 Verse 8 prophesies that the "destroyer" will come and not a town in Moab will escape, for the "valley," meaning either the area just west of the Dead Sea or the Jordan Valley north of the Dead Sea, also will be ruined. Even more difficult is v. 9, where the Heb. word ץיצ, ṣîṣ, is rendered "salt," on the basis of a similar word in Ugaritic. If this rendering is correct, then it may parallel the example of Abimelech, who scattered salt over the ground after he destroyed Shechem (Judg 9:45). Tiglath-pileser I (1115–1076 BC) did the same over the ruins of a conquered city.

Moab's Imminent Destruction (48:11–17)

48:11–12 Moab was famous for her wine, but in this example Moab is satisfied with not pouring the wine from one vessel to another. The figure is of wine left on its "lees/dregs" (v. 11b). The problem with not pouring wine from one vessel to another is explained well as follows:

> In making wine, first the grapes were stomped, then the juice was placed into bottles or skins and allowed to ferment. During this time the sediment, or dregs, would settle to the bottom. After 40 days

---

112. *COS*, §2.23.

113. See W. L. Reed and F. V. Winnett, "A Fragment of an Early Moabite Inscription from Kerak," *BASOR* 172 (1963): 1–9.

the fermented wine was carefully poured into another container to separate it from the dregs. If the dregs were allowed to remain, the wine became too sweet and thick and was spoiled. This object lesson from nature was ultimately applied to people who had become too complacent (cf. Zeph. 1:12). Moab had never felt the harsh reality of exile so, like the unpoured wine, her aroma was unchanged.[114]

Moab has become complacent and has not changed (for the better!), thus Moab will go into exile abroad. Moab was under the domination of Assyria, and she apparently always cooperated with her overlord. But that is going to change, as Yahweh will pour them out of their security, just as wine is poured from one vessel to another (v. 12). The Babylonians will be the decanters who will pour out the Moabites from the old wine jars. Wine left on its dregs or lees (which is the sediment that settles on the bottom of the vessel), when left undisturbed, would not be purified away as is required when it was poured from one jar to another.

48:13 One of the results of this stirring up Moab's complacency will be that she will realize that Chemosh is unable to deliver her from the hands of the conqueror—a real humbling of both Chemosh and Moab. Two centuries earlier, Israel realized the same truth, for her foolishness in worshiping idols at Bethel with its golden calf had ended up in the same kind of humbling then (1 Kgs 12:26-33; 13:1; Hos 8:5-7). Some think "Bethel" is an allusion to a Northwest Semitic deity that Israel worshiped. This deity does appear as a **cult** in the fifth-century BC Elephantine Papyri, from where the Jews had gone into exile.

48:14-16 Calamity will come to Moab shortly (v. 16), yet even in the face of imminent disaster, a challenge has to be issued to Moab: "How can you say, 'We are heroes'?" (v. 14). Moab is still as proud as always. Whatever their previous prowess was in military situations, such prideful bluster must now be halted. Moab will be invaded and her towns captured (v. 15), but the conqueror is still not identified. She will lose her "choicest young

---

114. C. H. Dyer, "Jeremiah," in *The Bible Knowledge Commentary: An Exposition of the Scriptures*, ed. J. F. Walvoord and R. B. Zuck (Wheaton, IL: Victor Books, 1985), 1:1195.

men" (v. 15b). This is certain because Yahweh of Hosts, who is here called the "King," is the One who says it will happen (v. 15c).

Moab's calamity was predicted as long ago as in Balaam's prophecy (Num 24:17), and then repeated in Amos 2:1 and Isa 15–16. Now there will no longer be a delay (v. 16); it will come quickly (v. 16b). This fall of Moab is only recorded in Josephus,[115] who places it five years after the fall of Jerusalem and in the twenty-third year of Nebuchadnezzar's reign.

48:17 All those who live around Moab are invited to mourn for her and her once well-known "fame" (v. 17), but that will all be gone very shortly.

The Moabite Cities Destroyed (48:18–28)

48:18 Ten more Moabite cities are named in a mocking and taunting manner. For example, the city of Dibon, a major walled city in Moab, is invited to come down from its perch as the capital of the country and sit on the parched ground (v. 18). Dibon, Mesha Inscription was found, was located about two miles north of the Arnon River near the King's Highway.

48:19-27 Less than a mile and a quarter southeast from Dibon was the town of Aroer, possibly modern Khirbet 'Ara'ir. It had a fortress that guarded the King's Highway. From that strategic point, they could stop persons fleeing and ask, "What has happened?" (v. 19d) / Therefore it could be announced by the "Arnon" River (v. 20), on Moab's northern boundary, that Moab is destroyed. The towns mentioned in vv. 21-24 are mostly unidentified in our day. The point by now is beginning to become very clear: "Moab's horn is cut off" (v. 25), which sums it all up very concisely. The horn, of course, is the usual metaphor for power and strength, along with the outstretched arm. But Moab's arm is also "broken" (v. 25b). The invader will strike Moab with such ferocity that the nation will stagger like a helpless drunk (v. 26). Moab had made herself great (defied Yahweh), but that is all gone now; she is like a drunk lying flat out on the ground and nothing but a laughingstock (v. 27).

115. *Ant.* 10.9.7.

48:28 Moabites are invited to leave their cities and go build their dwelling places up in the ravines, rocky clefts, and crevices, where they would be difficult to reach, just as "doves" often build their nests in such inaccessible places (v. 28). There perhaps they can moan like doves do as well.

Lament over Destroyed Moab (48:29–39)

48:29 God's prophets have heard over the years of Moab's hubris, which is here defined in six terms: Her "pride," "exceeding arrogance," "conceit," "pride," "arrogance," and "haughtiness of heart" (v. 29)—but all of that is gone now!

48:31–32 This is followed by five different verbs for weeping and moaning by Yahweh in vv. 31–32. Kir Hareseth (v. 31b) is singled out, for it was the ancient capital of Moab, modern-day Kerak, situated at three thousand feet, atop a mountain, some sixteen miles south of the Arnon River and eleven miles east of the Dead Sea.

48:33 The cutting off of joy and happiness is likened to the cutting off of the wine from the presses (v. 33). Instead of the shout that ordinarily would be coming from those tramping out the grapes in the wine press, a shout of a war cry has gone forth. The picture is reversed.

48:34–39 Some of the towns mentioned in v. 34 have been mentioned already, but the "waters of Nimrim," which are dried up, appear to be a reference to the River Nimrim that flowed into the Jordan River about eight miles north of the Dead Sea (v. 34b). God will also put an end to offerings that are made to the idols on high places (v. 35). In fact, Yahweh laments for Moab like the strains of a flute at a funeral (v. 35). Another cause for mourning is that Moab's wealth is gone (v. 36). The funeral customs can be seen all over Moab, such as shaved heads, beards cut off, and even the pagan practice of slashing their bodies with knives and the like (v. 37) as a sign of mourning. Moab has been broken like a jar by Yahweh (v. 38b). She is mocked and ridiculed by all who see her now, as compared to her former boasting and wealth. These neighbors turn their backs on Moab (v. 39).

Moab Destroyed and Restored (48:40-47)

48:40-42 The invaders are pictured as an eagle swooping down on Moab with its wings spread out in their majestic length and perhaps casting a shadow over the land. The person represented by the eagle is not identified in this context, but it is Nebuchadnezzar, for the same metaphor of an eagle for this man and his country is found in Ezek 17:3–5. This bird of prey rises high in the sky as it locates its prey with its extraordinary eyesight.

48:43-44 With a flurry of alliterative words all based on the same Heb. consonants ("terror," פַּחַד, *pahad*; "pit," פַּחַת, *pahat*; and "snare," פַּח, *pāḥ*), Jeremiah shows how trapped Moab is. Those fleeing in terror will fall into a pit, and those climbing out of the pit will be ensnared in a trap (v. 44). The language of v. 43 is almost identical to Isa 24:17. Likewise, the language of v. 44 is almost identical to Isa 24:18 (cf. Amos 5:19), where the "visitation" or "punishment" will be universal, but here it will be limited to Moab.

48:45-46 The language of vv. 45–46 is also adopted from earlier texts, that is, Num 21:28–29; 21:27; 24:17b from Balaam. So Moab's judgment picks up both ancient and recent oracles.

48:47 The prophecy against Moab ends with a divine promise of a "restoration of the fortunes of Moab in days to come" (v. 47).[116] This is a blessing originally given to the people of Israel and Judah, but here it is extended to Moab.

The national god of Moab, Chemosh, is no match for Yahweh; Chemosh is in fact nonexistent. But the point is that Moab will be destroyed as a nation for one key reason: it had defied Yahweh (v. 42). But once again the grace of God far outweighs all Moab's sin, so God promises that he will "restore the fortunes of Moab in days to come" (v. 47). Here is marvelous grace that is greater than all our sin!

---

116. Willis argues that the expression בְּאַחֲרִית הַיָּמִים should be simply translated "in the future," and it means "an indeterminate future." See J. T. Willis, "The Expression *be'acharith hayyamin* in the Old Testament," *ResQ* 22, nos. 1–2 (1979): 54–71.

AN ORACLE CONCERNING AMMON (49:1-6)

In this chapter of Jeremiah five more foreign nations are added to the previous three: Egypt (46:1-26), Philistia (47:1-7), and Moab (48:1-47). The messages in chapter 49 are generally much shorter than those featuring Egypt and Moab: Ammon gets just six verses (vv. 1-6); Edom gets sixteen verses (vv. 7-22); Damascus, though not a nation but a city, gets five verses (vv. 23-27); Kedar gets six verses (vv. 28-33); and Elam, modern Iran, gets six verses (vv. 34-39).

Amon is charged with seizing the territory that belonged to Israel (vv. 1-2) and with the sin of pride (v. 4). Ammon was located just north of Moab and, like Moab, was part of the progeny of Lot, through an incestuous relationship with Lot (Gen 19:38).

TRANSLATION

1 Concerning the Ammonites:

> This is what Yahweh has said:
> "Has Israel no sons?
>> Has he no sons at all?
> Why then has Molech[117] taken possession of Gad,
>> And his people dwell in his towns?
> **2** Therefore, Look out! The days are coming,
>> Declares Yahweh,
> When I will make Rabbah of the Ammonites[118]
>> To hear the shout of battle.
> She will become a desolate mound,
>> Her [surrounding] villages[119] will be set on fire.
> Then Israel will drive out those who drove him out,[120]
>> Declares Yahweh.[121]

---

117. The LXX, Syr., and Vg., and the current translation read מִלְכֹּם, "Milcom/Molech," where the MT has מַלְכָּם, "their king."

118. The phrase בְּנֵי־עַמּוֹן, "sons of Ammon," is absent in the LXX.

119. The LXX has καὶ βωμοὶ αὐτῆς, "and her altars," and the Tg. has וְיָתְבֵי כַּפְרָנְהָא, "and the inhabitants of her villages and her villages," where the MT has וּבְנֹתֶיהָ, "and her daughters."

120. The LXX has τὴν ἀρχὴν αὐτοῦ, "his ruler," where the MT has יֹרְשָׁיו, "his dispossessors."

121. The phrase אָמַר יְהוָה, "says Yahweh," is absent in the LXX.

3 Howl, O Heshbon, for Ai is destroyed.
    Cry out, your daughters of Rabbah!
Put on sackcloth! Lament!
    Rush here and there inside the walls,[122]
For Molech will go into exile,
    Together with his priests and officials.
4 Why do you boast of your valleys,
    Boast of your valleys so fruitful?[123]
O unfaithful[124] daughter—
    You trust in your riches:
    'Who will attack me?'[125]
5 Look here! I will bring terror on you
    From all those around you,"
    Declares Adonai Yahweh of Hosts.
"Each one of you will be driven away
    And no one will gather the fugitives.[126]
6[127] Yet, afterwards, I will restore the fortunes of the Ammonites,"
    declares Yahweh.

COMMENTARY

The message Jeremiah gives against Ammon is similar to that in Amos 1:13–15; Zeph 2:8–11; and Ezek 25:1–7.[128] The capital city of Ammon was Rabbah, now identified with Jebel Qal'ah (modern Citadel Hill), which is located in the center of the modern city of Ammon, about twenty-five miles east of the Jordon River and fourteen miles northeast of Heshbon. The city had a generous source of water from the Jabbok River (modern Zerqa River),

---

122. The phrase וְהִתְשׁוֹטַטְנָה בַּגְּדֵרוֹת, "rush here and there inside the walls," is absent in the LXX.

123. The LXX has τοῖς πεδίοις Εναχιμ, "the valleys of Enakim," where the MT has בָּעֲמָקִים זָב עִמְקֵךְ, "your valleys, boast of your valleys so fruitful."

124. Or "backsliding." The LXX has ἰταμίας, "bold"; Syr. has ḥbjbt', "loved"; and the Vg. has *delicata*, "delight," where the MT has הַשּׁוֹבֵבָה, "unfaithful."

125. A few mss add הָאֹמְרָה, "saying," before "Who will attack me?"

126. The word לַנֹּד, "the fugitives," is absent in the LXX.

127. Verse 6 is absent in the LXX.

128. For a critical analysis of the text of Jeremiah 49:1–6 see F. North, "The Oracle against the Ammonites in Jeremiah 49:1–6," *JBL* 65, no. 1 (1946): 37–43.

which empties into the Jordan River. The exact boundaries of this nation cannot be as easily identified as those of Edom and Moab, but some excavation of Citadel Hill shows that it was a thriving urban city in the Iron II period (900–586 BC).[129]

This land of Ammon was captured by Israel from the hands of King Sihon, who was king of the Amorites, and allotted to the Israelite tribes of Reuben and Gad, who both resided on the east side of the Jordan River. Ammon tried again and again to repossess their land from Reuben and Gad. During King David's time they were at first friendly to Israel, but then they later revolted against David, and David incorporated their land into his empire (2 Sam 10). Later, the Assyrian Tiglath-pileser III took Gilead and led the tribes of Reuben and Gad off into captivity and exile, in 734/33 BC (2 Kgs 15:29), with the result that the Ammonites were able to regain their land. But as Babylon rose to power in 605 BC, the Ammonites, who at first were loyal to Nebuchadnezzar, reversed their stand and, after the fall of Jerusalem, they offered sanctuary to the Judean refugees as their king successfully plotted against governor Gedaliah and had him assassinated (40:13; 41:15). Josephus notes that the Ammonites were conquered by Babylon in 582 BC and that later the Arabs invaded their territory and all traces of the nation were lost.[130]

49:1 This message to Ammon begins with two questions: "Has Israel no sons? Has he no heir?" (v. 1). This is a reference to when the people of the Israelite tribe of Gad were taken into captivity by the Assyrians. Why had the Ammonites reoccupied the lands that had belonged for so long a time to the Gadites? Did they think the Gadites would not have heirs or sons to possess the land? Were the Ammonites altogether forgetful of the promises God had made to Israel about the land they had possessed? The answers to these questions are unknown. The fourfold reference to "heirs" or "taking possession" in v. 2 is a further allusion to the point made in Judg 11:23–27. Why had "Molech," the god of Ammon (here standing for the whole nation),

129. Only here does Heshbon appear as an Ammonite city; usually it appears as belonging to Moab. See E. A. Knauf, "Jeremia XLIX 1–5: Ein zweites Moab-Orakel im Jeremia-Buch," *VT* 42, no. 1 (1992): 124–28.

130. *Ant.* 10.9.7.

not taken back his territory for the past three hundred years? Why make an objection after so many years?

Molech was the patron deity of the Ammonites. The **cult** of Molech is generally connected with the sacrifice of children by throwing them into a raging fire ("passed through [the fire] of Molech"—Lev 18:21; 2 Kgs 23:10; Jer 32:35). It is thought that this is the identical rite referred to in Deut 12:31; 2 Kgs 16:3; 21:6; 23:6; Isa 30:33; Jer 7:31; 19:5 (see "Excursus: Topheth"). Molech may also be connected to the religion at Ugarit. Canaanite tablets found at Ugarit in 1956 mention a deity called *milkm*. And it could also be connected to a type of similar sacrifice found especially in neo-Punic inscriptions (fourth to first centuries BC). Elsewhere in the Bible, King Solomon erected a shrine to Molech on the Mount of Olives (1 Kgs 11:5, 33), but good King Josiah tore in down (2 Kgs 23:13).

49:2 The days are coming (v. 2) when Yahweh will sound the shout of the battle cry against the capital of Ammon. The result will be that Rabbah, and the villages surrounding it, will be left a mound of ruins (v. 2d). Israel will then dispossess those who dispossessed them. What event this refers to is unknown.

49:3 Both the capital cities of Moab and Ammon, Heshbon and Rabbbah (v. 3), are told to start mourning because their day of judgment is certain and assured. Whether Ammon held Heshbon at this period is not known, but the boundaries between these territories in Transjordania went back and forth depending on the times and the battles. It is time to put on the sackcloth and observe the panic inside the city walls as all rush here and there with little rhyme or reason (v. 3d), seeking cover in the countryside. What the reference to "Ai" means cannot be determined with certainty, but it is not the well-known site of the west side of the Jordan (v. 3). If it is not a proper name referring to another location, then it means "heap of ruins" in this context.

Not only will the people go into exile (v. 3e), but so too will their god Molech, just as the god of Moab, Chemosh, was taken captive (48:7). This should demonstrate to the Ammonites and the Moabites that these gods are not worth even the material they are made out of. Molech will be accompanied into exile by his priests and officials (v. 3f).

49:4 Another reason for this calamity is stated in v. 4: her pride. She was complacent about her riches, apparently those crops derived from the Jabbok River Valley (v. 4). But Yahweh calls Ammon an "unfaithful daughter" (v. 4c), which is surprisingly similar to his calling Egypt (46:11) and Babylon (50:42) "daughter," and of course Israel is called a "daughter" as well (for example, 31:22). Instead of Ammon acknowledging that her greatest riches are to be found in Yahweh, she stupidly puts her trust in what she is able to produce on her own (v. 4d). She arrogantly boasts: "Who will attack me?" (v. 4e). She will soon find out.

49:5 God answers: He will attack them (v. 5) and bring terror on them from every side. Everyone will rush headlong as no one seems to be in charge of rallying the scattering and escaping community of Ammon into some unified action (v. 5c–d).

49:6 But once again, as in the case of Egypt (46:26), God has a message of hope even for Ammon. God will restore the fortunes of Ammon after he judges them (v. 6; cf. 48:47; 49:39). Just as Israel will be brought back and restored, so Ammon will be taken care of just as generously by God.

AN ORACLE CONCERNING EDOM (49:7–22)

This prophecy is unusual in that it shares several lines with the prophet Obadiah's word against Edom. For example, vv. 9 and 10a resemble Obad 5 and 6, while Jeremiah's vv. 14–16 resemble Obad 1–4. This has led to a variety of views as to which came first, Jeremiah or Obadiah's prophecy, or even perhaps that they both used a third source. No one has been able to mount a conclusive argument that definitively answers these questions. Edom appears in a good number of additional prophecies. They include: Ps 137; Joel 3:19; Obadiah; Amos 1:11–12; 9:12; Isa 21:11–12; 34:1–17; 63:1–6; Lam 4:21–22; Ezek 25:12–14; 35:1–15; and Mal 1:2–5. Jeremiah's prophecy against Edom consists of three parts: the inevitability of judgment (vv. 7–13), the method of destruction (vv. 14–19), and the consequences of Yahweh's judgment (vv. 20–22).

TRANSLATION

7 Concerning Edom:

> This is what Yahweh of Hosts[131] has said:
> > "Is[132] there no longer wisdom in Teman?
> Has counsel departed from the prudent,[133]
> > Or their wisdom been dispersed abroad?
> **8** Flee! Turn aside!
> > Hide in the deep caves,
> > You who live in Dedan.
> For I will bring disaster on Esau[134]
> > At the time I punish him.
> **9** If the grape-gatherers came to you,
> > Would they not leave gleanings?
> If thieves came during the night,
> > Would they not steal only what they wanted?[135]
> **10** But I will strip Esau bare,[136]
> > I will uncover his hiding places,
> > So that he cannot conceal himself.[137]
> His offspring, relatives and neighbors will perish,[138]
> > And he will be no more.
> **11** Leave your orphans, I will protect their lives;
> > Your widows can trust in me."

---

131. The word צְבָאוֹת, "of Hosts," is absent in the LXX.

132. The interrogative ה is absent in the LXX, which understands the following questions as statements.

133. The MT has מִבָּנִים, "from sons." The LXX has ἐκ συνετῶν, "from the prudent" (cf. Syr.), apparently reading the word from the root בין, "to understand." The current translation follows the LXX.

134. The LXX has ὅτι δύσκολα ἐποίησεν, "for he has done grievously," where the MT has כִּי אֵיד עֵשָׂו, "for the disaster of Esau."

135. The LXX has ἐπιθήσουσιν χεῖρα αὐτῶν, "they will lay their hand," where the MT has הִשְׁחִיתוּ דַיָּם, "would they not steal only what they wanted."

136. The Syr. has bṣjt, "I will search out" (Heb. חִפַּשְׂתִּי), where the MT has חָשַׂפְתִּי,"I will strip bare."

137. The LXX has κρυβῆναι, "to be hidden," where the MT has וְנֶחְבָּה, "and he was hidden."

138. The LXX has ὤλοντο διὰ χεῖρα ἀδελφοῦ αὐτοῦ, "they have perished by the hand of his brother," where the MT has שֻׁדַּד זַרְעוֹ וְאֶחָיו, "his offspring will perish and his brothers."

12 For this is what Yahweh says, "Look here! If those who did not deserve to drink the cup must drink it, why should you go unpunished? You will not go unpunished, but most assuredly will drink of it. **13** For I have sworn by myself, declares Yahweh, that Bozrah[139] will become a ruin and an object of horror, a taunt,[140] and a curse-word; all of its towns will be in ruins forever."

> **14** I have heard a report from Yahweh:
>> An envoy has been sent[141] to the nations:
> "Assemble yourselves to attack it!
>> Rise up for the battle!
> **15** I will make you small among the nations,
>> Despised among men.
> **16** Your horror has deceived you,
>> And the presumption of your heart beguiled you.
> You who live in the clefts of the rocks,
>> Who occupy the heights of the hill.
> Though you build your nest
>> As high as the eagle's,
>> From there I will bring you down, declares Yahweh.
> **17** Edom will become an object of horror;
>> All who pass by her will be shocked[142]
>> And will whistle [in awe] because of her wounds."[143]

18 "Just as Sodom and Gomorrah, and their neighboring towns, were overthrown, declares Yahweh, no more shall any person live there; no human being will settle there.

> **19** "Look! Like a lion coming up
>> From the thicket[144] of Jordan to the rich pastureland,
> So I will chase Edom from its land in an instant.

---

139. The LXX has ἐν μέσῳ αὐτῆς, "in its midst," where the MT has בְּצְרָה, "Bozrah."
140. The word לְחֹרֶב, "a taunt," is absent in the LXX.
141. The LXX has ἀπέστειλεν, "he has sent," where the MT has שָׁלוּחַ, "is being sent."
142. The word יִשֹּׁם, "he will be shocked," is absent in the LXX.
143. The phrase עַל־כָּל־מַכּוֹתֶהָ, "because of her wounds," is absent in the LXX.
144. The LXX has ἐκ μέσου, "from the midst," where the MT has מִגְּאוֹן, "from the thicket."

Who is the chosen one I will appoint for this?
Who is like me? And who can challenge me?
And what shepherd can stand against me?"

20 Therefore, hear the plan that Yahweh has planned against Edom,
and the schemes that he has schemed against the inhabitants of Teman:

"The young of the flock will be dragged away;
He will completely destroy[145] their pasture because of
them.[146]
21 The earth is rocked by the sound of their fall;
Their cry[147] can be heard in the Sea of Reeds
22 Look out! Like an eagle he will ascend[148] and swoop down,
Spreading out his wings over Bozrah,[149]
In that day, the hearts of Edom's warriors
Will be like a woman in labor.

COMMENTARY

The Inevitability of Judgment (49:7–13)

The name "Edom" means "red" (Gen 25:25) and no doubt refers to the red
soil and red sandstone so characteristic of the high plateau on which this
country sits (ca. six thousand feet above sea level). This rugged and mountainous land extended from the River Zered in the north to the Gulf of
Aqaba in the south. Its border on the west was the Arabah Valley, and on
the east it was the Syrian-Arabian desert.

---

145. The LXX has ἀβατωθῇ, "it will be destroyed," where the MT has יַשִּׁים, "he will completely destroy."

146. Because of the "predominantly pastoral language of the passage," Kselman suggest
translating the second part of v. 20, "Surely the little ones of their flock shall be dragged off,
Surely the nurslings of their pasture shall be appalled." See J. S. Kselman, "A Note on Jer 49,20
and Ze 2,6–7," *CBQ* 32, no. 4 (1970): 579–81.

147. The word קוֹלָה, "her cry," is absent in the LXX.

148. The word יַעֲלֶה, "he will ascend," and the following conj. are absent in the LXX.

149. The LXX has ὀχυρώματα αὐτῆς, "her fortresses," where the MT has בָּצְרָה, "Bozrah."

49:7 This section opens with another rhetorical question (v. 7), similar to the way the oracle against Ammon opened (v. 1). Edom is famous for her wisdom (Obad 8; 1 Kgs 5:1), but has that wisdom taken a leave of the people in Teman (v. 7c)? Did not Eliphaz, one of Job's so-called comforters, come from Teman as well (Job 2:11; 4:1)? Teman, meaning "south" or "south-land" (perhaps pointing to the center of Edom's territory being south of the Dead Sea), could refer to either a city or a region in Edom. Teman was the grandson of Esau (Gen 36:11). Therefore, this name is strongly associated with Edom.

49:8-10 The advice in v. 8 seems to be that the inhabitants of Dedan, a major trading post in the northwestern Arabian Desert, should keep their caravans away from Edom, lest they too come under the disaster that is about to fall of Edom. God continues to ask rhetorical questions in v. 9, which he then answers himself in v. 10 in two images, one of grape pickers and the other of thieves coming at night to steal. We are left with the question: how do these two images help us to know how God is going to deal with Edom/Esau?

49:11 The divine answer is disturbingly clear: He will strip the grape vines bare. Leaving no gleanings, he will also not leave any place for the people to hide. The "seed/offspring" will be destroyed, including the relatives and neighbors. So get up and get out of this area; leave orphans and widows to the trusting care of Yahweh (v. 11), who himself will "keep them alive" (v. 11a).

49:12-13 The reason for such drastic judgment is given in vv. 12-13. The "cup" that is referred to is the same one mentioned in 25:29; it is the cup of divine wrath. Certainly Judah deserves this punishment, as does Edom for their gross sins. So who then are those who do not deserve to drink it? Apparently this is a reference to those who happened to be in the land at the time of the impending disaster and who will be swept up in the awfulness of the coming invasion!

The capital city of Edom was Bozrah (בָּצְרָה, bāṣrâ), whose name is reminiscent of the word for "grape-pickers" (בֹּצְרִים, bōṣrîm), which may have been one reason why the image of grape pickers came to mind. Bozrah was about twenty-two miles southeast of the Dead Sea at a major set of crossroads in the King's Highway (v. 13). Yahweh will see to it that Edom will become a ruin, a place of horror, a taunt, and a curse word along with all the towns nearby.

The Method of Destruction of Edom (49:14–19)

49:14 Verses 14–16 are very similar to Obad 1–4. In this section, Jeremiah hears a message from Yahweh by means of an "envoy" (צִיר), which is an ambassador or may even be an angelic messenger. The difference between the prophets Obadiah and Jeremiah is that Obadiah has the words "we have heard," but Jeremiah makes this an address to all the nations that are guilty before Yahweh. The command from the envoy is: "Assemble yourselves to attack [Edom]! Rise up for battle" (v. 14b).

49:15–16 Edom has felt most secure because of her location, perched high up in the mountains, but the nations are called on by Yahweh to join together to face Edom and to "make [her] small among the nations" (v. 15). In place of Edom's once high regard and opinion of herself, she will now be humiliated in front of all the other nations (v. 15; Obad 2). So the one who "lives in the clefts of the rocks" (v. 16c), in those sandstone cliffs on the southeast side of the Dead Sea, will forget all about her arrogance for being set up for any eventuality and beyond all attack, for even though their settlement is as "high as the eagle's" (v. 16f), Yahweh will "bring them down" (v. 16g).

49:17–18 Edom will become an "object of horror" (v. 17a), similar to what happened to Jerusalem (19:8). She too will be overthrown, just as the close-by towns of Sodom and Gomorrah were once devastated to such an extent that their names have become proverbial for all such disasters thereafter (18; Deut 29:23; Amos 4:11; Zeph 2:9). So stunning will be the destruction of Edom that all who pass by will whistle in awe and shock at what had taken place there (v. 17c). Edom will remain uninhabited and desolate, just as the five cities of the plain remain ruined (v. 18b).

49:19 Yahweh will spring his attack on Edom with such impact that Jeremiah uses the simile of a lion (v. 19a). Elsewhere Yahweh is depicted as a fierce lion (Hos 5:14–15). So sudden will this be that Edom will be chased off their land "in an instant" (v. 19c), before anyone can blink an eye.

This is followed immediately with four questions that highlight the incomparability of our Lord:

1. Who is it that I, Yahweh, can appoint to do this for me?

2. Who is mighty enough to be my "chosen one" to carry out this task?

3. Who do you think is going to oppose me and stop me from doing this to Edom?

4. What shepherd of the sheep of Edom can stand up against me when I have decided to go ahead with my plan?

The answer to all four questions is that there is no one who can compare to the living God. He can appoint whomever he chooses and whichever ruler he pleases to carry out the attack, and no one can stop him and oppose him once Edom's sin has mounted up so high that there will be no escape. This prediction is fulfilled in 552 BC, when Nabonidus invaded Edom and ended the monarchy of that land, as Mal 1:3–4 also notes. The Arabs took over the land, and Edom has not been heard of since.

Complete Destruction (49:20–22)

49:20 Yahweh does have a plan that embraces everything, but here it is particularly for Edom (v. 20). In many ways his use of "Teman" (v. 20) is a return to v. 7, where Yahweh asks where the wisdom and counsel given to Teman have gone. Again, Teman stands for the whole country. The "young of the flock" (v. 20) refers to the people of Edom, just as "shepherd" in v. 19 refers to their ruler. The land of Edom, here called their "pasture," will be completely destroyed (v. 20c).

49:21 Edom's fall will be so astounding and so complete that the shock-waves will be felt far and wide (v. 21). The screams of the Edomites are figuratively depicted as going back into history, all the way to the time when Israel crossed over Yam Suph, the "Sea of Reeds," otherwise known as the Red Sea.

49:22 Even more graphic is the picture of the conqueror coming like an eagle that rises high in the sky only to finally swoop down to earth as it spots its prey (v. 22). So it will happen to Edom, as her warriors faint in their endeavors and become like a woman in labor (v. 22d).

This passage, which is so similar to the words of doom in the prophet Obadiah (Obad 1-6), does not end with a promise of restoration, as the prophecies against Moab and Ammon did. Edom will be overthrown just like Sodom and Gomorrah were overthrown (Jer 49:18), with the result that "no one will live there; no man will dwell there" (v. 18c-d). Their judgment will be without the extended grace of God. Can it be that they have offended God that seriously?

AN ORACLE CONCERNING DAMASCUS (49:23-27)

Instead of giving a prophecy against a nation, this, the shortest of the oracles against the nations, focuses on the city of Damascus in Syria. As the chief city of Syria, it represents the whole nation, just as Teman represents Edom or Samaria represents northern Israel. Syria was called "Aram" in those earlier days when there were frequent contests between Israel and Syria. There is no specific historical occasion that seems to have been the reason for this prophecy. Nor is any specific sin against God or an offense against the people of God listed in this short prophecy.

TRANSLATION

23 Concerning Damascus:

> Hamath and Arpad are dismayed,
>> For they have heard disastrous news.
> They are disheartened,
>> Troubled like a restless sea.[150]
> **24** Damascus has become feeble,
>> She has turned to flee,
>> And panic has seized her.
> Anguish and pain have grabbed hold of her,

---

150. The word בַּיָּם, "in a sea," is absent in the LXX. The current translation reads כַּיָּם, "like a sea."

Like a woman in labor.[151]

25 How has the famous city not[152] been abandoned,
    The joyous town.[153]

26 Therefore, her young men shall fall in her open plazas;
    And all her soldiers will be silenced in that day,[154] declares
        Yahweh.[155]

27 I will set fire to the walls of Damascus;
    It will consume the citadel of Ben-Hadad.

COMMENTARY

Damascus of Aram is not listed among the doomed cities in 25:18–26, but she does appear now in these oracles against the nations. The three cities mentioned here, Damascus, Hamath, and Arpad, had been at one time three Aramean city-states, each of which was overrun by Tiglath-pileser III of Assyria (Isa 10:9; 36:19; 37:13). These states seem to have been in the path that Nebuchadnezzar followed as he pursued the Egyptians south after defeating them at the Battle of Carchemish. Damascus was defeated in 732 BC by the Assyrians. Damascus served as the capital city of Syria from the tenth to the eighth centuries BC. It was during this time that she was often involved in battles with northern Israel.

This prophecy is very similar to two other prophecies against Damascus that were delivered in the eighth century: Isa 17:1–6 and Amos 1:3–5. However, what may have gotten the Syrian/Aramean nation into trouble in the seventh century was the apparent joining of her armies with the Babylonian armies as Nebuchadnezzar attacked Judah and Jerusalem in 597 BC (2 Kgs 24:2).

---

151. The LXX omits צָרָה וַחֲבָלִים אֲחָזַתָּה כַּיּוֹלֵדָה, "anguish and pain have grabbed hold of her like a woman in labor."

152. The word לֹא, "not," is absent in the Vg.

153. The translation of this line follows the LXX. The MT reads "The town of my exultation." α΄, σ΄, θ΄, the Syr., Tg., and Vg. read "of exultation," and the LXX has ἠγάπησαν, "they have loved," where the MT has מְשׂוֹשִׂי, "of my exultation."

154. The phrase בַּיּוֹם הַהוּא, "in that day," is absent in the LXX and in ms evidence from the Cairo Geniza.

155. The word צְבָאוֹת, "of Hosts," is absent in the LXX.

49:23 Hamath (v. 23) was located on the east bank of the Orontes River
in central Syria, 209 miles north of Damascus, which in former days had
functioned as a separate kingdom. Tiglath-pileser III (745-727 BC) conquered Hamath in 740 BC, and Sargon II (721-705 BC) later destroyed the
city completely. Arpad (v. 23) is usually identified with modern Tell Rif'at,
which is about twenty-two miles north of Aleppo in northern Syria. This
city is usually mentioned with Hamath in the Bible and in Assyrian documents, since both exhibit an unusual antiquity and influence until the
Assyrians brought a halt to their importance and significance. Both Hamath
and Arpad are dismayed over the disastrous report they have heard. This
may have been news about the Assyrian armies about to attack them. This
causes them consternation that is like that of the troubled sea (v. 23d).

49:24-25 Damascus also is affected by a spirit of panic (v. 24). Even though
Damascus resided comfortably in the fertile plain east of the Anti-Lebanon
Mountains and also on a major intersection of several international trade
routes, her anguish can be compared to that of a woman in labor when she
too hears the news of the approaching conqueror (v. 24). Apparently, the
news is so startling that the residents of Damascus cannot even summon
up enough courage and strength to flee before the invader gets there (v. 25).
The beauty of the city of Damascus was legendary; it was a town of fabu-
lous joy and delight.

49:26-27 Since the warriors are unable to leave the city, or even to rouse
themselves to go away from the city of Damascus, they will fall in the city
plazas, and the result will be both their defeat and their deaths (v. 26). The
walls of Damascus, even if they are made out of limestone blocks, will also
be reduced to powder when the flames get hot enough (v. 27)—it all will
burn up in the flames.

Verse 27 is an adaptation of Amos 1:4, which places the word "Damascus"
where Amos had instead used the expression "house of Hazael." Jeremiah
uses "Ben-Hadad" ("son of Hadad," the storm god worshiped by the
Syrians), a name more frequently associated with Damascus, since there
were no less than two rulers in Damascus with that name (1 Kgs 15:18-20;
2 Kgs 13:24).

No rescue or deliverance is set for Damascus in the day of Yahweh; it will just be a period of judgment. God is the one who will set fire to the walls of Damascus.

AN ORACLE CONCERNING KEDAR AND HAZOR (49:28–33)

Kedar and Hazor represent a group of nomadic Arabian tribes often mentioned in Mesopotamian texts such as the Arabian Annals from the times of Tiglath-pileser III (745–727 BC), Sargon II (721–705 BC), Sennacherib (704–681 BC), and Esarhaddon (681–669 BC).

TRANSLATION

28 Concerning Kedar and the kingdoms of Hazor[156] whom Nebuchadnezzar, king of Babylon, defeated,

This is what Yahweh has said:

"Arise, and attack Kedar!
Destroy[157] the people of the east.
29 Their tents and their flocks will be taken,
Their tent-curtains[158] will be carried off
with all their goods and camels.
[Men] will shout[159] at them:
'Terror on every side.'
30 Flee! Move out[160] quickly!
Stay in deep caves,
you who dwell in Hazor,[161] declares Yahweh.
For Nebuchadnezzar, Babylon's king,
Has plotted against you;

---

156. The LXX has βασιλίσσῃ τῆς αὐλῆς, "the queen of the court," where the MT has וּלְמַמְלְכוֹת חָצוֹר, "and the kingdoms of Hazor."

157. The LXX has πλήσατε, "fill," where the MT has וְשָׁדְדוּ, "(and) destroy."

158. The LXX has ἱμάτια αὐτῶν, "their garments," where the MT has יְרִיעוֹתֵיהֶם, "their tent-curtains."

159. The LXX has the impv. καλέσατε, "call out," where the MT has the pf. וְקָרְאוּ, "(and) they will shout."

160. The word נֻדוּ, "move out," is absent in the LXX.

161. The LXX has ἐν τῇ αὐλῇ, "in the courtyard," where the MT has חָצוֹר, "Hazor."

He has devised a plan against you."[162]

31 "Arise! Go up to a nation at ease,
Which lives securely, declares Yahweh;[163]
A nation that has neither gates nor bars.
Its people live alone.

32 Their camels will become plunder,
And their large herds will be booty.
I will scatter to the winds those who clip the hair by their
foreheads;
I will bring disaster on them from every side, declares
Yahweh.

33 Hazor[164] will become a lair for jackals,
A desolate place forever.
No one will live there;
No person will sojourn there!"

COMMENTARY

49:28–29 Kedar is mentioned quite frequently in the Bible. They were descended from Ishmael (Gen 25:13) and did not live in walled cities but preferred to live in tents (Isa 42:11; Ps 120:5). They also were excellent with the bow as well as in breeding sheep (Isa 21:16–17; 60:7). Kedar was defeated by the Babylonians in 599 BC according to the Babylonian Chronicle.

Hazor is not to be identified with the city in northern Israel but a desert group living in tents east of the settled areas of Transjordania and Syria. These desert tribes were almost a constant thorn in the side of settled kingdoms to the west of them, as they often raided them and robbed them of their crops just as they were ripening (for example, Judg 6:3). They also were a thorn in the side of the major world powers of Assyria and Babylon.

The people of Kedar and Hazor are now told to flee and get away as fast as possible (v. 30), for even though the appointed human invader is Nebuchadnezzar, Yahweh actually is the one who has commissioned him

---

162. Ms evidence from the Cairo Geniza, many Heb. mss, the LXX, Tg., Vg., and the current translation follow the **Qere** with עֲלֵיכֶם, "against you," where the MT has עֲלֵיהֶם, "against them."

163. The phrase נְאֻם־יְהוָה, "declares Yahweh," is absent in the LXX.

164. The LXX has ἡ αὐλή, "the courtyard," where the MT has חָצוֹר, "Hazor."

to serve in this capacity (v. 28). Nebuchadnezzar has not been referred to in these chapters on the oracles against the nations since 46:26. Only there and here in vv. 28, 30 is Nebuchadnezzar mentioned in chapters 47 through 49.

This news of the coming conqueror comes with the command to "destroy the people of the east" (v. 28d). This includes all that is associated with the nomadic style of life: their tents, their flocks, their tent curtains, their goods/possessions, and their camels (v. 29). This is quite an inventory for a desert group of peoples. All this is accompanied by the cry of calamity: "Terror on every side" (v. 29d). Who gives this shout, however, is not clear: it could be one given by their enemies, or it could come from the people themselves.

49:30 God's advice is to "Flee, move out quickly" (v. 30a). Reside in deep caves to escape detection (v. 30b). Once again the enemy is identified as being no less than Nebuchadnezzar (v. 30d). He indeed had a strategy, yet it is not his doing alone, for Yahweh God ultimately is the One who is bringing this disaster on them from every side (v. 32). Why this is the only place in these oracles against the nations that Nebuchadnezzar is identified is difficult to say.

49:31-32 So, to the once-prosperous and quite contented Kedar and Hazor, who felt so secure in their settings and surroundings that they needed neither bars nor gates around their land, destruction will come all of a sudden for those who think they are all alone (v. 31). These desert tribes will be scattered all over the place instead of being exempt from all the ravages of war. As part of the plunder, their camels will be taken, along with their large herds of cattle or sheep and goats (v. 32). Terror will come at them from every side (v. 32d).

49:33 Hazor will become a place where no one lives except jackals (as is said of Jerusalem in 9:11; 10:22 and of Babylon in 51:37). In place of an area of hospitality, the once-isolated setting will become even more desolate, a place where no one lives and no person will sojourn (v. 33).

AN ORACLE CONCERNING ELAM (49:34-39)

The next-to-last oracle against the nations is against Elam, which was located east of the Tigris River in the country we know today as Iran. Its capital was Susa (Shushan), which was defeated by the Assyrian king Ashurbanipal in 647/646 BC. In the LXX order of prophecies against the nations, the prophecy against Elam comes first. There also is a brief notice of this nation in Ezekiel's prophecies to the nations in Ezek 32:24-25. Elsewhere, Elam is noted by the prophet Isaiah as being famous for its "archers" (Isa 21:2b-4; 22:1-5). The peoples who occupied these areas were the Elamites and the ancient Medes. During the seventh century BC they carried on a constant conflict with the Assyrians.

TRANSLATION

34[165] What came as the word of Yahweh to Jeremiah the prophet concerning Elam, at the beginning of the reign of Zedekiah, king of Judah, saying:

> **35** This is what Yahweh of Hosts[166] has said:
> "Look! I am going to break the bow of Elam,
> > The mainstay of their might.
> **36** I will bring against Elam four winds,
> > From the four corners of the heavens.
> I will scatter them to all these winds,
> > And there will not be a nation
> > Where Elam's exiles do not go.
> **37** I will terrify them before their foes,
> > Before those who are seeking their lives;
> I will bring disaster upon them,
> > Even my fierce anger, declares Yahweh.
> I will send after them the sword,
> > Until I have consumed them.
> **38** I will place my throne in Elam,

---

165. The version of this verse in the LXX reads only ἃ ἐπροφήτευσεν Ιερεμιας ἐπὶ τὰ ἔθνη τὰ Αιλαμ, "The things Jeremiah prophesized against the nations, Elam." The remainder of the verse appears at the end of v. 39.

166. The word נִאבָצ, "of Hosts," is absent in the LXX.

And I will destroy[167] from there both king and officials,
declares Yahweh.[168]

39 But when it is all over, I will most certainly restore the fortunes of Elam, declares Yahweh."

COMMENTARY

49:35 This oracle is unusual in that it does not mention any cities of Elam, nor does it list any specific sins or evils they have done. God is the subject of the verbs here. There is a general statement about divine judgment, also mentioned in 25:15–38. Yahweh shows his military might by removing the very weapon that Elam boasted of as that which she depended on as the "mainstay of [her] might": the "bow" (v. 35b–c). The bow, when used properly, could be lethal, but it also could become most useless if broken by the enemy.

49:36–37 Verse 36 predicts that the enemy will come at Elam from every direction. With foe coming from every side and from every quarter, it is hard to see how the archers will be able to mount an attack. Moreover, the devastation that will attend such an invasion is great; Elam will eventually be scattered by God (using the agency of the Babylonian forces) to the four winds and to the four corners of the earth. There will not be a nation where their exiles do not go (v. 36c–e). God warns of more trouble in v. 37 as terror is spread among those being invaded and a great disaster is sent by God as a result of his fierce anger. Elam will be pursued relentlessly by the sword until it has consumed them all.

49:38–39 God will also set up his throne in Elam itself and will continue to destroy both king and officials by means of the human conqueror (v. 38). Surprisingly, however, when it is all over, God himself will, similarly to his promise to Israel and Judah, restore the fortunes of Elam (v. 39). This same divine promise is also made in 48:47 and 49:6 to two other nations. This promise is realized, at least in part, by the way in which Elam later

---

167. The LXX has καὶ ἐξαποστελῶ, "and I will send forth," where the MT has וְהַאֲבַדְתִּי, "and I will destroy."

168. The phrase נְאֻם־יְהוָה, "declares Yahweh," is absent in the LXX.

becomes the heart of the Persian Empire, with its capital at Susa. Even beyond that, Elamites are also present in NT times at the Day of Pentecost (Acts 2:9, 11). No distinct word is found in Scripture of what part Elam may play in the final day, but that may be part of the "not yet" aspect of this prophecy. Iranians are known to be exiled all over the world today in significant numbers, just as the Jewish people are scattered.

This prophecy predicts that God will scatter the people of Elam (modern Persia) to the four winds. Today a huge number of persons of Persian descent are taking up residency all over the world.

AN ORACLE CONCERNING BABYLON (50:1–51:64)

The ninth and final oracle against the nations is against Babylon, in chapters 50–51, which have almost as many verses in them as the combined eight other oracles in chapters 46–49 (110 verses in chaps. 50–51 as opposed to 121 in chaps. 46–49).[169] This demonstrates just how important a role Babylon plays for the nation of Judah and the prophet Jeremiah. It is true, of course, that Babylon has been given the role of conqueror by Yahweh himself. But that does not mean that she will not be called to account regarding how she carries out this assignment.

TRANSLATION

1 The word that Yahweh spoke concerning Babylon,[170] the land of the Chaldeans, through Jeremiah the prophet:

2 "Make it known among the nations,
  Proclaim it, lift up a banner;[171]
  Keep nothing back,
Say, Babylon will be captured!
  Bel[172] will be put to shame,

---

169. Aitken correctly points out that "the oracles against Babylon in Jeremiah 50–51 are not a loose and amorphous conglomerate of thematic elements tacked together at random ... they have structural organization and coherence." See K. T. Aitken, "The Oracles against Babylon in Jeremiah 50–51: Structures and Perspectives," *TynBul* 35 (1984): 25–63.

170. The LXX has λόγος κυρίου ὃν ἐλάλησεν ἐπὶ Βαβυλῶνα, "The word of the Lord that he spoke against Babylon," where the MT has הַדָּבָר אֲשֶׁר דִּבֶּר יְהוָה אֶל־בָּבֶל, "The word that Yahweh spoke concerning Babylon." The rest of the verse is absent in the LXX.

171. The phrase שְׂאוּ־נֵס הַשְׁמִיעוּ, "and lift up a banner, proclaim it," is absent in the LXX.

172. The LXX adds the phrase ἡ ἀπτόητος, "the fearless," for Bel.

Marduk[173] will be filled with terror,
Her images will be put to shame,
Her idols will be dismayed."[174]
3 For a nation from the north will attack her,
And lay waste her land,
With no one living in it;
Both man and beast will flee away.[175]
4 In those days, at that time, declares Yahweh,[176]
"The people of Israel shall come,
And the people of Judah together,
Will go weeping to seek Yahweh their God.
5 They will ask the way to Zion,
And turn their faces toward it.
They will come[177] and cleave to Yahweh,
In an everlasting covenant that won't be forgotten.
6 My people were lost sheep,
Their shepherds have led them astray
And caused them to wander on the mountains,
They roamed from mountain to hill
And forgot their resting place.
7 Whoever found them devoured them;
Their enemies said, 'We are not guilty,'[178]
For they sinned against Yahweh,[179]
Their true pasture,
The hope of their fathers.

---

173. The LXX adds the title ἡ τρυφερά, "the luxurious," for Marduk.

174. The LXX omits הֹבִישׁוּ עֲצַבֶּיהָ חַתּוּ גִּלּוּלֶיהָ, "her images will be put to shame, her idols will be dismayed."

175. The phrase נָדוּ הָלָכוּ, "they will flee away," is absent in the LXX.

176. The phrase נְאֻם־יְהוָה, "declares Yahweh," is absent in the LXX.

177. The LXX has the fut. indic. καὶ ἥξουσιν, "they will come," where the MT has the impv. בֹּאוּ, "come." The current translation follows the LXX.

178. The LXX has μὴ ἀνῶμεν αὐτούς, "let us not abandon," where the MT has לֹא נֶאְשָׁם, "we are not guilty."

179. The word יְהוָה, "Yahweh," is absent in the LXX from the end of the verse. The editors of *BHS* suggest that this occurrence of יְהוָה was originally הוֹי, "woe/alas," at the beginning of the previous verse (cf. Zech 2:6 [MT Zech 2:10]).

8 Flee from the midst of Babylon,

Go out[180] from the land of the Chaldeans!

And be like the male-goats[181] that lead the flock!

9 For, look! I am going to arouse,

And bring up[182] against Babylon,

An alliance of great[183] nations,

From the land of the north.

They will take up their positions against her;

She will be captured.

Their arrows will be like skilled warriors[184]

Who do not return empty-handed.

10 So Chaldea will be for plunder;

Her plunderers will all have their fill," declares Yahweh.[185]

11 "Because you rejoice, and because you are glad,

You who pillaged my inheritance,

Because you frisk about like a heifer threshing[186] grain,

And neigh like stallions![187]

12 Your mother will be greatly ashamed,

She who gave you birth will be disgraced.

Look![188] She will be the least of the nations—

A wilderness, a dry land, a desert.[189]

13 Because of the wrath of Yahweh,

She will not be inhabited,

---

180. The Cairo Geniza, the Syr., Tg., and Vg. follow the **Qere**, which has the impv. צֵאוּ, "go out," where the MT has the pf. יָצְאוּ, "they went out."

181. The LXX has ὥσπερ δράκοντες, "like the serpents," where the MT has כְּעַתּוּדִים, "like the male-goats."

182. The word וּמַעֲלֶה, "and bring up," is absent in the LXX.

183. The word גְּדֹלִים, "great," is absent in the LXX.

184. The MT, with many Heb. mss, α´, the Tg., and the Vg., has כְּגִבּוֹר מַשְׁכִּיל , "like a mis-carrying soldier." The current translation follows some Heb. mss, the LXX, σ´, and the Syr. in reading כְּגִבּוֹר מַשְׂכִּיל, "like skilled warriors."

185. The phrase נְאֻם־יְהוָה, "declares Yahweh," is absent in the LXX.

186. The LXX has ὡς βοΐδια ἐν βοτάνῃ, "like cows in vegetation," where the MT has כְּעֶגְלָה דָשָׁה, "like a heifer threshing."

187. The LXX has καὶ ἐκερατίζετε ὡς ταῦροι, "and gored like bulls," where the MT has וְתִצְהֲלִי כָּאַבִּרִים, "and neigh like stallions."

188. The word הִנֵּה, "look," is absent in the LXX.

189. The phrase צִיָּה וַעֲרָבָה, "a dry land, a desert," is absent in the LXX.

But will be completely desolate;

All who pass by Babylon will shudder

And whistle[190] because of all her wounds.

14 Take up your stations around Babylon,

All you who draw the bow!

Shoot[191] at her! Spare no arrows!

For she has sinned against Yahweh.[192]

15 Shout against her on every side![193]

She signals surrender,[194] her towers fall,

Her walls are battered down

Since this is the vengeance of Yahweh,

Take vengeance on her;

Do to her as she has done.

16 Cut off from Babylon the sower,[195]

And him who reaps with his sickle at harvest.

Because of the sword of the oppressor,[196]

Let everyone return to his own people,

Let everyone flee to his own land.

17 Israel is a scattered flock,

That lions have chased[197] away.

The first to devour him was the king of Assyria, and then the last to gnaw on his bones[198] was Nebuchadnezzar,[199] king of Babylon." **18** Therefore,

---

190. Or "hiss."

191. Some Heb. mss have ירו, "shoot," where the MT has ידו. This is the only occurrence of ידו in the qal in the MT, but it occurs in the piel ("to cast") and hiphil ("to praise/confess"). The verb ירי frequently occurs with the sense of "to shoot."

192. The phrase כִּי לַיהוָה חָטָאָה, "for she has sinned against Yahweh," is absent in the LXX.

193. The word סָבִיב, "on every side," is absent in the LXX.

194. The LXX has παρελύθησαν αἱ χεῖρες αὐτῆς, "her hands were weakened," where the MT has נָתְנָה יָדָהּ, "she signals surrender" (lit. "she gave her hand").

195. The LXX has σπέρμα, "seed" (Heb.: זֶרַע), where the MT has זוֹרֵעַ, "the sower."

196. The LXX has μαχαίρας Ἑλληνικῆς, "the Grecian sword," where the MT has חֶרֶב הַיּוֹנָה, "the sword of the oppressor."

197. The LXX adds αὐτόν, "him," as the obj. of the verb הִדִּיחוּ, "they have chased."

198. The word עַצְמוֹ, "his bones," is absent in the LXX.

199. The word נְבוּכַדְרֶאצַּר, "Nebuchadnezzar," is absent in the LXX.

this is what Yahweh of Hosts, the God of Israel,[200] has said: "Look, I am going to punish the king of Babylon and his land as I punished the king of Assyria. **19** But I will bring Israel back to his own pasture and he shall feed on Carmel and in Bashan.[201] His appetite will be satisfied on the hills of Ephraim and Gilead.

20 "In those days, at that time, declares Yahweh,[202] search will be made for Israel's guilt, but there will be none, and for the sins of Judah, but none will be found, for I will pardon the remnant I spare.[203]

> **21** Attack the land of Merathaim![204]
> March against the inhabitants of Pekod![205]
> Pursue, attack,[206] and devote to destruction, declares Yahweh,
> Do everything I have commanded you.[207]
> **22** The noise of battle in the land,
> [The noise] of a great collapse![208]
> **23** How broken and shattered,
> Is the hammer of the whole earth!
> How horrific is Babylon among the nations!
> **24** I have set a trap for you, O Babylon,
> And you were caught before you knew it.
> You were found and captured,[209]
> Because you opposed Yahweh.
> **25** Yahweh has opened his arsenal,
> And brought out his instruments of wrath;

---

200. The phrase צְבָאוֹת אֱלֹהֵי יִשְׂרָאֵל, "of Hosts, the God of Israel," is absent in the LXX.

201. The word וְהַבָּשָׁן, "Bashan," is absent in the LXX.

202. The phrase נְאֻם־יְהוָה, "declares Yahweh," is absent in the LXX.

203. The LXX adds the first three words of the following verse, ἐπὶ τῆς γῆς, "upon the land," and the phrase λέγει κύριος, "says the Lord."

204. The LXX has πικρῶς, "roughly," where the MT has מְרָתַיִם, "Merathaim."

205. The LXX has the impv. ἐκδίκησον, "avenge," where the MT has פְּקוֹד, "Pekod."

206. The LXX has μάχαιρα, "sword" (Heb.: חֶרֶב), where the MT has the impv. חֲרֹב, "attack."

207. The word אַחֲרֵיהֶם, "after them," is absent in the LXX and Syr. The current translation follows the LXX.

208. The LXX adds the phrase ἐν γῇ Χαλδαίων, "in the land of the Chaldeans," at the end of the verse.

209. The phrase נִמְצֵאת וְגַם־נִתְפַּשְׂתְּ, "you were found and captured," is absent in the Syr.

For Adonai Yahweh[210] has work to do
  In the land of the Chaldeans.
26 Come against her from afar.
  Open her granaries,
  Pile her up like heaps[211] of grain!
Put her under the ban,
  And leave her no remnant.
27 Slay all her young bulls;[212]
  Let them go down to slaughter.
Woe to them!
  For their day has come,
  The time for them to be punished.
28 The sound of fugitives and refugees,
  [Coming] from the land of Babylon,
To tell Zion of the vengeance of Yahweh our God,
  [Who has taken] vengeance for his temple.[213]
29 Summon archers[214] against Babylon,
  All those who draw the bow.
Encamp all around her;
  Let no one escape.[215]
Repay her for her deeds;
  Do to her as she has done!
For she has defied Yahweh,
  The Holy One of Israel.
30 Therefore, her youths shall fall in the open squares;

---

210. The word צְבָאוֹת, "of Hosts," is absent in the LXX.

211. The LXX has ἐρευνήσατε αὐτὴν ὡς σπήλαιον, "search her like a cave," and the Syr. has *'jk 'rṭljt'*, "like a naked woman," where the MT has סָלּוּהָ כְמוֹ־עֲרֵמִים, "pile her up like heaps."

212. The LXX has ἀναξηράνατε αὐτῆς πάντας τοὺς καρπούς, "dry up all her fruit" (reading פְּרִיהָ, "her bulls," as פְּרִיהָ, "her fruit"), where the MT has חִרְבוּ כָּל־פָּרֶיהָ, "slay all her young bulls."

213. The phrase נִקְמַת הֵיכָלוֹ, "vengeance for his temple," is absent in the LXX.

214. The current translation, with KJV, ESV, NET, NIV, NRSV, and the editors of *BHS*, reads רֹבִים, "archers," where the MT has רַבִּים, "many." The LXX and NASB follow the MT.

215. Many Heb. mss follow the **Qere**, which has אַל־יְהִי־לָה פְּלֵטָה, "let there be no escape for her."

All her men of war will be silenced in that day,"[216] declares
Yahweh.

31 "Look, I am against you, O arrogant one!" declares Adonai
Yahweh,[217]

"For your day has come, the time for you to be punished.

32 The arrogant one will stumble and fall,

And no one will help her up.

I will kindle a fire in her towns[218]

That will consume all that is around her."

33 This is what Yahweh of Hosts[219] has said:

"The people of Israel are oppressed,

And the people of Judah too.

All her captors hold them fast,

Refusing to let them go.

34[220] Yet their Redeemer is strong.

Yahweh of Hosts is his name.

He will vigorously defend their cause

So that he may bring rest to their land,

But unrest to those how live in Babylon.

35 A sword against the Chaldeans, declares Yahweh![221]

Against those who live in Babylon,

And against her officials,

And against her wise men!

36 A sword against her empty-talkers,[222]

---

216. The phrase בַּיּוֹם הַהוּא, "in that day," is absent in the LXX.

217. The word צְבָאוֹת, "of Hosts," is absent in the LXX.

218. The LXX has ἐν τῷ δρυμῷ αὐτῆς, "in her forest" (Heb.: בְּיַעְרוֹ), where the MT has בְּעָרֶיהָ, "in her towns" (lit. "in his towns").

219. The word צְבָאוֹת, "of Hosts," is absent in the LXX.

220. **34** The LXX version of this verse is καὶ ὁ λυτρούμενος αὐτοὺς ἰσχυρός κύριος παντοκράτωρ ὄνομα αὐτῷ κρίσιν κρινεῖ πρὸς τοὺς ἀντιδίκους αὐτοῦ ὅπως ἐξάρῃ τὴν γῆν καὶ παροξυνεῖ τοῖς κατοικοῦσι Βαβυλῶνα, "And their Redeemer is strong, the Lord Almighty is his name. He will enter into judgment toward his enemies in order that me may destroy the earth and provoke the inhabitants of Babylon."

221. The phrase נְאֻם־יְהוָה, "declares Yahweh," is absent in the LXX.

222. θ´, the Syr., Tg.[f. Mss], the Vg., and the current translation read בַּדֶּיהָ, "her empty-talkers," where the MT has הַבַּדִּים, "the empty-talkers."

They have become[223] fools![224]

A sword against her warriors,

  They will be filled with terror!

37 A sword against his horses and his chariots,

  And all foreigners in her ranks,

  They will become like women.

A sword against her treasures,

  They will dry up.

38 A drought[225] on her waters,

  They will dry up.

For it is a land of idols,

  Idols that will go mad with fright.[226]

39 Therefore desert creatures and hyenas will live there,

  And there the owl will live.

It will never again be inhabited,

  Or lived in from generation to generation.[227]

40 As God overthrew Sodom and Gomorrah,

  Along with their neighboring towns, declares Yahweh,

So no one will live there;

  No human being will sojourn in it.

41 Look! A people coming from the north;

  A mighty nation and many kings

  Are being stirred up from the remotest parts of the earth.

42 They are armed with bow and spear;

  They are cruel and without mercy.

They sound like the roaring sea,

  As they ride on their horses;

---

223. Or "they will become fools."

224. The LXX omits חֶרֶב אֶל־הַבַּדִּים וְנֹאָלוּ, "a sword against the empty-talkers, they have become fools."

225. The word חֹרֶב, "a drought," is absent in the LXX, which reads ἐπὶ τῷ ὕδατι αὐτῆς ἐπεποίθει, "on her waters she will be ashamed," where the MT has חֶרֶב אֶל־מֵימֶיהָ, "a drought on her waters, they will dry up."

226. The LXX has καὶ ἐν ταῖς νήσοις οὗ κατεκαυχῶντο, "and in the islands where they boasted," where the MT has וּבָאֵימִים יִתְהֹלָלוּ, "idols that will go mad with fright."

227. The phrase וְלֹא תִשְׁכֹּן עַד־דּוֹר וָדוֹר, "or lived in from generation to generation," is absent in the LXX.

They come like men[228] in battle formation,[229]
  To attack you, O daughter of Babylon.
43 The king of Babylon has heard a report about them,
  And his hands hang limp.
Anguish has gripped him,
  Pain like that of a woman in labor.
44 Look! Like a lion coming up from the Jordan's thicket,[230]
  To a rich pastureland,
I will chase them from upon it.
  Who is the chosen one I will appoint for this?
For who is like me? Who can challenge me?
  And what shepherd can stand against me?
45 Therefore, hear the plan that Yahweh has planned against
  Babylon,
  The schemes that he has schemed against the land[231] of
    the Chaldeans:
The young[232] of the flock will be dragged away;
  He will completely destroy their pasture[233] because of
    them.
46 At the sound of Babylon's capture,
  The earth will tremble;
  Its cry will resound among the nations."

51:1 This is what Yahweh has said:

"Look here! I will rouse against Babylon,

---

228. Emerton recommends repointing כְּאִישׁ, "like a man," to be, as in the LXX, כְּאֵשׁ, "like fire." See J. A. Emerton, "A Problem in the Hebrew Text of Jeremiah 6:23 and 50:42," *JTS* 23, no. 1 (1972): 106–13.

229. The LXX adds the phrase ὥσπερ πῦρ, "like fire," after "in battle formation."

230. The LXX only has ἀπό, "from," where the MT has מִגְּאוֹן, "from the thicket."

231. Some Heb. mss with the LXX read יוֹשְׁבֵי, "the inhabitants," where the MT has אֶרֶץ, "the land."

232. The LXX has τὰ ἀρνία, "the lambs," where the MT has צְעִירֵי, "the young."

233. The current translation follows the Syr., Tg., and Vg., as well as the MT of Jer 49:20 with נְוֵהֶם, "their pasture," where the MT of Jer 50:45 lacks the suf. and has נָוֶה, "pasture."

And[234] the inhabitants of Leb Kamai,[235]
     A destroying wind.

2 I will send to Babylon foreigners[236]
     To winnow and devastate her land,
     For they will[237] oppress her on every side in the day of her
         distress.

3 Let not[238] the archer draw[239] his bow,
     Nor[240] let him put on his armor.

Do not spare her youths!
     Put her army under the ban.

4 They will fall down slain in Chaldea's land,
     Pierced through in her streets.

5 For Israel and Judah have not been widowed,
     By their God, Yahweh of Hosts,[241]

Even though their land is full of guilt,
     [Before] the Holy One of Israel.

6 Flee from the midst of Babylon!
     Save your lives, each one of you!
     Do not be destroyed because of her guilt!

For it is time for Yahweh's vengeance;
     He will repay her what she deserves.

7 A golden cup was Babylon
     In Yahweh's hand,

---

234. Some Heb. mss and the LXX read וְעַל, "and against," where the MT has וְאֶל, "and to."

235. The LXX has Χαλδαίους, "Chaldeans," where the MT has לֵב קָמָי, "Leb Kamai."

236. α´, σ´, and the Vg. read זֹרִים, "winnowers," where the MT has זָרִים, "foreigners."

237. The LXX has οὐαί, "woe," where the MT has הָיוּ, "they will."

238. The word אַל, "to," is absent in the LXX. The current translation follows many Heb. mss, the Syr., Tg., and Vg. in reading אַל, "not," where the MT has אֶל, "to."

239. The MT has a second occurrence of יִדְרֹךְ, "he will draw," immediately following the first. The current translation follows many Heb. mss, versions, and the advice of the editors of *BHS* in deleting the second occurrence.

240. The word וְאֶל, "and to," is absent in the LXX. The current translation follows some Heb. mss and versions in reading וְאַל, "nor," where the MT has וְאֶל, "and to."

241. The editors of *BHS* suggest placing 51:5a, כִּי לֹא־אַלְמָן יִשְׂרָאֵל וִיהוּדָה מֵאֱלֹהָיו מֵיהוָה צְבָאוֹת, "for Israel and Judah have not been widowed, by their God, Yahweh of Hosts," after the second clause. Holladay accepts the change, seeing the "guilt" in v. 5b belonging to Babylon, but adds that if the guilt belonged to Israel, the conj. כִּי must be translated as "though" (Holladay 1990, 396n5a–a).

To make all the earth drunk.
From her wine the nations drank,
   Therefore, the nations[242] have gone mad.
8 Suddenly Babylon fell and was broken;
   Wail over her!
Get balm for her pain;
   Perhaps she can be healed.
9 We would have healed Babylon,
   But she cannot be healed;
Let us leave her[243] and each go to his own land,
   For her judgment reaches to heaven,
   It ascends to the skies.
10 Yahweh has brought forth our vindication.[244]
   Come, let us report in Zion
   What Yahweh our God has done for us.
11 Sharpen the arrows,
   Fill the quivers![245]
Yahweh has stirred up the spirit of the kings[246] of the Medes,
   Because his purpose is to destroy Babylon.
For Yahweh's vengeance is this:
   Vengeance for his temple.
12 Signal attack on Babylon's walls!
   Strengthen the watchmen!
   Station the watchmen, prepare an ambush![247]
For Yahweh has both planned and done
   What he spoke against Babylon's inhabitants.
13 You who live by many waters,

---

242. The second occurrence of the word גּוֹיִם, "nations," is absent in the LXX.

243. The LXX, with Syr. and Vg., has the subjunctive ἐγκαταλίπωμεν αὐτήν, "let us leave her," where the MT has the impv. עִזְבוּהָ, "leave her."

244. The LXX has τὸ κρίμα αὐτοῦ, "his judgment," where the MT has צִדְקֹתֵינוּ, "our vindications."

245. The LXX has τὰς φαρέτρας, "the quivers," where the MT has הַשְּׁלָטִים, "the shields." The current translation follows the LXX.

246. The LXX with Syr. has the sg. where the MT has the pl. מַלְכֵי, "kings."

247. The Syr. has wṭb'wh bmj', "and immerse it in water," where the MT has הָכִינוּ הָאֹרְבִים, "prepare an ambush."

> Rich in treasures,
> Your end has come,
> > The time for you to be cut off.[248]

14 Yahweh of Hosts has sworn by himself:[249]
> 'I will certainly fill you with men,
> As with [a swarm] of locusts.
> > And they will shout over you a triumph.'"

15 He[250] made the earth by his power;
> He founded the world by his wisdom,
> And by his understanding he stretched out the heavens.

16 When he thunders,[251] the waters in the heavens roar;
> He makes clouds rise from the ends of the earth.

He sends lightning with rain
> And brings the wind out of his storehouses.

17 Every person is stupid and without knowledge,
> Every refiner of silver is ashamed of his idol;

For his molten images are a fraud;
> They have no breath in them.

18 They are nothings, the objects of mockery.
> When their judgment comes, they will perish.

19 Not like these is the Portion of Jacob;
> For he is the Maker of all things,

Including the tribe[252] of his inheritance[253]—
> Yahweh of Hosts[254] is his name.

---

248. The LXX has ἥκει τὸ πέρας σου ἀληθῶς εἰς τὰ σπλάγχα σου, "your end has come, truly, into your bowels," where the MT has בָּא קִצֵּךְ אַמַּת בִּצְעֵךְ, "your end has come, the threshold of your cut-off thread" (this idiom has been translated here as "the time for you to be cut off"). For בִּצְעֵךְ, "your cut-off thread," the Syr. has *mḥwtkj*, "your bruise."

249. The LXX has κατὰ τοῦ βραχίονος αὐτοῦ, "by his arm," where the MT has בְּנַפְשׁוֹ, "by himself."

250. LXX[c], with the Arabic and Syr., identifies the subject as κύριος, "Lord."

251. The LXX has εἰς φωνὴν ἔθετο, "into a sound/voice he placed," where the MT has לְקוֹל תִּתּוֹ, "when he thunders."

252. Many Heb. mss, with LXX[L], the Tg., Vg., and 10:12 read וְיִשְׂרָאֵל שֵׁבֶט, "including Israel, the tribe," where the MT has וְשֵׁבֶט, "including the tribe."

253. The LXX has αὐτός ἐστιν κληρονομία αὐτοῦ, "he is his inheritance," where the MT has וְשֵׁבֶט נַחֲלָתוֹ, "including the tribe of his inheritance."

254. The word צְבָאוֹת, "of Hosts," is absent in the LXX.

20 "My war club are you,
  My weapon of war;[255]
With you I will smash to pieces the nations,
  With you I will destroy kingdoms.
21 With you I will smash in pieces horse and rider;
  With you I will smash in pieces chariot and driver.
22 With you I will smash in pieces man and woman;
  With you I will smash in pieces old man and youth,[256]
  With you I will smash in pieces young man and virgin,
23 With you I will smash in pieces shepherd and flock,
  With you I will smash in pieces farmer and team,
  With you I will smash in pieces governor and his officials.
24 "Before your eyes, I will repay Babylon and all who live
  Chaldea for all the wrong they have done in Zion," declares
  Yahweh.
25 "Look here! I am against you, O destroying[257] mountain,
  You who destroy the whole earth, declares Yahweh.
I will stretch out my hand against you,
  And roll you off the cliffs,
  And make you a burnt-out mountain.
26 Nevermore shall they quarry a cornerstone from you,
  Or a stone for a foundation.
For you will be a waste forever," declares Yahweh.
27 Lift up a banner in the land!
  Sound the trumpet among the nations!
  Prepare the nations for battle against her.
Summon against her these kingdoms:
  Ararat, Minni, and Ashkenaz.
Appoint a commander against her;
  Send up horses like bristling[258] locusts.

---

255. The LXX has διασκορπίζεις σύ μοι σκεύη πολέμου, "you scatter for me the weapons of war," where the MT has מַפֵּץ־אַתָּה לִי כְּלֵי מִלְחָמָה, "my war club are you, my weapon of war."

256. The phrase וְנִפַּצְתִּי בְךָ זָקֵן וָנָעַר, "with you I will smash in pieces old man and youth," is absent in the LXX.

257. The LXX has τὸ διεφθαρμένον, "destroyed," where the MT has הַמַּשְׁחִית, "destroying."

258. The LXX has πλῆθος, "a multitude," where the MT has סָמָר, "bristling."

28 Prepare the nations for battle against her:
> The king[259] of the Medes,

His governors and all his prefects,
> And all the lands they rule.

29 Then the land will tremble and writhe,
> For Yahweh's purposes[260] against Babylon stand,

To lay waste the land of Babylon,
> So no one will live there.

30 Babylon's warriors have ceased to fight,
> They remain in their strongholds,

Their strength is exhausted;
> They act like women.

Her dwellings are set on fire;
> The bars of her gates are broken down.

31 Runner after runner comes running,
> Messenger after messenger,

To tell the king of Babylon
> That his entire city is captured,

32 The river crossings are seized,
> The marshes set on fire,

And the soldiers are terrified.[261]

33 This is what Yahweh of Hosts, the God of Israel[262] has said:
> "The daughter[263] of Babylon is like a threshing floor at the time[264]
>> it is trampled;
>> Yet a little while and the time to harvest her will come."

34 Nebuchadnezzar king of Babylon has devoured us,[265]

---

259. The LXX and Syr. have the sg. where the MT has the pl. מַלְכֵי, "kings." Compare v. 11.

260. Some Heb. mss, the LXX, and Syr. read מַחְשֶׁבֶת, "purpose," where the MT has מַחְשְׁבוֹת, "purposes."

261. The LXX has ἐξέρχονται, "they are going out," where the MT has נִבְהָלוּ, "they are terrified."

262. The phrase צְבָאוֹת אֱלֹהֵי יִשְׂרָאֵל, "of Hosts, the God of Israel," is absent in the LXX.

263. The LXX has οἶκοι βασιλέως, "houses of the king" (Heb.: בָּתֵּי מֶלֶךְ), where the MT has בַּת, "daughter."

264. The word עֵת, "time," is absent in the LXX.

265. The verbs אֲכָלָנוּ, הֲמָמָנוּ, הִצִּיגָנוּ, בְּלָעָנוּ, and הֱדִיחָנוּ appear with a 1 c. pl. suf. ("us") in the **Kethiv** but appear with a 1 c. sg. suf. ("me") in the **Qere** and some Heb. mss.

He has thrown us into confusion,

He has made us like an empty jar,

    Like a dragon he has swallowed us up,

And filled his belly with delicacies,

    And then washed us out.[266]

35 May the violence done to our flesh be upon Babylon,[267]

    Say the inhabitants of Zion,

And may our blood be on those who live in Babylonia,

    Says Jerusalem.

36 Therefore, this is what Yahweh has said:

"Look! I will plead your case[268] and avenge you;

    I will dry up her sea and make her springs dry.

37[269] Babylon will become a heap of ruins,

    A lair for jackals, an object of horror and scorn,

    A place where no one lives.

38 All her people roar[270] like young lions,

    They growl[271] like lion cubs.

39 But while they are aroused,[272]

    I will set out a banquet for them,

And make them drunk,

    Then they will sleep[273] forever and not awake, declares

        Yahweh.

40 I will bring them down like lambs to slaughter,

    Like rams and goats."

---

266. The verb הֱדִיחָנוּ, "he spewed us out," is absent in the LXX.

267. The LXX has οἱ μόχθοι μου καὶ αἱ ταλαιπωρίαι μου εἰς Βαβυλῶνα, "my hardships and my troubles upon Babylon," where the MT has חֲמָסִי וּשְׁאֵרִי עַל־בָּבֶל, "may the violence done to our flesh be upon Babylon" (lit. "my violence and my flesh upon Babylon").

268. The LXX has ἰδοὺ ἐγὼ κρινῶ τὴν ἀντίδικόν σου, "look, I will judge your adversary," where the MT has הִנְנִי־רָב אֶת־רִיבֵךְ, "look! I will plead your case."

269. The LXX version of this verse reads only καὶ ἔσται Βαβυλὼν εἰς ἀφανισμὸν καὶ οὐ κατοικηθήσεται, "and Babylon will be a desolation and without inhabitant."

270. The word יִשְׁאָגוּ, "they roar," is absent in the LXX.

271. The LXX has ἐξηγέρθησαν, "they rose up" (Heb.: נֵעֹרוּ), where the MT has נָעֲרוּ, "they growl."

272. The Syr. has bḥmt', "with heat/venom," where the MT has בְּחֻמָּם, "while they are aroused."

273. Some versions have יֵעָלְפוּ, "they will faint," where the MT has יַעֲלֹזוּ, "they will exult."

41 How Sheshach[274] will be captured,
   The renown of the whole earth.
How Babylon has become
   A horror to the nations!
42 The sea has surged over Babylon;
   Its roaring waves will cover her.
43 Her towns will be desolate,
   A dry and desert land;
A land[275] where no one lives,
   Through which no person travels.
44 I will punish Bel in Babylon,[276]
   And make him disgorge what he has swallowed.
The nations will no longer stream to him,
   And the wall of Babylon will fall.[277]
45 Come out from the midst of her, my people!
   Each person must save his own life!
   [Run] from the fierce anger of Yahweh.
46 Lest your hearts grow faint,
   And you fear because of the rumors you have heard in
      the land—
One rumor comes this year,
   Another the next,
Rumors of violence in the land
   And of ruler against ruler—
47 Therefore, look here! The days are coming,
   When I will punish the idols of Babylon.
All her land will be humbled,
   And her slain will lie fallen in her midst.
48 Then heaven and earth shall exalt over Babylon,
   And all that is in them,

---

274. The word שֵׁשַׁךְ, "Sheshach," is absent in the LXX.
275. The second occurrence of the word אֶרֶץ, "land," is absent in the LXX and Syr.
276. The LXX has Βαβυλῶνα, "Babylon," where the MT has בֵּל בְּבָבֶל, "Bel in Babylon."
277. The LXX is lacking 44b–49a.

For out of the north destroyers will attack[278] her, declares
    Yahweh.

49 Yes, Babylon must fall because of Israel's slain,
    Just as the slain of all the earth have fallen because of
    Babylon.

50 You have escaped from the sword,
    Leave![279] Do not linger!
Remember Yahweh in a distant land,
    Let Jerusalem come to you mind."

51 We have been shamed, for we have been insulted;
    Reproach covers our face,
For foreigners have entered the holy places,
    The house of Yahweh.[280]

52 Therefore, look out! "The days are coming,"
    Declares Yahweh,
"When I will punish her idols,
    And throughout her land the wounded will groan.[281]

53 Even if Babylon were to reach the sky,
    And if [she were to] fortify her lofty stronghold,
    Yet from me will come destroyers against her," declares
    Yahweh.

54 The sound of a cry comes from Babylon,
    A mighty collapse from the land of the Chaldeans!

55 For Yahweh is destroying Babylon,
    He will silence her noisy din.
Their waves roar like mighty waters,
    The tumult of their crash resounds.

56 For a destroyer has come against Babylon;[282]
    Her warriors will be captured,

---

278. Several mss and v. 53 read יָבֹא, "they will come," where the MT has יָבוֹא, "he will come."

279. The LXX has ἐκ γῆς πορεύεσθε, "go out from the land" (Heb.: מֵחֲרָבָה לְכוּ), where the MT has מֵחֶרֶב הִלְכוּ, "from the sword, leave."

280. The LXX has εἰς τὰ ἅγια ἡμῶν εἰς οἶκον κυρίου, "into our holy place, into the house of the Lord," where the MT has עַל־מִקְדְּשֵׁי בֵּית יְהוָה, "into the holy places, the house of Yahweh."

281. The LXX has πεσοῦνται, "they will fall," where the MT has יֶאֱנֹק, "he will groan."

282. The LXX has ὅτι ἦλθεν ἐπὶ Βαβυλῶνα ταλαιπωρία, "for distress has come upon Babylon," where the MT has כִּי בָא עָלֶיהָ עַל־בָּבֶל שׁוֹדֵד, "for a destroyer has come against Babylon."

Their bows will be broken.
Yahweh is a God who requites,
   He will repay in full!

57 "I will make her officials and her wise men drunk,
   Her governors, prefects, and warriors as well;
They will sleep forever and not awake," declares the King,
   Whose name is Yahweh of Hosts.[283]

58 This is what Yahweh of Hosts[284] has said:
"Babylon's thick walls,[285] so shall be leveled
   And her high gates set on fire.
The peoples exhaust themselves for nothing,
   The nations' labor is only for the flames."[286]

59 This is the message Jeremiah, the prophet, gave to the quartermaster[287] Seraiah,[288] the son of Neriah, the son of Mahseiah, when he went to Babylon with Zedekiah,[289] king of Judah, in the fourth year of his reign. **60** Jeremiah had written on a scroll all the disasters that would come on Babylon—all that had been recorded concerning Babylon. **61** Jeremiah said to Seraiah, "When you get to[290] Babylon, see that you read all these words aloud. **62** Then say, O Yahweh, you have said you will destroy this place,

---

283. The LXX version of this verse reads καὶ μεθύσει μέθῃ τοὺς ἡγεμόνας αὐτῆς καὶ τοὺς σοφοὺς αὐτῆς καὶ τοὺς στρατηγοὺς αὐτῆς λέγει ὁ βασιλεύς κύριος παντοκράτωρ ὄνομα αὐτῷ, "and he will make her leaders and her wise men and her commanders completely drunk, says the King, the Lord Almighty is his name."

284. The word צְבָאוֹת, "of Hosts," is absent in the LXX.

285. Many Heb. mss, with the LXX and Vg., have חוֹמַת, "wall," where the MT has חֹמוֹת, "walls."

286. The LXX has καὶ οὐ κοπιάσουσιν λαοὶ εἰς κενόν καὶ ἔθνη ἐν ἀρχῇ ἐκλείψουσιν, "and the people will not labor in vain nor the nations fail in their rule," where the MT has וְיִגְעוּ עַמִּים בְּדֵי־רִיק וּלְאֻמִּים בְּדֵי־אֵשׁ וְיָעֵפוּ, "the peoples exhaust themselves for nothing, the nations' labor is only for the flames."

287. The LXX has ἄρχων δώρων, "ruler of the gifts," where the MT has שַׂר מְנוּחָה, "ruler of the resting place" (translated here as "quartermaster").

288. The LXX has the expanded phrase ὁ λόγος ὃν ἐνετείλατο κύριος Ιερεμια τῷ προφήτῃ εἰπεῖν τῷ Σαραια, "The word which the Lord commanded Jeremiah the prophet to say to Seraiah," where the MT has הַדָּבָר אֲשֶׁר־צִוָּה יִרְמְיָהוּ הַנָּבִיא אֶת־שְׂרָיָה, "the word which Jeremiah the prophet commanded Seraiah."

289. The LXX has παρὰ Σεδεκιου, "from Zedekiah," where the MT has אֶת־צִדְקִיָּהוּ, "with Zedekiah."

290. Many mss have בְּבֹאֲךָ, "when you get to," where the MT has כְּבֹאֲךָ, "when you get to."

so that neither man nor beast will live in it; it will be desolate forever.
63 When you finish reading this scroll, tie a stone to it and throw it into
the Euphrates. **64** Then say, 'So will Babylon sink to rise no more because
of the disaster I will bring upon her. And her people will fall.'" The words
of Jeremiah end here.[291]

COMMENTARY

Babylon's Doom and Israel's Release from Exile (50:1–10)

This section has a nice **inclusio** after a general superscription in v. 1,
wherein Babylon's doom by an enemy from the north brackets the whole
section in vv. 2–3 and vv. 9–10, with a proclamation of Israel's release from
exile in vv. 4–7 in between the two end brackets, as it were. Babylon is both
the name of a major city on the Euphrates River, some fifty-five miles south
of the modern city of Baghdad, Iraq, and the name of the country located
in what is now called southern Iraq. The land of the Babylonians was originally called "Chaldea," which goes back to the second millennium BC. The
Chaldeans/Babylonians lived south of the city of Babylon. Nabopolassar,
father of Nebuchadnezzar, gained power in 626 BC and founded a dynasty
that lasted until the empire fell in 539 BC, as Cyrus, king of Persia, accom-
plished a coup over the city of Babylon with very little killing, destruction,
or looting.

50:1-2 Interestingly, the word that Yahweh God speaks in this oracle
against the nation of Babylon comes "through/by the hand of" Jeremiah
the prophet (v. 1). It is unclear if this unusual phrasing means that Jeremiah
wrote the prophecy, but the word is genuinely from Yahweh and comes
under the aegis of this prophet's authentic oracles. Even though Babylon
has not yet fallen, her doom and her end are so certain that a proclamation
can now be made (vv. 2–3). Nothing is to be held back: all the nations of the
world (the call in v. 2 is pl.) can breathe a sigh of relief, for the Medes and
the Persians will bring an end to the Babylonian reign of terror.

---

291. The phrase וְיָעֵפוּ עַד־הֵנָּה דִּבְרֵי יִרְמְיָהוּ, "and they are weary; the words of Jeremiah end
here," is absent in the LXX.

Babylon's exalted god was Marduk, also rendered Merodach by Israel. This name and deity is related to the Canaanite god Baal. Originally Bel was the name reserved for the Sumerian god Enlil, the chief god of the Akkadian pantheon, but as the city of Babylon rose to its heights in the Neo-Babylonian period (626–539 BC) the Babylonians merged Marduk with Bel and called him Bel Marduk. This merger is best illustrated in the Babylonian creation account, *Enuma Elish* (lit. "when on high," the first words of the story), where Bel and Marduk are seen as one. Both terms used here, "image" (עָצֵב) and "idol" (גִּלּוּל), have a tone of disrespect. This is especially true in the case of the second term, which is derived from the word "dung" or "manure" (גָּלָל, *gālāl*). These idol gods are something like "shameful piles of compost," to put the translation as delicately as possible!

50:3 The enemy of Babylon, in one of the great ironies of this book, will come from the north (v. 3; exactly where Judah's enemy will come from, 1:13). The foe is not identified precisely at this point, but it is clear that the Persians, who lived to the east of them, and the Medes, who lived to their northwest, are the main enemies. But that leaves a problem: how can Jeremiah predict that the foe will come from the "north"? The best response seems to be that for the Jewish people the "north" had a sinister association, so it became a colloquialism for the direction from which all hostile action came. Others say that the Medes and the Persians did attack from the north.

50:4–5 Verses 4–7 promise the restoration of Israel and Judah, joined together once again, after being a divided nation since 931 BC. They will return to Yahweh by "seek[ing] Yahweh their God" (v. 4d) and turning from their wicked ways as worship is offered by them to Yahweh God. They will "cleave" to Yahweh their God, and the "covenant" he had made with them will not be forgotten (v. 5) as they ask which way they should take to go to Zion (v. 5). So two peoples, once divided (Israel and Judah), are now joined together and joined to Yahweh.

When will this happen? The time is set as "in those days" or "at that time" (v. 4a). Since it involves not only the return from the Babylonian exile but also the unification of the divided nation, an "everlasting covenant" (v. 5d), and a remembrance of their guilt no more, the action promised here must be spread out over a long period of time, into the days of the second coming.

50:6–10 The people are referred to under the figure of wandering or lost sheep that are destroyed because of poor leadership (v. 6a–c). Not only have their prophets and their priests given them poor leadership, but their kings and their officials done the same. However, the sheep have been on a spiritual wandering trip as well. This has made them helpless and vulnerable to all sorts of attack, away from God's protection. This is why their enemies claim they are not guilty of attacking Judah (v. 7b), "for they sinned against Yahweh" (v. 7c). So here is wicked Babylon calling the kettle black, when they are just as guilty before God for rejecting him and placing their idols in God's place. Such danger lies ahead for Babylon that Judah and the nations are exhorted by Yahweh to get out of that land as fast as possible (v. 8). The reason is that Yahweh is going to bring an alliance of nations from the north (v. 9b–d) so this Chaldean nation will be captured and plundered (vv. 9f, 10).

The Invaders Attack Babylon (50:11–16)

50:11–13 Yahweh speaks directly to Babylon in v. 11 and repeats the word "because" (כִּי) three times over as he gives the reasons he will take the action described in v. 12. These reasons are:

1. Babylon rejoices;

2. Babylon is glad as they pillage God's "inheritance," Judah; and

3. Babylon frolics about like heifers that are greatly excited.

Babylon enjoys conquering Judah too much. Therefore, the great empire of Babylon will be reduced to shame, disgrace, and being regarded as the least of the nations (v. 12). She will be so badly beaten by the conquering armies that all who pass by will whistle in amazement (v. 13).

50:14 Therefore, the hostile armies of the nations are ordered to take up their stations around Babylon. Now the tables will be turned on her as the order is given to "shoot at her! Spare no arrows" (v. 14c–d). She too "has sinned against Yahweh" (v. 14e).

50:15 "She has given her hand" (v. 15b) is used here as an idiom for surrender by means of stretching out the hand in submission. Down come her towers (v. 15b), and her walls are battered in (v. 15c). The reason for all this destruction is to be found in the "vengeance (נָקָם) of Yahweh" (v. 15d). Babylon is now reaping what she has sown. Babylon and the nations of the world are here taught that empires and nations must not think that, once they become so large, they have only themselves to answer to for all their acts, whether good or bad. In God's world there is a correlation between evil, sin, or unrighteousness and the punishment that follows. In this instance Yahweh's retribution will be realized through the invading nations.

50:16 The invaders cut the city of Babylon off from those who sow and harvest the crops in the rich alluvial plains surrounding Babylon (v. 16a-b), so the city should now brace itself for a period of starvation. Also, let all those who have been held captive in Babylon return home to their own lands, for there are many other exiles in Babylon besides those from Judah (v. 16d-e).

Yahweh Intervenes for His Scattered Flock (50:17-20)

50:17-18 Once again the focus of the passage shifts back to Yahweh's people Israel, who are here regarded as "a scattered flock" (v. 17a). Israel is seen as a flock of lost and scattered sheep who have been driven from their land, first by the lion of Assyria and now more recently by the lion Nebuchadnezzar, who has "gnawed on [Judah's] bones" (v. 17c). As a result of this oppression, God will bring disaster on Babylon, just as he had done already to Assyria (v. 18). But he will restore Israel to her own pasture, where they will feed on lush grass in four non-Babylonian sites: Carmel, Bashan, Gilead, and Ephraim. Carmel was located on the Mediterranean coast with hills covered with excellent vegetation. Bashan, in northwestern Transjordania, had a fine reputation for its fertile soil and stately oak trees that gave shade. Gilead was also known for its medicinal plants, and Ephraim in northern Israel had beautiful soil that produced grapes, wheat, and other crops.

50:20 But there is more: in the messianic era, called "in those days" (v. 20), God will so thoroughly forgive the sins of Israel that a "search will be made for Israel's guilt, but there will be none" (v. 20b-c). No longer will the guilt of Israel's sin or Judah's sin stand between them and God. Israel's return to the land also means spiritual renewal of both Judah and Israel.

Yahweh's Command to Attack and Destroy Babylon (50:21–32)

50:21 The unidentified hordes of soldiers are ordered by Yahweh to attack the land of "Merathaim" (v. 21a), which probably means "double rebellion" (a play on an Akkadian word *marratum*, which refers to the marshy area in southern Babylon where the Tigris and Euphrates Rivers merged with the salt waters of the Persian Gulf, but as a pun it also carries the idea of "bitter," "salt water"). They are also given orders to go against the "inhabitants of Pekod" (v. 21b), which is the name for an Aramean tribe settled along the east bank of the lower Tigris River. The term denotes the territory where the tribe lived, between sea land in the south and the Diyala River in the north. They were known in Babylonian sources as the Pukudu, but it also is a wordplay on the Heb. "punishment," "visitation" (פָּקַד, *pāqad*). Pekod and Merathaim are just another way to represent the whole nation of Babylon as hostile and treacherous.

50:22–25 The sights, sounds, and the laments of the ensuing battle are graphically depicted in vv. 22-25: "pursue, put to the sword, and put under the ban" (v. 21), commands Yahweh. The staccato commands are as if Yahweh is barking out orders to the armies attacking Babylon. However, it is unclear who the speaker is in vv. 22-25. It may not be Yahweh who sets the trap for Babylon (v. 24a); the third-person references at the end of vv. 24 and 25 suggest that this is Jeremiah's description of Babylon's future, now given in the form of a lament. Babylon has trapped herself by the same schemes she used on others. Babylon, once known as the "hammer of the whole earth" (v. 23b), is the receiver of the work of Yahweh in judgment (v. 25). Yahweh's treasure house is the arsenal from which he brings out the arms of the nations as they are summoned to attack Babylon (v. 25). Yahweh "has work to do in the land of the Chaldeans" (v. 25c).

50:26–27 What happens to the "granaries" (v. 26b) and the "young bulls" (v. 27a) selectively represents what will happen to all the city's resources and the population at large. It all will be destroyed, except for perhaps a very few who escape. The divine directives to Babylon's enemies are often repeated in this section (for example, vv. 26–27; cf. v. 14).

50:29–32 The reason for all this havoc is that Babylon "has defied Yahweh, the Holy One of Israel" (v. 29g–h). Babylon acted arrogantly and presumptuously as she brutally carried out her defiant acts of her military might. This is why God is against her: she is terribly "arrogant" (vv. 31a, 32a). But this nation will stumble and fall as a fire is lit in her towns and she too is consumed (v. 32).

The Unchangeable Purpose of Yahweh (50:33–46)

50:34 The oppressed people of Israel and Judah currently may be held fast by their captor Nebuchadnezzar, but Yahweh their "Redeemer is strong" (v. 34a). Yahweh will act in redemption as a kinsman redeemer, championing the cause of the oppressed people. (God as "Redeemer" is also found in Isa 41:14; 43:14; 44:6, 24; 47:4; 48:17; 49:2, 26; 54:5, 8; 59:20; 60:16; 63:16.) So vigorously will Yahweh press the case for Israel that he will finally bring rest to the land of Israel while he brings unrest to all who live in Babylon (v. 34c–e).

50:35–38 Meanwhile, Babylon can expect nothing but the "sword" (vv. 35–38). That sword will reach her officials, her false prophets, her warriors, her horses and charioteers, and her treasures stored up from her plundering conquests, and even "a sword" (here rendered "drought") "on her waters" (v. 38a). Babylon is a "land of idols" (v. 38c), but they too will go mad with terror (v. 38d), it is promised in a bold hyperbole.

50:39–43 Therefore, the land will return to desolation (vv. 39–40), without an inhabitant. That nation will be overthrown exactly as God overthrew Sodom and Gomorrah (v. 40), for they too suffered total annihilation. Now, Cyrus, king of Persia, is approaching from the north with many kings (v. 41a–b). In fact, v. 42 is like 6:23, with the one exception, that instead of it being an attack on the "Daughter of Zion," now it is an attack on the "daughter of Babylon." It will be just as treacherous and unmerciful as Jerusalem experienced. There are more changes made to the wording of 6:24 about how the people of Jerusalem will react to the enemy's forces barging into their city. With minor changes, 50:43 has the king of Babylon react almost in an identical way to how Judah did in 6:24, as his hands hang limp and anguish grips him.

50:44-46 In the closing poem of this section (vv. 44-46), these verses are virtually identical to a portion from the oracle against Edom (49:19-21). The only exception is that the news will travel much farther than to the Red Sea; here all the nations will hear and will tremble (v. 46).

Proud Babylon Judged (51:1-14)

51:1 This unit begins and ends with a judgment announced against Babylon (vv. 1-2, 13-14). God calls Babylon "Leb Kamai" (לֵב קָמָי; v. 1c), which means "the heart of those who rise against me." But this is also a cryptogram, known as an *atbash* (see 25:26 for an explanation), so that the Heb. consonants *lbqmy* are reversed to spell instead *ksdym*, a disguised form of Chaldea/Babylon. It is employed here not because the name of Babylon is a secret, for Jeremiah has already revealed that name (v. 1b), but so that the citizens of that land might realize that they are those who were opposing Yahweh from their hearts.[292]

51:2 Verse 2 has another wordplay: it is between the word for "foreigners" (זָרִים, *zārîm*) and the word for "winnow" (זֵרוּהָ, *zērûhā*). The agricultural metaphor of winnowing grain is used to speak of Babylon's coming destruction. As grain is thrown up in the air to let the heavy grains fall to the ground as the husks are blown away, so God will blow away Babylon like chaff. These foreign armies will oppose Babylon on every side (v. 2c).

51:5-10 At the center of attention are the exiles in vv. 5-10. Israel and Judah have not been widowed (v. 5a), but they must now flee the city in order to avoid the coming disaster (v. 6). This is true of all other exiles that Babylon has captured and forced into captivity. Apparently, God calls on the exiles to wail over Babylon and get balm for her wounds (v. 8b-c) in

---

292. Dahood is forceful in proposing that the verse be translated "Thus spoke Yahweh: Behold I am arousing against Babylon and against her inhabitants the courage of her assailants, the temper of the ravager." See M. Dahood, "The Integrity of Jeremiah 51,1," *Bib* 53, no. 4 (1972): 542.

a most amazing directive. But despite any efforts to these ends, Babylon cannot be healed (v. 9). It is time to quickly get out of the land, for Babylon's judgment reaches up to heaven. The exiles are now being vindicated; it is time to report what Yahweh has done back in Jerusalem (v. 10). Both Israel and Babylon have sinned, but Israel is the people of God, and they have been remembered by God himself.

51:11 In v. 11 the "Medes" are identified for the first time as Babylon's enemy. They are to get their weapons ready for war. The Medes were a federation of Indo-European tribes who around 1200 BC migrated to the highlands north and east of Babylon, in northwestern Iran. By the eighth century BC they had become a nation, with their capital at Ecbatana. In 612/611 BC the Medes were led by their king Cyaxares in a joint venture with the Babylonians to defeat the Neo-Assyrian capital of Nineveh. By this point she was becoming one of the four great powers of the ancient Near East (with Babylon, Lydia, and Egypt). By the middle of the sixth century BC Cyrus the Great brought the Medes under the umbrella of the Persian Empire.

The Incomparably Great God (51:15–19)

51:15–19 Once again we have verses that are repeats of earlier texts: 10:12–16, which in that earlier context functions as the prophet's polemic against idols. In this context it functions as a portrayal of Yahweh's incomparability over against the once-mighty empire of Babylon. God, the Creator, made the earth by his power and founded the world by his wisdom (v. 15). In this context, this poem functions as a hymn of praise. God is the judge over Babylon. In comparison to him, all others on earth are stupid and without knowledge (v. 17). Especially ridiculous are the makers of idols, for the inanimate images are just plain zeros, without breath in them (v. 18). What a contrast with the One who is the Maker of all things, including Israel (v. 19).

The Smashing War Club of Yahweh (51:20–26)

51:20–23 Nine times the phrase "with you I will smash" (מַפֵּץ, "to smash") is repeated in this section. Nothing will be able to stop the threatened judgment that will now rain down on Babylon (vv. 20–23). This speaks of the thoroughness with which God's judgment will finally come on the arrogant and wicked nation of Babylon. The verses are so straightforward that little explanation is needed except to identify the subject of "My war club are you" (v. 20a). The answer seems to be that just as Assyria and Babylon were God's "rod" and "club" (cf. Isa 10:5) in the past, so this is now the calling of the Median leader. He will be God's weapon to bring Babylon down, his "hammer" (50:23).

51:24-26 God will judge Babylon "for all the wrong they had done in Zion" (v. 24). Moreover, Babylon is called a "destroying mountain" (v. 25a), even though she lived on an alluvial plain; therefore the word is used metaphorically of the towering superiority by which she wreaked havoc worldwide (v. 25b). Added to this, God will hurl the Babylonians over a cliff and make them like a dormant volcano, that is, a "burnt-out mountain" (v. 25e). So pulverized will this city be that it will be impossible to salvage any stones/bricks to be used for foundations in this area that lacked stones or rocks of any kind (v. 26).

The Enemy Advances (51:27-33)

51:27-28 In a series of seven impvs., Yahweh gives the final command to advance (vv. 27-28) against Babylon. The city of Babylon is depicted as being miserably demoralized and severely weakened (vv. 29-32). Three additional kingdoms, north of Mesopotamia (Ararat, Minni, and Ashkenaz), are summoned to join the forces against Babylon. These kingdoms are from Armenia and northwest of Iran, in ancient times called Urartu. Their territory was east of Anatolia (present-day Turkey), near Lake Van. Minni lay west of Ararat, and Ashkenaz was further north of both of them and may be identified with those Herodotus called the Scythians. They are well-known kingdoms from Assyrian documents. They held power for a while, though they were beaten by the Assyrians and then later by the Medes, but were powerful enough by around 550 BC that they fell within the dominating forces of Cyrus of Persia.

51:29-33 The impact of this assault on Babylon is seen in vv. 29-32. The Babylonian soldiers just give up and stop fighting (v. 30a). They stay put in their strongholds (v. 30b), and they are described as being exhausted and as ineffective as women (v. 30d-e). Runner after runner comes with investigative intelligence from the field of battle to the king, but the news is not good: the entire city has been captured (v. 31c-d). The Medo-Persians now have control of the river crossings over the Euphrates and the Tigris Rivers (v. 32). The marshes are now on fire (v. 32b), and the time to "harvest" Babylon has arrived (v. 33).

Israel's Prayer Answered (51:34-44)

51:34-35 The use of the verb "to swallow" (בָּלַע) in vv. 34 provides an **inclusio** with v. 44. The "dragon" (תַּנִּין, v. 34d), who is Nebuchadnezzar, is depicted as having swallowed up Judah and the other nations he has conquered, but then after he so generously fills his belly, he spews them out (v. 34e-f). Like an animal that has eaten too much, so the king of Babylon vomits up Judah. Babylon is viewed as the very essence of evil; thus the prayer of the exiles is for God to avenge them (v. 35).

51:39-40 Yahweh promises to take up the case of those who have been wronged by this monarch. He will set a banquet for them and make them drunk (v. 39). Then he will bring them down like lambs to the slaughter (v. 40).

51:41-43 Like "Leb Kamai" in v. 1, "Sheshach" is also an *atbash* cryptogram for "Babel/Babylon." She, who once was the "renown of the whole earth" (v. 41b), has now become a "horror to the nations" (v. 41c-d). The seawater will surge over Babylon and cover her (v. 42); in contrast, v. 36 pictures the sea as drying up, so the use here must be metaphorical as v. 43b continues with the metaphor of a "dry and desert land." The invading army is seen as a monstrous series of waves that will engulf Babylon and her god Marduk.

51:44 The images for the overthrow of Babylon are numerous and graphic. Babylon's deity Bel will be punished along with the nation of Babylon (v. 44a). Her walls will come crashing down, and she will "disgorge" all she has ingested, and nations will no longer stream to her (v. 44b-c). In fact, the walls of Babylon were legendary for the strength of their fortifications. The inner wall of Babylon was some twenty-one feet thick, while an outer wall measured about twelve feet thick. This double wall of construction was called a casemate wall. These walls were not made of stone, as was true in Israel (for there were no stones in Babylon), but they were built from bricks made of clay found in the area and baked in the sun. The walls were further fortified by 250 towers.

To make the city even more secure, it had a moat dug around its walls and filled with water. One of the most famous of its eight main gates was the northern Ishtar Gate, its bricks enameled in pictures of dragons and lions in a golden color and blue faience. That Ishtar Gate has been reconstructed in Berlin's Pergamon Museum. This city was one impressive defensive structure, but Cyrus took the city without ever engaging it in battle.

Come Out of Babylon (51:45–49)

51:45 This section and the next begin with God's call to "come out" of her (vv. 45, 50). The best way to save themselves is to flee out of that country as fast as possible. God's wrath is now meant to be directed against Babylon, so the exiles must not linger or be fainthearted about leaving, for this is the only way they can save themselves. God calls the exiles "my people" (v. 45a).

51:46–49 When victory is announced over Babylon, a shout will go up that will be heard around the world (v. 48). But be careful about heeding one rumor after another rumor, for when the real victory comes, it will clearly be evident (v. 46). Babylon will surely be humbled (v. 47c). Babylon's slain will lie on the ground just as Judah's slain had at the hands of the Babylonians (v. 49).

Babylon's Final End and a Symbolic Act against Her (51:50–64)

51:50–55 "Leave, do not linger!" This section begins as the last one did in v. 45. Instead of recalling anything good about Babylon, the exiles are to fill their minds with Jerusalem and the land surrounding that city (v. 50c-d). Instead of the recalling the old guilt and shame, think about the holy places and the house of Yahweh (v. 51). God will surely bring down Babylon even if her towers reached the sky and she exalted in her fortifications (v. 53). The collapse of this city and nation will be heard all over the place (v. 54). The tumult she once raised as her warriors raised the alarm and attacked nation after nation will now be hushed (v. 55).

51:56–57 The invaders will break the bows of the Babylonians, and her once-hostile warriors will be captured, for God will now repay her for all the evil she has done to Judah and to the other nations (v. 56). All will be taken in battle: Babylon's king, governors, prefects, and warriors alike (v. 57). They will lapse into a never-ending sleep (v. 57 c).

51:59 The oracle against Babylon in chapters 50–51 is dated to the fourth year of Zedekiah (593 BC), which is just about the time when the first major group of captives was taken from Judah (v. 59). Jeremiah sent this document to Babylon with Seraiah, presumably a brother of Baruch, Jeremiah's scribe, since both are said to be sons of Neriah. Whether he went to Babylon with Zedekiah or he went by himself is a dispute the LXX has with the MT.[293] Had Zedekiah gone to Babylon, it would be difficult to say when and under what circumstances.[294]

51:60 Jeremiah concludes his oracles against these nine nations and tells how they were all written in a book (v. 60). This group of messages formed a unit that was used in an embassy type of message to Babylon.

51:61–64 Seraiah, governmental "quartermaster," is instructed by the prophet to read aloud all the words in these oracles to the nations (v. 61). After he finishes reading these words, he is to pray to Yahweh to fulfill these words by destroying Babylon and leaving it desolate and an uninhabited ruin forever (v. 62). Then in one last symbolic action, he is to tie a stone to the scroll and then throw it into the Euphrates (v. 63) and make this remark: "So will Babylon sink to rise no more because of the disaster I [God] will bring upon her. And her people will fall" (v. 64). With that, the words of Jeremiah end.

"Babylon must fall because of Israel's slain," argues Jeremiah on behalf of the Lord (51:49). Babylon has to be destroyed to repay her for all the evil she has worked on Israel and the nations around her. Her thick walls will

---

293. If the LXX is correct, the Heb. text may have read מֵאֵת rather than אֵת.

294. The curses intended for Jerusalem (Jer 36) are now aimed at Babylon. See B. Gosse, "La malédiction contre Babylone de Jérémie 51,59–64 et les rédactions du livre de Jérémie," *ZAW* 98 (1986): 383–99.

be leveled, and her high gates would be set on fire (51:58). All these disasters and more Jeremiah writes out on a scroll, and after he delivers the message to the Babylonian staff officer, he is to tie a stone around the scroll and throw it into the Euphrates River. In like manner, Babylon will sink.

But the question must be asked: Did the things prophesied by Jeremiah in chapters 50–51, namely, the collapse or destruction of Babylon (50:41–46) and the promises of a return home for the exiles (50:4–5), actually take place? If they did take place, when? It is not unusual for scholars to interpret "In those days" (50:4, 20), "latter days," or "in that day" as pointing to a time in the messianic age. While these phrases are often described in the biblical text as already having begun with the first coming of Messiah (for example, Heb 1:1–2), Jeremiah marks out both the event of the return and the event of the devastating attack on Babylon as already having been started even though they will not be completely fulfilled until the future. There is what is sometimes called the "telescoping" of widely separated events (for example, the first and second coming of Messiah) such that it is often impossible to sort out which of the events predicted belong to the first coming and which to the second coming.

When the Jews returned from the Babylonian exile, they were only a small portion of those who would return in the future. As of the time of the writing of this commentary, already almost *half* of the total number of Jewish people in the world (ca. thirteen to fourteen million) have returned to the state of Israel—6.5 million Jewish returnees out of a total Israeli population of some 7.5 million. Thus, the issue of the return from captivity in Babylon is just a small part of God's gathering the Jewish people from all the nations in the world "in that day" as a part of that complex of events surrounding the second coming of Messiah as described in chapters 50–51.

Cyrus, it is true, entered Babylon unopposed and did not need to destroy the city itself. If that is so, then what are we to make of the descriptions in these chapters of the slaughter and devastation that Babylon will face? It is a fact that Babylon did fall and has not risen since that day; the city of Jerusalem fell, but it did come back, as did the Jewish people, both then and now. How, then, shall we evaluate Jeremiah's words? It will not do to say these words are only as prophetic hyperbole. To do so is to verge on saying Jeremiah gave a false prophecy.

Our conclusion is that it is better to say that both these prophecies did come to pass and will come to pass, but in different time frames. Apparently, Babylon will yet come to a violent and devastating end; she will be left a wasteland and an uninhabited place. The way these chapters will be fulfilled will follow the pattern of the return of the Jewish people to the land of Israel. Jeremiah's words, then, not only came to pass in the historic records of the past, but they are still being fulfilled in the coming days, for they reflect the truth of God.

THE FALL OF JERUSALEM
(52:1–34)

I t is odd that this historical appendix in Jer 52 does not mention Jeremiah, but it does serve to bring closure to the immediate history of his prophecies. The content seems to be taken from 2 Kgs 24:18–25:30, and it is an expanded form of Jer 39:1–10. A similar passage describing the fall of Jerusalem is found in 2 Chr 36:11–21. Since Jer 51:64 notes that the words of the prophet have ended at that point, this chapter clearly is a supplement that came probably from a later hand. That much of the material is a virtual repetition of 2 Kgs 24:18–25:30 makes the suggestion that it is the work of another author appear even stronger. In the LXX version of Jeremiah, chapter 52 comes right after the word given to Jeremiah's scribe Baruch in chapter 45. This suggests that this chapter was added to the prophet's book. The LXX version of chapter 52 also does not include vv. 2–3, 15, and 28–30.

ZEDEKIAH'S REBELLION AND ITS CONSEQUENCE (52:1–11)

TRANSLATION

1 Zedekiah was twenty-one years old when he became king, and he reigned in Jerusalem eleven years. His mother's name was Hamutal,[1] daughter of Jeremiah of Libnah. **2**[2] He did evil in the eyes of Yahweh, just as Jehoiakim had done. **3** It was because of Yahweh's anger that all this happened to Jerusalem and Judah, until he cast them from his presence.

---

1. The **Kethiv**, with the LXX and Vg., has the variant spelling חֲמִיטַל, "Hamital," and the **Qere**, with the Tg. and 2 Chr 23:31, has חֲמוּטַל, "Hamutal."

2. Verses 2 and 3 are absent in the LXX.

Now Zedekiah revolted against the king of Babylon. **4** So in the ninth year of Zedekiah's reign, on the tenth day of the tenth month, Nebuchadnezzar king of Babylon with his entire army marched against Jerusalem. They encamped outside the city and built siege works against it on all sides. **5** The city came under siege until the eleventh year of King Zedekiah. **6** By the ninth day of the fourth month[3] the famine had gripped the city so that there was no food for the people to eat. **7** Then the city [wall] was broken through, and the whole army fled.[4] They left the city[5] at night through the gate between the two walls near the king's garden, though the Babylonians were all around the city; and they went off in the direction of the Arabah. **8** But the Chaldean forces pursued King Zedekiah and overtook him in the plains[6] of Jericho. All his troops[7] were scattered from him. **9** They captured the king and brought him to the king of Babylon at Riblah in the land of Hamath,[8] where he pronounced sentence on him. **10**[9] The king of Babylon executed the sons of Zedekiah before his eyes; in addition, he executed all the officials of Judah in Riblah. **11** Then he blinded the eyes of Zedekiah, bound him with bronze chains, and took him to Babylon, where he put him in prison[10] till the day of his death.

COMMENTARY

52:1 Verses 1–3 closely mirror the account of this final king of Judah found in 2 Kgs 24:18–20 and 2 Chr 36:11–14. He began his reign at twenty-one years of age, as an appointee by and under the control of the Babylonian government. His eleven-year reign fell between the first capture of Jerusalem in March of 597 BC and the final fall of Jerusalem in July 586 BC. This third son of Josiah had his name changed from Mattaniah to Zedekiah by Nebuchadnezzar (2 Kgs 24:17). His mother was named "Hamutal" or

---

3. The phrase בַּחֹדֶשׁ הָרְבִיעִי, "in the fourth month," is absent in the LXX and 2 Kgs 25:3. The Syr. has *wbjrḥ' dḥmš'*, "in the fifth month."

4. The word וַיִּבְרְחוּ, "they fled," is absent in the LXX.

5. The word מֵהָעִיר, "from the city," is absent in the LXX.

6. The LXX has ἐν τῷ πέραν, "in the beyond," where the MT has בְּעַרְבֹת, "in the plains."

7. The LXX has οἱ παῖδες αὐτου, "his servants," where the MT has חֵילוֹ, "his troops."

8. The phrase בְּאֶרֶץ חֲמָת, "in the land of Hamath," is absent in the LXX and 2 Kgs 25:6.

9. 2 Kings 25:7 is shorter and combines Jer 52:10–11.

10. The LXX has εἰς οἰκίαν μύλωνος, "in the millhouse," where the MT has בְּבֵית־הַפְּקֻדֹּת, "in prison."

"Hamital" (a variant reading provided by the Masoretic scribes; cf 2 Kgs 23:31), the daughter of Jeremiah from Libnah. Libnah has not yet been conclusively identified, but it was a town of some significance apparently located in the southern Shephelah, that is, the "low" country that was located between the mountainous region of central Judah and the coastal region.

52:2–3 His reign was not a good one, for v. 2 summarizes it as one in which he did evil in the eyes of Yahweh, just as his half-brother, King Jehoiakim, did. Neither one of these men follow in the footsteps of their father, King Josiah, who walked so conscientiously before God and was reigning when the book of the law was found in 621 BC, which was followed by a spiritual revival. So extensive is the evil of those days that it arouses the wrath of Yahweh to such a point that ultimately he casts Judah from his presence (v. 3). The casting out is a result of both what has gone on in the land of Judah and that they had degenerated to the point that the only course left was to throw them out of the land. To make matters worse, Zedekiah begins to feel his importance, so he later on decides to rebel against the king of Babylon, who appointed him and under whose control he reigned. Not only does Zedekiah rebel against Babylon, but he had given his word in an oath in the name of Yahweh that he would be faithful to Babylon (37:1–2; 2 Chr 36:13).

52:4–6 Nebuchadnezzar has had enough of Zedekiah, so on the ninth year of Zedekiah's reign, on the tenth day of the tenth month, Nebuchadnezzar and his whole army march against Jerusalem (v. 4). Later on, this day was commemorated by observing a new day of fasting in remembrance of the troubled time (not a biblically required fast; vv. 6, 12; Zech 8:19). The Chaldean king and his army build "a siege mound" (2 Kgs 25:1), a type of rampart, all around the city of Jerusalem. The siege of Jerusalem, along with the resulting famine, according to a shorter chronology, lasted eighteen months, from January 588 to July 587 BC, but if the calculation of this time has an autumn starting point for Zedekiah's regnal years, then his "eleventh" year began in the autumn 597 BC and the fourth month spoken of here fell in the summer of 586 BC, July 18. Thus, the siege actually lasted two and a half years, with a slight relief that came when the Egyptians advanced against Babylon, resulting in a temporary lifting of the siege. Conditions under the siege, when it was reestablished, became so severe that there was no food left for the people to eat (v. 6).

52:7-11 Then the city wall is broken through, and Zedekiah and his army flee, going out at night through a gate between the two walls near the king's garden (v. 7). However, the Babylonians come in hot pursuit and overtake King Zedekiah as he is headed for the Arabah, in the plains of Jericho (v. 8). Zedekiah is captured (v. 9) and taken before Nebuchadnezzar, who is stationed at Riblah in the land of Hamath. There the king of Babylon pokes out both of the king of Judah's eyes, after he executes all his sons before him (v. 10). Then he binds him in bronze shackles and takes him to Babylon, where he remains in prison for the rest of his life (v. 11).

THE DESTRUCTION OF JERUSALEM AND

THE SACKING OF THE TEMPLE (52:12-23)

TRANSLATION

12 On the tenth[11] day of the fifth month, in the nineteenth year of Nebuchadnezzar king of Babylon,[12] Nebuzaradan commander of the royal bodyguard, who stood before[13] the king of Babylon, came to Jerusalem.[14] **13** He set fire to the temple of Yahweh, the royal palace, and all the houses of Jerusalem. Every house of anyone great[15] he burnt down. **14** The whole[16] Chaldean army[17] under the command of the imperial guard broke down all the walls around Jerusalem. **15**[18] Nebuzaradan the commander of the guard

---

11. 2 Kings 25:8 has בְּשִׁבְעָ, "on the seventh," where Jer 52:12 has בֶּעָשׂוֹר, "on the tenth."

12. The LXX omits הִיא שְׁנַת תְּשַׁע־עֶשְׂרֵה שָׁנָה לַמֶּלֶךְ נְבוּכַדְרֶאצַּר מֶלֶךְ־בָּבֶל, "in the nineteenth year of Nebuchadnezzar king of Babylon."

13. 2 Kings 25:8 has עֶבֶד, "a servant," where Jer 52:12 has עָמַד לִפְנֵי, "he stood before." The LXX, with Vg., reads ἑστὼς ἐνώπιον, "he had been standing before."

14. 2 Kings 25:8 has יְרוּשָׁלָ͏ם, "Jerusalem," where Jer 52:12 has בִּירוּשָׁלָ͏ם, "in Jerusalem."

15. 2 Kings 25:9 reads וְאֶת־כָּל־בֵּית גָּדוֹל, "and every great house," as does the LXX of Jer 52:13, with καὶ πᾶσαν οἰκίαν μεγάλην, "and every great house," where the MT of Jer 52:13 has וְאֶת־כָּל־בֵּית הַגָּדוֹל, "(and) every house of anyone great."

16. The word כָּל, "all," is absent in Jer 39:8 and 2 Kgs 25:10.

17. The word חֵיל, "army," is absent in the LXX.

18. Verse 15 is absent in the LXX.

carried into exile[19] some of the poorest people[20] and those who remained in the city, along with the rest of the craftsmen[21] and those who had gone over to the king of Babylon.[22] **16** But Nebuzaradan[23] left behind the rest of the poorest people[24] of the land[25] as vinedressers and farmers.[26]

17 The Chaldeans broke up the bronze pillars, the moveable stands, and the bronze sea that were at the temple of Yahweh[27] and carried all[28] the bronze to Babylon. **18**[29] They also took away the pots,[30] shovels, wick trimmers,[31] sprinkling bowls, dishes, and all the bronze articles used in the temple service. **19** The commander of the imperial guard took away the basins, censers, sprinkling bowls, pots, lampstands, dishes, and bowls used for drink offerings—all were made of pure gold or silver. **20** The bronze[32] from the two pillars, the sea,[33] and the twelve bulls under[34] it,[35] and the moveable stands, which King Solomon made for the temple of Yahweh, was

---

19. Jeremiah 39:9 adds the location of the exile as בָּבֶל, "to Babylon."

20. The phrase וּמִדַּלּוֹת הָעָם, "the poorest people," is absent in Jer 39:9 and 2 Kgs 25:11.

21. Jeremiah 39:9, with the Syr., has הָעָם, "the people," while 2 Kgs 25:11, with the Tg. and Vg., has הֶהָמוֹן, "the multitude," where the MT has הָאָמוֹן, "the craftsmen."

22. Jeremiah 39:9 has נָפְלוּ עָלָיו, "they went over to him [that is, Nebuzaradan]," where the MT has נָפְלוּ אֶל־מֶלֶךְ בָּבֶל, "they went over to the king of Babylon."

23. The word נְבוּזַרְאֲדָן, "Nebuzaradan," is absent in the LXX and in 2 Kgs 25:12.

24. 2 Kings 25:12 has the collective sg. וּמִדַּלַּת, "and the poorest," where Jer 52:16 has the pl. וּמִדַּלּוֹת, "and the poorest ones."

25. The LXX has καὶ τοὺς καταλοίπους τοῦ λαοῦ, "and the rest of the people," where the MT has וּמִדַּלּוֹת הָאָרֶץ, "and the poorest of the land."

26. The meaning of the Heb. word וּלְיֹגְבִים is uncertain, and the word only appears here and in the parallel in 2 Kgs 25:12. The LXX has γεωργούς, "farmers." Cf. Jer 39:10.

27. Some Heb. mss have בְּבֵית־יְהוָה, "in the house of Yahweh," where the MT has לְבֵית־יְהוָה, "belonged to the house of Yahweh."

28. The word כָּל, "all," is absent in the LXX and 2 Kgs 25:13.

29. The list of items taken in vv. 18–19 differs between the accounts in the MT and LXX and the briefer version in 2 Kgs 25:14–15 (Holladay 1989, 437nn18–19a).

30. The LXX has τὰ σαφφωθ, which BHS suggests may mean "basins," where the MT has הַסִּפִּים, "the basins."

31. The LXX has τὰ μασμαρωθ, which BHS suggests may represent the "wick trimmers / snuffers," in v. 18 of the MT where the MT has הַמְזַרְקוֹת, "sprinkling bowls."

32. 2 Kings 25:16 has לִנְחֹשֶׁת, "of the bronze," where Jer 52:20 has לִנְחֻשְׁתָּם, "of their bronze."

33. 2 Kings 25:16 has הַיָּם הָאֶחָד, "the one sea," where Jer 52:20 has הַיָּם אֶחָד, "one sea."

34. The phrase וְהַבָּקָר שְׁנֵים־עָשָׂר נְחֹשֶׁת אֲשֶׁר־תַּחַת, "and the twelve bulls under," is absent in 2 Kgs 25:16, which adheres to 2 Kgs 16:8, 17.

35. The LXX, with Syr., adds τῆς θαλάσσης, "the sea." The MT does not signify what the twelve bulls were under.

more than could be weighed.[36] **21** Each of the pillars[37] was eighteen[38] cubits high and twelve cubits in circumference; each was four fingers thick and hollow[39].[40] **22** The bronze capital on top of the one[41] pillar was five[42] cubits high. One was decorated with a network and pomegranates[43] of bronze all around. The other pillar with its pomegranates was similar. **23**[44] There were ninety-six pomegranates on the sides; the total number of pomegranates above the surrounding network was a hundred.[45]

COMMENTARY

52:12-14 Another day that lodges deep in the memory of all Israel was the day Nebuzaradan, the commander of the imperial guard (lit. "chief of the cooks"), sets on fire the temple of Yahweh, the royal palace, and all the houses of any important people in Jerusalem: August 17, 586 BC (or the tenth day of the fifth month; vv. 13-14).[46] This becomes another unofficial day of fasting in Judah (Zech 7:3-5; 8:19). The severity and results of this fire can be seen from some of the excavations on the east side of Jerusalem, which overlooks the Kidron Valley. It is variously called the "burnt house" or the "house of Ahiel."

---

36. The phrase כָּל־הַכֵּלִים הָאֵלֶּה, "of all these vessels," is absent in the LXX.

37. The word וְהָעַמּוּדִים, "and concerning the pillars," is absent in 2 Kgs 25:17.

38. The LXX, with 2 Chr 3:15, has τριάκοντα πέντε, "thirty-five," where the MT has שְׁמֹנֶה עֶשְׂרֵה, "eighteen."

39. The LXX has κύκλῳ, "around" (Heb.: סָבִיב), where the MT has נָבוּב, "hollow."

40. וְחוּט שְׁתֵּים־עֶשְׂרֵה אַמָּה יְסֻבֶּנּוּ וְעָבְיוֹ אַרְבַּע אַצְבָּעוֹת נָבוּב, "and twelve cubits in circumference; each was four fingers think and hollow," is absent in 2 Kgs 25:17.

41. The word הָאֶחָת, "the one," is absent in 2 Kgs 25:17.

42. 2 Kings 25:17 has שָׁלֹשׁ, "three," where Jer 52:22 has חָמֵשׁ, "five."

43. 2 Kings 25:17 has עַל־הַשְּׂבָכָה, "with latticework," and the LXX has ὀκτὼ ῥόαι τῷ πήχει τοῖς δώδεκα πήχεσιν, "eight pomegranates to the cubit for the twelve cubits," where the MT has וְרִמּוֹנִים, "and pomegranates."

44. Verse 23 is absent in 2 Kgs 25.

45. The LXX has τὸ ἓν μέρος, "the one part," where the MT has רוּחָה, "to the wind.

46. For an analysis of the date discrepancy between 2 Kgs 25 and Jer 52, see M. Avioz, "When Was the First Temple Destroyed, according to the Bible?," *Bib* 84 (2003): 562-65; and R. F. Person, "II Kings 24,18-25,30 and Jeremiah 52: A Text-Critical Study in the Redaction History of the Deuteronomistic History," *ZAW* 105, no. 2 (1993): 174-205; and G. Fischer, "Jeremia 52—Ein Schlüssel zum Jeremiabuch," *Bib* 79 (1998): 333-59.

52:15–19 Nebuzaradan takes a second group of people into exile, including some of the poorest people, the rest of the craftsmen, and the deserters who had defected to Babylon (v. 15).[47] Over the years the temple was subject to a number of raids, with many of the key items removed, but now the heavy and larger items are broken up for their metallic worth of gold, silver, and bronze (v. 17). This includes the two twenty-seven-foot-high pillars of the temple, named Jachin and Boaz, which stood on the porch to the temple (1 Kgs 7:23–24), along with the moveable stands (1 Kgs 7:27–33) and the bronze sea, which was fifteen feet in diameter and seven-and-a-half feet high (1 Kgs 7:23–24). Verse 18 includes a large number of the bronze implements and v. 19 those things made of pure gold and silver. It all goes to Babylon as spoil to join those taken in 597 BC.

THE CAPTIVITY (52:24–30)

TRANSLATION

24 The commander of the bodyguard took Seraiah[48] the chief priest, Zephaniah[49] the second priest, and three of the doorkeepers.[50] **25** Of those still in the city, he took[51] the officer who was[52] in charge of the fighting men and seven[53] royal advisers. He also took the secretary who was chief officer[54] in charge of conscripting the people of the land and sixty of his men who were found[55] in the city. **26** Nebuzaradan the commander took them all and brought them to the king of Babylon at Riblah. **27** There at Riblah, in the land of Hamath, the king of Babylon struck them[56] and had

---

47. J. N. Graham, "Enigmatic Bible Passages: 'Vinedressers and Plowmen': 2 Kings 25:12 and Jeremiah 52:16," *BA* 47 (1984): 55–58.

48. The word שְׂרָיָה, "Seraiah," is absent in the LXX.

49. The word צְפַנְיָה, "Zephaniah," is absent in the LXX.

50. The LXX has τοὺς φυλάττοντας τὴν ὁδόν, "the keepers of the way," where the MT has שֹׁמְרֵי הַסַּף, "the keepers of the threshold." The phrase is translated as "the doorkeepers" here.

51. The phrase וּמִן־הָעִיר לָקַח, "and from the city he took," is absent in the LXX.

52. 2 Kings 25:19 has הוּא, "he was," where Jer 52:25 has הָיָה, "he was."

53. 2 Kings 25:19 has וַחֲמִשָּׁה, "and five," where Jer 52:25 has וְשִׁבְעָה, "and seven."

54. The word שַׂר, "chief officer," is absent in the LXX.

55. The Syr. has *(d)'šthrw*, "they were left," where the MT has נִמְצְאוּ, "they were found."

56. 2 Kings 25:21 has וַיַּךְ, "and he struck," where Jer 52:27 has the alternate spelling וַיַּכֶּה, "and he struck."

them executed.[57] So Judah went away into captivity, away from her land.[58] **28** This is the number of the people whom Nebuchadnezzar carried into exile: in the seventh year,[59] 3,023 Jews; **29** in Nebuchadnezzar's eighteenth year,[60] 832 people from Jerusalem; **30** in his twenty-third year, 745 Jews taken into exile by Nebuzaradan the commander of the imperial guard. There were 4,600 people in all.[61]

COMMENTARY

52:24–30 Verses 24–27 parallel what is recorded in 2 Kgs 25:18–21, but instead of this text going on to relate the governorship of Gedaliah, we are told the details of the number of those taken into exile at one time or another (vv. 28–30). Seraiah, the "chief priest," along with Zephaniah, the "second priest," and three of the doorkeepers are taken into captivity, since their positions represent influential types among the Judeans. Whether this list is a supplementary accounting rather than a full accounting cannot be determined at this distance from 597, 586, and 582 BC (with the numbers of 3,023, 832, and 745 respectively). Second Kings 24:14, 16 has ten and eight thousand, respectively, instead of 3,023, but this later number corresponds to the number given in the Babylonian Chronicle. The Babylonian Chronicle is only partially preserved, but it does mention King Jehoiachin of Judah being taken into captivity and his uncle Zedekiah being appointed and the destruction of Jerusalem in 586 BC.[62] One list may only include the males who were taken captive.

---

57. The word וַיְמָתֵם, "and he executed them," is absent in the LXX.

58. The phrase וַיִּגֶל יְהוּדָה מֵעַל אַדְמָתוֹ, "so Judah went away into captivity, away from her land," is absent in the LXX.

59. The Syr. adds *dmlkwth*, "of his kingdom."

60. Some Heb. mss, LXXᵒ, the Syr., and Tg.ᶠ add הֶגְלָה, "he sent into exile."

61. Verses 28–30 do not appear in 2 Kgs 25 or the LXX.

62. See D. J. Wiseman, *Chronicles of Chaldean Kings in the British Museum* (London: British Museum, 1956), 73.

KING JEHOIACHIN RELEASED (52:31–34)

TRANSLATION

31 In the thirty-seventh year of the exile of Jehoiachin[63] king of Judah, in the year Evil-Merodach became king[64] of Babylon, he released Jehoiachin king of Judah and freed him from prison on the twenty-fifth day[65] of the twelfth month.[66] **32** He spoke kindly to him and gave him a seat of honor higher than those of the other kings[67] who were with him in Babylon. **33** So Jehoiachin put aside his prison clothes and for the rest of his life he ate regularly at the king's table. **34** As long as he lived,[68] till the day of his death,[69] the king of Babylon[70] gave Jehoiachin, for his support, a regular allowance.

COMMENTARY

52:31–34 As a final note in this supplement, the calendar springs forward from 582 BC to 561 BC. This corresponds once again to 2 Kgs 25:27–30 as the focus is now put on King Jehoiachin (also called Coniah), who had a brief reign in Jerusalem from 598 to 597 BC. He is not represented as one who rejected the word of Yahweh as did kings Jehoiakim and Zedekiah. Thus, when Jehoiachin reaches about fifty-three years of age (2 Kgs 24:8), he has already been exiled for thirty-seven years, but then he is suddenly treated kindly by the new king of Babylon, Evil-Merodach (meaning "foolish Merodach" = Amel-Marduk, meaning "man of Marduk," or one who worships the god Mardul/Bel). This new Babylonian king reigns from 562 to 560 BC. Jehoiachin is released from prison and given a position higher than any of the other kings who were taken captive from the other countries. The document known as The Court of Nebuchadnezzar mentions

---

63. The LXX has Ιωακιμ, "Joakim," where the MT has יְהוֹיָכִן, "Jehoiachin."

64. 2 Kings 25:27, with the LXX, has מְלֹכוֹ, "he began to reign," where the MT has מַלְכֻתוֹ, "of his reign."

65. 2 Kings 25:27 has בְּעֶשְׂרִים וְשִׁבְעָה, "on the twenty-seventh," and the LXX has ἐν τῇ τετράδι καὶ εἰκάδι, "on the twenty-fourth," where the MT has בְּעֶשְׂרִים וַחֲמִשָּׁה, "on the twenty-fifth."

66. LXX[B] adds καὶ ἐκειρεν αὐτόν, "and he shaved him."

67. A few Heb. mss, 2 Kgs 25:28, the LXX, and the current translation follow the **Qere** with הַמְּלָכִים, "the kings." The **Kethiv** has מְלָכִים, "kings."

68. The phrase כֹּל יְמֵי חַיָּיו, "all the days of his life," is absent in the LXX.

69. The phrase עַד־יוֹם מוֹתוֹ, "till the day of his death," is absent in some Heb. mss and 2 Kgs 25:30.

70. 2 Kings 25:30 has הַמֶּלֶךְ, "the king," where the MT has מֶלֶךְ־בָּבֶל, "the king of Babylon."

the names of some of these other kings.[71] They included the kings of Tyre, Gaza, Sidon, Arvad, Ashdod, and so forth. Tablets were found when the Ishtar Gate was excavated by the Germans in 1900 that confirmed that Jehoiachin ate well from the king's table, as the biblical narrative records.

Evil Merodach was assassinated by Neriglissar, his brother-in-law, who came to the throne and ruled from 560–556 BC. It seems Jehoiachin's kind treatment continued under this new ruler as well. However, as Jeremiah predicted in 22:26, Jehoiachin died in Babylon, which ended the false hope of those in Judah who looked forward to the return of this king to continue the Davidic dynasty in Jerusalem. It never happened. God had other plans.

It is all over. Jerusalem has fallen. The only good news is that captured King Jehoiachin was released from prison in Babylon and treated well by his captors until the day he died in Babylon. Jehoiachin's treatment had its ultimate source in a kind and merciful God, who desired to bless the descendants of David. Israel has fallen, but the promise-plan of God has not come to an end. The Lord is still in control and occupied with the development of the next stage in that promise-plan. The ultimate son of David, Jesus (Matt 1:1), will enter the world in order to demonstrate that God will display his mercy, grace, and faithfulness in unimaginable ways.

---

71. ANET, 307.

EXCURSUSES

EXCURSUS: THE ARK OF THE COVENANT

The ark of the covenant is mentioned almost two hundred times in the OT, with over a third of the references occurring in the books of Samuel. Because it is so closely associated with Yahweh, it is called "the ark of God" in thirty-four instances (for example, 1 Sam 3:3). It is also known by other names such as "the ark of [God's] might" (Ps 132:8) or the "ark of his power" or his "splendor" (Ps 78:60, 61).

The ark was a box made of acacia wood of approximately five feet in length, three feet in height, and three feet in width. It was overlaid inside and out with pure gold. On top of the ark was what was called the mercy seat. Integral to this mercy seat were the two cherubim, whose spread-out wings touched either side of the holy of holies in the tabernacle and temple. The cherubim faced each other and looked down on the ark. There were four golden rings, one at each of the four corners of the box, through which were placed two poles with which the priests carried the ark. The poles were also overlaid in gold. Inside the ark were the two tablets of the law (the second set, after Moses broke the first set) that God gave to Moses at Sinai.

In the OT the ark is highly regarded and was used as a symbol of Yahweh's presence and power to rally the hopes and efforts of the Israelites. When they saw the ark move, then it was time for the troops of Israel to move (Josh 3:3). Accordingly, some affirm that when the Jewish people see the ark of the covenant restored when the new (rebuilt third) temple is built on Mount Zion, it will be time for all Jews to follow after the Messiah and go to a new location in the city of God.

Where is the ark at this time? No one has seen it or knows where it is. One tradition that speaks of it, recorded in the fourteenth-century work *Kebra Nagast*, begins with the queen of Sheba visiting King Solomon. The tradition says he gave her everything she asked for—including a child. That male child was Menelik I, the first of the long-lasting Abyssinian dynasty (which can be traced down to the somewhat recent Haile Selassie I [1892–1975], emperor of Ethiopia, whose full title was "King of Kings, the Lion of Judah, Defender of the Christian Faith, Emperor of the Ancient Kingdom of Ethiopia, the Chosen of God"). The tradition continues that, when Menelik was nineteen years old, King Solomon threw a going-away party for him after he had been educated in Jerusalem. Solomon had a replica of the ark of the covenant made for Menelik as a going-away present, but due to the drunkenness of the Jews at the party (or at some other occasion), Menelik was able to switch the two arks and take the authentic ark home, where it resides to this day, preserved in a church at Aksum, Ethiopia.

It is difficult to verify the substance as well as the details of this tradition, but it is true that after Solomon the ark, despite all its significance and glory, is simply not mentioned again after 2 Chr 35:3, which reports, "He [Josiah] also said to the Levites who taught all Israel and who were holy to Yahweh, 'Put the holy ark in the house which Solomon the son of David king of Israel built; it will be a burden on your shoulders no longer.'" This appears to be the last reference to the ark, almost four hundred years after the time of Solomon. Some conjecture that the ark was still around in 591 BC, the sixth year of King Jehoiachin's exile, since Ezekiel the prophet sees the Shekinah glory of Yahweh leave the temple and stop on the Mount of Olives (Ezek 10:18; 11:23). The presumption is that, since Yahweh resided on the throne between the wings of the cherubim on the ark of the covenant, the ark was still be the temple at this point. But was it the original ark?

There is also a tradition, based on the apocryphal account of 2 Macc 2:4–5, that the prophet Jeremiah removed the ark just before the city of Jerusalem was destroyed by Nebuchadnezzar. There is no listing of the ark of God as being one of the returned treasures.

It is possible that the ark will reappear in the end times. Isaiah 11:10–12 mentions two "banners" or "ensigns" that will be raised:

1. "The root of Jesse will stand as a banner for the peoples."

2. "[God] will raise up a banner for the nations" as he "gather[s] the exiles of Israel."

The word used for "banner" (נֵס) is the same word used for the pole that held the fiery serpent Moses lifted up in the wilderness, at which all who looked would live (Num 21:4–9; John 3:14–15). The second banner mentioned will be connected with the return of the Jewish people to the land of Israel, but more importantly with one of the final battles on earth. It is possible that this future ensign will be the ark of the covenant. We are not told that the Hebrew נֵס is equated with the ark, but we are told in Jer 3:16 that, in connection with the coming of Christ, Israel's numbers will increase greatly in the land.

Isaiah 18 continues this story and connects to the nation of Ethiopia. This prophecy speaks of another nation somewhere beyond the rivers that rise in Ethiopia (Isa 18:1) that will come on "whirring wings." If the Abyssinian Dynasty truly has Solomonic origins, then there has been a Jewish king from the house of David and Solomon and the tribe of Judah ruling and reigning over a remnant of the Ethiopian Jews all this time that the Davidic throne has been vacant. The little kingdom of Ethiopia is one of the oldest nations on record (mentioned in Gen 2:13 and Job 28:19), yet it is one of the few unconquered nations of the world!

Isaiah 18:3 says that at some point in the future a "banner" or "ensign" (נֵס, nēs) will be raised and a trumpet sounded.[1] We are not told the purpose, but if this is similar to the same "ensign" in Isa 11:12, then this may signal the turn in a final battle in Israel in connection with the return of the Lord, and it was the ark of the covenant that signaled victory for so many battles of Israel in the past. At this time the Ethiopians will bring a "present" (Isa 18:7) to Yahweh at Mount Zion, where the new temple (the third temple) by then will have been built. That "present" in all likelihood will be the ark of the covenant, returned to its former resting place! Thus, as the ark came in triumph to the holy land in the days of Joshua, this symbol of victory and the symbol of the presence of God will once more return to the land.

---

1. For this line of thought, I am indebted to A. E. Bloomfield, *The Ark of the Covenant* (Minneapolis: Bethany Fellowship, 1965), 1–36.

Along with the return of the ark will be the return of the Jewish people to the land, like the return to the land of Canaan from Egypt (Isa 11:11–12, 16).

EXCURSUS: THE QUEEN OF HEAVEN

The Queen of Heaven, an epithet for an ancient Near Eastern goddess, seems to have become an object of worship during the time of Jeremiah. Though she has not been conclusively identified, she is probably the goddess Ishtar, Astarte, and/or Ashtoreth. The prophet supplies most of the biblical information in Jer 7:18 and 44:17–19, 25. She was worshiped as the source of fertility and abundance and was probably introduced to Israel by King Manasseh (2 Kgs 21:1). Many of Israel's neighbors had female consorts for their male deities, though such a thought never arose in Israel, despite what some scholars claim.[2]

Jer 44:17 records how the people burned incense to the "Queen of Heaven" and poured out drink offerings to her in the towns of Judah and the streets of Jerusalem. In Assyria the goddess Ishtar was called the "lady of heaven," and in the Canaanite Ugaritic script she is known as the "queen of heaven." This goddess appears to be identical to the Canaanite Astarte, or perhaps the ubiquitous Ashtoreth, found throughout the Bible.

In the unusual texts found at Elephantine, Egypt, a certain Anat-Yahu is named as a consort of Yahu, whom some equate with Yahweh. This may have been the same **cult**, which by this time had reached Canaan, against which Jeremiah preached so vehemently. Anat was also known as a Canaanite female deity.

Some contend that the cakes that the women made were in the shape of female human beings, but others say they were flat and moon-shaped, while still others argue for star-shaped cakes. If the cakes were similar to abundant images and clay molds that have been found, then they were most likely shaped like women. The clay forms usually accent the sexual parts of the body.

---

2. Some scholars argue that Yahweh was indeed paired with a female deity. For a discussion of this view see W. G. Dever, *Did God Have a Wife?: Archaeology and Folk Religion in Ancient Israel* (Grand Rapids: Eerdmans, 2008).

EXCURSUS: SHUB SHEBUT

The promise that God will restore the nation of Israel back to their own land is wrapped up in this Hebrew expression שַׁבְתִּי אֶת־שְׁבוּת, *šabtî ʾet-šĕbût* (or *shub shebut*). If the second word, the noun שְׁבוּת, *šĕbût*, is derived from verbal root שָׁבָה, *šābâ*, then the phrase means "turning back from captivity," but if it is derived from שׁוּב, *šûb*, then the phrase means "turning back the turning" or "restoring the fortunes of the one being brought back."

This expression first appears in Deut 30:3 and then for the first time in the book of Jeremiah in 29:14. Jeremiah uses this expression eleven more times in his book (30:3, 18; 31:23; 32:44; 33:7 [2x], 11, 26; 48:47; 49:6, 39; also see Job 42:10; Pss 14:7 [53:7]; 85:2; 126:4; Joel 4:1; Hos 6:11; Lam 2:14; Zeph 2:7; Ezek 16:53 [3x]; 29:14; 39:25).

Regardless of which root it is taken from, it clearly indicates that there will be a homecoming of the whole nation of Israel in the coming days of the end times. It will be a time of the reversal of the divine judgments and the introduction of peace and prosperity as Israel and Judah are restored to covenant favor.

EXCURSUS: TOPHETH

The word "Topheth" (תֹּפֶת) is difficult to understand. It is most commonly identified as a play on an Aramaic word meaning "firepit" or "cooking stove" (תפת). Jeremiah takes the consonants of the Aramaic word and replaces the vowels with the vowels *o* and *e*, supplied from the Hebrew word *bosheth* (בֹּשֶׁת), meaning "shame," thus making it a deliberate deformation of the word and an object of contempt and scorn.

Topheth and its shrine were located in the Valley of Hinnom (later known as Gehenna) immediately to the south and west of the walls of Jerusalem, in the Wadi Rababi. Jeremiah refers to the valley as Ben-Hinnom. We do not know who Ben-Hinnom was, but it is likely that the valley was named after him before this evil practice had sprung up. Some conjecture that Topheth was situated in the open area where two valleys met, the Central or Tyropean Valley and Kidron Valley, on the east side of the old city of Jerusalem.

The name Topheth occurs in the Old Testament only in 2 Kgs 23:10; Isa 30:33; Jer 7:31–32; 19:6, 11–14. Here the Judeans "burnt their sons and their daughters in the fire" (Jer 7:31), a practice that is strictly forbidden in Lev

18:21 and Deut 18:10. This **cultic** activity involved the gruesome rite of sacrificing the firstborn infants to the god Molech. In 2 Kgs 16:3;[3] 21:6; and 2 Chr 28:3; 33:6, two kings of Judah, Ahaz (735–715 BC) and Manasseh (687–642 BC), consign their sons to the fires of Topheth. During the reforms of King Josiah these horrid practices were abolished (2 Kgs 23:10), then after were reintroduced. One would think hearing the screams of the children as they rolled into the fire would have been enough to shock Judah into turning back to Yahweh. But it was not.

A number of nonbiblical texts and archaeological data from the north African city of Carthage shed further light on Topheth. Archaeological excavations there in the 1970s found an open-air precinct dedicated to the goddess Tanit that demonstrate that infanticide was practiced there. Some scholars had claimed that Jeremiah was exaggerating in his condemnation of Topheth, but the burial urns found at the sanctuary of Tanit were filled with charred remains of children, demonstrating that the practice did exist. Infant sacrifice at Carthage increased, not decreased, in the fourth and third centuries BC. And if some in Judah had wanted to prove Jeremiah wrong, they could have called his bluff about the charge of infant sacrifice at any time, but never is there even one word to hint that he was not being truthful. Archaeologists have also discovered other such sites in Sicily, Sardinia, Cyprus, and Tyre.[4]

Later in Jeremiah, in 32:35, Topheth is connected to the worship of Baal instead of Molech, whereas other texts from the first millennium BC associate human sacrifices with the pagan Ugaritic god El. Therefore, the reference in Jer 32:35 may only be intended as a polemic against Baal and his **cult**.

---

3. This verse does not specifically mention Topheth, but it does describe the child sacrifices.

4. For further information, see King, *Jeremiah: An Archaeological Companion*, 136–39.

GLOSSARY

chiasm: A literary structure where parallel elements correspond in an inverted order (that is, A-B-C-C′-B′-A′).

cult/cultic: A system of religious worship, especially with reference to its rituals and ceremonies. This definition is to be distinguished from the more specific and common modern usage of the word in the sense of "a religion regarded as unorthodox or false."

dittography: The unintentional duplication of a word or phrase in the copying of a manuscript.

hapax legomenon: (pl. *hapax legomena*) A lexical item that occurs only once within a designated body of literature.

inclusio: A literary framing device by which the same word or phrase occurs at both the beginning and the end of a linguistic unit.

Kethiv: Aramaic for "what is written." The written text of the MT, as opposed to what the Masoretic scribes read. See also *Qere*.

paronomasia: A figure of speech involving the combination of words with similar sounds, though not similar meanings, in order to call attention to the point being made.

provenance: Place of origin.

Qere: Aramaic for "what is read." A marginal notation in the MT made by scribes when the written text was confusing or unclear. See also *Kethiv*.

stanza: The main subunit of an entire poem, consisting of multiple **strophes**.

strophe: Poetry units of one or more cola. Multiple strophes comprise a **stanza**.

synecdoche: A figure of speech in which one idea is exchanged for another; for example, the whole for the part or the part for the whole.

terminus ad quem: "limit until which." The latest time an event could have happened.

Vorlage: An original document; the manuscript from which a scribe copied a text.

GENERAL BIBLIOGRAPHY

TECHNICAL MONOGRAPHS

King, Philip J. *Jeremiah: An Archaeological Companion*. Louisville: Westminster John Knox, 1993.

Nicholson, E. W. *Preaching to the Exiles: A Study of the Prose Tradition in the Book of Jeremiah*. New York: Schocken, 1971.

Rata, T. *The Covenant Motif in Jeremiah's Book of Comfort: Intertextual Studies in Jeremiah 30-33*. New York: Peter Lang, 2007.

Schmid, K. *Buchgestalten des Jeremiabuches: Untersuchungen zur Redaktions- und Rezeptionsgeschichte von Jer 30-33 im Kontext des Buches*. WMANT. Neukirchen-Vluyn: Neukirchener Verlag, 1996.

ARTICLES AND ESSAYS

Aberbach, D. "W'tn lhm Y'brwm (Jeremiah VIII 13): The Problem and Its Solution." *VT* 27 (1977): 99-101.

Aejmelaeus, A. "Jeremiah at the Turning-Point of History: The Function of Jer. XXV 1-14 in the Book of Jeremiah." *VT* 52, no. 4 (2002): 459-82.

Aitken, J. K. "ΣΧΟΙΝΟΣ in the Septuagint." *VT* 50 (2000): 433-44.

Aitken, K. T. "The Oracles against Babylon in Jeremiah 50-51: Structures and Perspectives." *TynBul* 35 (1984): 25-63.

Aharoni, Y. "Ramat Raḥel." In *The New Encyclopedia of Archaeological Excavations in the Holy Land*, 4:1261-67. Edited by Ephraim Stern. New York: Simon & Schuster, 1993.

Althann, R. "The Inverse Construct Chain and Jer 10:13, 51:16." *JNSL* 15 (1989): 7-13.

———. "Jeremiah IV 11-12: Stichometry, Parallelism and Translation." *VT* 28, no. 4 (1978): 385-91.

Anderson, B. W. "The New Covenant and the Old." In *The Old Testament and Christian Faith*, 225–42. Edited by B. W. Anderson. New York: Harper & Row, 1963.

Archer, G. "The Relationship between the Septuagintal Translation and the Massoretic Text of Jeremiah." *Trinity Journal* 12, no. 2 (Fall 1991): 139–50.

Avioz, M. "When Was the First Temple Destroyed, according to the Bible?" *Bib* 84 (2003): 562–65.

Bailey, K. E., and W. L. Holladay. "The 'Young Camel' and 'Wild Ass' in Jer. II 23–25." *VT* 18, no. 2 (1968): 256–60.

Becking, B. "Baalis, The King of the Ammonites: An Epigraphical Note on Jeremiah 40:14." *Journal of Semitic Studies* 38, no. 1 (Spring 1993): 15–24.

———."Does Jeremiah X 3 Refer to a Canaanite Deity Called Hubal?" *VT* 43, no. 4 (1993): 555–57.

———."Sour Fruit and Blunt Teeth: The Metaphorical Meaning of the *MĀŠĀL* in Jeremiah 31,29." *SJOT* 17, no. 1 (2003): 7–21.

Behar, D. M., et al. "Multiple Origins of Ashkenazi Levites: Y Chromosome Evidence for Both Near Eastern and European Ancestries." *American Journal of Human Genetics* 73 (2003): 768–79.

Ben-Dov, J. "A Textual Problem and Its Form-Critical Solution: Jeremiah 10:1–16." *Textus* 20 (2000): 97–128.

Bergman, A., and W. F. Albright. "Anathoth?" *BASOR* 63 (1936): 22–23.

———."Soundings of the Supposed Site of Old Testament Anathoth." *BASOR* 62 (1936): 22–26.

Berlin, A. "Jeremiah 29:5–7: A Deuteronomic Allusion." *HAR* 8 (1984): 3–11.

Boda, M. J. "From Complaint to Contrition: Peering through the Liturgical Window of Jer 14,1–15,4." *ZAW* 113 (2001): 186–97.

Bowen, N. R. "The Quest for the Historical *Gĕbîrâ*." *CBQ* 63, no. 4 (2001): 597–618.

Büchner, D. "Boshet in Jeremiah 3:24: Disenfranchisement and the Role of the Goddess in Seventh-Century Judah." *JTS* 59, no. 2 (2008): 478–99.

Büsing, G. "Ein alternativer Ausgangspunkt zur Interpretation von Jer 29." *ZAW* 104, no. 3 (1992): 402–8.

Brueggemann, W. "At the Mercy of Babylon: A Subversive Rereading of the Empire." *JBL* 110, no. 1 (Spring 1991): 3–22.

Cazelles, H. "Israel du Nord et Arche D'alliance (Jer. III 16)." *VT* 18, no. 2 (1968): 147–58.

Chavel, S. "'Let My People Go!' Emancipation, Revelation, and Scribal Activity in Jeremiah 34.8–14." *JSOT* 76 (1997): 71–95.

Christensen, D. L. "In Quest of the Book of Jeremiah: A Study of Jeremiah 25 in Relation to Jeremiah 46–51." *JETS* 33, no. 2 (1990): 145–53.

———. "'Terror on Every Side' in Jeremiah." *JBL* 92, no. 4 (1973): 498–502.

Clendenen, E. R. "Discourse Strategies in Jeremiah 10:1–16." *JBL* 106, no. 3 (1987): 401–8.

Cohen, S., and V. A. Hurowitz. "חקות העמים הבל הוא (Jer 10:3) in Light of Akkadian *Parṣu* and *Zaqīqu* Referring to Cult Statues." *JQR* 89, nos. 3–4 (1999): 277–90.

Cohn, H. "Is the 'Queen of Heaven' in Jeremiah the Goddess Anat?" *JBQ* 32, no. 1 (2004): 55–57.

Cook, J. "The Difference in the Order of the Books of the Hebrew and Greek Versions of Jeremiah—Jeremiah 43 (50): A Case Study." *OTE* 7 (1994): 175–92.

Cramer, G. H. "The Messianic Hope of Jeremiah." *BSac* 115, no. 459 (1958): 237–46.

Dahood, M. "The Integrity of Jeremiah 51,1." *Bib* 53, no. 4 (1972): 542.

———. "Word and Witness: A Note on Jeremiah 29:23." *VT* 27, no. 4 (1977): 483.

———. "The Word-Pair *'ĀKAL* || *KĀLĀH* in Jeremiah XXX 16." *VT* 27, no. 4 (1977): 482.

de Hoop, R. "The Meaning of *pḥz* in Classical Hebrew." *ZAH* 10 (1997): 16–26.

DeRoche, M. "Israel's 'Two Evils' in Jeremiah II 13." *VT* 31, no. 3 (1981): 369–71.

———. "Jeremiah 2:2–3 and Israel's Love for God during the Wilderness Wanderings." *CBQ* 45, no. 3 (1983): 364–76.

Di Pede, E. "Jérusalem, Ebed-Melek et Baruch : Enquête narrative sur le déplacement chronologique de Jr 45." *RB* 111 (2004): 61–77.

———."La maniìre de raconter et l'enjeu du récit: Jérémie présente Ananias en Jer 28,1 TM et 35,1." *BibInt* 16, no. 3 (2008): 294-301.

———."Le récit de la prise de Jérusalem (Jr 46 LXX et 39 TM): son importance dans le récit et son impact sur le lecteur." *Biblische Zeitschrift* 52, no. 1 (2006): 90-99.

Dijkstra, M. "Prophecy by Letter (Jeremiah XXIX 24-32)." *VT* 33, no. 3 (1983): 319-22.

Edelman, D. "The Meaning of *QIṬṬĒR*." *VT* 35, no. 4 (1985): 395-404.

Ehrman, A. "A note on בוטח in Jer. XII. 5." *JSS* 5, no. 2 (1960): 153.

Emerton, J. A. "Notes on Jeremiah 12:9 and on some suggestions of J. D. Michaelis about the Hebrew words *naer, æbrā, and jadă*." *ZAW* 79, no. 2 (1967): 225-28.

———."A Problem in the Hebrew Text of Jeremiah 6:23 and 50:42." *JTS* 23, no. 1 (1972): 106-13.

Feigin, S. "The Babylonian Officials in Jeremiah 39:3, 13." *JBL* 45, nos. 1-2 (1926): 149-55.

Feuillet, A. "Note sur la Traduction de Jer 31:3c." *VT* 12, no. 1 (1962): 122-24.

Finley, T. J. "Dimensions of the Hebrew Word for 'Create' (בָּרָא)." *BSac* 148, no. 592 (1991): 409-23.

Fischer, G. "Jeremia 52—Ein Schlüssel zum Jeremiabuch." *Bib* 79 (1998): 333-59.

Foreman, B. A. "Strike the Tongue: Silencing the Prophet in Jeremiah 18:18b." *VT* 59, no. 4 (2009): 653-57.

Fox, M. V. "Jeremiah 2:2 and the 'Desert Ideal.'" *CBQ* 35, no. 4 (1973): 441-50.

Fretheim, T. E. "Is Anything Too Hard for God? (Jeremiah 32:27)." *CBQ* 66 (2004): 231-36.

Frick, F. S. "The Rechabites Reconsidered." *JBL* 90, no. 3 (1971): 284-85.

Ginsbury, P. N. "*DOVÉR* and *M'DABER*." *JBQ* 33 (2005): 40-46.

Gordon, T. C. "A New Date for Jeremiah." *ExpTim* 44 (1932-33): 562-65.

Gosse, B. "Jérémie 17, 1-5aa dans la rédaction massorétique du livre de Jérémie." *Estudios Bíblicos* 53 (1995):165-80.

———."Jérémie xlv et la place du recueil d'oracles contre les nations dans le livre de Jérémie." *VT* 40 (1990): 145-51.

———. "La malédiction contre Babylone de Jérémie 51,59-64 et les rédactions du livre de Jérémie." *ZAW* 98 (1986): 383-99.

———. "The Masoretic Redaction of Jeremiah: An Explanation." *JSOT* 77 (1998): 75-80.

———. "Le prophéte Jérémie en Jer 11, 18-12,6 dans le cadre du livre de Jérémie et en rapport avec Psautier." *ZAW* 118 (2006): 549-57.

Graham, J. N. "Enigmatic Bible Passages: 'Vinedressers and Plowmen': 2 Kings 25:12 and Jeremiah 52:16." *BA* 47 (1984): 55-58.

Grossberg, D. "Pivotal Polysemy in Jeremiah 25:10-11." *VT* 36, no. 4 (1986): 481-85.

Grothe, J. F. "An Argument for the Textual Genuineness of Jeremiah 33:14-26." *Concordia Journal* 7 (1981): 188-91.

Habel, N. "The Form and Significance of the Call Narratives." *ZAW* 77, no. 3 (1965): 297-323.

Harris, S. L. "The Second Vision of Jeremiah: Jer 1:13-15." *JBL* 102, no. 2 (1983): 281-88.

Hasel, G. F. "The Meaning of the Animal Rite in Genesis 15." *JSOT* 19 (1981): 61-78.

Hayes, K. M. "Jeremiah IV 23: *Tōhû* without *Bōhû*." *VT* 47, no. 2 (1997): 247-49.

Henderson, J. M. "Who Weeps in Jeremiah VIII 23 (IX I)? Identifying Dramatic Speakers in the Poetry of Jeremiah." *VT* 52, no. 2 (2002): 191-206.

Herr, L. G. "Is the Spelling of 'Baalis' in Jeremiah 40:14 a Mutilation?" *AUSS* 23, no. 2 (Summer 1985): 187-91.

———. "The Servant of Baalis." *BA* 48, no. 3 (September 1985): 169-72.

Herrmann, W. "Zu Jer 33,11." *BN* 123 (2004): 41-44.

Hess, R. S. "Hiphil Forms of QWR in Jeremiah VI 7." *VT* 41, no. 3 (1991): 347-50.

Heyink, B. "Jeremiah the Prophet." In *The Lexham Bible Dictionary*. Edited by J. D. Barry et al. Bellingham, WA: Lexham, 2012, 2013, 2014.

Hicks, R. L. "*Delet* and *Megillāh*: A Fresh Approach to Jeremiah xxxvi." *VT* 33, no. 1 (1983): 46-66.

Hobson, R. "Jeremiah 41 and the Ammonite Alliance." *Journal of Hebrew Scriptures* 10 (2010): 1-15.

Hoffman, Y. "Aetiology, Redaction and Historicity in Jeremiah XXXVI." *VT* 46, no. 2 (1996): 179–89.

Holladay, W. L. "Covenant with the Patriarchs Overturned: Jeremiah's Intention in 'Terror on Every Side' (Jer. 20:1–6)." *JBL* 91, no. 3 (September 1972): 305–20.

———. "Jer. XXXI 22B Reconsidered: 'The Woman Encompasses the Man.'" *VT* 16, no. 2 (1966): 236–39.

———. "Jeremiah 2:34b—A Fresh Approach." *VT* 25 (1975): 221–25.

———. "The Priests Scrape Out on Their Hands: Jeremiah V 31." *VT* 15, no. 1 (1965): 111–13.

———. "The So-Called 'Deuteronomic Gloss' in Jer. VIII 19b." *VT* 12, no. 4 (1962): 494–98.

———. "Structure, Syntax and Meaning in Jeremiah IV 11–12A." *VT* 26, no. 1 (1976): 28–37.

Huffman, H. B. "The Covenant Lawsuit in the Prophets." *JBL* 78 (1959): 285–95.

Hyatt, J. P. "The Deuteronomic Edition of Jeremiah." In *A Prophet to the Nations*. Edited by L. G. Perdue and B. W. Kovacs. Winona Lake, IN: Eisenbrauns, 1984.

———. "The Original Text of Jeremiah 11: 15–16." *JBL* 60, no. 1 (1941): 57–60.

———. "The Peril from the North in Jeremiah." *JBL* 59, no. 4 (1940): 499–513.

Isbell, C. D., and M. Jackson. "Rhetorical Criticism and Jeremiah VII 1–VIII 3." *VT* 30 (1980): 20–26.

Jacobson, H. "Jeremiah XXX 17: ציון היא." *VT* 54, no. 3 (2004): 398–99.

Joosten, J. "Les Benjaminites au Milieu de Jérusalem: Jérémie vi 1ss et Juges xix–xx." *VT* 49 (1999): 65–72.

Kaiser, W. C., Jr. "False Prophet." In *The Evangelical Dictionary of Biblical Theology*. Edited by W. Elwell. Grand Rapids: Baker, 1996.

———. "'Massa,' II. A Burden." In *Theological Wordbook of the Old Testament*. Edited by R. L. Harris, G. L. Archer Jr., and B. K. Waltke. Chicago: Moody, 1980.

———. "The Old Promise and the New Covenant: Jeremiah 31:31–34." *JETS* 15 (1972): 11–23.

Kapelrud, A. S. "The Interpretation of Jeremiah 34,18 ff." *JSOT* 22 (1982): 138–41.

Katzenstein, H. J. "'Before Pharaoh Conquered Gaza' (Jeremiah 47:1)." *VT* 33, no. 2 (1983): 249–51.

Kipper, J. B. "Ein übersehenes Fragment Aquilas in Jr 38(31),22b." *Bib* 66, no. 4 (1985): 580–81.

Kitchen, K. A. "The Philistines." in *Peoples of Old Testament Times*. Edited by D. J. Wiseman. London: Oxford University Press, 1973.

Kline, M. "Double Trouble." *JETS* 32 (1989): 176–77.

Knauf, E. A. "Jeremia XLIX 1–5: Ein zweites Moab-Orakel im Jeremia-Buch." *VT* 42, no. 1 (1992): 124–28.

Kselman, J. S. "A Note on Jer 49,20 and Zc 2,6–7." *CBQ* 32, no. 4 (1970): 579–81.

Lalleman, H. "Jeremiah, Judgment, and Creation." *TynBul* 60, no. 1 (2009): 15–24.

Lemaire, A. "Jérémie XXV 10B et la stèle araméenne de Bukân." *VT* 47, no. 4 (1997): 543–45.

Lemke, W. E. "The Near and Distant God: A Study of Jer 23:23–24 in Its Biblical Theological Context." *JBL* 100, no. 4 (1981): 541–55.

———."Nebuchadrezzar, My Servant." *CBQ* 28, no. 1 (1966): 45–50.

Leuchter, M. "The Temple Sermon and the Term מקום in the Jeremianic Corpus." *JSOT* 30, no. 1 (2005): 93–109.

Lewin, Ellen Davis. "Arguing for Authority: A Rhetorical Study of Jeremiah 1:4–19 and 20:7–18." *JSOT* 32 (1985): 105–19.

Lipiński, E. "Prose ou Poésie en Jér 34:1–7." *VT* 24, no. 1 (1974): 112–13.

———."באחרית הימים Dans les Textes Préexiliques." *VT* 20, no. 4 (1970): 445–50.

Low, K. "Implications Surrounding Girding the Loins in Light of Gender, Body, and Power." *JSOT* 36, no. 1 (2011): 3–30.

Lundbom, J. R. "The Double Curse in Jeremiah 20:14–18." *JBL* 104, no. 4 (1985): 589–600.

Maier, V. C. I., and E. M. Dörrfuß. "'Um mit ihnen zu sitzen, zu essen und zu trinken' Am 6,7; Jer 16,5 und die Bedeutung von *marzea*." *ZAW* 111 (1999): 45–57.

Margaliot, M. "Jeremiah X 1–16: A Re-examination." *VT* 30 (1980): 295–308.

Martin, J. D. "The Forensic Background to Jeremiah III:1." *VT* 19 (January 1969): 83.

Mavinga, J. N. "Jeremiah's Royal Book: A Twofold Aspect Applied to the Royal Oracle (23:1-8; 33:14-26)." *Journal for Semitics* 18 (2009): 105-30.

McCord, H. "The Meaning of *YHWH Tsidhkenu* ('The Lord our Righteousness') in Jeremiah 23:6 and 33:16." *ResQ* 6, no. 3 (1962): 114-21.

McKane, W. "The Construction of Jeremiah Chapter XXI." *VT* 32 (1982): 59-73.

———. "Jeremiah (20th and 21st Century Interpretation)." In *Hebrew Bible: History of Interpretation*. Edited by J. H. Hayes. Nashville: Abingdon, 2004.

Michel, W. L. "Şlmwt, 'Deep Darkness' or 'Shadow of Death'?" *Biblical Research* 29 (1984): 5-20.

Migsch, H. "Die Interpretation von Jeremia 35,14a und die Vulgatalesart." *BN* 111 (2002): 28-33.

———. "Zur Interpretation von *We'et Kål-bêt Hārekābîm* in Jeremia XXXV 3." *VT* 51, no. 3 (2001): 385-89.

Miller, P. D. "Sin and Judgment in Jeremiah 34:17-19." *JBL* 103, no. 4 (1984): 611-13.

Motyer, J. A. "Jeremiah VII, 22." *TynBul* 1 (1965): 4-5.

Mowinckel, S. *Zur Komposition de Buches Jeremia*. Kristiania, 1914.

Müller, H.-P. "Das »Haus des Volkes« von Jer 39,8." *ZAW* 114, no. 4 (2002): 611-17.

Müller, V. H. "'Der bunde Vogel' von Jer 12:9." *ZAW* 79, no. 2 (1967): 225-28.

Mulzac, K. D. "*ŚRD* as a Remnant Term in the Context of Judgment in the Book of Jeremiah." *Asia Adventist Seminary Studies* 7 (2004): 39-58.

———. "*YTR* as a Remnant Term in the Book of Jeremiah." *Journal of the Adventist Theological Society* 19, nos. 1-2 (2008): 3-17.

North, F. "The Oracle against the Ammonites in Jeremiah 49:1-6." *JBL* 65, no. 1 (1946): 37-43.

Novick, T. "עקב הלב מכל ואנש הוא מי ידענו (Jeremiah 17:9)." *JBL* 123, no. 3 (Fall 2004): 531-35.

O'Day, G. R. "Jeremiah 9:22-23 and 1 Corinthians 1:26-31: A Study of Intertextuality." *JBL* 109, no. 2 (1990): 259-67.

Oded, B. "Where Is the 'Myth' of the Empty Land to Be Found?" In *Judah and the Judeans in the Neo-Babylonian Period*. Edited by O. Lipschits and J. Blenkinsopp. Winona Lake, IN: Eisenbrauns, 2003.

Ossom-Batsa, G. "The Theological Significance of the Root *ŠWB* in Jeremiah." *Andrews University Seminary Studies* 39, no. 2 (2001): 223–32.

Person, R. F. "II Kings 24,18–25,30 and Jeremiah 52: A Text-Critical Study in the Redaction History of the Deuteronomistic History." *ZAW* 105, no. 2 (1993): 174–205.

Peters, J. P. "Notes on Some Difficult Passages in the Old Testament." *JBL* 11, no. 1 (1892): 38–52.

Pinker, A. "The Semantic Field of עשׂה in the Hebrew Bible." *VT* 57 (2007): 386–99.

Rata, T. "Notes on Leviticus 19:28." In *Holman Christian Study Bible*. Nashville: Broadman & Holman, 2010.

Reed, W. L., and F. V. Winnett. "A Fragment of an Early Moabite Inscription from Kerak." *BASOR* 172 (1963): 1–9.

Reid, G. "'Thus You Will Say to Them': A Cross-Cultural Confessional Polemic in Jeremiah 10.11." *JSOT* 31, no. 2 (2006): 221–38.

Reimer, D. J. "A Problem in the Hebrew Text of Jeremiah X 13, LI 16." *VT* 38 (1988): 348–54.

Renkema, J. "A Note on Jeremiah XXVIII 5." *VT* 47, no. 2 (1997): 253–55.

Rom-Shiloni, D. "The Prophecy for 'Everlasting Covenant' (Jeremiah XXXII 36–41): An Exilic Addition or a Deuteronomistic Redaction?" *VT* 53, no. 2 (2003): 201–23.

Roshwalb, E. H. "Jeremiah 1.4–10: 'Lost and Found' in Translation and a New Interpretation." *JSOT* 34, no. 3 (2010): 351–76.

Rottzoll, D. U. "Die *KH 'MR* ... -Legitimationsformel." *VT* 39, no. 3 (1989): 323–40.

Rudman, D. "Creation and Fall in Jeremiah X 12–16." *VT* 48, no. 1 (1998): 63–73.

Sawyer, J. F. A. "A Note on the Brooding Partridge in Jeremiah XVII 11." *VT* 28, no. 3 (July 1978): 324–29.

Schiller, J. "Jeremia und das Tofet: Bemerkungen zur grammatischen Interpretation von Jer 19,11–12." *ZAW* 123, no. 1 (2011): 108–12.

Schmitt, J. J. "The Virgin of Israel: Referent and Use of the Phrase in Amos and Jeremiah." *CBQ* 53, no. 3 (1991): 365–87.

Seybold, K. "Der Löwe von Jeremia XII 8: Bemerkungen zu einem prophetischen Gedicht." *VT* 36, no. 1 (1986): 93–104.

Sharp, C. J. "'Take Another Scroll and Write': A Study of the LXX and the MT of Jeremiah's Oracles against Egypt and Babylon." *VT* 47 (1997): 487–516.

Shiloh, Y., and D. Tarler. "Bullae from the City of David: A Hoard of Seal Impressions from the Israelite Period." *BA* 49, no. 4 (1986): 204.

Smit, J. H. "War-Related Terminology and Imagery in Jeremiah 15:10–21." *OTE* 11 (1998): 105–14.

Smith, G. V. "The Use of Quotations in Jeremiah XV 11–14." *VT* 29, no. 2 (1979): 229–31.

Smith, M. S. "Death in Jeremiah, IX, 20." *Ugarit-Forschungen* 19 (1987): 289–93.

———. "Jeremiah IX 9—A Divine Lament." *VT* 37, no. 1 (1987): 289–93.

Snaith, N. H. "Jeremiah XXXIII 18." *VT* 21, no. 5 (1971): 620–22.

Snyman, S. D. "A Note on *PTH* and *YKL* in Jeremiah XX 7–13." *VT* 48, no. 4 (1998): 559–63.

———. "A Structural-Historical Investigation of חמס ושד in Jeremiah 6:1–8." *HTS* 58, no. 4 (2002): 1593–1603.

Soggin, J. A. "Einige Bemerkungen über Jeremias ii 34." *VT* 8, no. 4 (1958): 433–35.

Southwood, C. "The Spoiling of Jeremiah's Girdle (Jer xiii–xi)." *VT* 29, no. 2 (1979): 231–37.

Stager, L. E. "The Fury of Babylon." *BAR* 22, no. 1 (1996): 56–77.

Steiner, R. C. "Incomplete Circumcision in Egypt and Edom: Jeremiah (9:24–25) in the Light of Josephus and Jonckheere." *JBL* 118, no. 3 (1999): 497–526.

Sternberger, J. "Un oracle royale à la source d'un ajout rédactionnel aux 'confessions' de Jérémie: Hypothèses se rapportant aux 'confessions' de Jérémie XII et XV." *VT* 36, no. 4 (1986): 462–73.

Stipp, H.-J. "Jeremia 24: Geschichtsbild und Historischer Ort." *JNSL* 25, no. 1 (1999): 151–83.

Stone, A. "Does 'Shadow of Death' Mean 'Deep Darkness'?" *BR* 51 (2006): 53–57.

Strawn, B. A. "Jeremiah's In/Effective Plea: Another Look at נער in Jeremiah I 6." *VT* 55, no. 3 (2005): 366–77.

Taylor, M. A. "Jeremiah 45: The Problem of Placement." *JSOT* (1987): 79–98.

Thelle, R. I. "דרש את־יהוה: The Prophetic Act of Consulting YHWH in Jeremiah 21,2 and 37,7." *SJOT* 12 (1998): 249–56.

Thomson, J. G. S. S., and J. G. McConville. "Jeremiah." In *New Bible Dictionary*. Edited by D. R. W. Wood et al. Downers Grove, IL: InterVarsity Press, 1996.

Tov, E. "Exegetical Notes on the Hebrew Vorlage of the LXX of Jeremiah 27 (34)." *ZAW* 91, no. 1 (1979): 73–93.

van der Wal, A. J. O. "Jeremiah II 31: A Proposal." *VT* 41, no. 3 (1991): 360–63.

van der Westhuizen, J. P. "A Stylistic-Exegetical Analysis of Jeremiah 46:1–12." *JBQ* 20 (1991–92): 84–95.

van Lingen, A. "*BWʾ-YṢ*ʾ ("To Go Out and to Come In") as a Military Term." *VT* 42, no. 1 (1992): 59–66.

Vischer, W. "The Vocation of the Prophet to the Nations: An Exegesis of Jeremiah 1:4–10." *Interpretation* 9, no. 3 (1955): 310–17.

Walton, J. H. "Vision Narrative Wordplay and Jeremiah XXIV." *VT* 39, no. 4 (1989): 508–9.

Werblowsky, R. J. Zwi. "Stealing the Word." *VT* 6, no. 1 (January 1956): 105–6.

Wessels, W. J. "Jeremiah 22, 24–30: A Proposed Ideological Reading." *ZAW* 101 (1989): 232–49.

———. "Jeremiah 33:15–16 as a Reinterpretation of Jeremiah 23:5–6." *Hervormde Teologiese Studies* 47 (1991): 231–46.

Whitney, G. E. "Alternative Interpretations of Lōʾ in Exodus 6:3 and Jeremiah 7:22." *WTJ* 48 (1986): 151–59.

Wiebe, J. M. "The Form of the 'Announcement of a Royal Savior' and the Interpretation of Jeremiah 23:5–6." *Studia Biblica et Theologica* 15 (1987): 3–22.

Willis, J. T. "Dialogue between prophet and Audience as a Rhetorical Device in the Book of Jeremiah." *JSOT* 33 (1985): 63–82.

———. "The Expression *beʾacharith hayyamin* in the Old Testament." *ResQ* 22, nos. 1–2 (1979): 54–71.

Willis, T. M. "'They Did Not Listen to the Voice of Yahweh': A Literary Analysis of Jeremiah 37–45." *ResQ* 42 (2000): 65–84.

Wilton, P. "More Cases of *Waw Explicativum*." *VT* 44, no. 1 (January 1994): 125–28.

Yardeni, A. "Remarks on the Priestly Benediction on Two Ancient Amulets from Jerusalem." *VT* 41 (1991): 180.

Yates, G. E. "Jeremiah's Message of Judgment and Hope for God's Unfaithful 'Wife.'" *BSac* 167 (April–June 2010): 144–65.

Young, R. C. "When Did Jerusalem Fall?" *JETS* 47, no. 1 (2004): 21–38.

Zogbo, L. "Enallage: Shifting Persons in Old Testament Texts." Paper presented at the United Bible Societies Triennial Translation Workshop, May 1994.

GENERAL BOOKS

Achtemeier, P. J. *Harper's Bible Dictionary*. San Francisco: Harper & Row, 1985.

Barstad, Hans. M. *The Myth of the Empty Land: A Study of the History and Archaeology of Judah during the "Exilic" Period*. Oslo: Scandinavian University Press, 1996.

Bloomfield, A. E. *The Ark of the Covenant*. Minneapolis: Bethany Fellowship, 1965.

Briggs, C. A. *Messianic Prophecy*. New York: Scribners, 1889.

Bright, J. *Covenant and Promise*. Philadelphia: Westminster, 1976.

Carroll, R. P. *From Chaos to Covenant*. New York: Crossroad, 1981.

Cowper, W. *Poems by William Cowper, Esq., of the Inner Temple*. 10th ed. New York: William L. Allison, n.d.

Dever, W. G. *Did God Have a Wife?: Archaeology and Folk Religion in Ancient Israel*. Grand Rapids: Eerdmans, 2008.

Driver, S. R. *Deuteronomy*. ICC. New York: Charles Scribner's Sons, 1895.

Hegel, G. W. F. *The Philosophy of History*. New York: Collier and Son, 1837.

Hindson, E. E. *The Philistines and the Old Testament*. Grand Rapids: Baker, 1971.

Kaiser, W. C., Jr. *Preaching and Teaching the Last Things: Old Testament Eschatology for the Life of the Church*. Grand Rapids: Baker Academic, 2011.

Kurt, A. *The Persian Empire: A Corpus of Sources from the Achaemenid Period.* New York: Routledge, 2013.

Negev, A., and S. Gibson, eds. *Archaeological Encyclopedia of the Holy Land.* Rev. ed. New York: Continuum, 2001.

Thomson, J. G. S. S. *The Old Testament View of Revelation.* Grand Rapids: Eerdmans, 1960.

Wiseman, D. J. *Chronicles of Chaldean Kings in the British Museum.* London: British Museum, 1956.

SCRIPTURE INDEX

Old Testament

New Testament

Other Ancient Documents

2 Maccabees

Dead Sea Scrolls

Talmud

Megillah